University of
Hertfordshire **UH**

College Lane, Hatfield, Herts.  AL10 9AB
**Information Hertfordshire**
*Services and Solutions for the University*

For renewal of Standard and One Week Loans
please visit the web site http://www.voyager.herts.ac.uk

This item must be returned or the loan renewed by the due date.
A fine will be charged for the late return of items.

# COMMERCIAL AND INVESTMENT BANKING AND THE INTERNATIONAL CREDIT AND CAPITAL MARKETS

# COMMERCIAL AND INVESTMENT BANKING AND THE INTERNATIONAL CREDIT AND CAPITAL MARKETS

A Guide to the Global Finance Industry and Its Governance

## BRIAN SCOTT-QUINN

ICMA Centre for Financial Markets, Henley Business School, University of Reading, UK

First published 2012 by
PALGRAVE MACMILLAN

Palgrave Macmillan in the UK is an imprint of Macmillan Publishers Limited,
registered in England, company number 785998, of Houndmills, Basingstoke,
Hampshire RG21 6XS.

Palgrave Macmillan in the US is a division of St Martin's Press LLC,
175 Fifth Avenue, New York, NY 10010.

Palgrave Macmillan is the global academic imprint of the above companies
and has companies and representatives throughout the world.

Palgrave® and Macmillan® are registered trademarks in the United States,
the United Kingdom, Europe and other countries.

ISBN: 978–0–230–37047–0

This book is printed on paper suitable for recycling and made from fully
managed and sustained forest sources. Logging, pulping and manufacturing
processes are expected to conform to the environmental regulations of the
country of origin.

A catalogue record for this book is available from the British Library.

A catalog record for this book is available from the Library of Congress.

10  9  8  7  6  5  4  3  2  1
21 20 19 18 17 16 15 14 13 12

Printed and bound in Great Britain by
CPI Antony Rowe, Chippenham and Eastbourne

# CONTENTS

# TABLES

# FIGURES

# ABOUT THE AUTHOR

Professor Brian Scott-Quinn is Chairman of the ICMA Centre for financial markets at Henley Business School, where he is Director of Banking and Strategy Programmes. He worked in the fields of investment banking, securities trading, asset management and stockbroking prior to founding the ICMA Centre in 1994 as a specialist university finance school. It is focused on securities markets and banking and is sponsored by the International Capital Markets Association (ICMA), which is the trade association and market regulator for some 400 banks, investment banks and asset managers active in the international capital market (www.icmagroup.org).

Originally a financial manager with Coats Viyella, the FTSE 100 multinational textile company, his career in the City of London started as a trainee with the merchant bank Hill Samuel. He then became a fixed income analyst with Kidder Peabody Securities Ltd. Along with three others he was a founder of Ross & Partners Securities Ltd – a privately owned international bond trading house. After negotiating the sale of Ross & Partners to Drexel Burnham Inc. he became finance director of Drexel Burnham Lambert Securities Ltd, responsible for funding and risk management. He then moved to Security Pacific Bank (now part of Bank of America Merrill Lynch), a Californian bank with an office in London. Initially a portfolio strategist he subsequently became strategy advisor to the Group CEO, working on issues relating to the commercial bank, the securities trading operation and the stockbroker Hoare Govett.

In 1994 he proposed to ICMA the concept of a business school devoted exclusively to issues related to the financial services industry. The board of ICMA agreed to allocate £3 million from their capital account for constructing a purpose-designed building to house the ICMA centre at the University of Reading, near London (in the *2012, Times Higher Education Student Experience Survey* 'league tables', Reading was ranked 12th in the UK). ICMA has since donated a further £5 million to the university which enabled the construction of a second facility that includes some 100 Thomson Reuters terminals with associated trading, valuation, risk management and asset management software. He was Director of the Centre from the time he founded it until 2006 when he took up the newly created post of Chairman. Today, the ICMA Centre is one of the largest university finance schools in Europe and is part of the triple-accredited (AMBA, EQUIS and AACSB) Henley Business School, the UK's oldest business school which is home to some 7,000 students from over 140 countries.

His main area of consulting and executive education is business unit and corporate strategy in the financial services industry, which will be the subject of his next book.[1] He has been a consultant to, amongst many others, Westpac Bank, NM Rothschild, Canada Life Insurance, Australian Mutual Provident (AMP), Investec Bank, Shuaa Capital (Dubai), the London Stock Exchange and SWX Europe (the Swiss exchange). He was a member of the Financial Services Authority (FSA) industry working group on Secondary Bond Market Transparency. He has been a consultant to the US Treasury and in 1978/79 he was a monetary policy advisor to Margaret Thatcher's first Chancellor of the Exchequer (finance minister), Lord Howe of Aberavon (Sir Geoffrey Howe). He is also a director of the holding company for LendLoanInvest.co.uk, a peer-to-peer social lending platform infrastructure provider.

He and his civil partner live in Notting Hill, London and also near Exeter in Devon. He welcomes suggestions for new content for the next edition of this book and his proposed new book. He can be contacted at bsq200@me.com

---

[1] *__Management of Complex Financial Institutions__: The Economics of, and Strategy Development in, Wholesale and Investment Banking, Asset Management, Insurance and Financial Infrastructure Companies'*

# PREFACE

In most areas of employment, professionals learn about their industry by starting with a text which gives a broad sweep of the whole industry and provides a guide as to how all the working parts fit together. They then advance to specialised texts. Finance, unfortunately, has become so focused on its various 'silos' that most people in the industry *start* by focusing on a specialised text relevant only to the narrow area they will be working in, without first developing an overall mind map of the industry, its functions, its inter-connections and its structure. They may learn the intellectual underpinnings of finance – EMH, CAPM, M&M, Black-Scholes, etc. – at university, but without gaining any real understanding of the limitations of models as nothing more than 'idealised' representations of the real world. They are also likely to have learned only about a world in which risk can be 'calculated' mathematically rather than about today's world of increasing uncertainty.[2]

In this new world, finance theory is less useful than it once was. Indeed, once rational expectations theory and the efficient market hypothesis have been mastered, the most valuable practical insight today may be to understand the circumstances in which these theories may lead to entirely wrong investment conclusions as a result of market failure and the consequent misallocation of resources. It is unlikely that at university many people would have covered the new world of developed market sovereign finance, which has moved into the difficult territory of structured finance, voluntary write-down and collective action clauses. Today even politicians need to try to understand these arcane concepts; thus I have written some chapters and case studies to give at least a flavour of the issues in this political/financial area.

I have focused on trying to fill a 'gap in the market' for a book on the industry as a whole and thereby to produce a text that combines the needs of both industry

---

[2] Frank Knight, in his key work *Risk, Uncertainty, and Profit* (1921) Boston, MA: Hart, Schaffner & Marx; Houghton Mifflin Company, established the distinction between risk and uncertainty: 'uncertainty must be taken in a sense radically distinct from the familiar notion of risk from which it has never been properly separated. It will appear that a measurable uncertainty or risk proper, as we shall use the term, is so far different from an unmeasurable one that it is not in effect an uncertainty at all'. Thus Knightian uncertainty is unmeasurable, i.e. it is not possible to calculate uncertainty, while risk is in principle measurable. The impact of the financial crisis and the eurozone sovereign debt crisis would both fall into the territory of uncertainty rather than risk. In such an environment, investors tend to shun all risky securities, which hence can be substantially mispriced.

professionals and those undertaking the study of finance at university. There should, of course, be no divorce between these two groups – professionals and students – who are indeed often one and the same but at different stages in their career. Their needs are similar in that both need an understanding of markets (credit and capital) of organisations (commercial and investment banks, asset managers, insurers and financial infrastructure providers) and of governance and regulation.

What I have tried to do in this text is to cover the three interrelated aspects of the business[3] of finance:

- *how markets should work*: competition and price discovery, but also *market failure*;
- *how organisations should work*: cooperation and integration within and between companies, but also *company (bank) failure*;
- *how governance should work*: the social, political, corporate governance, risk management and regulatory framework within which markets and organisations are permitted by society to function, and which are designed to ensure that markets and organisations function as they should, *but also the implications when they fail.*

Today we also have an additional issue: that of the governance of nation states and of the eurozone grouping of nation states not working as was intended and the impact of this failure feeding back to markets and banks. This destructive feedback loop between states and financial firms, particularly in the eurozone, is one of the key unresolved issues of our age and impacts all major countries including the US and China.

Professionals, in particular senior executives, regulators and parliamentarians with responsibility for the finance industry, need to understand not just particular job functions, products or markets but this complex industry as a whole. They need to think in terms of all three of the above aspects individually but equally in terms of their interrelationship. At the same time they need to understand the elements of specialised areas with which they are not conversant and in particular recent developments such as securitisation, synthetic ETFs, dark pools, algorithmic trading, peer-to-peer lending as well as more traditional areas such as risk management, private equity, M&A, IPOs and derivatives, all of which are covered in this text. Finally, as new regulations such as Basel III raise the cost of bank intermediated finance, I cover the disintermediation of credit intermediaries (banks), the consequence of which is an ever-increasing proportion of financing being provided through capital markets and also through the so-called shadow banking system.

---

[3] This is a modified version of the way in which the Dean of the Yale School of Management, Edward Snyder, sees the world of business in general, not specifically finance. He has been quoted as saying that business schools have taught the first two of these aspects very successfully but that the third is the real challenge.

This book is a guide for those industry professionals who are:

- about to move into a managerial role and, although well-established and successful in a single area of finance, understand that they will not succeed without a good understanding of the industry as a whole, new products and markets, regulatory pressures and issues relating to strategy development but also for;
- those who are just entering the industry, such as those on a graduate training programme, who need an industry-wide perspective plus an understanding of new developments, before focusing on their speciality.

It is also intended to assist students and their teachers:

- on an MBA programme, which may in the past have used traditional finance textbooks which ensure an understanding the EMH, CAPM, M&M and Black-Scholes but may not provide an understanding of how the industry works in practice, the limitations of financial models or issues related to governance;
- on an MSc in Finance programme which has a wide range of specialist theory courses, but which also requires an understanding of the practical application and limitations of that theory;
- in the final or penultimate year of a BSc business or management programme where students need to understand the finance industry as potential users of its services, rather than as potential employees in the financial services industry who also require highly specialist programmes.

Last, but by no means least, it is for those who have a *need to know*, such as lawyers and accountants who service this industry, regulators (and parliamentary committees) who oversee it and, importantly, financial services industry employees who are not in the 'front office' but in key functions such as financial control, product control, operations management, treasury, IT and compliance and who need to understand the industry, its products, the risks it creates and how to minimise them.

This is a 'modern' text in the sense that it covers all the major developments in markets in the period from the year 2000 – the year which seems to have been the starting point for many of the developments which led to the global financial, eurozone and US government debt crises – up to the start of 2012. But by the term 'modern' I also mean a contrast with the past when the credit and capital markets were treated separately in different texts, since authors frequently had experience of one side of the financing business but not the other. Hence we had texts on 'money and banking' and others on 'capital markets' but with the 'cross-over' areas of securitisation and shadow banking being omitted. Today it is important to see credit and capital markets in an integrated way which is manifest in the new organisational structure of some investment banks where lending and capital markets are both within the investment banking department.

In a book of this nature, chapters on regulation of firms and markets are as important as chapters on the firms and the markets themselves. I therefore have one chapter on regulation of firms and one on regulation of markets. The re-regulation of both areas following the financial crisis and the failure of existing regulation to avert it, has led amongst other things to what is known as Basel III, the Volcker Rule (the Dodd Frank Act), ring fencing of the UK's retail banks, regulations requiring the majority of derivatives transactions to be undertaken on exchange and cleared through a clearing house and may possibly lead even to taxes on financial trading in the EU. That regulation of risk taking is necessary (if the financial crisis alone was not sufficient to suggest this) is probably exemplified by the recent case[4] of the large loss ($2.2bn over just a few weeks and possibly a much higher loss by the time positions are unwound) in the unit of JP Morgan which was supposed to hedge the bank's exposures to risk (the Chief Investment Office). JP Morgan is believed by many to be the best managed bank in the United States with the best risk management systems yet at the time of writing; this loss suggests that risk management is still as much an art as a science and, worryingly, probably even less effective in many other banks than in JP Morgan.

A book of this nature can be no more than an introduction to the issues in today's financial markets. This is a dynamic industry and always in rapid flux. Any reader who really wants to understand it needs to ensure that they follow developments throughout their career. It is only by doing this that a person will stand out in the corporate environment as someone who understands the theory[5] but also has his or her ear 'close to the ground'. It is such people who are likely to be singled out for promotion or for a management role. The *Financial Times* (FT) has by far the best analytical articles of any newspaper and is, of course, also very up to date. For those who are unable to purchase paper copies, it is also available electronically worldwide and can be read easily on an iPad. You will notice many references to the FT in this book, and these represent some of the best insights into the issues in today's markets. The other publication is *The Economist*. This is a weekly publication which has an excellent finance section. It also publishes special reports on, amongst other areas, finance. It too is available electronically.

Today I would say that we are in The New Age of Uncertainty. This is a similar phrase to that used by one of the world's best-known economists, Professor John Kenneth Galbraith of Harvard University. *The Age of Uncertainty* is a 1977 book and also a television series, co-produced by the BBC. Galbraith acknowledges the successes of the market system but associates it with instability and social inequity. Today we once again have to face these same issues of financial and economic instability and social inequity but on a much greater scale than in 1977. But more specifically in the field of finance we are facing a world in which the financial models which have pervaded the mindset of bankers and regulators and governed decision-making for some 50 years, and in particular our framework for

---

[4] Reported in the press on 10/11 May 2012.

[5] I cover the necessary finance theory, though relatively briefly, in particular the rational expectations hypothesis and its cousin, the efficient market hypothesis (though I also cover market failure), the capital asset pricing model and its application in contributing to the reduction of the risk premium in new financing, and Modigliani and Miller's theory of capital structure and the issues it raises in relation to bank capital structure and moral hazard resulting from the 'too big to fail' doctrine. These theories are all essential to understanding finance, but as many readers will have already covered them I will *not* go into the depth that some specialised textbooks do.

risk management, no longer provide the certainty we once believed they gave us. We have shifted, as we noted earlier in this Preface, from a world of measurable risk to Knightian uncertainty.

Another major difference between this book and many others is that it has a fully global perspective rather than just covering the US markets with a brief nod to the existence of 'overseas' markets, as is still the case with many older texts. Clearly my own experience is European though; as I have worked for a number of US commercial and investment banks, I have a good understanding of their modus operandi. I have also taught Chinese, Korean, Thai and other Asian students at Henley Business School for many years and provided teaching and consulting services to investment banks and asset managers in Beijing, Shanghai, Shenzhen, Seoul, Taipei, Dubai and Riyadh which I hope has given me a more global perspective than many authors. Today there is a symbiosis between the Western world, which is short of savings and in particular of risk capital, and the Asian and Middle Eastern worlds, which have surplus savings and may be willing to act as 'patient investors' with a long-term horizon provided the expected return on such investments is commensurate with the risk involved. Their sovereign wealth funds are increasingly becoming the investors of last resort for equity-starved banks and other financial institutions. This symbiosis has become a key feature of the second decade of this century, but it also brings new risks to both sides.

**Parts I–III** cover the core of the banking/investment banking business and in particular capital allocation and liquidity creation through bank credit, shadow banking and primary and secondary capital markets. Collectively, these three sections are relatively self-contained. **Parts IV–VII**, which comprise the remainder of the text, are essentially on risk management, governance and control. Risk management covers managing risk in both investor portfolios and financial-sector firm balance sheets. Governance and control covers internal firm governance but also, and importantly, external control over the internal capital allocation process via the market in corporate control. This is the mergers and acquisitions market and, closely related to it, the private equity business with its unique governance and control structure. In the most regulated industry in the world an understanding of regulation is important and is a key aspect of governance and control. Finally I cover fundamental changes in the industry structure, ethos, ethics and performance which has been ongoing over the past quarter century but has been manifest most dramatically since the year 2000.

# ACKNOWLEDGEMENTS

My interest in the global financial system arose in the first instance from my experience of working in the international capital market in the 1980s and 1990s. I am particularly grateful to Emeritus Professor Sam Hayes, of Harvard Business School, who encouraged me, at that time, to write an earlier book on Investment Banking. Sam has also inspired me to write this one. One of my biggest supporters in this project has been John Langton, chief executive of the International Capital Market Association from 1991 to 2005. John was the driving force within ICMA in its efforts to improve its global education services for the international capital markets, including the creation of the ICMA Centre itself. The continuing support of ICMA under its subsequent leadership has allowed us to create a centre dedicated to financial markets within Henley Business School, which is second to none.

Those who have helped me in rethinking how credit and capital markets actually work, given what we have learned from market failures since 2007, are numerous. But I would particularly like to thank Tim Clarke, formerly a global financials analyst for his help throughout the creation of this book and in particular for his suggestions on structure. My thanks to Louis Trincano of Access Capital Partners, a private equity fund-of-funds, who reviewed the chapter on private equity, to Professor Charles Goodhart of LSE, who cleared up some important points for me in relation to bank credit – something that is ever more important these days for understanding how financial markets work, and to Con Keating, who gave me advice on issues relating to the meaning of liquidity. Mark Casson from the University of Reading has, as always, given me good advice in this project as has Konstantina Kappou, a new colleague at the ICMA Centre who has joined us after 10 years working in sales and trading in the City of London.

Most importantly, my partner Tony Stokoe, without whose support I could not have written this book, has been very patient with me and allowed me to spend more time in my office than is probably good for anyone.

# ABBREVIATIONS

| | |
|---|---|
| ABS | asset backed security |
| AFME | Association of Financial Markets in Europe |
| AIG | American Insurance Group |
| ALM | asset and liability management |
| AP | authorised participant |
| ATSs | alternative trading systems |
| BATS | Better Alternative Trading System (registered name of an exchange) |
| BCBS | Basel Committee on Banking Supervision |
| bp | basis point(s) |
| CAC | collective action clause |
| CAPM | capital asset pricing model |
| CBT | computer based trading |
| CCP | central counterparty |
| CDs | certificates of deposit |
| CDO | collateralised debt obligation |
| CDSs | credit default swaps |
| CSDs | domestic central securities depositories |
| DB | defined benefit |
| DC | defined contribution |
| DDM | dividend discount model |
| DMA | direct market access |
| ECB | European Central Bank |
| ECNs | electronic communication networks |
| EMH | efficient market hypothesis |
| ESM | European Stability Mechanism |
| ETFs | exchange traded funds |
| FICC | fixed income, currency and commodities |
| FSA | Financial Services Authority |
| GLBA | Gramm–Leach–Bliley Act |
| HBOS | Halifax Bank of Scotland |
| HFT | high-frequency trading |
| ICMA | International Capital Markets Association |
| ICSDs | international central securities depositories |
| IDB | interdealer-broker |
| IIF | Institute of International Finance |
| IMF | International Monetary Fund |

| | |
|---|---|
| IPMA | International Primary Market Association |
| IPO | initial public offering |
| ISD | Investment Services Directive |
| ISMA | International Securities Market Association (renamed ICMA) |
| LBOs | leveraged buy outs |
| LGD | loss given default |
| LIBOR | London Inter Bank Offer Rate |
| LIFFE | London International Financial Futures Exchange |
| LOLR | lender of last resort |
| LSE | London Stock Exchange |
| M&A | mergers and acquisitions |
| M&M | Modigliani and Miller hypothesis |
| MiFID | Markets in Financial Instruments Directive |
| MMMFs | money market mutual funds |
| MTFs | multilateral trading facilities |
| MTM | mark-to-market |
| NAV | net asset value |
| NBBO | national best bid and offer |
| NMS | National Market System |
| NPV | net present value |
| NRSRO | Nationally Recognized Statistical Rating Organizations |
| NYSE | New York Stock Exchange |
| OMS | order management system |
| OTC | over-the-counter |
| OTF | organised trading facility |
| P&I | principal and income; principal and interest |
| PD | probability of default |
| PE | private equity |
| QE | quantitative easing |
| RMs | relationship managers |
| ROE | return on equity |
| SEAQ | Stock Exchange Automated Quotation (LSE) |
| SEC | Securities and Exchange Commission |
| SEF | swap execution facilities |
| SETS | Stock Exchange Electronic Trading System (LSE) |
| SIFI | systemically important financial institution |
| SIVs | securitised investment vehicles |
| SMEs | small and medium sized enterprises |
| SPV | special purpose vehicle |
| SSS | securities settlement system |
| SWFs | sovereign wealth funds |
| UCITS | undertakings for collective investments in transferable securities |
| VAR | value at risk |

# THE FUNDAMENTALS OF FINANCE, MARKETS, VALUATION AND FINANCIAL FIRMS

**PART**

# 1 THE PRICE MECHANISM AND THE THREE PILLARS OF FINANCE

## WHAT IS FINANCE?

If the 'man in the street' were asked 'What is finance?', some of the possible answers might be: 'It's to do with money'; 'It's about getting a mortgage'; 'It's what banks do'; 'It's about saving for retirement'. All of these answers would be correct. But what they all omit is two important words: **risk** and **price** . Finance is about assessing risk, pricing it and then transferring it through credit and capital markets. A new issue of shares, for example, is about pricing the riskiness of the company concerned and then transferring that risk to new investors through the capital markets. If that company subsequently goes to a bank to raise a loan for expansion, the bank manager's job is to assess the risk of a loan to that particular company, price that risk as an interest rate to be charged and then transfer that risk on to the bank's own balance sheet.

## THE LIFECYCLE VIEW OF FINANCE

A more intuitive, and personal, understanding of the role of the finance industry would have as its starting point the **human economic lifecycle**. This starts with the observation that people's income is highly variable during their lifetime. In the early years of adulthood, students (or their parents) will have to find a means to finance their education at a time when their income is small or zero. Once employed their income would, in least in previous generations, increase year by year. But their income will fall to zero or close to zero if they lose their employment, if they are ill for a long period and, with certainty, when they retire from employment. If income falls short of essential spending on food and accommodation, an individual has a problem. To overcome this potential problem, people build up a 'cushion' of wealth by spending below their income when times are good, i.e. by **saving**. The greatest need for saving is to finance consumption in retirement a period when it is known, well in advance, that there will be no, or little, income generation. Saving for retirement involves regular month-by-month saving throughout working life in order to build up a large cash sum often known as a 'pension pot'.

It is these cushions of wealth that individuals build up which provide the raw material for the whole finance industry. They are built up, i.e. **accumulated**, during times when income exceeds spending and **decumulated** during periods when income falls short of day-to-day expenditure. We call this saving and dis-saving the **intertemporal transfer** of spending power, which simply means moving spending power backwards or forwards in time. Thus the finance industry enables each individual or household in the economy to **store surplus income as capital** during good times and **convert capital back into income**, i.e. 'releasing' it again, during bad times. In aggregate across all individuals in a country, it is the **pooling** of these relatively small cushions of wealth into large sums which finances industrial expansion, i.e. provides large capital sums for investment, which in turn should enable the growth of GDP and full employment in a modern economy. . Saving by one sector of the population also enables other sectors of the population to borrow against their future expected income for purposes such as financing a house purchase – another key role of the finance industry.

The cohort of the population that tends to save most consists of those from age 40 and above up to the point of retirement. The group that tends to borrow most on credit cards, loans for purchasing a motor-car and a mortgage for a house purchase is the younger age group. Thus the inter-temporal transfer process is also an inter-generational one.

## AN INFLUENTIAL POLITICIAN'S VIEW OF FINANCE

The following may not be a definition of finance but it is a clear indication of what one very senior politician in Europe, Germany's finance minister Wolfgang Schäuble, thinks the function of the finance industry should be and also what it should not be. It probably reflects the thoughts of many other politicians as well as many voters. As the banking industry can only exist within the framework of a 'social contract' with society, what he says is likely to become a key battleground between the finance industry and democratically elected governments, not only in the eurozone but also in the US, the UK and many other countries:

> I believe it is in the interest of the financial sector itself that it should concentrate more on its *proper role of financing the real economy* and ensuring that *capital is allocated in the most intelligent way*, instead of banks conducting the bulk of their trading on their own account.[1]

What is very clear from this statement is the potential conflict that society and politicians see between the role of the financial sector in **facilitating economic growth and full employment through the provision of finance** and the **trading activities** undertaken within this sector. This conflict, which is a fundamental issue covered in this text, has risen to the top of the political/regulatory agenda and has led, amongst other things, to proposals from the European Union for a tax on trading activities. This would be designed to reduce trading activity as well as to raise substantial tax revenue.

---

[1] *Financial Times*, 31 October 2011. This statement was issued just prior to the G20 summit in November 2011 to be held in Cannes, France (author's italics and emboldenment).

## A VIEW FROM ANCIENT EGYPT

At the level of **saving by a country rather than by an individual**, a good example comes from ancient Egypt. Pharaoh (the king of Egypt) asked Joseph to interpret a dream about seven fat and seven thin cattle, and seven fat and seven thin ears of grain. Joseph interpreted the dream as a warning to make preparations for seven years of hardship and to act pre-emptively during the seven years of plenty by filling the granaries (saving) so that people would not starve when crops failed and famine hit. He therefore advised Pharaoh to store surplus grain during the years of abundance. As economies may also follow seven-year business cycles, such advice would also be relevant to modern times. It is in fact the basis of what is known as counter-cyclical fiscal policy and also macroprudential financial regulatory policy.

Had Pharaoh not taken Joseph's advice, and thus had the country not been able to feed itself, Pharaoh would have had to visit a neighbouring country and ask its leader if he could help by lending grain until the harvest improved. In return, he would have promised to repay more grain than had been 'borrowed'. Today, of course, if a country has not been prudent in its spending and has overspent its income, the same appeal to other countries is made but via the international capital markets. Thus, for example, the US has borrowed massively from China through the first decade of this millennium to make up for its own negligible savings rate. Within the eurozone, Germany, which has high savings relative to its investment in productive capacity, lent substantial sums to other eurozone countries, such as Greece, Spain and Italy, by way of its banks providing loans to customers in these other countries where, on balance, the population spends more than it earns and saves less than is required to finance industry. At some point lenders may take fright when they believe that a country to which they have lent will not be able to service its debts. At this point, we have crises like those from which the eurozone has been suffering since 2010.

## FINANCE AS A SCIENTIFIC PROFESSIONAL TOOL

As we are studying **finance as a professional discipline**, we also need a more scientific definition than those given above. A possible definition is:

- Finance is the science of money. It is the scientific discipline that enables us to study, in a rational way, **how to allocate scarce resources** in society. This allocation problem – how best to use labour, capital, raw materials, intellectual property rights and other scarce resources – is key to ensuring the highest level of output, the highest rate of economic growth and the highest levels of employment.
- The finance discipline covers the financing of companies (corporate finance), the financing of government expenditure (public finance), the provision of mortgage finance, pension provision, etc. (household finance), and the financing of payments imbalances between countries (international finance) through the intermediation of the credit and capital markets. While the mechanical processes of finance involve the transfer of investor cash to companies, governments, households and countries, in the other direction they involve the transfer to

investors of economic risk after a process of risk assessment and risk pricing in the credit and capital markets.

In a market economy, the allocation of **consumption goods** – food, clothes, iPhones etc. – is achieved through the price mechanism. Everything we buy has a price which rises (and may fall) over time to ration it so that supply always equals demand. The price mechanism also operates in the credit and capital markets to ration capital (savings) to be allocated to:

- **Companies** wishing to buy **investment goods** such as machinery, offices, factories, patents, etc. by investors trying to confirm in advance that the company can pay interest and dividends and repay loans from the surplus between sales and costs;
- **Households** wishing to purchase a home by only lending to those believed to have the ability to **service** their loan, i.e. to pay interest and repay the loan;
- **Governments** wishing undertake higher current and capital expenditures than they are willing to try to raise from citizens through taxation.

**The interest rate is the most important rationing mechanism in an economy and operates through the PRICE of credit.** The starting point for the price of credit is that set by the central bank of a country, which is a short-term rate and which may be called *base rate (UK), repo rate(EU) or, in the case of the US, the Fed Funds rate*. From this rate, **all other interest rates are determined by market forces not by the central bank or the government**. The banker, financier or investor has to estimate, and then price, uncertain (risky) future expected cash flows. The rate which he or she determines as appropriate for this purpose will vary as the central bank rate varies. The central bank rate is, therefore, a key determinant of the demand for credit, hence the amount of real investment in the economy and in consequence the growth rate of the economy. Changes in the central bank rate are also the main instrument used by the central bank to try to manage the inflation rate through the impact of interest rates on levels of demand and on the exchange rate. From our point of view, the key importance of interest rates is that these are what determine asset prices – and **asset prices are what finance is mainly about**. Asset prices include those of securities trading in equity markets and bond markets and of real assets such as residential property.

## THE MARKET PRICE AS THE MEANS OF ALLOCATING RESOURCES IN SOCIETY

In finance, **price is the key to almost everything**. For this reason, in a book on investment banking, bank credit, shadow banking and capital markets, we need to examine the **price mechanism** and how it operates through markets – not just financial markets, but markets in a wider sense.

The price mechanism operates in three different types of market, all of which are related:

- Markets in goods and services;

- Labour markets;
- Financial markets (credit, securities and derivative contracts).

Adam Smith[2] was the first to consider the problem of how the production of goods and services is coordinated so that the 'correct' amount of each is produced (markets in goods and services) and that all of those who want to work can obtain employment (labour markets). Smith believed that the market system ensured that prices moved towards their 'natural' level and would thereby direct human and physical resources to where they were most needed. There was an automatic correction mechanism. If a shortage developed, the price of finished goods would rise and supply would expand as producers attracted more resources (labour and materials) to the production of their particular goods by raising the price offered for these resources. Conversely, if demand fell, the producer would reduce the wages he offered and bid less for (physical) resources and thus both labour and resources would move out of producing his particular goods and move to the production of those where final-market prices were higher. Such a system would be self-equilibrating and resources would thus always be employed fully because prices adjust to changes in supply and demand for resources.

You may notice that no reference is made in this paragraph to financial markets. This is because many people, economists and also the man in the street, have assumed that the financial system and the markets of which it is comprised, are merely a 'veil' covering the 'real' economy. They take the view that a country's output of goods and services is determined by its state of technical knowledge and its access to natural resources. It is somewhat surprising that this has been such a common view since it is also widely acknowledged that economic development is a process of capital accumulation.

Long-term capital enables:

**capital widening** which is financing to enable the employment of a growing labour force and

**capital deepening** which involves additional capital being available to each employee, thereby increasing the capital available to each employee and hence (hopefully) productivity.

In addition, the provision of **venture capital** is critical in ensuring that new ideas can be developed into saleable products or services. Thus economic development depends on financial markets – credit and capital – to allocate investment capital amongst competing projects.

In the first decade of the new millennium, there has been considerable evidence that the credit and capital markets have not, in practice, allocated capital in the most appropriate way. In addition, the cost of running the 'capital allocation machinery',

---

[2] Adam Smith was the world's first economist. He was a great thinker and published the first analysis of the functioning of the market economy when he was a professor of philosophy at the University of Glasgow. His most famous book, *An Inquiry into the Nature and Causes of the Wealth of Nations*, was published in 1776, the same year as the American Declaration of Independence.

i.e. the cost of the whole financial system, would seem to have increased substantially over this period. The Turner Review,[3] for example, gives a figure for value added (percentage of GDP) of monetary and other financial institutions of just 3.5% in the year 2000 but increasing to almost 6% by 2007. That suggests that the industry became less efficient in its role of intermediation even if we allow for some of the increase involving exported financial services or increased demand for financial intermediation by households. It also reflects, of course, the massive increase in remuneration (including bonuses) over this period paid out to many of those employed in this industry. These issues of 'appropriate' capital allocation and the cost of the mechanisms which enable this allocation are discussed further in Chapter 15 on Market Failure and in Chapter 28 on the Future Structure of the Industry.

A number of economists since the time of Adam Smith have developed what is known as **general equilibrium theory** which posits that competitive markets are efficient and ensure that companies produce the things that people want in the right quantities and at the lowest cost. General equilibrium theory would also posit that any unemployment in an economy must be voluntary since labour is sold in a market and if there is an excess supply this can be overcome by people simply offering their labour for a lower price. We will not enter into discussion of this proposition except to note that throughout Europe and the US in 2012, unemployment is much higher than in many past periods and those who are unemployed would be very unlikely to claim that it was voluntary! We call this market failure – resources of labour which are available are not being utilised to maximise output of goods and services.

When we 'lift the veil' covering the 'real' markets we can look at the issues raised by possible mispricing in the credit and capital markets. When we analyse such pricing what we are in fact pricing is two things:

• The willingness of people to delay gratification today in return for possibly greater gratification in the future (the so-called **time value of money**).
• The risk involved in delaying gratification which is a function of the risk of the underlying investments that people are undertaking and which is measured as the **risk premium** in excess of the time value of money. One risk investors take is that, by deferring consumption, they will have less to consume in the future rather than more (as a result of their investments losing value).

Friedrich Hayek, an Austrian economist wrote in his book *The Use of Knowledge in Society* that 'we must look at the price system as … a **mechanism for communicating information** if we want to understand its real function'. In making their investment decisions, individuals generally have in their mind some model of the financial asset **price determination process** – for example a model of what determines share market prices. The hypothesis to which many market participants and many market regulators adhere – one might call it their mindset – is known as the **efficient market hypothesis (EMH)**. This asserts that financial markets are, in general, **informationally efficient**. This means that prices change instantaneously

---

[3] The Turner Review was a regulatory response to the global banking crisis, published in March 2009 by the FSA.

to reflect new and relevant information. This is an example of Hayek's view of the price mechanism – that it transmits information.

We call this process of price adjusting to new information the **impounding of information**; and if the EMH is correct then not only does the price change to reflect the impact of the new information on the asset's future expected cash flows and risk but it happens almost instantly. In consequence, an investor cannot, on a consistent basis, achieve returns in excess of the market return for a financial asset with this level of risk. Another way of putting this is that financial assets are always correctly priced or, to use a common expression in finance, **there is no free lunch**. This means that there is nothing for nothing in this world – no possibility of expected returns above those appropriate for the level of risk. Despite this belief, however, it can be observed that investors still commit substantial resources to trying to 'beat the market', which suggests that they do not believe the hypothesis to be true, at least for them. Logically, analysts in the City of London and so-called active investors must believe that the EMH is false.

Above, we used the expression '**always correctly priced**'. However, this can mean two things:

- It may mean that every financial asset is correctly priced **relative** to other financial assets, such as Google shares relative to Intel shares;
- It may also mean correctly priced in relation to **fundamentals**, which means expected future cash flows from the asset and the risk of them not materialising.

In Chapter 15 on **market failure** we will consider in some detail whether credit and capital markets do in fact seem to misprice financial asset classes in terms of fundamentals, leading to the mispricing of whole asset classes such as housing, the stock market, structured assets and peripheral eurozone debt. Such mispricings, when market prices rise beyond what a scientific valuation based on fundamentals would suggest to be appropriate, are known as **bubbles**. Under the assumptions of the EMH such mispricings should not happen.

The reason why it is important that we know if markets are informationally efficient in **both** the above senses is that if markets always price asset classes correctly, for example equity shares as a whole (not just one equity relative to another) based on fundamentals, then we may assume that the resulting set of prices will also result in **allocative efficiency**. This type of efficiency means that the credit and capital markets will allocate capital (savings) to their most productive use and thus, other things being equal, the output of the economy and household utility will be maximised. Allocative efficiency implies that the price of an asset accurately reflects the (appropriately risk-adjusted) discounted stream of future earnings that it is expected to yield over its lifetime.[4] Thus even if markets are informationally efficient, if they fail to satisfy the allocative efficiency condition, then resource allocation decisions (such as residential construction prior to the house price collapse in the US or spending by some peripheral eurozone governments prior to 2010)) can result in significant economic inefficiencies. There is evidence that the risk adjustment to the discount rate that has been undertaken on

---

[4] I cover the concept of discounting and risk adjusted discount rates, below.

the pricing of a number of asset classes in, for example, US housing, US mortgage debt and peripheral eurozone sovereign debt, has not been appropriate for the risks that could have been foreseen. These risks were, in all cases, foreseen by a not-insignificant number of key analysts in central banks and research institutes. However, their views were not incorporated into market pricing. When times seem good, nobody wants to hear bad news!

## NON-MARKET ALLOCATION MECHANISMS

An alternative means of rationing goods and services and deciding on the allocation of capital is through bureaucratic decisions such as those that were made by state bureaucrats in societies operating under communist principles. In such societies, Karl Marx said that the rule for allocation should be '**From each according to his ability, to each according to his needs**'. This clearly requires a bureaucratic system to assess such needs and allocate goods and services (motor car and iPhone allocation, for example) on the basis of this assessment. It also then requires the necessary investment in industry, yet without a mechanism to suggest what goods and services industry should be producing. In addition to questions about the efficacy of such an allocation process there also arose the difficulty of motivating people to be more productive if the financial benefits of working to the maximum of one's ability did not, in large part, flow to the person putting in the effort. Thus fairness was by no means guaranteed. In states with such allocation mechanisms there is little incentive to innovate or work hard.

Until the late 1950s, China had a system of resource allocation based on central planning. But in 1957, Hsueh Mu-chiao, who was then chairman of the State Statistical Bureau, advocated that central economic agencies should retain planning responsibility for only a few areas, mainly macroeconomic, and that other decision-making on resource allocation should be decentralised. Apart from a few key products, production planning for all other products, he said, should be determined by individual enterprises according to supply and demand. Decentralisation of decisions on resource allocation and rationing by price, based on supply and demand, is a key feature of capitalist economies. In China this early step towards a greater use of the **pricing mechanism** as distinct from central bureaucratic fiat was an important one in starting the process which transformed the country's' economy. However, it was not until after Chairman Mao's death, when Deng Xiaoping took over the leadership of the country, that economic reform moved ahead rapidly. His leadership led to ongoing reforms which have resulted in a dramatic increase in China's GDP

In China, until quite recently, housing was allocated by the state, not through the market system. In an analysis of the Chinese property market[5] the author notes:

> Before 1998, China did not have a residential real estate market to speak of and there was no need for such exotic financial products (mortgages). In urban areas all housing was built and allocated by the state through the ubiquitous 'work unit'.

---

[5]  Jamil Anderlini, 'A Lofty Ceiling Reached', *Financial Times*, 14 December 2011.

Even today, however, the People's Republic of China is not a pure capitalist economy. There remains much direction of credit and capital from the centre. Even the major banks in China, while they have quotations on the stock market, remain subject to a considerable degree of direction from the state as it remains a majority shareholder.

## OPTIMAL ALLOCATION OF RESOURCES OVER TIME IN AN UNCERTAIN ENVIRONMENT

The word 'resources' in the expression '**optimal allocation of resources**' generally means real resources – labour, raw materials, finished goods and services, etc. But prior to this stage in the resource allocation process, the finance field is concerned with the optimal allocation of savings, i.e. cash, from those who save to those who can make a good case that they can use the savings in an 'appropriate' way. The finance process is about ensuring that only those who can make the 'best' economic use of the real resources that cash can buy are allocated savings belonging to others to enable them to acquire such resources. A company, for example, has to be able to demonstrate that it will make good use of the financial resources provided by investors; and thus one of the functions of the 'scientific' financial system is to provide a means of deciding what is a 'good' or 'appropriate' use.

A good example of effective resource allocation would be the start-up of the Apple Corporation by Steve Jobs. He was able to create what is now a large and successful company by persuading others to provide the cash necessary to expand it from its origins in the 1970s as nothing more than a 'clever idea' he developed at home to becoming the world's most valuable company. The individuals who provided the initial financing must have believed that parting with their cash by investing in Apple could generate an acceptable return to reward them for giving up spending power now (time value of money) **and to compensate them for the risk** they were taking. The first 50 Apple 1s were built in Job's parents' spare bedroom. Just a few months later Apple moved upscale – to Job's parents' garage!

There were two types of resource allocation in the process of Jobs scaling up his 'brainy idea' into something that could become a real company. One involved investors allocating their scarce savings to provide the cash needed to buy shares issued by Apple. The other was the use of the cash realised from the sale of shares for the purchase of real assets and the payment of wages by the company. However, these two types of allocation must be linked. Investors will only allocate their savings if they know what these resources will be used for and if they believe that they will generate a satisfactory return, given the risks involved. Thus there are two stages in the investment process.

### Financial investment

In the first stage, households allocate their spare financial resources (savings) to **financial** assets such as buying shares in Job's start-up venture. A financial asset is simply a **contract** in the form of a document – the **prospectus** – issued at the time of a new share issue (an initial public offering of shares generally known as an IPO) or at the time of a bond issue (a debt contract). The contract agrees the transfer of household cash directly to companies in exchange for shares or bonds at prices based on the future cash flows that the real assets are expected to generate and the risk of these case flows not materialising.

However, households will only transfer resources through share or bond purchases if the information provided in a prospectus convinces them that the company will make 'good' use of the resources. Thus the company has to lay out a business plan detailing the use to which the proceeds of the financing will be put, i.e. the real assets to be purchased, the output expected from the use of these real assets, the number of units expected to be sold and their expected price. From this it is possible to estimate **future cash flows**. There then needs to be a **scientific means of evaluating** whether this is a 'good' use of resources which will also involve trying to assess the degree of certainty that we can have that these cash flows will actually materialise. I cover methods of analysis under 'the three pillars', below.

### Real investment

In the second stage, companies allocate the cash raised from investors to purchasing scarce **real** resources, i.e. investment goods such as factories, power stations, machinery, research and development, as well as hiring labour on the basis of the business plan which they put to investors. As decisions on real investment are simply the counterpart to decisions on financial investment, methods of analysis are also covered under 'the three pillars', below.

## TIME SHIFTING OF CONSUMPTION

While finance is widely taught as being principally about how to finance new investment in industry (as in our Apple example above) it is also, and very importantly, about **changing a household's consumption pattern relative to its pattern of income earning**. Optimal resource allocation over time for a household may involve the time shifting of consumption, i.e. changing an individual or household's allocation of consumption resources over a lifetime by borrowing and investing. For households, therefore, **optimal resource allocation over time** means **maximising household utility** over time, i.e. achieving the greatest satisfaction from income over a lifetime through borrowing and lending/investing. This may mean, as we noted earlier, borrowing when young and when income is low in order to have more to spend on holidays, a motor car, housing, etc. and paying the price of consequently having a lower proportion of a (higher) income to spend in mid-life due to interest payments and capital repayments. It also means increasing saving in mid-life in order to have an income in retirement from investments.

## RISK BEARING

In addition to considerations of consumption, different people have different attitudes to risk bearing and therefore to the question of how much of society's risk they are willing to absorb by, for example, buying risky shares. Thus, in addition to enabling an optimal allocation of financial resources (cash), finance is also about the optimal distribution of **society's economic risks** away from those who do not want to bear them to those who have some comparative advantage in bearing them in exchange for an appropriate expected rate of return to compensate for risk bearing. Undertaking the pricing of risk, i.e. determining the price at which risky shares, bonds, companies, etc. should be bought and sold, is a key activity of people working in the finance industry. Those who buy shares or bonds are taking on society's economic risks so others do not need to bear them. The major economic risks manifest themselves as credit risk, equity risk, currency risk, interest rate risk and commodity price risk.

A problem to which I allude in the text is the increasing unwillingness of Western financial institutions and individuals to bear all the equity risk necessary to finance the hoped-for rate of economic growth in the West. In consequence, the equity risk of Western economies is being increasingly borne by financial institutions and individuals in Asian and OPEC countries.

## THE THREE PILLARS: THE SCIENTIFIC TOOLS OF FINANCE[6]

Finance has become a scientific discipline since academic finance research began in the United States in the 1950s. This has resulted in finance changing from being a field where there was no 'scientific' way of making evaluations to one where scientific evaluation is central to the whole business. There are three essential elements to this science. The three pillars are: first, a means to **optimise over time**, i.e. to analyse the trade-off between having money now and having more in the future; second, a means of **measuring and managing risk**; and third, based on these first two, a means of **valuing financial assets**, i.e. pricing shares and bonds, which has the role of effecting the allocation of scarce resources in society and effecting the trade-off between having money to spend now or having more to spend in the future.

### Pillar 1: optimisation over time; the time value of money; discounting and compounding

The key financial decision that has to be made by decision-makers in firms is whether spending money now on something which will only bring benefits in the future is justified by the expected future benefits. If they are spending money on, for example, an expansion in productive capacity, their hope is that they can sell the additional output in the future at a price which will reward appropriately those who financed the company.

The same type of decision-making process is also used by individuals, as in the example below. But for individuals, as well as having to make decisions on investment (buying a house or investing in education), they also have the possibility of **consumption shifting decisions** – borrowing to consume now in exchange for paying interest and repaying a loan in the future and therefore having less

---

[6] This is the approach taken by Merton and Bodie in *Finance* (Prentice Hall, 1998).

consumption in the future. This is something companies do not do as they do not consume. Governments also have this option of bringing consumption spending forward. Government borrowing represents a decision to finance expenditure, perhaps on unemployment benefits or health care, not from taxes raised from today's taxpayers but from future taxpayers. It is thus what is known as **inter-generational transfer**.

## Example: an individual's investment in his or her own human capital

An example of an investment decision that an individual has to make is one where someone who is 21 years old and has completed a bachelor degree is considering whether or not to take a second degree, perhaps an MSc in Finance. The course fee is, say, £18,000. The additional cost of accommodation and food for a year compared with living with parents is, say, £6,000. As an alternative to undertaking the MSc, the person could choose to take a job immediately after his or her first degree with a salary of £21,000. Thus the **cash cost** of undertaking the degree programme for one year is £24,000 plus an **opportunity cost**, i.e. income fore-gone, of £21,000, giving a total investment in the project (obtaining an MSc) of £45,000. If money is borrowed to finance the programme, then there is also an explicit interest cost to be considered. If the money does not need to be borrowed and is already available, then the alternative would have been to invest it in a bank deposit or in the stock market. There is thus an **opportunity cost**, i.e. a potential return that is lost, to be added here also.

To make that investment worthwhile, the investor has to estimate the increase in future earnings that this investment in **human capital** will bring and over what period those additional earnings will accrue. If, for example, the higher earnings did not accrue until the person was very senior, perhaps not until he or she was over 50 years old, this would be very different from a situation where the higher income commenced immediately after graduation – **timing of cash flows is very important**.

The decision on whether or not to undertake the degree and other decisions of this type involving future cash flows and time can be aided by taking account of the **time value of money**. This simply means that money today is more valu-able than the same amount at a future date. Mainly this is because money can earn interest or, looking at it the other way, we can obtain money now (spending power) if we are willing to pay interest on that money in the future. In effect, a loan is a way of buying **liquidity** now, i.e. spending power for which the price we pay is the interest cost for each year the loan is outstanding and the loss of spending power sometime in the future when we have to repay the loan. But equally the time value of money enters the equation since most people would prefer to benefit from a higher income immediately, rather than have to wait until they are 50 years old for the higher salary to be paid.

## Example: corporate finance, a capital budgeting decision by managers

Companies have to make decisions on what projects to invest in. A mobile phone company, for example, might have more demand for existing phones than its maximum output but may also want to develop new phones, for example a smartphone. It thus has *two* investment opportunities – to lay out money now for a capacity expansion or alternatively for a new product (or, in an ideal world, both). The **capital budgeting department** has to estimate the investment cost involved in each and the likely revenues to be generated each year until the project comes to an end. On the basis of these projections of future cash flows they can then discount them to a present value. The discount rate that will be used is the firm's **cost of capital** which is normally taken to be a weighted average of the cost of equity and debt and which reflects how risky the firm is. A good example of such investment decisions can be seen in the case of Nokia, once the world's largest mobile (cell) phone maker. It invested heavily in developing a 'smartphone' to compete with the Apple iPhone. Despite a very large investment, it did not succeed and, believing that the project would not generate the required return for its investors, abandoned it in 2011 in favour of buying in technology from Microsoft.

Another case study of a different manufacturer of mobile phones is LG Electronics, the world's third-largest handset maker by sales, which planned to raise about 1,000 billion won ($892 million) in a rights issue to help turn round its troubled smartphone business:

> 'The stock sale is aimed at securing financing for investment in our core businesses. We plan to revive our global competitiveness in key areas such as smartphones through steady investment,' the company said. Although its cross-town rival Samsung Electronics has caught up fast in the high-margin smartphone segment to become the world's largest smartphone manufacturer, LG remains a marginal player in the competitive market. LG did well with so-called feature phones before Apple shook the market with the iPhone. But it has fallen behind in recent years as it misread the mobile market and is still suffering from its late arrival. 'Investors are concerned more about its fundamental competitiveness, rather than its short-term cash flow,' said Choi Nam-gon, analyst at Tongyang Investment Bank. 'And the stock sale plan has sparked fears that its handset business may be in worse shape than they thought.' The announcement sent shares in the company down 13.7%.[7]

Clearly the above case suggests that investors (one side of the savings/investment symbiosis) do not have confidence in management's resource allocation decision (the other side of the symbiosis). Allocating a huge amount of financial resource to revive LG's global competitiveness in a highly competitive business sector must be thought by investors to be inappropriate given the share price fall on its announcement. 'Inappropriate' means unlikely to generate investors' required rate of return and hence be likely to reduce what is known as **shareholder value**. Capital market pricing should prevent such misallocation of real resources. In this case the company seems to be going ahead even though investors clearly do not think it is in their interest as the owners of the company.

---

[7] Song Jung-a, 'LG Eyes Rights Issue for Smartphone Turnaround', *Financial Times*, 3 November 2011.

### Capital budgeting

Investment decision-making in a company, such as investing in developing a new phone to try to compete with Apple, should be undertaken using a **capital budgeting** process. This involves calculating the **net present value (NPV)** of a project. This is an amount calculated by deducting the present value[8] (which means allowing for the timing of cash flows) of the real investment (outflow) from the present value of all future cash (inflows) generated by the project. To **maximise shareholder value or wealth**, the investment decision-making criterion would be to accept all projects which generate a **positive net present value**, which means that the project would increase **shareholder value** (note that the word 'net' means the present value of future cash inflows minus the present value of cash outflows). This means that such projects should increase the value of the company's shares. If two projects have a positive NPV but the company does not have sufficient internal resource (retained profit) to finance both, then, other things being equal, it should raise additional funds on the primary capital market or from a bank.

Making corporate finance decisions, such as whether to invest in the design and manufacture of a new type of cell phone or financial investment decision on how much to put aside to provide a secure income in retirement, involves discounting (bringing to a present value) and compounding (to a future value), respectively. An obvious question, however, is what rate of discount should be used. In essence this is asking, first, what is the **pure time value of money** (i.e. the cost of money for a particular period of time if there were no risk at all of it not being repaid) and, second, what is the **risk premium** (i.e. the extra return in excess of the **pure time value of money**, necessary to persuade investors to take on any particular risk). The pure time value of money is generally taken to be the yield on government bonds for the period in question. The reason for this is that government bonds, at least those of developed countries, have in the past been assumed to be risk free. We now know of course, since the eurozone crisis, that this is no longer true. For the eurozone, we would instead take the yield on German government bonds (bunds) as the risk free rate of interest. We then need to add to this the additional amount of return that investors require to compensate them for the risk of the particular financial assets they are considering buying, which we call the risk spread.

**Pricing risk** to assess the appropriate risk spread is the key function in finance, and from that comes the ability to price shares, bonds, loans, insurance policies, options, corporate acquisitions, etc. In the financial intermediation industry, pricing is everything – indeed it is what most of the industry is about. Get the price right (for the risk involved) and you make money. Get the price wrong and you lose your job! If prices are very wrong, they may cause global financial instability such as we have seen since 2007.

### Pillar 2: risk management

Risk is the **possibility of unexpected outcomes**. In finance, risk is generally measured as variability of return, i.e. the likelihood that the **actual return** on an

---

[8] See a textbook for more on present values, discounting and capital budgeting.

asset will be *either* higher or lower than the **expected return**. The expected return will generally be estimated by taking historical returns on the asset as a starting point. Uncertainty as to the actual return that will be generated is known as **variance**. The wider the range around the expected value of cash flows or prices that are expected, the riskier is a project, an investment or a portfolio.

### How do different people view risk?

Return is good; risk is bad in the sense that it raises the possibility of doing much worse than expected and indeed of losing everything. But generally we expect that the higher the estimate of risk on an investment, the higher will be its expected return. Risk management can be defined as a method of identifying risks, measuring and assessing them, formulating the cost–benefit trade-off from risk reduction and deciding on what actions to take. These actions in turn depend on individual attitude to risk, which is known as the degree of **risk aversion** of an individual or a company. This is a measure of how willing someone is to pay to reduce their exposure to risk (for example by taking out insurance versus remaining uninsured).

For risk-averse individuals and households, some form of risk management may raise their utility by reducing the uncertainty of future income and hence consumption. Thus risk management techniques and products available to households, including insurance, can increase overall welfare.

Given that investing now for expected future returns is risky, the second pillar of finance is a set of methodologies for controlling the risk to which an individual, household, firm, government or financial institution is subject as a result of holding financial assets. This may involve, for example, **portfolio diversification** as employed by asset managers as well as self-directed investors, **insurance** against risk involving a payment to someone else to take on a particular risk, or the **hedging** of the risk by offsetting it in some way. The financial services industry can help individuals and companies with assessing and managing risk.

While financing is often thought of as the transfer of cash between investors and firms, in fact it can equally and often more usefully be thought of as the transfer of risk. Investors want to take on the various risks that exist in society because **society rewards risk taking** and they wish to participate in that risk/reward system. But as risk means the possibility of loss, risk management to minimise the possibility of **catastrophic loss (such as could result from investing all one's wealth in a single company which goes into liquidation)** is important for most people and also for most financial firms.

## Pillar 3: asset pricing

The key function in finance is pricing assets and, most importantly, pricing them correctly for the level of risk. For an intermediary, '**getting the price right**' is the key to success. Correct pricing is necessary in the provision of bank loans (the price in this case being the interest rate charged for the level of risk on a particular loan), in initial public offerings of shares and bonds (the offer price), in secondary market transactions in shares and bonds (bid and offer prices), and in making acquisitions in the merger and acquisition market (the acquisition bid price).

## Cash market instruments (capital assets)

These are assets, the value of which derives from the cash flows they generate – either interest or dividend payments. These cash flows can be valued using discounted cash flow techniques. The main capital assets are equities, bonds and loans. Equities and bonds are traded in **cash** markets (so-called to distinguish them from derivative markets). Loans are also traded, particularly amongst banks and institutional investors, but there is no public market as there is for equities and bonds. Cash market instruments are also known as **capital assets**, which always have value provided they are generating cash or can be sold to realise cash.

A government bond is a liability issued by a government (an asset to the holder, i.e. the investor) on which the government promises to pay a fixed amount of interest each year for an agreed number of years and at the end of the agreed period to repay the original amount (the capital or **principal**). Such a bond which provides regular income is known as a **coupon** bond, a term which derives from bonds originally being paper certificates with small coupons attached (rather like small banknotes) which could be clipped off the bond and taken to a bank (a paying agent) for payment in cash.[9] When an investor asks what the coupon is on a bond, he or she is asking what is the original rate of interest promised on the bond. The original investor in the bond receives the annual coupon in return for paying the **issue price** or **par value** of the bond. It has conventionally been assumed that the cash flows arising from a government bond are free of risk since governments of developed market countries (sovereigns) are conventionally assumed to be extremely unlikely to default on payment though today that assumption may not be valid.

A corporate bond is a liability issued by a company (an asset to the holder) on which the company promises to pay a fixed amount of interest each year for an agreed number of years and at the end of the agreed period to repay the principal. In this case, however, there must be some degree of risk involved as we cannot be sure that the company will in fact meet all its financial obligations. This is known as **credit** risk. In consequence, investors expect to receive an amount of interest in excess of that on an otherwise comparable government bond. The additional amount received is known as the credit risk premium. A key issue in valuation is how to assess the risk premium required on any liability being issued in order to make it attractive to investors.

Financial assets, i.e. liabilities issued by governments or companies, have value to investors only because they can or actually do generate income (cash flow). These cash flows are known as **P&I** flows which can stand for either **principal and income** or **principal and interest**, where 'principal' means the repayment of part, or the whole, of the original investment, and 'income' means interest and dividends. There are three sources of P&I available which can service loans, bonds and shares. However, if we include real estate assets, which are also a very important class of asset, then there is a fourth (which is listed last in what follows). They are:

- **Income from employment** by individuals (to service mortgages, credit card debt, etc.). This is income generation from **human capital**. We assume that if

---

[9] Karl Marx in *Das Kapital* referred disparagingly to 'mere coupon clippers', i.e. financiers, in contrast to genuine entrepreneurs.

someone invests in, say, a Master's degree in finance, his or her human capital is increased and thus the expected future income flows from employment rise.

- **Cash flow from the operations** of a company or business (to service loans, bonds and equity).
- **Tax revenue** raised by the finance ministry of a country (to service government debt).
- **Rental income** from property (to service the mortgage on the property or to provide income to the owner).

### Derivative market instruments (contingent claims)

This is another type of financial instrument which is closely related to capital assets. These are instruments which derive their value from the value of the **underlying** assets on which they are based, which may be a capital asset or a real asset such as oil or wheat. They are a means of exchanging risks and are thus not assets in the traditional sense. They are not capital assets as they do not generate cash flows. At their **expiry** they generate either a profit or a loss depending on the change in the value of the underlying asset. They are often known as **contingent assets** as their value is based on developments in the future, i.e. future economic conditions and the impact this has on the underlying asset (capital or real). They are a way of 'placing a bet' on an outcome with, for example, two people with opposite views taking opposite sides of a derivative contract. There is no generation of principal or interest or dividends. There is a simply a transfer of cash between two traders when a contract expires.

### Real assets

Finally, there are **real assets**. This category includes real estate which we covered above. But it also includes commodities. There are two main categories of these. Soft commodities are mainly foodstuffs, and hard commodities includes metals and plastics (e.g. copper, aluminium, steel, steel bar, oil, polypropylene, polyethylene) used as inputs to the manufacturing, transport and building industries. There is also oil which is a major input to manufacturing, transport and home heating. Commodities are traded on specialised commodities exchanges such as the Shanghai Futures Exchange and the London Metal Exchange. But in addition there are assets which are principally just **a store of value**, such as works of art, gold, silver and precious stones. Such assets have **no cash flows associated with them** and have only very limited value as inputs to other processes. Most gold is held as a store of value which may be in the form of jewellery and not for utilitarian purposes such as the plating of electrical contacts. The value of such assets is derived from subjective visual enjoyment or belief in the value of the asset as a store of value in times of uncertainty. Their value cannot be calculated in the way we scientifically calculate the value of a capital asset from its expected cash flows and risk. Such assets are, therefore, **purely speculative assets**, unlike company securities which generate cash flows.

In finance a key function is estimating the value of an asset. This is a complex matter and one to which whole modules in finance degrees are devoted. For those who have not covered these issues elsewhere I would recommend referring to a good textbook on valuation.[10]

# THE UNIVERSE OF FINANCIAL ASSETS IN WHICH WE ARE INTERESTED

Figure 1.1 shows the global stock of financial assets held by investors, i.e. liabilities issued by companies, banks and governments and, indirectly, by households as of year-end 2006, just before the financial crisis hit, resulting in a great reduction in these asset values. This is the global set of assets in credit and capital markets which is the focus of this book.

# ASSET VALUATION MODELS

## The Law of One Price, arbitrage and the price of financial assets

The **Law of One Price** is a statement that, in a competitive market, if two assets are essentially the same they will trade at the same market price. This result comes about because of the ability of **economically rational** traders to conduct **arbitrage trades**, meaning the purchase of one asset and the immediate sale of another equivalent asset in order to generate a riskless profit from the price difference between them. This is a form of **pairs trading** where two transactions, involving a sale and a purchase, are undertaken at the same time. For example, if the price of foreign exchange (**forex**) in London is different from that in New York then, since there are no transport costs involved, it is very easy and cheap (apart from commission payments) to buy in the cheaper market and immediately resell in

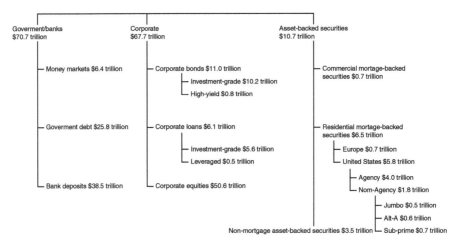

**Figure 1.1**   Global financial assets as of year-end 2006

*Sources*: Bank of England Financial Stability Review (FSR), October 2007 (p. 20), http://www.bankofengland. co.uk/publications/Documents/fsr/2007/fsrfull0710.pdf (accessed, 2 February 2012). BIS, Board of Governors of the Federal Reserve, European Securitisation Forum, Eurostat, Fitch Ratings Ltd, McKinsey Global Institute, ONS, Securities Industry and Financial Markets Association, Standard and Poor's, World Federation of Exchanges and Bank calculations.

---

[10]  For example, Zvi Bodie Alex Kane, Alan J. Marcus, *Essentials of Investments* (McGraw Hill/Irwin, 7th edition, 2008).

the higher priced market. We can use the law of one price to make the assumption that **arbitrageurs will ensure that this 'law' holds in relation to the values of assets that are not just identical but are similar to each other** and which can be easily and cheaply traded. Of course arbitrageurs may not have sufficient capital available to undertake the required volume of pairs trades to ensure that this 'law' always holds. If so, this would be likely to result in the law of one price not in fact always holding in practice and consequently to the mis-pricing of assets.

The Law of One Price is the most fundamental valuation principle in finance. In the case of bonds, the 'law' would say that if two bonds have exactly the same cash flows and the same degree of risk, even though they may have been issued by different companies, they should trade at the same price (or more correctly, yield, which is the expected return), because if one were trading at a higher yield than the other, investors would buy it (it has a lower price) and sell the one trading at a lower yield (it has a higher price), thus bringing about an equality of yield.

## Valuation models

If we were always comparing an asset with others that were identical to the one we were trying to value, we could use the Law of One Price directly and easily. In practice we are unlikely to find an asset which is exactly the same as the one we are trying to value. We must, therefore, employ some quantitative method to estimate value from **the prices we do know** which are of comparable but not identical assets. Quantitative methods that we use to **infer** the value of an asset, based on information about the price of a comparable asset or asset type and market interest rates, are known as **valuation models**.

## Valuing real estate

Real estate valuers, when they visit a domestic residence to undertake a valuation, consider information on the value of houses in general in the particular area (is it a high or low-valued part of town?), the floor area, the condition of the house, but most particularly the transaction prices at which sales have been achieved on **comparable** houses in that area. If a house next door which is virtually identical has sold for a particular price, then that would be the starting point. The next step would be to consider the relative condition of the two houses. The step after this would be to take the difference in timing between the two sales and adjust for the general change in house prices in the area over this period. In practice, of course, two houses are seldom very similar (or two office blocks or shopping centres) and thus the process is much more complex. Thus real estate valuers have to undertake an extensive education programme to gain their professional qualification from, for example, the Royal Institute of Chartered Surveyors.

## Valuing equity shares – the price/earnings (PE) valuation approach

One approach to the valuation of a company's shares is by comparison with similar companies using what is called the price/earnings multiple approach. The **price/earnings (P/E) ratio** is the market price of the share divided by this year's actual or next year's expected **earnings**, i.e. profit, not dividends. This can be thought of as the number of years it would take this company to generate profit per share equal to today's price per share (assuming no growth in profits). If profits are likely to grow fast, this number will be large (high P/E) compared with a company which is not expected to grow fast (low P/E) since, in a growth company, by definition earnings (profits) are expected to grow very rapidly, thus quickly reducing the number of years needed to generate the price of a share from its earnings.

If we are using this approach to value one company which is not yet trading on the market, for example if it is going to make an initial public offering of its shares, we look for other companies which are trading on the market and which are comparable – same industry, growth prospects, etc. On the basis of the law of one price we simply multiply the current (or next year's expected) earnings by this multiple to obtain a price. If the two companies really are comparable, then when the company is floated on the primary market at this price, this will also turn out to be the price at which it continues to trade in the secondary market i.e. the price will be right

If we look in the Companies and Markets section of the *Financial Times* we can find the average price earnings ratios of a wide range of countries and companies. For example, in the UK, the price earnings ratio for the market as a whole at the time of writing was 10.8. This means that an average company would take 10.8 years to earn in profits an amount on one share equal to the value of that share (assuming no growth in earnings). At the time of writing, Peru had a P/E ratio of 38 while Portugal's ratio was only 4.8 – both very different from the UK.

It is possible that these three countries, UK, Peru and Portugal, all have similar companies to each other which are expected to grow at similar rates (though it is not actually very likely). However, the investors in each country may put very different valuations on these similar expected profit streams. This may be because investor **attitudes to risk differ** by country. Of course it is actually more likely that the reason for the different P/E ratios is that Peruvian companies are expected to grow much faster than Portuguese companies, with UK companies somewhere in between.

Firms with a high price earnings multiple are expected to have a high rate of growth of earnings and hence of dividends. This must mean that they have excellent new high return (i.e. higher than their cost of capital) investment opportunities available to them. When the managers of such firms undertake a capital budgeting exercise, they will find many projects that have a positive net present value and hence which should be undertaken. Apple Corporation would be an example of such a company.

## Valuing equity shares – book value multiple

If you own a portfolio of shares and revalue them daily, then the value recorded in your company accounts (book value) will be the same as market value, which is the price at which they are currently trading on the stock market. If you don't revalue, book value and market value will diverge. The same logic applies to companies.

Book value is the amount at which a company's assets were originally recorded in its accounts. This is also known as **historical cost**. Over time book value (historical cost) and market value (i.e. the value of the company on the stock market) may get out of line. We would expect that the stock market value would be at least equal to, or above, book value (provided book values are correct values), since if it is below it could be profitable to wind-up (liquidate) the company if its assets could actually be sold for book value. The proceeds, which would then exceed the share price, would be returned to shareholders.

We generally expect the share price to be higher than book value since any company is supposed to have some competitive advantage in using its assets to make them worth more in terms of enterprise value than simply as stand-alone assets of various types. Another way of putting this is that companies should have **franchise value**, which is the amount of value their brand name, reputation and skills add to the company value beyond the cost of their assets.

## Discounted cash flow valuation of bonds and equities

An asset's fundamental value arises simply from expected future flows of cash back to the investor from the asset. To value these, we have to consider the time value of money and the likelihood that the asset will in fact generate these cash flows (risk). Thus we have to use an appropriately risk-adjusted interest rate to discount these cash flows back to a present value.

A bond is just a contract between a government or a company and an investor. In the case of a fixed interest bond (the most common type) the contract specifies that the borrower will pay the investor the same fixed amount of interest each year of the bond's life and, at the end of its life, the initial investment will be repaid.

Let's start with (supposedly) riskless cash flows from a government bond rather than a company (corporate). Such a bond involves an investment now of perhaps $1000 in return for annual interest payments, known as **coupon payments** of, say, 5% i.e. $50. However, although we paid $1000 for this bond, during its life, its price will change continually as a result of **market** interest rates changing. We have to consider why this happens when the cash flows from the bond have not changed. We might, for example, want to know what our bond is worth 2 years after buying it i.e. 8 years before the government pays us back our $1000 because we need to sell it as we want the cash to go on holiday.

We know the annual interest rate on the bond i.e. that a payment of $50 will be made every year regardless of the price of the bond in the market and we know the **redemption value** i.e. the **face value** of the bond (1000) that will be repaid at maturity i.e. in 10 years' time for a 10 year bond. Thus we know all the cash flows for **certain**. What we don't know is the **rate** at which cash flows should be discounted (the discount rate) to calculate the value of the bond **today**, let's say 2 years after issue.

This rate depends on the time value of money over the remaining life of the bond (8 years) which can vary day by day. We can find this rate in the market. Market interest rates are the current rates that can be observed for comparable bonds and which will provide us with valuations of **comparable assets** to enable us to price our particular bond by using the Law of One Price. Thus, if we look at the prices at which other government bonds with a remaining life of 8 years are trading (comparable assets), we can find the rate at which investors are discounting future cash flows which are **certain** in order to come to the market price. If other government bonds with a remaining life of 8 years (or new bonds being issued with an 8 year life) are giving a yield of 7%, we then know that for our particular bond to be attractive to investors, it too must **yield** 7% i.e. give a return over its remaining life of 7%. If it didn't, no one would be willing to buy it from us. Since the **coupon** on our bond is only 5%, i.e. the annual interest payment, we know that we can no longer be sold for its purchase price (1000). However, when it is **redeemed** i.e. paid back by the government, the **redemption value** also known as **face value** or **par value** will still be 1000 i.e. the investor to whom we sell it will be repaid 1000 by the government as this was the original issue price. Thus the new investor will receive $50 of interest for each remaining year of life of the bond plus a capital gain at redemption which, **in combination** in present value terms must give a return of 7% per annum. The price which achieves this is approximately $880.[11] At this price, the bond gives a **current yield** (or **running yield**) of around 5.7% annually but when the future value of the additional repayment amount above the purchase price is factored in at its present value, the **yield to redemption** of the bond is found to be approximately 7%. In theory investors are indifferent between receiving a current yield of only 5.7% followed by a capital gain at maturity of $125 and receiving a running yield of 7% and no capital gain at maturity. This is because once the time value of money is allowed for, both sets of cash flow have the same value to the investor.

## Remember: the price of a bond moves inversely to the market rate of interest

As our example above shows, if the interest rate for eight-year money **rises** above 5%, the price of our bond will be **falling** so that anyone now buying that bond will obtain a higher yield (return on amount invested) than we who bought it at its par value as a result of paying less for it yet is still receiving only 5% fixed interest (based on the issue price of 1000). If there is no 8 year bond to which we can look to find the market yield for this term, we can extrapolate from rates on bonds with a final maturity on either side of 8 years.

We can apply the same principle to risky corporate bonds. We can look at the rate at which investors must be discounting expected cash flows on a bond of similar final maturity date and similar risk (a bond with the same rating from a credit rating agency) and then discount the cash flows on the bond that interests us at the same (risky) discount rate. If this bond is not trading in the market this enables us to calculate the price we should be willing to pay for it. It is very difficult to cover bond valuation in a few, condensed) paragraphs such as those above and probably even harder to feel comfortable from reading those paragraphs.

In the case of equities, there are a number of discounted cash flow approaches to valuation such as the dividend growth model. For the sake of brevity we will not cover these here. For a full treatment of valuation of equities and bonds you might wish to refer to a standard finance text such as Bodie, Kane and Marcus *Essentials of Investment* published in 2008 (7th edition) by McGraw Hill.

---

[11] Calculator available at http://www.montegodata.co.uk/scripting/bondvalue calculator.htm

# ISSUES IN BANK ASSET VALUATION AND VALUATION OF BANK SHARES

As we are studying financing institutions, banks are a particular type of company in which we have an interest. A key problem with valuing financial assets held on the balance sheet of financial intermediaries and banks in particular is that their value depends not simply on objective facts, i.e. cash flows and risk adjusted discount rates, but also on accounting and regulatory rules. In fact, there are two quite different ways of valuing financial assets, such as loans and securities when these are held on bank balance sheets.

## Historic or amortised cost

The first, and more traditional, method is amortised cost – an accounting rule based on the historical cost of acquiring the asset. Using the historical/amortised cost principle, the value of an asset would *not* be increased if its market value rose, since under this principle we use acquisition cost (historic cost) as the basis of valuation. Equally, accountants within banks do not need to reduce the value of the asset from its historic cost, i.e. amortise it, unless there has been an **impairment** to its value. Impairment is something which reduces the value of the asset. It is in trying to define what counts as impairment that the difficulties in the area of valuation have arisen.

The traditional rule has been that for loan assets held on the bank balance sheet and **intended to be held to maturity** there has to be some 'event' that **triggers** a reconsideration of the loan (or other asset's) value – something that suggests that the asset has become impaired. But provided a borrower continues to pay interest, even if we know that he or she will be unable to repay the loan, we do not recognise impairment. Equally, even *if* the loan could to be sold to another bank and we know that on sale it would have a value lower than the historic cost, if we don't **actually** sell it, we still may *not* recognise this as a diminution or impairment of value. Instead we continue to value the asset at the historic cost. Also, if an asset is worth less because interest rates have risen and therefore the discount rate that should be applied to the expected cash flows has risen (this makes the asset worth less), we do not recognise this as impairment either. If, however, there has been some trigger event, such as a delayed payment of interest by a borrower or a declaration by a rating agency that there has been an event of default (in the case of a corporate loan), then it would have to be written down to its appropriate amortised cost.

## Mark-to-market (MTM) and fair value

In contrast to the historic or amortised cost basis for valuation, mark-to-market (and fair value which is a version of MTM) uses market prices as the starting point for valuation. Pure MTM simply takes the price in a market or the price at which a similar asset has been sold as the basis for value. **Fair value** has been defined as the amount at which the asset could be bought or sold in a current transaction between willing parties **other than in a liquidation sale**. This latter over-ride – other than in a liquidation sale – is extremely important. The reason is that in times of market stress, assets sold in a market tend to sell for much less than their **funda-mental value** which is defined as the value of expected cash flows discounted at the appropriate risk adjusted discount rate. This is known as the **discounted cash flow** valuation or DCF value. There is often a substantial discount on the DCF value as a result of market selling pressure.

## Trading book and banking book

Having considered the possible rules for valuation – historic/ amortised cost or fair value – the next question is which of these two rules should be used for each class of asset on a bank's balance sheet. The regulators have decided that the appropriate rule depends on the **intention** of a bank with respect to its assets. If its intention is to **hold assets to maturity** there is one set of rules; if its intention is to **trade its assets** there is a different set of rules.

The regulatory rules therefore require banks to categorise their balance sheet assets into two classes:

- Assets intended to be held to maturity, such as loans, are allocated to the **banking book** and held there until maturity at the price paid for them unless, as we noted above, there has been some trigger event which requires us to write the asset down in value.
- Assets which the bank may have an intention to sell or trade and therefore does not intend to hold to maturity have to be allocated to the **trading book**, i.e. the part of the balance sheet for assets which may be sold in market transactions and have to be revalued to reflect market prices daily.

## The relationship of market price to historical (book) cost for bank shares

When we consider the value of bank shares we can also compare with market price at which the bank's own shares trade in the market with the historical (balance sheet) value that the accountants put on the assets of the bank. This should give us some idea of how valuable investors think a bank's assets are compared with the view taken by the accountants working for the bank. If the price/book ratio is below one this suggests that investors don't believe that the accountant's valuations are realistic. If they are well above one, this suggests not only that investors think the asset valuations are appropriate i.e. not overvalued, but also that they believe the bank has a '**franchise value**' i.e. it can generate a return on its shares above the cost of its capital. I cover these ideas in more detail in Chapter 28.

Figure 1.2 shows price/ book ratios i.e. stock market price of the bank's shares/ historical cost valuation of the underlying assets for major banks up to early 2011. In good times the book value multiple as it is called, may rise to as high as four times. Since the crisis, few trade much above 1 and, in 2011, many were trading well below book with some in Europe even as low as 0.1. At the time of writing, Lloyds Bank was trading at around 0.33 and its price/earnings ratio on expected profits in 2012 was around 5.

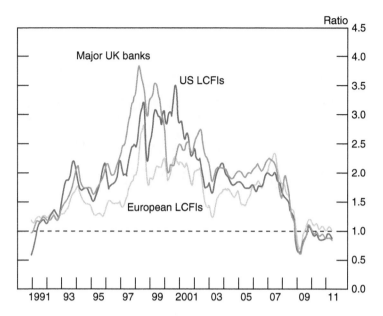

**Figure 1.2**   Major UK banks' and Large Complex Financial Institutions' price to book ratios

*Sources*: Bloomberg, DataStream and Bank of England calculations, Financial Stability Review June 2011 (p. 33), http://www.bankofengland.co.uk/publications/fsr/2011/fsr29sec3.pdf (accessed, 2 February 2012).

# BALANCE SHEETS: THE KEY TO UNDERSTANDING TRANSFORMING FINANCIAL INTERMEDIARIES

**2**

'Intermediation' means standing between. There are two ways of standing between. The first involves simply acting as a means of bringing two people together after which the intermediary drops out and the two sides then conduct their business. For example, a dating agency which brings together people of the opposite sex drops out as soon as they have been introduced. Similarly a stockbroker introduces a buyer and a seller of a security then drops out as they transact with each other. This kind of intermediation does not require that the intermediary has a balance sheet. I discuss this kind of intermediation, known as broker or agency intermediation, in more detail later.

The second type of intermediation is known as **balance sheet or transforming intermediation** because by creating a balance sheet between investors and companies it enables both sides to benefit from the difference in nature between the assets and liabilities on the balance sheet. The benefit comes from overcoming some of the inherent conflicts between the two sides. Companies want to have long-term funds that don't have to be repaid at short notice. They also want the lowest cost of funding. Investors on the other hand want to have liquidity i.e. be able to liquidate their investments at any time. They also want to have the minimum risk and the maximum return. In intermediated finance the two sides of a transaction are not brought together directly. Instead, each side transacts separately with the intermediary. The intermediary, in consequence, needs to have a balance sheet on which the outcome of transactions with others can be entered. As a result of these transactions, the intermediary creates asset positions on one side of the balance sheet, which are financed by liability positions on the other side.

Understanding balance sheets is crucial to understanding financial intermediation, the banking system, investment banks and the issues relating to the financial crisis. It is the balance sheet that tells us most about the particular type of institution we are looking at and the specific types of risk it faces. I examine below, balance sheets in general, not specifically bank balance sheets, since similar issues apply to all companies, and it is important to understand that there is nothing special about financial company balance sheets. The differences with **corporates** i.e. non-financial companies are ones of degree only. Specifically, banks employ much more debt than corporates (are more highly leveraged) and employ much shorter maturity debt to achieve this leverage than most other companies. In addition, of course, they hold financial assets, not real assets, which often makes valuation of their assets difficult.

## BALANCE SHEET MANAGEMENT

Companies (apart from financial companies) have mostly **real assets**, i.e. tangible things on the left-hand side of their balance sheet. Financial companies have mostly **financial assets**, on the left-hand side of their balance sheet. Either type of asset holding has to be financed in some way. The right-hand side of the balance sheet shows how the acquisition of the assets has been financed by the issue of financial liabilities.

● **Balance sheet management is about minimising the cost of this financing without causing the company to take on too much financial risk.**

In the first example below, the real assets of the manufacturing company are financed solely by the owners of the company, i.e. the stockholders or shareholders. They hold the **equity** of the company, which is the company's liability to its owners. That liability is defined in a contract, which is detailed in the **prospectus** at the time of issue. A balance sheet (see Box 2.1a) simply shows the different types of participation, i.e. the liabilities that a company has issued to those who finance it. Liabilities are simply legal contracts specifying rights and obligations. In this case there is only one type of contract, namely equity. In addition to the balance sheet, companies have a profit and loss account which shows by how much the revenue generated by the company exceeds its expenses.

---

### Box 2.1a

| Balance Sheet as at start-up of company: 1 March 2011 | | | |
|---|---|---|---|
| **Assets** | | **Capital and liabilities** | |
| Real assets belonging to the company | | Financial assets (financial capital) owned by investors) | |
| Real assets (buildings machinery etc.) | 80 | Common Stock (Equity/ shares) | 80 |
| **Total assets** | 80 | **Shareholder funds** | 80 |
| **Profit and loss account for first year of trading from 1 March 2011 to 29 February 2012** | | | |
| Revenues | | 300 | |
| Expenses | | 280 | |
| **Profit for the year** | | **20** (transferred to shareholder funds on the balance sheet) | |

---

As a result of the generation of profit which has not been paid out to shareholders as dividends, at the end of the first year of trading the company balance sheet will have expanded by 20 as shown in Box 2.1b. This is because the surplus cash generated by trading has enabled the company to purchase additional real assets to expand the company. The resources invested by the company in additional assets are reflected as an addition to shareholder funds in the form of retained profits. Note that the company could have chosen to pay out the 20 as dividends to the shareholders in which case shareholder funds would have remained at 80.

---

**Box 2.1b**

**Balance Sheet as at 29 February 2012**

| Assets | | Capital and liabilities | |
|---|---|---|---|
| Real assets (buildings machinery etc.) | 100 | Common Stock (Equity/ shares) | 80 |
| | | Retained profit | 20 |
| **Total assets** | **100** | **Shareholder funds** | **100** |

---

Retained profit is the main source of finance used to expand most businesses, i.e. most expansion is not financed through bank loans or from the capital markets but from the success of the firm in previous years at generating profit. Indeed, some firms pay no dividends for their first ten or fifteen years because they believe that the investment opportunities available within the firm are greater than any shareholder is likely to find outside the company.

In the above example the shareholders have done very well. The initial capital employed in the company (80) has expanded by 20 over the course of the year. An important measure of the performance of companies is the ratio of profit to base capital, known as the return on equity (ROE). This company made a profit of 20 on a base capital of 80, giving an ROE of 25% – an unusually high rate of return.

An example of a company that in most years has paid no dividend is Apple Corporation. The reason, one presumes, is that they believe shareholders will obtain a better return from profits being retained and reinvested in highly profitable new projects. Only when they no longer have so many internal investment opportunities are they likely to start again to pay dividends to shareholders. In the meantime, shareholders can realise the increase in shareholder funds that arise from the retained profits by selling shares at a profit, i.e. they can convert capital to income through secondary trading markets. In March 2012, Apple announced that it would pay its first dividend since 1995 as reported by the company in the press release below[1] (and also repurchase shares as a way of reducing the company's equity capital thereby increasing its ROE):

**Apple Announces Plans to Initiate Dividend and Share Repurchase Program Expects to Spend $45 Billion Over Three Years**

CUPERTINO, California—March 19, 2012—Apple® today announced plans to initiate a dividend and share repurchase program commencing later this year. Subject to declaration by the Board of Directors, the Company plans to initiate a quarterly

---

[1] http://www.apple.com/pr/library/2012/03/19Apple-Announces-Plans-to-Initiate-Dividend-and-Share-Repurchase-Program.html

dividend of $2.65 per share sometime in the fourth quarter of its fiscal 2012, which begins on July 1, 2012.

Additionally, the Company's Board of Directors has authorized a $10 billion share repurchase program commencing in the Company's fiscal 2013, which begins on September 30, 2012. The repurchase program is expected to be executed over three years, with the primary objective of neutralizing the impact of dilution from future employee equity grants and employee stock purchase programs.

'We have used some of our cash to make great investments in our business through increased research and development, acquisitions, new retail store openings, strategic prepayments and capital expenditures in our supply chain, and building out our infrastructure. You'll see more of all of these in the future,' said Tim Cook, Apple's CEO. 'Even with these investments, we can maintain a war chest for strategic opportunities and have plenty of cash to run our business. So we are going to initiate a dividend and share repurchase program.'

If a company suffers losses, then its shareholder funds will diminish. If a company is wound up, i.e. liquidated, the equity holders have a right to any residue left after meeting any other liabilities. This is known as the **residual interest**. Thus shareholders are always 'at the bottom of the heap' and only get what is left after all other obligations have been met, which is also described as **taking the first loss**, since any losses accrue to shareholders first before affecting the interests of debt holders (liability holders). In the case above, there are no other liabilities such as tax debts, supplier debts, bank loan debts or bonds and thus there is a perfect equivalence between the value of the assets and the value of the equity.

## INTRODUCING DEBT LIABILITIES INTO THE CAPITAL STRUCTURE

Balance sheet management is about trying to reduce the cost of financing a company's assets (lowering its average cost of capital) by employing other types of contract with suppliers of capital. In particular it means employing debt capital rather than equity capital. In contrast to equity which is never repaid and has no mandatory dividend payments, debt must be **serviced**, i.e. interest and capital repayments must be paid when due. Thus there are mandatory P&I payments that must be met by the company out of its revenues. If the company fails to make any mandatory payment, the contract it has with the supplier of that funding permits the supplier (the debt-holder) to force the company into liquidation. This is why debt financing, otherwise known as financial leverage, is potentially destabilising to a company.

Most companies employ debt financing either in the form of a bank loan or in the form of a bond (normally a fixed interest rate security). The reason for using debt is that the explicit cost of debt capital (the interest rate) is much lower than the cost of equity capital, i.e. the expected return on equity. This is because equity takes more risk, i.e. it takes the first loss, since debt has preference over equity. It is generally thought that introducing debt will lower the *average* cost of capital that a company employs (although this is much disputed)[2] and thus most companies

---

[2] According to finance theory this is not the case. See Modigliani and Miller (M&M) discussion below.

make use of debt in their **capital structure**, i.e. the right-hand side of the balance sheet (the liability side; see Box 2.2a and Box 2.2b), which show debt as well as equity being used to finance the same assets.

---

## Box 2.2a

**Opening Balance Sheet as at start-up of company: 1 March 2011**

| Assets | | Capital and liabilities | |
|---|---|---|---|
| Real assets (buildings machinery etc.) | 80 | Common Stock (Equity/ shares) | 60 |
| | | Debt (annual interest rate 10%) | 20 |
| **Total assets** | **80** | **Equity and liabilities** | **80** |

**(Net assets, i.e. total assets net of liabilities, also known as shareholder funds, 60)**

**Profit and loss account** for first year of trading from 1 March 2011 to 29 February 2012

| | |
|---|---|
| Revenues | 300 |
| Expenses | 280 |
| Interest on debt | 2 |
| **Profit for the year** | **18** |

---

In this example where the company is partly financed by debt, the shareholders have not made as much profit – only 18 as against 20 previously. However, they have only employed capital of 60. As a result the ROE has risen to 18/60, i.e. 30% compared with 25% without the use of debt. The closing balance sheet for this company is shown below.

---

## Box 2.2b

**Closing Balance Sheet as at 29 February 2012**

| Assets | | Capital and liabilities | |
|---|---|---|---|
| Real assets (buildings machinery etc.) | 98 | Common Stock (Equity/ shares) | 60 |
| | | Retained profit | 18 |
| | | Debt | 20 |
| **Total assets** | **98** | **Equity and liabilities** | **98** |

**(Net assets i.e. total assets net of liabilities also known as shareholder funds, 78)**

---

Much of the dispute over whether or not debt reduces the average cost of capital arises from the fact that as debt is introduced into the capital structure, the return to shareholders becomes more variable – higher if the company does well but lower if it does badly. Since volatility of the share price is how risk is measured, it may be that the higher ROE that we observe above is simply the extra return required by shareholders for bearing the additional volatility caused by debt (i.e.

risk). If this is so, then in practice the average cost of capital may not be reduced through using lower-cost debt except as a result of the tax-shield benefit discussed below.

Once debt is introduced, the surplus of revenues over costs is reduced by the interest payable on the debt. But of course, by employing debt as well as owners' equity, the business can expand to a larger size than might be possible without this additional source of financial capital. Thus if the owners had only 60 of funds available but needed 80 for the business to be set up, this additional capital provided by a lender would enable the business to commence. Alternatively, even if the owners do have the cash available, they do not need to invest as much of their own cash in the equity of the company since part of the financial capital is provided by lenders. As there would then be less shareholder capital financing of the firm, provided the cost of debt is lower than equity, the ROE would rise. The drawback is that paying interest on debt and making capital repayments according to the schedule in the prospectus for the bond is mandatory and gives rise to financial risk which leverages up business risk. Thus companies are subject to two types of risk:

- **Business risk:** which is the risk that the venture has revenues below the level of its costs (it is making losses) and therefore the value of the business is declining.
- **Financial risk**: which is the risk introduced by adding debt to the capital structure. Whereas, without any debt, a company has to meet only its day-to-day running costs, once there is debt in the capital structure it must also pay interest and make any required repayments of the loan (P&I payments). Thus total cash outflow in any period increases if a company has debt in its capital structure. If a company fails to make such P&I payments, its debtors can force it into liquidation. Thus debt introduces a second risk, financial risk, on top of business risk.

The use of debt is also described as using **leverage** or **gearing** in the capital structure, which means that the total assets of the company can be increased by using debt finance. Leverage is generally measured as the debt/equity ratio, but it can also be measured as the ratio of debt to **earnings before interest, tax, depreciation and amortisation**, which is the approach used in leveraged financing of private equity acquisitions.

The capital structure of a company reflects the **revenue and risk sharing contracts agreed between the holders of the various financing instruments and the company**. The equity holders (as the owners of the company) accept that if they ask others to provide financial capital in the form of debt then these others will have **priority over them in terms of cash flow distribution and also in any distribution of the assets if the company has to be liquidated**. Thus when things are going well, the fixed-income bond holders, for example, obtain a **fixed return** (hence the expression **fixed interest securities**) or, in the case of bank loans, the bank receives the agreed rate of interest, while any surplus accrues to equity (the **residual**, variable return). But when things are going badly, if there is no **surplus**, i.e. profit after debt holder liabilities have been met, then shareholders will make nothing. If things are going very badly and there is insufficient cash even to meet all the payments required to service the debt (default), then debt holders can force the company into liquidation and claim their share of the proceeds from the sale of assets (a liquidation sale).

## IS THERE AN OPTIMAL AMOUNT OF DEBT

The Modigliani and Miller hypothesis (M&M) states that in the absence of tax benefits the capital structure of a company does not affect the average cost of capital (see Figure 2.1(a)). If correct, adding lower-cost debt to the capital structure would simply mean that the cost of equity would rise (because it would become more risky) and thus the weighted average of these two sources of capital would remain constant. The reason why tax makes a difference is that the expense of servicing debt (interest payments) is considered by the tax code in almost every country to be a business expense, whereas the expense of servicing equity (dividend payments) is not considered to be a business expense and hence is not tax deductible. If this is the case then it might seem that the optimal capital structure would be, say, 99% debt. However, the M&M theory assumes no bankruptcy costs, i.e. if the company goes into liquidation and its assets are sold off, it assumes there are no losses suffered in such a 'liquidation' sale. In the case of a bank closure the losses on liquidation are particularly high. With high bankruptcy costs, there is a point at which additional debt starts to result in a trade-off between the tax-shield benefit of debt and the increased risk of bankruptcy. As a result there is a D/E ratio, D/E* (see Figure 2.1(b)), at which the cost of capital is minimised. Any further increase in debt would cause the cost of equity[3] to rise so rapidly that it would outweigh any tax-shield benefit.

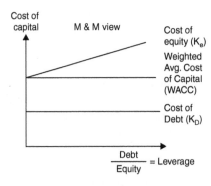

**Figure 2.1(a)**   Modigliani and Miller view

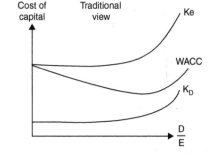

**Figure 2.1(b)**   The traditional view

## SUBORDINATION

Not all debt is the same. There are different 'classes' of debt. The diagram below has two arrows at the side which read **seniority/priority** on the up arrow and **subordination/risk** on the down arrow. What this means is that each component

---

[3]  The cost of debt would also be likely to rise sharply as bondholders saw a likelihood of losing all, or a part of, their investment as a result of bankruptcy costs.

of the capital structure has a different contract between the company and the supplier of capital. The contract with shareholders at the time of an initial public offering (IPO) specifies that this financing component has the **residual interest** in the company. This means that it has no rights to any cash flow of the company. It will never be repaid and need not receive dividends. It does, however, have the ownership rights to any retained profits in the company, though it can only access these profits if the company chooses to pay a dividend. In the event of bankruptcy the shareholders will be the last to receive anything. Instead, debt holders have first rights to any cash generated by the sale of assets in bankruptcy. Any residue then accrues to, flows to, the shareholders.

The key feature of a 'structured balance sheet' is that each lower level in the capital structure protects those above it. The top slice, the senior debt, has first call over any cash generated by the business because that is what is specified in the contract between the senior debt holders and the company. This means that interest on senior debt, and any capital repayments, are made first. Another way of looking at it is that if the available cash is insufficient to meet the interest and capital repayments on all liabilities, then these are not met *pari passu*, i.e. proportionally or without preference. Instead, there is a **cash flow waterfall** of payments cascading down the capital structure with cash being abstracted at each level as it flows down.

It can be seen in Figure 2.2 that common stock (equity) has the greatest risk and the least seniority. But, to compensate, equity has the highest **expected return**, while senior debt has the lowest.

**Senior debt** has absolute preference and thus, even if no other level in the capital structure has its obligations met, the senior debt will be paid out to the full extent of any cash available from on-going business activities. Also, if the company is forced into liquidation, the senior debt has priority over every other level in being repaid from the proceeds of liquidation. If the senior debt amounts to, say, 10% of the total capital structure then it is **protected** by the remaining 90% of the capital structure which is subordinate to it and which is at higher risk of not receiving interest or capital repayment or, in the event, of liquidation, the proceeds from such a liquidation. It is this subordination of each layer to the ones above, i.e. the absence of pari passu payments to all layers, that provides this protection or, in effect, **insurance**.

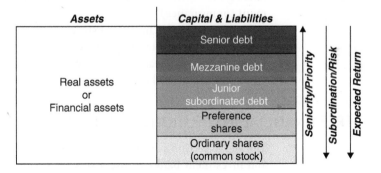

**Figure 2.2**   Structured balance sheet

**Mezzanine debt** is an intermediate level of debt in terms of risk and expected return. It is less secure than senior debt but more secure than subordinated (junior) debt whose interests are subordinated (more junior rank) to the more senior mezzanine debt – (a mezzanine floor in a building being an intermediate level floor between two main floors.)

**Subordinated (junior) debt** is superior to preference shares in terms of seniority but inferior to mezzanine.

**Preference shares** pay dividends but only if interest payments and capital repayments (P&I) on higher ranking tranches of the capital structure have been made. Equally, in liquidation, they will receive any cash due after all debtholder liabilities have been met but before the common stockholders (ordinary shareholders).

Finally, **common stock** (the US term) or **ordinary shares** (the UK term) or just **equity,** as distinct from preference shares, i.e. the owners or shareholders of the company, are on the bottom rung because the company does not have a fixed obligation to them as it does to the other layers but instead any residue (whether large or small) accrues to them as owners. However, in the event of the residue being negative, this does not accrue to them, provided the company has limited liability. This means that the liability of the shareholders to meet the liabilities due to debt holders and others is limited to the face value of their shares. Thus shareholders cannot lose more than their investment in a limited company. This is in contrast to individuals who incur debt. They are always liable for all of it. Limited liability companies in the UK are either plc (public limited company) or Ltd (private limited company). In the US the term 'Incorporated' or 'Inc.' is used. Equity is a liability of the company, as is debt. The difference is that equity is a liability to the owners of the company, whereas debt is a liability to creditors.

Equity is the cushion that protects all creditors, i.e. the debt liability holders, who, in the case of a bank, includes its depositors. It can be thought of as providing insurance to the classes of liability above it. It takes the **first loss** if the company starts to lose money and, since it has the last claim on any cash, the more equity there is and the less debt, the safer the debt and the less the likelihood of the firm going into liquidation. Each form of financial capital thus provides a cushion to any class of liability above it. Any form of financial capital in the seniority/priority ranking below the one being considered is providing a form of **credit enhancement** (or insurance) to it.

Understanding balance sheet structures is important in all areas of finance but particularly in understanding collateralised debt obligations – the type of balance sheet structure that caused so many problems in the credit crisis. We cover this type of structure in a later chapter.

## DEBT-FREE FINANCIAL INSTITUTIONS FINANCED ONLY BY EQUITY

The above section considered leveraged companies which would include banks and investment banks whose assets are financed on the foundation of a small share capital on which is built a large superstructure of debt securities issues with different levels of subordination and also maturity. This is sometimes known as a **structured finance** balance sheet, though this term is generally reserved for financial intermediary balance sheets and not other companies. However, not all financial institutions operate in this leveraged fashion. Some have a balance sheet financed by equity shares only.

Mutual funds are the key type of intermediary whose balance sheets generally have no debt. Instead they have only equity shares known as **units** (hence the term **unit trust** for a mutual fund operating in the UK). Funds of this type have a balance sheet on which all the assets held are financed by equity and where an equity share or unit represents an **undivided interest**, i.e. all the interests of the providers of capital are the same. Such funds are also known as pass-through funds because the income generated from the assets is passed through to investors on an equal basis, i.e. *pari passu*, meaning that every investor in the fund is on an equal footing or ranks equally with all the others. This is different to structured finance or most companies, where there are different categories of investor, such as shareholders, bond holders and bank lenders, each with a different set of rights to the cash flow generated by the financial assets.

A company/mutual fund/unit trust with an unleveraged balance sheet, i.e. financed only with equity, is much less likely to suffer from financial distress than a leveraged one in the event that the assets on the balance sheet unexpectedly lose value, since it would need a 100% fall in the value of assets to wipe out the equity. This is one reason why a financial system in which a high proportion of assets is held by unleveraged institutional investors rather than by banks is likely to be much more stable. In the eurozone crisis, a major problem has been the extent to which highly leveraged banks have been holding eurozone sovereign debt and loans to private sector borrowers based in countries such as Greece, Portugal, Ireland, Spain and Italy. . A small loss on such assets (say 3%), if realised, i.e. if the accounting for the asset suddenly has to recognise a diminution in value (mark-to-market), has the potential to make the bank insolvent if, like many banks, it was financed by only 3% equity capital. In this event shareholders would lose 100% of their equity in the bank and debt holders would be next to suffer some loss. If, however, sovereign debt assets were held in a mutual fund structure or any unleveraged structure, each unit holder in the fund would suffer only a loss **proportional to the loss suffered by the whole fund**. Thus a 3% loss on the fund as a whole would result in each investor losing 3% of his or her investment, whereas in the case above of a bank leveraged 33 times (as many banks were prior to the 2007 financial crisis), a 3% loss would result in a 100% loss of investment for every shareholder and the consequent collapse of the bank.

For an investor analysing financial institutions, analysis of the balance sheet is a key activity. Examining leverage, maturity mismatch (short term debt financing long term assets), subordination terms, type of asset, etc. will give an indication of the risks borne by the particular financial institution. These issues will be covered in more detail in later chapters.

# 3

# FINANCIAL INTERMEDIATION: INDUSTRY SECTORS, PRODUCTS AND MARKETS

## FINANCIAL INTERMEDIARIES AS AGENTS OR PRINCIPALS

An intermediary stands between the two sides in a transaction and thus creates an indirect relationship between them. In order to survive and prosper, intermediaries need to provide some service that is of sufficient value that those on either side are willing to pay for it. But before we can understand intermediation or disintermediation we need to understand the two basic types of intermediaries that we introduced in the previous chapter. These two quite distinct types are:

1. **Agency** (brokerage) intermediaries which don't have financial assets (except perhaps customer accounts) on their balance sheet; for example a stockbroker
2. **Principal** (balance sheet) intermediaries which do have very large holdings of financial assets on their balance sheet. Within this category we also need to distinguish:
   a. **Unleveraged** intermediaries financed purely by equity capital (e.g. a mutual fund);
   b. **Leveraged** intermediaries financed by a high proportion of debt capital (e.g. a bank or investment bank).

An example of an agency intermediary is a stockbroker (a company or partnership) which brings together those with equal and opposite needs and matches them. A principal intermediary on the other hand must have a balance sheet; on one side of this it holds financial assets which it has acquired, and on the other side it issues liabilities which finance these asset holdings. In the first form of financial intermediation (brokerage) the nature of the assets involved is not changed by the intermediation process – they are simply transferred without involving ownership by the agent. The broker acts like eBay by conducting a search for the other side, introducing the two sides to each other and enabling them to transact. Balance sheet intermediaries, on the other hand, **change the nature of the assets offered to investors** (the intermediary's liabilities) compared with **the assets held on their balance sheets**. Note that a **financial liability** issued by any company is a **financial asset** in the hands of an investor.

If intermediaries cease to provide a value-for-money service, it is likely that the activity will cease or be disintermediated. An instance of this in the banking field is when intermediated financing moves from bank balance sheets (principal intermediation) to agency intermediated financing through capital markets.

## HOW AGENTS AND PRINCIPALS DIFFER IN THEIR RELATIONSHIP WITH CLIENTS

An **agent** is someone (or a company or partnership) who acts on behalf of his **client** and only in the interest of his client, not in his own or his company's interest. He is thus an advisor who executes the best deal for his client. He would normally be remunerated either through a commission payment or from a flat annual fee (perhaps based on assets under management). Note that we use the word 'client' in the context of agency business, whereas below, when we look at business undertaken as principal, we use the word 'counterparty'. Brokers operate as agents as do salespeople, and in fact the terms 'broker' and 'salesperson' are often used synonymously.

A stockbroker in most countries is required by the terms of his registration with the regulatory authority to provide his client with **best execution**. Traditionally this meant the best price, although today other features, such as speed of execution, settlement cost, size of transaction, etc., may also be relevant. The stockbroker also has to have systems in place which can enable him to demonstrate to regulators that he actually has obtained competing quotes (prices) and that he has selected the best quote (price), i.e. the highest one (customer sell order) or lowest one (customer buy order).

A **principal**, on the other hand, acts in his (or in his company's) interest in transactions. Thus, for example, a dealer (marketmaker) in an investment bank operates purely as a principal. He has an inventory of securities (bought and sold positions) on the bank's balance sheet from which he transacts with other traders to whom he provides buy and sell prices. He is a **price maker**. He transacts with **counterparties**, i.e. those on the other side of a transaction, with the objective of generating profits for his employer. We call them counterparties rather than clients because they are finance professionals. As a result, the relationship is one where regulators do not require the best execution rule to be implemented. The higher the price at which a dealer can sell to a counterparty and the lower the price at which he can buy, the better he is doing his job for his employer. The remuneration to the firm is not from a commission or fee but simply from the difference between buying and selling prices known as the **spread**.

## EXAMPLES OF PRINCIPAL AND AGENCY FUNCTIONS
### Brokerage and advisory intermediaries

Brokerage or agency intermediaries and advisors don't commit capital to transactions and do not take financial market risk. **They are *not* balance sheet, transforming, (principal) intermediaries** since their balance sheets are small and generally they hold few financial assets (apart from monies owing to clients, for example).

## Stockbroker

A **stockbroker** is a good example of this, the simplest type of intermediary. All such a person does is to find the two sides to a transaction (buyer and seller) and bring them together, either directly (two of his own customers) or through an execution venue such as an exchange or market maker. He neither changes the nature of the securities in which he acts as agent nor does he commit capital to them. He is simply acting like eBay to match two sides – buyer and seller.

## Corporate finance advisor

A corporate finance broker acting for a company will advise the company on the best way to structure its liabilities, i.e. should it obtain new capital by raising more equity or through a bond issue or through bank finance? The corporate finance broker would then search for the commercial bank or investment bank best able to provide the appropriate origination services. He neither changes the nature of the securities nor commits capital to them.

## Social lending and borrowing: person-to-person lending

Banks which function as principal (balance sheet) intermediaries between those who want to lend and those who want to borrow provide clear benefits to both sides. However, banks have high cost structures and regulatory capital requirements. If it were possible to use agency intermediation which does not involve a balance sheet (hence is not regulated as a banking business) to bring borrowers and lenders together, this could lower the cost of intermediation substantially. Recently we have seen the creation of direct person-to-person (also known as peer-to-peer) lending websites which cut out balance sheet intermediaries. The first of these in the UK was Zopa.com. Another provider of lending platforms to 3rd parties is LendLoanInvest.co.uk (the author is a director of its parent company), which enables lenders and borrowers to be brought together directly. They act as introducing brokers. The higher are the capital charges and liquidity requirements (Basel III based regulations), the higher the cost of commercial bank balance sheet intermediation. In consequence direct lending through peer-to-peer (brokerage) networks becomes relatively more attractive in terms of lowering the cost of intermediation. There are also peer-to-peer sites such as Crowdcube, which provides a means for companies to raise equity without having to use an investment bank as an intermediary. Civilized Money is another company intending to set up peer-to-peer banking and equity funding provision.

## Investment bank new issue origination (primary market financing): agency basis

An investment bank arranging a financing for a company, but acting purely as the organiser of a new share issue (IPO) or a new bond issue for a company on what is known as a **best efforts basis** (as distinct from an **underwritten** basis as explained below), simply introduces investors to the company's securities and tries to interest them in buying. If they do not buy them, the company does not receive fresh capital. The investment bank neither changes the nature of the securities nor commits capital to them.

## PRINCIPAL (CAPITAL) INTERMEDIATION

### Investment bank new issue origination (primary market financing): principal basis

Principal intermediaries are balance sheet intermediaries. Thus, whereas a broker would provide no help if an issue of securities could not be sold to investors, an investment bank operating on a principal basis, i.e. an **underwritten** deal or **bought deal**, would put itself at risk of having to invest in the securities by putting them on its balance sheet. In the case of the **underwritten** issue it would be required by its contract with the issuer to purchase any securities that it could not sell to investors. In the case of the **bought deal** it would actually buy the whole issue from the issuer (as principal) and then hope to resell to investors. If it was unable to sell all the securities, those which were unsold would have to be held for a longer time on its own balance sheet, using its own capital or borrowed funds until investors were willing to buy them or until it reduced the price sufficiently to make them attractive to investors. If it does have to hold these securities it then has to be able to find additional financing quickly to enable it to hold them on a longer-term basis. It is thus subject to price risk (the risk of a fall in price) during this period.

### Secondary market trading: dealing function

A dealer in securities **makes prices**, i.e. provides quotations to professional investors and brokers. If a dealer has a contract with a stock exchange to provide dealing services, he or she is known as an official **market maker**. Dealers and market makers have a **dealing book**, i.e. a balance sheet of securities positions (bought and sold positions) from which the dealer transacts, thereby providing a service to brokers or institutional investors which enables them to deal instantly (in the broker's case, on behalf of a client), even if no investor counterparty is available immediately on the other side. He or she does this by quoting prices to brokers and institutional investors, and committing capital and hence taking risk.

So what intermediation services do dealers provide for which people are willing to pay the dealing spread? They don't provide advice! Those who transact through a dealer have to know what they wish to buy. If they want advice, they have to go to a broker who will obtain advice from a securities analyst and then go to the dealer to have a transaction executed on their behalf. **What dealers sell to investors is immediacy** – they enable investors to achieve immediate executions (buys and sells) when there might be no investor on the other side at the time when the client wants to transact. By providing this liquidity they hope to make a profit from the spread between the price at which they buy and the price at which they sell. Brokers, on the other hand, can only operate if they can find both sides of a transaction at around the same time or pass the order on to a multilateral trading centre, such as an exchange, or find a dealer to take the other side. A dealer, in contrast to a broker, is willing to take the risk of committing capital to a trading position **to facilitate client trades** in the hope of making a good risk-adjusted return on capital employed. Thus dealers, like their investment banking primary market colleagues, also need immediate access to short-term financing if their dealing inventory suddenly increases. This is normally obtained through what is known as the **repo market**(see Chapter 8).

## Broker/dealer

Investment banks are often described in the industry as the **sell side**. It should be noted that today this expression does not mean that they only sell securities. This name comes from the fact that originally the **only** function of investment banks was organising new issues of securities through the primary market (the market for new issues) and thus they only ever **sold** securities (to investors). But today, as they also have a secondary market department (the market between investors in existing shares) they are continually involved in both buying and selling. The department that undertakes this buying and selling in the secondary market is the broker/dealer part of the investment bank and, indeed, investment banks are often just called **broker/dealers**. In the secondary market they obviously both buy and sell. In practice almost all sell-side firms combine broking and dealing.

In the UK this was illegal until 1986 due to the perceived, and very real, conflict of interest. Since then the regulatory authorities have permitted broking and dealing, i.e. agency and principal businesses, to be combined, though with some safeguards. The other side of the industry is the **buy side**, which means the institutional investors who transact through the broker/dealer division of the investment banks, i.e. the sell side. They are the people who purchase (buy) the new issues of securities (in the primary market) which the investment banks are selling on behalf of companies and governments. Of course, they also sell and buy in the secondary market, so once again the word is slightly misleading.

## Commercial banking

Banks are principal intermediaries in that they take in deposits from one set of customers and transform these into loans to another set of customers. Thus the balance sheet and the relationships between the two sides of it is key to understanding the nature of their intermediation function.

# STRUCTURE OF THE INDUSTRY – FIRMS, PRODUCTS AND MARKETS
## Financial firms
### The banking sector
This comprises:

- *Commercial banking*: deposit taking (safekeeping of funds), financing through credit provision (bank lending) and money transmission (payment) services (fee-based agency service).

- *Investment banking*: raising finance (equity and bond) through markets and on behalf of companies and others and subsequently providing liquidity in the securities issues it arranges (the trading and sales function). It also undertakes financial asset structuring (for example securitisation) and provides risk management services through, for example, the creation of, and trading in, derivative contracts.

## Other financial institution sectors

- **Asset management**: creating portfolios of assets for clients to help them achieve their risk management objectives at minimum cost.
- **Wealth management**: advising individuals on how to structure their wealth holdings to achieve a desired risk profile (this may be purely advisory without even brokerage intermediation).
- **Insurance**: the provision of risk management services involving pure risk of loss but also financial risk services structured from derivative products:
  - **Life insurance**: mortality risk (the risk of early death) and its opposite, longevity risk (the risk of outliving one's savings);
  - **General insurance**: insurance of property risks such as home insurance or car insurance;
  - **Financial derivative products**: such as credit default swaps issued by American Insurance Group (AIG) and other guarantees on securities such as those on US municipal bonds.

The above list of financial intermediaries looks like a straightforward set of financial activities. Indeed, the industry in the first half of the twentieth century, and even until the mid-1980s, was relatively simple, and the most striking feature of it was that each of these sectors was generally quite clearly defined. Most companies in the industry would restrict themselves to one or at most two of these sectors.

Today investment banking and commercial banking have mostly been combined within a single holding company; asset management may be part of such a group or in some cases today has since been spun-off or sold; insurance may also be in a larger group, either attached to a bank(so-called **bancassurance**) or as part of an asset management group. The industry structure in the US, the UK and to a lesser extent in other countries that has developed since deregulation started in the early 1980s has resulted in the creation of what are known as **financial conglomerates**, i.e. firms which cover most, or all, of the activities listed above. Regulators also use the term **complex financial institution** to describe such firms. They have another set of acronyms to describe certain financial institutions: if a firm is so large that its collapse would be likely to impact on other financial firms in a very adverse way, and if society at large (the taxpayer) is at substantial risk from such a collapse, then such a firm would be known as a **systemically important financial institution** (**SIFI**); or, if it is a global firm, it would be known as a **G-SIFI**.

## Firms providing infrastructure

In addition to the main industry sectors above, there is a very important set of companies involved in providing the necessary infrastructure without which the industry could not operate. These companies are important because essentially the financial intermediation industry is one in which **the main activity is processing information and sending electronic messages between parties**. These messages enable prices to be discovered and agreed either between dealers and customers (known as over-the-counter or OTC) or on exchange, then for contracts to be exchanged (normally under a master agreement, such as the ICMA General Master Repo Agreement, covering all similar transactions) or ISDA rules and, finally, for securities and funds to be transferred. At each of these stages, sending appropriate messages through a network is the means by which this industry operates.

These providers of messaging and other electronic services may be grouped conveniently under the following generic headings: trading centres, data providers and network providers.

## Trading centres

These are of two main types:

(1)  **Systems companies** that provide a means for traders to meet and execute a trade but **without any capital provision by the trading centre organiser** (a stock exchange such as the London Stock Exchange);
(2)  **Financial intermediaries** (broker/dealers) who provide a trading centre facility by acting in the role of a **capital intermediary using their own proprietary capital**.

Under these two headings we find:

- **Traditional stock exchanges** or derivatives exchanges (systems companies);
- **Other trading centres** such as multilateral trading facilities (MTFs), alternative trading systems (ATSs), electronic communication networks (ECNs) and crossing mechanisms (systems companies) (see Chapter 13);
- **Swap execution facilities** (SEF) and organised trading facilities (OTFs)[1] (systems companies);
- **Dealers and market makers** who provide prices in cash and derivative products to **clients** (financial intermediaries)(see Chapter 12);
  - **Interdealer brokers (IDBs)** who provide mechanisms for dealers to trade between themselves, i.e. not with the public but in an 'inside' market (systems companies).

---

[1]  Legislative bodies in the US and Europe are planning to increase regulation of the OTC derivatives market. In the US the Dodd-Frank Act defines an SEF as 'a facility, trading system or platform in which multiple participants have the ability to execute or trade swaps by accepting bids and offers made by other participants that are open to multiple participants in the facility or system'. Compared with OTC trading, this would provide pre- and post-trade transparency, encourage competitive execution and ensure an audit trail of trades. In Europe, the regulatory term used to describe an SEF is organised trading facility (OTF).

## Data providers

These are firms which collect and distribute the data required by traders in order for them to establish prices at which to trade (the price discovery process). These are of three main types:

(1) **Trading centres** themselves, such as exchanges, which provide their own data on pre-trade opportunities and post-trade executions directly to traders.
(2) **Data consolidators**, such as Thompson Reuters or Bloomberg, which collect data from all trading centres and provide traders with a so-called 'consolidated tape', i.e. price and quantity information from all trading centres offering trading services in the same securities.
(3) **Pricing and index providers**, particularly for non-exchange products, where prices are not easily available. For example Markit, which provides price data and financial infrastructure to reduce risk and improve operational efficiency in lightly traded products. Another example is Standard and Poor's Corporation, which, as well as providing ratings services, also provides index services, such as the S&P 500 index.

## Network providers

These are firms which enable the messages generated by traders and infrastructure providers to be routed appropriately. For example:

**Equinix**, which connects businesses with partners and customers around the world through a global platform of data centres and a broad choice of networks.

**BT Radianz**, which is designed exclusively for the financial services community and provides fast, secure connectivity and hosting. It has more than 400 service providers to which they give access to pretrade, trade and post-trade and cross-asset applications over the entire electronic trade cycle, connecting a global community of more than 14,000 financial customer locations.

**Society for Worldwide Interbank Financial Transfers**, (SWIFT) which provides messaging services to enable large cross-border payments to be made. This company enables all the large payments involved in securities transactions (payments between banks) to be conducted safely. It is owned principally by the major commercial banks.

# Clearing and settlement infrastructure

Trades have to be cleared and settled, since trade execution simply means agreeing a contract of sale. Agreeing the contract terms has to be followed by agreeing the amount owing, the place of delivery, etc. This is covered in Chapter 14.

In addition to these providers, there is also an infrastructure of legal, accounting and other firms providing services to financial intermediaries.

At one time financial institutions operated almost exclusively in a single country (or in a few closely related countries). Today we have many truly global financial institutions – both financial intermediaries and electronic market centres. Whereas, not long ago, financial markets could be accessed only by someone actually located on the market trading floor (the New York Stock Exchange, for example, did not allow true electronic access to its market until 2006), today it is almost as easy to access markets based in London from anywhere in the world as it is from within the City of London itself; and similarly with New York markets. Financial products are ideal to sell globally, as today the cost of transporting them to foreign countries is virtually zero.

The International Capital Market (previously known as the Eurobond market[2]) was the first truly international market which came into existence in the 1960s. It was never a domestic market regulated by the authorities in a particular country. It was always a so-called 'off-shore' market, even though those working in it were based principally in the City of London, i.e. the financial district of London, which today also includes London Docklands.

## FINANCIAL PRODUCTS AND SERVICES

All financial products are simply contracts between two parties. I will describe only the simplest of such contracts. In the case of commercial banks, the main products are deposit accounts (a bank issued liability) and, on the other side of its balance sheet (the asset side), it issues loan contracts.

In the case of an investment bank, one of its main products is arranging a contract between issuers, such as companies, and investors which facilitates the transfer of resources (cash) from investors to companies. Such contracts can be in the form of equity or debt securities. The contract is in the form of a **prospectus** which lays down the liability to which the company has committed itself. In the case of a debt contract the liability the company creates is an obligation to pay interest and to repay the loan. On the other side of the contract, from the point of view of the investor buying the loan, it is an asset. This is because it provides a flow of income and repayment of the investment at maturity. An asset is something that is valuable and clearly this company issued liability (promise to pay) is valuable to the investor and is thus an asset in his or her hands.

Investment banks also offer contracts in which they themselves are on one side of the contract and an investor or trader is on the other side (a bilateral contract). Derivative contracts offered by investment banks are of this nature. Investment banks also provide a means by which investors can convert their investments back into cash, i.e. they provide secondary markets in securities and derivatives. All such trading transactions are covered by some type of **master agreement**, i.e. a contract covering multiple transactions.

In the provision of trading services(secondary market services) investment banks make a distinction between so called **flow trading**, which means servicing clients needs day-by-day, and **proprietary trading**, which means the bank trading for its own account rather than on behalf of a customer. Being a large flow trader is the objective of any bank wishing to be in the top league. Barclays CEO Bob Diamond has said being one of the world's '**flow monsters**' has been important for

---

[2] Note that the word 'Eurobond' in this context has no connection with the current discussion of *a* Eurobond (a common bond issued by eurozone countries) which at the time of writing is simply a concept.

it in achieving its profit goals. Every investment bank wants to be a flow monster, but only a handful (the so-called bulge-bracket firms) can be leaders in the high volume institutional investor flow dealing in bonds, interest-rate swaps, foreign exchange and the major equities. Recall from the start of Chapter 1, the view of the German finance minister in respect of bank trading activities. In his view trading should be an activity limited to servicing client needs i.e. flow trading and should not involve proprietary trading.

Asset management houses offer **collective investment fund** (see Chapter 18) contracts in which they issue shares or units in a 'fund'. Such units are equivalent to equity shares in most respects.

Insurance companies issue contracts to those who wish to manage risks in some way. For example, a home insurance policy (contract) would provide that, in the event of a house burning down, the insurer would pay for the cost of rebuilding.

## FINANCIAL MARKETS

Markets are mechanisms through which people can exchange assets. But when a financial asset is exchanged for cash, essentially what is being exchanged is a set of risks. Thus, for example, when a share is sold, the risks of holding that share are exchanged with someone who wishes to take on its risks and in exchange is willing to provide to the seller of the share, the riskless asset, cash. Of course they will only take on those risks if they believe that the potential reward from so doing will make it worthwhile.

There are two types of market:

(1) **Primary market**: this provides **funding liquidity**. A **corporate** (meaning a non-financial company) or other issuer such as a government will raise capital (long-term finance) in a market by issuing financial liabilities which offer to those on the other side of the market (**investors** who are buying a financial asset) the possibility of financial returns. The actual returns realised by investors will almost certainly, over time, prove to be more or less than the return expected at the time the contract was agreed, i.e. the returns are risky. Thus when we talk about future return we use the expression **expected return**.

(2) **Secondary market**: this provides **market liquidity** once new securities have been issued. An investor holding a financial asset who needs to convert it back to cash will contract to sell it to another investor through the infrastructure of a **trading centre**, i.e. a place to buy and sell shares such as a stock exchange but normally via an intermediary such as a broker. The secondary market transfers liquidity **between two investors** (or between their financial institution intermediaries). As in the primary market, this is the exchange of one asset for another asset (cash for shares in both), but in this case between two investors.

Financial markets, both primary and secondary, **enable** transactions, i.e. enable the transfer of liquidity (cash) in one direction and a risk/return opportunity in the other. But the **key function** of a secondary market is to discover the **fair** price at which this should happen. Fairness in this case simply means a price at which, at a particular point in time, all demand to buy can be matched against all demand to sell. This means that a secondary market is a mechanism in which supply and demand, if not already in balance, can be brought into balance through a price change. This process is known as **price discovery**. The secondary market is, therefore, the mechanism though which a price is found at which supply and demand balance. This is known as the **market price** and, provided a sufficient number of participants are active on both sides of the market, is considered to be the fair price for transactions. However, this does not imply that it truly reflects the underlying **fundamental** value of the asset,[3] particularly as many participants in the market will have a different view of the fundamental value of the asset being traded.

In the absence of a market with many competing traders, known as **multilateral trading** such as on a stock exchange, the alternative, which is transactions between just two people, known as **bilateral trading**, might be expected to be more limited in number because of the difficulty two people would have in coming to an agreement on what something was 'worth'. In fact bilateral trading volumes exceed multilateral trading volumes. Whether the prices which are discovered in these markets are fair, is another issue. I will cover bilateral markets in more detail when we consider dealer markets in Chapter 12.

The relationship of secondary financial markets to financial intermediaries is that the latter are the participants most actively involved in markets, either on their own behalf (as principals) or on behalf of their clients (as agents). The market is the mechanism through which buy and sell orders can interact and thereby, the fair price can be discovered. All that happens on a market is that contracts are made, i.e. there is agreement on:

the item being transferred (the particular security);
the quantity;
the price;
where it is to be delivered;
where the cash in payment should be deposited.

Subsequently, another part of the market infrastructure enables the actual cash to be exchanged for the financial asset, and the final settlement of the transaction can be completed with one party having a financial asset delivered to an agreed location and the other party receiving cash in an agreed bank account (**clearing and settlement**).

The International Capital Market (previously known as the Eurobond market) is a good market to use to exemplify the distinctions between firms, products and markets. The International Capital Market is a debt market in which the **financial product** is corporate, sovereign and supranational bonds. Dealing takes place between **financial firms** (banks, investment banks and asset managers) through the banks' own **technology infrastructure** using bilateral trading rather than on a multilateral exchange and under the rules of ICMA.. Each transaction is a legal

---

[3] 'Fundamental value' means the value calculated scientifically (using discounted cash flow techniques) using an investor's or trader's forecast of cash flow and their estimation of the risk of those cash flows.

contract but it is normally undertaken under a **master agreement** signed by both the transacting parties at the start of their relationship. Subsequent to this, each transaction would be covered by this agreement.

## THE CHANGING NATURE OF THE INVESTMENT BANKING FIRM SINCE THE YEAR 2000: A BRIEF SUMMARY

Traditionally, investment banks were contrasted sharply with commercial banks since the former were involved in a different area of business from the latter. Indeed, investment banks traditionally operated in almost the opposite way to commercial banks in that their commitment of capital was seldom long-term and even their short-term commitment was limited. A major reason for this was that, until quite recently, investment banks were operated as partnerships financed by capital provided by the individual partners. Such partnerships generally also had unlimited liability, unlike limited liability companies (plc, Ltd, Inc. GmbH, etc.) where the liability of owners is limited to the capital they have paid in. Thus investment banks had very small balance sheets relative to the volume of business they undertook. In the corporate finance field, capital commitment was unusual as relatively few **originations** (new issues) required that the investment bank take up unsold securities. Additionally, investment banks were not involved in lending since they did not have a deposit base.

As investment banks changed from being private partnerships to being public companies quoted on a stock exchange, they had access to much more capital and, with limited liability, were much more willing to take risks with outside capital. One reason for this was that the directors hoped that increased risk would bring higher returns and their own remuneration, being linked to returns, would be enhanced. This resulted in them changing from financial institutions with small balance sheets (compared with commercial banks) to being public companies with highly leveraged balance sheets comparable in size to many commercial banks. Goldman Sachs, for example, chose to become a public company only in 1999. By 2007 it had a balance sheet of over $1 trillion. A balance sheet of that size is larger than many large commercial banks and is not required simply to support customer business. Thus investment banks have changed from being institutions which posed no **systemic risk**, i.e. a risk to more than just their own shareholders, to being a substantial source of such risk because of their absolute size, the nature of their asset funding and their close interconnections with the commercial banking industry through borrowing from banks and derivative contracts with banks.

Over the decade from the year 2000, broker/dealers have been cutting their capital commitment in some areas such as client trading services (flow trading). They have been able to do this because there are two ways in which a client trade execution can be achieved:

(1) **Capital facilitated**: employing capital to enable the trade
(2) **Agency** only: acting as a broker without capital commitment.

They have shifted from the former to the latter as capital has become more scarce and alternative uses have provided higher returns. Thus large institutional clients have found that the broker dealer will not undertake large trades as dealer (i.e. committing capital) and instead will act only as a broker to break up their order into smaller pieces to send the smaller orders on to a multilateral trading venue such as an exchange.

The 'more profitable use' to which investment banks have instead been putting their capital is their own **proprietary trading and investment** activities, i.e. trading on their own account using their own capital. In many instances they also set up large hedge funds and private equity funds **off-balance sheet**, i.e. as separate companies, financed partly by their own capital and partly with investor funds. The result of the huge volume of capital commitment by investment banks to these activities has been to change the nature of many of them from being mainly **client-focussed** (and acting on the one side as a broker to corporates and on the other side as a broker to investors) to being **own-capital institutions** (acting as principal in a high proportion of their activities). This has, in turn, led to potential and actual conflict with their corporate clients (companies) and their investment clients (hedge funds, investment funds, private equity firms and others) which I will cover in Chapter 29. Thus today, in addition to acting as both **agents and principals** in trade execution for clients, investment banks also act as principal traders to invest the investment bank's **own funds**. This activity is undertaken by the **trading and principal investment department**[4] which means that it trades for itself as principal and not as an agent for its clients. This is a department which uses the bank's own funds, i.e. not client funds, to invest in assets such as private equity, hedge funds and structured equity and to undertake proprietary trading using the bank's own funds. Thus investment banks have, as clients:

investors;
issuing companies; and also
in-house departments.

Given that the interests of each of these classes of client are likely to have different objectives, there may be conflicts of interest in an investment bank with such a structure. Indeed, investment banks have increasingly chosen to take advantage themselves of the best investment opportunities that they spot, rather than offering them to clients, something which may be quite legal but may not be appreciated by clients who may be on the other (losing) side of the trade.

A good example of an investment bank with a large principal trading division is Goldman Sachs. Before the credit crisis Goldman, as we noted earlier, had a balance sheet size of over $1 trillion, i.e. a balance sheet with $1 trillion of financial assets financed by capital raised by issuing equity and a range of debt securities (liabilities) to investors in the amount of $1 trillion. A balance sheet of this size is clearly not required just to provide trade execution services to clients. Instead it is structured to try to allow the firm to take first advantage of its own expertise and incoming information flows across a wide range of financial markets rather than simply giving the best ideas for potentially profitable trades to clients. If a good investment opportunity is spotted, it may be logical from a profit perspective for

---

[4] This was the term used until recently by, for example, Goldman Sachs.

any investment bank to use its own funds to participate. Thus rather than simply earning commissions and fees (from agency business) and spreads (from principal business with counterparties) it aims also to make capital gains from its own principal investment positions. One reason why it may be more successful than average in achieving a high return on its capital is quite simply the huge information flow it obtains from its on-going interaction with clients worldwide (flow business), which puts it in a very good position to be '**ahead of the market**'.

Principal investments by commercial and investment banks including Goldman Sachs were one of the main sources of loss in the financial crisis. One proposal to prevent a recurrence of such losses in the banking system is the 2010 so-called Volcker[5] proposal in the United States which would force financial institutions with a banking licence to withdraw from principal investing activities (apart from traditional lending and market making) because of the risk such activities are deemed to pose to the taxpayer. Aspects of this were included in the Dodd-Frank Wall Street Reform and Consumer Protection Act ('DFA')in the United States which came into force in 2010 with the following purposes:

> An Act to promote the financial stability of the United States by improving accountability and transparency in the financial system, to end 'too big to fail', to protect the American taxpayer by ending bailouts, to protect consumers from abusive financial services practices, and for other purposes.

## A WIDER PERSPECTIVE ON FINANCIAL INTERMEDIATION

The purpose of this chapter has been to help readers to understand the role of intermediation in finance. But there is a much wider question to which attention should also be devoted. Financial intermediation is an industry which has grown dramatically in size over the past 20 years and, most particularly, in the decade from the year 2000. In the UK it has grown substantially in terms of its 'contribution' to GDP and in terms of numbers of highly skilled and highly paid people employed. An important question is whether or not the growth in this industry has helped achieve the objectives of society as a whole, which are employment, economic growth and the achievement of the personal financial aspirations of individuals and their comfort in retirement. Many would say not.

It may be that the costs of increasing amounts of intermediation are greater than the benefits. Most of the additional revenue being generated, rather than improving the outcome for companies and households, may be **economic rent** which is the extra return above the normal profit level that would be observed in a perfectly competitive market. This may result from, for example, **asymmetric information problems** between clients and financial intermediaries as a result of the intermediary being much more knowledgeable about the features of the product it is selling than is the client. If this is the case then the additional intermediation may

---

[5] Paul Volcker (born 1927) was chairman of the Federal Reserve Board (the US Central Bank) from 1979 to 1987. He was the chairman of the Economic Recovery Advisory Board under President Obama from 2009 until January 2011.

be subtracting from welfare. This is a very fundamental issue which has come to the fore in the aftermath of the financial crisis.

In the UK, in June 2011, the Secretary of State for Business in the United Kingdom, Vince Cable, announced that Professor John Kay would undertake an independent review to examine investment in UK equity markets and its impact on the long-term performance and governance of UK quoted companies. The *Kay Review of UK Equity Markets and Long-Term Decision Making* will be published in 2012. In a recent speech, John Kay noted that:

> A fundamental issue for the review will be whether the growth of intermediation has achieved this objective [improving company performance and saver/investor returns]. Or has the proliferation of intermediaries added to the costs faced by savers, what I describe as the 'wedge' between the underlying return earned by the company and that received by the investor? Has it interposed agents with their own objectives which may differ from those of either companies or savers? And, if all these things – more professionalism, higher costs, multiplication of potential conflicts of interest – are true, have the costs of increased intermediation justified the benefits? That is a core issue on which we shall be seeking evidence, both through submissions and from our own research.

# FINANCIAL INTERMEDIATION: COMMERCIAL AND INVESTMENT BANK STRUCTURE

## THE FIRST BANKS

In medieval times, merchants who traded between regions of a country or between countries needed to be able to change one currency in the form of gold or silver coins into other currencies. Merchants also needed to be able to keep their wealth somewhere they believed to be safe (gold and silver are very heavy to carry and 'keeping it under a mattress' was not safe). They grew to trust particular money-changers with whom they would deposit their money, i.e. their gold and silver coinage, for safekeeping. The moneychanger would then make a book entry in his accounts showing who had *deposited* money and would give them a **receipt**. When merchants wanted to pay each other large sums, this could then happen across the books of a moneychanger rather than in coinage. If the person being paid did not have an account with that moneychanger, he could either *open an account* with him or the transaction could be settled between his moneychanger and that of the seller. This **settlement** could easily be undertaken physically between moneychangers if they worked in the same area. All that was required would be a short walk at the end of the day to settle any outstanding balances amongst the competing moneychangers. Similar services could also be provided by goldsmiths and even by monasteries and innkeepers – if they were trusted. The receipt that a moneychanger issued when a merchant deposited money was in effect a **debt**, i.e. a liability of the issuer (the moneychanger) and an asset to the holder (the merchant).

Over time, the certificates issued by certain trusted goldsmiths came to be accepted by people other than the creditor and thus creditors came to be able to use such receipts, evidencing their holding of a sum of money with a particular moneychanger or goldsmith, as a means to pay other merchants, i.e. they became **privately issued transferable debt certificates** (paper currency) rather than just receipts which were not transferable. The person receiving the certificate could, at any time, go to the moneychanger or goldsmith and ask for the coins or bullion which underlay the certificate. And thus banks came into existence since such certificates were, in principle, little different from a large denomination dollar bill or pound sterling note. It should be noted, however, that such banks were not involved in **financial intermediation**, i.e. they did **not** offer to lend money which is now such a key function for banks and other financial intermediaries. They therefore did not provide credit and thus were not involved in **maturity transformation**, i.e. borrowing short term and lending long term which contemporary banks do. They were what are known as **cloakroom banks**, i.e. they let you leave money with them for safekeeping for a fee and gave you a 'cloakroom ticket' or receipt which enabled you to reclaim the money later.[1]

## BANKS AS FINANCIAL INTERMEDIARIES

Over time, moneychangers and goldsmiths realised that, provided they retained the confidence of their customers, it was very unlikely that everyone to whom they had issued receipts would arrive at the door at the same time and demand that their wealth be returned. They thus started to **use deposits as a way of making loans** and thus invented the **fractional reserve system** of banking, i.e. there was much less than 100% cash (gold) backing for deposits since much of the gold was now being lent out. **The fractional reserve system (less than 100% of assets held as gold or cash) is what makes banking systems inherently unstable in the event that investors panic. It has been at the root of numerous banking crises.** On the other hand it is what enables the high level of credit provision in modern society without which economic growth and employment would be lower than it has been in the past.

Before the banks started to offer credit (loans), a tradesman, farmer or merchant would have been able to raise finance only by going to a person with surplus wealth and 'borrowing' this wealth in exchange for a promise to repay, i.e. by issuing a private debt in exchange for money (gold or silver) in a process known as **direct financing**, i.e. financing without the use of a financial intermediary.

Direct financing without intermediation has four limitations:

1. It is limited by the amount of wealth (gold) that is available and that people are willing to lend;
2. It requires a 'credit assessment' and 'risk pricing', i.e. price discovery – something which most people would not be good at, which means they will only lend to those they know personally;
3. It ties up a lender's money until final repayment of the loan;
4. If principal and interest are not paid when due, the lender has to apply to the courts for redress which is both expensive and difficult for an individual to do.

The innovation which turned early banks into **financial intermediaries**, as we know them today, was for the moneychanger, goldsmith or merchant (some merchants started to specialise in financing and became merchant banks), rather than the person whose wealth it was, to arrange the lending. This had numerous advantages. The **'banker'** could specialise in banking and in evaluating how creditworthy potential borrowers were and what **'credit spread'** (risk premium) to

---

[1] A very good coverage of the development of banks can be found in *The Ascent of Money: A Financial History of the World* by the UK-born Harvard professor Niall Fergusson, published by Penguin Press in 2008 and adapted as a television documentary for Channel 4 (UK) and PBS (US).

charge any particular borrower (the credit assessment or pricing function). The cloakroom bank thus became an **intermediary** between the owner of wealth and the person to whom it was lent. But more importantly, by creating a **diversified portfolio of loans**, i.e. not just lending out to one borrower but to many, the risk[2] of the portfolio of loans of a banker, compared with the single or small number of loans that could be made by the original holder of the wealth, was greatly reduced. This reduction in risk meant that loans could be made for a lower rate of interest since there was much less chance of losing all one's wealth from a single large loan (catastrophic risk). This is the same benefit that is achieved from holding a diversified portfolio of shares. Like so many innovations in finance, it reduced the cost of financing and thus increased the volume of financing available.

Risk reduction is one of the principles of modern banking and should provide one of the great benefits of this type of intermediation compared with direct lending. However, **leveraged balance sheet lending** which is what banks do, financed from short-term customer deposits and only a small amount of shareholder equity capital, creates a substantial risk both of insolvency (losses causing liabilities to exceed assets) and of illiquidity (inability to pay cash back to depositors). Even if a bank is not in fact insolvent, depositors may fear that it is and thus rush to remove their deposits. In an unstable economic or political environment this can cause a liquidity crisis (a bank run) unless the bank holds a high proportion of liquid assets.

In terms of the balance sheet, which is the key feature of what are termed '**principal**' type financial intermediaries (in contrast to agency type), on one side (the liability side) the banker takes in deposits from many people on the assumption that most will not want their money back at the same time. On the other side (the asset side) the banker assumes that he can estimate what proportion of his many borrowers will not repay (perhaps 3%). By charging a credit spread (an additional amount above the interest rate he is paying on his deposits) to cover such potential losses (**expected losses**) he can avoid making a loss overall. But most importantly, when a customer who made a deposit wants to have it returned, it can be returned even though it has been lent out, since the banker always keeps a sufficient quantity of reserves (on the asset side of the balance sheet) for those **few** customers who want to take repossession of their money. Of course if **every** customer wanted his or her money back, this would cause a **bank run** – such as happened to Northern Rock bank in the UK in 2008.

Today we use the expression **reserves** or **liquid reserves** or **liquid assets** for the assets that banks keep in reserve to allow for temporary differences between deposits coming in and deposits going out. Indeed, in some countries such as the USA, Australia and India, the central bank is known as the Reserve Bank, i.e. the central bank is the final source of cash reserves for a commercial bank which has run short of liquid assets. As we noted above, this is on the **asset side** of the balance sheet. This is not 'capital' which is on the **liability side** and is also sometimes called a reserve, but is a measure of how much of the total financing of a bank is provided by its owners. Capital reserves on the liability side of the balance sheet protect lenders from loss.

---

[2] This is just an application of old adage, 'don't put all your eggs in one basket'.

# TYPES OF BANK TODAY

## Central banks

The first type of bank is the **central bank** of a country which is a single institution normally owned by the government. An example is the Bank of England which is the central bank for the United Kingdom. It was founded in 1694 to act as the government's banker and debt manager. Although privately owned for much of its life, the activities it undertakes are determined by its governing legislation and by its relationship with government. Surprisingly, it was not nationalised until 1946 and was thus a private company owned by shareholders until that date.

The central bank provides **central bank money**, i.e. liabilities issued by the central bank (partly notes and coins but principally **deposits at the central bank**). In practice, only banks and other financial institutions have access to central bank money in the form of central bank deposits, i.e. only they have bank accounts with the central bank. Central bank money is the means by which the settlement of transactions **between** commercial banks takes place. For this reason central bank money is known as the **settlement asset** and results in what is known as **settlement finality**, i.e. a transaction settlement that cannot be rescinded, unlike, for example, a payment by cheque where the cheque might 'bounce', i.e. fail to be paid by the bank. Central banks thus create a much less risky type of money, in theory riskless, than the second type of bank, the commercial bank. Commercial banks promise to convert commercial bank money in the form of demand deposits (also known as credit money) into central bank money (notes and coin) at any time and at a 1:1 exchange rate. Thus commercial bank money (bank deposits) should be as good as notes and coin.

Central banks no longer keep the promise on their notes 'to pay the bearer on demand' which is written on the face of many bank notes. This originally meant that the bank note would be exchanged for gold at any time. The statement is now just a historical legacy. In the United States where the central bank is known as the Federal Reserve System or simply the Fed, the expression that people rely on is that dollar bills are said to have 'the full faith and credit of the United States' backing them.

Instead of exchangeability into gold, we look for three things from a central bank in respect of the currency or **fiat** money as it is also called:

1. That the currency of a country will be accepted by everyone in that country in exchange for goods and services (trust);
2. That its value within the country will not decline at an unacceptable rate over time (inflation will be held to a low level);
3. That its value in international trade, as distinct from domestic transactions, will not decline at an unacceptable rate, i.e. there will be a limit on the amount the currency might depreciate against other currencies (maintenance of international value, meaning the exchange rate).

The importance of the maintenance of value arises from one of the roles of a currency, which is that of being a **store of value**, i.e. a means to hold savings safely. If it cannot maintain its purchasing power both domestically and internationally, it is not performing as holders of currency might expect. Currencies have two other roles – **unit of account** (to allow things to be priced relative to each other) and **medium of exchange** (to facilitate transactions). The US dollar is the most used currency internationally in all three roles. It is used as a unit of account not only in the United States but also for pricing globally traded commodities (gold, oil, wheat, etc.) and a high proportion of international trade. It is used not only in transactions within the US and between the US and other countries but frequently in transactions between third parties as a suitable 'neutral' currency. It is also used as an **international store of value**, not only by households who fear that their own currency is about to devalue (for example it was often used by residents of South and Central America when their own currencies were falling in value), but also in the role of **reserve currency**, i.e. one held by governments or central banks to provide foreign currency liquidity for the private sector in the event of an **imbalance in international trade** (a current account deficit). China, for example, has almost $3 trillion in reserves, a high proportion of it in US dollar assets.

## Commercial banks

The second type of bank, the **commercial bank**, is normally a shareholder-owned company quoted on a stock exchange, though in some countries the government owns the commercial banks. Even in China, where banks have been 'privatised' and their shares are quoted on the Shanghai market, the government is still the majority shareholder in most of them. While the central bank provides notes and coin (which no longer have any intrinsic value), the private banks provide the major part of the money supply of a country in the form of their deposit liabilities. For an individual, most of his or her spending power will be held not in the form of bank notes in a wallet and coins in a pocket (it would be too bulky, just as gold is) but in the form of bank deposits which can be transferred by the use of a cheque, a debit card, a contactless payment system or direct transfer using e-banking. Thus an individual holds some of his or her spending power, also known as **transaction balances**, in the form of central bank money (the promise of the central bank that its notes and coin will be accepted by others in payment) and the remainder in **commercial bank money** (the promise that the liabilities issued by a company, a commercial bank, will be accepted in payment).

Commercial bank money is simply bank deposits, and thus it is the **commercial banks which create the major part of the money supply**. Modern commercial banks are obviously involved in lending (provision of credit) as well as the safe-keeping of money (store of value function) and in the transfers of funds between customers (payment function). But in the same way as a goldsmith by granting a loan expanded the money supply, so does the provision of a loan by a commercial bank. There are, of course, constraints on how much money a bank can lend out. In economic terms, it will lend until the marginal cost of funds equals the marginal rate at which it can lend. But more importantly, a bank has to ensure that it has the ability to repay depositors (from the asset side of the balance sheet) when they ask for their money back (**liquidity**). Banks thus have to manage their **liquidity risk**, i.e. the risk that they are unable to repay depositors on demand. They also have to be sure that, in the event that some borrowers do not repay, they have sufficient shareholder capital (on the capital and liability side of the balance sheet) to absorb the loss without affecting the value and safety of their deposits (**solvency risk**).

In the period starting in the year 2000 up to the start of the financial crisis in mid-2007, banks were running down their reserves against loss – i.e. their equity capital (again, this is on the liability side of the balance sheet) relative to their total assets, thus creating the risk of insolvency – and also running down the liquid assets they had available (on the asset side of the balance sheet) to meet increased demand by depositors and other lenders for liquidity i.e. for the return of their cash. As a result of these reductions in cash reserves (asset side) and in equity capital (liability side), they started failing. Initially the problems seemed to be due to a liquidity shortage but with the benefit of hindsight it became clear that many banks were also insolvent i.e. had insufficient capital. In consequence, regulators worldwide are now **recalibrating** the rules, i.e. changing the required amount in terms of shareholders' equity capital/asset ratio on the liability side of the balance sheet (to protect from insolvency risk) and liquid assets/total assets ratio on the asset side of the balance sheet.

## Investment banks

The key feature which distinguishes commercial banks from any other type of financial institution is that a bank must have a banking licence. This permits it to accept deposits from the public. The price of being allowed to accept deposits (which are generally accepted to be risk free for savers due to deposit insurance) is that banks must subject themselves to stricter regulation and more intrusive official supervision than any other type of financial institution, including investment banks. However, this 'privileged' position also gives them access to liquidity at the central bank discount rate which is a facility not generally available to investment banks.

Unlike commercial banks, investment banks do not have a banking licence. As a result they may not accept deposits from the public. The advantage of this status is lighter regulation. Traditionally they focussed on arranging securities issues (equity and bond) for companies. It could be argued that they should not be called banks at all since, traditionally, they do not lend or take deposits from the public. Equally they should not have the word 'investment' in their title since they do not traditionally invest. However, in their role as arrangers of financings through capital markets, they can be considered to be bankers.

In the past most investment banks were separate companies from commercial banks (with the exception of those based in Continental Europe). Today most '**complex financial institutions**', as they are sometimes known by the regulators, have as their foundation a combination of investment and commercial banking. To this many have added asset management, wealth management and, sometimes, insurance.

The list below[3] is of those firms which have a major presence in the investment banking business. In 12 out of these 16, commercial and investment banking have been merged. These are **universal banks**, i.e. they are commercial banks with

---

[3]  See www.investmentbanksguide.com for brief descriptions of many investment banks.

large investment banking subsidiaries. Only three (those in bold) are essentially pure investment banks,[4] even though they also undertake lending (financed not by deposits but by other types of borrowing) and may also own a commercial bank subsidiary:

- Bank of America (Bank of America Merrill Lynch);
- Barclays (Barclays Capital);
- BNP Paribas (BNP Paribas CIB);
- Citigroup (Citi Institutional Clients Group);
- Credit Suisse;
- Deutsche Bank;
- **Goldman Sachs;**
- HSBC;
- JPMorgan Chase (J. P. Morgan Investment Bank);
- **Morgan Stanley;**
- **Nomura Holdings;**
- UBS (UBS Investment Bank);
- Royal Bank of Canada (RBC Capital Markets);
- Royal Bank of Scotland;
- Wells Fargo (Wells Fargo Securities)
- Jefferies and Company Inc,

Prior to 1933, commercial banks in the United States were actively involved in investment banking, i.e. arranging securities issues as well as deposit-taking and lending. However, in the wake of the stock market crash and the Depression in the United States which started in 1929, many banks collapsed, causing retail depositors to lose their savings. This led to the **Glass Steagall Act (GSA)** of 1933, which drew a line between commercial banking and securities activities and forced banks to choose which side of the fence to operate on. **J. P. Morgan**, for example, was forced to split into **J. P. Morgan** (the commercial bank) and **Morgan Stanley** (the investment bank). It was believed that such splits would prevent failing banks using depositors' funds to purchase failing securities issues which could lead to losses for depositors. Thus it was an attempt by the regulator to try to overcome conflict of interest and moral hazard issues that led to the split – issues which today are once again at the fore in the wake of the financial crisis.

Despite the ban, many US commercial banks retained quite extensive investment bank activities since debt underwriting and derivatives trading continued to be allowed. In addition, all the major US commercial banks set up subsidiaries in the United Kingdom in the City of London from the late 1960s onwards to enable them to gain experience of all investment banking activities, including

---

[4] Note that in order to obtain support from the Federal Reserve System at the time of the banking crisis, Goldman and Morgan Stanley both converted to Bank Holding Company status. This in effect made them into commercial banks. However, they do not operate as commercial banks. This change in legal structure was just to ensure the availability of help from the Fed.

equity underwriting. They hoped to use the skills gained in the UK in their operations in the United States if and when the Glass Steagall Act was removed from the statute book.

They also hoped to benefit from the upsurge in international business in London after 1967. Investment banks such as Kidder Peabody (which latterly belonged to General Electric Corporation), for which I worked at one time, was one of the early US firms to use London as a base to build up its international business followed by Merrill Lynch, Goldman Sachs and Morgan Stanley. All these firms were very active in the Eurobond[5] market (now the International Capital Market whose trade association and market regulator is ICMA), organising the underwriting of bond issues for companies and others – something which was illegal in the US. In practice, the actual work on such primary market issues was, for many years, undertaken in New York. Only the actual offering documents came out of London. Thus, as is so often the case with regulations, firms found a way to beat the spirit of the Act.

The Glass Steagall Act was repealed only in 1999 when the **Gramm–Leach–Bliley Act** (GLBA) was passed. This allows US commercial banks to operate in securities markets in a very similar way to investment banks but through a subsidiary under a holding company structure. The new Act resulted in many commercial banks moving strongly into investment banking. One consequence of this was greater competition and thus falling margins in a number of product areas. This may have been one reason why, to compensate for falling profits, investment banks (and also commercial banks) increasingly entered the **principal investing business** from 1999 onwards. Since the passing of the GLBA, there has been an increasing similarity of the activities of commercial and investment banks. However, commercial banks have always had the advantage of being able to accept deposits – a low cost form of funding compared with the money market funding that investment banks have to use – but at the cost of tighter regulation. Since 2008, however, when the last remaining large, pure investment banks in the United States (Goldman Sachs and Morgan Stanley) converted to bank holding company status in order to obtain implicit state support, it has become even harder to distinguish commercial and investment banking companies.

China still has a legal separation of commercial banking from securities activities which is likely to remain in force after the experience of Western banks in the financial crisis. In Japan there has been the equivalent of the Glass Steagall Act since 1945. That separation is now also ending, partly as a result of legislative change but also from the close connections that have developed between banks and brokers.

In Continental Europe, in contrast, the so-called **universal bank** model, i.e. combined commercial and investment banking (often with insurance as well creating a bancassurance company), has been the standard business model, particularly in Germany and Switzerland through banks such as Deutsche Bank, UBS

---

[5]  Note once again that this original use of the word Eurobond is different from today's use, which means the theoretical concept of a bond issued by the eurozone, guaranteed by all eurozone governments but used to help finance specific countries in the zone.

and Credit Suisse. However, in practice the Continental banks had little involvement in what today we consider to be the business areas of a typical investment bank. It was not until they set up investment banking operations in the City of London, mostly in the 1980s, and started to compete much more strongly in the rapidly growing Eurobond market, that they started to look quite similar to US investment banks. Today, of course, Deutsche Bank, UBS, Credit Suisse and BNP Paribas are major investment as well as commercial banks with all four having their major investment banking activities in London. Although UBS seemed initially to be successful in the run-up to the financial crisis in breaking into the so-called **bulge bracket**, i.e. major investment bank league, in August 2011 it reported that it was cutting back its investment banking activities very substantially and limiting them to essentially those which it deemed necessary to support its private banking and wealth management franchise. A loss of $2.3 billion in its Delta 1 trading department in September 2011 has also caused yet further retrenchment in the investment banking division of the company.

In the UK, prior to 1986, investment banking activities, i.e. organising new issues of shares and bonds for companies, was undertaken by so-called merchant banks which came into being in earlier times as a result of some merchants choosing to specialise in banking. This resulted in the creation of banks such as Hill Samuel & Co. (founded in 1832 as a company trading with the Orient), for which I worked at one time in the fixed-income primary market department. Such banks had a deposit-taking banking licence but did not have retail operations, only corporate financing which could be provided either in the form of the provision of credit (a bank loan) or a securities issue (shares or bonds). Merchant banks were a separate category of bank from retail high street banks but the division of business in this way between the two types of bank was not mandated by law, only by custom. Such banks did not trade securities. That service was provided by brokers and dealers. But in the UK, commercial banks could not own brokers and brokers could not own dealers (market makers who provided prices) until 1986. Thus a customer wishing to buy securities would approach a broker, the broker would ask competing dealers in the market for their prices and would then execute the trade with the best priced dealer.

## INVESTMENT BANKS AND INVESTMENT BANKING: HISTORY

The first investment bankers were the merchant banks of Europe with names such as Warburg, Baring, Lazard, Rothschild, Hill Samuel and Schroder. These were originally merchants who moved into the business of financing trade, in particular the grain trade, in Europe. Through their contacts with wealthy families they started to provide investment management services. This generated funds which they were able to use to provide financing for trading and other ventures. Today the names still exist but the ownership or activities have changed. Warburg is now part of UBS, Barings became part of ABN Amro after a rogue trader in Asia, Nick Leeson, bankrupted it and it was sold to ABN for one euro. ABN Amro, in turn, was acquired by Royal Bank of Scotland (ABN's losses caused RBS to collapse shortly after the acquisition). Rothschild remains independent but provides only corporate banking, venture capital and private banking services, while Schroder is principally an asset management and corporate finance advisory company having sold its merchant banking activities. Lazard describes itself on its website thus:

> Lazard, one of the world's preeminent financial advisory and asset management firms, operates from 41 cities across 26 countries in North America, Europe, Asia, Australia, Central and South America. With origins dating back to 1848, the firm provides advice on mergers and acquisitions, strategic matters, restructuring and capital structure, capital raising and corporate finance, as well as asset management services to corporations, partnerships, institutions, governments, and individuals.

The term 'investment bank' is a US one, though it is now common parlance in many countries. Traditionally, the investment bank was an institution **which facilitated the issue of securities (equity and debt) by companies**. Thus investment banks were concerned only with the **primary market**, i.e. the market for the issue of new securities. It is only much more recently that investment banks also started to provide advice to companies on matters such as acquisitions and to set up specialist merger and acquisition (M&A) departments. The various activities with which the traditional investment bank was involved are classified as **corporate finance**, i.e. everything related to the companies to which they provide services. As **customer-facing institutions**, it was **corporates** they faced, not households. Traditionally they would not be involved in investment of their own capital in securities. **They also did not trade securities for customers and would often not be members of a stock exchange as this is required only for trading.**

Traditionally investment banks, such as Morgan Stanley, **had only one office** which would be located on Wall Street. The reason for this was that they had relatively few clients – just the major companies across the United States. The chief executives of these companies would come to New York if they wished to discuss financing or the corporate financiers would visit them at their headquarters. As corporate facing institutions, investment banks were not concerned with **brokerage**, i.e. the provision of liquidity in the secondary market to asset managers or individuals. They were also not trading houses and therefore did not make markets as dealers. In 1972, Morgan Stanley employed only 110 people! It had only \$12 million of capital![6] It has changed out of all recognition since then. By 2007, it employed around 50,000 people, had around \$35 billion of capital and a balance sheet size of over \$1 trillion.

On the other hand, brokerage firms such as Smith Barney, Dean Witter Reynolds and Merrill Lynch, were known principally as **wire houses**, i.e. firms with branches across the country providing **brokerage and asset management services** and linked to head office by telephone and telex wires (cables). As they dealt with '**Main Street** customers', they needed to have offices in major towns and cities. Their telex network then linked every Main Street office to Wall Street, i.e. to the head office in Manhattan, enabling the New York office to access the investment banks on Wall Street (to source new issues of shares and bonds) and the New York Stock Exchange for secondary market trades. As **customer-facing**

---

[6] The source of this information is Professor Emeritus Sam Hayes, interviewed in *Inside Job*, a film on the 2008 financial crisis which is a 'must see' for anyone studying finance.

**institutions**, they faced **individuals** and to a lesser extent institutions since, prior to the 1960s, institutions were relatively less important than individuals as customers. Smith Barney later became part of Citigroup.[7]

In addition to brokerages and investment banks there were also specialised **trading houses** to which brokers could go for trade execution. For example, Spear Leeds & Kellogg Specialists LLC, which was a so-called **specialist** on the New York Stock Exchange which acted as a market maker[8] or Salomon Brothers (now part of Citigroup). Such dealers and market makers were the firms which risked their own capital (dealt as principal) to make prices (provide price discovery) to others on a wide range of markets.

## THE STRUCTURE OF THE TYPICAL INVESTMENT BANK

We noted above that investment banking (corporate facing) and brokerage (investor facing) services were originally provided by different companies. The typical, integrated, investment bank today has two main divisions reflecting this historical, and logical, split:

1. **Corporate facing**: the **investment banking** side, also known as the **banking** side or **corporate finance** department, which arranges new securities issues (and may also arrange **mergers and acquisitions**) and provides advice to companies;
2. **Investor facing**: the **broker/dealer** side (brokerage, trading, market making, distribution of new issues, provision of secondary markets).

While these two activities are the key ones in any modern investment bank, in practice investment banks have added a number of other financial intermediary activities which are not integral to their client-facing activities as bankers or as broker/dealers. These non-client related activities are known as **principal** (or **proprietary**) trading and investment as we noted earlier. . Principal activities involve using their own capital for generating profit (or loss) directly without providing client services. **Principal investing** is own funds' investment in hedge funds, debt assets and private equity in order to try to generate capital gains. The dealer side of the broker/dealer part of the business is also a principal business in that it has to commit capital to trading positions, though these positions are supposed to be taken simply to enable the trading desk to service its clients.

---

[7] Citigroup sold 51% of Smith Barney to Morgan Stanley after the financial crisis hit as part of Citigroup's effort to raise money to provide fresh capital after its huge losses. The wealth management arm of Morgan Stanley, previously based on Dean Witter Reynolds (another large US broker), was merged with Smith Barney to become Morgan Stanley Smith Barney. At the time of writing, Morgan Stanley is proposing to buy out the Citigroup interest.

[8] SLK is now a wholly owned subsidiary of Goldman Sachs and Co., having been acquired in the year 2000 in order to provide Goldman with access to its technology and automated market mechanisms, RediBook.

In addition to principal activities, investment banks may also offer private banking/wealth management services and many undertake asset management for clients. Investment banks, despite the fact that they do not raise deposits, also provide loan financing in competition with the commercial banks. They do this from funds raised in the short-term money markets. This lending, however, is only to high-risk (and therefore potentially high-return) borrowers, such as private equity companies. Investment banks may, in addition, have a commercial bank subsidiary and therefore have a sister company (under a bank holding company structure) which is raising deposits from the public and companies, though it is very unlikely to have branches. Some investment banks also offer insurance services.

## Structure of a 'simple' investment Bank

Banks have a number of divisions to reflect their diverse activities. We will start by considering just the investment banking and securities (broker/dealer) divisions, as these are the key ones in any modern large investment bank. However, I have included an asset management division to show where this would be located, although a number of banks will not have an asset management division and many have recently sold off such divisions.

In Figure 4.1, the first thing to note is that there are three product divisions in this bank: corporate finance; securities trading and sales (which includes research and middle and back offices) and asset management.

**Corporate finance** is the original activity in a typical investment bank and is indeed, as we noted earlier, the original meaning of the term 'investment banking'. The two main activities under this heading are the organisation of financings for companies and the arranging of mergers or acquisitions. Both of these activities can be conducted on an **agency** basis but, in practice, competition between investment banks for this type of business has led to a situation in which it is

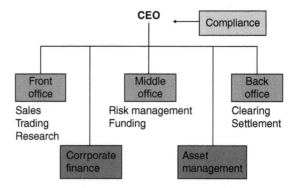

**Figure 4.1**   Typical investment bank structure
*Source*: David Lascelles[9]

---

[9]   David Lascelles was a banking editor of the *Financial Times* writer and co-founder of the Centre for the Study of Financial Innovation (CSFI). See: csfi.org

normal for an investment bank to **underwrite** securities offerings, i.e. to make a commitment to buy the issue by employing its own capital, if investors will not. In the case of mergers and acquisitions, they may provide not only advice but also bridge financing to enable the acquisition to go ahead quickly before permanent financing has been arranged by them.

It is argued by some that the easier access to customer deposits in a universal bank, through the retail banking arm as compared with **a pure play** (one without a banking licence) investment bank, has advantaged the former due to its being able to offer lower cost lending to potential clients and to finance securities holdings through customer deposits. Indeed, some would argue that clients will always turn to firms having funds available to finance deals as well as having the expertise in arranging them. Using customer funds for large leveraged loans and investment in securities may, however, put customer deposits at risk. In the case of UBS, the new chairman who took over after the financial crisis admitted that using private banking/wealth management client deposits to finance the investment bank (which many believed was in fact insolvent during the crisis), was not an appropriate structure for the business as it put wealth management clients funds at excessive risk.

This would suggest to many commentators that commercial banking and investment banking should be in separate companies. Indeed in the UK, the government will pass legislation in 2012, based on the Vickers Report, to separate UK retail banking from investment and wholesale banking by means of 'ring fencing'. **'Ring fencing'** means that retail banking on the one hand and investment and commercial banking activities on the other would have to be undertaken in separate companies with separate boards of management and with separate capital and liquidity to support them. Both companies could, however, be owned by a single 'bank holding company'. Many would argue that today's financial conglomerates have too many conflicts of interest and should go further than simply ring fencing retail banking. They would argue that advisory (agency) services should always be separate from financing (principal) services and that investment banking should be separate from private wealth management. This was the structure of the industry in the UK prior to 1986.

It can be seen in Figure 4.1 that corporate finance (and also asset management) is separated from the sales and trading department by reporting independently to the CEO. These departments may also be in a separate building or, if not, there will be a so-called 'Chinese wall' between them. This is designed, in theory, to minimise the conflicts of interest which can arise if these departments are all under the same management.

**Sales, trading and research (equity, bonds and derivatives)** is the **broker/dealer** part of the business. The broker undertakes sales (agency business) while the dealer makes markets, i.e. makes prices and takes positions as principal. While trading and sales is not an area that the investment banks used to be involved in, today they all provide this service. Trading and sales is divided into three 'offices' in order to minimise risk, particularly the risk of collusion between people within the firm.

The **front office** is the trading floor of the bank where brokers and dealers sit and do business on the telephone or by computer with their investor clients (both retail and wholesale clients).

The **middle office** has the function of providing risk measurement and management systems, ensuring compliance with the levels of risk taking that the firm permits (such as maximum long or short positions) and providing the treasury function, i.e. ensuring the availability of the funding (such as arranging repo financing) required to finance constantly fluctuating **positions** (holdings of securities). There is also a function called 'product control'. Although product control typically falls within the middle office division, its role is distinct. This is the department that can spot the mis-bookings of rogue traders. The product controller 'recreates' a trading book from scratch on a daily basis just to verify that the price updates and valuation models in the front office reflect the correct levels of risk assumed by the traders. In some banks, product control is now located on the trading floor to ensure that communication with traders is more effective.

The **back office** is responsible for ensuring that the trades are cleared and settled. This means ensuring that clients have paid the cash required to settle a trade before the securities are delivered to them, or that clients have been paid the appropriate amount of cash when the bank receives securities purchased from them.

It is critical for a bank to ensure independence between the three offices involved in sales and trading to minimise the risk of deception. In the well-known case of Barings Bank, a very junior trader, Nick Leeson, undertook trades which bankrupted the bank resulting, as we noted earlier, in it being sold to ABN Amro. The ease with which he did this was due to the back office in Asia, where he traded, reporting to him (clearing and settlement staff reported to a trader) and thus he could control the behaviour of employees in this department. In the more recent (2007) case of Jerome Kerviel at Societe Generale, it would also seem that controls were ineffective[10] and as a result the company lost $5 billion. No bank robber has ever got away with as much as this, though it is also the case that this was a trading loss, not theft. The most recent case (2011) involving Kweku Adoboli, a trader in UBS who lost $2.3 billion, would also seem to have involved some cross-over between the front and back offices, as Adoboli had previously worked in the back office and understood well the systems used there. Today back offices, for reasons of lower labour and rental cost, are normally at some distance from the front office which is in the City of London or on Wall Street. In the UK the back office may be in Bournemouth or Glasgow, and in Wall Street it may be in New Jersey. Increasingly, however, many back office tasks have been **offshored** to India.

In addition to front, middle and back office, investment banks have always traditionally had a research department. Research is today supposed to be an independent department (though only because regulators have recently required this)

---

[10] 'Using his knowledge of SocGen's back office and control systems – a computer system called Eliot – Mr Kerviel was able to enter false hedging contracts to make it appear as if he was taking minimal risks. By logging into the system under different names, he then cancelled the fake contracts before they were settled, replacing them with new ones. "He was always rolling one transaction into another. If he was ever caught, he just said it was a mistake and would start putting the trade somewhere else," says Mr Mustier.' ('How Kerviel Exposed Lax Controls at Société Générale', *Financial Times*, 7 February 2008.)

and not a tool of the sales side.[11] The fear of regulators is always that researchers will be 'persuaded' to recommend shares in which the investment bank itself has a proprietary interest or for which it is the company advisor, even if it believes they are mispriced, i.e. too expensive relative to their worth. Some researchers have been fined by the regulator or banned from the industry from this behaviour.

The **trading function** provides the means for holders of financial assets to turn their securities into cash or vice versa (the provision of liquidity). Investment banks have sales and trading departments which offer trading services in equity and fixed-income securities, foreign exchange, commodities and also in over-the-counter derivative instruments (contracts based on the prices of other assets as explained below). However, the actual business organisation varies widely between banks and also over time. In some banks equity and bond trading are under the same management. In others, equity and equity derivatives are placed together. In most banks today, however, fixed income **rates** are separated from fixed income **credit**. 'Rates' means 'government bonds', (hence traditionally implying no credit risk) plus interest rate swaps (swapping fixed interest rate flows for variable interest rate flows), whereas 'credit' covers corporate bonds and credit default swaps (See Chapter 9) which allow credit risk to be transferred separately from the underlying cash investment in a bond.

In most investment banks, there is a **fixed income, currency and commodities (FICC)** division which in the last decade has been the most profitable side of the business (though most of the seeming profit was offset by equivalent losses in the financial crisis).. Equities and related derivatives trading would normally be in a separate department from FICC, though some banks have now combined these departments. On the investment banking side, it is increasingly common to have equity financing, debt financing and lending (use of loans for financing a company) all in a single financing department (investment banking in its traditional meaning).

---

[11] 'On July 31, 2008, the Secretary of State of Massachusetts filed a complaint against Merrill Lynch for allegedly co-opting its "supposedly independent" research department to help in sales efforts. "Specifically, Merrill Lynch permitted its Sales and Trading, including Auction Desk, managers to unduly influence and pressure the Research Department in a number of ways. The actual research report is said to contain the expression 'conservative's conservative security' as a description of ARS. But only 8 days after this report was distributed to clients, Merrill pulled out of the ARS market. As a result, investors were no longer able to liquidate their investments. Other banks have also had complaints filed against them by the State in connection with ARS.

Merrill has responded to the legal action thus: "We are disappointed that Massachusetts filed this action because it ignores the only reason our advisors sold auction rate securities. They believed they were good investments for clients willing to trade some liquidity for higher return. The inarguable fact is the number of auctions that had failed in nearly two decades of ARS sales was small. In 2007 there were no failed auctions of securities sold to retail clients and, in fact, none to these clients until late January 2008."' (Fox News. com, 'Mass. Regulators Accuse Merrill Lynch of Fraud' 31 July 2008 http://www.foxnews.com/printer_friendly_wires/2008Jul31/0,4675,MerrillLynchFraud,00.html)

The **asset management** department in the diagram above is the part of the investment bank which provides portfolio investment services to clients. This function is covered in Chapters 17 and 18.

An example of an actual investment bank structure is that of Barclays Capital (see Figure 4.2). The two different sets of clients can be seen with the bank intermediating between them.

## DERIVATIVES TRADING: RISK MANAGEMENT SERVICES PROVIDED BY INVESTMENT BANKS

Included in the trading activities of banks is the trading of derivative securities – futures, swaps and options on equities, bonds, long and short-term interest rates, exchange rates, energy prices, etc. Derivatives trading is undertaken in considerable part as a means of offering clients **risk management products**.

**Risk is the chance of loss.** All human activities involve risk – day-to-day life has risks such as crossing the road (loss of life or limb). Owning a house presents the risk of it burning down (loss of property). All business activity involves risks such as claims against directors and officers of the company (D&O liability), the risk of claims for pollution damage, the risk of a factory being destroyed, the risk of an oil spill in the Gulf of Mexico, etc., which generate losses for a company.

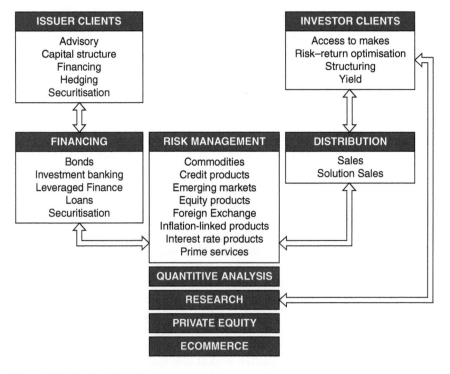

**Figure 4.2**  Barclays Capital corporate structure
*Source*:  Barclays website (2010).

These types of risk are known as **pure risk** which is the type of risk most people are aware of in their daily lives. This is a type of risk where there are only two possible outcomes – either a loss or no loss (rather as in digital information, either 1 or 0). Generally there is no possible upside to such pure risks. The financial companies which provide risk management services in the field of pure risk are insurance and re-insurance companies. The **underwriting** function in insurance, i.e. the evaluation of pure risk, remains a somewhat separate part of the financial services industry and generally requires actuarial skills. Actuaries are the people who estimate risks in the field of life insurance which requires, for example, the estimation of the premium to be charged for life insurance of a person given his or her age and gender (see p. 314).

Pure risk is in sharp contrast to another type of risk – one with which we are most concerned in this book – which is **financial risk**, i.e. the risk of loss in the value of financial instruments. Financial risk also covers the risk from changes in the prices of inputs needed to create products and services, e.g. fuel costs for an airline or grain costs for bread manufacturing companies or in the price of a currency such as dollars for a large exporter like Rolls Royce aero engines which prices its output in US dollars but whose costs are mostly in sterling (£). The difference between financial risk and pure risk is that while in the case of the latter there is no possibility of an upside, in the case of financial risk there should be **as much chance of an outcome being positive as negative**. An investment in shares, for example, is as likely to rise in value as to fall (shares are priced in the market according to the balance between those who think they are more likely to rise in price against those who think they are more likely to fall in price). This assumption follows from the EMH which we covered in Chapter 1. Equally, the price of gold or oil is as likely to fall (to the benefit of airlines) as to rise at any particular point in time, even if, over longer periods, both have shown a secular (on-going) rise in price. Financial risk or commodity price risk is also known as **speculative risk** – it involves an outcome where there is (*ex ante*) as much possibility of gain as of loss in a particular period. While a share rising in price might not seem like a risk – only a fall seeming to be such – because of the statistical properties of share price movements (or commodity price movements) it is potential variability of returns (or prices) that we use to measure risk.

## RISK MANAGEMENT INVOLVING THE USE OF FINANCIAL INDUSTRY PRODUCTS

### Hedging using cash markets

Hedging means reducing one's exposure to financial risk by eliminating the risk of a downside price movement. But hedging also causes the elimination of any possibility of a gain from an upside price movement. An outright sale is the basic method of hedging risk. If someone sells some shares because they are afraid that that they may decline in value, this is hedging their risks. But it also means that if they are wrong and the shares actually increase in price, they don't benefit from this price rise. By selling the asset and putting the cash proceeds in the bank (risk-less deposit), an investor has used the simplest method to achieve the elimination of risk: selling the risky asset (the share) in exchange for a low risk asset, cash.

Such a transaction transfers the risk of the shareholding to another investor who is more willing to bear that risk. For example, when share prices were reaching an all-time high in 2007, some investors decided that they were no longer willing to bear the risk of a setback in the market. Other investors, for whatever reason, were willing to accept this risk. The sale of shares from one category of investor to another achieved the objectives of both sides to the trade: for the sellers, a reduced risk; for the buyers, an increased risk. This is known as **gains from trade**. Both sides gain from the transaction in terms of their perceptions of risk at the time of trade but, clearly, after the transaction, one side has gained financially while the other has lost. Asset sales of this type involve the use of the **cash market** for shares (as distinct from the derivatives market). In the case of foreign exchange the cash market is known as the **spot** (foreign exchange) market. Cash markets are those in which assets are sold for cash and delivered immediately, in contrast to transactions in forward and futures markets where there is no sale, but simply an exchange of contracts.

From August 2007 many banks realised that the large portfolios of mortgage backed securities they were holding were highly risky. Many of them were willing to sell these to investors, even at the cost of a large loss, since they were not willing to take the risk of the portfolios falling even further in value, as this could wipe out the bank's capital. An example of this was Merrill Lynch's sale of such securities for what might be described as a 'knockdown price'.[12]

It is important to note that in a spot market transaction, the risk that is eliminated is that of a price change **at any time in the future**. This is achieved in a transaction which is completed immediately (or almost immediately). In contrast, in derivative markets (see below), risk is only hedged for the period of the derivative contract and comes back to both parties when the contract is closed.

Cash markets, however, are not the only means of hedging risk and they may also have relatively high transactions costs, partly due to illiquidity.. An alternative to cash markets is to use markets which, rather than transacting spot, transact for future contract completion and do not require sale of the underlying asset. These are the derivatives markets.

## Hedging using forward and futures markets

Hedging in a derivatives market involves offsetting one type of risk against another. The major markets for this type of activity are the forward, futures and swaps markets. The forward contract is the fundamental type of contract in this type of hedging. A **forward contract** commits the buyer of the contract to buy a specified quantity of an asset on a specified date for a specified price. Conversely, the seller of such a contract is obligated to sell the same quantity of an asset on the same date at the same price. Forward contracts are known as derivative contracts because the price at which the transaction is struck is **derived** from that of the **underlying**.

---

[12] On 28 July 2008, Merrill Lynch issued a press release in which it describes a sale of '$30.6 billion gross notional amount of U.S. super senior ABS CDOs to an affiliate of Lone Star Funds for a purchase price of $6.7 billion'. These CDOs had already been marked down to $11.1 billion, thus resulting in a further loss to Merrill Lynch of $4.4 billion.

The underlying can be an asset such as a share, a basket of assets or an index such as the Standard and Poor's 500, i.e. an index which shows the average change in value of a portfolio of 500 US companies weighted according to market value. In practice, in most contracts, the actual underlying is not bought and sold, i.e. the actual commodity is not transacted at contract closing. Instead, cash settlement is used where one side pays the other the difference between the price at the initiation of the contract and the price at the expiry date.

In contrast to a cash market transaction, a forward contract is not completed until the date specified in the contract **and the risk returns to the hedger at that point**. Equally, it is important to understand that at the time of contract there are no payments either way – **there is no insurance being provided, only an exchange of risks**. It is only subsequently when market prices change that it becomes clear that one party has gained at the expense of the other and a transfer of cash to reflect this takes place. While the original purpose of forward contracts is hedging, in practice many market participants use them for speculation. This use is not necessarily bad, as many might think. Without speculators, who act in a similar way to market makers or dealers, the other side of a contract – the counterparty – might not be available to trade at a fair price and thus liquidity might be reduced.

A good example of a forward contract is the **natural hedge** which might be transacted between a wheat farmer and a bakery group. Many months elapse between planting and harvesting. During this time, the market price of wheat will vary depending on how successful the **global** harvest is likely to be. The farmer wants to guarantee a price which will enable him to have a reasonably stable income over time. The bakery wants to ensure that it will not suddenly be forced to increase the price of its bread (with a consequent sales slump) if the harvest is bad and prices in the cash (spot) market shoot up. By effecting a forward transaction between them, both parties can improve their welfare (gains from trade). In a **bilateral contract** like this, i.e. between two such parties only, the forward price of their derivative contract will depend on negotiation between them. It will be based on the market price of the underlying at the time of the transaction and expectations of both parties as to the likely cash market price at the time the contract matures. **The forward price in such a bilateral contract that is agreed will depend on the relative bargaining power of the two parties to the trade**. A big bakery can probably achieve a contract price which is more favourable to them than to a small farmer can.

Today very few transactions actually take place directly between two parties such as a farmer and a baker. In practice they are almost all undertaken through a **financial intermediary**, in this case an investment bank, which transacts **independently** with each side. However, the investment bank dealer will not necessarily have an exactly offsetting contract with each side. He holds a **dealing book** which is a list of transactions he undertakes on each side of the market. In this respect he is performing the same function as the dealer in equity markets. Using a dealing book results in the dealer creating a portfolio of risks, some of which may offset each other, but where he may take on a net risk, either intentionally or not, which may give him either a net long (bought) or a net short (sold) position. This risk-taking activity of dealers is a necessary part of being a dealer, unlike that of a broker who does not take on such risk. The type of market in which these transactions take place is known as an **OTC** market (also called a dealer market). The expression OTC simply means **bilateral transactions** between a single dealer and a single market participant, rather than transactions on exchange where there is competition between multiple parties on both sides of the market – known as **multilateral trading**. Such competition is likely to lead to a 'fair' price being discovered and also to the spread between the buying price and the selling price being reduced. OTC is also the market structure for most foreign exchange, corporate bonds, treasury bonds and many other securities.

In addition to transactions in the OTC market, there are also forward transactions in **exchange-based** (multilateral) markets. Such forward transactions when on an exchange are known as **futures** rather than forwards. An example of such a market is the Chicago Mercantile Exchange. A futures market is simply a forward market but on a multilateral exchange, rather than being based on a bilateral contract between a trader and an investment bank dealer (OTC market transaction). Rather than involving contracts negotiated between two traders (bilateral trading), there are many traders making competing bids and offers – hence the expression **multilateral trading** as we noted earlier. Provided in Table 4.1 as an example, are the futures prices for wheat on 6 July 2009 in Chicago for transactions maturing up to 10 March 2010.

This book was completed after 10 March 2010 so we do actually know the prices in the spot market for wheat on that date. If the futures price was a good estimate of the actual price in the future, the 10 March 2010 futures price would be close to the spot (cash) price on that date, i.e. $569. If this was the case, the contract could be closed without either side winning or losing. In practice it is likely to be a different price and thus one side makes a gain and one side makes a loss.

In fact the price on 10 March 2010 was only $494. Thus whoever was long of the contract at the price of $569 lost money, whereas whoever sold forward (the short side) could close the contract by buying in the cash market at only $494 and thus would make a profit of the difference between $569 and $494. This calculation is only an approximation since it is necessary also to consider interest costs, but it does provide a general idea of how futures markets operate.

The above example was in the commodities market – the first market to be created for forward and futures transactions. But let's say we are using a so-called single stock futures contract, i.e. a forward contract on the shares of one particular company rather than on an index. Like all futures contracts they are just like bets. I bet the market will go down by, for example, the end of the day; and you, the reader, bet it will go up. If we agree the terms of the bet, i.e. we write a contract at an agreed settlement price, then at the end of the day if the market has gone down,

**Table 4.1**  Futures prices of wheat, 6 July 2009

| 9 July 2009 | $497 |
|---|---|
| 9 September 2009 | $524 |
| 9 December 2009 | $551 |
| 10 March 2010 | $569 |

you have to pay me the difference between the price we agreed and the actual price. However, whether or not this trade is speculation or hedging depends on whether or not each of us undertook the transaction because of:

- a belief that we knew better than the market which way it would move by the close (speculation); or
- because we had already bought shares in the market prior to taking on the bet and wanted to reduce what we saw as a short-term risk of a fall in price (hedging).

If I already hold the shares and they fall, then the amount you pay me simply makes up for the losses on my portfolio. Of course if I lost the bet, I would have to pay you, but provided my shares have risen in line with the futures contract, I would not be out of pocket. Equally, if you were short of the shares (had sold without actually owning them), and if the price fell, you would gain on the holding in the share even though you lost on the contract.

In settling a forward or futures contract, one side pays the other the difference between the spot price and the contracted futures price. Although one side 'loses' and the other side 'wins', in fact both sides achieve a gain in **utility if** the objective was to reduce risk. In practice over a lifetime, each side probably wins as often as it loses (though there is a net cost to each in the form of transactions cost to support the running of an exchange and brokers' fees). The objective of undertaking the contract for a hedger is not to achieve winnings but to **smooth out income over time** in order, perhaps, to minimise the risk of bankruptcy due to price movements – and this is achieved by both sides. This should increase the utility of both parties. If one of the parties was merely gambling, then it is different. A key feature of a forward (or futures) contract is that there is an **opportunity cost** of eliminating the possibility of a loss. What this means is that the opportunity to make a gain, if the price rises, is also lost. Another way of putting what I am explaining in this paragraph is that by engaging in such a contract, both sides, if they are hedgers, gain **certainty** – and that has a value (it should **increase their welfare**), which is why they are transacting.

To summarise the two motives for entering a derivative contract:

1. A **hedger** would be one who took a position (normally in a derivative market) to reduce his or her exposure to risk.
2. A **speculator**, on the other hand, would adopt a position in a derivative market to take on exposure to a particular risk with the aim of increasing his or her wealth through knowing better than the market (or by being lucky) where the price would end the day. Speculators provide an important service in the markets by taking the other side when there might otherwise be no one there. Dealers can be considered to be speculators, though they try to minimise the extent to which they are speculating. Hedge funds frequently use the market for speculation (rather than hedging) since they believe they are better at forecasting than others operating in the market. It is important not to think of speculators as bad and hedgers as good. There is no moral judgement in markets.

**Swaps** are simply a set of forward contracts which oblige the two parties to exchange cash flows at predetermined intervals. The most common type is the interest rate swap that allows a company which, for example, borrows money from a bank at a floating interest rate (which changes every three, six or twelve months), to convert it into a borrowing which has a fixed rate for the total period of the loan – perhaps five, seven or ten years. For the company, this reduces the uncertainty as to one type of cost to which it is subject, namely the rate of interest it has to pay on its borrowings. It is thus a way of hedging the risk of volatility in profits caused by sharp changes in interest rates over the years. It **changes the nature of risk but does not eliminate risk**. The new risk is that interest rates fall sharply and remain low for many years but the company is tied into a long-term swap at a much higher rate. Indeed, chief executives of companies have lost their jobs for hedging such a risk and then having to continue paying a high rate of interest when their competitors, who had not, had lower costs (and thus lower prices) as a result of interest rates having fallen.

## Option contracts – options as insurance

We noted that forward and futures markets do not involve any upfront cash payment by either side. The reason is that no insurance is being provided by either side. A forward or futures contract involves taking on risk by both sides – the risk that the contract moves in the opposite way to that expected. It is not an insurance policy.

Options are different from forward/futures contracts in that they **do** provide insurance. For this reason, the person who provides the insurance has to be paid. The person who creates the option contract is known as the option **writer**. His or her counterparty is the option **holder**. An option involves you paying someone a **premium**, i.e. an upfront payment like an insurance premium, in return for which you can transfer to him or her the risk of either a downward or upward price movement, while still retaining the 'risk' of the opposite movement, i.e. upward or downward. Downward price movement protection from an option contract is thus like an insurance contract in the sense that you pay a premium in advance for protection against loss. This is known as a **put** contract. In the event of a fall in price of the underlying, the option contract specifies that the writer of the option will pay you an amount equal to any fall during the contract period. Alternatively, a **call** is an option contract in which the writer pays you the amount of any rise in the price of the underlying which would provide you with protection against a share, which you wanted to buy in the future, rising in price before you can buy it.

## Diversification

Diversification is a key means of reducing risk. In equity investment, for example, it is a means of exchanging risks amongst a large group of people by each taking a small amount of the risk of each venture (equity share in a company). This is simply the practical application of the age-old injunction 'not to put all one's eggs in one basket'. Diversification is a 'costless' means of reducing the variance (variation in value) of an investment portfolio, whereas the other techniques above all involve some cost – either an explicit cost (option) or an opportunity cost (future). Diversification can be achieved by an investor him or herself without the need to employ a financial intermediary (though most people do employ an asset manager), unlike futures and options which generally require an investment bank or an exchange to arrange the transaction.

The importance of risk management through diversification is not only that it reduces risk for investors. It is also that, by so doing, it makes risky assets more attractive to investors, thereby raising the price at which they can be sold, i.e. **lowering the cost of capital**. This is because risk is not just a function of the variance of the particular firm's shares but of how risky they are **when held in a portfolio**. Portfolio management through diversification is covered in more detail in Chapter 17.

# PART II

# PRIMARY MARKETS: FUNDING LIQUIDITY AND EXTERNAL CAPITAL ALLOCATION THROUGH CREDIT AND CAPITAL MARKETS

# 5 LIQUIDITY: WHAT IS IT?

Liquidity is a much used word yet it has various meanings which are often not distinguished. The financial crisis which commenced in 2007 was, in considerable part, and by any definition of the term, a liquidity crisis, though it quickly became apparent that it was also a bank solvency crisis.

The two words 'liquidity' and 'money' are very closely connected but not interchangeable. Our starting point in trying to understand them is in fact a more general word – 'asset'. An asset is anything that has value. Thus a domestic residence is an asset but a real asset because it is tangible (has a physical presence). Financial assets are valuable things which are intangible and are in the form of financial contracts. Cash (notes, coin and bank current account) is an asset and is the only asset which is immediately acceptable by anyone as a medium of exchange in a contract. By contrast, a house or a motor car or a valuable painting, while all are assets, are not generally acceptable as a medium of exchange. Their value depends on their first being sold for cash in a transaction and the price at which that transaction is undertaken. Cash on the other hand has a fixed value and is immediately available for transaction purposes at its face value.

However, we also have other assets that are not quite money/cash but are close to it for which we use the expression **near money** (synonym: **quasi-money**) which is a term used in economics to describe highly liquid assets that can easily be converted into cash including:

- savings accounts;
- holdings in money market mutual funds;
- bank time deposits (certificates of deposit);
- short-term government treasury securities (such as T-bills);
- bonds near their redemption date.

An obvious question then, when considering the difference between assets, is the degree of 'moneyness' that such assets have, which gives rise to the question of what is moneyness or liquidity.

**Moneyness or liquidity** generally refers to how quickly and cheaply and in what size of transaction an asset can be converted into cash with little loss of value. Money (in the form of cash) is the most liquid asset, meaning it is something that will **always be accepted by others in payment of debts**. An asset is more liquid if it is 'more certainly realisable at short notice without loss'. The key difference between money in the form of notes, coin and bank deposits (credit money as explained below) on the one hand (which are the most liquid of all assets) and every other type of asset on the other hand is that money has a **fixed (par) value**. 'Par' means its original value at issue, i.e. when the bank issues the liability known as a deposit in the amount of, say, £100, that is the par value of the deposit and that is the amount that will be returned to the depositor. In fact, as we noted earlier, a bank agrees in the terms of business in its contract with depositors that it will always exchange deposits (commercial bank money) for central bank money (notes and coin) at an exchange rate of 1:1. All other assets are subject to price risk otherwise known as market risk. Assets which take time to sell, and where an attempt to sell quickly or in large size will almost certainly lead to a substantial fall in the realised selling price, would be defined as illiquid. Thus assets lie on a spectrum between completely liquid and having a fixed (par) value and very illiquid and having a variable value. An illiquid asset has a variable (uncertain) value depending on the speed of sale (a forced sale undertaken quickly will lower the selling price), the demand for that type of asset at the time of sale, the ability to find a buyer, etc.

Two types of money exist today:

1. **Central bank money** in the form of notes and coin which have replaced gold, silver and other precious metals which were once used as money, i.e. as the **settlement asset** to meet payment obligations:
2. **Credit money** which represents a claim on a financial intermediary and is in practice a much more important settlement asset than cash in the form of notes and coin.

Credit money is typically divided into two types: **commercial bank money** and **central bank money**. Commercial bank money arise as a result of money being placed on deposit with a commercial bank. The depositor of the funds receives in return a demand deposit account that can be used as a settlement asset in his or her business transactions and is much more convenient than specie or notes and coin. Central bank funds (money) are simply bank accounts held by commercial banks at the central bank. Financial institutions can deposit funds at their central bank and receive in return a settlement asset in the form of central bank funds. A financial institution can then direct its central bank to move these funds from its own account to that of another financial institution to settle its payment obligations, either to that financial institution or to a customer of that institution.[1]

Central bank money is the most secure means of making a payment, which normally means extinguishing a liability. It is 'the ultimate settlement asset at the apex of the payment hierarchy'.[2]

---

[1] See C. Johnson and R. Steigerwald, Legal and Policy Aspects of the Central Bank's Role in the Payment System: Some Costs and Benefits of the Choice of Settlement Asset (Federal Reserve Bank of Chicago, 2007).

[2] S. Millard and V. Saporta, 'Central Banks and Payment Systems: Past, Present and Future', Background Paper, Bank of England Conference on 'The Future of Payments', London, May 2005.

## DO BANKS CREATE LIQUIDITY?

One question which is often asked in respect of bank credit creation and maturity transformation is whether or not banks actually **create** liquidity. The answer is that as the money supply of a country, apart from notes and coin, is comprised of the **deposits of the banking system**, i.e. the liabilities issued by private companies (banks), then, if deposits increase, the money supply and hence liquidity has increased. **Deposits increase if banks increase their lending** since a loan **automatically** creates a corresponding deposit. This is because, just as central banks can create money just through the 'magic' of double entry bookkeeping (quantitative easing by central banks is simply the creation of money), so too can private commercial banks. When a commercial bank accepts, from a customer, a promise to repay a loan it puts this promise (a valuable asset which will bring an investment return to the bank) on the asset side of its balance sheet. The corresponding double entry on the liability side of the balance sheet is the bank's own promise to pay out on demand i.e. a demand deposit which it puts into the bank account of its customer. As bank balance sheets thus expand through additional lending in the economy, so too does the money supply of the country. If, of course, there is no **net** new lending, i.e. new lending minus loan repayments, then, other things remaining equal, the money supply will remain constant.

Another way of looking at this strange conundrum of how banks create deposits (money) simply by lending is that a bank loan involves a borrower creating a liability (a promise to repay a loan) which he or she exchanges for a bank liability, i.e. a bank demand deposit which he or she can then spend. All the bank is doing is providing what is traditionally known as the **acceptance function**. The bank is assessing the 'credit' of the borrower and, if it thinks it is good, it is exchanging the borrowers promise to pay (which non-banks will not accept as payment for goods and services) with its own credit (a bank deposit) which non-banks **will** accept as a means of payment. Thus automatically both the asset (the borrower's promise to repay the bank which is risky and others would not accept in payment for goods and services) and the liability (the bank's deposit liability which is not risky and others do accept in payment for goods and services) are simultaneously put on the balance sheet. Subsequently, of course, as the borrower uses the deposit to make payments, and as the deposit flows to other banks, the lending bank needs to raise adequate resources to meet these outflows. It does this either through attracting new deposits (perhaps by offering a higher interest rate than other banks) or by issuing other types of liability to investors who then provide it with cash. Ultimately, therefore, a bank can only continue lending if it can raise funds at a cost below the rate it generates from such new lending.

The 'trick of banking' is that those who have demand deposits in their account whether from their own saving or from a loan, believe they have retained their liquidity (they do after all have the same amount of cash in **their** demand deposit account) even though **their** liquidity has, in effect, been transferred to borrowers who now also have cash in **their** demand accounts. In this sense, depositor and borrower are 'sharing' the same liquidity. This is similar to the capital markets where liquidity is transferred between investors through the secondary market. This understanding of what banks do is the view of someone who thinks in terms of capital markets. Those who come from a money and banking background might analyse it somewhat differently from me.

This system of lending is known as the **fractional reserve banking system**. While lending creates its own financing in the short-run, in practice it can be more useful to consider the bank as lending out to one set of customers (its borrowers) most of the cash which its other set of customers (its depositors) put with it. The bank retains only a small amount of the original cash, as reserves, which are held as the bank's own demand deposit with the central bank (Bank of England in the UK), cash in the till and other liquid assets, and lends out the rest. Rather than creating liquidity, in the steady state banks are simply transferring it between those who temporarily have more of it than they require to those who have a temporary need for it. What banks do is to enable the economy to make the most economical use of a given amount of cash through the mechanics of the fractional reserve system. If however the central bank puts more **reserves** into the system (central bank money say from a quantitative easing programme as discussed below) **and** banks lend more, the very act of lending creates additional deposits and hence increases the money supply.

While banking might seem mysterious compared with capital markets, the key thing that it is necessary to understand is that while corporates (non-financial companies) issue liabilities (debts) just as banks do, these liabilities are not accepted as a medium of exchange. Bank current account deposit liabilities on the other hand are. Company liabilities, while being valuable assets, are not money because they are unlikely to be accepted by anyone as payment for the purchase of goods or services or for the extinguishing of a debt. Thus while companies can increase the liabilities outstanding in an economy by creating debts just as banks do, unlike the debts created by banks or by the central bank, these debts do not provide the medium for transactions in an economy (liquidity).

Banks cannot expand their lending unless they have adequate reserves with their central bank. Reserves are the liquidity that banks themselves need to hold to satisfy customers' demand for cash in the event that they have insufficient notes and coin in their tills. Banks can expand their balance sheets by a multiple of the reserves they hold. The **money multiplier** is the maximum amount that deposits can expand on the basis of an increase in reserves. If we assume a reserve requirement of 10% then an initial increase in reserves of $100 can ultimately lead to the creation of an additional $900 of deposits through additional lending, leading in the final stage of credit expansion to a total of $1,000 of deposits. This happens since the deposit that the bank has created for its borrower is then spent by the borrower and ends up in other banks (and some back in the original bank).[3]

It is in fact the public's demand for **par value liquidity** (par means of **fixed** value instantly convertible into currency) that creates the raw material (demand deposits) for the banking system. Without this demand for assets which have a low rate of return but high liquidity, it would be difficult for banks to earn the interest spread they need as intermediaries. Indeed, from early times, fractional reserve banking has been built on the simple proposition that the public's collective

[3] As the money multiplier is a complex idea, I recommend that you refer to a good banking textbook for a more detailed explanation.

*ex ante*[4] demand for at-par liquidity is greater than its collective *ex post* need for such liquidity.[5] The main reason for this is that in practice people are lazy and prefer to just leave funds idle in demand deposits and accept the loss of interest. The alternative would be to spend time and effort moving funds in and out of demand deposits from higher yielding assets, just as a corporate treasurer is paid to do, in order to hold the minimum transaction balance possible.

What this means, therefore, is that households believe they need, or prefer to have, more liquidity than they actually do. This perceived liquidity need is for both **transactional needs** (buying things) and also for **precautionary needs** (unexpected contingencies). It may also be for **speculative needs**, i.e. having cash available in case a good bargain turns up and is available for purchase only by those with cash. An example would be a house which is offered at a bargain price but only to cash buyers, not those who have to seek out bank financing. In turn, this means that much of the liquidity that demand deposits give to households is not, in practice, used. As it is not being used, it can be transferred to long-term borrowers for consumption purposes or for the acquisition of assets such as stock in trade, trade financing, expansion of a venture etc.

The explanation above of the money multiplier is the traditional explanation and it is correct in saying that the **maximum** amount that deposits can expand is a function of the reserve requirement. Today, however, the multiplier is much lower than in the past, due to what is known as **quantitative easing**. QE, as it is known (in the European Union the facility that is designed to provide an equivalent economic effect is known as the Long Term Refinancing Operation or LTRO), involves the central bank of a country purchasing securities from the private sector (or directly from the government treasury) and paying for these purchases by the creation of new central bank reserves (deposit accounts held by commercial banks at the central bank). By increasing the availability of central bank reserves held by the commercial banking system, commercial banks are enabled to expand their lending without breaching their reserve ratios.

Unfortunately bank lending is not just a function of available reserves. It is also a function of the evaluation of the risk of lending and also of the amount of capital (equity) which the bank holds relative to required capital ratios. In times of uncertainty, banks are likely to reduce lending, since any lending becomes more risky. Also, in times of capital ratios being below those which the regulatory agency requires (see pp. 389–391), banks are unlikely to want to increase their balance sheet size even if they have surplus reserves. Thus, increasing reserves will not, of itself, increase bank lending and thus help to keep the economy growing, which may be the objective of QE. Instead what happens is that the ratio of deposits to reserves falls. Thus the traditional view of the money multiplier, while it may tell us the maximum amount by which deposits can increase, does not in fact guarantee that they will increase by anything like this

---

[4]  *Ex ante* means before the event and *ex post* means after the event.
[5]  *The Paradox of De-leveraging Will Be Broken*, Paul McCulley, November 2008, PIMCO. (The largest fixed income asset manager in the US). http://www.pimco.com/EN/ Insights/Pages/Global%20Central%20Bank%20Focus%202011-08%20McCulley%20 Paradox%20of%20Deleveraging%20Will%20Be%20Broken.aspx

amount. In fact, in the UK and other countries which have had QE programmes in 2009/2010/2011, money supply growth has been minimal or negative. Thus the credit necessary to stimulate the economy has not been growing as hoped. Figure 8.4 shows the huge rise in bank reserves during the period of QE in the UK. This implies that the banks which have received the central bank funds from QE have been unwilling to lend most of it to other banks or to potential borrowers.

Banks can finance themselves by creating deposits or other non-deposit liabilities (securities) such as certificates of deposit (longer-term deposits) or commercial paper (short-term tradable securities). However, the regulatory authorities like to see banks being financed by a high proportion of retail customer deposits rather than by the money markets (wholesale investors). This is because retail deposits are often described as **sticky** funds, i.e. they don't tend to be redeemed in practice and, rather than being left on demand deposit for only a few days, are actually held by customers in aggregate, almost perpetually. In addition, of course, to the extent that one depositor does remove their funds, another is likely to deposit theirs into that same bank or another bank. The **law of large numbers**[6] should result in bank deposits being relatively stable as withdrawals closely match deposits, at least for large banks. Of course, the law does not guarantee that, at any moment, any particular bank will have exactly the same funds coming in as going out. There is a need for a buffer to ensure against mis-matches between funds in and funds out. One such buffer is the interbank market, i.e. the market in which one bank can lend funds which are surplus to its needs to another which is temporarily short. In addition to this, banks hold assets which are liquid, such as treasury bills, which can easily be turned into cash if they are short of liquidity.

Traditionally, the liquidity of a bank was viewed as the proportion of its total assets that were liquid. Liquid assets include deposits at the central bank (this is the ultimate form of credit money and should be free of all credit risk or market price risk) and short-term government bills or bonds (theoretically free of credit risk but which may have some market price risk). By selling government securities that it is holding, i.e. obtaining liquidity by using a market to sell its assets (**market liquidity**), these liquid assets should enable a bank to repay depositors on demand even if its reserves at the central bank are temporarily insufficient due to sudden demand. However, if all depositors demand that their deposits be returned in the form of notes and coin, or that all their deposits be transferred to other banks (which is effected through the transfer of deposits via the central bank), the bank

---

[6] This is the theorem that describes the likely outcome of performing the same experiment a large number of times. The law predicts that the average of the results obtained from a large number of trials should be close to the expected value. Not only that but it will become closer as more trials are performed. In the case of bank lending it allows the use of the 'expected loss' concept based on historical losses on similar portfolios of assets. If it always held, it would 'guarantee' stable long-term results for random events. However, in practice events are often not as random as we believe and therefore the outcome may be much higher or lower than the expected value.

would suffer a **bank run**. An example of this was the run on Northern Rock Bank in the UK in 2007, the first run on a bank in the UK since 1878.[7]

## FUNDING (BORROWER) LIQUIDITY

Liquidity is often explained as the ability to convert a financial asset such as shares into **cash** at minimum cost and with minimum loss of value, which is how we analysed it in the section above. In turn, cash is something that is universally accepted in exchange for goods and services. This is only one concept of liquidity, known as **market liquidity** or **investor liquidity**; it is relevant for assets being sold in a secondary market.

Liquidity, in fact, begins one stage back from the concept of market liquidity with the raising of funds in a primary market by a borrower to provide **borrower liquidity**. This is more usually known as **funding liquidity** or **financing.** In fact every sector of the economy requires access to liquidity from financing (funding liquidity) on a continuing basis.

### Households

A household trying to coordinate the sale of one house and the purchase of another has the problem that, unless the sale of one and the purchase of another are coincident in time, there will be a need for **bridging finance**, i.e. a temporary loan to cover the entire cost of the new house until such time as the old house can be sold. This type of transaction reflects the difference between wealth and liquidity – the house represents wealth (a valuable asset holding) but not liquidity. While cash and a house are both assets (wealth), only cash can be used to pay for purchases. Someone selling a house is unlikely to agree to take another house as part of the payment since that transfers liquidity and price risk to the seller.

Wealth is a measure of total assets, i.e. valuable things that a person owns. Cash (or liquidity) is the part of this wealth that is available for immediate use in a transaction (**transaction balance**). If you go out to purchase goods in a store and, on reaching the cash desk, realise that you have left your wallet at home, a storekeeper is unlikely to be convinced by your story that you have sufficient wealth (assets) to pay for the goods. His only interest when transacting with you is whether or not you have a means for paying now, i.e. have the liquidity of cash, a debit card or a stand-by line of credit, such as a credit card, in order to meet the amount owning.

---

[7] On 2 October 1878, one of Scotland's biggest banks crashed. A hastily scribbled telegram from the head office instructed its branches: 'Bank has stopped payments. Close your door at once and pay nothing whatever.' The liquidity crisis that hit Britain's financial sector in 1878 ensured the City of Glasgow Bank's ruin. The Bank was also insolvent and, once rumours of this started, it had little chance of surviving. Other banks in the United Kingdom were able to survive the liquidity shortage by drawing on the Bank of England's reserves. See *The Times Online*, 22 October 2007.

## Corporates

Liquidity is a day by day concern of companies as there will always be a mismatch between expenses (costs) such as materials, wages and tax payments on the one hand and sales (revenues) on the other hand, which means that on some days a company will have surplus cash and on other days it will have a cash shortage. Also, when goods are sold this may not bring in cash, just a promise to pay within 30 days (a liability issued by the customer but certainly not as good as cash). The payment may not even come in on time and such a delay in payment (the conversion of a promise to pay into a bank deposit) can cause companies to collapse. If a company wants to expand output, it may need to raise additional funds in the form of **working capital** to finance the additional spending on raw materials, wages, etc. prior to actually selling the additional output and finally receiving cash from the sale.

When a company raises money for working capital from a bank, the shorter the term of the loan the less **borrower liquidity** it provides, since it needs to be **redeemed**, i.e. paid back, in a short period of time. If at the repayment date the company still needs the cash (perhaps a customer has failed to pay), a new bank loan needs to be arranged – which is described as **rolling over** the loan. However, if conditions in markets have changed in that time (for example a financial crisis breaks out), it may not be possible to refinance (to roll-over) the funding, and hence the company may suffer a liquidity crisis. If the company had taken out a much longer-term loan, this would have provided greater borrower (funding) liquidity, i.e. a longer time before the liquidity had to be returned to the investor.

## Countries

Countries can also have liquidity crises. For example, the South East Asian countries or ASEAN (Association of South East Asian Nations) member nations, in particular Thailand, suffered a liquidity crisis in 1997/98. Earlier inflows of short-term foreign capital, seeking high returns (hot money), left the country suddenly when investors feared devaluation and a sharp drop in economic growth. What happened was similar to a traditional **bank run**, i.e. when depositors fear for their wealth and pull it out as quickly as they can. Bank runs or a country liquidity crisis are quite likely when borrowings are for short periods of time. Longer-term loans increase borrower liquidity/funding liquidity and reduce the chance of a run. Since then many Asian countries have followed a policy of building up foreign exchange reserves to provide insurance against such an event happening again. These countries' foreign exchange reserves have, in fact, increased massively since the 1997/98 crisis.

The 2007 credit crisis hit Iceland particularly hard and, in October 2008, the country had to accept an International Monetary Fund (IMF) loan (bailout) of around \$6 billion (£3.49 billion). That is a lot for a country with only just over 300,000 people. The IMF is the **international lender of last resort**[8] or provider

---

[8] A lender of last resort (LOLR) is either the central bank of an individual country that will lend to commercial banks when no private sector lender is willing to do so or, if the central bank itself does not have the resources, the IMF will step in to help the country by acting as lender of last resort. The LOLR does so because it believes that the economic consequences of not doing so are substantial and might threaten the country's or the global economy's growth.

of liquidity, i.e. the institution to which a country has to appeal for a loan when no other lender, not even the central bank, can provide sufficient funds in its role as LOLR. In return for the loan, the borrower has to accept certain conditions, normally including a reduction in public spending and possibly also a rise in taxation. Such terms in a loan are described as **conditionality**.

## PRIMARY MARKET FINANCING: FUNDING LIQUIDITY

The essential problem in trying to finance a modern, capital intensive economy is that the real assets which underlie its productivity, economic growth and job creation, and generate the (**P&I**) cash flows to service loans, are inherently illiquid. Many real investment projects such as new nuclear power stations take many years of investment in real assets before they start to generate cash. To generate sufficient cash to compensate the providers of capital, and also to repay the capital they have lent (i.e. to service the P&I payments on the funding), may take 20 years. While there is some **patient capital** available, it is relatively scarce. There are, for example, **buy and hold investors** who have the intention of holding bonds to maturity and holding equities for many years, such as life insurance companies and pension funds which have long-term liabilities. But in practice, even these investors are unlikely to hold all their financial assets to maturity or to be willing to buy assets such as long-term bonds if there is no way of realising their value by trading on a market after the initial purchase. In addition, there are relatively few such patient investors relative to the need for long-term capital. Most lenders don't want to wait this amount of time and would thus not buy long-term securities.

The problem of a society which is trying to invest in new ideas and to generate economic growth is that the projects that help achieve this are almost always, by physical nature, illiquid. This means that once cash (liquidity) has been invested in them in the form of labour and raw materials, the process cannot easily be reversed to convert the project back into cash. Also, because such projects don't provide immediate benefits in terms of additional goods and services for consumption, they require those who finance them to reduce their current consumption of goods and services in order that their resources can, instead, be committed to real investment projects, **i.e. someone has to give up consumption now (save) in order that more consumption goods are available in the future**.

Very few households are willing to have their cash tied up for long periods of time in a form which prevents them from having access to it for many years – their needs may change and they may want to consume now rather than wait for many more years to increase their consumption of goods and services. Thus a basic problem in financing new projects is that few people will finance them unless they can reverse their initial financial investment decision at a time of their choosing. It is this **irreversibility of financing** in the short run which potentially gives rise to financing and liquidity problems.

While the objective of much of the finance industry is to provide mechanisms which allow liquidity to be transferred easily and at low cost from households to new investment projects (primary market financing or funding), this will only be possible if there is also a mechanism to allow the initial investor in the project subsequently to transfer his or her interest in the project to another investor, i.e. to exchange his or her shares or bonds for cash (liquidity) with another investor.

Secondary markets are the mechanism that enable this subsequent transfer of liquidity. Without secondary markets to provide **market liquidity (investor liquidity)**, primary markets which provide **funding liquidity (borrower liquidity)** would barely function, as few individuals would be willing to accept the illiquidity that long-term projects would otherwise force on them. There is thus a symbiosis between primary and secondary markets.

For most investors, an illiquid investment would be unacceptable, and to get them to accept this illiquidity would probably require such a high expected rate of return on investment as to make the proposed project unviable. Thus the more the securities industry can do to provide investors with the confidence that their investment will be liquid at any time in the future, then **the lower will be the price (rate of return) at which they are likely to be willing to lend or invest**. This means that one of the main functions of the finance industry is to **reduce the liquidity premium** that investors would otherwise demand on a project to as close as possible to zero. The liquidity premium is simply the additional return that an investor demands to compensate for the risk that he or she may not be able to liquidate the investment easily. The lower the liquidity premium, the lower the cost of financing and therefore the larger the number of projects that can go ahead.

The liquidity conflict between the interests of investors in real assets (firms) and the interests of investors in financial assets (households) is one which financial systems and institutions have in considerable part resolved. Primary market liquidity, i.e. funding liquidity from credit markets (bank and shadow bank loans) and from securities markets (equity and bond finance), is the starting point for a venture. But it is liquidity offered through a financial intermediary to savers and investors after they have acquired financial assets that provides the confidence that persuades them to hold their wealth in credit intermediary liabilities (bank deposits) and securities (equities and bonds) rather than in gold or notes and coin and thus to provide primary market financing. Their savings can thus become productive for the economy rather than being stored 'under the mattress'. Thus liquidity in financial assets is vital for a primary market to work well.

This liquidity is achieved in two ways, one through the intermediation of banks and the second through secondary markets in securities:

**Banks (provision of demand deposits).** A bank transforms savers' short-term deposits into long-term loans such as mortgages or financing for companies. The 'secondary market' in these deposits is provided by the bank itself. A depositor has the right to demand redemption (conversion into central bank money i.e. notes and coin) of his or her deposit at any time on request. Although the deposit will be matched on the balance sheet with a relatively illiquid loan to a borrower, the bank maintains arrangements whereby net withdrawals of deposits can be met by sales of liquid assets or by borrowing from other sources, including the central bank in its role as LOLR.

In effect, the bank is providing a secondary market mechanism whereby the loans it makes (its assets) can be **'refinanced'** continually during their life. More generally, as one depositor withdraws his funds (to recover his liquidity) another will be depositing (to temporarily store his liquidity). Thus the bank stands between (intermediates between) savers, continually transferring one way and then the other from those who wish to postpone consumption by acquiring a deposit and others who wish to recover their deposit, perhaps to spend on consumption. This is similar to a stock market where shares are exchanged for cash. There is one big difference, however. The exchange of a bank deposit for cash is always at the amount of the original investment (deposit). The exchange of a share for cash is unlikely to be at the amount of the original investment: it may be at a greater or smaller amount. The operation of this bank secondary market mechanism is considered in Chapter 7.

**Secondary markets (provision of liquidity in securities).** Stock exchanges and OTC markets enable investors to transfer liquidity between themselves, so that when one investor wishes to recover her liquidity she can search (a stock exchange provides a search function like e-bay) for another investor willing and able to provide that liquidity. The investor providing the liquidity must wish to reduce her liquidity by swapping cash for a security, while her counterparty in the transaction must wish to increase her liquidity. Secondary security markets are covered in detail in Chapter 12.

Primary markets provide a range of financing much wider than simply equity finance (initial public offerings), which is the example often chosen when discussing new financing. Thus financing in the modern economy can provide all of the following:

- a means for households to obtain the use of residential housing services through long-term mortgage finance (bank loan) as an **alternative to rental** of housing services;
- a means for households to smooth out the normal daily or monthly variability of cash inflows and outflows through the provision of short-term loans, such as those to finance the purchase of a new car, and **stand-by liquidity**, such as overdrafts and credit card facilities, which become available on demand;
- a means for companies to smooth out the daily difference between cash inflow and outflow (resulting from the time lag between buying raw materials to make goods and receiving cash from sales) through **stand-by facilities** such as an overdraft and lines of credit;
- **initial public offering** services for private companies wishing to raise funds from the public;
- **finance for expansion** for growing companies (debt and follow-on equity issues);
- **leveraged financing** for private equity funds which are arranging the **buy-out** of a company;
- financing for new companies at the innovation end of financing through **venture capital**;
- a means for governments to bring spending forward from the future (and thus from future tax payers) to the present time through **public borrowing**, also known as **sovereign borrowing**.

## MATURITY OF FUNDING: BORROWER LIQUIDITY

Whereas financial investor liquidity (bank provided and secondary market liquidity) is about the ability of a lender to turn his or her investment back into cash with immediacy, borrower liquidity is the reverse of that, i.e. it is the freedom **not to have to return that liquidity to the investor (or the bank) for a long period of time**. The ideal type of financing from the point of view of borrower liquidity is equity financing. This is **irredeemable**, i.e. never repaid,[9] and in addition it need not pay any dividend. Thus equity financing **does not incur any contractual P&I cash outflows**.

The next best type of financing is where the expected cash inflows from the real assets match the contractual cash outflows from the liabilities. Thus, for example, in constructing a power station with an expected life of 30 years, the best financing apart from equity would be 30-year **zero-coupon bonds**, i.e. bonds where the interest is paid back along with the initial sum borrowed only at maturity of the bond and of the project and not in the intermediate period. The next best might be a bond with an **interest rate holiday** for the first five years and with no mandatory principal payments until final maturity. The interest rate holiday would allow the power station to be completed and generating revenues (P&I) before any interest had to be paid.

In terms of borrower liquidity there is, unfortunately, a very important trade-off. Generally, the longer the maturity of the borrowing, the higher its cost. This relationship is shown by the **yield curve** on the financing date. Figure 5.1 shows the interest rate against the period of borrowing The good news is that the longer the term of borrowing (30 years instead of six months, for example), the longer the borrower can put off the thought of having to return liquidity of which he or she has temporary use. But it might be that 30-year interest rates are very high. As

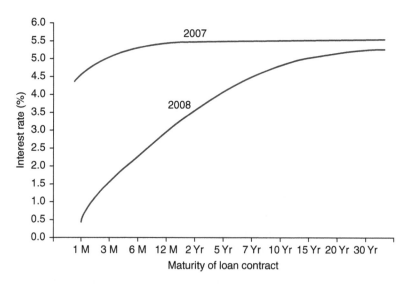

**Figure 5.1** Hypothetical yield curves a year apart in time: upper curve end 2007, lower curve end 2008

*Source*: Data US Treasury Department. http://www.treasury.gov/resource-center/data-chart-center/interest-rates/Pages/TextView.aspx?data=yieldYear&year=2007 (accessed, 29 March 2012).

---

[9]  Companies do buy back their shares in the market but this is not redemption.

can be seen in Figure 5.1, for any company borrowing at the end of 2007, 30-year money would have been almost 3.5% more expensive than six-month money. On the other hand, had the company waited and gone to the market in October 2008 it would have paid an interest rate of only just over 0.5% more for 30-year money than borrowing at a maturity of six months. When there is a **steeply upward sloping yield curve**, i.e. the price of long-term money is well above short-term, there is a temptation to borrow at six-month maturity in order to reduce the cost of borrowing – even though this risks the problem of not being able to refinance the loan in six months' time, i.e. **roll-over risk**.

If the borrower chooses to finance at six-month maturity, then in six months' time he or she must repay the borrowing, regardless of the fact that the underlying investment has not generated the principal amount that is necessary to repay it. The only way to pay off the loan is then to take out a new one and use the proceeds of the new one to redeem the old one. The borrower then faces what is called **roll-over risk** or **funding risk** which is the risk that when roll-over is necessary, either he is in financial difficulty or banks have increased their own liquidity preference (they want to hoard cash) and will not renew loans even to sound borrowers. This has been a problem in bank markets since the financial crisis. Thus he finds he is unable replace funds which have run-off. If this happens he is likely to have to **default** on the loan repayment.

Because of this risk, borrowers who are not willing to subject their company to a high roll-over risk aim to push maturity dates as far forward as possible and to have a spread of maturity dates so that they are less likely to have a sudden liquidity crisis. The same principle applies to governments. The UK government, for example, has a relatively long average maturity of its debt – almost 12 years whereas some countries, including some eurozone countries, have an average maturity of less than half of this. It is this latter group of countries that may have difficulty rolling over their sovereign debt as it matures.

The section above has been designed to impress on readers that it is important to appreciate that liquidity concerns exist as much on the part of borrowers as on the part of lenders and investors. Indeed this is one of the central problems in finance – how to reconcile the **different needs of the two side of the primary market** – the issuers (who want borrower liquidity) and the investors (who want investor liquidity). Essentially finance is about finding the price (expected rate of return) at which these conflicting desires can be equated. The existence of secondary markets can greatly reduce this mis-match. Also, the fact that most (rational) investors hold portfolios of many shares rather than just a single one means that if that company's shares collapse in price due to some cause unique to that company, this has a greatly reduced impact on the total value of the investor's assets than if only that one company's shares comprised all of his or her assets. Both these factors – the available of good secondary markets and the ability to diversity risk – enable primary market financing to be much lower in cost than it otherwise would be and hence enables a much higher rate of capital expansion and, hopefully, economic growth.

# FINANCING THE FOUR SECTORS: COMPANIES, HOUSEHOLDS, GOVERNMENTS AND OVERSEAS THROUGH CREDIT AND CAPITAL MARKETS

## CORPORATE FINANCING (PRIMARY MARKET FUNDING LIQUIDITY FROM BANKS OR CAPITAL MARKETS)

Financing involves two stages:

1. First, project evaluation, which means calculating whether or not a proposed project is financially viable, i.e. will it, probabilistically, generate the returns that a bank lender or investors expect for the level of risk it presents? This is generally done using the discounted cash flow approach to project evaluation which in the case of a company is part of the capital budgeting process.
2. Second, the pooling (collection) of small savings into a unit of financing large enough to meet the needs of the project.

### Project evaluation

When a financier such as a commercial banker or investment banker is considering providing finance for a corporate project, he or she is concerned with four things:

1. estimated cash outflows of the project from the initial investment and from running costs during the life of the project;
2. estimated cash inflows from revenues;
3. the time value of money (pillar 1);
4. the appropriate risk premium to apply to the expected inflows, given that they are uncertain (pillar 2).

The last of these four, pricing of risk, is as we have noted a key function in finance because of its contribution to optimal resource allocation. This risk premium has to be added to the pure time value of money to give an appropriate rate at which to discount cash flows. When the company does this discounting to evaluate an investment project it is known **as capital budgeting**. When the financier does it, it is known as **investment appraisal** and its purpose is to value the project or company in terms of how likely it is that any loans can be repaid (debt) or how much it is likely to increase shareholder value (equity). If the company and the financier agree the calculations, the financier will confirm that he or she believes the project can make its P&I payments without too much risk, and will arrange the financing at the appropriate risk-adjusted expected return.

## Pooling of funds (household assets and corporate assets)

Individually, households have relatively small savings – perhaps just 2,000 euros, dollars or pounds. On the other hand corporates, governments and even mortgagors (those with a mortgage secured on a home) have a need for large financings of a size which may be hundreds of thousands or billions of dollars. Thus a key function in finance is the **pooling** of small-scale savings to create financings large enough for the needs of corporates, governments and mortgagors.

Pooling can be achieved in two different ways, one being through depository intermediaries and the other being through capital markets:

### Depository institutions: commercial banks

Commercial banks perform a key role in terms of **pooling of funds**. By taking in deposits from most households and companies across a country, they can aggregate many small amounts of saving to create large pools of cash for industry. Their mechanism for doing this is their **branch network**, i.e. the availability of branches in every high street which makes it easy for people to access the deposit system. Increasingly, of course, banks have also been able to gather deposits using the internet and electronic transfer from depositors, which makes raising deposits at a distance much easier without the need for local branches. Indeed, some banks such as ING Direct gather deposits entirely without branches.

### Capital markets: two pooling models
#### *Retail brokerage model*

Capital markets also enable pooling. The traditional mechanism for achieving this is the brokerage community. For example Merrill Lynch was originally a nationwide stockbroker in the United States which could gather funds for investment in shares, bonds and other assets from its hundreds of branches across the country each with hundreds or thousands of individual retail accounts. These were first pooled by each branch office, which would then transfer the total amount to Merrill's head office on Wall Street from where the aggregate of all pooled funds from all the branches would be pooled again and transferred into investment in large corporations across the United States.

Merrill Lynch, along with other similar institutions, was known as a **wirehouse** because it had so many branches all connected by telegraph wires (before telephones were invented) which allowed orders for shares and bonds to be transmitted to their Wall Street office. **Wirehouse brokers** are individuals who work for such nationwide firms rather than operating as independent brokers or financial advisors (wealth managers).

### Investment institution model

Many investors do not feel that they have the expertise to select investment assets for use as savings vehicles (store of wealth function) and prefer to use **pooled investment vehicles** such as **mutual funds** into which they will invest. In addition, there are financial services which cannot be provided by an individual but only by an institution which undertakes pooling. These include, importantly, the provision of annual pension payments until death (**an annuity**) and **insurance**. A pension fund is a means of pooling monthly deductions from salary into a pension fund pool (the accumulation phase) to provide retirement income from a future date (decumulation phase). Insurance policies enable the collection of small sums of money from across a nation for investment in an insurance fund which provides protection from risks such as property damage or insurance against early death. Money market mutual funds, which I will cover under shadow banking, are a hybrid type of institution between depository (but without a deposit-taking licence) and investment (mutual funds) and have been an important means of pooling funds into highly liquid assets (quasi-money), particularly in the United States.

Figure 6.1 shows these three routes through which funds can flow.

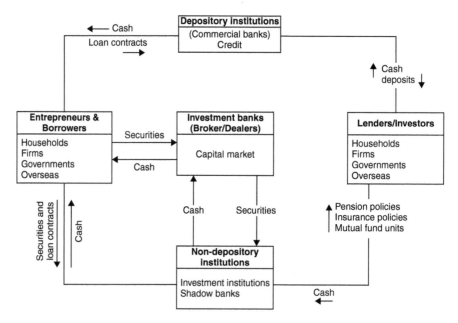

**Figure 6.1** The three financing routes

As well as pooling funds, the financing industry is also transferring funds in time and space.

### Transfer across time

Transfer across time is the basic function of the capital market. An example of this is saving through a company pension scheme which involves an employee moving liquidity, i.e. immediate spending power, forward in time by lending it, through the pension fund, to others who can use it now for spending purposes, such as companies which are expanding through capital investment. From the point of view of companies that raise funds from banks, equity and bond markets, the process is the opposite – the company is using liquidity which others want to 'store', i.e. the store of value function, and is using that liquidity for long-term real investment projects by spending it now before returning it to the lenders at a later date if it is redeemable debt. If it is equity, of course, it is never returned by the company and the investor can only recover his or her liquidity by finding another investor to sell to.

### Transfer across space

There is no particular reason why the most attractive investment projects should be only in the local area in which the funds have been pooled. Capital markets, therefore, also perform the function of assessing projects being undertaken at a distance and offering them to investors as risk/expected return investments. Thus, for example, when the US railroads were first built in the 1800s, much of the investment came from Europe. Equally, in the period 2000–07, many German banks financed US mortgage debt by purchasing US structured debt securities. They did this because they seemed *ex ante* to be offering much higher yields than investment opportunities in Germany. We now know, of course, that the *ex post* yield on these securities was highly negative as the collapse in their prices was a key cause of the financial crisis.

The duration of the loan (or equity investment) and the terms on which liquidity is made available to companies (or households or governments) are laid out in the form of a contract between the provider of the funds and the user of the funds. This defines:

- the **period** for which the funds are to be made available;
- at what **price**, i.e. interest rate or expected return on equity (ROE);
- with the provision of what **security** (if any);
- the rules to be followed if the contract is broken (what rights does the supplier of funds have in this event?), and;
- under which country's legal system.

In the case of an equity or bond investment, the contract is defined by the information in the prospectus and other documents issued at the time, an initial public offering of shares or a bond origination.

Publication of the prospectus should give investors the information they need to try to evaluate a project or a company and decide if they think that allocating cash to it will be the best use of their savings or whether there other investment opportunities available with better risk/return prospects. The company will have undertaken a discounted cash flow analysis of its existing and projected future projects and made its calculations available to investors,who will attempt to confirm that the company has made an appropriate evaluation. They, or their agent, will test the calculation to see if they agree with its assumptions . This latter process is known as investment analysis. In practice, most investors will, of course, rely on their agents, i.e. investment bankers and analysts, to undertake this evaluation.

# FINANCING SECTORAL IMBALANCES

Primary market financing is about transferring cash (liquidity) between those with a surplus of it for current transactional and contingency needs and those with an economic requirement for it either for consumption or investment. In the section above we looked at this at the micro level, i.e. the individual firm, the individual saver or the individual investor.

At the macro level we look at this in terms of the private sectors of the economic system, (**households** & **enterprises**) and the public sector (**government**). There is a fourth sector: the rest of the world (**overseas**). To the extent that a country spends more than it earns, this has to be financed by the overseas sector. The ability to spend (on consumption and real investment) more than a country earns arises from the willingness (or otherwise) of the overseas sector to provide more goods and services to the country (its imports) than the country provides to the overseas sector (its exports). This creates a balance of payments current account deficit which must, of course, be matched by balance of payments current account surpluses in other countries. I will now consider each of these sectors in turn before examining how the balances between them are equilibrated.

## Households

The term **household** refers to any economic unit comprised of **natural person,**[1] i.e. human beings, whether a single person, two people and their children living as a unit, a married couple or civil partnership or an extended family including grandparents. In respect of financial services companies, such households or individuals are known as **retail customers**, **retail clients** or **retail investors**. **Institutional investors**, i.e. the investment management firms such as pension funds, hedge funds, mutual funds, insurance companies and others which employ professionals to manage money, may seem to be the largest investors and, of course, are the principal clients of investment bank trading and sales departments. However, they are, in fact, only the **proximate source of saving**, i.e. the closest to the investment process, as they are simply investing savings which they have **pooled** on behalf of households. End-investors are ultimately always households.

All wealth in a country is ultimately held by the household sector (both domestic and overseas households) since households own all companies and all other assets in an economy either directly or indirectly through financial intermediaries. Not only is all wealth held by this sector, **all economic risk in society is absorbed by it**. Economic risks, such as crop failure, terrorist destruction, flood damage, asbestos claims, over-investment in global telecoms (early 2000s), the cost of the BP oil spill in the Gulf of Mexico, the cost of the earthquake and nuclear meltdown in Japan, etc., are all absorbed by the household sector, though frequently mediated by the risk management services of the financial sector. Thus even if an insurance company pays out on a claim by a company for, say, unexpected earthquake damage in Japan or unexpected flooding damage in Thailand, households ultimately bear the cost, since insurance company shares are held either directly by households or indirectly through pension funds, mutual funds, etc. by investors worldwide.

---

[1]  The other type of person is the **legal person**, which is generally a company.

When we say that households hold all wealth, this means not just equity shares but also includes all debt in an economy, since debt is an asset to its holder. Whether it is household debt (credit card debt, mortgage debt, etc.), government debt or corporate bonds (senior debt, mezzanine debt, junior debt or bank debt, it is all, ultimately, held by the household sector. Thus any diminution in the value of such debt falls on households.

If expenditure, whether on consumption or investment, exceeds income there is a need to borrow in the financial markets to finance the difference. Conversely, if expenditure is less than income, the household is saving and its savings can be invested in financial (or real) assets. While households are almost always, in aggregate, net providers of savings, many individual households have net financial liabilities rather than net financial assets. The UK saw its household savings rate decline from the year 2000 onwards towards a level close to zero until the financial crisis hit. Since then households have been reducing spending relative to income in order to generate resources to repay borrowing. This is often known as household balance sheet deleveraging.

## Household financial decisions

There are three sets of financial decisions that households have to make:

### Consumption versus saving

Households are likely to have periods when their current income is less than their desired expenditure and vice versa. The **life cycle hypothesis** would suggest that when people are young they borrow to finance the purchase of a motor car and the 'shelter' services of a residential property asset (a house), but as their incomes grow and particularly when their children leave home they start to think about saving for retirement. After retirement, savings fall as they are consumed in the absence of earned income. **Saving and borrowing are a consequence of surpluses or deficits in the household's income and expenditure accounts**. Borrowing implies bringing spending power forward in time, i.e. having more to spend now at the price of having less to spend in the future. Saving and investing involve reducing spending now in the expectation of having greater spending power in future time periods, i.e. shifting spending back to a later date. This **time shifting of liquidity** (cash) is a key function of the financial sector. It can be seen in Figure 6.2 below that US, UK and Japanese households have been dramatically reducing their saving and therefore increasing their consumption as a percentage of their income from around the year 2000 (and also before). This has been an important factor in creating the conditions for a financial crisis, as the consequence must be large inflows of capital from abroad. Germany, it will be noted, has maintained a very high rate of saving and consequently, in contrast to the US and UK, has run large surpluses on its balance of payments on current account.

### Risk management decisions

Given the risks involved in life, i.e. the uncertainties as to future income, the unexpected arrival of a child, the risk of hospitalisation, etc., how much insurance should be taken out to reduce such risks? How much cash should be held for everyday transactions (**transactional balances**)? How much for unexpected

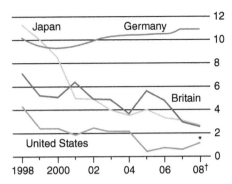

**Figure 6.2**   Household savings as a percentage
of disposable income for various countries

*3.
†Forecast.

*Source*: Data from OECD: US Bureau of Economic
Analysis.

contingencies (**precautionary balances**)? Some households will also hold cash
balances in order to be able to take advantage of investment opportunities that
might arise (**speculative balances**).

On the investment side, a key risk management question is whether the household should invest in a widely diversified basket of securities to minimise risk or
hope for a big win by investing in a few well-researched companies. Another risk
management question is whether capital protection securities should be purchased
which minimise downside risk at the cost of a lower upside potential.

### Financing decisions

Given the household's income, should it borrow to finance additional consumption or investment in a real asset such as a home or save until it has sufficient cash?
Another example would be whether it should acquire investments in securities
through a **margin loan**, i.e. borrowing from a broker, even when it may have sufficient cash to purchase these without a loan? Should it, alternatively, use **derivative contracts**, such as futures, options or contracts for difference, to invest in
potential securities market returns rather than investing through the **cash market**,
i.e. the market which involves buying the actual securities, since derivatives would
use up less cash which could be employed for other purposes, including increasing
total financial investment? Both of these means of financing involve **leverage**, i.e.
using only some of the investor's own resources and borrowing the remainder
from others, giving rise to the possibility of **negative equity**, i.e. the value of the
investment falling by more than the amount of cash put into it, leading to a net
loss when the lending is repaid. Negative equity is an expression also used in the
housing market. If a house buyer acquires a property, the price of which falls below
the amount he or she has borrowed, they are then in a position of negative equity
e.g. if they had borrowed 80% of the cost of a £100,000 house but the house falls
to a value of only £70,000; if they repaid their borrowing at that point, they would
realise a loss of £10,000.

These decisions are ones that all households must make either explicitly or implicitly. However, asset allocation decisions and security selection decisions and other risk management decisions may be sub-contracted to a pension plan provider or a financial planner or wealth manager, i.e. an agent with specialist skills.

For households, saving and investment through the acquisition of financial assets and their associated risks are not objectives in themselves but simply means of **achieving a desired consumption pattern over a lifetime** (including consumption of housing/shelter services), given their expected lifespan, income pattern, spending pattern (including such things as financing university education for children) and the availability and prices of goods and services. Equally, borrowing to allow investment in a home, a motor car, shares or any venture is not an objective in itself but a means of achieving long-run consumption services, including the use of owner-occupied housing through deferred purchase (mortgage) rather than rental or the use of transport services (through purchase of a motor vehicle rather than car rental).

Finance, from the household viewpoint, therefore, is concerned with how households make saving/borrowing, lending, investment and risk management decisions to optimise their lifetime consumption possibilities, given their expected lifetime income pattern, any intergenerational transfers (from parents or to children) received or expected to be made, risks including those involved in asset holdings (including domestic property), transaction costs and the liquidity available in different asset markets.

Although we have viewed households as being the ultimate holders of all financial assets, they also have financial liabilities just as companies do. The distinction between the two, however, is that households, unlike enterprises, are unlikely to access the capital market directly when they create financial liabilities. Households access banks and other financial intermediaries involved in lending. There is still a connection with the capital market, however, in that household debt (mortgage, credit card, student loan, etc.) may ultimately be **securitised** and sold into the capital market and thus, indirectly, the capital markets including foreign investors are financing households (see Chapter 9 ).

Lending to individuals involves a substantial amount of risk. To cover this, lenders may require insurance or **collateral** which, as we noted earlier, is the pledge of an asset that enables the ownership of the asset to be transferred to the lender in the event of the contractual terms of a loan being breached. A mortgage on a house involves such a pledge, as this gives the lender greater security, i.e. it protects the capital repayment.

Compared with **unsecured lending**, i.e. lending with no asset available to the lender to be liquidated in the event of a breach of loan terms, **secured lending** with collateral will be at an interest rate that is lower than it would be without (a reduction in lender risk reduces the risk premium charged). In addition, the lender will normally also require insurance on the property itself (to protect the holder of the collateral in the event of fire or other risks). It may also require the income earner in the household to take out **payment protection insurance** to ensure that interest payments can be maintained even during a period of unemployment. They may also require **life insurance** where the beneficiary, in the event of the death of the debtor, is the mortgage company. This saves the mortgage company having to arrange the sale of the property (thus taking on price risk) provided the life insurance is in an amount sufficient to cover the outstanding capital amount.

## Enterprise financial decisions

The term **enterprise** is one of many expressions used to cover a wide range of organisational forms whose function is to produce goods and services. This range includes **corporations** (a US term) or **companies** (a UK term) which in finance are known as **corporates, partnerships, sole proprietorships, cooperatives** and the generic term **firm**. But in addition there are **state owned enterprises** (often utilities) and **mutual companies** owned by account or policy-holders (traditionally insurance companies and UK building societies had this form of organisation). A **public company** is one whose equity shares are available in a market accessible to the general public. A **private company** is one where the equity shares are not freely available on any public market, though they can be transferred informally in private markets.

We generally distinguish two sets of companies. First, the **corporates**, which includes all companies. Second, the sub-set of **financial intermediaries**, which is frequently separated out from other corporates because their role is simply to 'stand between' by employing their balance sheets rather than providing goods or non-financial services.

Once we talk about a company we are talking about an economic construct in which the owner of the firm is separate from the firm itself. We are assuming that the firm has its own **legal personality** separate from its owner, i.e. it is a legal person in contrast to what is known as a **sole trader**, which is a business enterprise owned and managed by one individual where there is no legal or financial separation between the owner and his or her business. This concept of separate legal personality is a key one in business without which we could not have the type of capital markets and large-scale financings we have today.

In the Western world, the earliest firm resembling what we call a corporation was the joint stock company founded in 1553 as the 'Russian Company'. In that endeavour, 28 persons each invested £6,000 in the common stock of the company to open up trade routes to Russia and China. What distinguished this entity is that it was defined as 'one bodie and perpetuall fellowship and communalitie', and that *it held legal rights of an individual.* It could hold title, sue and be sued *under its own seal.*[2]

It was this development of the **joint stock company** or **corporation** that allowed the pooling of funds through a capital market which, in turn, enabled the development of much larger enterprises. A joint stock company is a **legal person** in which two or more **natural persons** come together for a venture and the **company** (a legal person) issues to them certificates of ownership (share certificates). This mechanism enables funds to be pooled not just from the local region but from across a nation and, increasingly, internationally from people with

---

[2]  Dwight Crane *et al*, *The Global Financial System* (Harvard Business Press, 1995 ), pp. 82–83.

whom the borrower has no direct relationship. It facilitates financing from a wider geographical area.

Like households, enterprises have to make a set of financial decisions. There are three main types of corporate decision:

### Investment decisions

In the case of enterprises this generally involve real asset investment decisions, not decisions on holdings of financial assets (though for financial firms, this is clearly not the case). Thus firms need a process to decide what investment projects to undertake. This process is called **capital budgeting** and uses the discounted cash flow approach of evaluating investments to ensure that they would add to corporate value.

**Financing** decisions have to be made as to how any new real investment will be financed. There are two sources of such financing. The first is the savings of the firm (defined as the amount of profit it retains (retained profit) rather than paying out to shareholders) which I cover in Chapter 20 under the heading 'the internal capital market'. To the extent that this is not sufficient, it needs to access the second source which is the capital markets or the banking system in order to raise additional finance. Thus the financing decision implicitly incorporates the dividend (pay-out) decision.

### Risk management decisions

Risk management decisions have to be taken by companies just like households in respect of real asset insurance, e.g. property. Like households taking out a mortgage, they also have to make risk management decisions on matters such as whether to choose finance in which the interest rate varies frequently in line with market rates (floating-rate finance from a bank) or fixed-rate finance (fixed income bond finance). They may also choose to transfer the risk of price changes in raw material (oil, metals, etc.) by taking out hedging contracts with financial firms. Airlines, for example, often hedge their future fuel costs up to a year ahead using forward contracts which fix costs for that period.

## Government

A government's principal source of income is taxation – personal tax, corporate tax, sales tax and inheritance tax being the main ones. Like households or companies, governments have to plan to ensure they can meet the contractual payments incurred on their debt. However, while humans have a limited lifespan and companies seldom survive in their original form for even as long as a century, **sovereigns**, i.e. the authority which has the right to govern a country by making and enforcing laws and extracting taxation, are normally considered to have an infinite life (unlike a sovereign in the sense of a particular king or queen or president). As a result, it is generally expected at the time of a debt issue that while **sovereign debt** will pay interest, **repayment of the debt will be effected not out of revenue but from issuing new debt (roll-over)**. Sovereign debt is almost never secured since governments generally do not have large asset holdings, i.e. most governments are technically insolvent in terms of their balance sheet. But in the case of some European countries which are having difficulty in refinancing government debt, it has been suggested that they might use one of their islands as collateral for a loan (funding liquidity) or even sell some of their islands to raise cash (market liquidity)!

If a country has issued more debt denominated in its own currency than it can **service**, i.e. make good on P&I obligations, it can increase taxation to meet such payments. An alternative is to reduce the real value of the debt by causing the value of money to decline, i.e. through allowing inflation to accelerate. Zimbabwe for example, has an inflation rate of millions of per cent and has thus wiped out any real value in its debt. The Weimar Republic in Germany did the same. Inflation reduces the value of outstanding debt since debt has a fixed nominal value. If, however, the debt is mostly held by overseas investors this policy is likely to make future debt issues very difficult for that country. Also, in the case of a country which is a member of a single currency area and thus has no control over the value of its currency, it is not possible for one country to inflate its way out of excessive debt or indeed to effect a currency depreciation in order to reduce the value of its debts. This applies to Greece which is a member of the eurozone and thus, if it does repay its debt, it must always repay in what is, in effect, a foreign currency. It should be noted, however, that one of the reasons for setting up the eurozone as a single currency area was to prevent competitive devaluations amongst European countries which some believe is not an acceptable practice amongst close trading partners. What has happened instead is that very large payments imbalances have developed within the eurozone due to changes in the relative competitiveness of its member country, balances which then have to be financed. This has been the source of the eurozone crisis in the view of many observers.

## Overseas sector

The overseas sector, as we noted earlier, is the one which offsets the net balance of all the other (domestic) sectors, i.e. **the net domestic balance** of (government + household + corporate). Figure 6.3 gives a good global picture of the imbalances that were building up rapidly in the period from 2000 to 2008. Oil exporters were clearly running very large surpluses. China's export surplus grew while the US deficit increased.

Many would argue that these gross imbalances in world payments have contributed towards the conditions in which financial instability can suddenly arise. The Bank of England,[3] for example, notes that 'while the proximate causes of the (financial) crisis lie within financial markets, the build-up of substantial global macroeconomic imbalances over the past decade (from 1999) may also have contributed significantly'. The Bank goes on to note that one reason for the large financial surpluses that China and other Asian countries have generated in this period has been the build-up of large 'precautionary' savings by households in the

---

[3] *Global Imbalances and the Financial Crisis* in Bank of England, Quarterly Bulletin, 2009 Q3. http://www.bankofengland.co.uk/publications/Documents/quarterlybulletin/qb090301.pdf

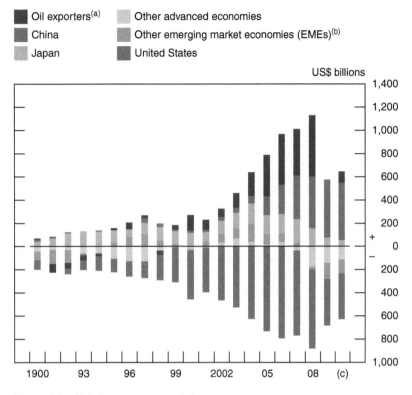

**Figure 6.3**  Global current account balances

(a) The sum of the ten largest oil exporters in 2004: Algeria, Iran, Kuwait, Mexico, Nigeria, Norway, Russia, Saudi Arabia, United Arab Emirates and Venezuela.

(b) Other EMEs includes the newly industrialised Asian economies.

(c) IMF World Economic Outlook (April 2009) forecast for 2009 and 2010.

*Sources*: Bank of England calculations (Chart 3.11 FSR June 2009) with data from IMF World Economic Outlook (April 2009) (p. 48). http://www.bankofengland.co.uk/publications/Documents/fsr/2009/fsr25sec3.pdf (accessed, 2 February 2012)

absence of government provision of health, education and social security services in a number of these countries.

In contrast to Asian country, the UK had a large current account **deficit** in the period leading up to the economic crisis in 2007. This deficit expanded again through the first quarter of 2010.

## CAPITAL FLOWS WITHIN AND BETWEEN THE FOUR SECTORS

Financing is about intra-sectoral (within), inter-sectoral (between) and inter-country (cross-border) financial flows, i.e. within and between the four sectors. For example:

- domestic intra-sectoral flows e.g. from household bank deposits to household mortgages;
- domestic inter-sectoral flows e.g. between households and firms;

● inter-country flows which equilibrate the export surpluses of China, Saudi Arabia and Germany (amongst others) on the one hand with the corresponding current account deficits of the United States, the United Kingdom and other deficit countries.

The household sector is generally a net provider of funds (liquidity) to the other sectors of the economy, while other sectors (corporates and government) are frequently net users of funds (liquidity). However, if the household sector itself is in net deficit, as has been the case in the United States at periods since the year 2000, and the other sectors cannot balance the household sector deficit with a corresponding surplus, then funds **must** flow in from the overseas sector. This reflects a simple accounting identity. If foreign investors are reluctant to invest, the exchange rate will fall and interest rates will rise until the point at which such an investment becomes attractive.

The need to import funds on a large scale raised issues of **international imbalance** for a number of countries in the lead-up to the credit crisis. For example, Figure 6.4(a) shows that the 'Rest of the world' became a very substantial lender to the UK economy through, for example, the inflow of interbank deposits from abroad reflecting the fact that both central government and households have gone into substantial deficit.

Customer funding gap is customer lending less customer funding, where customer refers to all non-bank borrowers and depositors.

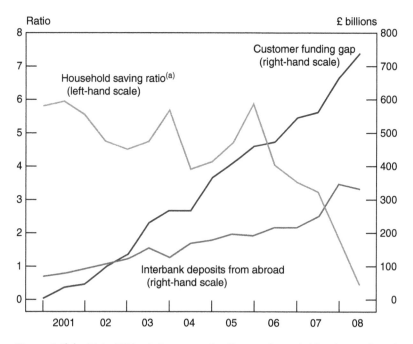

**Figure 6.4(a)** Major UK banks' customer funding gap, household savings ratio and foreign interbank deposits

(a) UK household savings as a percentage of post-tax income.

*Sources*: Bank of England (FSR October 2008, p. 9). http://www.bankofengland.co.uk/publications/Documents/fsr/2008/fsrfull0810.pdf (accessed, 2 February 2012). Dealogic, ONS, published accounts and Bank calculations.

Figure 6.4(b) shows that the customer funding gap has declined since 2008, from over 25% of total lending to around only 8% in 2011.

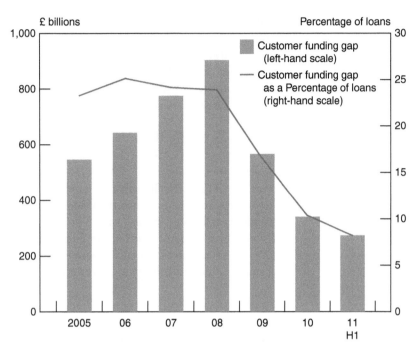

**Figure 6.4(b)**   UK banks' customer funding gap

*Note*: H1 means first half.

*Sources*: Bank of England (FSR December 2011, p. 17). http://www.bankofengland.co.uk/publications/fsr/2011/fsrfull1112.pdf (accessed, 2 February 2012); published accounts and Bank calculations.

## THE FINANCING OF INTERNATIONAL FINANCIAL (IM)BALANCES

To finance an excess of spending over income requires a capital inflow to a country equal to the current account deficit. This counterpart is the capital account surplus which is equal and opposite to the current account deficit. This capital inflow arises from overseas banks and governments purchasing financial assets from the over-spending country. Examples would be the Chinese government purchasing US Treasury bonds which finance US spending in excess of income, or German banks purchasing Italian government bonds or lending to Greek or Portuguese companies which finances these countries spending in excess of income. Clearly, to do this, China and Germany must run surpluses on their own current accounts. Thus capital flows between countries are a key element in analysing the global financing mechanism.

In accounting terms the sum of the balances of the three sectors, public, private and overseas, must equate to zero as we noted before. Indeed, if the balance of payments on current account was zero, then the private sector balance and the government balance would be mirror images of each other. If the private sector chooses to go into surplus, then the government must automatically go into deficit by an equal amount.

Let's examine the sectors in terms of the accounting relationships that must hold between them.

- *Private sector balance*: this is the sum of the balances of the enterprise and household sectors. Real investment by the enterprise sector (I) is financed by household sector savings (S). If savings fall short of (or exceed) the investment need, other sectors have to finance the balance, whether positive or negative. The private sector balance is equal to investment minus savings $(I - S)$.
- *Government sector balance*: this equals government spending minus taxation $(G - T)$.
- *The domestic balance*: this is the sum of the balances of the private and government sectors, i.e. $(I - S) + (G - T)$. If there is no balance of payments surplus or deficit then $(I - S) + (G - T) = 0$. If one is negative, the other must be of the same size but positive. If the balances of the private and government sector (the domestic sectors) do not exactly offset each other, there must be a balance of payments deficit or surplus between the domestic and overseas sector.
- *Overseas sector balance*: this is the difference between exports and imports $(X - M)$. The sum of the balances of the three sectors must logically (as an accounting identity) always equal zero. Thus $(I - S) + (G - T) + (X - M) = 0$.

The globalisation of world trade and finance has led to an increasing importance of the overseas sector in the twenty-first century and has also led to the **global financial imbalances** which were one of the factors in the financial crisis. Thus in the period since the year 2000, net deficits in the US, the UK and other countries have been financed by capital inflows from net surplus countries such as China, Germany, Japan and OPEC countries. We have also had substantial **regional financial imbalances** in the eurozone which have led to a sovereign debt crisis for some members of the single currency zone.

The US was in reasonable payments balance in the year 2000. But by 2008 (the height of the financial crisis), the US government balance had plunged to a massive 10% of GDP. This deficit was, in turn, financed by the three sectors in surplus – households, business and foreign. In the case of the UK the massive government deficit through 2009 was financed by a large surplus in the business sector and a shift from deficit to surplus by the household sector caused by reduced spending and paying off borrowings. The other financing component of the government deficit was, of course, the foreign sector, and its contribution (a capital account surplus) is simply the counterpart to the balance of payments current account deficit.

Some would argue that the problem in both countries is the huge government deficits incurred in recent years. Equally, however, it can be argued that if the private sector (households and business) goes into surplus, which means that it cuts back its spending dramatically (deleveraging its balance sheets by paying off debt through increased saving), then, unless the government steps in to take up the slack in the economy by boosting spending, the country will simply go into a deep recession or an economic slump. Thus the government deficit is simply the accounting counterpart of the other sectors choosing to go into surplus.

## GLOBAL IMBALANCES: THE WORLD'S LARGEST CURRENT ACCOUNT SURPLUSES AND DEFICITS

Until 2011, China had a large current account surplus with all other countries in the world almost equal to the total deficit of the US with all countries. The net imbalance between these two countries, while not quite as large is nearly of the same size. This imbalance is believed by some to have been a major contributor to the financial crisis. If we now consider eurozone surpluses and deficits one set of eurozone countries (Spain, Italy, Portugal, France and Greece, for example) has surpluses while another (Germany Netherlands, Austria and Finland, for example) have deficits. The eurozone as a whole, however, happens to have a virtually zero net balance with the rest of the world. This is only by chance, however. But what this tells us is that the eurozone problem is one of a failure of internal financing rather than a need to finance the zone externally. There is really no need to ask China to help with financing the eurozone as a whole, - a request which was made in November 2011.

The real problem in the eurozone is that its major surplus countries, Germany and the Netherlands, are unwilling to continue financing the deficits of Greece and the others as they now consider this too risky. The problem which became manifest in 2010 is a political one rather than a pure financial one and results from the inherent contradictions of the Maastricht Treaty which set up the eurozone structure. The single currency was not set up according to economic 'laws' on how single currency zones can be a long-run success. There was a common currency and a single central bank but no coordination of spending and taxing policy across the zone nor any 'lender of last resort' for countries suffering liquidity problems. In the long run, for a currency union to function effectively, there needs to be a high degree of political union and a willingness by some countries to finance other countries for the foreseeable future. For this to be agreeable to the countries being financed, they would have to agree to submit to extra-territorial control of their taxation and spending policies. It seems unlikely that voters in the deficit countries would agree to transfer the degree of sovereignty required to make such financing possible. Equally it would seem unlikely that voters in surplus countries would agree to open-ended financing commitments without a sound 'business plan' laying out how the country planned to return to balance

# 7 BANKING: CREDIT INTERMEDIATION THROUGH DEPOSITORY INSTITUTIONS

Commercial banks are **the key type of financial intermediary in any economy**. They are central to the functioning of the economic system in contrast to many other financial businesses which are of lesser centrality. Most commercial banks have a **retail** and a **wholesale** banking operation. In their retail operations as **high street** or **main street** banks, they offer deposit, lending and money transfer services (cheques, debit card, e-transfers) to households and to small and medium sized enterprises (SMEs). Included under loans would be consumer loans, mortgage loans, credit card loans and business development loans. The retail part of a commercial bank may have some thousands of branch offices. The wholesale part, on the other hand, is likely to be a single office on **Wall Street** (in the case of the US), in the **City of London** (the UK financial district), in **Shanghai** (in the case of mainland China) or **Hong Kong**. The wholesale part is likely to be involved in large scale lending, including cross-border lending, normally as part of a lending syndicate with other banks.

A commercial bank as we noted earlier, as distinct from an investment bank, is a specific type of financial intermediary which is probably best identified as **an institution which holds a banking licence**. This may seem tautological but it is an important distinction from all other financial institutions. This licence allows a company (which is what a bank is) to solicit deposits from the public. A deposit is defined as a **fixed value asset** which will be returned in full to the depositor, either on demand (demand deposit) or at the end of a defined period (time deposit) of normally not more than a year. More precise definitions will normally be found in legislation in any particular country.

A key feature of a deposit is that, except in the event of bank failure, its value is contractually fixed, i.e. the amount returned will be not less, or more, than the amount deposited. This is in sharp contrast to money invested with a mutual fund, for example, where the value (price) is re-calculated every day, based on prices in markets Thus deposits are **fixed value assets**, whereas mutual fund holdings are **variable value assets**. Understanding this distinction is critical in understanding many of the problematic issues in contemporary finance, including those raised by shadow banking (see Chapter 10).

Bank deposits in most countries are covered by some type of **deposit insurance**. Mutual funds, on the other hand, do not benefit from deposit insurance (though such insurance was extended to money market mutual funds in the US during the financial crisis). The insurance fund is either a government sponsored or a private sector scheme which pays back deposits to customers (sometimes only partial repayment up to a maximum) in the event that the bank fails and cannot or will not honour its par value promise. If a large part of the banking system failed, deposit insurance schemes would be unlikely to have sufficient resources to repay all depositors. Thus even with deposit insurance schemes, the government of a country may remain the insurer of last resort. This applies particularly in democracies, since governments don't want to alienate voters by announcing that they will not save depositors from the consequences of failure of their bank.

In summary, the features of banks which make them special in any economy are:

- the **fixed nominal**[1] **value** of their liabilities (deposits);
- the **instant** redeemability of a high proportion of their liabilities (demand deposits);
- the fact that bank demand deposits are by far the largest component of the **money supply** of a country and thus the money supply is mainly the liabilities of private companies;
- the provision of **essential credit** to lubricate trade and commerce;
- they are key players in the **payments system** which, if it broke down, could result in all commercial activities (shopping, travel, salary payments, purchase of raw materials, etc.) ceasing.

In recognition of the critical importance of this specific type of financial intermediary and its 'fragility' due to high leverage and maturity mismatch, banks have always been much more closely regulated than other financial institutions. Banks are risky, i.e. liable to collapse, because they invest in risky assets (loans) financed mainly by customer deposits (debts), and they may lose much more than they expect on these loans (unexpected loss). Thus, while their liabilities (deposits) have a **fixed value**, their assets can collapse in value due to losses. It is somewhat odd that banks have been allowed to operate until recently with relatively little shareholder capital to bear the risk of such losses – given the repercussions on the wider economy if a bank fails.

There are regulations on the amount of shareholders' equity (**capital**) they need to have on the liability side of their balance sheet and, on the asset side, how much of their assets they must hold in liquid form (**reserves** to enable them to meet customer demand for cash). But what has been clear from the crisis is that in many cases neither the capital requirements nor the liquidity requirements were adequate to prevent collapse. Nor was the detailed regulation and supervision of banks adequate. Only government intervention with taxpayer resources was able to prevent the collapse of some of the world's major

---

[1] We use the word **nominal** to mean that the amount is fixed in terms of an amount of money (a number of pounds or dollars), but of course money may not retain its **real** value due to inflation and thus investors still take on inflation risk.

financial intermediaries from 2008 onwards. Some, however, such as Dexia Bank, a Franco/Belgian bank, have had to be rescued a second time in 2011 due to eurozone sovereign debt losses.

The authorities, i.e. government and regulators, have always believed that the collapse of a bank, or at least a large bank, is potentially very damaging to the economy. Such a collapse could cause a chain reaction, leading to other banks also collapsing, since if one bank is seen to collapse, depositors and lenders to all banks are likely to wonder whether their bank might also collapse. Even just one large bank collapsing would lead to a sharp fall in the provision of credit and, if a number collapsed, this would lead to a recession due to the lack of credit available to 'lubricate the wheels of the economy'. Governments, therefore, are always aware that they might need to bail out banks even at a high cost to taxpayers. The purpose of regulation, therefore, is to minimise the likelihood of collapse and hence the need for taxpayer support and, in the event of bank collapses, to minimise the cost of bailout to the state. Today, regulators worldwide are trying to calibrate new rules (Basel III) to try to minimise the risk of another financial crisis resulting from banks collapsing.

## THE FUNCTIONS OF COMMERCIAL BANKS

I list below what banks do in their role of accepting deposits, raising funds in securities markets and making loans, i.e. the commercial banking deposit and loan functions. Banks do of course undertake other activities such as dealing in foreign exchange, providing access to mutual funds and other investments, and selling insurance policies. But we are looking, at this point, at the commercial banking function, not at what any particular commercial bank may do in addition to its main role as a provider of commercial banking services, i.e. deposit taking, provision of credit and money transfer.

### The liability side of the balance sheet

This involves issuing liabilities (creating assets) for investors, savers and other banks to hold in order to finance bank lending. These are:

1. **Deposit taking**, i.e. accepting money 'over the counter' in a branch and by electronic transfer and internet banking.
2. Borrowing in the global interbank markets, i.e. markets such the **London Interbank Market** – the wholesale market in short-term deposits and loans in major currencies between banks, investment banks, asset managers, corporates and others with short-term liquidity available for investment.
3. Issuing domestic and foreign currency **certificates of deposit (CDs)** to retail and wholesale customers to raise funds for lending purposes. CDs are a hybrid between deposits and securities as they are tradable deposits.
4. Issuing **commercial paper** which is a short-term security, though similar in many ways to CDs.
5. Issuing **fixed income medium- and long-term bonds**.
6. Issuing **equity** which reduce the bank's leverage ratio (debt/equity).

## The asset side of the balance sheet

This involves creating household and business liabilities to provide these sectors of the economy with financing and thereby creating financial assets for the bank (liabilities of households and businesses). These are:

1. Lending to **households** for house purchase (mortgages), consumer goods purchase, student loans, credit card lending, etc.
2. Lending to **investment grade** companies, i.e. companies with an investment grade rating from one of the ratings agencies.
3. Lending to small and medium sized enterprises (**SMEs**).
4. Providing **leveraged loans** to non-investment grade companies. A leveraged loan simply means a loan of such a size relative to equity that it will result in that company having very high leverage, i.e. debt/equity ratio. A high proportion of such lending has, in the past, been to **private equity funds** to finance large buyouts of companies or divisions of companies.
5. Lending to **other banks** in the global interbank markets.
6. Lending to the **public sector** (in part through forced investment as a result of the regulatory requirement to hold governments bonds and bills for liquidity purposes).
7. **Overseas lending** which has been particularly important to, for example, German banks as German household and corporate savings were in excess of the country's real investment requirements $(S > I)$.

Rather than holding customer liabilities on their balance sheet for the full duration of such lending, banks may choose to **securitise** existing consumer loans, mortgages and corporate loans, which means taking them off the bank balance sheet through sale to other financial institutions or to their own off-balance sheet securitised investment vehicles (SIVs). This eliminates the need for on-going financing as such asset sales raise fresh cash for a bank. Such activities have also given rise to the shadow banking sector (see Chapter 10).

## BANKS' BALANCE SHEET TRANSFORMATIONS

As well as providing **size transformation**, i.e. pooling services, by collecting small deposits to convert into large loans, there are two other dimensions of **transformation** that banks provide through their balance sheets.

### Credit risk transformation

Banks offer depositors fixed value liabilities which are nominally 'riskless' assets and use the proceeds to make risky loans, i.e. loans that borrowers may not repay. Credit transformation is the process of lowering the risk of doing this. They achieve this transformation by two means:

First, through the benefit of portfolio diversification, i.e. a large pool of loans, which is well diversified over type of borrower and geographical location. This reduces **idiosyncratic risk** which is the risk that one large borrower or one particular type of borrower or a class of borrowers in one region of the country defaults and creates a large percentage loss on the portfolio. Thus a large portfolio of loans benefits from the statistical properties reflected by the **law of large numbers**,[2] i.e. in this case the average expectation of loss on a large number of loans can be calculated and allowed for in pricing. Further diversification is achieved by syndicating loans with other banks, i.e. each bank takes a participation in the loans which others make;

Second through creating liabilities on their balance sheet which use **priority of claims**, also known as **subordination** to provide protection to deposit holders. Thus equity takes the first loss, junior debt takes the next loss, then senior debt and deposits. This is the same technique as we discussed in Chapter 2 under the heading 'subordination'. Deposits may safer than senior debt, despite having the same priority in many countries, since they may also be covered by deposit insurance.[3] Thus each level in the capital structure is protected by claims which are junior to it in the prioritisation of pay-out in the event of insolvency. I cover these issues in more detail in the next chapter.

The question that must be asked in respect of this use of subordination is whether or not the average cost of financing the asset book of such a company (a bank) can be lowered, compared with simpler liability structures. Modigliani and Miller's capital structure irrelevance theorem as we noted earlier would suggest not, but only if there is no tax deductibility of interest and no costs involved in bankruptcy. Practice would suggest it can – though only if so-called black swan[4] events (once in a thousand year events, also known as tail events, i.e. the tail of the distribution of returns), which give rise to a very occasional but very large loss, are not incorporated into pricing. Thus such balance sheet structuring may not actually lower the cost of funds if we allow for the cost of financial crises when the financial system is hit by a black swan event.

## Maturity transformation

This is achieved through a bank's ability to offer long-term loans (the bank's assets) even though its deposits (the bank's liabilities) are short-term, i.e. banks have the seeming ability to **create liquidity** for the corporate and household sectors by making themselves **illiquid**. Provided the yield curve is upward sloping (as it is more often than not), then this also reduces the cost of long-term funding.

One of the main functions which banks provide to society – credit intermediation by borrowing at short maturity and providing risky loans at long-term

---

[2]  See Note 6 in Chapter 5.

[3]  Under current law in many countries, while deposits have greater priority than junior debt they have the same priority as senior debt, not a higher priority, and thus the safety of deposits in practice is in large part a function of deposit insurance. Some countries are now considering giving deposits priority over senior debt as this would reduce the extent of calls on the insurance fund and, in the event of systemic losses exceeding the resources of the insurance fund, the taxpayer.

[4]  See Nassim Taleb, *Black Swan* (Penguin, 2008).

maturity – can only be undertaken through banks taking on three main types of risk:

- the risk that they will not be repaid (**credit risk**);
- the risk that the cost of their liabilities rises above the yield on their assets (**interest rate risk**);
- the risk that the short-term liabilities they issue will not be 'rolled-over' by savers or investors (**roll-over risk** or **liquidity risk**).

Thus two of the main risks to which they are subject are:

- *Solvency risk.* Banks, as we have noted already, offer their liabilities as highly liquid, **fixed value** deposits with a high level of safety. In return for these features, depositors are willing to accept a lower rate of return than on other assets which do not have these features. Thus a bank has **liabilities** which have **certain value**, i.e. there is no uncertainty about how much they are worth, whereas the bank's **assets** have **uncertain value** due to credit risk, as borrowers may default on their payments causing the bank to lose up to 100% of asset value. This gives rise to the possibility of the bank losing more on its assets than it has capital and thus becoming insolvent.
- *Liquidity risk.* A bank has liabilities that are mainly **due on demand** (demand deposits), while its assets (loans to customers) become due for repayment only on specified dates, which in many cases are as much as 20 years or more in the future. Thus a bank, as well as being subject to **solvency risk**, i.e. the risk of the value of its assets falling below that of its liabilities due to credit losses, is also subject to **liquidity risk**, i.e. the risk that its mandatory cash outflows exceed its cash inflows.

Given these substantial risks, banks, like any company, have to manage their risks to try to avoid bankruptcy (insolvency) or illiquidity (inability to meet demand for cash). While corporates are also subject to these risks, they are much more acute for banks, particularly given how highly leveraged and maturity-mismatched banks are.

Banks can only take on these risks with reasonable safety as a result of having two mechanisms available to them to control risk:

A **viable business model**. requiring an adequate spread between borrowing and lending rates, careful and appropriate risk management (such as ensuring that borrowers do have the income they claim to have), and good business practice. This model involves:

- a bank's skill in assessing the risk of loans and pricing these correctly;
- economies of scale in both **pooling of funds** (liabilities mainly in the form of deposits) and in **origination of loans** (assets), compared with **direct** lending by households to corporates or between two households;
- a reduction in the risk per unit of value lent from diversification as a result of the pooling of **independent risks** (an application of the law of large numbers provided the risks actually are independent);
- appropriate use of **subordination** in the capital structure.

**A social contract with society** which is the socially designed structural under-pinnings which provide support to the banking business model in the event of liquidity stress and the legislative framework which a country has in place to enable recovery of debts through the courts in the event that borrowers try to avoid repayment of loans. This involves the provision by a country of a political, legal, regulatory and supervisory framework to try to ensure that the likelihood of illiquidity or insolvency are minimised. This includes:

- The availability of **stand-by liquidity** in the form of the central bank **LOLR** facility.
- **Deposit insurance** provided either by the government or, under a legislative requirement, a private sector deposit insurance scheme.
- A set of **rules**, in particular **solvency and liquidity rules**, such as Basel II and III, which the Basel Committee of Banking Supervisors suggests the major countries should implement within their bank regulatory framework.
- **Bank examiners** (supervisors) from a regulatory agency who overview the activities of the bank to try to ensure that the business model is safe and that the solvency and liquidity rules are being followed.
- **Market discipline** which requires a country to have a legal, accounting and regulatory framework which tries to ensure that financial and other informa-tion relevant to the liquidity and solvency of the institution is made available to the public (including rating agencies, bond investors and share analysts). This is intended to enable interested parties to take appropriate action to protect their wealth in the event that the financial institution is following an inappro-priate business model or otherwise taking too much risk. Market discipline is intended to support the activities of regulators and supervisors in helping to ensure the safety of financial institutions.

The business model framework should enable the bank to intermediate at a lower cost than direct lending from households to firms or between households (but not necessarily at a lower cost than direct capital market financing). The social contract and political and regulatory framework are designed to minimise the risk of insolvency or illiquidity of banking institutions as a result of their busi-ness model. Insolvency or illiquidity could result in the event that the assump-tions made on expected losses from default by customers, or on the demand for liquidity from customers, prove to be wrong and thus the bank is unable to meet its promises as to certainty of value and immediate (or prescheduled) redemption of its deposit liabilities.

The key question today in relation to the social contract is whether or not it needs to, or should, involve the state, through the taxpayer, underwriting what is known as the **too big to fail**[5] doctrine. This doctrine says that if a financial insti-tution is very large, it cannot be allowed to fail (i.e. be forced into liquidation) because the impact on the economic stability of a country is too great. Therefore, there is an implicit taxpayer guarantee that such financial companies, even if they

---

[5] The book *Too Big to Fail* by Andrew Ross Sorkin (Penguin Books, 2009) became a film of the same name in 2011 and is certainly worth watching to learn about this issue.

become insolvent, will always remain **going concerns**, i.e. will not become **gone concerns**, which means to fail.

## MINIMISING THE RISK OF INSOLVENCY BY PRICING RISK APPROPRIATELY

Banks lend money (their raw material) in the expectation of receiving regular P&I payments from borrowers according to a schedule laid down in a **loan agreement**. This is the contract between the borrower and the lending bank. However, it is expected that some borrowers will default on the terms of the agreement – either by being late in making interest payments or capital repayments, or failing to pay at all within a reasonable time. Of course, the bank does not know *ex ante* (in advance of making a loan) which particular borrower will default or it would not lend to them. If default is due to unwillingness to pay, the bank may use the courts to enforce repayment and therefore may not suffer a loss. But if it is due to inability to pay, the bank will suffer a loss.

Banks believe they can estimate from previous years' experience what proportion of their total borrowers of each type will default or, more precisely, the expected default rate on loans as a percentage of total lending of each type. It is this ability to estimate future losses statistically on a portfolio of loans based on historical experience that *should* enable banks to manage the risk that arises from lending. Also, their large portfolios of loans give banks a great advantage over individuals who might make only one loan and could therefore lose everything due to a single default as they cannot benefit from the law of large numbers. It is the portfolio effect of a large loan book which enables banks to calculate a relatively stable **loss ratio**. This loss ratio is known as **expected loss** and is a particularly important concept in banking. Unfortunately, in practice, in the period from 2000 onwards, banks did not seem to price loans correctly to take account of actual risks and therefore actual losses were much greater than expected losses. The historical loss models of banks were based on only a few prior years when defaults were low (the global economy was very strong) and the models assumed, wrongly, that this meant that defaults would continue to be low for a long time ahead. This period was known as the **Great Moderation** – a period of low volatility in markets and low loan losses in the banking world.

Banks price their loans in order to cover expected loss which, to a bank, is simply **a normal cost of doing business**. The bank will make an estimate of expected loss on a loan based on two things:

- **probability of default (PD)**, i.e. what is the percentage likelihood, based on historical data, that this particular type of borrower will get into financial difficulty in the economic conditions expected to pertain over the period of the loan.
- **loss given default (LGD)**, i.e. what percentage of the defaulted loan is the bank likely to be unable to recover from, for example the liquidation or bankruptcy of a corporate borrower or from reselling an individual borrower's home. The PD multiplied by the LGD gives the **expected loss** which is a measure of the risk of the loan.

The basis of these statistics is historical information on loans made by the bank to the particular type of borrower in the past. A borrower's profile is created in terms of historical factors which the bank has in the past found to correlate well with subsequent credit performance for this type of borrower. For example, has the person or the company paid interest when due and repaid loans on the due date? In the case of consumer lending, there are a number of agencies such as Experian or Equifax in the UK which will produce a **credit score** for any individual, which will then be the basis for the risk premium that the person will be charged by a lender (or if the score is too low, credit will be refused).

For each type of borrower the bank then sets an interest margin (above its cost of funds) for its lending rate, which includes this **expected loss**, i.e. the percentage of its assets of this type that it expects to lose in the year ahead, as a cost of doing business (a business expense). Thus its lending rate would be calculated as its average (or marginal) borrowing rate, which is the cost of its liabilities plus expected loss plus a margin to cover costs and profit. If **outcomes match expectations**, i.e. its expected loss equals its actual loss, then its profit will be the amount expected, defined as **normal profit**. Banks will often target a rate of return on their capital at the start of a year (based on their cost of capital) and then use a pricing formula based on historical experience that is expected to generate that return. For example, some banks target a return on equity capital of 12% which, is after all costs including expected loss.

## A CONSUMER CREDIT LOAN PRICING EXAMPLE

Major UK banks at the end of 2011 were offering unsecured credit on their credit cards at a typical rate of 19.9% per annum. The cost to a bank of raising funds through current account deposits in the UK at that time was between 0 and 0.5%. The **marginal cost** of one-year funds (i.e. the highest cost source) at that time was around 3.5%. Thus the interest rate spread for banks is at least 16.5%, perhaps more. The major UK banks need to generate a return after expected loss and costs of around 2% on assets (which gives the required 12% return on equity if the ratio of equity to debt on the balance sheet is 1:6). Thus, after deducting the required return on assets, banks have around 14.5% to cover expected losses and costs. If we took another 2% to be the administrative costs involved, that still leaves 12.5% for expected loss. Are losses likely to be as high as that or higher?[6]

Figure 7.1 indicates the level of losses on various asset classes in the UK over an extended period of time. On the basis of this chart, 13% to cover expected loss on unsecured credit card debt, as in the example above, may look about right at the present time and includes some safety margin to protect against defaults increasing. In fact credit losses had risen to about 10% by 2010.

What happens if losses are higher than expected, i.e. an **unexpected loss**? Many banks worldwide have experienced very large unexpected losses during the financial crisis and in this situation the role of equity capital is critical. Capital, which means shareholders' funds, is the ultimate protection for **creditors** of a

---

[6] It is worth noting at this point that Greece, at the time of writing, would have to pay a lot more than this credit card rate to raise money. In fact it was unable to raise money at all from private sector lenders.

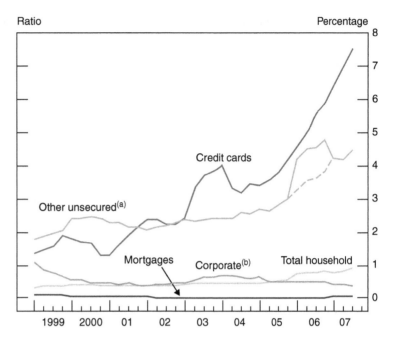

**Figure 7.1**  Credit losses on various asset classes

*Note*: Calculated quarterly as write-offs over previous year divided by average stock of lending.
(a) Dashed line shows the rate excluding a one-off write-off of £0.7 billion in 2005 Q4, which distorted the series.
(b) Data exclude Nationwide.

*Sources*: Bank of England (FSR October 2007, p. 36).
http://www.bankofengland.co.uk/publications/fsr/2007/fsrfull0710.pdf (accessed, 2 February 2012), FSA regulatory returns and Bank calculations.

bank, i.e. depositors and bondholders. Protection means that any losses fall first on shareholders.

Expected losses are met out of **revenue**. Unexpected losses are taken by **shareholder funds**. Understanding these two sentences is key to understanding much of banking.

The second sentence above means that if losses beyond expectation are no greater than the amount of the shareholders' funds (capital) then the other providers of financial capital (depositors and other creditors) will not lose money. Thus **the more equity capital a bank has the more protection other capital providers have**. This is because if a bank makes a loss, the first to lose are the shareholders. Their equity or **shareholder funds** take the **first loss**. But if the loss is greater than shareholder funds, i.e. the shareholders are wiped out, then each of the other classes of security holder suffers in their turn. First the preferred shareholders, then the subordinated debt holders, then the mezzanine debt holders, then the senior debt holders and finally, or in some jurisdictions at the same time, the depositors start to incur losses or may even be wiped out. Well before this, however (i.e. well before a bank has lost all its capital), it would have been put through a **restructuring and resolution process**, i.e. the regulator would arrange either that it is acquired by a stronger institution, or it raises more capital, or it is nationalised or it is wound up (liquidated). This is covered in Chapter 16 .

If a bank has fewer **write-off** charges (reductions in value to reflect expected loss) and write-offs than expected, then it will generate a higher return than targeted and is likely then to be earning what is defined as **supernormal profit**:

> US credit card losses are falling faster than expected, positioning the six largest card issuers to earn nearly $10bn more than had been predicted only months ago, a new Moody's study says. Historically US credit card write-offs have tracked the unemployment rate. The divergence from past experience reflects bank efforts to weed out risky borrowers, moves by consumers to pare back debts after the excesses of the past decade and new rules intended to discourage reckless lending. 'We are getting back to an old-fashioned basis of lending – that is providing credit only to people who have the ability to repay'.
>
> *Financial Times*, 27 August 2010

## PRICING INVESTMENT GRADE LOANS TO CORPORATES AND LEVERAGED LOANS

Whereas in the fixed income markets loans are priced on the basis of a spread above the treasury yield for a government bond of comparable maturity in the same currency, in the loan market they are generally priced above an interbank rate, i.e. a rate at which banks borrow and lend to each other, or above the central bank rate. In the UK and for international loans, the most usual reference rate is the London Inter Bank Offer Rate (LIBOR) in the appropriate currency, for example dollars or sterling, for the appropriate maturity. LIBOR is often said to be the AA rate, i.e. the rate at which companies rated AA by the rating agencies would be able to borrow, in this case AA-rated banks.

Interbank rates are generally priced as loans for 1, 3, 6 or 12 months. They are thus relatively short-period rates. Banks, of course, lend for much longer periods. In order to overcome this mismatch, most bank lending is provided on the basis of what is known as a **floating rate**, i.e. the rate of interest changes every 1, 3, 6 or 12 months to match the changing underlying bank borrowing rate. Thus although the bank may be lending for a much longer period (it has a long-term commitment), it may not be taking an **interest rate risk**, i.e. the risk that the rate at which it lends is below that at which it borrows. Thus bank lending is not true long-term lending of the type which is provided by a fixed income security issue (up to 30 years at a fixed rate). However, bank borrowers can convert their floating rate loan to a fixed-rate loan for longer periods through the use of the **interest rate swap** market. This is a market in which an obligation to pay a short-term variable interest rate is exchanged with those who want to pay a long-term fixed rate. The interest rate swap market is the largest of all derivative markets.

**Investment grade loans** are loans made to high-grade corporations which have a relatively high credit rating. This high rating is likely to arise partly from the fact that they have relatively little debt in their capital structure. These loans are held mainly by banks since only they (and not investors such as hedge funds) have a sufficiently low cost of funds (the deposit rate) to make such high quality (low return) lending profitable. Banks, after all, have to borrow at the AA interbank rate (the average bank is AA-rated) and therefore when lending have to charge a rate higher than this. AAA corporations, for example, would not be willing to pay the AA rate or worse for such borrowing, since they could go directly to the capital market (without using a financial intermediary) and borrow at a rate which better reflected their own credit rating. **One of the reasons for the dis-intermediation of banks by capital markets is that bank credit ratings have been falling relative to corporates.** Thus banks are likely to lend to AA borrowers (at best) but mostly to lower rated ones.

Even for banks, such high-grade loans may not be profitable purely from the spread income (bank borrowing rate minus lending rate and other costs) that can be earned since from around 2007, banks have had to pay more to raise funds in the bond market than corporates. Thus, for the corporates which can access bond markets it would generally be preferable for a bank to arrange a bond issue for them rather than offering a loan.

If they do choose to offer a loan, they may charge an arrangement fee to help make the loan more profitable. Generally, however, banks have increasingly had to accept that such lending is only likely to be viable as part of a client relationship. Banks now look at the overall profitability of their relationship with an issuer, including non-credit income such as cash management services, capital market services (IPOs and bond issues), merger and acquisition advice, etc. Thus banks which can offer a full range of services to customers (universal banks or investment banks with lending capabilities) are more likely to be successful in such lending than pure commercial banks which don't have capital market activities. Such cross-subsidisation does, however, raise competition issues. It is also very relevant in the debate amongst regulators as to whether universal banks should be split into two quite separate companies in the form of an investment bank and an independent commercial bank, as was the case in the US under the Glass Steagall Act until 1999. In fact, in the UK it seems likely that this will happen, based on the so-called Vickers Report, which is considered in the final chapter.

**Leveraged loans**, which means loans to companies with a relatively low credit rating generally as a result of a high debt to equity ratio, might be offered at LIBOR + 150 basis points or above. In addition, as structuring such loans is complex, there will also be an arranger[7] fee paid to the arranging bank(s) which may be up to 2.5%. Investing in such loans can be attractive, not only to other banks but also to institutional investors such as hedge funds. Banks have increasingly had to resort to such higher-risk lending, as lending to the best credits has migrated to the capital markets. Such disintermediation is increasingly happening in Continental Europe where, until the banking and sovereign debt crises, bank lending was seen as the natural way to raise debt finance.

## SYNDICATION

Most large bank loans are syndicated. A syndicated loan is one in which the funds supplied to the borrower come from a group of lenders rather than simply one bank. The syndicated market grew rapidly in the 1980s as a way of financing

---

[7] While we talk about origination in the capital markets, in lending markets banks have traditionally used the term 'arranging'.

early large leveraged buy outs (LBOs), such as the record $13 billion raised by **Kohlberg Kravis Roberts** for their 1989 LBO of RJR Nabisco. Such a loan would have been far too large for one bank to risk its capital on or even to be able to pool that volume of funds. Thus to spread the risk and to pool from a wider geographical area there was a need to syndicate it to a large group of US and international banks.

## THE PRICE, QUANTITY AND ALLOCATION OF, CREDIT

In Chapter 1 we reviewed the role of the price mechanism in allocating resources. In the bank credit market, it might be assumed that it is the price of credit, the interest rate, that results in credit being allocated to its most productive use. However, the mechanism of credit allocation is not as simple as that.

In the study of economics we consider that there can never be a shortage or a surplus of anything which is priced in free market. Price will always rise to equate supply and demand. Thus if there is a shortage of some item, the economist would say that this is because the price is wrong. However, if we look at the issue of tickets for a concert for a very popular band or the men's final at Wimbledon or for the 100m sprint final of the London Olympics, there is only a limited number of such tickets available. The fact that there is difficulty getting hold of one is a result of non-market allocation. The price is not continually raised in order to reduce demand until it matches the fixed supply.. Instead, the majority of tickets for Wimbledon are allocated through the Public Ballot with applications for the 2012 Ballot beginning on 1 August 2011. The Club could, of course, simply charge what the market can bear, i.e. rationing by price rather than by a ballot but chooses not to.

In the case of bank credit, banks are essentially allocating credit to three different types of activity: lending for activities which have the potential to increase the GDP of an economy, such as for investment in a factory extension; credit to enable the transfer between people of a high value asset such as a house (mortgage); or credit intended to be used for consumption goods and services, such as that provided by credit cards. There is some evidence that banks in the UK, and perhaps other countries, favour asset based lending (lending where there is underlying collateral) simply because it is easier and believed to be safer. If this is so then real estate lending in particular will be attractive. This may lead to less credit being allocated to firms which have the capability to expand a country's GDP (but little collateral to offer) and instead cause proportionately more credit to be allocated to existing real and financial assets and in consequence to lead to asset price inflation (a bubble).

# BANK LIQUIDITY MANAGEMENT

## THE PROBLEM OF BANK RUNS

The City of Glasgow Bank collapsed in 1878, and Northern Rock would have collapsed by 2008 without government intervention. In both cases, when too many depositors came to the bank and demanded the return of their deposits, as fractional reserve banks they were unable to meet the full amount of their customer demand. It is the fractional reserve nature of banking, i.e. the small proportion of liquid assets relative to total assets, that is the principal cause of the fragility of the banking system and which consequently makes it subject to crises. Another way of putting this is that it is the highly leveraged nature of banks which makes them risky.

A bank 'run', i.e. a demand for the return of deposits by a higher proportion of depositors than the liquid assets available to the bank, can be set off by a fear that the bank is heading towards insolvency. This was the case with the City of Glasgow Bank. In the case of Northern Rock it was said to be the revelation that wholesale lenders were not rolling over their loans, which made even insured retail depositors nervous. This nervousness was exacerbated by reports on television suggesting a possible crisis at the bank. The nervousness led to a liquidity crisis. However, after the event it would appear to have been the case that the bank was, indeed, heading towards insolvency. A genuine liquidity crisis can also easily set off a solvency crisis because if a bank ceases to operate as a going concern. The reason is that the market value of its assets in a liquidation sale may easily fall below their value on the balance sheet and this may be below the value of its liabilities. At that point a bank becomes a so-called gone concern.

There are three mechanisms that can be used to try to reduce the likelihood of bank runs:

• The first mechanism is for a country to have **effective bank regulation and supervision** to try to ensure that the directors manage the bank in a prudent way.
• The second is to reassure depositors that their funds are not at risk, even if the bank collapses. This can be achieved through a deposit insurance system, organised either by the industry or by the regulator. Thus in the event of a bank going into liquidation, depositors would be **made whole**, i.e. repaid 100%

on their deposits (or up to a pre-announced limit). Having this reassurance makes depositors less likely to initiate a run on deposits. While such insurance applies to retail depositors it generally will not apply to wholesale deposits by companies.

- The third method of trying to reassure depositors is for it to be known that the government has a **too big to fail** policy under which it would rescue a bank which was in difficulty. As well as in many Western countries, this would apply in a country such as China which does not have deposit insurance but where it is 'assumed' by everyone that the government would not let a large bank collapse.

The protection of a particular bank's depositors is the ostensible reason for regulators providing or requiring deposit insurance. But even more important is the fact that if a single bank has a run on its deposits and has to shut, depositors in all banks in that country may panic and rush to take their deposits out, regardless of how safe the authorities might say other banks are. To put it another way, an **idiosyncratic**[1] problem at one bank very quickly becomes a **systemic** problem, i.e. a problem for all banks, even if all other banks are actually safe. Thus deposit insurance helps to ensure **financial stability**. It should be noted, however, that Northern Rock still suffered a bank run, despite the UK having deposit insurance. Unfortunately deposit insurance introduces the problem of **moral hazard**.[2] What this means is that if depositors have no chance of loss from depositing in a bank which is unsafe, then they are likely to choose to deposit with the bank which offers the highest deposit rates regardless of risk. An example of this was UK savers making deposits with Icesave, an Icelandic bank which set up an internet based deposit collection facility in the UK and offered above average rates. Shortly after, however, the parent company bank became insolvent. Unfortunately the banking system of Iceland was too large relative to a country of only 300,000 people for the Icelandic government to save the banks. On the other side of the equation, a bank which is paying more for deposits has to lend to riskier borrowers in order to make an adequate spread. This is a bet that riskier lending will provide the expected risk-adjusted return. If it does not, as was the case with Icesave, the insurance fund and borrowers in general (banks contribute towards the fund) and the taxpayer or overseas taxpayers in the case of Iceland, have to pay the price of this type of behaviour.

## BANK LIQUIDITY MANAGEMENT TO MINIMISE THE LIKELIHOOD OF A BANK RUN

To understand liquidity management let's start with a type of bank that does not exist in Europe but is common in the United States – the **unit bank**, i.e. one that

---

[1] An idiosyncratic problem is one which is unique to a particular company with no reason to believe that the same problem is relevant to any other.

[2] **Moral hazard** arises when an individual or institution such as bank does not take full responsibility for the consequences of its actions, and may in consequence act less carefully than it otherwise would. As a result, another party, such as a country's taxpayers, may be forced to suffer some of the costs of its decisions.

has no branches, just one office. Such banks are highly subject to the risk that, on any particular day, depositors take out more cash than they pay in. Such variations in cash flows are to be expected in a unit bank. To minimise liquidity risk, such a bank would look at the historical pattern of cash inflows versus cash outflows to estimate the likely peak **mismatch** of these flows. It would then hold sufficient liquid assets, such as deposits at the central bank, government bills and government bonds, relative to illiquid loans to enable it to generate liquidity by selling these if cash outflows were likely to exceed cash inflows. It would then repurchase them when inflows and outflows came into balance. It might also have access to the surplus funds of other banks when they had excess deposits over withdrawals on a particular day. Such funds would be accessed through the interbank market which, in the United States, is known as the **Federal Funds Market**.

In practice, most banks are not unit banks but multibranch banks. They rely on the **law of large numbers** for the major part of their liquidity. This 'law' which we covered earlier is central to much of finance and will reappear in many guises in other parts of this book. The 'law' in this case means that on average a multibranch bank is likely to receive around the same amount of money being deposited as withdrawn on any particular day because it has thousands or millions of depositors. It is only when the numbers are not large enough (as in a unit bank for example) that a need for substantial external liquidity may arise in normal times.

It is important to note, however, that cash inflows and outflows do not arise just from customers depositing or borrowing money. They also arise from the need to repay wholesale money market loans that the bank may have used to finance its loan book, and these may be very short maturity loans which require continual refinancing in the money markets (rolling over). If wholesale lenders do not refinance the bank by renewing the loans they have made, the bank suffers a 'run' very similar to that which occurs if depositors all try to redeem their deposits at one time. Investors in bank-issued **securities** have none of the 'security' that insured **depositors** have and thus provide much less **sticky** funds. As a result, they are in fact much more likely to run than traditional depositors. Thus while deposit insurance was brought in by governments to prevent bank runs, in practice banks have had to move away from financing their asset holdings mainly from such sticky, insured funds and increasingly use funds from securities markets which are **much more likely to run** – making deposit insurance of much less value in stopping runs. This has been due to the much greater increase in demand for credit than in the supply of deposits. This is one of the fundamental problems that has arisen from changes in the structure of bank balance sheets worldwide and that led to the liquidity crisis and subsequent solvency crisis in the Western banking system.

One reason for the shortage of deposit funds relative to borrower demand is that depositors have become less willing to provide 'free' or low cost deposits to banks when other financial intermediaries are offering seemingly more attractive, liquid assets. This **dis-intermediation of the banking system**, an important aspect of which has been the increasing attraction to households of **money market mutual fund accounts** compared to bank deposits, has been a particular feature of the US. But a second reason is that UK and US households, in particular, cut their savings rate to almost zero in the years prior to 2007 but at the same time increased their demand for credit for house purchase (mortgages) and other types of loan. Thus banks, faced with excess demand by borrowers, raised funds from abroad (indirectly from high saving households in other countries). Generally this is only possible through cross-border interbank lending and on global capital markets. Thus banks were obtaining liquidity from markets, i.e. **funding liquidity** (liability side of the balance sheet), whereas traditionally they had always obtained it by selling assets to generate **market liquidity** (asset side of the balance sheet). It was a loss of funding liquidity that caused many banks to fail in recent years, rather than just a shortage of market liquidity.

Banks need to search for liquidity all the time to fund their existing balance sheet as deposits and other liabilities **run off** (mature) and as their asset books grow. They may also need to increase their liquidity either because their customers want to increase *their* liquidity or because they themselves may want more liquidity if their own **liquidity preference** increases, i.e. the extent of their desire to be liquid increases despite the loss of income that may result from reduced lending. This may be because they believe that it will be hard to find adequate funds in the future or because they believe demand by customers for cash will increase in the future.

## HOW BANKS MAINTAIN THEIR LIQUIDITY AND REGULATORY CAPITAL RATIOS: BALANCE SHEET LIQUIDITY MANAGEMENT

Banks can increase their own liquidity by acting on either the asset or the liability side of their balance sheet, i.e. obtaining market liquidity (asset side of the balance sheet) or obtaining funding liquidity (liability side of the balance sheet). These changes in liquidity also give scope for changing the bank's regulatory capital (equity) ratios.

### Asset side of the balance sheet

#### Self-liquidating assets (loan assets convert to cash)

A **fundamental** type of liquidity arises when loans are repaid or partial repayments are made. Cash flows in from loans on their **maturity date** or at intermediate partial repayments dates. However, this liquidity is available only to a **hold-to-maturity** investor who buys an asset when it is issued and holds it until redemption. Traditionally banks were such investors. **Thus in this definition of liquidity, clearly the longer the maturity of the asset, the less liquid it is**.

Most loans have an **amortisation** schedule, i.e. dates on which intermediate and final loan repayments must be made. From this schedule, a bank can work out the cash inflow (P&I) that will arise each day from its total portfolio of loans. Banks aim to ensure that they have a portfolio of loan assets in which a steady proportion is **self-liquidating** each day. It is estimated that for many banks around 20% of their loan assets self-liquidate each year.

#### Reducing the acquisition of new loan assets

If, when existing loan assets **run off** (are repaid), the bank keeps the cash that results rather than lending it out again by making new loans, then the bank is becoming more liquid. Its balance sheet may be the same size but it has more cash instead of loans on the asset side. Alternatively it may use the cash which is generated to pay off some of its liabilities, thus reducing total balance sheet size and directly improving its capital ratio.[3] Thus if regulators require banks to increase their capital ratios to give greater protection to depositors and taxpayers, this can be achieved either by increasing the numerator (more equity) or by reducing the denominator (fewer loan assets). If the latter, while the *bank* would become more liquid, this may result in the *economy* becoming less liquid as a result of the bank not providing credit that may be needed by the corporate and household sectors. If this happens, economic activity may decline (a decline in GNP) and unemployment may rise.

In times when banks think bank equity is too expensive a source of funds (when bank shares are trading at very low book/market ratios), it may lead to them being forced to accept new equity injections from governments in order to enable them to maintain their lending and minimise the risk of a recession.

## Selling assets for cash: market liquidity

### Sale of assets held as liquid reserves

We have already noted above that a bank will hold liquid assets such as deposits at the central bank. Central bank deposits are money (cash). However, such deposits earn little, if any, interest. Therefore banks keep most of their liquid reserves in the form of short-term government securities which can be sold easily in the market for cash and should have little market risk. Banks may also have other assets which trade in a market and can be sold.

### Sale of loan assets

Loans to customers can be sold as assets to other banks, asset managers, hedge funds, etc. which pay for them in cash. Selling loans allows the recovery of funds which have been lent. These funds can then be used to increase the liquidity of the bank or to meet other loan commitments. **Whole loan sales** can be made where one investor is willing to buy the whole of a loan rather than just a part. Of course, when markets are stressed, loan sales may become impossible as all banks may be trying to sell. Thus in a systemic crisis when all banks are trying to sell loan assets, prices will plunge.

### Securitisation

Sales of assets, such as mortgages, credit card debt and auto loans, can be achieved by securitisation, i.e. made into a form in which they are more easily saleable because they can be traded in a market. They become more liquid and can then be sold to other balance sheet investors, such as other banks, pension funds or insurance companies. Unfortunately during times of stress, such as during the financial crisis from 2007 onwards, the securitisation market collapses thus closing this route to obtaining liquidity.

---

[3] Capital ratios can be calculated as equity relative to liabilities, or relative to total assets, or relative to 'risk weighted assets'. This latter measure is normally used by regulators. Thus even just allowing loans to turn into cash (risk weighted assets fall even though total assets and total liabilities remain unchanged) will improve a bank's regulatory capital ratio.

When assets are sold, all that happens is that one type of asset held on the balance sheet (perhaps government bonds) changes into cash. In turn, that cash could be used to make new loans, or in times of liquidity problems it can be kept on the balance sheet to make the bank more liquid. Alternatively, it may be used to pay down liabilities in which case **the balance sheet falls in size on both sides as both assets and liabilities are reduced**.

## Liability side of the balance sheet

### Funding liquidity

The alternative to selling assets to generate cash is to issue liabilities. This increases balance sheet size – both liabilities (debt issue) and assets (cash).

### Unsecured borrowing

Unsecured fund raising by a bank means that the lender is not given any asset to hold as security (**collateral**) in the event that the loan is not repaid.

**Equity is the ideal type of unsecured funding**. As it is unsecured it does not **encumber** any of the bank's assets, i.e. the bank does not have to hand over control of any assets by providing collateral to lenders. There is also no need for it to pay a dividend (if the bank is in financial difficulty) and it is only redeemed in the event that the bank itself is **liquidated** (closed down), in which case it might have little value. Unfortunately this ideal type of funding is believed by bank directors to be expensive. Much of this belief results from the fact that dividend payments do not attract tax relief, as we noted earlier, while interest payments do. In addition to subsidising debt issues from such tax relief, governments *also* subsidise bank debt through the implicit 'too large to fail' guarantee that they give to bank debt. This reduces the cost of bank debt substantially but not the cost of equity. When the UK announced that it intended to ring-fence UK retail banks from their wholesale and investment banking arms, the rating agencies reduced their ratings on UK banks. This was done because the implicit government guarantee through the 'too large to fail doctrine' would apply only to the UK retail bank subsidiary in a ring-fenced structure and not to all the liabilities of the bank holding company which would include the wholesale and investment banking arms.

Figure 8.1(a) shows how much lower the ratings of bank debt would be if banks did not have 'implicit' support from governments in the form of the too large to fail doctrine. For example, if Irish senior bank debt was not protected by the Irish state, meaning that the Irish government would not rescue failing Irish banks, then Irish bank debt would be rated Ba2. This is well below investment grade. Instead it is rated A2 on the scale used above, which is well above the border between investment and non-investment grade. As a result, banks can fund much more cheaply in debt markets *relative* to equity markets due to this subsidy. What this means is that the cost of debt for a bank does not rise nearly as much as it logically should as it becomes more highly leveraged (the assumption behind the Modigliani and Miller model) as a result of investors making the assumption that this high leverage does not make the debt much more risky. This is a clear example of moral hazard. The state takes on the additional risk rather than the investors in bank debt taking it. For the UK Figure 8.1(b) shows the implicit subsidy estimated by the Bank of England to be over £100 billion in 2009, a saving of around 2.5% on funding cost.

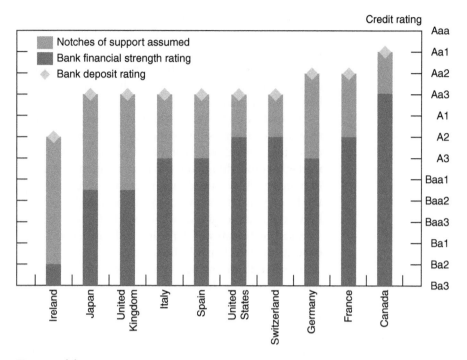

**Figure 8.1(a)**   Implicit subsidy to bank debt financing cost from government support

*Sources*: Bank of England (FSR June 2010, Slide 25 Chart 3.21), http://www.bankofengland.co.uk/publications/fsr/2010/FSR10Jun3.ppt#302,25, Slide 25 (accessed, 2 February 2012), Moody's.

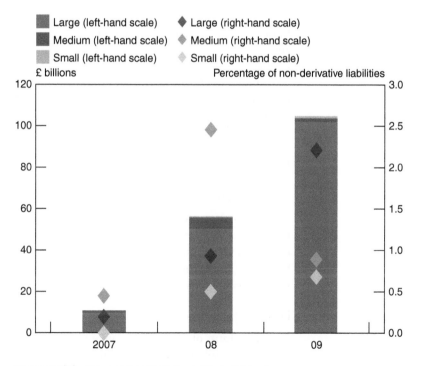

**Figure 8.1(b)**   Value of this implicit subsidy to UK banks

*Source*: Bank of England (FSR December2010, Chart 5.9 (p. 51)), http://www.bankofengland.co.uk/publications/fsr/2010/fsrfull1012.pdf (accessed, 2 February 2012), Bank of America Merrill Lynch, Bankscope published by Bureau van Dijk Electronic Publishing, Moody's and Bank calculations.

**Fixed income bonds.** Other types of unsecured funding include senior and junior fixed income securities. The cost of debt funding is a function of how risky the bank is overall compared to other companies in the capital market and also on the seniority of the debt, i.e. the extent of its subordination (as well as the implicit government guarantee). Preference shares can also be issued which are a hybrid between debt and equity.

**Deposits** from the public are an important type of unsecured funding. A bank may be able to increase its funding by, for example, raising interest rates offered to depositors above those of competitors. A bank may also use the internet and heavy marketing expenditure to try to raise additional deposits beyond those raised in its branches. As we noted earlier, Icesave, which had no branches in the UK, did this by offering rates above competitors in the UK market and marketing its offer heavily. This attracted a large volume of additional deposits. Banks can also issue so-called **certificates of deposit** which are generally for larger and longer-term deposits and which may be tradable.

**Interbank borrowing** is another example of what has, traditionally, been unsecured funding. The London Interbank Market is where sterling funds are lent between banks at LIBOR. Unfortunately, this market can dry up (become illiquid) in times of market stress because it is unsecured and therefore puts lenders at risk. During the early stages of the credit crunch before banks were rescued by governments, banks refused to transfer their liquidity to other banks. If they were already lenders in the market, then, when loans expired, they refused to renew them, i.e. to roll-over short term lending. They thus kept the cash that the other bank had repaid. The only means by which money could be transferred between banks was through the central bank acting as a financial intermediary, accepting deposits from one bank and lending to another. Today, some interbank lending is secured and to the extent that this practice becomes more common, the freezing of the interbank market might not happen so quickly in future crises.

**Commercial paper** is a form of short-term security (less than one year maturity) which can be issued by banks. Buyers of such assets include **money market mutual funds (MMMFs)**, which I will cover later. If these funds are concerned about the safety of a bank they are unlikely to renew their purchases of such paper. This has been a problem for eurozone banks trying to fund themselves in 2011 as US MMMFs ceased buying such securities.

## Secured borrowing

A creditworthy entity (borrower) can **pledge** assets to a lender, i.e. the lender can take control of the assets if the borrower defaults and thus raise funds against their **collateral value**, such as in the case of mortgage lending. In the case of a bank borrowing in the money and capital markets, the mechanism that is frequently used is the repurchase agreement.

## Repurchase Agreement

A specific form of secured borrowing is the **sale and repurchase agreement** market, generally known as the **repo** market. A **repurchase agreement** allows a borrower to use securities as collateral for a loan. The borrower agrees to sell securities to a lender but at the same time contracts to buy them back (repurchase them) on an agreed future date at an agreed, higher, price (which reflects an implicit interest rate). In effect it is the equivalent of a cash transaction combined with a forward contract which transfers cash to the borrower while the lender receives the security of the collateral. The difference between the selling price and the repurchase price creates an implicit interest rate. Figure 8.2 shows a simplified repo transaction using government securities as collateral.

Repo transactions almost always involve a **haircut**, i.e. a reduction in the collateral value from market value in order to protect the lender from a possible decline in market value during the period of the repo. What this means is that a lender might provide only 90% of the value of an asset of which it takes control, as security for the loan. The other 10% of its value has to be financed by the bank from its own resources, i.e. its own equity. This is very similar to the position of a household wishing to take out a mortgage on a house. The bank might lend 90% of the value of the house but the household has to provide the other 10% from its own resources (own equity). In the case of repo, if the collateral value falls below the initial haircut value, the borrower will be asked for additional collateral or to repay part of the loan. In the case of a mortgage, lenders do not require additional collateral if the value of the home falls below the amount borrowed. Instead the borrower moves into a position of **negative** equity in which he or she owes more to the lender than the value of the home. When this happens the lender may be at risk of loss depending on the legal framework of the country in which the asset is located.

Repo transactions are frequently as short as overnight (or at most for a few days at a time) but they are generally rolled over each morning on a continuous basis in the amount required. If a lender will not rollover the following morning the borrower may be forced into default.

Table 8.1 shows that even secured lending is a very unreliable source of funding during a financial crisis. It illustrates the huge increase in 'own equity' demanded by lenders, i.e. the haircut, that a bank had to provide to borrow against various types of collateral between April 2007 (just before the crisis) to August 2008 (during the crisis). Banks simply did not have sufficient spare cash of their own to

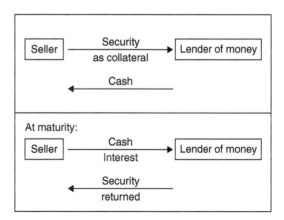

**Figure 8.2**   Repo transaction

**Table 8.1**   Change in repo market haircuts from 2007 to 2008 (%)

| Asset | April 2007 | August 2008 |
|---|---|---|
| US Treasury bonds | 0.25 | 3 |
| Investment-grade corporate bonds | 0–3 | 8–12 |
| High-yield corporate bonds | 10–15 | 25–40 |
| Equities | 15 | 20 |
| Investment-grade credit default swaps | 1 | 5 |
| Senior leveraged loans | 10–12 | 15–20 |
| Mezzanine leveraged loans | 18–25 | 35+ |
| Collateralized loan obligations (AAArated) | 4 | 10–20 |
| Prime mortgage-backed securities | 2–4 | 10–20 |
| Consumer asset-backed securities (ABS) | 3–5 | 50–60 |
| ABS collateralized debt obligations (AAArated) | 2–4 | n.a. |
| ABS collateralized debt obligations (AArated) | 4–7 | n.a. |
| ABS collateralized debt obligations (Arated) | 8–15 | n.a. |
| ABS collateralized debt obligations (BBBrated) | 10–20 | n.a. |
| ABS collateralized debt obligations (equity) | 50 | n.a. |

*Note*: n.a. means the particular class of collateral is not acceptable to lenders.

*Source*: Bank of England. Financial Stability Report October 2008 (p. 36), table 5.B; datasource: IMF. http://www.bankofengland.co.uk/publications/fsr/2008/fsrfull0810.pdf (accessed, 2 February 2012).

finance their portfolio of assets using repo when haircuts were so sharply increased and were thus forced to try to sell assets. Ultimately central banks had to step in and provide repo finance at lower haircuts and against collateral which officially they should not have accepted, as it was of low quality (high risk).

The financing of dealer inventory holdings in a trading department was the original use of repo. It is particularly suitable for such financing the requirement for which varies sharply in amount day-by-day. But in the build-up to the financial crisis it was also used to finance longer-term holdings of assets, such as positions held on the **proprietary trading book**, These positions were held, not to enable the servicing of client needs i.e. flow trading, but as **principal positions** financed by the bank's own funds (and borrowed funds) and held purely with a view to profit for the bank. Borrowing on repo works well except during times of financial crisis. In such times, if the securities pledged as collateral against the loan are becoming more risky, the lender may require an ever larger haircut. This means that the bank has to provide a higher and higher proportion of the value of the securities from its own resources, which means it could suddenly be short of cash. On the other hand, the great advantage of repo financing is that, because it is very short term, it is relatively inexpensive if the **yield curve** is upward sloping, i.e. when the rate of interest paid is lower, the shorter the period of the loan. When we cover securitisation in the next chapter we will see that one reason for the banks suffering such large losses was that they were holding large volumes of high risk securitised assets on their balance sheets, financed by overnight repo for which, suddenly, they were unable to obtain funding. Initially such holdings had provided a very profitable interest rate arbitrage which involved borrowing at a low rate of interest (short-term) and investing (long-term) at a high expected return but taking on substantial liquidity risk.

## Covered bonds

A covered bond is one where there is specific security (collateral) for a loan but in addition, in the event that the collateral turns out to have a value below that of the loan, the investor also has recourse to the general assets of the company, in liquidation, for any balance still owing. It is thus a kind of 'belt and braces' type of protection. However, if all lenders demand security, a bank would not have sufficient **unencumbered** assets to provide this protection, i.e. assets not already pledged as specific collateral. In addition, beyond a certain percentage of encumbered assets on the balance sheet, the safety of unsecured creditors falls sharply and thus unsecured credit would cease to be available or only at a price so high as to make it unattractive.

## Lender of last resort: the central bank as provider of liquidity insurance

If liquidity is important for banks, then why do they not simply hold sufficient liquid assets to ensure that they can meet customer demand at all times? The answer is simply that there is an **opportunity cost** of so doing, i.e. resources invested in central bank deposits or short-term government securities will not earn nearly as much as loans. Banks thus have an incentive to economise on liquidity and to assume that 'the worst' will not happen. They tend to assume that there will be no **black swan** events that will result in their being unable to provide the cash their customers demand, as detailed in a stand-by liquidity agreement such as an overdraft.

There will, however, be times when **particular banks** (not the banking system as a whole) will be short of liquidity and, due perhaps to market perceptions, cannot obtain liquidity from any of the sources listed above. In addition, there may also be times when commercial banks are, **in aggregate**, short of liquidity, i.e. there is a systemic liquidity shortage as happened during the financial crisis. Because banks perform such an important role in the economy – money transmission and the financing of investment and trade – governments in all countries, as we noted earlier, regulate and supervise them more closely than any other type of financial enterprise to minimise the likelihood of collapse due to liquidity or solvency problems. Indeed, there is no other sector of the economy in which governments regulate the capital structure of companies in such a way – and that includes nuclear power.

There is usually a minimum required **liquidity ratio** of some type to give the bank a liquidity cushion in the event of a liquidity squeeze. In the UK in the 1960s this ratio was around 30%. However, new rules in 1971 reduced this to 12.5%. In 1981 the Bank of England replaced its reserve ratio regime with a cash ratio deposit regime. However, this did not directly require a minimum level of liquid assets. The regime introduced in 1996 focussed on holding sufficient liquidity to meet a particularly severe cash-flow funding stress. This was designed to ensure that they had enough highly liquid assets to meet their outflows for the first week of a liquidity crisis without recourse to the market for renewed wholesale funding. This was to give the authorities time to explore options for an orderly resolution. Today, the Basel Committee is formulating new and more onerous liquidity ratio rules which will be implemented in Basel III (see Chapter 24) and which are designed to reduce liquidity risk.

Figure 8.3 shows clearly how liquidity ratios have declined over the decades in the UK. This decline is comparable to that in most other countries. The financial crisis demonstrated clearly that liquidity buffers had been run down too far.

During the financial crisis, those UK banks which had liquidity available to them in the form of deposits at the Bank of England were unwilling to lend those deposits in the interbank (unsecured) market to other banks. As a result balances of those banks at the Bank of England rose dramatically (see Figure 8.4). One of the roles of the central bank during a period of crisis, therefore, is to act as a financial intermediary in the interbank market by being willing to lend the resources deposited with it by one commercial bank which has surplus funds to another which has a shortage of funds. The Bank of England was therefore acting in a principal capacity as a financial intermediary (like a commercial bank) and taking on the credit risk (counterparty risk) of lending to commercial banks. It did take collateral in return but, given that other commercial banks would not accept this same collateral except at unacceptably high haircut ratios, the Bank of England was clearly accepting a degree of credit risk.

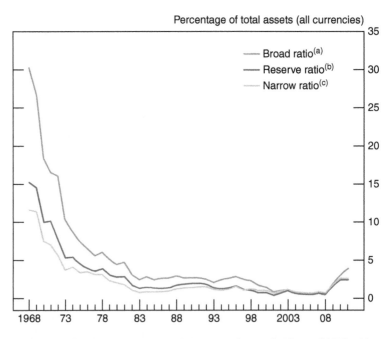

**Figure 8.3**  Sterling liquid assets relative to total asset holdings of UK banking sector

(a) Cash + Bank of England balances + money at call + eligible bills + UK gilts.
(b) Proxied by: Bank of England balances + money at call + eligible bills.
(c) Cash + Bank of England balances + eligible bills.

*Source*: Bank of England (FSR June 2011, Chart 3.12, Slide 14). http://www.bankofengland.co.uk/publications/Documents/fsr/2011/FSR11jun3.ppt (accessed, 2 February 2012).

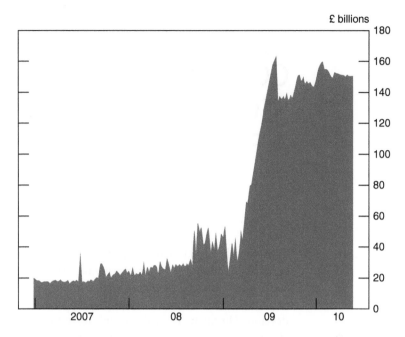

**Figure 8.4** Current account balances (reserves) held by commercial banks at the Bank of England

*Source*: Bank of England (FSR June 2010, Chart 1.5 (p. 15)). http://www.bankofengland.co.uk/publications/Documents/fsr/2010/fsr27sec1.pdf (accessed, 2 February 2012).

In the event that a bank does run out of liquidity, the central bank stands-by as **lender of last resort** willing and able to provide a loan **against the security of the bank's assets**, i.e. a collateralised loan. The central bank fills this role if private sector lenders and asset buyers are unwilling or unable to do so. This role of the central bank as provider of liquidity has been key in minimising the impact of the credit crisis. But central banks only have a mandate to provide liquidity if the bank is suffering a liquidity crisis, not a solvency crisis. But it may be difficult for the central bank to distinguish between insolvency and illiquidity, particularly at a time of crisis.

The problem with a central bank providing liquidity insurance (liquidity provider of last resort) is that banks may come to rely on this (cheap) insurance and therefore minimise their own holdings of low-yielding liquid assets. This makes them more likely to suffer from a liquidity crisis. The new regulations introduced during the crisis by, for example, the Bank of England have tried to reduce the extent of this **moral hazard** by making the price of such support much higher. Equally, banks try to avoid using finance from the central bank at a penalty rate since, if it becomes known in the market that a bank needs such finance, the 'stigma' the bank would incur might make it even more difficult to raise funds from private sources.

# 9 CONVERTING LOANS TO SECURITIES: SECURITISATION AS A FINANCING TOOL

Traditionally capital market financing (direct transaction between issuers and investors via a broker/dealer intermediary) is distinguished sharply from balance sheet intermediated financing (bank financing). But the distinction between loans and securities is not as sharp today as in the past as a result of techniques developed by financiers which enable loans to be converted into securities. In this chapter I examine how assets that a bank or other lender **originates** (i.e. loan arranging) can be converted into securities that are attractive to non-bank investors, such as pension funds, insurance companies, hedge funds and, importantly, non-domestic investors. This conversion process is one aspect of the disintermediation of the banking system which has been a critical development in the finance industry, particularly since the year 2000. Initially it brought considerable benefits to banks, investors and society but latterly it was fraudulently misused and became the central cause of the Western world's bank financial crisis.

## WHY DID BANKS CHOOSE TO SECURITISE?

Securitisation involves pooling various types of debt, such as residential mortgages, commercial mortgages, car loans and credit card debt obligations, and selling the resulting pooled debt as bonds or collateralised debt obligations (CDOs) to different classes of investor.

A key to understanding securitisation is to realise that the traditional model of banking that is taught in textbooks is one that, in developed economy markets, has changed qualitatively as well as quantitatively. As we have already noted, the traditional model of the commercial bank is that of organisations that borrow funds from depositors (accept deposits) and use these deposits to fund loans to companies and households. The loans which the bank originates are then held on its balance sheet until maturity when they are repaid, allowing the bank to re-lend the funds. This model of banking is known as the **originate to hold** model. If a bank operates this way and both originates mortgages (and other loans) **and** funds these from deposits only, **its lending and hence its balance sheet size is constrained by its ability to raise deposits**. Such a bank can expand beyond its deposit base in two ways, and indeed banks such as Northern Rock used both simultaneously.

First they can issue increasing volumes of securities (as distinct from deposits), some of which will be sold abroad, to finance their lending, given the absence of adequate deposits. If they do this their balance sheet will increase in size and, given the additional risky assets they are holding, they will require additional equity capital in order to meet regulatory ratios (Basel capital ratios). A bank such as Lloyds Bank in the UK had a loan to deposit ratio in 2011 of 148%, which logically must mean that a lot of their funding came from obtaining funding liquidity in the capital markets. HSBC on the other hand had a ratio of only 78% and therefore would have had much less need to access capital markets.

Second, they can take assets right off their own balance sheets (securitisation) rather than holding them and funding them by issuing securities on these balance sheets. This reduces total balance sheet size (or at least stops it growing in size) and thus minimises the need to find additional shareholder funds (equity) to meet regulatory ratios.

In an era of loan demand growth exceeding deposit growth banks used both techniques. First, they could turn to the capital markets and obtain funding liquidity by issuing debt securities. But if this was not sufficient to meet the ability of their mortgage lending department to originate new mortgages, then securitisation provided a *deus ex machina*[1] to the dilemma faced by bank chief executives who wanted to expand faster than other banks in the country (for example, Northern Rock in the UK). It allowed expansion beyond the constraints of:

- deposit gathering ability;
- capital market willingness to lend;
- the regulators' requirement for additional equity capital to back increases in assets.

Thus, provided originators of mortgages could find a means to profit from **securitisation fees** and ongoing mortgage **loan administration fees**, it could be a more profitable business model than just plain old-fashioned lending i.e. the 'spread' business of borrowing at one rate and lending on at a higher rate.

Bringing in a new set of investors – investment institutions – which enabled a net transfer of credit assets to these (non-bank) investors was the objective of securitisation. In theory this meant reducing the amount of risk held by *leveraged* financial institutions (banks) and increasing the amount held by *unleveraged* and hence less risky institutions (pension funds and other institutional investors). Such investment institutions don't have to hold capital against their investments because they are not leveraged. Thus, as well as reducing financial instability, selling risky assets to investment institutions can be financially attractive for both sides, as such institutions may be more competitive than banks for the purpose of HOLDING credit-risky assets. On the other hand retail banks are more competitive than institutional investors at ORIGINATING mortgages as they are in contact with thousands or millions of potential borrowers through

---

[1] A solution to a dilemma provided by a 'god on high' descending to provide a means of escape from the dilemma. On stage, in the form of a 'machine' descending from above the stage to, for example, rescue someone from the clutches of another.

their nationwide branch network. This could thus be seen as an example of gains from specialisation according to comparative advantage – a key principle in the theory of gains from trade.

**Originate to distribute** is the name given to the process we have just described by which a bank first arranges loans (originates) – mortgages or other loans – and then, after creating securities from the loans (securitisation), sells them to investors (distributes). In the new model, a bank originates new loans, not with the intention of holding on to them (**originate and hold**), but with the intention of selling them once they have **warehoused** a sufficient volume of them, i.e. pooled a sufficient amount. In some securitisations, they might warehouse up to £5 billion of loan assets prior to securitisation in order to have a sufficient size of issue to ensure good liquidity and to reduce the unit cost of the securitisation process (which is not insignificant). Banks were able to make very good returns on this business model from securitisation fees, from on-going mortgage or credit card servicing fees and because they were frequently able to sell the securitised assets for a higher price than the historic cost at the time of issue, i.e. they were able to make a capital gain.

## HOW DOES A SECURITY DIFFER FROM A LOAN ASSET?

One aspect of securitisation is that it involves the pooling of household and other **liabilities** in distinction to the previous type of pooling which we covered which was the pooling of household and corporate **assets** (cash). A key distinction between a securitised asset (an asset-backed security or ABS) and the underlying assets which back it is that the ABS should be relatively liquid and able to be traded in a market, whereas the assets backing it will not be liquid and will not trade. For an asset to be tradable, i.e. for it to be possible to buy or sell it easily in large size on a public market or a well-established private market, it has to have **predictable cash flow characteristics**. The government (sovereign) bonds of major countries such as the US trade well in the public market because they are issued in very large size, which means there will always be some investors wanting to buy and sell. In addition, each individual bond within such an issue has the same characteristics as all the others (homogeneity).

In contrast to most sovereign bonds, mortgage loans (or credit card loans) are relatively small and have **idiosyncratic cash flows**, i.e. each mortgage has a different principal amount, may have a different interest rate, a different start and end date, different interest payment dates, different level of credit risk, etc. No institutional investor would buy such small, idiosyncratic assets. Apart from the fact that it is inconvenient, the main reason is the **asymmetric information problem**. There is no way the institutional investor can know the true credit quality of individual loans as they have had no contact with borrowers. As a result, it is traditionally banks and similar credit institutions which arrange mortgages by meeting potential borrowers in the bank's office, checking the facts on their mortgage application and only then agreeing a loan (the mortgage **underwriting** process). After this they are happy to hold loans on their balance sheet since they have sophisticated software to enable them to '**service**' the debt, i.e. ensure that borrowers make their payments on the due date and that the information on payments is added to the borrower's record at the bank – something which institutional investors do not have. They also have a process to enable them to **foreclose**, i.e. repossess and resell properties, which are seized from a defaulting borrower.

An institutional investor does not have facilities to service mortgages, but will only purchase an asset which has **predictable cash flows**, meaning that he or she expects to receive regular coupon interest payments on the dates specified in a contract (the prospectus) and to receive redemption payments on the due dates. The institutional investor also requires independent and external verification of the quality of the asset, such as that (supposedly) provided by rating agencies. Also, for many institutional investors, high credit risk is not acceptable. However, by pooling a large number of relatively small and heterogeneous mortgages in a portfolio and financing the pool by issuing securitised assets where each bond issued is identical to all the others, known as **undivided interest**, the resulting securitised asset should have little **non-systematic risk**, i.e. individual borrower risk or regional risk (provided the mortgages are diversified by region, type of borrower, etc.). The level of **systematic** risk, i.e. risk of all mortgages in the loan pool suffering a decline in value due to a similar cause, can then be assessed by, for example, an 'independent' rating agency in order to give investors a measure of risk. It should be noted, however, that if the individual loans have not been carefully underwritten in the first instance, i.e. this process was not undertaken properly or it was undertaken fraudulently, then any assessment of the systematic risk will be faulty. Thus if, for example, most of the loans have been made to those who do not have the necessary income to service their mortgage, then the underwriting has not been effective.

Let's assume at this point that the underwriting process has been correctly carried out and that there has been no fraud (as happened frequently when both lenders did not check whether borrowers did actually earn what they said they did). In this case, by **smoothing** cash flows i.e. making them into regular payments on fixed dates, the securitisation process enabled investors or rating agencies to evaluate the pooled asset easily and cheaply (enables statistical risk assessment) and hence made investors more willing to invest in this new type of asset. In summary, securitisation takes idiosyncratic cash flows from a wide range of small borrowers, which individually are of no interest to institutional investors and, through **pooling,** changes them into a **smoothed income stream** that can be attractive to such investors.

Many institutional investors are not permitted by their mandates to acquire loans i.e. assets which are not classed as securities. They may also not be permitted to acquire unlisted securities, i.e. those not on the official list of an exchange (or the official listing authority). However, they will be permitted to acquire securities which do have an official listing. Thus securitisation would normally also involve obtaining a listing on a market, such as the Luxembourg Stock Exchange, which specialises in such listings. Listing does not, however, imply trading. Most issues listed on the Luxembourg exchange do not trade there and indeed do not trade at all, even in dealer markets. Thus 'being listed', 'being tradable' and 'actually trading on a market' are separate features of a security.

# AGENCY SECURITISATION IN THE US

The first institution anywhere in the world which was set up specifically to securitise mortgages was the Federal National Mortgage Association (known as Fannie Mae). It was created by the US government in 1938 with the intention of making it easier and cheaper for US citizens to obtain funds to purchase a home. In 1970, a similar entity – The Federal Home Loan Corporation, known as Freddie Mac, was set up. These two companies are known as (government) **agencies** and the securitised assets they issue are known as **agency bonds**. Fannie Mae was set up as a private company able to issue securities on the capital market. However:

When it was set up by the US government, Fannie had an 'explicit guarantee' from the government; if it had financial problems, the government would bail it out to enable its investors to avoid loss. In 1968 Fannie became a private corporation, with only an '**implied guarantee**'. There was no official promise that the government would bail it out. The industry, government officials, and investors simply assumed it to be so. The absence of any documented guarantee was what enabled the US government to achieve one of its objectives which was for Fannie and Freddie to be taken off the balance sheet of the government; this made the US National Debt appear, falsely, lower than it actually was.

While securitising mortgages from a wide range of borrowers across all 52 US states can provide protection from non-systematic (idiosyncratic) risk, such securities still have substantial **systematic risk**, i.e. the risk of mortgages as a whole suddenly generating large unexpected losses on a portfolio. But with the implicit credit backing of the US government – '**the full faith and credit of the US**' – systematic credit risk could be eliminated for the investor by, in effect, being transferred to the government. Such securities would then trade at yields very close to those of US Treasury bonds. Of course, as there was no actual explicit guarantee after 1968, in law the bonds were not guaranteed.

All prospectuses for Fannie Mae securities (certificates) include the following statement:

The certificates and payments of principal and interest on the certificates are not guaranteed by the United States, and do not constitute a debt or obligation of the United States or any of its agencies or instrumentalities other than Fannie Mae. We (Fannie Mae) will issue and guarantee the certificates. Each certificate represents an **undivided ownership interest in a pool** of residential mortgages.

Thus it is Fannie Mae which actually guarantees the securities it issues, not the US government. Thus if Fannie Mae became insolvent investors in its agency bonds would lose money. However, investors continued to believe that Fannie Mae was 'too large to fail' just like large banks and would be bailed out by the government. In consequence its securities, in practice, traded at prices that reflected US government guaranteed bonds. It did in fact collapse in 2008 and investors were indeed bailed out by the US government – a good example of moral hazard coming back to bite the US taxpayer.

Fannie raises funds in the securities markets to enable them to purchase and hold mortgages themselves. They also use these funds to acquire mortgages for a short holding period while they securitise them and then sell them on to investors.

This securitisation process enables what were once mortgages to be sold in the form of standardised securities and thus to be purchased by investors. In addition, however, Fannie's intervention in the mortgage process was believed to **credit enhance** the securities, thus enabling them to be sold for a higher price (lower yield) than if they were securitised by banks. The key to the credit enhancement was, and perhaps remains, the guarantee that Fannie provides on the securitised mortgages which investors believed was really an explicit guarantee of the US government.

Large losses were realised on the underlying mortgages in 2007/08. With only 3% of equity capital, any losses above 3% of its portfolio of mortgages would cause Fannie to become insolvent. This happened in 2008, at which point Fannie was put into **conservatorship**, i.e. nationalised. It proved to be **too large to fail**. Some would say this was because one of the largest investors in Fannie's own securities and also in the mortgage backed securities (MBS) which it created was the Chinese government through its sovereign wealth and other funds. Failure of Fannie, and consequent loss for such funds, would have had severe consequences for the US (see Figure 9.1).

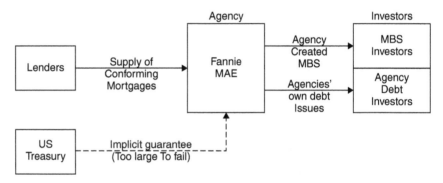

**Figure 9.1**  The use of an Agency in financing US mortgages (in this case Fannie Mae)

## NON-AGENCY SECURITISATION

A bank can convert mortgages to securities just in the same way as the agencies. Indeed almost any type of cash flow can be turned into a security.[2] All that this means is that the value of future cash flows from, for example, mortgages, credit card debt and student loans is brought forward in time – the opposite of **financial**

---

[2] A rather unusual securitisation, which in practice has been a poor investment, was the so-called 'Bowie bond'. This securitised the expected future royalty payments from the singer David Bowie's past song catalogue. All the bond did was to **bring forward all the expected royalties** from his work to give him a large cash sum now (but discounted at an appropriate rate) in exchange for giving up that same stream of revenue in the future. For investors, of course, it did the opposite. He took their cash, i.e. their liquidity, and, from their point of view, it was sent forward to be returned over the course of future years from future royalties, but with an implicit rate of interest. Investors did badly which, of course, means that the issuer, David Bowie, did well.

**investment** where cash is **sent forward in time**. Indeed, any equity or bond of a company is simply a securitisation – i.e. bringing forward expected future cash flows of that company.

The difference between Fannie (or Freddie) and commercial banks is that the latter cannot obtain either an explicit or implicit guarantee from a government. In consequence, the key problem for banks when they started to securitise mortgage and other debt and to compete with the agencies was **how to create a financing mechanism which could mimic the ability of the agencies to offer high quality (AAA) debt even though the underlying (asset backing) mortgages or credit card debt were certainly not AAA.**

The importance of achieving such a mechanism lay in the fact that many institutional investors such as pension funds and insurance companies would not purchase A-rated investments (which might be the average of all mortgages), only AA or AAA. Equally, another class of investor, hedge funds, would also not buy single A but, equally, would not buy AA or AAA (the yields were too low for them). They wanted higher yielding BBB or BB. The answer to this **market segmentation** lay in a form of financial engineering, a mechanism known as **prioritisation of claims** or **tranching**, which involves issuing different classes of securities with each class having different risk/return characteristics. This is in sharp contrast to agency debt which states that 'each certificate represents an **undivided** ownership interest in a pool of residential mortgages', i.e. every security issued to finance Fannie mortgages has the same characteristics and none has preference in payment over any other. Such securities are also known as **pass-through** since all P&I payments by borrowers pass through to all investors equally. Fannie could achieve this through the government 'implicit' guarantee. Commercial banks could not, as they had no such guarantee.

In securitisations, a securitised asset is a financial asset which represents a claim on the cash flows pooled from a collection of non-tradable financial assets held in a segregated **vehicle** also known as a special purpose vehicle (SPV) which takes the form of a company or a trust. The word 'vehicle' means that the company or trust is a mechanism created simply to help in the conversion of loans into securities and does nothing else. It has no staff or offices of its own and is simply a **brass plate** company. One further requirement in making the securities issued by such vehicles attractive to institutional investors is to have them listed on a stock exchange. Surprisingly, as we noted before, this does not mean that these securities actually trade on a market. In practice many were totally illiquid, which became a problem when valuations were required by auditors.

## COLLATERALISED DEBT OBLIGATIONS (CDOS)

CDOs are **ABSs**, just like the MBS issued by the agencies. The key difference from agency MBS is that they are **tranched**,[3] which means that they are split into slices, where each tranche is more risky than the one above. Thus, instead of being financed by one class of MBS, there are multiple classes, each with a different combination of risk and expected return. Thus unlike Fannie, which states in its

---

[3] 'Tranche' is the French word for slice, as in a slice of cake.

prospectuses that 'each certificate represents an undivided ownership interest in a pool of residential mortgages', CDOs have **divided** ownership interests in the underlying mortgage assets due to the vehicle (the company or trust) issuing a range of securities with different risk/return characteristics resulting in **subordination**.[4] In this regard CDO balance sheets are very similar to any corporate or bank balance sheet (as covered in Chapter 2) since companies also issue securities with a divided ownership interest in the underlying assets. This is because they issue equity and also junior debt and senior debt, i.e. debt issuance is divided between two classes of debt.

**CDOs use this structure to achieve credit risk transformation through subordination** in their capital structure just like banks do through their capital structure, i.e. some tranches are subordinate to others – equity is subordinate to junior (mezzanine) debt, which is subordinate to senior debt. **Subordinate** means ranks below other securities with regard to claims on cash flows or assets (in an event of default). It is the use of subordination that enables some of the liabilities issued by a CDO to have a higher rating than the underlying assets (mortgages or credit card debt) which back it (the assets of the asset-backed securities), and in consequence others must have a lower rating. Before studying how this is achieved, we will look at the structuring of a CDO.

In Figure 9.2 we can see the assets being moved from the originating bank's loan portfolio by means of sale to another company, the SPV, which in this case is known as a CDO. To pay for the purchase of these assets the SPV has to issue its own securities, known as ABSs, since their value is backed by the value of the assets on its balance sheet. Like any company it issues a range of securities – equity, junior debt and senior debt.

Structures like this cannot provide an explicit guarantee of the type that the US government gave to the agencies before they were privatised in 1968. They also have no implicit guarantee from anyone. But the structure provides what is known

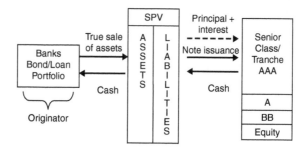

**Figure 9.2**  Structure of a CDO

*Source*: Adapted from Global Financial Markets Institute (GMFI) figure, www.gfmi.com/newsletters.0610.html (accessed, 6 February 2012).

---

[4] For completeness, it should be noted that another vehicle to hold assets and issue tranched securities is the securitised investment vehicle (SIV) which is similar in many regards to a CDO. We are not covering SIVs which were set up by banks to hold securitised assets off balance sheet for the simple reason that they have been closed down as they became illiquid or insolvent.

as **credit enhancement**, i.e. the credit rating of some parts of the divided structure can be higher than that of the underlying collateral and, conversely therefore, the credit rating of some parts must be lower than that of the underlying collateral.

Figure 9.3[5] shows a CDO (meaning the balance sheet of the SPV or company used to hold the assets and issue the liabilities). As can be seen, this balance sheet looks just like that of any company – on one side are the assets and on the other side the means of financing them with shareholder funds and borrowed money.

On the asset side we have financial assets (perhaps credit card loans, student loans, mortgages, loans to companies) which on average yield LIBOR + 85 basis points (a basis point is one hundredth of one per cent). These assets are rated AA. However, some investors are not willing or permitted to buy AA rated securities but will buy AAA. On the other hand, there are a lot of investors who will not buy AAA (because they consider the yield too low) but who will buy BBB (the lowest investment grade rating). The economic logic is that by transforming AA securities which may have a limited market into AAA and BBB securities (plus the equity residual), it is possible to widen the market and thereby to sell the new securities for a lower average yield (a higher price) than the yield on the underlying financial assets, i.e. to make an interest arbitrage profit. It was this ability to issue the liabilities for a lower average yield than the interest generated from the asset side that enabled such companies, i.e. the CDO, to seemingly make a profit for their sponsor or for whoever held the equity, or both. The residual profit, of course, accrues to the equity. As we now know, of course, the equity investors failed to reap this profit because of unexpectedly high losses on the underlying assets.

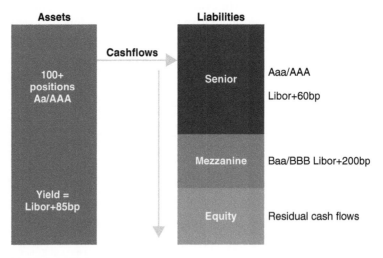

**Figure 9.3**  CDO structure

*Source*: Minyanville.com, http://www.minyanville.com/businessmarkets/articles/S-Credit-consumer-ECB-treasuries-deflation/6/23/2008/id/17677 (accessed, 6 February 2012).

[5]  http://www.minyanville.com/businessmarkets/articles/S-Credit-consumer-ECB-treasuries-deflation/6/23/2008/id/17677

By taking all the 'spread', i.e. the interest payment above LIBOR generated by the assets and reallocating it in different proportions to two different sets of liabilities (senior and mezzanine), it is possible to create securities that are more attractive to investors and to have some cash left at the end available for the equity. In this example, the AAA asset backed security gives up only 25 basis points (¼%) compared with the underlying AA assets, though this enables the smaller mezzanine tranche to offer a yield spread of 200 basis points, i.e. 115 basis points (BP) more than that of the underlying AA assets which is LIBOR + 85. The equity tranche will benefit from any interest received from the assets that does not need to be paid out to the debt tranches. You should think about how this 'magic trick' can be done by doing some calculations.

## THE TRANCHE STRUCTURE OF A CDO

Table 9.1 indicates a possible tranching and subordination structure for a CDO. In this particular case there is 5% equity in the capital structure of the CDO. This means that any losses in the value of the underlying collateral on the asset side of the CDO up to 5% is borne by whoever holds the equity (it could be the **sponsor**, i.e. the arranging bank, or it could be a hedge fund – these often buy the equity piece). The next 1½% of losses (from 5% up to 6.5%) would be borne by what is called the junior mezzanine holders, the next 6.3% would be provided by the mezzanine. It is assumed that there is virtually no possibility of more than 12.8% of losses on the portfolio (based on historical analysis of loss rates on the underlying type of ABS) and thus the final tranche (the remaining 87.2% of the whole structure) is AAA – i.e. virtually no chance of loss. As we now know, that was not the case and many such structures lost more than 50% of their value, thus eating very severely into the value of the so-called super-senior tranche.

The start-point and end-point of these ranges are known as the **attachment** and **detachment** points respectively, i.e. the points at which losses attach and detach. These are just the boundary points of the different tranches. What these two words mean is the points in the structure where the credit losses attach to a tranche. You could even imagine the credit losses as resulting from a crocodile which is trying to get its jaws on the structure and is eating into the lower tranches. The crocodile will eat the equity first then, if it is still hungry, the junior mezzanine, then the mezzanine and, finally, if it is still not satisfied it will eat part or all of the super-senior. Thus equity takes the first loss (as in any company), i.e. from the zero level up to 5% and after that the losses attach to the junior mezzanine tranche, then each

**Table 9.1** Attachment and detachment points for an actual CDO

| Tranches | % of credit losses (Lower and upper attachment and detachment points) |
|---|---|
| Super–senior | 12.8–100 |
| Mezzanine | 6.5–12.8 |
| Junior mezzanine | 5–6.5 |
| Equity piece | 0–5 |

successive tranche in turn. Once the crocodile has worked through the equity, the junior mezzanine and the mezzanine, and if these (i.e. 12.8% of the structure) are not sufficient to fill its stomach, it detaches its jaws from the mezzanine (which has been swallowed) and attaches them to the super-senior. Thus provided losses do not exceed 12.8% the crocodile will be satiated. If losses exceed this level, however, it carries on eating up the super-senior and it will not let go until it is satiated or the whole structure has been eaten. This will be at the point at which further losses stop, which could be anywhere between the 12.8% level and 100% (if every borrower defaulted and made no interest or capital payments).

Figure 9.4 is valuable in showing the different characteristics of each tranche in terms of the trade-offs that each class of investor is making – who bears first loss, who takes the highest risk and the expected yield for each level of risk assumption.

## CREDIT DEFAULT SWAPS (CDSS): SEPARATING THE 'TIME VALUE OF MONEY' FROM CREDIT RISK BEARING

Normally CDSs would be covered in a textbook on derivative securities. However, they have been central in allowing the rapid development of the so-called synthetic CDO market, which has been at the core of issues relating to the financial crisis. The use to which they have been put has enabled a quicker and, for the investment banks, more profitable method of structuring a CDO to meet specific client needs. They also, unfortunately, introduced some unexpected risks into the financial system compared with those of cash CDOs.

We normally think of financing as a single, homogeneous activity, i.e. raising money. But in fact it is two things. The first is simply the resource transfer when

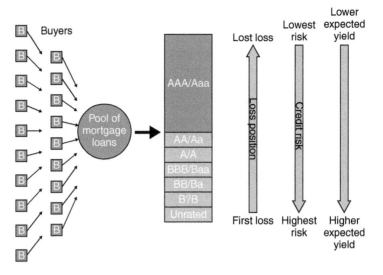

**Figure 9.4**   Creating mortgage-backed structured securities

*Source*: Wikipedia; Author of figure from Wikipedia is Thomas Splettstoesser, http://en.wikipedia.org/wiki/File:Risk%26ReturnForInvestors.svg (2 February 2012).

we believe there is no risk of our funds not being returned on the due date. For example if we lend to the US Treasury it is (was once) assumed that there is virtually no risk of not receiving interest or being repaid. If we lend to the US Treasury, we lend at the **pure time value of money** for the period for which it is lent, i.e. somewhere on the US Treasury yield curve. But, second, if we lend to any other borrower then there is an element of credit risk. To compensate for this we demand a risk premium. In pricing new corporate bonds, we have already noted that this is done by assessing the required **spread over Treasury**, i.e. the amount in excess of the time value of money element to induce lenders to take the risk of corporate lending.

So we have taken the total return on a loan or a bond and identified two components of that return – the first is simply the time value of money (the transfer over time function), while the second is the reward for taking on the risk that we don't get our money back. A key financial innovation was the development of a market which allowed these two components of return to be separated through the **CDS** – a derivative instrument which can transfer credit risk between parties. The existence of credit derivatives enables the **separation of funding and credit risk bearing** – market functions which are normally combined in a funding instrument such as a loan or a bond. They allow those who want to take on **credit risk as a distinct asset class** to do so without also needing to provide funding – their own funding (borrowing) cost may be too high for this if, for example, they are a hedge fund. It may seem strange to want to take on risk, but doing so is **the essence of investment**. An investor will take on a risk if he or she thinks the reward for bearing this risk is appropriate. As we noted before, pricing securities and derivative contracts is of the essence in finance. What that means in practice is evaluating risk and then pricing it.

The CDS market, like all markets, has traders on both sides. In this case, on one side are the **protection sellers**, i.e. those willing to **assume** credit risk (**risk assumption**), and on the other side are the **protection buyers**, i.e. those who wish to **transfer** risk to another party (**risk transfer**). Clearly a market cannot function without there being traders on both sides, on the one side wishing to hedge credit risk and, on the other, willing to invest in credit risk as an alternative means of taking on corporate bond risk or lending risk.

A CDS is, in effect, an insurance policy contract against what is known as a **credit event**. The contract has to specify **triggers** which are events considered to be credit events and which initiate the process whereby the protection buyer is compensated for his or her loss. These credit events may include:

- default on a payment, i.e. interest or principal;
- a rating downgrade by a rating agency;
- bankruptcy or restructuring.

Credit events are defined in relation to either a **reference asset**, i.e. a particular obligation of an issuer, or to a **reference entity**, i.e. a particular issuer.

Figure 9.5 shows how the market works in practice. The party which is providing the guarantee is the **protection seller**. It receives quarterly payments (the credit spread premium) to reflect the risk of default of the particular borrower. If there

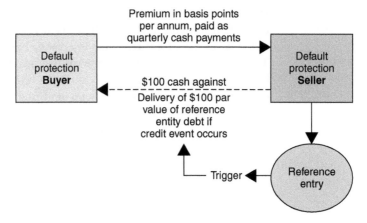

**Figure 9.5**   How the credit default swap market operates

is no **credit event** then the seller simply keeps all the premium income generated from the CDS contract. If there is a credit event such as a default, then the protection seller needs to pay out the par value, i.e. the issue price of 100, in cash and in return receives the actual bond which may or may not have a value (recovery value given default).

Subordinated debt of banks is risky. Bank risk is traded in the CDS market. Figure 9.6 shows that the cost of insuring such debt rose from around one-fifth of 1% (20 basis points) before the crisis to almost 2½% (250 basis points) by 2009. Of course, in the case of specific banks, the rate could be very much higher indeed.[6]

While we assumed earlier that Treasury debt was perfectly safe, in practice **sovereign debt** as it is called is also risky. Table 9.2 gives an indication of the level of risk of a number of countries as assessed by CDS investors, hedgers and speculators. It is well known that Greek debt is risky and indeed the country has suffered a 'voluntary' haircut on its debt. However, it can be seen that even before the sovereign debt problems of 2011 other countries also had large risk premia.

The US and Germany have low CDS premia. This is despite the fact that both countries have large outstanding public sector debts and large annual deficits, and thus we cannot be completely certain that all debt servicing will happen as per the contractual terms on which the debt was issued. The table shows that Irish government debt had a premium of 2.85% in June 2010. However, by February 2011 the premium had moved up to 570 bp (5.7% per annum) to guarantee Irish government debt against default – and that was not the peak level to which the spread rose.

Unfortunately, as was discovered at the time of the eurozone summit agreement to help Greece (in October 2011), if investors are deemed to have accepted

---

[6] If the CDS spread of a borrower is 50 basis points (0.5%), then an investor buying $100million worth of protection from a AAA-Bank must pay the bank $500,000 for that amount of insurance on the debt.

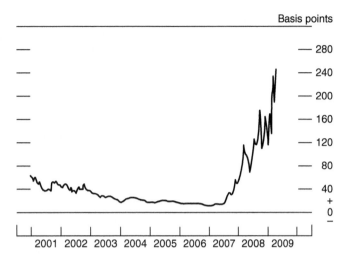

Basis points

**Figure 9.6** Bank CDS premia to 2009 (Federal Reserve Board and Markit)

*Note*: The data are weekly and extend through 15 April 2009. Median spread of all available quotes.

*Source*: Markit, www.markit.com; http://www.federalreserve.gov/pubs/bulletin/2009/pdf/bankprofits09.pdf (accessed 6 February 2012), Federal Reserve Board, Bulletin, Vol. 95, 2009.

**Table 9.2**  Sovereign CDS spreads increase from 2008 to 2010 (premia in bp)

|  | January 2008 | June 2009 Report | December 2009 Report | June 2010 Report |
|---|---|---|---|---|
| United Kingdom | 9 | 87 | 70 | 93 |
| United States | 8 | 45 | 32 | 43 |
| France | 10 | 38 | 24 | 95 |
| Germany | 7 | 34 | 23 | 50 |
| Greece | 22 | 155 | 182 | 762 |
| Ireland | 13 | 220 | 150 | 285 |
| Italy | 20 | 105 | 85 | 245 |
| Portugal | 18 | 77 | 70 | 358 |
| Spain | 18 | 98 | 86 | 269 |

*Sources*:  Bank of England Financial Stability Report June 2010, table 2a (p. 21), http://www.bankofengland.co.uk/publications/Documents/fsr/2010/fsrfull1006.pdf (2 February 2012), Thomson Reuters Datastream.

the default 'voluntarily', then there is no 'trigger' and therefore no payout on the default swaps. It's rather like someone who has insurance against his house burning down. It does burn down, he informs the insurance company, a loss adjuster visits and discovers a petrol can and matches nearby and realises that the owner has burned down his own house. The destruction was voluntary and therefore cannot be compensated by insurance. Similarly, if investors 'voluntarily' accept a 50% loss on their investment, insurance will not compensate them. However, most holders of Greek debt would not have insurance (CDS contracts), as the yield pickup from holding risky Greek debt compared with German debt would be virtually wiped out by having to pay the CDS spread. As you can see from the following, the representative of the banks holding Greek debt was offered two possibilities: either the banks could voluntarily accept a 50% loss or they could choose an involuntary 100% loss:

### October 26th, 2011, Eurozone Summit

Shortly after midnight, Dallara, Managing Director of the Institution of International Finance[7] (representing all the major banks) was called into the summit room and offered an ultimatum. If the banks would not agree to a 50% cut on their Greek bonds Europe would let Athens default. Luxembourg's prime minister said 'that if a voluntary agreement with banks was not possible, we wouldn't resist for one second, to move toward a scenario of the total insolvency of Greece'. Such a move 'would have cost states a lot of money and would have ruined the banks,' he added. After the summit, the banks issued the following statement indicating that they had acquiesced to political demands.

### Press Statement on Euro Area Stablization Measures October 27, 2011

The following statement was issued by Mr. Charles Dallara, Managing Director of the Institute of International Finance:

On behalf of the private investor community, the IIF agrees to work with Greece, Euro Area authorities and the IMF to develop a concrete voluntary agreement on the firm basis of a nominal discount of 50% on notional Greek debt held by private investors with the support of a 30 billion euro official package. This should set the basis for the decline of the Greek debt to GDP ratio with an objective of reaching 120% by 2020. The structure of the new Greek claims will need to be based on terms and conditions that ensure an NPV loss for investors fully consistent with a voluntary agreement.

*Financial Times*, 27 October 2011

## CREDIT DEFAULT SWAPS AND SYNTHETIC CDOS

Securitisation is essentially a means to enable a bank to finance increased lending. But clearly it is also a means for an investor to take on credit risk by investing in these securities. Investors take on credit risk because the market should reward those who take risk. They expect to realise a **credit risk premium** (over the default-free interest rate) just like equities are expected to generate an equity risk premium (over the default-free interest rate).

Synthetic CDOs are created using CDSs which allow the assumption of credit risk without having to obtain the **reference assets** – bonds or other assets – in the marketplace. Instead of buying these bonds, the underlying assets (the collateral) are other securities which for whatever reason are easy to source. The collateral

---

[7] The Institute of International Finance Inc. is the world's a global association of financial institutions. Created in 1983 in response to the international debt crisis, it has evolved to meet the changing needs of the financial community. Members include most of the world's largest commercial banks and investment banks, as well as a growing number of insurance companies and investment management firms.

may be, US Treasury securities which are easy to obtain and on which **the returns reflect purely the time value of money**. Alternatively it may be any securities which the investment bank has in its inventory and which the investor is willing to accept as collateral. The additional return for taking on credit risk is then added by buying credit risk (**selling protection**) through the CDS market which is generally much more liquid than the market in the underlying bonds. This is because a CDS contract can be written anytime by an investment bank provided it can find both sides to the trade or is willing to take one side itself. It can thus create additional (synthetic) credit risk beyond the amount represented by the total par value of the bonds at issue.[8]

Because it is often difficult to source bonds in illiquid markets, the synthetic approach has made the creation of CDOs based on bond credit risk much easier than if it required the purchase of the actual bonds. One of the main protection sellers was the insurance company American Insurance Group (AIG). When the issuers of many insured assets defaulted (a trigger event), AIG had an obligation to make up the losses to the protection buyers. Unfortunately it was unable to do so with the resources it had available to it as it had insufficient reserves for the risks it had assumed. Thus counterparties which had bought protection had contracts which AIG could not fulfil. However, thanks to the 'generosity' of US taxpayers, AIG was rescued by the US Treasury which provided sufficient funds to enable it to make good on its obligations. Had it not done this, it was feared by the US government that a collapse of AIG could have bankrupted many banks and other financial institutions, including Morgan Stanley and Goldman Sachs. The risk that they would not receive payments on their CDS contracts as a result of AIG defaulting is an example of **counterparty risk**. The extent of the US taxpayer's 'generosity' can be seen in Table 9.3. This shows the largest beneficiaries (institutions which were **made whole**) from the $40 billion that was paid out by the US Treasury.

**Table 9.3**   AIG's largest counterparties at the time of its collapse

| Bank | $ billions |
| --- | --- |
| Société Générale | 11.0 |
| Goldman Sachs | 8.1 |
| Deutsche Bank | 5.4 |
| Merrill Lynch | 4.9 |
| UBS | 3.3 |

---

[8] Note that the creation of this additional synthetic credit risk is offset by the creation of an exactly opposite position in credit risk, i.e. the two sides of the contract net out. Someone who wants to take on credit risk can do so and someone who wants protection from credit risk can also do so. If the investment bank cannot find the other side to its contract it will hold it in its own (risky) trading portfolio.

## CASE STUDY OF A SYNTHETIC CDO FOR AN INSURANCE COMPANY INVESTMENT PORTFOLIO

This is an example of a synthetic CDO that was offered to a major UK life insurer, just as problems were emerging in this asset class, which was said by the structurer to have an expected return higher than equivalent assets of the same rating class. This particular CDO was one on which I was involved in advising the UK insurer which was seeking assets in which to invest but which would provide a yield slightly higher than the assets it traditionally acquired such as corporate bonds. The insurance company (the investor) requested a minimum return of 40 bp over LIBOR at seven-year maturity with an AA rating. Table 9.4 shows the range of tranches offered by the investment bank based on CDSs on European corporates (non-financial companies). The prospectus stated that the underlying collateral could be either US Treasury bonds (riskless collateral) or any other type of collateral such as mortgage-backed securities (potentially very risky).

The major investment bank which offered these securities was able to offer two different classes (tranches) to the investor, based on the seven-year portfolio **average spread of 51.5 bp**. Class I, although it was of a higher credit rating than required (AAA), was still able to offer a yield above LIBOR of more than the minimum required by the insurance company, i.e. 71 bp rather than only 40. Indeed the yield being offered on the AAA was higher than the portfolio average yield. Was there a 'Super AAA' tranche above the AAA at a lower yield? There would have to be. Was the collateral in fact a higher yielding asset such as mortgage securities rather than US Treasuries? Yes indeed it was. When the structurer was informed that the investor wanted US Treasuries as collateral rather than any bonds which the structurer chose, the response was 'that's no problem but of course the yield you will receive on the CDO will fall to perhaps less than your target.'

If we work through the structure we can see that the tranches being offered are very 'thin' – each is only 1% of the whole structure. In Class 1, the lower attachment point is at 6.2% and the upper attachment (detachment) point is at 7.2%. Beneath this AAA tranche, protection is being provided by other investors in the capital structure who are buying the more risky tranches, which amount to the first 6.2% of the capital structure. Thus if the P&I cash flow waterfall is insufficient to service all the tranches, these investors take any shortfalls up to the amount of 6.2%. To simplify, if there are defaults in the amount of exactly 6.2% of the asset value of the whole structure, all the losses will be borne by the other investors, including equity investors, while any investors above this level will lose nothing.

**Table 9.4**  Illustrative corporate CDO

| Rating | Class I: AAA | Class II: AA |
|---|---|---|
| Lower attachment point | 6.20% | 5.20% |
| Upper detachment point | 7.20% | 6.20% |
| Indicative coupon | 3M £L + 71 | 3M £L + 104 |

*Note*: This was a seven-year synthetic CDO, shown to the investor on 26 March 2007.

Thus our AAA investor is protected up to this point. If there are losses beyond this point (6.2% of the underlying loan portfolio) the AAA investor will have to bear some degree of loss. However, if we look at the position of the AA investor in the event of a 6.2% loss, he or she will lose everything as they start bearing losses at the 5.2% level in the structure and have lost everything by 6.2%.

The problem raised by these **narrow tranches** is that it leverages losses. If the loss on the underlying assets increases from 6.2 to 6.7% (a ½% additional loss), the AAA loses 50% of its value, which is a dramatic leverage. If losses reach 7.2%, the AAA loses 100% of its value just as the AA tranche has. This 'leverage' in the impact of a small additional loss is a feature of many CDOs that may have been intentional on the part of the structuring investment bank, but it is unlikely that the risks it created for potential investors were well explained to them.

Why then is part of the structure from 6.2 to 7.2% (a 1% tranche) called AAA, and who says it is AAA? The AAA designation comes from a rating agency. Rating agencies, known officially in the United States as **Nationally Recognized Statistical Rating Organizations (NRSRO)**, give what in law is classified as an 'opinion' on the credit risk of a security. As an opinion it should not subject the agency to the risk of being sued for misleading investors, should it cause them to buy a 'safe' investment which then suffers large losses. Thus the rating agency does not have the responsibility that other providers of financial services may have in respect of the implied quality of their product (an opinion). Making the value of the rating even more suspect is the fact that NRSROs do not act as agents of investors. They are the agents of, paid by and work for the benefit of, the structurer or issuer. There is therefore a conflict of interest in the role of the rating agencies. In fact, according to the Bank for International Settlements, while only 20% of outstanding debt in 1991 was rated AAA, by 2009 an extraordinary 55% of outstanding debt was rated AAA. Quite apart from the fact that many of these AAA ratings were virtually fraudulent, it is also the case that, as the total debt burden in an economy rises, the risk of such debt would be expected to rise and thus a lower proportion of total debt would be in the top rating class.

We now know that the highly conflicted status of rating agencies caused them to suffer from 'poor judgement', i.e. to produce ratings that were not based on an appropriate means of evaluating these new instruments in comparison to the traditional corporate bonds which they have always rated. Some have suggested that the agency that rated so many of the defaulting CDSs must have been called Moody and Poor! That has certainly been the outcome for many investors who did not work out the fine details of these structures for themselves.

The US investment bank which offered this synthetic security to the UK investor (the life insurance company) also offered Class II: AA tranche as we saw above. The yield of LIBOR plus more than 1% looks impressive. But we do have to ask: if LIBOR is the interbank unsecured lending rate and banks are rated AA (as most banks were), how can it be that this security which is AA yields 1% more than that?

The reason we should ask is that the whole theory of finance says that you should have the same expected return for the same level of risk. This, of course, is because investors will arbitrage away the excess return by borrowing at LIBOR and investing in the AA tranche of such structures until the discrepancy disappears.

Alternatively the explanation of why this tranche offers 1% more is quite simple. It is not AA as understood in terms of a conventional credit such as a corporate bond. Thus the level of risk is not the same and therefore the 1% extra expected return is for bearing a risk that is actually equivalent to a corporate credit of, perhaps, BB rating or lower. A key difference as we have noted lies in the thinness of the tranche, which means that in fact it is very possible for the investor in this tranche to get wiped out completely. In contrast, if a corporate AA bond defaulted, the **loss given default** is likely to be much less than 100% of the investment. Thus the investor would not lose everything.

There is **no free lunch in finance**. Higher expected return should always mean higher risk, which may mean much lower actual return. If there really were such a 'free lunch', then banks would have been borrowing in the interbank market at LIBOR and investing heavily in these CDOs at more than 1% above LIBOR. That's a great arbitrage! In fact they were and in very large size! That is one reason why so many banks ended up holding CDOs even though securitisation was supposed to be a way of bringing in outside investors, i.e. the opposite of what they were actually doing. In summary, they were greedy. In the case of UBS, the losses they incurred on their portfolio of such securities was around $50bn. The consequence of the loss was to take them close to collapse.

An important 'flaw' in the design of synthetic CDOs as we noted above was that the collateral might not, in fact, comprise 'riskless' US Treasury bonds. The **collateral can be anything that the investment bank might choose to use**. The possibility that such collateral could be used *was* noted in the offering documentation. It stated that collateral could include US Treasuries, mortgage backed securities and various other types of security. In fact, one of the attractions to the investment banks of synthetic structures was that they could use the cash provided by investors as a low cost means of financing their proprietary holdings of mortgage bonds and other illiquid assets, which were otherwise very expensive and difficult to finance in the repo market. Thus they were not in practice going to use high quality, low risk, US Treasuries unless the investor client spotted the 'fatal flaw' in the structure and demanded US Treasuries. But if this happened the supernormal return vanished just like the Cheshire cat in Alice in Wonderland.

The issue of fiduciary responsibility[9] to investment clients/counterparties came to the fore in April 2010 when the Securities and Exchange Commission (SEC) issued a suit against Goldman Sachs in connection with an issue of CDOs known as Abacus that was sold to, amongst other investors, IKB, a German bank. Goldman settled with the SEC by paying a $0.5 billion fine, though not admitting guilt. In this particular case it was claimed that the investment bank itself, or another client, was **actually betting against the securities it had sold its client**. The Goldman

---

[9] A fiduciary duty is a legal relationship of trust between two or more parties. In such a relationship, one person, in a position of vulnerability perhaps due to lack of knowledge (asymmetric information), vests confidence, good faith, reliance and trust in another whose aid, advice or protection is sought,, normally in a financial matter. In such a relationship a fiduciary is required to act at all times for the sole benefit and interest of the one who has placed trust in him or her. An example would be a stockbroker acting as agent for his or her principal (the client)

response was that **in any swap transaction there must be a long and a short side, and their client**, IKB, had chosen to be long of these securities and was a professional investor while another professional client, a hedge fund which was shorting real estate assets and made some billions of dollars of profit during the financial crisis from so doing, was **quite entitled to take a contrary position**. In essence Goldman would seem to be claiming that it did not owe the client a fiduciary duty of trust because it was not a retail client. However, it would seem that the hedge fund client was actually involved in **choosing** which particular assets to use and was naturally keen that Goldman include assets that would quickly lose value.

It was not only to 'sophisticated' investors that similar securities were sold. They were also sold to retail investors. As I have indicated before, securities salespeople have a greater duty of care towards 'innocents' than towards other professionals – 'big boys' as they are known. In the case below the ability of a credit derivative to create 'winners' and 'losers' is quite clear. What has to be uncovered is whether or not Morgan Stanley intentionally created these securities using underlying assets, – the reference assets – that they knew at that time would fall in value and thus create profits for Morgan Stanley. Only after the court case will the issues be clarified. It is quite possible and indeed likely, that Morgan Stanley will, settle out of court to avoid being found guilty.

### Investors Win the Right to Sue Morgan Stanley

A group of Singaporean investors who claim Morgan Stanley sold them opaque financial products that were designed to fail have won the right to sue the US investment bank in New York. These were so-called Pinnacle Notes – complex products that were sold in 2006 and 2007 before losing almost 100 per cent of their value during the financial crisis.

Investors alleged that Morgan Stanley had designed the notes in such a way that they would generate losses that would then produce a corresponding profit for the bank. Morgan Stanley has denied any allegations of wrongdoing. The complaint alleged that the Pinnacle Notes were marketed as 'conservative investments' while in fact being 'specifically designed to wipe out the ... $154.7m investment' that would be redirected 'into Morgan Stanley's coffers'. The investors allege that Morgan Stanley used synthetic collateralized debt obligations that it had created as collateral to underpin the notes, rather than safe securities, such as US Treasuries, as is common industry practice. According to the complaint, Morgan Stanley deliberately linked the CDOs to risky companies, including Icelandic banks and companies with high exposure to a US housing market downturn. 'The synthetic CDOs that Morgan Stanley created were not merely bets, but bets Morgan Stanley rigged, in which it placed itself on the side guaranteed to win (the "short" side) and placed Plaintiffs on the side guaranteed to lose (the "long" side),' the suit said.

*Financial Times*, 4 November 2011

## THE BANKS WERE NOT DISTRIBUTING: THEY WERE NOT DOING WHAT THEY SAID THEY WERE DOING

It might seem odd that it was not just institutional and retail investors which suffered from the collapse in price of structured securities. It might have been expected that the banks would have been saved from loss since they were supposedly selling these securitisations. Banks, in fact, suffered more than most with UBS, for example as we have already noted, having to write off over $50 billion as a result of losses on CDOs. Unfortunately, what the regulators discovered after the financial crisis hit was that banks were in fact:

- originating and then distributing in large part to each other and to other parts of their bank;
- holding large amounts of about-to-be-securitised debt (warehousing) on their balance sheets as investors stopped buying when they became aware of the risks of CDOs;
- creating vehicles (companies) known as securitised investment vehicles (SIVs) to hold their own securitised mortgages off-balance sheet, 'hidden' from the regulators.

Thus in practice, risk and the need for funding were not leaving the global banking system as a whole to the extent that regulators had believed. The true size of the banking system after including banks' own off-balance-sheet financing (part of the shadow banking system which is covered in the next chapter) was also not diminishing. Banks were in fact **originating to arbitrage**, as this model has been called, meaning that they were borrowing low-cost short-term funds in the repo market to invest in higher-yielding longer-maturity securities (securitised mortgages, credit card debt, etc.) which is an interest rate differential arbitrage.

**Project financing** is very similar to ABS financing. In this case the sponsor of the project (which may be a construction company or a government or local authority) is not the borrower. Instead the project is operated through a company set up specifically for this purpose (off-balance-sheet financing) and it is the project company that takes out the necessary loans and therefore bears the risk. A good example of project finance was the Channel Tunnel – a project sponsored by the UK and French governments. To avoid risk to taxpayers in these countries, the project was undertaken through a ring-fenced limited liability company, i.e. a special purpose vehicle. When the Channel Tunnel Company was clearly unable to meet its P&I payments on the major part of its €6 billion debt the loss was taken by the banks and investors holding Eurotunnel debt and not by the sponsors (the UK and French governments). Governments often resort to off-balance-sheet financing in order to try to pretend that the debt issued by such entities is not really government debt. In the case of the Channel Tunnel this proved to be so, but often governments still provide an implicit guarantee as they so clearly did for the agencies Fannie and Freddie.

## SECURITISATION IN CHINA

While securitisation is generally thought of as a purely Western finance phenomenon, it was reported to have come to life in China in 2007, just as it was being reduced in importance in the West. It is still alive and well according to the report below:

> The China Banking Regulatory Commission, China's banking regulator, has told lenders they must put all loans sold or transferred to lightly regulated Chinese trust

companies back on their books and stop using 'informal securitization' to evade regulatory requirements.. ...

The repackaging of loans into securitized products has been blamed for exacerbating the global financial crisis in the West but such complex instruments had been little used in China. Yet in the last year, and especially in the last six months, a largely unregulated market in securitized loans has proliferated as banks have strained to get around the government's attempts to rein in rampant lending growth ... .

The total outstanding credit sitting off banks' balance sheets in trust company products is around Rmb2,300bn, up nearly 10-fold from the end of 2007, according to government and independent estimates. Putting this back onto the banks' books will strain capitalization and loan to deposit ratios and could force some banks to turn to the capital markets even before an ongoing massive round of fund-raising has been completed. 'The transfer of a growing amount of credit off banks' balance sheets and out of the purview of market participants is the most disconcerting trend Fitch has observed in China's banking sector in recent year' according to Charlene Chu, a senior analyst at Fitch Ratings. ...

Three major banks all said on Tuesday that they had suspended sales of trust company products but one, China Merchants Bank, was still offering a product based on the securitized loan of a Chinese coal miner that promised a minimum annual return of 8 per cent. According to the bank's salesman: 'There's hardly any risk to this investment because the company's assets are a lot bigger than the Rmb800m it's borrowing; it's quite safe I assure you.'

Jamil Anderlini, 'China banks Told to Account for Loans',<br>Financial Times, 10 August 2010.

Do you believe this salesman?

# 10 SHADOW BANKING: CREDIT INTERMEDIATION THROUGH NON-DEPOSITORY INSTITUTIONS AND MARKETS

In the chapter on credit intermediation by banks we looked at financial institutions (financial companies) which accepted deposits and made loans and we classified these institutions as banks. We identify a financial institution as a 'bank' if it is a company which has a banking licence and is therefore permitted to accept deposits. The function of this type of company is **credit intermediation**, i.e. intermediation between lenders and borrowers through the use of a balance sheet in order to provide lenders with attractive savings vehicles and borrowers with loans. However, there are other institutions that also perform credit intermediation but which, in law, are not banks. They are not banks for the simple reason that they are not permitted to accept what in law is defined as a deposit. They therefore do not hold a banking licence and are **not regulated as banks**.

I devote a separate chapter here to the shadow banking system for two interrelated reasons. First, the shadow banking system is very large. Second, this sector was an important 'actor' in the financial crisis. Figure 10.1 shows that in the period since 1994, the US shadow-banking system (as it is defined by the New York Fed) became larger than the traditional credit intermediation system (the banking system). In China, as we note at the end of this chapter, there is a danger that the same issues will arise with shadow banking as occurred in the US.

Essentially the shadow banking system is a set of institutions and markets which provide credit intermediation services in which the assets of the intermediaries are securitised loans (rather than just the loans themselves, which is what banks traditionally hold) and the liabilities they issue are securities rather than being deposits (which is what banks traditionally use to finance their assets). The shadow banking system is a mechanism that also involves many more links in the chain of intermediation between the initial borrower and the final investor than in the case of bank intermediation where all the intermediation takes place on the balance sheet of the bank itself. It is this intermediation chain that binds the various components into a network which is the shadow banking system and also gives rise to shadow banking's vulnerabilities. The intermediation chain is complex and therefore I will not attempt to cover it in detail.

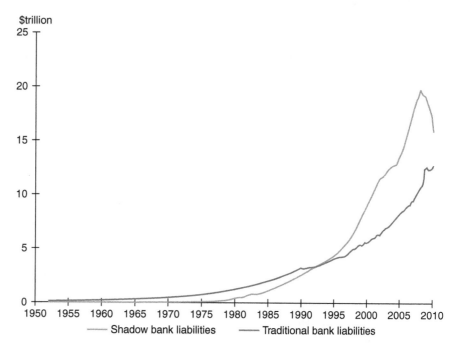

**Figure 10.1**   Shadow banking industry size compared with traditional banking industry size ($ trillions)

*Sources*: Z. figure 1, 'Shadow Bank Liabilities vs. Traditional Bank Liabilities, $ trillion' in 'Shadow Banking' by Zoltan Pozsar, Tobias Adrian, Adam Ashcraft and Hayley Boesky (Staff Reports No. 458, July 2010),, http://www.scribd.com/doc/34118631/Federal-Reserve-Bank-of-New-York-Staff-Report-No-458-July-2010 (8 February 2012).

The key to understanding the implications of shadow banking is that most of its institutions, just like commercial banks, perform maturity transformation and are, therefore, potentially fragile in the same way as commercial banks, though they do **not** have the **'liquidity and solvency support mechanisms'** that banks have available to them, nor are they regulated as to capital and liquidity ratios as banks are. This fragility came to the fore during the financial crisis when it resulted in dramatic instability in the global financial markets.

The major components of the shadow banking system are:

- **Private sector finance companies**, for example General Motors Acceptance Corporation (GMAC), which used to be a large provider of financing for mortgages, or GE Finance and GE Capital, which are both subsidiaries of General Electric, the US electrical company. GMAC (no longer owned by General Motors but mostly by the US Treasury) was larger than many banks and operated globally before it collapsed in 2008 and was nationalised.
- **Public sector (or quasi-public) mortgage companies** such Federal National Mortgage Association (Fannie Mae) and Government National Mortgage Association (Ginnie Mae) in the United States which held trillions of dollars in assets before they collapsed in 2008 and had to be rescued by the US Treasury.
- **Asset management companies**: conduits and securitised investment vehicles (SIVs) which may be used for off-balance-sheet credit intermediation by banks

and CDOs which are also asset management companies, all of which had been liquidated by 2010 as they had become unable to rollover their funding.

- **Investment banks**: which undertake substantial maturity transformation on their balance sheets, originally only in their trading book but latterly by financing long duration asset holdings through the overnight repo market and providing 'structuring services' to originators of loans to enable securitisation, some of which, such as Bear Stearns and Lehman Brothers, collapsed in 2008.
- **Securities lenders such as fund managers**: who lend out equities to short sellers such as investment banks and thus generate cash that has been provided as collateral against their securities loans. They need to find a profitable use for the cash during the securities lending period. In the short term they might lend into the repo[1] market, more properly known as the **sale and repurchase market**, or for longer term lending they would invest in MMMFs (money market mutual funds).
- **MMMFs**: which offered apparently 'fixed par value deposits' to retail, corporate and other investors but at higher interest rates than offered by the commercial banks on assets of seemingly similar risk until the largest fund in the world, the Reserve Primary Fund, collapsed in 2008.
- **Hedge funds**: which may hold long-term assets financed by short-term loans, for example Long Term Capital Management, the hedge fund which collapsed in 1998 with losses of $4.6 billion, and the new fund run by the same management, JWM Partners, who announced its closure in early 2009 after suffering a loss of 44% in the main fund between September 2007 and February 2009.

## A REPRISE OF HOW COMMERCIAL BANKS MANAGE THEIR LIQUIDITY AND SOLVENCY RISKS

I described in Chapter 7 how a commercial bank undertakes various types of transformation in order to provide credit intermediation services to its customers. These transformations enable a reduction in the cost of credit relative to direct lending. The problem with this intermediation process, as we noted before, is that it is inherently fragile and subject to **runs**, i.e. a sudden outflow of deposits that can cause the intermediary to fail.

The fragility of commercial banks results from the use of short-term liabilities to fund illiquid long-term assets. As the failure of a credit intermediary can give rise to adverse effects on the real economy, governments since the 1930s have generally provided two facilities which reduce the chances of such failure.

First, liquidity insurance (liquidity put) is the provision of **liquidity-backup facilities** in the form of access to the **discount window** (the US and UK term) of the Fed or the Bank of England or the **standing facilities** (the eurozone term) of the European Central Bank ECB. This enables banks to obtain cash by borrowing from the discount 'window' at the central bank in exchange for (putting) collateral to the central bank. The borrowing rate is normally

---

[1] Repo lending generally involves an ongoing relationship between the borrower and lender (or buyer and seller) and thus usually involves a master agreement to be in place (typically the SIFMA/ICMA commissioned Global Master Repo Agreement).

substantially above the interbank rate (often 1% above) to discourage excessive use of the facility, but if the interbank market is frozen, then it may be the best source of liquidity for commercial banks. This facility is described as a liquidity put option, i.e. it enables banks to source liquidity at their option (though the price of the option is the higher interest rate) by 'putting' securities to the central bank in return for cash.

Second, insurance against depositor loss from insolvency is the provision of **deposit insurance** which also operates like a put option in that it enables depositors to obtain a full reimbursement of their deposit from the deposit insurer in exchange for giving up their claim on the assets of the bank in liquidation. Depositors simply 'put' their right to a return of their deposit back to the insurer which then reimburses them in full or in part. The insurer then becomes the creditor in respect of deposits in any winding-up procedure (resolution).

If all companies which undertake credit intermediation are inherently fragile, then we need to consider whether it should be the **function** of credit intermediation that should be regulated, rather than simply a subset of companies which undertake the function and which happen to be defined in law as **banks**, i.e. companies which hold a banking licence. Just as the commercial bank credit intermediation system is fragile, so too is the so-called shadow banking system,[2] and indeed more so, and it may, therefore, have similar liquidity backup and asset holder insurance **needs** as the banking system.

In principle, this liquidity backup and credit insurance was provided by banks (liquidity support) and other financial institutions such as AIG (credit risk insurance) that offered lines of credit, backup facilities and credit insurance. But as McCulley observes (see Note 2), what this means is that shadow banks were in fact relying on other potentially fragile companies to bail them out, but in the case of banks, ones with taxpayer support. Hence they too relied on the 'real' banking and insurance companies and ultimately on taxpayers.

An obvious question is why the shadow banking system exists in addition to the traditional, commercial, banking-based, credit-intermediation system. The first reason is **regulatory arbitrage**. This means taking advantage of the fact that regulations that apply to deposit-taking banks don't apply to 'shadow banks'. For example, shadow banks, as they are not classed as banks, do not have to comply with the Basel II requirements on the amount of capital they employ relative to their risk-weighted assets. The second reason is that the shadow banking system is more specialised in each component and may offer advantages from such specialisation which give it a **comparative advantage from cost savings** compared with deposit-taking banks.

---

[2] Paul McCulley was the first person to use this term when he coined the term 'shadow banking system' in August 2007 at the Federal Reserve System's annual symposium in Jackson Hole. He noted that 'unregulated shadow banks fund themselves with uninsured commercial paper which may or may not be backstopped by liquidity lines from real banks. Thus the shadow banking system is particularly vulnerable to runs – commercial paper investors refusing to [roll-over their loans] when their paper matures leaving the shadow banks with a liquidity crisis – a need to tap their back-up lines of credit with real banks and/or to liquidate assets at fire sale prices'.

## WHAT IS 'SHADOW CREDIT INTERMEDIATION'?

Traditional credit intermediation involves three types of transformation, as we noted in the last chapter: size transformation, credit transformation and maturity transformation. In addition to, or as an alternative to, these three types of credit transformation, shadow banks can also use third-party enhancement to provide insurance against liquidity risk and credit risk.

Liquidity enhancement is likely to be provided by the 'official' bank sector which provides **a backup line of credit** to the shadow bank. This is a guarantee that if the shadow bank is unable to raise funds in the securities markets (the manifestation of rollover risk) the bank providing the line of credit will step in and provide alternative financing. Many shadow banks were in fact SIVs set up and managed by a conventional bank as a means of taking assets off-balance sheet and hence into the asset management sector which was regulated quite differently from the banking sector. Thus the shadow bank obtained liquidity insurance from its sponsor and therefore was implicitly relying on liquidity support from the lender of last resort, i.e. the central bank.

## THE ROLE OF MONEY MARKET MUTUAL FUNDS

A money market mutual fund is a mutual fund (a collective investment fund) which holds a diversified portfolio of assets within a particular asset class which, in this case, is short-term securities issued by commercial banks and shadow banks. Like any mutual fund the assets it holds must by law be highly liquid, and thus when there is a net demand by investors for liquidity by the fund's shareholders (those who hold units in the fund) this can easily be generated by selling some of the underlying assets.

Traditionally, mutual funds invest in equities or bonds, the value of which changes minute by minute during the day. A mutual fund, therefore, makes its promise to redeem units in the fund but only at the **net asset value** of the fund at the time of redemption. Thus a mutual fund provides **variable value** assets, unlike a bank which provides **fixed value** assets. In practice, however, MMMFs have seemed to offer investors fixed value assets and, indeed, US law permits this, because:

- The assets are short term and hence their market value does not vary much.
- Credit risk on the assets is small since most of them are liabilities issued by banks and investment banks and are considered to be safe due to the 'too big to fail' doctrine employed by most governments.

As a result of these features, the Securities and Exchange Commission qualifies certain funds as MMMFs under SEC Rule 2a-7 pursuant to the Investment Company Act of 1940.

As a result of what seemed to be a safe business model, MMMFs made an implicit promise **not to break the buck** – an American expression which means always to repay 100 cents on the dollar (a buck being slang for a dollar). Only if the value of units fell by more than 0.5% did they need to publish the fact that they could not redeem at par. The problem is that if they do suffer a default on an asset they may be unable to meet this **implicit** promise of redemption at par.

This happened to **Reserve Primary** money market fund. On 15 September 2008, the news of Lehman Brothers' bankruptcy caused investors to try to redeem the money they held in Reserve Primary Fund – the world's first ever MMMF which opened for business in 1970 and held $62 billion in assets before losing $785 million when Lehman collapsed as a result of holding $785 million in short-term liabilities in the form of commercial paper, issued by Lehman Bros. The Reserve Fund's board valued the securities at zero, causing the fund's share price to fall to 97 cents. The fund also put a seven-day hold on all redemption requests.

If the entities issuing any of the liabilities held by such a fund default then the value of the fund must fall.[3] Thus such funds present exactly the same risks as bank deposits – liquidity risk and credit risk – yet have no official liquidity or credit risk insurance. Nor do they have equity capital to use as protection for the holders of units in the fund. Today, regulators are considering forcing MMMFs to offer **variable value funds** or alternatively severely limiting the types of asset they may hold if they wish to claim that they are fixed value funds. This, of course, raises the issue of whether MMMFs should have been regulated as credit inter-mediaries in the first place since they conduct a business very similar to that of deposit-taking banks. Indeed, many people referred to money they put into such funds as 'deposits', even though legally they were quite different. It should also be noted that during the financial crisis the Fed arranged for all MMMF assets to be guaranteed by the government, thus creating moral hazard in the future if such a crisis was repeated.

It is not only independent shadow banks which have been raising funds in the securities markets, either directly or indirectly. The banks themselves have been doing so as a way of growing at a faster rate than would be possible on the base of deposit growth. Northern Rock, for example, was utilising the securities markets in two ways, as we noted earlier. First, like all banks it was issuing securities to increase its total financing. The securities issued by Northern Rock were called **securitised notes** and were purchased by MMMFs, corporate treasurers with spare cash, hedge funds, etc. Second, it was securitising assets in off-balance sheet vehicles, seemingly to reduce the size of its balance sheet and selling the resulting ABSs to investors, and in particular to MMMFs.

By investing in both these types of security, the MMMFs were acting as a conduit between the banks and the public. But what they were also doing was undertaking **maturity transformation**. They were taking in funds which were notionally at least repayable 'on demand' but investing the proceeds in longer term securitised notes issued by banks.

---

[3] On 15 September 2008, Lehman Brothers Holdings Inc. filed for bankruptcy. On Tuesday, 16 September 2008, Reserve Primary Fund broke the buck when its shares fell to 97 cents, after writing off debt issued by Lehman Brothers. On 19 September 2008, the US Department of the Treasury announced a programme to 'insure the holdings of any publicly offered eligible money market mutual fund that pays a fee to participate in the program'. The insurance guarantees that if a covered fund breaks the buck, it will be restored to $1 Net Asset Value (NAV). This programme is similar to deposit insurance, in that it insures deposit-like holdings and seeks to prevent runs on funds.

It is clear that these MMMFs are balance sheet intermediaries providing maturity transformation – just like banks. They offer what look like demand deposits – they seem to promise **fixed value** assets, just like banks – but offer higher interest rates than bank deposits. However, they are not regulated in the way banks are and thus their promise to pay out what was paid in (their **fixed value** promise) may be suspect if they suffer any defaults on their portfolio.

## HOW CREDIT INTERMEDIATION HAS CHANGED

A key feature of banks as we have noted has been the shift of the industry from an **originate and hold** business model to an **originate, securitise, distribute or retain** (arbitrage) model, through off-balance-sheet asset-management vehicles. This has caused the banking industry to change from a credit risk intensive business funded by deposits and making its income from the spread between its cost of funds and the yield on its loans, to one which is market risk intensive, is funded by wholesale funds and makes income mainly from fees. Table 10.1 summarises this change.

As a result of this change, banks became more like manufacturers, creating products and selling them in the market to the highest bidder.

## WHAT WAS WRONG WITH THE SHADOW BANKING SYSTEM?

The shadow banking system and the innovations it represents has the potential to be a very useful adjunct to traditional banking. Securitisation, in particular, is a great innovation if used appropriately. But even if many experts and society in general were not previously aware of the risks of these 'innovative' instruments, we now know that the instruments were, in considerable part, responsible for the financial crisis. One reason was the **information asymmetries** that exist in the **new paradigm of innovative finance**, i.e. a new model which it was generally believed had created a superior, and even less risky, system of credit intermediation than traditional banking. It was also believed that it could economise on capital and liquidity and thus generate higher profits for financial firms. In retrospect, it is clear that the financial system was operating with insufficient capital or liquidity. In addition, the asymmetries were such that it is surprising that the model had such a relatively long life before collapsing under the **skewed incentive structures** that were created. Not only were there severe information asymmetries but, in addition, the models that were being used to design these structures had severe model errors, i.e. mistakes in the design (which some would actually call intentional 'mistakes'). This arose in part from the close collaboration between the

**Table 10.1** Differences between licensed banks and shadow banks

|  | **Traditional (licensed) banks** | **Shadow banks** |
| --- | --- | --- |
| Main risk | Credit loss | Market price movement |
| Funding | Retail deposits | Wholesale markets |
| Income | Spread | Fees |

structurers and the rating agencies who, **some** would say, colluded to create structures that they knew to be highly risky, yet had AAA ratings attached to them.

## CHINA'S SECURITISED PRODUCTS, OFF-BALANCE-SHEET PRODUCTS AND MMMF EQUIVALENTS

It is clear now that the securitisation practices in China described at the end of the previous chapter are continuing. In a report in the *Financial Times*, more than a year after the one quoted on p. 154/155, the following was written:

> A scramble to retain customers pulling their money from traditional deposit accounts is causing Chinese banks to use a growing number of alternatives that regulators fear could undermine the financial underpinnings of the economy. China places a ceiling on deposit rates as a way of limiting competition among banks and to fortify the capital positions of institutions that had effectively been insolvent a decade ago. But with inflation nearly 3 percentage points above the rate ceiling many depositors are hungry for better returns, forcing banks to come up with new ways to retain deposits.
>
> Their main technique has been the issuance of wealth management products, which typically are loans repackaged as short-term investment vehicles and are held off-balance-sheet. Annualised rates can be as high as 8 per cent, more than double the one-year deposit rate. Official media have reported in recent weeks that the nation's biggest banks had seen a net outflow of traditional deposits in the first half of September. A more accurate reflection of the importance of wealth management products was found in the monetary growth data released by the central bank on Friday. The broad M2 measure of money growth, which includes deposits but not wealth products, was nearly 1 percentage point below forecasts. 'M2 should have increased more, considering the increase in the monetary base and the multiplying effect. We suspect depositors continue to switch to wealth management products and that slowed the growth of traditional deposits,' said Citi economist Shuang Ding.
>
> 'Fears Grow as Chinese Banks Fight for Deposits', *Financial Times*,
> 17 October 2011

# 11 CAPITAL MARKET EQUITY INITIAL PUBLIC OFFERINGS AND CORPORATE BOND ORIGINATION

Capital markets are much more **impersonal** than bank lending, and the investor in such markets is unlikely to have any personal knowledge of the management of the firm to whom he or she is providing financing, unlike a bank manager who is likely to have met a corporate borrower. As a result, there have to be other mechanisms to try to ensure that the potential investor is not investing in an excessively risky company, has the necessary information to enable an effective evaluation of risk and that he or she is kept informed regularly of developments in the company. Essentially, therefore, for capital markets to function effectively, there have to be mechanisms to overcome **asymmetric information problems**.

## INFORMATION DISCLOSURE

At the time of a new issue of shares or a bond issue a **prospectus**, i.e. a document which discloses information to potential investors, has to be issued with the required content detailed (in the case of the European Union, in accordance with the Prospectus Directive of the EU). In addition, the sponsors of the issue, i.e. the investment banks which have the **mandate** (the contract to arrange the issue and distribute it to investors), will be adding their name and hence reputation to the issue. One might assume that they would not do this without having a strong belief in the issuer and the likelihood of the issue performing well. But in practice some investment banks have 'promoted' issues where it was quite clear that there were serious problems with the company.[1] It has to be assumed that the issuing

---

[1] The most famous analyst who nearly went to jail for dishonesty was Henry Blodget. He was disbarred from the industry and paid a $2 million fine. 'Blodget became an emblem of bubble era dishonesty by maintaining "Buy" recommendations for stocks he privately described as "worthless" or "PoS" (for "piece of shit").' It was partly due to such actions that the US suffered the dot.com crash. Very similar issues have arisen more recently in the CDO market with salespeople privately describing some CDO tranches in very similar terms to the above. This behaviour is also thought, therefore, to be one of the causes of the CDO market collapse. Source: http://www.theregister.co.uk/2004/08/09/google_ipo_jeopardy/

house promoted such companies because of the revenue it generated for them, even though they knew that it was likely that investors would lose a high proportion of their investment.

At the time of capital raising, and on an ongoing basis, the filing of company accounts at a registry, such as **Companies House** in the UK, is a legal requirement in all countries for both private and public companies. In the US, public companies are required to report quarterly on their results in order to ensure that investors can take appropriate action at an earlier point than would be the case with six-monthly accounts.

Another mechanism to try to overcome the information asymmetry problem is the reports issued by Nationally Recognised Statistical Rating Organisations (NRSROs) such as Standard and Poors. The U.S. Securities and Exchange Commission permits financial firms to use the ratings from such agencies for certain regulatory purposes. The Basel Committee on Banking Supervision also allows the ratings of these agencies to be used in capital calculations by banks. Both these uses have become contentious since the financial crisis and the subsequent eurozone sovereign debt crisis.

Ratings were designed to enable investors, who do not have the skills necessary to evaluate an issue, to make an invest/don't invest decision based on the rating allocated to the issue by the agency. Unfortunately the conflict of interest in the business model that the agencies employ, i.e. they are the agents of the issuer/structure not of the investor to whom they seem to owe no duty in law, would seem to have been one of the main reasons for the collapse of the subprime and the collateralised debt obligation markets. One has to consider that, in human nature, greed is a strong driving force and that, without the constraints provided by regulation, supervision and enforcement, situations with inherent conflicts of interest have led to unsatisfactory outcomes throughout history.

## RATING AGENCIES AND PRICING

Ratings agencies rate both countries (sovereigns) and the securities issued by private entities such as corporations. A corporate bond has a degree of credit risk which is generally reflected in its credit rating, i.e. a designation given to it by a rating agency (note it is the issue which is rated not the company itself, though the two are clearly related). The lead manager of the issue will price it on the basis of the yield on the Treasury bond closest in maturity to the proposed corporate issue plus the **credit risk premium** required to compensate the investor for the additional risk he or she is taking, which is known as the **spread over Treasury**. There are a number of rating agencies of which the best known are Moody's, Standard and Poors, and Fitch. They provide ratings both at the time of issue and during the life of the issue should their view of the appropriate rating change.

Ratings are 'opinions' of the relative credit risk of fixed-income obligations with an original maturity of one year or more. They address the possibility that a financial obligation will not be honoured as promised. Such ratings reflect both the likelihood of default and any financial loss suffered in the event of default.

Moody's Long-Term Rating Definitions:

**Aaa**  Obligations judged to be of the highest quality with minimal credit risk.

**Aa**  Obligations judged to be of high quality and subject to very low credit risk.

**A**  Obligations considered to be upper-medium grade and subject to low credit risk.

**Baa**  Obligations subject to moderate credit risk. They are considered medium grade and as such may possess certain speculative characteristics.

**Ba**  Obligations judged to have speculative elements and subject to substantial credit risk.

**B**  Obligations considered speculative and subject to high credit risk.

**Caa**  Obligations considered to be of poor standing and subject to high credit risk.

**Ca**  Obligations considered to be highly speculative and likely to be in, or very near to, default, with some prospect of recovery of principal and interest.

**C**  Obligations that are the lowest rated class of bonds and typically in default, with little prospect for recovery of principal or interest.

The other major rating agency is Standard and Poor which uses the ratings AAA, AA, A, BBB, BB, B, CCC, CC and C, corresponding with those above. In both scales, the first four ratings, i.e. down to Baa or BBB, are known as **investment grade**, while the ratings lower than this are known as **junk bond** or, less pejoratively, **high yield**. It would normally be expected that the spread over treasury of a bond would be a function of its rating, i.e. the lower the rating, the higher the expected yield. The difference between the ten-year treasury bond and the yield on the **high yield index** (index reflecting a wide range of high yield bonds) at the time of writing was around 7%.

## STANDARDISED MARKET PRACTICES – HISTORY OF ICMA

A key factor in enabling the growth of the international (debt) primary and secondary capital markets (the Eurobond market as it was known) in its early stages was the creation in 1969 of the Association of International Bond Dealers (AIBD) which is both a **trade association** (i.e. a collection of firms with a common interest) and a **self-regulatory organisation**. The International Primary Market Association (IPMA) was set up in 1984, out of its original incarnation as a committee of AIBD, as a separate organisation to enable a standardisation of rules and regulations in the primary (new issue) international bond market. In the secondary market AIBD had as its principal function in the early days the standardisation of bond trading practices in the international capital market. In 1992, AIBD changed its name to the International Securities Market Association (ISMA). In 2005 IPMA and ISMA joined together again and the new joint association was renamed the **International Capital Market Association (ICMA)**.[2]

---

[2]  See www.icmagroup.org

Without standardisation of practices, the market could not have grown to the size it has today. More particularly, it could not have become so international. The **International Swaps and Derivatives Association**, ICMA's equivalent in the derivatives markets, has as its main role the standardisation of contracts and trading procedures in the global swaps and derivatives markets and has enabled these markets to grow much faster than they otherwise could. Other market sectors have their own market regulators and trade associations which aid the process of standardisation. In addition, the market developed a new type of settlement organisation which enabled multi-currency clearing and settlement of trades in a more efficient and safer manner than would have been possible with the existing infrastructure in domestic markets. The two organisations which were created were Euroclear and Clearstream (formerly known as Cedel).

## INITIAL PUBLIC OFFERING OF EQUITY

An equity IPO involves a company changing its status from private company to public company. Public status results in changes in the financial reporting requirements (transparency), in the format of the annual general meeting, in press coverage of corporate events and other aspects of corporate life. There are a number of reasons why a company would choose to convert to a public company status despite its drawbacks:

- First, it enables the owners of the private company to '**cash out**' their investment in their company and realise cash for their shares. They may, for example, have reached retirement age. This has been a motivation in the case of private equity companies set up in the 1970s where the owners are of an age at which they wish to cash out.
- Second, it means that the company can **raise additional equity** capital either at the time of going public or subsequently in order to expand. This can facilitate the financing of acquisitions.

In addition to the above reasons there are a number of others:

- When there is a **privatisation**, i.e. the conversion of a company from **state ownership** (ownership by the government or a state agency) to **public company status**. An example would be the US Treasury which acquired AIG, the large insurance company, during the financial crisis. The government then offers it back to investors in an IPO (or may sell it to another company) at the time which it believes to be optimal to raise the most cash for the Treasury. The prime minister of the UK, Mrs Margaret Thatcher, was the first leader of a major country to commit to privatising almost all its state-owed companies. At the time (1979) this included British Petroleum (BP), British Gas, British Telecom and electricity. In the case of electricity, the whole industry was restructured at the same time so that instead of one company owning all the links in the vertical chain required to get power to consumers – gas, coal, oil, nuclear, wind and solar generation, national grid high voltage distribution (which was given monopoly rights), retail distribution – the three activities

were separated. In addition, any company could participate in retail distribution even though it had no power generation capacity. The privatisation rules
required all producers to sell to retailers at 'fair' prices.

• When a **private equity** company needs to realise its investments in portfolio
companies in order to return cash to fund investors and undertakes an IPOs
(and also what are known as trade sales which I explain below) of its various
businesses.

• When a public company wishes to dispose of a **division** of the company. This
may be because it has become so successful that it is believed to be worth
more than the total market capitalisation of the whole company but its value
is believed not to be reflected in the valuation of its shares on the market.
Alternatively it may be that the division no longer fits with the activities of the
rest of the company. Such disposals are often referred to as **carve outs, spin-
offs or demergers**. They involve creating another quoted company. After this
has been done, either the company can give the shares away at no charge to
its own shareholders (who are already the indirect owners) or it can float the
company in an IPO and keep the proceeds to use for reinvestment (on behalf of
its shareholders) in other new projects or return the proceeds to shareholders.
The case of AIA, the Asian arm of AIG, is one where initially management
decided to realise cash through an IPO in Hong Kong, then agreed to a trade
sale to Prudential Insurance of the UK. When this fell through they reverted to
their plan for an IPO.

• In the case of the large Chinese commercial banks an important reason for
obtaining a quotation on the Shanghai stock exchange and allowing a small free
float (most of the shares are still held by the Chinese state) was to help improve
corporate governance of these banks by introducing a limited degree of market
discipline.

While IPOs are a common way of realising cash from a private investment, from a
state-owned company or from a division of a public company, there is a very clear
alternative way of undertaking a cash realisation. This is to arrange a **trade sale**,
i.e. to sell the company to another company (public or private) which is willing
to pay a price comparable to, or higher, than the likely realisation from an IPO
(as was expected in the case of the planned sale of AIA to Prudential, referred to
above). At some points in the economic cycle a trade sale may realise more than
an IPO. At other times, the reverse is the case. Equally, a sale to a private equity
company (also frequently known as a buyout fund) may realise the highest offer
for a division of a company at times when the cost of capital to the private equity
industry is low. Once reason for the frequently higher valuation by potential investors in the case of a trade sale rather than an IPO is that an investor from the
same industry is likely to be able to realise economics of scale or scope from the
purchase. One reason why private equity companies (see Chapter 22) are sometimes willing to pay a higher price than trade investors or public investors in an
IPO is that if they have access to low cost debt, they may be willing to leverage the
acquisition so much that the effective cost of purchase to them is actually lower
than for other bidders. The benefit of such leverage may, however, turn out to
be illusory if interest rates rise (raising funding costs) or the economy goes into

recession (revenues fall). If this happens, the private equity firm may realise a loss when it sells the investment.

## HOW IS AN IPO UNDERTAKEN?

Normally the expression '**origination**' is used for the process of bringing together the two sides in a primary market (in contrast to the loan market where the term '**arranger**' is traditionally used) and thereby originating a first time issue of shares. Companies may also have subsequent issues of shares in order to increase the equity shares available on the market – called a **secondary offering**. Such issues do not raise the same problem as occurs with an IPO, namely of having to discover the price at which to issue them. As the shares are already trading in the secondary market, there is already a market price on the basis of which subsequent offerings (normally at a small discount to market price) can be sold.

Origination can be achieved by three different means:

1. direct financing between households and enterprises where the pooling of funds is achieved by the company itself (non-intermediated financing);[3]
2. brokerage (agency) intermediation between the two sides (intermediated financing);
3. capital intermediation (principal) between the two sides (intermediated financing).

Direct negotiation between a company and potential investors is unusual. In an intermediated offer, the first step is for the company to choose which investment bank will be the **lead manager**. This is the investment bank which organises the IPO. It is also known as the **bookrunner** as it manages the **book**, i.e. the list of all clients who are interested in the issue, the number of shares they wish to buy and what price they may be willing to pay. In the US domestic market managers are often called **underwriters**, a term which traditionally means that they take on price risk when they are involved in the management of an issue.

The department of the lead manager that coordinates the whole origination process is the **Equity Capital Markets** desk or, in the case of a debt issue, the **Debt Capital Markets** desk. The staff in the origination department (the Investment Banking Division) liaise principally with the issuing company's own staff to agree the structure of the deal. The people working in the origination department may also be known as corporate financiers or just 'bankers'. They don't liaise with investors (see Figure 11.1). On the other side of the market (the investor side) the distribution and syndication staff in the Sales and Trading Division liaise with investors to assess the market clearing price i.e. the price at which supply and demand will balance. Sales and Trading (secondary market) departments talk daily to institutional investors about a wide range of company shares. As it is these

---

[3] The John Lewis Partnership (one of the UK's largest store groups) in 2011 pooled funds directly from its staff and customers by issuing a retail bond which was not available to institutions and did not involve an investment bank underwriter.

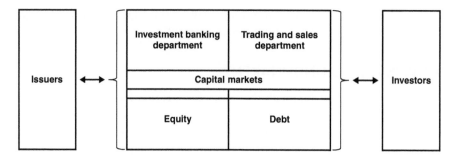

**Figure 11.1**   Bringing together issuers and investors within an investment bank

same investors who buy new issues, then it is easy for the sales people to talk also about a new issue and to gauge the likely price at which investors might buy.

New issues are normally offered not by one bank alone but by a **syndicate** (a group) of banks. Traditionally the reason for creating a syndicate was to pool funds from investors who otherwise could not be reached easily by the lead manager. Syndication also enabled risk spreading. In the past syndication was employed because lead managers (investment banks) were private partnerships and not highly capitalised and certainly not global in their reach. In order to widen their reach in the home market, reduce underwriting risk and sell overseas they would organise a syndicate of banks which enabled them to pool funds from a wider geographical region by accessing investors with whom they had no contact.

Today, the number of large institutional investors worldwide is relatively small compared to the size and global nature of the major investments banks, which today can access all the major institutions themselves. These institutions are, in turn, pooling funds from large numbers of households (from pension contributions, insurance premia and mutual fund purchases) and from smaller institutions. The 'distribution' reason for syndicates is therefore less strong than it was before. In terms of risk spreading, the major broker/dealers today all have sufficient capital to be able to take underwriting risk on all but the very largest of issues. In addition the time period between the announcement of the price of the issue and its sale is much shorter than in the past and continues to be shortened, thus greatly reducing the risk of a price fall between announcement and investor commitment. This reduces the likelihood of the underwriters having to take up unsold shares.

If syndicates are less important today in terms of the traditional reasons for forming a syndicate – widening the pool of investors to be tapped for funds and spreading the underwriting risk – then what is the reason for syndicates? It would seem to be the case that members of a syndicate are likely to allocate a researcher to an IPO when they are members of the syndicate. Doing so is important to the issuer and is likely to be helpful in supporting the price of the share in the secondary market. Issuers therefore like to see a number of banks in a syndicate as they believe it is beneficial to them to have as much current and future research output on their company as possible. This helps to avoid a company disappearing from public view shortly after the issue.

Perhaps most importantly, issuers who are trying to sell a 'difficult' issue at what may be too high a price, may try to involve (suborn) every major investment bank in order to try to avoid any negative research being published at the time of issue. This has been an important criticism of the new issue market structure in recent years when an issue has all the large investment banks within the syndicate and therefore none is likely to write a negative report for investors.

## Fees

Fees for IPOs vary greatly between international issues traded out of London and US domestic issues issued and traded out of Wall St. In the US the normal fee level for small company issues is 7% but falling as the size of the issue increases. Arranging IPOs is clearly potentially a very profitable activity provided the flow of new IPOs is sufficient to keep the investment bank's staff fully employed all the time. In the international market the fees are normally in the range of 3–5%, which still gives scope for substantial profits provided there are regular IPOs to structure.

These fees may seem high. One of the questions which competition authorities ask is whether or not there is any collusion between investment banks in the setting of IPO fees. It would seem that one reason fees are not generally competitively set is that companies value having a prestige underwriter to bring their issue to market and there are relatively few such **bulge bracket** investment banks today, i.e. the top seven or eight in the market, or more recently rather fewer. The term 'bulge bracket' is less used today than in the past, but today's bulge bracket firms would be Goldman Sachs, Morgan Stanley, JP Morgan, Bank of America Merrill Lynch, UBS, Deutsche Bank and, since its acquisition of the US interests of Lehman, Barclays. However, even UBS has found it difficult to remain, profitably, in the bulge bracket, at least in debt origination, and has already scaled back its ambitions in the global capital markets. Royal Bank of Scotland was attempting to enter the bulge bracket but has failed and is also scaling back very substantially.

The total fee represents a return for three services provided in connection with an IPO (with the figure in brackets the approximate percentage of the total fee for each service):

- management fee (20%);
- underwriting fee (20%);
- selling commission (60%).

The **management fee** rewards the bookrunner and any other lead managers for the work they do in bringing the company to market. However, in many instances, the bookrunner also takes what is known as a *praecipium*, which is an over-ride on the management fee before any other managers are given a share. This can be up to 50% of the management fee and thus makes being the bookrunner potentially a very profitable role.

The **underwriting fee** is, in theory, compensation for taking on the risk of guaranteeing the company an agreed price for the shares. At one time the risk was substantial but today, with most issues priced on the basis of a book-building process, the risk is relatively small. However, much of the underwriting fee may be taken up with the cost of what is known as **stabilisation**. This is the process whereby the bookrunner may buy back shares from the market in order to support the price in the days (up to 30 days) after the issue to minimise any price fall. The price at which the bookrunner is willing to do this is known as the **syndicate bid**. However, in some markets it is illegal to undertaken such price support as it is viewed as market manipulation by the regulatory authorities. If it is allowed, there will be strict rules as to how it is achieved.

The **selling commission** is paid to all those in the syndicate and not only the selling group (co-managers). Those who are in the selling group receive only selling commission and not underwriting or management fees as they are not involved in taking risk or management. However, in many syndicates there will be no selling group as this category is no longer considered so necessary, given that most banks have access to a wide range of clients.

## IPO PRICING

In a secondary market, there are many buyers and sellers who interact in a **double-auction**, i.e. buyers compete against each other to offer the best price to sellers and sellers compete against each other to offer the best price to buyers. This interactive auction process results in a continuous **price discovery process**. In an IPO, in contrast, as the shares have not traded before, there is no history of the price which balances supply and demand, no market from which to discover the price, and only one seller facing multiple buyers. There are essentially three methods by which price can be determined, each of which is analysed in what follows.

### Fixed Price Offer

In order to determine the price at which the issue should be made, the manager will undertake comparison of the company with other 'comparable' companies. For example, if it is a food distributor which is being priced, other food distributors which are already trading in the secondary market can be used to suggest an appropriate **price earnings multiple (P/E)**, i.e. the price of the share as a multiple of profits, for this type of company. The company can then be priced based on these 'comparables'. This approach was explained in the Appendices on valuation in Chapter 1. However, this type of exercise, though it may result in successful pricing, frequently does not. It is a type of exercise that can be conducted by an intern in an investment bank who has a good technical training in finance but no feel for markets.

The essential feature of a fixed price offer is that the offer price is set without any **price discovery process**, i.e. a process in which supply and demand interact in order to determine the **market clearing** price (the price at which demand takes up all the supply).

### Book building

It is the extent of investor interest at any particular price level which will determine the **market clearing price**, i.e. the price at which supply and demand are in balance. If the true market clearing price is discovered, then the issue would be expected to trade in the secondary market, immediately after the issue, **at the issue price** – neither above nor below.

One way to try to discover the market clearing price is to create a pseudo-market by asking potential investors to provide the issuing house with their **demand schedule**, i.e. how much they would buy at various price levels. In theory this method should result in prices closer to subsequent equilibrium than the fixed price method. In practice it is also the most commonly used method. Normally, using this method, the issuing house suggests an indicative price range, say 210–250p, rather than a single price, and then asks potential investors at which end of the range they would be likely to bid. It might be thought that investors would not give an honest answer to such a question. In practice, however, because investors want to keep good continuing relationships with issuing houses, they generally do not try to mislead. This is similar behaviour to that on eBay where those who want to transact in future want to build a good reputation for honesty and reliability in their ongoing transactions.

## Auction

Neither the fixed price method of pricing nor bookbuilding can guarantee an issue price close to equilibrium. There is, however, a third method that should properly equate supply and demand. This is the auction. In an auction, investors, whether retail or wholesale, simply indicate the number of shares they wish to purchase and the price they will pay. The auctioneer (the lead manager) then simply works down the demand schedule, descending in price, until the **clearing price** is reached at which the whole issue can be sold. The actual price paid by investors can be either on the basis of **pay as bid** (the investor pays the amount he or she has bid) or it can be a **uniform price** (each bidder pays the clearing price, not the price he or she bid). The largest such auction to date was Google (in 2004). In this case, Google itself ran the auction, not an investment bank, though one was involved in advising on the prospectus for the issue. Auctions are not popular with investment bankers as it cuts them out of a substantial fee income.

If there is no **money left on the table**, i.e. the price at the end of the first day's trading is the same as the issue price, investment bankers feel their investor clients have not done well. Jay Ritter[4] quotes a first day **premium** (mean first day return) of 23% on US IPOs for the period 1990–2004. This means that an investor who received an allocation of all new issues in this period and sold them the same day as he or she was allocated them, would have made a mean return of 23% from less than a day's investment. On the other hand, those selling the shares, i.e. the owners of what was a private company, who are, in fact, the **actual** clients of the issuing department of the investment bank who are paying for the issuing service, are receiving approximately 23% less than the company could have been sold for. Thus pricing is a contest between the sellers, i.e. the owners of the company, and the investors (who are also clients of the issuing house), in which it would seem that the investors almost always do well, at least initially. One reason for this is

---

[4]  See Jay Ritter's homepage (http://bear.cba.ufl.edu/ritter/).

that institutional investors are long-term clients of the investment bank whereas the issuer undertakes an IPO only once. Thus the investment bank may be more concerned with rewarding its investor base in order to keep them as clients than with ensuring that the issuing company receives the market equilibrium price for the shares it is selling. Although 23% was the average over the 14 years from 1990–2004, during the dot-com boom, under-pricing was frequently much more dramatic – sometimes over 200%. The modern, integrated, investment bank, as we have already noted, faces both ways – it has two or more masters, not, as in the past, clients on only one side of the gap across which it is intermediating. It also, of course, has the in-house proprietary trading desk as a client.

## THE WORLD'S LARGEST IPO – AG BANK – A CASE STUDY

**AgBank IPO Raises $19.2 Billion: July 7, 2010**

It was established by Mao Zedong for China's rural peasants. But on Tuesday, the Agricultural Bank of China embraced a capitalist's dream: it went public. In a move that would have been unimaginable in Mao's time, the Chinese bank sold $19.2 billion of stock in Hong Kong and Shanghai, The New York Times's Michael Wines reports. The offering could grow to $22.1 billion – the largest in history.

The Agricultural Bank was the latest in a long series of Chinese companies to go public since China reopened its stock markets 20 years ago. But its sale, which defied the running turmoil in the world's financial markets, cemented China's position as this year's leader in initial public offerings and, by extension, underscored its economic and financial might. The sale valued the Agricultural Bank at about $128 billion – more than Citigroup or Goldman Sachs.

The bank's shares were sold simultaneously in Hong Kong and Shanghai. In Hong Kong, the stock was priced at about 3.20 Hong Kong dollars each, in the middle of the expected range. In Shanghai, the Class A shares – which only Chinese nationals can buy – were priced at 2.68 renminbi,[5] the high end of expectations. The shares start trading in mid-July. The sale had been widely seen as a measure of confidence in China's economic prospects, and was once believed capable of fetching $30 billion. But the reception was dimmed by a rout in the Shanghai stock market, growing worries about a slowdown in China's economy and concerns about the bank's assets and growth prospects.

For now, the honour of the largest I.P.O. remains with another state-controlled bank, the Industrial and Commercial Bank of China, which raised $21.9 billion in October 2006. Diminished or not, Tuesday's sale continued a string of I.P.O.s by companies in emerging markets, which have underscored both the economic weakness of rich nations and the rising economic clout of developing countries. Virtually all the biggest I.P.O.s of 2010 have been outside the United States and Western Europe. It also

---

[5] The price in May 2012 was 2.76 renminbi.

continues China's winning streak in global markets. More than one-third of new listings this year have come from Chinese companies, up from one-quarter in 2009.

Most economic experts on China predict that the big banks will be saddled with another wave of nonperforming assets as the wild lending spree of the last two years produces a new crop of sour loans. Investors know this. Yet the Agricultural Bank I.P.O., like the ones preceding it, has been heavily subscribed, in part because virtually everyone believes the government is locked into ensuring the bank's success. Major government-controlled corporations are among the early subscribers to the issue.

*New York Times* 'Dealbook', 6 July 2010

In fact, the shares reached a high of 2.98 renminbi but in Sept 2011 were trading below the issue price at 2.46 renminbi.

## GLENCORE

The IPO of the commodities house Glencore in May 2011 is one where the price range suggested prior to fixing the actual price would seem to have allowed the possibility of a substantial premium as the shares moved to secondary market. The initial price range was between 480p and 580p per share, giving it a mid-point valuation of $61 billion (£36.5 billion). The CEO, Ivan Glasenberg, was said to want to ensure a good after-IPO performance, implying that he had instructed the issuing house to underprice. One banker is quoted in the *Financial Times* as saying 'there is huge demand from institutional investors but Glencore is ready to leave money on the table to secure a great deal.' A little later the price range was narrowed to 520–550p. The offer price was 530p. At the end of the first day's trading the price was still 530p – i.e. a perfectly estimated equilibrium price. Within a month of issue the shares were trading at only 452p. So what was the correct price? Was it the floatation price or was that (artificially) supported by the issue manager buying in the market? The floatation was **London's largest**, and the shares are also quoted in Hong Kong. In May 2012, the shares were trading at 340p.

## FACEBOOK

Facebook came to market just before this book went to press. Valuation of such a company is particularly difficult and was much discussed in the press[6]. One problem with such businesses is that competitors can easily enter the market. If they happen to offer something slightly different which millions of people world-wide prefer, the new company may become the 'cool' one to use and growth will cease at the old one. Even a company such as Facebook with 900 million customers is vulnerable to this phenomenon.

There is another equally fundamental problem with companies such as Facebook. While they do not need have factories and machinery as traditional manufacturing companies do, they nonetheless have huge capital investment needs in terms of servers (and also capitalised research and development costs).

---

[6] See, for example, 'Lex in Depth – Facebook' *Financial Times* 3 May 2012.

At the time of the issue, capital expenditure was consuming half of revenues – an unusually high proportion.

The IPO price was initially set to be within the range of $28-$35 at which levels, the company would be worth between $70bn and $87.5 bn. This is less than many analysts expected with some estimates being as high as $100bn. To be worth this latter sum would require that the company maintain its 50% sales margin, cut back capital spending as a percentage of revenue, and increase revenues by around six times today's level within five to seven years – possible but is it likely? In fact, just before the issue on 18 May, 2012, the underwriters raised the price range to $34 - $38 and also increased the number of shares on offer. At the time of issue, the price which was set was at the top of this range i.e. $38. The reason was said to be the huge amount of retail investor interest. So many people with Facebook accounts also wanted to own the shares almost regardless of the fact that 'scientific' pricing would suggest that this price was too high for this number of shares.

In fact, Facebook shares only maintained their price on the day of issue as a result of the lead underwriter, Morgan Stanley, buying back substantial volumes of shares in the market (price stabilisation function). Within a few days the price had fallen as low as $32. You should look up Facebook on Google to find out more about the issue and its subsequent price performance.

## BOND ORIGINATION: SOVEREIGN AND CORPORATE

There are substantial differences between government issuers (sovereigns) and corporate issuers. Governments normally have the highest rating in a country (except perhaps in times of crisis) and therefore should command the finest borrowing rates in their own currency. Of course, if they are not borrowing in their own currency they may not be able to borrow at the best rates. If they are members of the eurozone, for example, they are borrowing in a currency over which they have little, if any, control. In the eurozone it has been noticeable that some companies have been able to borrow at lower rates than the government.

All government bond issues from a particular country have equal credit standing, unlike corporate bonds where different bonds can have different levels of priority/seniority in the cash flow waterfall (divided cash flow). Government issues are also generally much larger than corporate issues, which makes them more easily tradable and, indeed, much more widely traded.

Governments are also generally unwilling to pay high fees to investment banks for providing issuing services of the type they provide to corporates. Instead, most governments designate what they term **primary dealers**, which are the members of the 'elite' group of investment banks who provide assistance to the country's finance ministry at the time of an issue. Normally an auction would be held at which the primary dealers would bid for the bonds on offer.

In the case of a government bond, there are no specific assets backing it, nor is there a process for recovery of any value if the government refuses to make good on its contract with investors. Also unlike a company which can declare bankruptcy or where liability holders can force it into liquidation, there is no bankruptcy process for countries. In an era when the possibility of default on government debt issued by a number of sovereigns is high, a study of the sovereign default process is critical for investors (see Chapter 16). Corporate bonds, on the other hand, may have collateral behind them. All companies have assets which can be liquidated to meet obligations to creditors. In addition, so-called covered bonds issued by Continental European banks and others have specific security (collateral) as well as full rights to asset realisations in any liquidation. Thus when evaluating a corporate bond it is necessary to estimate the probability of default and also the potential loss of value, i.e. the LGD. I cover the questions that arise in the event of default in more detail in Chapter 16.

# PART III

# SECONDARY MARKETS: MARKET LIQUIDITY AND MARKET FAILURE

# 12 MARKET LIQUIDITY: ORDER-DRIVEN AUCTION MARKETS AND QUOTE-DRIVEN DEALER MARKETS

## WHAT IS TRADING AND WHY TRADE?

Any asset – real or financial – whether a motor car, a house, shares or an item on eBay, can be **traded**, i.e. bought or sold in exchange for cash. Motor cars can be bought and sold, relatively slowly, through newspaper 'small adverts' or eBay or an immediate sale can be achieved through sale to a motor dealer; a house by advertising in the property section of a newspaper or through an estate agent (realtor). Any of these means of sale are, in effect, '**search engines**', i.e. a means by which those who wish to buy or sell something can search for each other and, having found each other, agree a price for sale then execute the sale by the exchange of the asset for cash. There are two problems with such transactions. The first is how to agree on the price, which is difficult when an advertisement in the newspaper is used and only one person may respond but which is relatively easy on eBay if an auction is used and many people bid. The second problem is credit risk, i.e. handing over goods before receiving money, or handing over money before receiving goods. Systems like PayPal, as used by eBay, aim to minimise such problems in web-based transactions. In securities markets, mechanisms such as **payment against delivery** (see Chapter 14) are used try to minimise this risk.

The ownership interest in any small private business or company can be bought and sold by the owners privately, provided they can find someone willing to take up their offer to buy or sell. Searching for 'the other side of a trade' can be undertaken by talking to friends, making one's interest known through, for example, a trade association, using a website, or by employing an agent (a broker) who specialises in organising such sales or purchases. In the case of a **public company** (plc in the UK) or **publicly held company** (corporation in the US), where the registration requirements of some agency have been complied with (for example, the Securities and Exchange Commission in the US), the securities will be **listed**. Listing standards normally cover matters such as the minimum capital that the company must have, the number of years since business commenced, the percentage of capital that is free to trade, and the financial reporting requirements (i.e. publication of accounts). Buying and selling of ownership interests then takes place on a market to which the public have access, rather than in the informal way in which owners of private companies might buy and sell.

**Listing** is simply the addition of the name of a company to a 'list' under which the company agrees to follow a set of rules and in return can have its ownership interests traded under those rules. In some countries the listing authority is quite separate from any 'stock exchange', particularly when there are multiple stock exchanges. This is the case in the UK where the agency is the FSA. If such is the case, then a company will normally also require to be **admitted to trading**, i.e. obtain permission to have its securities traded on a **regulated market** (an exchange which is formally recognised as such by the regulatory authority)[1] However, once a company is listed its shares can then also be traded on other execution venues, even without the permission of the company. Companies usually have a **primary listing exchange**, i.e. the one on which most of their trading, at least initially, takes place, but they may also have secondary i.e. additional listings, often in overseas markets such as New York or Hong Kong. However, such listings are becoming rarer as it has become easier to trade from anywhere in the world without the need for a local listing. One type of secondary listing is that of foreign shares in New York using American Depository Receipts (ADRs). These are certificates evidencing the underlying holding of foreign shares but the certificates are denominated in US dollars and dividends are also paid in dollars.

## TRADERS: BUY-SIDE AND SELL-SIDE

### Buy-side trader: working for an investment institution

The first traditional distinction between trader types is between those operating on the so-called buy-side from those operating on the so-called sell-side. Mostly, those on the **buy-side** work for asset management houses. These houses buy new securities issues (IPOs and new debt securities) and that is why they are called buy-side. But they also **buy *and* sell** from their investment portfolio in the secondary market in order to try to achieve their investment objectives. Thus the term 'buy-side' is actually quite misleading but remains the market terminology. It came into existence because the investment banks were the selling side of IPOs who sold new issues to investors who were thus the buy-side of the transaction.

It is important to distinguish two separate functions within an asset management house:

- The **portfolio manager** is the person who makes decisions on which securities to include in, or remove from, a portfolio. He or she is concerned with the long-term prospects of the security, based generally on the use of **fundamental analysis**, i.e. examining the macro-environment for the industry and the particular prospects of a company in that industry.

---

[1] Issuers apply to the UK Listing Authority which is part of the FSA for admission to the Official List and to the London Stock Exchange for admission to trading on their markets.

- The **buy-side trader** is the person who actually executes the transactions that the portfolio manager has decided on. One of the key skills required by a buy-side trader is the ability to achieve a good execution of the trade.. The buy-side trader is concerned only with short-term movements in the price of the security in order to try to buy and sell at the most advantageous point(s) in the trading day(s) using the most appropriate order types and, if necessary, splitting large orders into smaller parts (known as **slicing and dicing** or **shredding**). The initial large order is sometimes called the **parent order** and the smaller parts into which it is split, the **child orders**. Order placing strategies have had to become much more sophisticated with the advent of multiple execution venues, the availability of limit orders as well as market orders, and the possibility of using dark pools as covered in the next chapter.

A common distinction made by sell-side traders in the investment bank, when they are transacting with the buy-side, is between retail clients and professional or wholesale clients. **Retail** clients are traditionally small investors who are assumed not to be highly knowledgeable about markets and securities and who do not derive a high proportion of their total income from trading. **Wholesale** clients, on the other hand, are deemed to be **professionals** who are assumed to have an expert knowledge of markets and securities and earn their living from working in the markets as asset managers. Retail clients are likely to make relatively small trades (retail sized) which are not likely to have any impact on prices in a market. Professional clients on the other hand are likely to be transacting in large size as they work for institutions which are investing funds aggregated by pooling from hundreds or thousands of individuals. They are sometimes known in official documentation as **Big Boys** meaning that they can take care of themselves. Their large trades can easily affect market prices in a direction which is detrimental to their investment performance. They are also known as **counterparties** rather than clients because they are fellow professional traders.

A second buy-side distinction is between **long-term investors** and **professional traders**. The SEC distinguishes between these thus:[2]

- **Long-term investors** are the market participants who provide capital investment to companies and are willing to accept the risk of ownership in listed companies for an extended period of time.
- **Professional traders** generally seek to establish and liquidate positions in a shorter time frame, even as short as microseconds. Professional traders often have different interests than investors who are concerned about the long-term prospects of a company. However, the expression 'shorter time frame' is difficult to define in practice.

## Motivations for buy-side trading

It is important to understand that there is no absolute need for the trading of securities. Investors could simply **buy-and-hold**, i.e. employ a strategy that, once

---

[2]  See 'SEC Concept Release on Equity Market Structure', January 2010.

a security had been purchased, it would be kept for the income derived from it (dividends or interest income). This is the strategy employed by someone who is thought to be the world's most successful investor, Warren Buffet of Berkshire Hathaway. He has seldom been known to trade shares which he has bought for his fund.

Debt securities in particular are often bought by buy-and-hold investors. Because they have a fixed life, when they mature the principal amount of the investment is returned to the investor in cash. This cash can then be reinvested in new securities of the same issuer, i.e. **rolled-over**, and these new securities held until they mature. In the case of equity securities held by an individual, these could be kept until death and then passed on as part of the deceased's estate to the next generation. Indeed, in many countries, a high proportion of investors do operate this way as buy-and-hold investors. As a result the markets in such countries are not liquid simply because those who hold securities have no wish to trade them. This applies particularly to emerging markets in countries where wealth is unevenly distributed and the holders of securities comprise a very small proportion of the population. As ownership of a certain proportion of equity securities also gives rights of control of a company, many holders who are also actively involved in the management of a company may be unwilling to trade their securities and thereby risk losing management control. Where a family or other grouping has a large holding which is not traded, the amount that is free to trade in the public market is known as the **free float**.

For the purpose of analysis and when using a trading simulation, motivations for investor trading can be dichotomised as either:

- **Liquidity-motivated**, which means that an investor simply wants to exchange securities for cash or vice versa for **idiosyncratic** reasons, i.e. reasons peculiar to that investor, such as investing funds from inheritance or disinvesting in order to pay for a child's university education or, in the case of a derivative contract, to close it because the risk management need for the derivative is no longer relevant. Liquidity-motivated investors are known as **price takers** as they accept the price in the market as the price at which they must deal.
- **Information-motivated**, which implies that the investor is trading into or out of a security or contract because of a belief that it is either underpriced or overpriced. These are generally **price makers**. Fund managers who aim to generate an investment performance superior to the market as a whole (outperformance) only deal in what they believe to be mispriced securities, i.e. they invest in specific securities if they believe they are underpriced, and sell only if they believe any particular security is overpriced. In theory at least, liquidity-motivated traders lose out to such information-motivated traders if the information the latter have is correct.

In the case of liquidity-motivated traders, there is normally likely be an approximate balance between those who wish to invest and those who wish to disinvest for their own, idiosyncratic reasons. However, if they do no research to try to estimate the value of the securities in which they wish to transact, they have to accept the price on the market. In consequence, the price on the market is determined by the information-motivated traders – those who do have a view on the 'true' value of the security. They are the ones who are **price makers**, whereas the liquidity traders have to be **price takers**. The function of a trading centre or execution venue is to enable price makers and price takers to interact in a **price discovery process**.

The key theory of markets – **the EMH** – states, as we have noted earlier, that the current price of an asset represents the best estimate of the **true** price of the asset on the basis of all known public information. Thus, a security is as likely to rise in price as fall over a future period, i.e. price movements follow a **random walk**. As a result, the best estimate of the future price of any particular security is its current price. Traditionally we would also add that prices follow a random walk with a **positive drift component**, which means that we expect markets to trend secularly upwards over time. This has not, however, proved to be the case over the period from 2000 to 2011. The expression 'random walk' does not imply that markets are random or irrational. Indeed it is the consequence of investors being rational and reacting immediately to unpredictable news which has implications for the value of the asset, which is equally as likely to be positive as negative. Thus, if, in the absence of new information about its value, it deviates from this price – let us call this the **fundamental value** or **true value** – then traders will enter the market and drive it back to the price that reflects its fundamental value. This is based on the assumption of the rational expectations hypothesis, i.e. that investors act in their own best economic interest and hence ensure that markets are 'efficient', meaning assets trading on it are correctly priced.

While a belief that the trader has information that others do not have may be the reason for someone trying to execute a trade, equally a trade may simply be a liquidity trade. For the trader potentially on the other side, therefore, there is a problem of trying to discern the **motivation** of the trader in order to avoid trading with a **better-informed counterparty**. If the better-informed counterparty was correct in his or her view of the direction in which prices would move, then whoever he or she has traded with will subsequently lose money on the trade or at least suffer an opportunity loss – a trade which would not have been executed (at least not at that point in time or at that price) if he or she had also had the relevant information. These two motivations for trading – as a result of a need to change an investor's liquidity profile or trading on the basis of fundamental analysis – both lead to transactions based on **exogenous** factors, i.e. factors external to the trading market itself.

There is a third motivation for trading which is based on what is known as **technical analysis**. This is based on **endogenous** factors, i.e. factors within the market itself. Technical analysts believe that past patterns of prices can indicate future movements and, if such a trading style is profitable, refutes the efficient market hypothesis.

Technical analysis involves studying charts of past price patterns to try to predict future ones. This is the reason why technical analysis is also known as **chartism**. Chartists do not believe that markets are random and instead believe that there is a certain amount of predictability about them. The fundamentals of a company are thus largely ignored. Many traders can be found who use both fundamental and technical analysis. I myself do not believe that traditional chartism can lead to superior investment performance for a given level of risk over a sustained period of time but over shorter periods of time it can be remarkably successful.

Momentum traders, who are to some extent at least chartists, believe that they can detect when prices are moving up because other traders see an upturn and are buying into it. There is some evidence that such traders win over time in actively traded markets. There are also similarities between technical traders and high-frequency traders who are also looking at patterns but in a shorter time frame – patterns caused by 'frictions' in the trading process itself.

## The sell-side trader: working for a broker/dealer

Within an investment bank the sell-side trader is the intermediary between the market and the investor. There are two capacities in which someone on the sell-side may be transacting with a client – either as an agent or as a principal. First, as an **agent**. This means someone who has a **fiduciary** duty to his or her client. This is the duty to act, not for their own or their firm's profit, but to safeguard the interests of the client. A broker does not take **principal** positions, i.e. ownership of investments on his or her or the firm's account but trades purely on behalf of clients. He or she would thus try to source the required security (if the client wished to purchase) or find a buyer for it (if a sell) at the best possible price for his or her client or counterparty. This would be achieved by going to whichever market(s) traded this security and attempting to find the best price at which the trade could be executed (**best execution**). This is the traditional definition of best execution, though today it means the best set of features, depending on client wishes. Features include speed of execution (known as **immediacy**), maximum size of transaction that is possible at the price, willingness to wait to transact at a later time at a better price, lower commission percentage and lower settlement cost. Normally a sell-side person operating as an agent would be called a broker or, more frequently today, a salesperson.

Brokers have an additional function beyond simply helping a client to access a market indirectly. This is the **trade guarantee** function. A market will not normally allow those without known credit reputation (i.e. ability to pay) to deal in the market. If they were unable to pay or to deliver securities, trades would fail and the market would suffer reputation loss. Thus brokers take on this important role of ensuring trades do not fail because of customer credit or other problems. Providing this guarantee function, just like the function of finding buyers for sellers and sellers for buyers, aids the creation of liquidity. Electronic brokers for retail investors do not, of course, have this problem since they can confirm the credit status of a trader before executing a trade simply by requiring the client to first deposit with them the funds which they intend to use for trading.

The second capacity in which someone on the sell-side may be transacting with a client is as **principal**. In this case the sell-side trader is acting as a **dealer**, i.e. someone who trades in securities, not to generate investment returns from holding the securities for long periods, but to generate short-term gains from selling to and buying from buy-side counterparties in such a way that he sells on average at a higher price than he buys. He trades with the intention of making a good return on capital employed through providing a service to buy-side counterparties, i.e.

**the provision of liquidity**. He does this by making **quotes**, i.e. two prices – a buy (**bid**) price (quote) and a sell (**offer** or **ask**) price (quote), separated by the **spread** from which he hopes to make a margin. For this reason, this type of market is often known as a **quote-driven market**. Such markets as we have already noted are also called **dealer markets, OTC markets** or **bilateral markets**. The essential feature of dealer markets is that they are bilateral and not multilateral. The dealer normally does not have fiduciary responsibilities to its counterparties as these are almost always professional traders, not retail clients who would transact through a broker.

Normally when a buy-side trader asks a market maker for a price, she expects the dealer to give her a two-way price, for example 93–94, meaning the dealer is willing to buy from her at 93 or sell to her at 94. This minimises the risk of exploitative pricing, i.e. guessing or knowing which way the counterparty wants to trade, and worsening the price quoted on that side of the market. However, when markets are illiquid, a dealer will ask what the counterparty wants to do, i.e. which side of the market, buy or sell and then offer to try to do it at the best price he or she can.

The investment bank trading division is known as the **broker/dealer** business, i.e. it employs people who operate as salespersons (brokers) as well as those who make markets in securities for clients to trade against. This is known as **dual capacity** to distinguish it from **single capacity**, i.e. offering only a broking service or a dealing service, which was the normal market structure in many countries until relatively recently.[3] In addition, investment banks employ sales/traders who may perform both functions simultaneously but must inform the client in which capacity they are acting. Investment banks are often simply called broker/dealers as a shorthand term even though they perform many other functions.

The term (official) **market maker** generally refers to a dealer who operates under a set of rules, such as those of a **regulated market** (traditionally a stock exchange), and who is bound by its rules. Market makers may have **affirmative obligations**, i.e. things they are obliged to do for the market as a result of their role. These obligations would generally require the official market maker to maintain **two-way quotes**, i.e. a bid and an offer in a certain minimum size in those securities in which he or she is registered as a market maker during official market opening hours. Thus dealers and market makers are performing the same role. The only difference is in their obligations, if any.

A dealer or market maker is a professional (short-horizon) trader and not a long-term investor. Today, market makers are increasingly not humans but 'robotic' dealers that use computer algorithms to initiate trades and use high frequency trading and low latency technology to enable them to act as market makers and provide liquidity on exchanges. I will cover this in the next chapter. Human dealers are now rare in equity markets in Western countries for standard

---

[3] A principal outcome of the transformation of the London Stock Exchange market at the time of Big Bang in 1986 (when fixed equity trading commissions were abolished) was the conversion of the market from single to dual capacity and the entry into the market for the first time of the large US broker/dealers who already had extensive experience of this market structure.

trades and are increasingly disappearing from other markets. However, the algorithms have to be programmed by people who understand trading extremely well. Thus the algorithmic programmers are the new dealers.

# TYPE OF TRADER: PASSIVE AND ACTIVE – LONG, SHORT AND ARBITRAGE

## Passive

Some traders operate by simply accepting the market price as the 'true' price. They don't look for under- or overpriced shares (or other securities). They are liquidity investors seeking either to increase their liquidity by converting securities to cash or to reduce their liquidity by converting cash into securities. They are quite likely to use passive indexed investment funds (see Chapter 18) to realise their investment objectives rather than **stock picking**, i.e. actively selecting individual shares. Such funds, in turn, are managed on a passive basis and simply involve buying the shares that are in a particular index at whatever price they are trading at on the market.

## Active

The other type of trader, the **active** trader, is looking for mispricing. Generally this means mis-pricing of individual securities but it can also, as we will see shortly, mean the mispricing of one security relative to another. Only if a security is mispriced, either over or under, is he or she likely to be interested in it. 'Mispriced' means that the trader disagrees with the market consensus, which is what determines the market price. Such a trader will only buy shares which he believes are underpriced. He then hopes to sell them when they reach the 'true' price. Thus he is betting against the market and saying to the other traders in that market 'you have got it wrong but when you come to agree with my view, I will sell the security to you at the "true" price'. Thus he hopes to buy when the security is mispriced at too low a level and sell when it reaches the 'true' price, take his profit and reinvest the proceeds of the sale in another mispriced security.

There are also traders, generally within hedge funds, who will look, additionally, for securities which they believe to be **overpriced**. They will then sell these short and buy them back later when, or if, the market comes to agree with them and the price moves down to the trader's estimate of the true price. **Going short** on a share, i.e. selling something you don't own and only buying it later at a lower price, will be covered in Chapter 17.

Another type of trader looks for arbitrages. Arbitrage traders are active traders who believe that:

- two securities which generally have a close relationship to each other are mispriced **relative** to each other and that by buying the underpriced and selling (shorting) the overpriced (known as **pairs trading**) and waiting until the prices move back to their historical equilibrium to reverse the trade, a profit will be made or;
- the same security which trades in two different market centres can be bought in one at a lower price (perhaps on the BATS market as discussed in Chapter

13) and sold immediately in the other (perhaps the London Stock Exchange) at a higher price or;

- a basket of shares such as that contained in units of an exchange traded fund can be purchased and then broken up into the underlying individual shares which can then be sold for more than the unit cost or;
- the cash market security and the future or option on that same security are mispriced relative to each other and thus create an arbitrage profit opportunity.

## Exogenous and endogenous factors in mispricing

We have to distinguish two different reasons for mispricing.

First, there are factors exogenous to the market, i.e. fundamental economic and company specific factors. It is the function of securities analysts to try to examine fundamental factors and to evaluate how they will impact on particular countries, industry sectors, specific firms and specific securities issued by that firm. Each analyst will have his or her own view on what are the important factors and how these impact on any particular company and hence on the 'true' share price. Analysts will come to different views as to the 'true' price. If others trade on the basis of their analysis some will buy because the analyst they employ believes the security to be underpriced, some will sell because the analyst they employ believes it is overpriced, and others will not trade because they believe it is correctly priced.

Second, there are factors endogenous to the market, i.e. features of the market mechanism and the resulting frictions within the trading process itself which give rise to opportunities to buy at one price and sell at another price over short periods of time. We must recognise that the markets in which traders are active are not simply black boxes of the type that economists call a **perfect market**. This hypothetical (and very useful) construct is one without any trading **frictions**. It is assumed, for example, that all participants have perfect knowledge and the same knowledge. It is also assumed that no one participant has the market power enabling him or her to set prices. In such a market, also, there is no concept of a bid-offer spread nor of orders being large relative to the normal market trading size and thus likely to influence the equilibrium price.

The conditions of the perfect market result in what is known as **perfect competition**. In real markets, however, the assumptions of the perfect market do not hold and so we do not have perfect competition in real securities markets and hence there may be temporary short-term mispricings which traders may be able to exploit for profit.

Dealers and market makers are a class of trader who exploit the fact that competition in markets is not perfect and therefore that there are frictions. The existence of dealers tells us there are frictions since they aim to buy at a lower price and sell at a higher one in a short time.

I have also mentioned so-called technical trading or chartism. This too involves trading on factors endogenous to the market, namely price patters over some previous time period. This is, however, quite different from dealer market activity. Dealers exploit market frictions, which are unrelated to whether or not the EMH describes market pricing correctly. Chartists believe they can exploit **historical** patterns, i.e. they do not believe in the EMH.

## Time period between purchase and sale

Another distinction between types of trader involves the time span over which they expect their trading strategy to realise a profit, thereby allowing them to unwind their position(s). There are no clear dividing lines between these time spans or even between the strategies employed. But while strategies all differ, trading always involves (or should involve) a preplanned strategy which is designed to exploit either fundamental data (exogenous) or analysis of market data itself (endogenous), i.e. prices at which it is possible to trade (pre-trade transparency), prices at which trades have been executed (post-trade transparency) and trading volumes in particular securities over some short period of time.

We have already noted one distinction that the SEC uses – that between long-term investors and professional traders – though that distinction does not detail time spans. But a rough set of criteria would be as below:

### Traders concerned with the fundamentals of an asset

**Long-term investors** such as pension funds and mutual funds may have a time horizon of 12 months or more between the time they open a position (buy) and close it (sell). The turnover of their portfolio would then be 100% per year. They hope that within their time horizon the share will outperform the market. Thus it is being purchased below what they consider its true value and being sold when it has reached what they believe to be its true value. Investors who try to detect shares which are mis-priced are known as active investors. However, amongst this group there are very different strategies employed. Thus some may turn over their portfolio only once every four years or even more, while others may turn it over four or more times per year. Warren Buffet of Berkshire Hathaway is a long-term investor but with an average holding period of many years. He is considered by many to be the most successful investor of his era. His philosophy is to buy (the correct securities) and then hold on to them. He is a buy-and-hold investor, not a trading investor. In consequence his transaction costs are very low.

**Medium-term institutional investors** such as hedge funds employ strategies which may, amongst other things, concern fundamental values, but also relative values, of two assets. If their strategies are successful, their positions can be closed within a relatively short period of time (within a day, week, weeks or months) and profit realised. (For more on hedge funds, see Chapter 18.)

### Professional traders not concerned with long-term fundamentals

**Short-term traders** are those who might hold positions for a period of from a few hours to overnight to possibly a few days. Traditionally, a good example of such traders would be retail 'day-traders' who were once able to make small profits during a day and might operate from a trading 'arcade', i.e. a company which offers access to markets and clearing and settlement services. Market makers are short-term traders who hold positions open for as short a time as they can before closing them with another client or, if this is not possible, with another market maker. They may of course be forced to hold positions for longer than this if they cannot close-out within a day.

**Ultra-short-term traders** (high-frequency traders) are those who enter orders into a trading centre (such as BATS) and aim to close the position they took on within microseconds, or a few seconds at most. They may provide market-making type services but, unlike traditional market makers, they do not have clients. This is because they do not trade bilaterally with clients (as traditional market makers do) since they simply post their limit orders – bids and offers – anonymously (as all traders do) on a multilateral exchange.

Unlike institutional investors who are concerned with fundamentals, professional traders, such as high frequency traders, are not concerned with fundamentals nor with whether the EMH correctly describes the price formation process. Because of this, high frequency traders may have different interests from investors such as fund managers who are concerned about the long-term prospects of a company. High frequency trading is often about exploiting **very short-term mispricings** in a market due, perhaps, to short-term mismatching of supply and demand, i.e. trading frictions which real markets have in contrast to the 'perfect market' of an economics textbook. Long-term active fund managers are concerned with exploiting what they believe to be long-term mispricings. Thus perceived mispricing is key to both types of trading but each with quite different causes.

One reason professional traders can generate profit over short time horizons arises from the existence of the first type of trader – the long-term investment institutional trader who is trying to trade in and out of **large** positions over a reasonably short period of time. Inevitably such trades move prices away from 'fundamental' values in large part as a result of '**information leakage**'. This happens traditionally when, for example, a buy-side trader talks to his or her broker. The broker then talks to his or her dealer (who may, illegally, front-run directly by buying ahead of the client) who then will also talk to other dealers or to an inter-dealer broker (see below). The broker then talks to other investment institutions who he or she knows have an interest in the particular security, and very soon the whole market knows that there is a large order in the market. What this means in practice is that long-term investors are giving away money to professional traders in order to get their trades executed. Today when most equity market making is undertaken electronically and most buy-side order desks use an order placement engine of some type, there may be no voice leakage of information. However, the electronic execution systems are always trying to work out who is doing what in order to try to generate revenue from institutional traders attempting to execute large trades.

One question to be answered is whether or not active trading by investment funds improves their investment performance, despite the costs of trading with others[4] or whether the gains they make by exchanging one company's shares for

---

[4] Tabb Group (http://www.tabbgroup.com/) estimates suggest that around 300 securities firms and hedge funds specialise in this type of short-term trading, from which they generated roughly $21 billion in revenues in 2008.

another with each other are greater than the costs of such an exchange (trading costs). It is important to be clear that trading must be a zero sum game for the players as a whole, i.e. there can be no net winners. In fact it must be a negative sum gain because of trading costs. However, some traders may benefit from trading while others lose from it. Regardless of the fact that most funds fail to match market indexes over a period of years despite active trading, trading is important. First, it provides liquidity to passive investors; and this is the markets' key role. But second, without active trading and the underlying market analysis that drives it, security prices would not be at all 'efficient', i.e. they would not be based on underlying fundamentals. They could move up and down in a fashion quite divorced from the economic or company fundamentals. The conundrum of the efficient market hypothesis is that one conclusion to be drawn from it is that 'it is not worth while devoting resources to researching stocks since such research will not generate additional return'. On the other hand if no one undertook any such stock research it would be very worthwhile undertaking since prices would be quite out of line with fundamentals. This remains a fundamental conundrum at the heart of securities pricing.

Morningstar, which tracks fund performance, has produced statistics which suggest that the average mutual fund has around a 100% annual turnover. It is, however, almost impossible for mutual fund holders to detect the costs of such turnover, since they are not included in fund management charges as measured by the Total Expense Ratio (TER) that funds quote to investors. Instead such costs are deductions from the value of the fund, i.e. taken directly from the assets in the fund. Some estimates suggest that total trading cost including both explicit transactions costs, exchange fees, broker fees, clearing and settlement costs, etc. plus implicit costs, **market impact costs** which result in a large trade moving the price against the trader, could amount to 1% of assets per annum, thus reducing fund value by this amount annually. Over long periods of time, due to compounding, such losses result in a much greater loss of asset value than simply 1% per annum.

## MARKET MECHANISMS

We are going to focus initially on what is known as an **order-driven market**. This is the most common design for equity markets worldwide. This market mechanism is also known as a **limit-order market**, an **auction market** and as a **consolidated limit order book or CLOB**. But in order to understand how it works, we need to start with the very simplest type of transaction.

### Bilateral trading

In buying and selling items in everyday life between **two people**, a second-hand motor car, for example, the process operates with the seller stating his offer price, say $5,000. This price is likely to be based on the seller sounding out the market by looking at the prices car dealers are charging for a similar model. He would then adjust for the condition of his car and for the fact that unlike a car dealer he is not offering a guarantee or the 'stamp of approval' of a dealer. However, the potential buyer says 'that's too high a price' and proposes $4,000. The seller says, 'that's too low' and proposes a small price concession to bring his price to $4,800. The buyer then also offers a price concession, a somewhat larger one perhaps, and says $4,400. We now have a market in which the highest buying price that someone is willing to bid is $4,400 and the lowest selling price at which someone is willing to sell is $4,800 (a bid/offer spread of $400), so there cannot yet be a transaction (a trade) since buyer and seller still disagree on price, even though both have come closer to each other.

At this point, each side how keen he or she is to transact. Should they jump to the price the other wants or wait until the other gives in or simply drop out of the contest, i.e. either the buyer is so keen to buy that he says 'OK, 4,800', or the seller says 'OK, I accept 4,400', or one or both walk away. At $4,400–4,800 there is no agreement on the price, so no transaction can take place. These are **limit prices**, i.e. each side has said '**I will go that far but no further, you have reached my limit**'. But as soon as one side jumps to meet the other, there is a trade, which may go through at either $4,400 or $4,800.

To enable a trade to take place one of them has to agree to accept the price of the other. He has to become what we call a price taker and shift his position from being someone who says 'That's my limit' to being someone who says 'OK, I accept the price you're making'. It's a bit like arm wrestling. Let's say the buyer desperately needs this particular car and there is no other such car available locally. He then has to accept the limit price of the seller and agree to pay $4,800. In such a market mechanism, however, there is no competition between buyers and sellers – there is only one trader on each side. Thus we cannot really call the price discovered from the bargaining process a true **market price** what we earlier called a fair price. It is just the price agreed when one side gives in to the other. But at least both sides can attempt to determine the price, i.e. both can set limits on the price they are willing to offer and then wait to see if the other will agree.

Bilateral trading of the type just described is used in some markets, including bond markets, and indeed is a very common form of trading everywhere. Its drawback is that without competition between sellers it is difficult to know if the price that is agreed is a 'fair' one. Thus bilateral trading really needs multiple traders competing with each other and a means by which buyers can compare prices of competing bilateral traders.

A good example of competing bilateral traders is a fruit and vegetable market, such as the one on Portobello Road in Notting Hill, London, near where I live and shop on Saturday mornings. Each trader has a stall with oranges, plums, tomatoes, potatoes, etc. with prices displayed for the potential customer to see just by walking along. Thus the customer can purchase from the trader with the best prices. In practice you might expect that all traders would sell at the same price unless of course those at the very far end of the market charge lower prices just to ensure that some customers will walk further to them. Traders may accept bargaining; so, for example, if we buy large quantities or we are a regular customer, they may give us a discount. We also have to consider the possibility that traders collude to keep up prices, which may be why they are all much the same. They may also have agreed not to give any discounts to anyone. We may also find that if we walk along Portobello Road to check prices to find the cheapest and then return to that market stall, the trader tells us that the item has now sold out. By delaying our purchase to find the best price we may find that we cannot actually trade at that best price anymore.

## Auction markets: single auction

An **auction** is a process in which there is competition to trade on at least one side of the market. The auction of a painting by one of the 'great masters' at an auction house such as Christie's or Sotheby's is organised in a market with many **potential buyers** but only one potential seller. We call this a **single auction** because there is competition on only one side of the market. The seller's agent, the auctioneer, makes a starting **offer price** after which all the potential buyers start competing against each other to discover who will make the highest **bid** – i.e. a competitive **auction**. The bidders continue competing until no one will bid to match the last offer from the auctioneer. At this point, if the auctioneer wants to complete the transaction, he has to stop price making, become a price taker and come back down to accept the best bid available. He is thus acknowledging that the auction market has discovered the highest limit which becomes the market price, i.e. the highest bid from anyone in the room. We have reached the keenest buyer's limit. We call this the **price discovery process**. It may be, of course, that this price is below that which the seller is willing to accept, i.e. the limit price of the seller of the painting. In this case the seller will have put in a **reserve price** (a minimum price at which he will trade), which is his lowest **limit**. If his limit is not reached, then the best bid does not obtain a trade execution, i.e. does not succeed in buying the painting.

## Auction markets: double auction

In the case of securities markets, the only difference from the above scenario is that the auction (the competition) is not only between the **potential buyers but also between potential sellers**. This type of auction is a **double auction**, meaning that it takes place on both sides of the market. Buyers compete to be the best bid in the market. Sellers compete to be the best offer in the market. We can have multiple buyers and sellers because the item that is being traded – a share or a bond – is homogeneous, i.e. all are the same and are indistinguishable one from another which is not the case in a second-hand car sale or the auction of a painting since each is different (heterogeneous). In the case of securities the feature of being identical is called **fungibility**, i.e. traders don't really care which security they have delivered to them when they buy, since they are all identical.

An auction, as we noted above, is what we call a **price discovery mechanism** which enables supply and demand to be matched through order interaction (an order is a quantity and a price) resulting in the best-priced buy order being matched against the best-priced sell order to achieve **order matching** at the **market price**. In contrast to **dealer markets** (covered below) which are **bilateral** this price discovery process is **multilateral**, i.e. involve more than two parties. We use the expression '**order-driven**' or **central limit order book (CLOB)** for this type of market since the price is discovered through the **interaction of multiple traders' orders** in an auction mechanism (the order book).

The order-driven securities market is a very simple construct – it is merely an auction mechanism where people put in orders at the price they are willing to transact at. A **bid order** is an order to buy and an **offer** (also known as an **ask**) is an order to sell. Such orders are called **limit orders** (like the reserve price in the old master auction discussed above) and indicate willingness to trade at a price that the trader herself has set but not at a worse price. In the case of a bid which the trader has entered into the system, this means she will buy at a price equal to (or below) her limit (bid) price. In the case of an offer she will sell at a price equal to or above her offer price. We call this **price making** because the trader is willing to put her money behind a price she is making.

But to make such a market work also requires **market orders**. A **market order** indicates a willingness to trade **at a price that someone else has determined** (the trader who placed a limit order). Market orders simply accept the price in the market, i.e. they are **price taking**. This is like the purchaser of the motor car at the start of this section. He wanted the car sufficiently that he was willing to move from the price he bid to the price that the owner of the car was offering to sell at. He accepted the other side's price as being the market price in the absence of any other offers of the same type of car by other traders. He changed from being a price maker to being a price taker. **Understanding these order types and the differences between them is key to understanding trading on a market.**

When a trader sells at the market price using a **market order**, this is known as **hitting the bid**, meaning accepting the best bid on the order book. On the other side of the book when a trader wants to buy, if he **takes the offer** this means accepting the best offer by putting in a market order to execute against it (also known as **lifting the offer**). The best bid and offer are at slightly different prices (just as in the car sale we started with) and the difference between these prices is known as the **spread**. The offer (ask) price must always be above the bid price since, if it were equal to it or below it, a transaction would occur immediately because a transaction will always occur as soon as two people agree the same price for executing a transaction. **The only way in which a trade execution can take place is when a limit order meets a market order**, i.e. a priced order on the order book meets an unpriced order entering the market. This is the same as in the car case since, to achieve a trade, one side has to accept the 'market price', i.e. the price which the other side (the price maker) is sticking to, namely his or her limit price.

In an order-driven market, all the orders that come in are lined-up in columns. There are two common formats for this that show the same information but in different ways. In Table 12.1, **the market** is 50 bid at 99 and 50 offered at 100 or 99 to 100 in 50 as it would be said in the market and is shown in two slightly different layouts.

In this particular market for a recently issued corporate bond for the Trio Corporation a number of traders are willing to buy the bond from anyone who wishes to sell. The **best bid** is 99 (i.e. 99% of the face value of this $1,000 bond). The size in which this trader is willing to transact is 50 bonds, i.e. $50,000. On the other side of the market the trader who is offering to sell at the best price has an offer (the **best offer**) of 100, i.e. the full nominal price of the bond, also in a size of $50,000. These orders, along with all the other orders on the 'screen' in Table 12.1

**Table 12.1**  An order-driven market screen as available to investors: two possible layouts are shown both of which give identical information but are laid out slightly differently.

*Order Book Layout 1*

| Time: 09.21: 36 | | | |
|---|---|---|---|
| ORDERS for Trio inc. US$ 100m 4.5% of October 2015 | | | |
| quantity | bid price | offer price | quantity |
| | | 102 | 25 |
| | | 101 | 30 |
| | | **100** | 50 |
| 50 | **99** | | |
| 25 | 98 | | |
| 35 | 97 | | |

Below is the same information but laid out differently.

*Order Book Layout 2*

| Time: 09.21: 36 | | | |
|---|---|---|---|
| ORDERS for Trio inc. US$ 100m 4.5% of October 2015 | | | |
| quantity | bid price | offer price | quantity |
| 50 | **99** | **100** | 50 |
| 25 | 98 | 101 | 30 |
| 35 | 97 | 102 | 25 |

are **limit** orders, i.e. the trader behind them is willing to trade, not at any price available in the market, but only up to the limit he or she has specified. For example, the trader behind the best bid will offer any price up to 99 but not above. However, nothing at all is happening in this market – there are no trade **executions** (transactions). The reason is simply that the traders behind the best bid and best offer have a different view of the value of this security (or at least of the price at which they are willing to transact). For a transaction to happen, there needs to be agreement on the price. Alternatively, it may be that both the best bid and the best offer are from the same trader who is willing to trade either way and hopes to make a profit by buying at one instant from someone else at 99 and quickly selling on to someone else at 100 – known as market-making.

There are three ways in which an execution can take place in this 'stalled' market:

1. The trader with the **best bid** (99) can decide either that he now thinks the bond is worth 100 or that he can wait no longer (he has become impatient) to execute, so he is **willing to move his price up to match the best offer** (100), i.e. he changes his mind and now agrees that he will pay the price which the trader making the best offer has put on the bond, in which case he withdraws his limit order and enters a **market order**, meaning 'I accept your offer (100) as being the best available now' or;.

2. The trader with the **best offer** can decide, either that he now thinks the bond is worth only 99 or that he can wait no longer (he has become impatient) to execute, so he is **willing to move his price down to match the best bid**, i.e. he

is now willing to agree with the trader behind the best bid that at a price of 99 he will transact (change his limit order at 100 to an unpriced market order) or;

3. A new trader enters the market and says 'I want to buy' or 'I want to sell' and 'I am willing to do so at the price in the market now because I am impatient'. Let's say he wants to buy. Rather than placing a limit order he tells his broker to enter a market order to buy 50 bonds at the best offer price in the market (the **market offer**). As this is a price of 100, the transaction is executed at this price and the offer of 50 bonds at 100 disappears off the screen. Thus a market order gives **immediate execution**.

In the above example, in the first two cases one or other of the traders behind the best bid and the best offer (limit orders) decides that he is no longer what we call a **patient trader** and instead he wants **immediacy**, i.e. he wants to trade now even if he has to trade at a worse price than his original limit price. Such a trader is also called the **aggressor**. To trade, all he has to do is to move his price to match that on the other side, i.e. **to change from a limit order to a market order**. What the trader has done is to **buy liquidity** (i.e. the ability to transact now rather than later), whereas before he was **offering liquidity** to others with his limit order. He has become willing to pay the higher price as the price of getting the deal done now (buying liquidity which means trade execution now). Perhaps he now has some information on the value of the bond (**an information trader**) and believes that if he does not transact now the price will soon reflect that information and move up anyway. So it becomes best to execute now.

Let's say that the trader with the best bid in the market at 99 becomes tired of waiting for whatever reason (perhaps he now believes the bond is actually worth 101), so he gives in and agrees to transact at 100, i.e. he changes his order from a limit bid of 50 at 99 to a market order (he does not enter a price since he is now accepting someone else's best price in the market). His order does not appear on the screen but simply hits the best offer of 50 at 100. A trade is then immediately executed and appears in a line above the order book as shown in Table 12.2. You should also note that the original bid of 99 has disappeared (it was withdrawn) and the offer at 100 has also disappeared since it has executed against a market order.

After the trade, the screen looks as in Table 12.2 with **transactions** displayed at the top so that those who wish to trade subsequently know how the market has traded earlier.

**Table 12.2** An order-driven market screen as available to investors (after a trade has gone through)

| Time: 09.22: 56 | | | |
|---|---|---|---|
| ORDERS for Trio inc. US$ 100m 4.5% of October 2015 | | | |
| Transaction: 50 at 100 at 09.22:32 | | | |
| quantity | bid | offer | quantity |
| | | 102 | 25 |
| | | **101** | 30 |
| 25 | **98** | | |
| 35 | 97 | | |
| 50 | 96.5 (new bid) | | |

In this market, the spread has increased (because both the best bid and the best offer have gone) and will remain at 3 points until someone enters an improved market bid or offer. In practice this is likely to happen almost immediately.

It is important to learn from this example that there are **two ways of buying**. You can buy on the left or the right hand side of the order book. On the left-hand side of the order book you trade by offering to buy from anyone who wants to **hit your bid** (you are a passive participant) and then waiting and hoping they do so. On the right-hand side of the order book you trade by accepting someone else's price, i.e. accepting their offer or **taking the offer** by placing an unpriced **market** order which executes immediately. You also, therefore, pay a worse price, but this is simply the price you pay for **immediacy**, i.e. for immediate and certain liquidity. You should work out what happens if the trader with the best offer in the market becomes more urgent in his or her desire to trade and so changes his or her order to a market order instead.

When a potential trader first looks at the screen on an order-driven/order matching market, he or she has to decide on a trading strategy, i.e. to put in a limit order and wait or to put in a market order which will transact immediately. This is a key decision in trading. Patient traders will almost always trade at better prices against impatient traders and, provided the market does not move against them while they wait, will realise a superior investment performance.

If you remember back to our analysis of trading, we noted two different motives for trading: liquidity motivated and information motivated. The trader who is impatient (the market order placer) is more likely to be the information motivated trader who feels that he must transact before the information he believes he uniquely has becomes general knowledge and is impounded[5] in the market price. The liquidity motivated trader (the limit order placer) on the other hand is able to be patient since he simply wants to increase or decrease his liquidity at the lowest cost. In practice, however, while this dichotomisation might sometimes be right, at other times it is not.

When there is a trade, it is sometimes asked 'was it a buy or a sell?' Well of course it is both – one trader buys and one sells. However, there is always the question of whether it was **buyer initiated** or **seller initiated**. It is always the market order which initiates the execution. In the case above it was the buyer who initiated or was the **aggressor**. As the aggressor, he or she had to accept the higher of the two prices (i.e. the offer). He or she had to pay the spread (1%). Thus the trade takes place at the higher of the two prices in the market. During a trading day, even if the bid and offer prices of a security do not change during the day, there will still be a **bid-offer bounce**, i.e. the price will move up and down between the bid and offer prices depending on whether the aggressor (the market order placer) is a buyer or a seller.

It should be clear from this example that **the market order pays the bid/ask spread** – i.e. this is the **price of buying liquidity** while the **limit order receives the bid/ask spread**. The difference in price between the two types of order simply reflects the degree of patience displayed. We talk about buying liquidity and, in the example above, our trader actually wanted to sell shares. But whether he wanted

---

[5] Impounded in the market price means reflected in the market price.

to buy or sell if he was urgent, he would still have been **buying liquidity** (while either selling or buying the shares) since this simply means transacting urgently against a more patient counterparty. Buying liquidity is also known as **taking out liquidity**. The passive side, in contrast, is **providing liquidity**.

An alternative way of looking at market and limit orders is that market order placers are **price takers**, i.e. they accept the price on offer in the market, while limit order placers are **price makers**, i.e. they say 'this is the price I am willing to transact at with you – this is **my price**'. Price makers, whether investors or dealers, should normally be able to transact at a better price. In fact when a market order is entered into a market, it is by definition **unpriced**, whereas a limit order is **priced**.

It is important to note that:

● if only market orders are entered into a market, there can be no executions.
● if only limit orders are entered into a market there can be no executions.
● executions happen only when a limit order (or dealer quote) executes against a market order, the result of which is price discovery in the market price at that moment.

## A SUMMARY OF THE DIFFERENCES BETWEEN LIMIT AND MARKET ORDERS

**Limit orders** have to be entered first into the market mechanism (since otherwise there is nothing for market orders to execute against). The features of the limit order are:

● limit orders provide pricing information to other market participants;
● limit order traders are price makers and provide liquidity to other market participants;
● limit orders traders may pay lower fees to the exchange (or even receive a payment from the exchange for executions) as liquidity providers;
● limit orders may take the spread on a transaction
● limit orders provide a (free) option to other traders and are therefore risky to those placing them;
● limit orders do not provide guaranteed execution – they require patience;
● limit orders have to be watched in case prices move.

**Market orders** can only execute against limit orders and therefore can only be entered after a limit order on the opposite side is in the market. The market order:

● does not contribute to price discovery.
● trader is a price taker and may pay the exchange a higher execution fee.
● takes out liquidity.
● initiates the trade since a trade requires a market order to be entered.
● pays the spread.
● always gets executed if there is any limit order at all on the opposite side, as it is classified as an 'execute at market' order.

The terminology used by the SEC in its analysis of markets extends the above terminology:

- **A marketable order (immediately executable order)** can be either a market order **or** the best-priced limit order.
- **A non-marketable order** is a limit order which is not the best-priced order, i.e. is not at the top of the order book.

The double-auction market is a **price discovery mechanism**. This means that it is through the interaction of supply and demand (orders), i.e. prices and quantities in the auction mechanism, that it is possible to discover the price at which a transaction can take place at a particular moment to the satisfaction of both sides – the buyer and the seller. **Price discovery is the key output of a market** and results from bringing orders from buyers and sellers together to interact in one place. A market can be either a physical place, like an exchange floor, or the computer of an electronic marketplace, which has a program allowing bids and offers (orders) to interact. All that is happening in a market is that the price at which there is neither a surplus of the particular share nor a shortage is being discovered, i.e. **it is a rationing mechanism, as is all pricing**. A good quality market (small spread) and fair price discovery is a consequence of competition in a market between bidders trying to offer the highest price to buy and those on the offer side of the market offering the lowest price to sell. The best bid and offer are **the market**.

Auction markets almost always work on the principle of price and time priority. **Price priority** means that the best price already in the market always wins which is, of course, the idea behind an auction. In contrast, in a fragmented dealer market (where traders cannot see competing quotes or cannot execute on competing quotes after having obtained them),this is often not the case as other dealers may be quoting a better price than the one against which a trader is executing. The second rule – **time priority** – means that if the quantity (size) available on the side on which the trader wishes to transact is greater than the size in which he or she wants to transact, the trader who placed his or her limit order in the market first will get the execution rather than a pro rata transaction amongst everyone with an order at that price.

Figure 12.1 is an example of what was once one of the best-known order-driven markets in the United States – Island, which was an electronic communications network, ECN) operating as a competitor to the established markets) and which changed its name to Inet and became part of NASDAQ when that exchange purchased the company.

Here it can be seen that **the market** (the best priced bid and offer) in Altair (a computer company) on 15 November 2003 at 10.01 and 40.949 seconds, is

| quantity bid | price | quantity offered | price |
|---|---|---|---|
| 3000 | 1.29 | 125 | 1.30 |

However, if someone wishes to sell say, 6,000 shares (execute against the buy orders in the market), the bid price is lower for the second 3,000 as the next best bid in the market is at only 1.27. As can be seen on this screen, a large order has

| LAST MATCH | | TODAY'S ACTIVITY | |
|---|---|---|---|
| Price | 1.2900 | Orders | 98 |
| Time | 10:01:40.949 | Volume | 61,027 |

| BUY ORDERS | | SELL ORDERS | |
|---|---|---|---|
| SHARES | PRICE | SHARES | PRICE |
| 3,000 | 1.2900 | 125 | 1.3000 |
| 3,000 | 1.2700 | 8,000 | 1.3090 |
| 4,000 | 1.2600 | 3,000 | 1.3100 |
| 5,000 | 1.2500 | 1,600 | 1.3200 |
| 4,000 | 1.2500 | 3,024 | 1.3400 |
| 4,000 | 1.2500 | 2,500 | 1.3400 |
| 1,000 | 1.2400 | 1,000 | 1.3500 |
| 3,000 | 1.2300 | 2,100 | 1.3600 |
| 6,000 | 1.2100 | 2,500 | 1.3700 |
| 1,000 | 1.2000 | 900 | 1.3800 |
| 8,000 | 1.1910 | 3,000 | 1.3800 |
| 1,300 | 1.1900 | 2,000 | 1.3800 |
| 5,173 | 1.1620 | 1,000 | 1.4400 |
| 600 | 1.1000 | 2,000 | 1.4700 |
| 5,000 | 1.0900 | 840 | 1.4800 |
| (8 more) | | (19 more) | |

*As of 10:06:22.452*

**Figure 12.1**    Island order book for Altair

*Source*: Island (now part of NASDAQ), however, website no longer available.

to execute against successively worse priced limit orders, i.e. ones which are away from the market price if the trader wants a quick execution. This is also known as **walking the book**. What is also clear from this page is the large number of orders which are well off-market, i.e. 8 more orders on the bid side (willing to buy from a seller) and 19 more on the offer-side (willing to sell to a buyer). These will execute only if the price is very volatile during a trading day.

## USE OF 'CALL AUCTIONS'

Very active markets with a continuous flow of buy and sell orders function very effectively using continuous order-driven technology, i.e. multilateral trading. In the case of securities where there is relatively little desire by investors to trade, it may be that if the double auction were held throughout the day (continuous trading), there would be too few buyers and sellers (and perhaps only sellers or only buyers) and thus the price discovery process would not work well. This could lead to the price being well away from its 'true' value. For such securities, one solution is to have an auction only once per week or once per month. This would result in a concentration of buy and sell interest at this time and would lead to much improved price discovery – but only weekly or monthly pricing on the share would be available.

While no longer used much as the only exchange mechanism, the call market, also known as *a la crié* (the French for 'at the call'), is now used as a component of the European and other continuous electronic auction market mechanisms. It is used to **open the market** as a means of collecting together, before the opening, all the orders that people want to execute at the opening and is also used as a means of **closing markets**. In fact, in continuous markets, a high proportion of total daily volume generally trades at the opening and closing call auctions. Thus periodic call auctions help consolidate the market by achieving temporal consolidation and better pricing. Pricing at the open is likely to be better since a large number of traders are agreeing to execute at the opening call price. It is also generally better at the close and, since this is the price used by mutual funds and others for their end of day valuation, it is a particularly important price. If only the last trade on a continuous market was used as the closing price, this could easily be manipulated, whereas this could not be achieved in a closing call given the large numbers of orders likely to be in the system.

## TEMPORAL FRAGMENTATION: QUOTE-DRIVEN/DEALER/OVER-THE-COUNTER MARKETS/BILATERAL TRADING

A second solution to overcome the problem of infrequent trades is the use of dealer markets, also known as **quote-driven markets** or **over-the-counter (OTC) markets** which operate on a **bilateral** basis (dealer to counterparty) and are designed to enable traders to have their orders executed when they wish, without having to wait for the other side. Some exchanges have **designated dealers** with so-called 'affirmative' obligations to make bid and offer prices in an agreed size throughout market opening hours. These are known as (official) **market makers**. Bilateral trading of this type was the first form of trading we considered earlier in the case of two people agreeing the sale of a second-hand car.

A dealer essentially uses his or her own capital to bridge any time gap when there are insufficient orders to ensure that buyers can always find sellers quickly. The dealer acts as a counterparty to any customer, even though at that moment he or she may not have a customer counterparty for the trade. Thus dealer markets are designed to overcome the problem that infrequent trading causes **by providing immediacy** rather than the alternative which is for a trader to post a limit order on an order-driven auction market and wait for an eventual execution, or post a market order and accept what might be a very unattractive price. The dealer solution has a cost for traders – the cost of immediacy which, as in order-driven markets when a trader places a market order, is the spread. In dealer markets, however, the spread tends to be larger than in order-driven markets if only because trading volumes, except in markets such as sovereign debt of major countries or foreign exchange, are likely to be lower and hence the risk to a dealer, that the price might change before he or she finds a counterparty, is higher.

Dealers provide a market just as order-driven markets do. If we take the example we used above, Table 12.3 shows what a dealer might display on his or her screen when providing quotations in this bond in competition with the order-driven market.

**Table 12.3**   Single dealer quotation screen for a particular bond

| Time: 09.21: 36 | | | |
|---|---|---|---|
| Goldsmith Sach quotations for Trio inc. US$ 100m 4.5% of October 2015 | | | |
| quantity | bid | offer | quantity |
| | | 100 | 50 |
| 50 | 99½ | | |

In a dealer market, rather than calling these 'orders', we call them **quotes, though they are in fact limit orders**, but of course there is only one bid and one offer from any one dealer in any particular security. However, if one looked at all dealer quotations, there would be a range of bids and offers, just as in a limit order matching market. Thus conceptually there is less difference from an order-driven auction market than might be imagined, provided there are competing dealers and there is a screen on which all traders can see the competing dealer quotes.

The key difference between an order-driven and a dealer market, however, is that in a dealer market a buy-side trader **cannot enter a limit order** and must, therefore, pay for immediacy whether desired or not by placing a market order, i.e. price taking. He or she cannot suggest a price to the dealer and ask 'do you accept my price?'. Those who trade with dealers have to place market orders and not limit orders. However, it is also the case that dealers may improve the price particularly for good customers and therefore in telephone trading customers may always ask 'can you improve the price?'

In Table 12.3, the particular dealer (Goldsmith Sach) makes a quote of 50 bonds bid at 99½: 50 bonds offered at 100. When we look at the market as a whole, however, we can see all the dealers who make a market in that particular security. Such screens are provided by, for example, stock exchanges, Bloomberg and Thomson Reuters. The Stock Exchange Automated Quotation (SEAQ) system was the London Stock Exchange (LSE) equity market Competing Dealer Quotation System until recently.

## Competing dealer quote screen

Based on the prices shown on the screen in Table 12.4, any trader who wanted to **buy** would go to Morgan Stanhope. Any trader wanting to **sell** would go to Goldsmith Sach or American Lynch. If prices of competing dealers are as far apart as this it suggests that Morgan Stanhope are keen to sell these bonds, i.e. to reduce the inventory of bonds they are holding. On the other hand, both Goldsmith Sach and American Lynch would seem keen to acquire bonds. This suggests that these two dealers may have **short positions**, i.e. they have sold bonds they don't already own and are trying to encourage traders to sell to them to move to a less short position and thus reduce their risk exposure. Alternatively, of course, they may simply be bullish, i.e. they think the market is going up.

**Table 12.4**  Competing dealer quote screen in normal market size

| Trio inc. US$ 100m 4.5% of October 2015 | |
| --- | --- |
| Goldsmith Sach | 100–101 |
| American Lynch | 100–101 |
| Nomurage | 99–100 |
| Barcle | 98.5–99 |
| Morgan Stanhope | 97–98 |

Let's examine what dealers or market makers actually do. They stand ready to execute orders from other traders against the quotations they make. This means that their function is to provide liquidity to those who demand it and are willing to pay for it. A key feature of dealers is that they, rather than the continuous auction market, have to **make the price**, i.e. they are the price discovery mechanism. They have to do this at one remove from aggregate supply and demand, as in a concentrated (single exchange) multilateral market they have to **infer** the 'true' price from the arrival of orders from **their** clients alone – which is just a subset of the total market.. As they offer liquidity, they have an **inventory**, i.e. they have a balance sheet with a stock of (a **long** position in) the securities they deal in or, if they think prices are likely to fall or have been taken short by a client purchase, a negative position (a **short position**) in the security. A short position means that the dealer has sold securities he does not currently hold in the hope that he can buy them back later, hopefully at a lower price.[6] Of course a dealer may be **taken short** when he would rather not be as a result of executing a trade with a customer. In this case he needs to offer a competitive bid price, i.e. above that offered by other dealers, in order to buy from another trader and **close** his short position.

Essentially dealers provide **immediacy**, which is the ability of another trader to trade when he or she chooses. The traders they transact with are, in theory, **impatient traders** who are willing to pay a price for their impatience. However, in a market where there are no other execution mechanisms allowing traders to **interact directly** with each other, i.e. all trading is **capital intermediated**, then all traders have to become impatient as there is no benefit in being patient.

The LSE market both before and after its reform in 1986 (Big Bang) was a pure dealer market. In this, it was unusual in Europe as most markets there were brokered or auction markets rather than dealer-based. London was a dealer market because dealers had long been able to persuade the regulatory authorities that London investors (mainly institutional investors) demanded immediacy, i.e. they always wanted to have liquidity immediately available (and were willing to pay the price demanded for it) and were not willing to risk waiting for a better price. NASDAQ in New York was also a dealer market with no possibility of traders themselves offering liquidity to the market through placement of limit orders. In reality, of course, many traders do not require highly priced immediacy at all. However, it took until the mid-1990s to overcome the hold that dealers had on the London market and the hold that NASDAQ dealers had on theirs.

---

[6] The ability to borrow to allow short positions is a key aspect of liquidity creation in dealer markets.

In the mid-1990s I was a consultant to the CEO of the LSE when it was designing its electronic order matching market, the Stock Exchange Electronic Trading System (SETS). It was clear then that the large investment banks saw such a trading system as a direct (and powerful) competitor to themselves as dealers since the stock exchange did not have its own market, only an electronic display board on which traders could see dealer prices. It was dealer opposition that caused a delay of many years both on the LSE and NASDAQ until eventually electronic order driven systems were introduced. As one stock exchange official put it to me at that time, 'the dealers, as the owners (previously members) of the exchange, will not allow the exchange to become a competitor to them by introducing its own market mechanism'. And that was correct – it took many years for London and NASDAQ to convert from pure dealer markets to mainly order driven markets. Ultimately London introduced the SETS market while still maintaining the old SEAQ market.

On the SEAQ system, all the LSE did was to provide a screen in brokers' offices which enabled them to see the prices of all market makers which were providing quotations in each share listed on the market. They did not provide a 'market mechanism' as they do today in the form of an order-driven market.

An example on the screen in Figure 12.2 shows what are called Level II prices from the LSE. Today, not only can brokers receive this information, but it is also

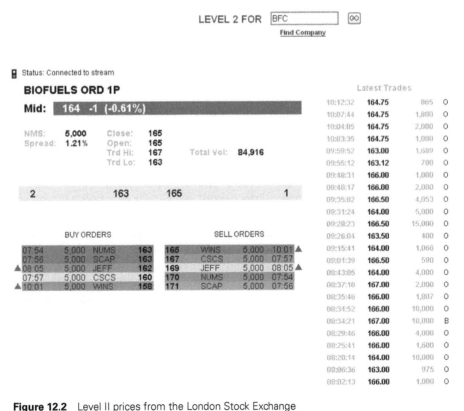

**Figure 12.2**  Level II prices from the London Stock Exchange

*Source*: MoneyAM.com, http://www.moneyam.com/help/?page=level2 (accessed 8 February 2012).

possible for retail clients to subscribe. As a result, retail clients can see the **depth** of the market, not just the **top of the book**. In the figure we see the information on the ordinary shares of 1 penny nominal value of Biofuels.

The screen displays prices from five market makers

1. Numis Securities (NUMS);
2. Shore Capital (SCAP);
3. Jefferies (JEFF);
4. Collins Stewart (CSCS);
5. Winterflood (WINS).

In this case the normal market size is 5,000 and that is the size they are all quoting. However, their prices are quite different. The **yellow strip** on the LSE SEAQ screen shows the best bids and offers at the top of the book, i.e. best prices on each side, otherwise known as **the market**. At the top of the book on the **bid** side are Numis and Shore Capital (SCAP) at a price of 163 pence, each in a size of 1x NMS giving the number '2' on the bid side, meaning two lots of NMS are available at that price. The best offer is not from either Numis or Shore Capital but Winterflood at 165. Numis is actually quoting 163–170 which is a very wide spread. The conclusion one might draw from this is that Numis is probably **short**, i.e. has probably sold earlier in the day and is now trying to attract the other side. Alternatively Numis might just be very bullish and looking to take a long position. Shore has an even wider spread and is bottom of the book on the offer side. Clearly neither of them wants to sell.

Looking now at the trades which have already gone through by 10.12 a.m., the first which was at 8.02 a.m. was at a price of 166. This was probably a customer buying (i.e. the dealer selling) since the price is closer to the best offer. The next trade is at 163, which was probably a customer selling, which means that his broker would enter a market order to sell, i.e. hitting the best bid which, since 7.54 in the morning, has been Numis which is bid at 163.

## CONCENTRATION AND FRAGMENTATION OF MARKETS

The idea of the **central market** is a very well established one. Concentrating all orders in a particular security in one place, to enable all buy orders to interact with all sell orders, has been a guiding principle of market design and market regulation for many years. Traditionally most countries have had only one **equity** stock exchange (though at one time some had regional exchanges). In some European countries there was even a law which prevented competition between equity markets. This was known as the **concentration rule** which was effective in, for example, France until it was banned by the European Union's new regulatory framework for markets, known as the Markets in Financial Instruments Directive, MiFID.

While Europe had a concentration rule for equities, it did not have one for bonds. Bonds have always been traded in bilateral dealer markets, which by definition are not concentrated but fragmented. One reason for this is that corporate bonds, being buy-and-hold investments which self-liquidate at maturity, do not turn over as frequently as equities. As a result, their liquidity from shortly after issue until their **redemption**, i.e. paying back in cash, at maturity, is relatively low. Dealers therefore provide a useful function in **bridging the time gap** between one side of a trade wanting to transact and the opposite side becoming available, thus **overcoming temporal fragmentation**. However, one consequence is that dealer markets are instead **geographically fragmented**. In fact each broker-dealer which offers a trading service is in effect offering its own 'mini-market'.

What this means in practice is that even within the time frame of my own experience of working in a bond dealing house, a client had great difficulty in knowing whether the quotation we gave her was the best available. She could, in theory, having called us and asked a price, then have called a couple of other dealing houses to ask their prices. Then, if our price was the best, she could call us back and ask to do the deal. As a result of her calling back we would then know that our price was the best of the three which probably meant it was the *wrong* price. So at that point we would say 'sorry, the price has moved – it's now ...' and quote a worse price. Thus clients came to realise that if they phoned a particular dealer, they would have to trust that dealer to offer the best price since there was, in practice, no way to check prices. On floor markets, in particular derivative markets, the expression used was that the price quote was good only as long as 'the breath is warm', in other words for a few seconds with no time to check the price '**away**'.

It was only in the late 1970s that the Reuters screen started to come into dealing houses and it was this electronic mechanism that allowed clients, for the first time, to see dealer quotes. This also meant that dealers could see each other's quotes. To avoid other dealers knowing the actual prices at which they were doing business, the prices quoted on the Reuters screen were generally not the actual dealing prices and were known as **indicative** prices. Real prices could only be obtained by calling the dealer and asking what the real price was (price improvement). Thus, even the display of **competing dealer prices** did not actually make much difference to genuine transparency and price competition. In addition, in the international bond markets, quotations still had large spreads – often as much as one point, i.e. 100 bp or 1% for lightly traded bonds.

## INTEGRATING DEALERS INTO A COMPETITIVE MARKET STRUCTURE

In this section we describe how the competing quote screen for equity trading on the LSE, the SEAQ screen and the interdealer broker (IDB) mechanisms for London equities did help to overcome the fragmentation of the equity market. But it must be realised that these mechanisms did not prevent dealers keeping good control of the prices their clients actually paid.

The starting point in Figure 12.3 is the box at top left – Concentrated Markets. This shows the two types of naturally concentrated trading venues – a floor market and a central electronic market. It also shows a completely fragmented dealer (bilateral) market in which there is really no concept of 'the' market price. In such a market it is quite possible that one dealer has matching buy and sell orders, another has more buys than sells, while a third has more sells than buys. As a result they will be quoting different prices to clients.

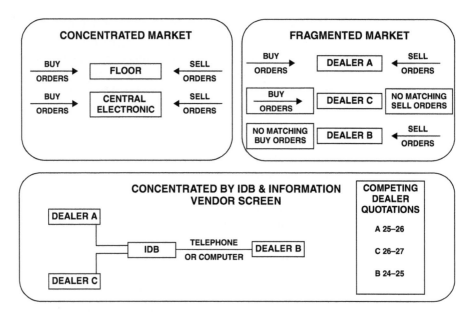

**Figure 12.3** How a fragmented bilateral dealer market becomes a concentrated competing dealer market

To make such a market more like a true central market, in which there is competition between quotes just as there is competition between orders in a multilateral market, it is necessary to provide mechanisms that enable traders to see the prices available across all marketplaces, i.e. across all dealers, and for dealers to be able to trade amongst themselves to eliminate imbalances that individual dealers may have between supply and demand from their particular clients. What we need to do is to create competition between the dealers to create a single **competing dealer market** rather than having a **set of many independent bilateral markets**. This is achieved principally through pre-trade transparency, which means that the prices of all dealers are on display to traders. There are essentially two mechanisms that can create a relatively concentrated market out of a fragmented dealer market.

*Competing quote screen.* The first is the provision of a single screen on which all dealer quotes are listed with the best bid and offer indicated in some way to make them easy to identify. On the LSE, the SEAQ system was used to provide this unified quotation mechanism in equities for the 20-year period after Big Bang in 1986 when the LSE was first reformed. Clearly, anyone wishing to deal in this market is likely to wish to execute at the best bid or offer as indicated, which was called the 'yellow strip' (as shown in Fig. 12.2) with the best prices on it being known as 'the **touch**'.

*Interdealer broker mechanisms.* The second is the **IDB** mechanism that allows dealers to trade with each other rather than with the public. This is a **private market** or **inside market**, i.e. one that only particular traders (dealers on the sell side) may use. Without such an inside market, one dealer could have clients most of whom wished to sell, while another had clients most of whom wished to buy. Unless these two sets of orders could be brought together, there would be no transactions. This is similar to the interbank market in deposits and loans which allows those banks with surplus liquidity to trade with those with insufficient liquidity.

The IDB market works in a similar way to a 'dark liquidity pool' (see the following chapter). It is not a true price discovery mechanism but is simply a means by which a broker can match two dealers who have equal and opposite interests. It is important to understand that it is a brokerage mechanism and not a dealership mechanism, i.e. a **broker** who transacts between dealers only.

When we look at Figure 12.3 .we see on the Competing Quote Screen that dealer C has the lowest prices and dealer B has the highest. This suggests that C wishes to sell and is willing to offer at a low selling price (only 25) while C wishes to buy and so is offering to buy at 26 (his bid). Clearly no one who wanted to buy would go to C; therefore his bid of 24 is really irrelevant as no rational person would trade at this price. Equally B's offer at 27 is not a price at which anyone will transact. Given the equal and opposite imbalance in supply and demand at dealers C and B (compared with A), if these two dealers contact the IDB, it will be able to broker a deal (indirectly) between them to even out the imbalance.

You might think that you, as a buy side trader could arbitrage this market – you should work out what the arbitrage on the screen is (note you make a profit of only 1). But in practice you would never see these prices on a screen since dealers don't want to disclose that they are long and wrong or short and caught. Thus a competing dealer screen will, in practice, never show a profitable arbitrage that another trader can exploit.

Dealers can, of course, transact with each other directly. However, such transactions are not anonymous, i.e. they let the other dealer know the problem his competitor has; for example that he is what is known as **long and wrong** or **short and caught** (he has a long or short position which he does not want to have). If a dealer announces this to other dealers, he is likely to have to pay a disadvantageous price to close his position. Thus most markets use the anonymous mechanism of the IDB to get out of unwanted positions. IDBs can be **voice brokers** or **electronic brokers**. By linking up dealers, they smooth out the potential effects of random order arrivals at individual dealers and thus make the market much more efficient and more like a concentrated market. Note that IDBs do not themselves deal in or take positions in securities. The IDB business is a large one. The largest of all in Europe is ICAP, which is an FTSE 100 company and is very successful.

## HOW DO DEALERS DISCOVER THE PRICE?

Just as the order-driven market auction mechanism constantly discovers the price, i.e. the price which creates an equilibrium between supply and demand at a moment in time, each dealer has constantly to discover the prices that he will quote. This means that he needs to be able to **infer** levels of demand and supply and to move his bid and offer prices appropriately. Appropriately means adjusting prices so as to try to maintain the desired **inventory level**, either as long positions (holding stock) or as short positions (having sold without having any stock), depending on how he thinks the market may move in the short run. Dealers operate by buying from clients and adding the purchase to their inventory or selling to clients from inventory (or by **going short**).

Dealers make profits by selling at a higher price than they buy and by mini-mising the time between buying and selling to reduce the risk of an adverse price change. Dealers are unlikely to be able to hold on to the whole of the spread between bid and offer since there will always be times when they suffer a loss from prices moving against their inventory holdings. On average they might hold on to 50% of the spread. They are not investors, so they hold inventory only to enable them to profit from the provision of liquidity. They are investing based on a company's fundamentals, i.e. they are not researching companies before taking positions. Thus many dealers like to go home in the evening with a **flat or square book**, i.e. they either have no positions, long or short, or the long positions hedge (as best as possible) the short positions, thus minimising overnight risk. Any dealer who approaches the end of day long but not wishing to hold long positions will be forced to sell those positions at the bid price in the market, not the offer price (think why this is so), and thus he loses the spread. He is seeking immediacy (whereas normally he offers immediacy) and therefore he has to pay the price of immediacy in order to trade urgently.

How then do they infer supply and demand? They do it from the **direction of trades** which they receive, i.e. whether they are buys or sells, which tells them whether demand by other traders from them is exceeding supply to them at their current prices or vice versa or is evenly balanced. For example, a simplistic way of looking at it would be that if a dealer quotes a two-way price (which gives the client the option to buy or to sell) and the first client buys from him, this would not necessarily give him any information but would either reduce his inventory or **take him short**. If the second client also buys, it is possible that the price he is offering at is too low. If the third order he receives is also a buy it is very likely that he is quoting too low a price and he will move his prices up to discourage further purchases. On the other hand, as he also moves his bid price up he will hope to attract more sellers and so **cover the short** position that he may have built up from the earlier sales. Thus **inventory management**, i.e. controlling the level of inven-tory to keep it as close as possible to the desired level, is a key skill of a dealer.

It should be noted that when a buy-side trader contacts a dealer, the dealer will not ask which way he or she wants to deal. He or she is expected to quote a two-way price. Indeed, on being given a two-way quote, a buy-side trader might even decide to change which side of the market he or she deals if the price on the other side is very attractive. The following is an example of how a market (dealer) in London might open 'his' market:

- 7.30 a.m. dealer enters **HIS** prices on screen at 98 - ½; (bid at 98, offered at 98 ½)
- Why those prices?
- His starting point is the previous night's closing prices; he then looks at closing prices on the same or similar securities in New York, Singapore and Hong Kong, looks at the news on Bloomberg or Reuters and listens to the bank's economist at the morning meeting in the dealing room;
- 7.31 orders start to come in;
- Order 1 buy, order 2 buy, order 3 buy;
- Changes quote to 98½–99 to reflect information on supply and demand;
- Hopes that, having gone short, the next few orders will be sell (to him).

The first fundamental rule about being a dealer is to understand that dealing is not about investment, i.e. there is no intention to hold stocks of securities for long periods for investment purposes. A standard rule in some trading houses is that if it has not turned over within a certain number of days, it must be sold regardless of any loss that may be involved. The popular way of putting this is **if in doubt, chuck it out!**

The second fundamental rule is that dealers are not interested in the type of investment analysis undertaken by securities analysts, i.e. long-term fundamental analysis. Essentially their price adjustments are designed to reflect two things that may result in price changes during the trading day:

● unexpected new information which has not, by definition, been previously incorporated into the price;
● short-term changes in the balance of supply and demand in the market that cause temporary, relatively small changes in the price of the security.

These two types of price change are quite different from each other in that the first relates to a **change in fundamentals** that was not expected, while the second is a price change caused by **frictions in the trading process**. Neither of these causes contradicts the EMH. If the latter, then dealers (and other traders) may make the assumption that prices will **mean revert**, i.e. return to their previous efficient market value, which is the basis of many trading strategies, known as **mean reversion strategies**.

In addition to price changes due to these two causes, the transaction prices also move as a result of the bid/offer spread, i.e. if the first transaction is a sale to a client (a client purchase) and the second a purchase (from a client) then it might look like the price has declined over the period between the trades. In fact the **price quotations** may not have changed at all. This, as we have already noted, is also known as the **bid/offer bounce**.

Dealers and exchanges argue that they are the means of providing liquidity to a market. However, it is neither exchanges nor broker/dealers who provide liquidity but traders/investors, i.e. **it is the DESIRE of traders/investors to transact that provides liquidity**. This is a very key point in terms of understanding how markets work. It is only if there are traders/investors on both sides of a market who want to transact that there can be a market. No amount of market making can make a market if investors do not wish to transact. What markets do is to facilitate the interaction of those who want to trade. But it is only the willingness of some traders (limit order placing investors or dealers) to provide an option to other traders by **making a price**, i.e. a limit order, that enables willing traders to execute their trades by enabling the discovery of the price.

It should be noted that dealer quotes are little different from limit orders – both offer liquidity which is then taken by someone wanting immediate liquidity by placing a market order. In the new market structure dealers, rather than operating a separate, bilateral market in the same securities as an order-driven market, simply put their market making bids and offers into the multilateral limit order market. Thus when looking at 'the screen' it is generally impossible to tell which are dealer quotes and which are investor limit orders – they are the same thing.

# THE NEW SECONDARY MARKET STRUCTURE: COMPETITION, DARK POOLS, ALGORITHMIC AND HIGH-FREQUENCY TRADING

**13**

There has been a dramatic change in equity market structure in the last ten years, not just in the UK and the US but throughout Continental Europe and Asia. Understanding the new structure is difficult and, for a trader, executing in the new structure is much more complex than in the past, i.e. under a single 'Stock Exchange' using order-driven trading alongside broker/dealers offering OTC market-making. To put it in the language of the SEC, the market structure today is **fragmented and complex**.

## WHAT ARE THE MAIN CHANGES AND WHAT HAS DRIVEN THEM?

The biggest change in markets has been the almost complete shift from 'manual' trading to electronic trading. Manual trading originally meant undertaking transactions on the floor of an exchange and also by telephone between a trader and a dealer. The role of the broker in such exchanges was to bring orders to the floor of the exchange for execution by dealers/ market-makers. But even when exchanges became electronic they were still accessed mainly through traditional brokers. The access mechanism was the telephone. Thus an order would be telephoned to a broker who would then enter it into an electronic system. Alternatively, in the London market, traders could view **indicative prices**, i.e. not dealing prices, on the Stock Exchange SEAQ screen and then telephone a dealer to obtain an actual quote for a transaction of the size he or she wanted. The price might be better (price improvement) or could be worse (for a large order) than the price on the screen.

It is important to appreciate that the world's largest market, the New York Stock Exchange, did not allow full electronic access to its market until 2006. It is the growth in the capability of computers and computer programs (algorithms), the development of global financial trading networks and permissive legislation that have combined to enable this revolution. The outcome has been:

• A huge increase in the number and variety of trading centres;

- A dramatic decline in average trade size;
- A dramatic rise in the number of trades and in total dollar volume;
- The development of electronic institutional block crossing networks (dark pools);
- A need for complex buy-side trade execution strategies, due to multiple trading centres and types of execution venue;
- The shift in many markets from human to electronic market-making;
- The growth of trading firms employing strategies that, for success, require low latency trading (quick access to execution venues) and high trading frequency (large numbers of orders and trades).

## BACKGROUND TO THE GROWTH IN THE NUMBERS OF, AND VARIETY OF BUSINESS MODELS EMPLOYED BY, TRADING CENTRES

Equity markets, since their inception until relatively recently, operated on the principle that concentrating all orders in one market centre (execution venue) would lead to superior market performance. For equity trading, this centre was **the** stock exchange, for example the LSE or the New York Stock Exchange (NYSE). In New York there was a second exchange, NASDAQ. But it competed with the NYSE for listings only, not on trading NYSE stocks. It specialised in IT and high tech company listings.

The logic of a single execution venue was that the more buy orders and sell orders there were which competed with each other to be best priced (the double auction market), the more accurate the price discovery process would be and the smaller the spread between best bid and best offer. In addition, the process would be fair, in that every participant order would have the same opportunity to be executed at the best price at any point in time. Such stock exchanges tradition-ally were mutually owned organisations, i.e. they were owned by the brokers and dealers who operated in them. Note that the users of the market were not part of the mutual ownership structure. As a result, markets were monopoly providers of trading services, generally run in the interests of brokers and dealers without necessarily full regard for the interest of users, i.e. the investment community.

In the past the objection raised to competition between trading centres had always been that if order flow fragmented, two trading centres could be executing transactions in the same security at different prices at the same time. This would happen if, in one market centre, there were relatively more buys than sells compared with another market centre. Then one market centre would be likely to discover a higher price than the other. This is very similar to the problem of competing dealers (as discussed in the previous chapter). In addition, the fewer orders there are on each side of the market competing to be the best priced order on that side the higher the market spread is likely to be. Thus competition for order flow could lead to market fragmentation and deterioration in market quality (price discovery, market spread, market depth) as well as unfairness.

## WHAT SHOULD THE OBJECTIVES OF MARKET REGULATORS BE?

A key objective of regulators is the 'economically efficient execution of securities transactions'. However, this is difficult to define since there may be a trade-off between the cost and innovation benefits of **competition** *for order flow* and a possible consequent drawback of loss of **competition** *between orders*, leading to a loss of pricing efficiency. As a result of this dilemma, regulators have had to consider whether or not to permit competition and, if so, whether it is also necessary to mandate some type of integration between market centres – similar in concept to the integration mechanisms provided by IDBs and multidealer quotation screens).

Under EU regulations, which were in force until 2007, a member state was permitted to grant a stock exchange a monopoly. In EU law this was known as the **Concentration Provision**. While the UK did not take advantage of this permission, i.e. it allowed competition, other countries such as France enforced it very strictly, requiring all trading in French shares in France to be undertaken on the Paris Stock Exchange.

The objection to a concentration rule is that it prevents competition between trading centres, i.e. places where orders can interact. The reason that competition between trading centres should be important is that a monopoly exchange has no incentive to innovate in terms of market order types or speed of execution or to minimise costs and hence trading fees. The members of the UK stock exchange (broker/dealers), for example, as we noted earlier, even refused to allow the LSE to introduce a low-cost electronic market until the mid-1990s. The reason for this was that it would compete with the dealers' own in-house markets and an order-driven market competitor built by the LSE would almost certainly drive down trading spreads in the dealer market. Thus it was argued there was no need for an order-driven market and indeed it was claimed that investors would not use it.

It was not until Tradepoint, a private venture order-driven market[1] set up by former LSE employees was about to open for trading in London stocks, that the members finally permitted the LSE to open an order-driven market – SETS. The LSE did, however, retain the SEAQ dealer market and thus London at that point had both an order-driven and a dealer market. However, Tradepoint was the only competing trading centre anywhere in Europe until after the new EU regulation framework, Markets in Financial Instruments Directive (MiFID), was introduced in 2007. This, amongst other things, required all member states to permit competing trading centres to be established. It was this permissive legislation which enabled pan-European equity markets to be opened for the first time, providing a single trading screen to access trading capability in all major European equities.

In the United States, until 1971, virtually the only equity market was the NYSE. It was thus *the* central market. NASDAQ, the other main market in the US today, was a new one which came into existence only in 1971. But it is important to appreciate that, until quite recently, the NYSE and NASDAQ competed, as we noted above, principally for listings of new companies (for example Apple, Microsoft, Dell and Cisco chose to list on NASDAQ as has Facebook, but they did not compete in the trading of each other's stocks. Thus the principle of the central

---

[1] I was a member of the Tradepoint Market Advisory Panel whose function was to try to introduce traders to the concept of multiple trading venues and the benefits of competition.

market was maintained because NASDAQ specialised in 'high tech' stocks and new companies, not in the traditional stocks such as GM and GE. Today, however, with electronic trading the NASDAQ market in particular has gained a substantial volume of trading in NYSE-listed stocks.

So why was the principle of the central market so entrenched? The reason is what economists refer to as externalities, in this case positive order flow externalities. An externality is related to the network nature of markets. When one person joins a network (like a dating agency network to enable people to meet members of the opposite sex) it is not only the person who joins who gains benefits but half the people in the network. Potentially everyone of the opposite sex gains from the new person joining. Equally, an Orange mobile phone is of practical use only if friends who might be on the Vodaphone or O2 network can interconnect to its network. This is in contrast to motoring where an extra car on a road network causes negative externalities, i.e. while the additional car owner obtains (private) benefits from having the use of a car on a road, this imposes congestion (public) costs on every other user of the road network and reduces their utility.

The greater the proportion of total potential orders that arrives at an execution venue, i.e. the more concentrated the market is, the more likely it is that a buy order of a certain size will be able to meet a sell order of the same size and that the price of the trade can be agreed. In the jargon of the marketplace, orders beget orders. If, in contrast, there are many trading venues (which are simply networks linking traders) trading the same securities and there is no connection between them, it is quite likely that while one venue has an excess of buyers, another has an excess of sellers and thus few transactions take place in either, or the price that is discovered does not reflect 'fundamentals'. Such a market might have time and price priority within its own venue but there would not necessarily be price or time priority across the venues. Such a market is said to be fragmented. If markets do become fragmented, then there have to be technical mechanisms to recombine them into something closer to a central marketplace such as we saw earlier in the case of dealer markets. This may happen through market forces, i.e. a company sees a profit opportunity to provide a consolidated screen or it may have to be mandated by law as it is in the United States through Regulation National Market System (Regulation NMS).

## ALTERNATIVE TRADING SYSTEMS: ATSs, ECNs AND MTFs

Alternative trading systems (ATSs), meaning trading centres providing an alternative to traditional exchanges and to broker-dealer market making, started to come into existence in the mid-1990s. A traditional order-driven exchange as we noted in the last chapter uses a relatively simple technology – the double auction mechanism using an order matching engine – to match incoming orders, according to a set of rules normally based on price and time priority. The best price wins and if two orders are at the same best price, the first one to be entered into the system wins. In the 1990s it became relatively easy, and inexpensive, to replicate such an engine outside the conventional exchange.

In the United States, these trading centres were known as electronic communication networks (ECNs), while in Europe under the EU regulatory framework they became known as multilateral trading facilities (MTFs), with the word 'multilateral' being used to distinguish them from the bilateral trading facilities offered by dealers. These facilities in terms of their technology were no different from exchanges. Only the regulatory framework under which they operated and thus provided competition to the traditional exchanges was different.

In Europe, the first and indeed only ATS in the 1990s, as we noted above, was Tradepoint, which started operation in 1995 and which the UK authorities classified as an 'other market'. It merged with SWX Swiss Exchange in 2000 and was renamed 'virt-x'. The ultimate parent of virt-x (SWX Group) merged with two other companies in 2008 and virt-x was renamed SWX Europe.

In the U S, the first new trading centre to come into existence was Island (subsequently called Inet). It started operation in 1996 aided by some changes in regulations. Today Island (Inet) is part of NASDAQ which acquired it in 2005. The screen grab of an order book showing orders for Altair on Island (see Figure 12.1) was taken by me when Island was an independent company (before becoming the core of the NASDAQ electronic order matching market).

Although these new mechanisms came into existence in the 1990s, it was only in the new millennium that they started to pose a threat to the 'traditional' exchange. Alternatives to the traditional exchange became viable for a number of reasons. First, price discovery had become electronic in most markets and therefore this concept became accepted, which it was not initially by many market participants. Second, it was not only the price discovery process that had become electronic. Order transmission from customers to brokers or from customers to trading centres had become increasingly electronic rather than by voice over the telephone to a (human) broker. Electronic order transmission and electronic order matching through low cost matching engines suddenly made the threat to existing exchanges much greater and also made the regulators realise the need for a regulatory framework which took account of competition for order flow. However, within Europe it was not until a new trading centre could offer the benefits of pan-European trading that such new trading centres suddenly took off as, in this multi-market feature, they had an edge over traditional nation state exchanges.

In the US the outcome of the regulators' consideration of the issue of competition between venues was Regulation NMS (Regulation National Market System), which came into force in 2006. In Europe it was the MiFID which, as we have already noted, came into force in 2007, which recognised that the existence of competing market centres required a new framework to ensure fair and orderly markets. While both of these regulatory frameworks are quite recent, they are both now rather out of date due to the speed of development in market technology. As a result, the SEC, the EU and also the Australian Securities & Investment Commission have recently carried out reviews of market structure and the implications of market developments for regulation. In the case of the EU, this will lead to MiFID II.

The screen grab in Figure 13.1 is an early example of a screen which consolidates the prices on a number of exchanges, ECNs and broker/dealers in the US and was used by traders following a particular stock, in this case Dell. It shows all the places it trades, including Island. We can judge from the fact that Dell is trading around its highest ever level that this screen grab is from the year 2000. At this time the competing trading centres were all order-driven markets and not crossing networks/dark pools which we will discuss shortly.

We can see in Figure 13.1 all the bids and offers in the market. For example, on the ask side:

SNDV is Soundview Technology Group

ARCHIP is Archipelago, which is the ECN that the NYSE bought in order to provide itself with modern technology;

MADF is Madoff Securities (Mr Madoff, who was the biggest Ponzi crook[2] in the world in recent years, also owned a brokerage);

BRUT is another ECN;

NITE is Knight Capital Group.

MSCO, which is best offer, is Morgan Stanley.

All these venues compete for business in Dell and other quoted companies. It can be seen that, at the time of the screengrab, Soundview is top of the book on the bid side, whereas Morgan Stanley (MSCO) has the best ask (offer). Soundview and Morgan Stanley are shown at the top of the book because they were the first to enter limit orders at this price and, in a market with price and time priority, they will be the first orders against which the next market order will execute in preference to those at the same price below them.

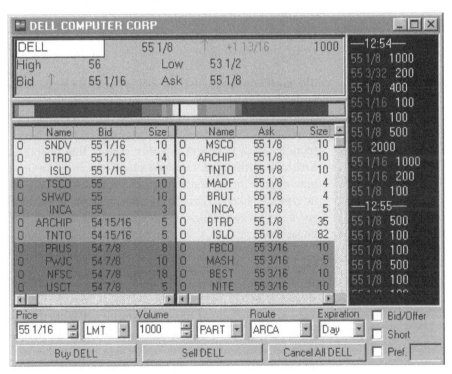

**Figure 13.1** A consolidated order book showing best bids and offers (asks) from all multilateral trading centres and dealers in Dell

---

[2] Ponzi financing is explained in Chapter 15.

# THE TRADER'S PROBLEM

A trader's job is to execute a trade. The availability of multiple venues and new types of venue resulted in a need for traders to reconsider the trade execution strategy that should be employed, compared with that which would have been appropriate prior to the market structure becoming fragmented and complex.

The factors traders have always had to consider when defining order placement strategy include, importantly, the need to minimise trading cost, which covers:

- Commissions;
- Bid/ask spread;
- Market impact cost.

In addition employers have to consider the cost of paying human traders, which can be substantial.

The existence of new market centres has increased the number of parameters that a trader has to consider when trying to minimise trading costs. He or she has to consider:

- The optimal order size;
- Whether to place a market or a limit order;
- Whether to enter most orders at the opening and closing single price auctions rather than all through the trading day;
- Which particular order-driven market(s) to trade on;
- To what extent he or she should use a broker to help with execution.

The **market impact cost**, the last of the costs in the list above, is the effect of a trade on the market price which causes the trade to be undertaken at a worse price than that which seemed to be available pre-trade. Market impact is unlikely to be an issue for a 'small' trade but, for a large trade, we have to assume that trading friction is likely to impact cost of execution. This is because a large trade is likely to have to 'walk the book' to obtain a large execution, i.e. buy (or sell) at increasingly unfavourable prices, and also because of **information leakage**. Large institutional investors are likely to have to execute trades which are multiples of normal market size and thus such investors have a particular interest in the question of market impact cost.

The first problem with a large trade is whether or not the trader has to give a price concession to the other side in order to attract sufficient orders on that side. This would be an example of market impact cost. The reason he or she might choose to do this is that there is always undisplayed liquidity potentially available in a market, i.e. holders of securities who will trade if the price offered to them is better than the market price. But in addition to the purely practical issue of how to attract sufficient size on the other side, there is the issue of trading with better informed counterparties and those who are trying to front-run a large order, i.e. to buy in front of such an order so as to sell immediately after the large order has moved the price up. For most large traders today and in the past, this is the key problem in trading and potentially gives rise to the highest of the costs (market impact costs) in the trading process.

The problem of large trades is not a new one. It has always existed and tradition-ally one way to try to reduce market impact was by employing a trusted broker who could search out liquidity without allowing too much information leakage into the market. Most of these strategies would involve executing the trade, the so-called **parent order** as we noted earlier, through trading in smaller sized pieces, so-called **child orders**. This is known as slicing and dicing. The problem with doing this is that other traders are trying to detect order patterns in a security's trading to determine if it is likely that there is an order in the market with **more to go**. If they think they have detected such a pattern they will enter transactions into the market to try to exploit the balance of the large order which has not yet been executed in smaller trades. Thus the trader's dilemma is unchanged in the new market environment – he or she still needs to employ trading strategies, but now has to employ them in a multiple trading centre environment. It is as if the trading problem has gone from being two dimensional to being three dimensional.

## THE NEW COMPETITORS TO TRADITIONAL EXCHANGES

When we look at what has happened in practice to trading of large company stocks since the advent of competition, the NYSE provides a good example of a tradi-tional exchange which has lost market share, not only to the new order-driven trading centres but also to a new type of electronic execution venue – the dark pool – that we will consider shortly. The statistics in Table 13.1 show just how dramatic has been the loss in market share by the NYSE in its own listed stocks since it first offered electronic access to its order book in 2006. We also see that the time taken to execute an order has fallen dramatically, as has the average order size.

An obvious question is where has the 75% of volume in NYSE-listed stocks that is not traded through the exchange gone? The answer, of course, is that it has gone to other trading centres.

Figure 13.2 shows the venues where trading is taking place. NMS stocks are all major stocks trading in the national market system. It can be seen that there are more than 200 dealer internalisation venues and 32 block trading type dark pools. It should also be noted that NYSE and NYSE Arca should be combined since the latter is simply the volume traded on the NYSE using the Archipelago system

**Table 13.1**  NYSE statistics

| NYSE stocks | 2005 | 2009 |
| --- | --- | --- |
| Daily volume (billions of shares) | 2.1 | 5.9 |
| Volume (%) | 79.1 | 25.1 |
| Daily number of trades (millions) | 2.9 | 22.1 |
| Average trade size (number of shares) | 724 | 268 |
| Speed of execution (seconds) | 10.1 | 0.7 |

*Source*: Data from Securities and Exchange Commission, 'Concept Release on Equity Market Structure', 2010.

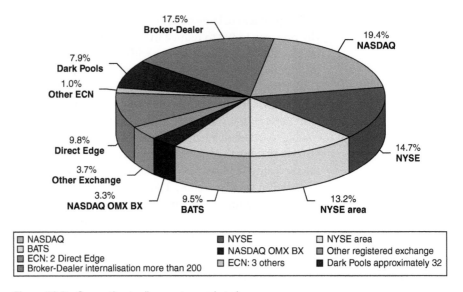

**Figure 13.2**   Competing trading centre market share

*Source*: Securities and Exchange Commission, Concept Release on Equity Market Structure 2010.

which the exchange purchased some years ago and which appeared in Figure 13.1 as ARCHIP.

To give some idea of the types of new market centre that have been growing in the US and the UK, I will discuss two – BATS and chi-x. In fact, BATS agreed in 2011 to acquire chi-x from its current owners, who are the major high frequency traders, along with some broker/dealers. At some point, therefore, it is likely that BATS will be a single marketplace operating as one of the largest and most successful exchanges in both the US and across almost all equity markets in Europe. As of the start of 2012, the two exchanges between them had 25% of European trading volume.

## THE PROBLEM OF CREATING A COMPETING EXCHANGE

'Liquidity begets liquidity' is a well-known aphorism. What this means is that investors will seek to trade wherever they think they will find liquidity. If there is no liquidity available they will not trade. Thus for a new exchange, the problem is how to attract customers when there is no guarantee that they will find liquidity. Indeed the biggest problem is how to attract liquidity providers to a new trading venue. As a result of this – the chicken and egg problem – most attempts to create new exchanges have failed. The solution for recent new entrants to the market, such as BATS and chi-x, has been threefold:

● First, by taking advantage of the rapidly falling cost of exchange technology, they have been able to leapfrog older exchanges which have high costs, thereby enabling the newcomers to offer very much lower trading fees.
● Second, by designing their systems from scratch as high speed systems, they have offered traders the ability to trade **ahead** of those using the slower, more traditional exchanges.

- Third, by devising a completely different pricing structure, they have attracted liquidity providers. This new pricing structure is known as 'maker-taker' pricing. Those who place limit orders (liquidity providers) who are price makers are either charged much less than those who place market orders (liquidity takers) or are actually paid for placing a limit order if it is executed against, i.e. results in a trade. Thus, for example, if the liquidity taker was charged 0.003% of the value of a trade for an executed order, two-thirds of this fee (0.002%) would be rebated to the liquidity provider. This was clearly an incentive for liquidity providers to enter the market and, indeed, is a major source of income to electronic high-frequency trading (HFT) market makers. Those who took liquidity, market order placers, paid the fee with no rebate and were, in effect, paying the limit order trader for his or her service.

## BATS (Better Alternative Trading System)

The BATS exchange (founded in Kansas City in 2006) is a good example of a new exchange. It was set up as an ECN but converted from ECN regulatory status (an exchange in all but name) to registered exchange status in 2008. It is now the third largest equity market in the US with a 9.5% market share. BATS has grown rapidly in competition with existing exchanges – the NYSE and NASDAQ – by offering low-cost trading, in part through state-of-the-art technology, very high speed execution, good order routing systems and maker-taker pricing. It is this latter concept that has been important in helping BATS break into the market.

Maker-taker pricing, which is now used by a number of exchanges, acknowledges that a market is a mechanism for providing liquidity to investors who desire it at that particular moment. Thus in every execution, one type of market participant (someone entering a limit order) is providing liquidity to another who is taking it (the market order placer). The most valuable service is considered to be the provision of liquidity, i.e. posting limit orders (passive) against which market orders (aggressive) can be executed. The reason is that the liquidity provider is effectively giving other traders a free option to trade at a price which may be the wrong one for it (the price may immediately move against it). BATS and other exchanges and trading centres have used a liquidity taker/price taker fee and a liquidity provider/price maker rebate as a way of attracting the initial liquidity providers. The pricing structure enables any firm which posts more limit orders (and has these executed against) than market orders to make a net return from the trading centre operator. Such market centres have thus become very attractive to a certain type of trader – one whose business model is to provide liquidity to the market and be rewarded for it, just like a traditional market maker. These are known as electronic liquidity providers.

Chi-x is a pan-European MTF set up in 2007 just as the 'Concentration Provision' in European market regulation was dropped in the MiFID regulation which came into effect in that year. Chi-x was the first market centre to take advantage of this new freedom to trade stocks from all European countries on a single MTF. By the end of 2011, chi-x had the largest share of European trading of any Regulated Market or MTF with an average 25% market share across the major EU countries. At the end of 2011, chi-x was acquired by BATS thus strengthening

BATS and creating an even more formidable competitor to Regulated Markets (stock exchanges) in Europe.

Chi-x, as well as offering an MTF market (order-driven double auction or visible book) also offers a dark pool or dark book as it is called in. Figure 13.3.

Chi-x thus has two 'books'. On the 'lit' side is its visible book i.e. it has pre-trade transparency, which accepts orders from traders in the form of limit orders or market orders. On the 'unlit' side, which it calls its dark book (Chi-Delta), is an order crossing mechanism which does not have pre-trade transparency i.e. executable prices are not displayed. Both books are connected to a central counterparty which takes over the trades by 'novation' before passing them to a securities settlement system. These processes – central counterparty novation and clearing and settlement are discussed in Chapter 14.

## LARGE TRADES AND INFORMATION LEAKAGE

Competition between order-driven trading centres and other technological developments such as HFT have resulted in the average trade size on most exchanges falling quite dramatically, making it much harder for the largest fund managers to execute their trades.

In the US, the following figures have been quoted for the average size for trades in IBM shares:

- 1998: 1,400 shares;
- 2006: 400 shares;
- 2010: 250 shares.

Table 13.2 shows the dramatic drop in trade sized since the start of the millennium in the UK.

Using a broker to execute large trades almost always leads to information leakage into the market. On receiving a large order, the broker will ask his dealer how much of the order he could fill immediately; the dealer will then go to other dealers or to an interdealer broker to see how much more he can fill by that means; the client's broker will also talk to his other clients and other brokers in order to

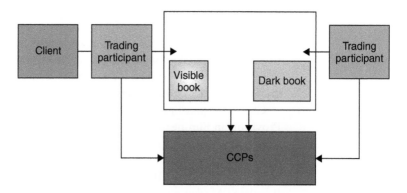

**Figure 13.3** Structure of chi-x Europe markets

**Table 13.2**  Number and value of trades and average trade size on the LSE SETS

| Year | Trades | Value traded (£bn) | Avg. trade size (£) |
|------|--------|--------------------|---------------------|
| 2000 | 8,593,453 | 531 | 61,751 |
| 2001 | 15,753,730 | 650 | 41,282 |
| 2002 | 23,834,026 | 670 | 28,119 |
| 2003 | 32,889,548 | 714 | 21,723 |
| 2004 | 40,853,969 | 877 | 21,458 |
| 2005 | 51,385,063 | 1,050 | 20,435 |
| 2006 | 78,186,752 | 1,509 | 19,295 |
| 2007 | 138,750,727 | 2,145 | 15,459 |
| 2008 | 194,313,207 | 2,055 | 10,578 |
| 2009 | 156,441,563 | 1,131 | 7,227 |

*Source*: LSE.

try to find the other side by transacting as much as possible with each counterparty. Inevitably price will move against the initial client. This broker information leakage problem, along with the dramatic decline in average trade size, has worsened the problem for institutional traders who are trying to execute large orders and has been a factor in the development of another type of new trading centre, the block crossing network, also known as a 'dark pool' or 'dark book' or 'unlit venue'.

## Dark pools/Crossing networks

In contrast to order-driven markets which we covered in the last chapter, where the key function is price discovery, these alternative trading systems do **not** discover the price, i.e. **they are not markets** – they are simply trading centres/execution venues. Instead of discovering the price, they use derivative pricing – which has nothing to do with derivatives but simply means that the price at which transactions are undertaken is based on the price derived from quotations available or transactions taking place on a different venue at the same time (normally the main central market or the best of a range of competing market prices). Thus they normally execute at the mid-price on the trading screen, which shows the current national best bid and offer (NBBO) in the US, or in Europe the European best bid and offer in the market. Access to these prices, for example LSE Level II prices, is available to anyone willing to pay the requisite fee to the exchange.

These venues focus on what is called 'quantity discovery', a term that has been coined by Bob Schwarz[3] to describe the process by which a trading venue can enable a private transmission of information on what counterparties actually want

---

[3]  See Robert Schwarz, Reto Francioni and Bruce Weber, *The Equity Trader Course* (Wiley Trading, 2006).

to do, in particular the size, rather than just what they are initially willing to reveal, i.e. a small child order of the parent order. Essentially they invite traders to send in indications of what they wish to do. If both a buy and a sell interest in the same security are in the system, the system will cross the two indications of interest (IOI) to create a trade. Similar mechanisms have existed (in non-electronic form) for many years as manual broker crossings when a broker has two orders from clients which match and he or she matches them in-house, taking a commission from both sides, rather than doing it through the exchange and paying an exchange fee.

Block crossing networks allow large orders to meet and (hopefully) execute without the rest of the market becoming aware of them until after the trade. They function by inviting traders to enter their orders for execution either at a fixed time, say noon, or at any time of day, depending on the system. Thus all orders that can cross against each other are executed totally anonymously and at the mid-price on the reference market (or somewhere between bid and offer) and without anyone except the counterparties knowing until the trade has been executed. They are, in fact, the 'perfect broker'. The system operator charges a fee, like any broker who effects a cross.

A drawback of such mechanisms is that because they are not auction markets there is no reason why supply and demand should balance. There is frequently a substantial imbalance which would simply fail to execute. This is either because of some supply/demand imbalance or simply because there is nothing at all on the other side (complete imbalance). Execution rates at one time were as low as 5–10% but today are closer to 15–25% as crossing networks gain popularity.

The Liquidnet institutional crossing mechanism is a good example of such a venue. It was launched in the US in 2001 and in Europe in 2002 and, as a crossing network, does not have a price discovery process. Instead it is a quantity discovery process with the option of using negotiation between counterparties to agree a price within the spread on the reference market. It is designed for institutional investors only, i.e. broker-dealers may not participate.

If the Liquidnet system detects that two participants are both interested in the same security but on opposite sides of the market, i.e. one wants to buy and one wants to sell, it sends a message to both parties which enables them to negotiate. Rather like eBay, it also lets each side know how often they have successfully negotiated with this particular counterparty in order to decide whether to try to negotiate and to encourage parties to develop a good execution record. Also, to avoid misunderstandings over size, it is possible to specify that the potential counterparty should only be signalled if its order is at least a specified percentage of the size that the other party wishes to transact. No information about orders or executions is transmitted to anyone except the parties themselves. The execution price is that agreed between the parties and would normally be at or within the market spread at the time of the trade. After the trade, however, the execution has to be reported to the relevant reporting authority. Thus such markets, while they do not have pre-trade transparency, do have post-trade transparency. Because they do not have it pre-trade they are also known as unlit markets, in contrast to order-driven markets, which are called lit markets because they have pre-trade transparency, i.e. pre-trade display of the order book.

Liquidnet's latest system is called Supernatural. On their website they describe its use as follows:

> When you use our Supernatural block trading strategies, you don't need to face the trader's dilemma – try to get an order done quickly but risk incurring market impact costs or play it safe by exposing less to the market but risk missing trading opportunities. It doesn't matter how you trade. Supernatural effortlessly handles your institutional-sized orders while delivering the highest crossing rate, resulting in substantial cost savings. The bigger the order, the better the results. When you use our block trading strategies, you are no longer constrained by ADV.[4] Amazingly, the larger the Supernatural order size as a percentage of ADV, the greater the cost savings, thanks to a higher crossing rate.

Figures taken from their website show that the average trade size is almost 42,000 shares – very much larger than average. Also the fill rate, i.e. the success rate in having an order executed, is almost 50%, which is much higher than for crossing networks in the past. They also have a large number of members – 637, who are institutional investors that use the system and operate in 39 different markets.

## DARK POOLS AND BROKER-DEALER INTERNALISATION

The institutional block trading centres of the type we have just looked at are also known as **unlit venues** or **dark pools** or **undisplayed liquidity**. They have acquired this name, not because of the lack of a price discovery mechanism, but because they do not disclose pre-trade orders. As this is required in most countries in order to provide pre-trade transparency, systems of this type require some type of 'waiver' (exemption) from the transparency regulations. They are allowed this because they are designed to provide an important service to institutional investors. If they were not able to hide from the market what a customer was trying to do, prices would simply move against the customer and there would be no benefit in trying to use the system.

Undisplayed liquidity in markets (dark liquidity) is not, in fact, something new. Traditionally a broker/dealer tries to match large orders internally (in-house crossing) which simply means that they cross trades internally between their customers without exposing these internal crosses to the public markets. Regulators, however, have considerable concern about undisplayed liquidity of any type since, by withdrawing orders from the public markets, such orders are not contributing to price discovery. This has become a central issue for regulators as such venues have attracted ever more volume. Regulators on both sides of the Atlantic are researching the issue of whether there comes a point at which so many orders are being executed in the dark (perhaps around 30% of the total) that the price discovery mechanism provided by the remaining orders which are routed to auction markets is insufficient to achieve satisfactory price discovery. If they found this to be so, they would make the rules for 'off-market trades' much stricter than they are currently.

The provision of dark liquidity, traditionally known as hidden orders/internal order crossing/off-exchange trading, was a traditional role for brokers. When

---

[4] Average daily volume (on main market).

venues such as Liquidnet came into existence, it was clear to brokers that such independent crossing networks would be likely to compete strongly for business against their internal crossing systems. As a result, virtually all the large broker-dealers have now set up their own electronic crossing systems (which often have the word 'cross' or 'X' in their name). However, these systems are not specifically designed for large institutional orders. The average order size is much smaller. Thus dark pools distinguish themselves as either block crossing networks mainly for institutional investors or as simply crossing networks for any size of order. On block crossing networks such as Liquidnet, the average trade size as we noted is almost 50,000 shares, whereas the average size of trade on broker/dealer crossing networks is little different from that on the public markets.

Broker-dealer dark pool crossing networks are sometimes thought to operate in the same way as independent pools operated by companies such as ITG (Posit) and Liquidnet. However, this is not the case. Whereas the system operator in the case of ITG and Liquidnet should not have a position-taking trading book (or trading affiliate) and thus not undertake any proprietary trading, broker-dealers, almost by definition, do. Thus in a broker-dealer pool, the counterparty is likely to be the broker-dealer itself which may enable the broker-dealer to take out the spread on two customer orders which it is 'crossing'. So although they come under the same heading – unlit venues – they are conceptually different. The similarity is that neither type provides any pre-trade information to the market.

Table 13.3 gives an indication of the range of venues and also of the volume going through each in early 2010. You can see clearly the difference in average trade size between Pipeline (now called Aritas) and Liquidnet on the one hand and the broker-dealer crossing networks.

## Algorithmic trading

At this point we are going to look only at automated **routing** of buy-side orders to trading centres **and** automated **execution** of trades. We are not examining

**Table 13.3** The major dark pools

| Name | % of total US equity volume | Average trade (shares) |
|------|---------------------------|----------------------|
| **Credit Suisse Crossfinder** | 1.55 | 332 |
| **Goldman Sachs Sigma X** | 1.44 | 450 |
| **Knight Link** | 1.23 | 426 |
| **GETCO Execution Services** | 1.11 | 365 |
| **Level** | 0.53 | 292 |
| **Pipeline Trading** | 0.12 | 51,210 |
| **Liquidnet** | 0.28 | 49,193* |
| **ITG POSIT** | 0.24 | 6,000 |

*Excludes Liquidnet's H20 product.

*Source*: Rosenblatt Securities.

automated **generation** of trades, i.e. the decision on what to trade, which I will cover shortly under HFT. We are only concerned with **how the buy side has coped** with the new multiplicity of venues, numerous order types and complex execution strategies.

The need to use algorithms, i.e. computer programs for trade execution, arises from the fragmentation of markets and falling trade size that has occurred in both the United States and in Europe as a result of technological innovation and falling costs and the permissive (in the sense of now permitting) legislation such as MiFID which has enabled alternative trading centres to establish themselves. Without some help, a buy-side trader could not make rational decisions on how to execute a trade quickly enough. The use of algorithms enables a computer to 'search out liquidity' and send an order or part of an order to a trading centre that has the requisite liquidity at that time. The SEC describes an execution environment as one where there is a need for systems to integrate all trading centres, dispersed rather than fragmented, with the word 'dispersed' not having negative connotations, whereas 'fragmented' in this context does.

For buy-side traders, the multiplicity of venues raises the issue of execution strategy, which we have covered briefly, but which now also involves questions relating to crossing networks:

- On lit venues, which one(s) to choose?
- To use market orders or limit orders?
- Over what time period to execute an order?
- Whether to execute most of the order at the opening and closing periodic auctions or throughout the day?
- What size of order to enter into trading centres?
- On unlit venues, which one(s) to choose?
- How to split an order between lit and unlit venues?
- How long to leave an order sitting passively in an unlit venue (dark pool) before transferring it to a lit venue?

Execution strategy is now a highly complex field. To help traders execute orders, a number of suppliers have developed systems that aid this complex task. These systems are known as **algorithms**, i.e. programs designed to replicate human decision-making and enable a scientific approach to parent order execution to be employed. Generally they involve an **order management system (OMS)** which can pass orders to the algorithmic engine which, on the basis of order flow information from the various venues, follows an appropriate execution strategy. Such systems rely on having information feeds from all the venues which enable them to 'detect liquidity' and direct part of an order to the location where they find that liquidity. Liquidity, in this case, simply means a matching order against which at least part of the total order can be executed. This type of algorithm can be provided by a **broker** or by an **independent firm**. A good example of broker-provided systems are those available through Goldman Sachs[5] as described in the extract from their website below:

---

[5]  Full details available at http://gset.gs.com/offering/execution.asp

Algorithmic (algo) strategies

Goldman Sachs offers a global, multi-asset suite of algorithms, which includes equities, futures, synthetics and options. The goal of each algorithm is to seek optimal execution based on user-specified trading parameters. To do so, the algorithms access both displayed and non-displayed sources of liquidity via our SIGMA$^{SM}$ smart router. Clients can also interact with non-displayed liquidity through SIGMA X (US, Japan, and Hong Kong) and SIGMA (EU). In addition, algorithmic trading gives clients access to a range of resources, including analytics, transaction cost analysis and execution strategy consulting.

## SIGMA$^{SM}$ & SIGMA X

Goldman Sachs Electronic Trading (GSET) has a global liquidity offering which consists of SIGMA X (US), SIGMA X (Asia), and SIGMA$^{SM}$ (Europe). Clients trading US shares can cross orders with non-displayed liquidity in our SIGMA X crossing network. One of the largest Broker Dealer ATSs in the US, SIGMA X allows customers to benefit from the aggregated source of liquidity that flows through the firm's infrastructure. In Europe, we offer our SIGMA suite of products: liquidity-seeking algorithms, smart order routing and aggregation tools, sophisticated crossing logic and a comprehensive set of analytics. The SIGMA suite enables you to access multiple liquidity sources, both displayed and dark, with no change to your existing workflow.

## INDEPENDENT BROKER ORDER EXECUTION ALGOS AND ROUTER

Weeden and Company, a pure broker without any dealing or proprietary trading, along with Pragma, a provider of trading solutions, has developed a **liquidity aggregation algorithm** known as ONEPIPE, which is shown in Figure 13.4 as an example of such a system. Systems like this ensure that no broker or financial institution ever sees the **parent order**, i.e. the original full-sized order, only the **child orders**, i.e. the parts of the order which have been broken off for execution (offspring).

ONEPIPE employs an allocation methodology that allows customers to source both dark and displayed liquidity, including block liquidity. The new methodology monitors liquidity conditions and dynamically adjusts attributes, such as minimum fill size, to take advantage of the type of liquidity available at each venue at any given time. It allows users to express the trading rate they want to achieve. The ability to trade at user-defined participation rates provides traders with more control and greater flexibility in how they utilise dark and displayed venues. It also incorporates anti-gaming and information leakage protection logic.

In Figure 13.4, the client site is the company with trade execution needs. It has an order management system (OMS) to enter orders, to keep track of orders placed and to follow order execution. Orders have to be routed to 'the Street' (Wall Street) and, with perhaps 40 different trading centres available, there is a need for algorithms which work out where liquidity is to be found and to execute a parent order, broken down into child orders, based on the parameters set by the trader. These algos are on the Pragma Algo Server in the figure.

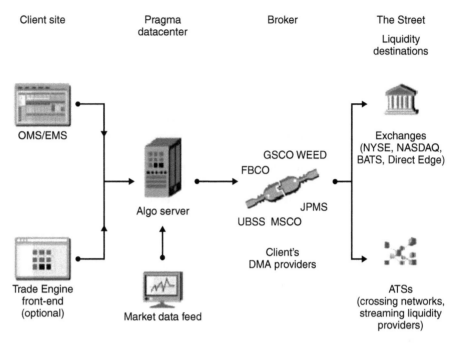

**Figure 13.4**   The Weeden/Pragma OnePipe™ hostedalgos™ system for algorithmic trade execution

*Source*: Weeden/Pragma trading. http://www.pragmatrading.com/products/hosted-algos (9 February 2012).

These algos can operate only if they are able to see what is happening in all the 'liquidity destinations' on the Street, i.e. there is appropriate transparency in both lit and dark venues. Thus market data feeds are critical in supplying the algos with the information they require to make decisions based on the trader's parameters, such as participation rate, time to execute and price limits.

A trader could be a member of all the liquidity destinations which it desires to access and have network connections to each. But that would be expensive. Instead the trader will work with a set of brokers, each of whom will have a contractual agreement (a broker agreement) to enable it to use the brokers' direct market access (DMA) facilities to access the Street. This is a means of avoiding brokers becoming aware of a large trader's trading intentions while still using a broker's 'pipes', i.e. its fibre optic cables. It also involves 'piggybacking' on a broker's membership of some dozens of exchanges and other trading centres without the institutional investor having to purchase expensive memberships. DMA should enable the buy-side to keep their trading strategies out of view of the broker and prevent brokers front-running them by knowing their trading intentions. Thus the brokers are acting not as agency advisors or providers of research but simply as providers of routing technology.

The broker identifiers in Figure 13.4 are GSCO (Goldman Sachs), WEED (Weeden), JPMS (JP Morgan Securities), MSCO (Morgan Stanley) FBCO (Credit Suisse First Boston) and UBSS (UBS Securities).

Part of the Weeden/Pragma system involves a means of benefitting from the huge number of dark pools available in the US, most of which are operated by broker-dealers. Thus, rather than simply choosing a preferred dark pool provider and sending all orders there, systems such as this can manage the orders in such a way as to optimise available liquidity in any dark pool at any particular time. This part of the whole order management system is described thus:

> While the new system is not aggregating the dark pools themselves, it's applying mathematics and optimization techniques to help buy-side traders efficiently manage their orders across a comprehensive list of dark pools – while preserving their anonymity. 'It's almost a central nervous system for dark pools.' Instead of needing direct connectivity to 30 separate dark pools, this allows a buy-side client 'to send their order through a single point on their OMS and have their order managed in an intelligent manner within all the passive sources that we have available to us.' The problem is now that there are so many of them, we're getting liquidity fragmentation.
>
> Wall St. & Technology.[6]

The Pragma TradeEngine™ screen grab in Figure 13.5 shows the interface which the trader would see. This gives an indication of some of the parameters that a

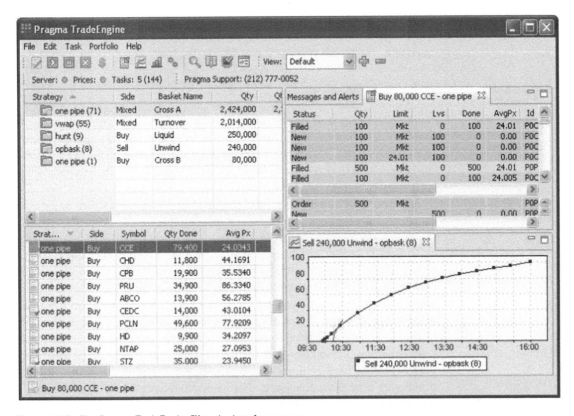

**Figure 13.5**  The Pragma TradeEngine™ trader interface screen

*Source*: Pragma website. http://www.pragmatrading.com/products/tradeengine-front-end (9 February 2012).

---

6  Pragma and Weeden to Launch OnePipe to Manage Fragmented Liquidity Across Dark Pools http://www.wallstreetandtech.com/articles/227000945

trader would set before asking the system to start the execution. This screen would also keep the trader up to date with progress on all executions.

The following report on a new algo produced by SocGen bank indicates the type of problem that traders today face and the type of solutions that are being developed to overcome them:

### New SocGen algo highlights information leakage risks

French investment bank Société Générale has announced the details of Eclipse, its new liquidity-seeking algorithm, which analyses the quality of liquidity that can be found in dark pools.

The algorithm, which is available in Europe and is in the final stages of development in the US, hunts dark and lit liquidity across a variety of venues including multilateral trading facilities, exchanges and broker-owned crossing engines.

'We developed a Quality of Venue Measure to look at the level of information leakage and adverse selection from each dark pool, and designed the logic for Eclipse based on our results.'

For example, one measure used looks at the volatility of the mid-price of a stock on a displayed exchange, after it has been traded in the dark. If, on a regular basis, the price of a stock moves adversely in the lit venue following a dark execution, one can infer that the trading counterparty is looking for information, rather than liquidity.

Using this type of analysis, clients can adjust the behaviour of Eclipse to suit their trading strategy, e.g. by posting larger portions of orders in those dark pools that are considered safe, or excluding those venues that have the most information leakage.

*The Trade News*, 2 August 2011

## HIGH FREQUENCY TRADING

A special class of algorithmic/automated trading is 'high frequency trading' HFT. It is difficult to define a high-frequency trader but one definition would be one which entered more than 1,000 orders per second into a market. Most of these might not result in trade executions as they may be 'fill or kill' ('immediate or cancel') orders with a high proportion not filling. Indeed 90% of orders may not lead to a 'fill' (execution). Such trading takes place in equities, options, futures, ETFs (exchange traded funds), currencies and other financial instruments that have electronic trading capability. It is important to be clear that **HFT is not a strategy**. It is a means of undertaking trades at high speed in order to generate profits from frequent small trades based on one of the underlying strategies.

The SEC in its Concept Release on the US equity market structure noted five characteristics that are often attributed to high frequency trading firms:

- They use very high speed and sophisticated computer programs for generating, routing and executing orders;
- They use co-location services, i.e. the trading engines of the HFT are next to the trading centre's servers;
- They have very short time frames for establishing and liquidating positions;
- They submit numerous orders that are cancelled shortly after submission;
- They end the trading day in as close to a flat position as possible.

Given that the HFT servers need information from the trading centre itself in order to initiate orders, because they are looking continuously at the bids and offers in the market and the executions that have happened in the last few microseconds, they have different needs than long-term investors who are making their own decisions based on fundamental factors (exogenous to trading centre data). HFTs, however, are making their trading decisions based on information which is endogenous to the trading centre(s), i.e. they are looking for short-term mispricings within or between markets or related products. As many of the trading opportunities which HFTs try to take advantage of are extremely short-term, the time taken to receive trade data from the trading centre, input it to the algorithms in their server and then send it an appropriate order to the trading centre (latency) is critical to their success.

HFTs are thus keen to reduce latency in their systems, i.e. the delay due to the distance that electronic messages have to travel. Even though messages travel at close to the speed of light, microseconds of difference between the arrival times of orders at the trading centre server will determine which order matches first. This latency concern is not the latency between their office and the exchange but between the HFT server (wherever it is located) and the server with the information their algorithms need to use to make decisions on order generation. Since the source of much of that information is data generated by the market centre itself, e.g. information such as trade execution prices and quantities, the closer the HFT servers are to the data –source, the faster the algorithms can generate orders. When a trader's servers are next to a market centre's own data centre this is known as co-location (or 'co-lo').

Table 13.4 shows the latencies in different trading centres. It shows that chi-x own latency, **if** the trader has his or her server co-located in the chi-x facility, is

**Table 13.4** Latency of various trading venues

| X Chi-X internal latency is approximately 350 microseconds | |
|---|---|
| **Trading venue** | **Median latency (milliseconds)** |
| Chi-X Europe | 0.4 (co-located) |
| Turquoise | <4 |
| LSE SETS | <6 |
| NASDAQ OMX Europe | 10 |
| Euronext | 13 |
| Deutsche Börse Xetra | 37 |
| OMX | 43 |
| Borsa Italiana | 106 |
| SWX | 216 |
| SWX Europe | 230 |

*Notes*: These internal figures are for round trip latency message acknowledgement based on sending an average number of messages to the exchange system and obtaining a response back to the participant's system over the course of a normal trading day. These figures are provided for illustrative purposes only and are not intended to represent an independent performance measure of latency.

*Source*: chi-x website.

only 400 millionths of a second , of which the time within its own system is only 350.

Many HFTs wish to arbitrage across markets and therefore the greater the number of markets in one location in which the HFT servers could be co-located, the better, since cross-market arbitrage will then not be slowed down by latency.. Since 2010 the Paris Stock Exchange has actually been located in a warehouse in Basildon in England (near London) rather than in a fine stone building in Paris. . Also located there are the Amsterdam Exchange, the Lisbon Exchange, the Brussels Exchange and the London International Financial Futures Exchange (LIFFE)! They all belong to the NYSE Euronext Group. Such exchanges now are simply servers in a building on an industrial estate in Basildon (rents are low compared with Paris or London or Amsterdam or Brussels). Euronext also sells 'rack space' to its customers and, by having all these exchanges and their customer servers in one location (co-location), latency is greatly reduced, enabling trading positions to be taken at the same micro-second within any one of these markets or between any two of them in a pairs-trade. Of course they also charge substantial fees for co-location and this income has now become an important profit centre for exchanges. In addition, it is more efficient for exchange operators to have all their servers in one location.

Figure 13.6, which is from NYSE Technologies, the company within the group which provides technology to NYSE Euronext and to co-location customers, shows the layout of the Basildon facility. It notes that the Colo Hall 1 alone provides more than 3,000 square metres of floor space and has 320 racks for traders' co-located computers. We don't know which exchange is in which hall, but it could be that Hall 7 is LIFFE, Hall 6 ,Paris and Hall 5 Amsterdam.

## Atlantic crossing

In HFT, milliseconds matter. A saving of just six milliseconds in transmission time is all that is required to justify the laying of the first transatlantic communications

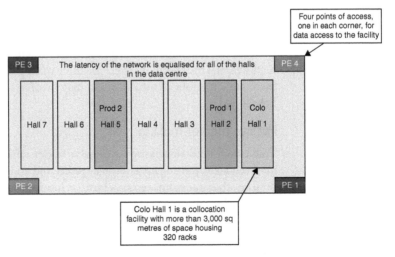

**Figure 13.6** European market centres divided into individual halls within the facility

*Source*: NYSE Technologies.

cable since 2001 at a cost of more than $300m. The existing best time across the Atlantic is 65 milliseconds, and the provider of this older cable is likely to lose all the HFT business when the new one becomes available. The British firm laying the cable, Global Marine Systems, is plotting a new route that is shorter than any previously taken as it will follow 'the great circle' flight path followed by London to New York flights. They expect almost every HFT and other transatlantic traders to become customers for the switch-on in 2013. Satellite which many people once thought would be faster is in fact too slow as the signal has to go up to the satellite and then back down to earth which makes for a very long journey.

## What strategies are employed by HFTs?

I start this section by noting that all HFTs employ computer based trading (CBT). The only difference between computer based trading (CBT) in general and HFT is that the HFTs execute their trading strategies at a higher speed than others and thus may be ahead of them in being able to spot short-term trading opportunities in markets.

CBT, like HFT, is not a strategy; nor do all CBT systems have the same characteristics. A useful taxonomy is as follows:[7]

CBT systems can trade on an agency basis, i.e. attempting to get the best possible execution of trades on behalf of clients, or on a proprietary (prop) basis, i.e. trading using one's own capital;

CBT systems may adopt liquidity-consuming (aggressive) trading styles or liquidity-supplying (passive) trading styles;

CBT systems may be classified as engaging in uninformed trading or informed trading.

HFT involves an automated trading strategy in which decisions on what to trade and when are made by an algorithm rather than by a person, and where reducing 'latency' in trading to a minimum is of the essence. In order to analyse HFTs as a specific class of trader within the taxonomy of the CBT universe above, it is necessary to understand the strategies they might use to try to generate a return on the capital they employ. There are three main groups of such strategies (though there are a number of others which may involve what is described as predatory behaviour):

### Passive market-making

Traditional market making involved a trader who we designate as a dealer or market-maker, putting up a two-way price (bid and offer) on a screen and waiting until another trader hits or takes him, i.e. hits his bid or takes his offer. Such a business is risky – it is offering a free option to other traders to transact at a price the dealer has made and which may be wrong. The risk is that the trader knows more

---

[7] From DR5, a study commissioned by the UK Government Office for Science Foresight project 'The Future of Computer Trading in Financial Markets' (Office for Science, 2011).

than the dealer about the 'true' price of the security and at worst he could be an insider (illegally informed) trader. The longer the dealer leaves his price on the screen (an option to be traded against) the greater the risk that he is exploited by someone with more information. To reduce the risk of exploitation by an information trader a dealer makes a wide spread, e.g. he might quote 97–97½ to give him the best chance of avoiding losing money. Nonetheless, a dealer may make only around 40–50% of the gross spread of the dealer quote – the rest he loses from price changes in his inventory. With electronic market making, as a result of low latency and the ability to cancel a trade within micro- or milliseconds, an HFT automated dealer can make much **finer prices**, i.e. tighter spreads without as much risk of losing on a trade. He also trades in smaller size than traditional market makers and will generally not hold any inventory positions overnight. Thus by using algorithms rather than human traders, the whole business of providing liquidity to other investors can be made less risky than in the past.

The speed with which such (algo) traders can look at the market order book (because their servers are co-located with the exchange's servers) means they see pre-trade prices first and can thus step in front of other traders who see the prices some milliseconds later. Thus access is not equal. The order size offered by such electronic market markers is smaller than that which would be offered by traditional ones since they operate on a basis that if they are losing on any trades they will quickly adjust the price. Thus they prefer not to trade in large size. As a result this type of market making may be less effective in providing liquidity to institutional investors who need to execute large trades. On the other hand executing large trades with a traditional market maker was easier for a buy-side institutional trader but more costly due to the large spreads they had to maintain to cover their risk of transacting with informed traders.

In addition to hoping to take out the spread on trades, electronic market makers also receive the liquidity rebate from the market centres which operate on the maker-taker pricing model we discussed earlier. Thus they are being paid for liquidity provision. There are two different types of relationship that an HFT which provides liquidity may have with an exchange or market centre. It may be the traditional type of relationship where the HFT has affirmative obligations in respect of the market centre, e.g. an obligation to provide a quote in a certain size on both sides of the market at all times during market opening hours. The HFT would then be called an (official) market maker on that particular market. Alternatively, the HFT might be doing the same type of transacting but without any obligations or benefits from the exchange. Such an HFT would be called a dealer rather than an official market maker.

But perhaps the biggest difference from traditional market makers or dealers is that HFT market makers/dealers do not have investor customers in the way that traditional OTC (bilateral) market makers/dealers do, since they simply interact with a multilateral market venue and not directly with investors in bilateral trading. Thus although we think of market-making as being a bilateral trading process, in this case it takes place on a multilateral platform. Thus electronic dealers do not need to be concerned about pressure from customers to provide a continuous liquidity service, even in difficult market conditions. HFT market makers may thus be more likely to be '**fair weather market makers**' than traditional market makers. It is much easier for HFT market makers to withdraw liquidity almost instantly if they feel it is in their interest and therefore they may be less likely to meet the needs of long-term investors. Such behaviour is like the traditional market-maker tactic of avoiding having to provide liquidity in a sharp market downturn, yet without breaking an exchange's rules, which they achieve by simply not answering the phone, putting it on hold or taking it off the hook.

## Arbitrage trading

### Intermarket arbitrage

One type of arbitrage trader seeks out pricing anomalies between two markets trading the same security. For example, such traders arbitrage price differences in the same security trading on the LSE and, say, BATS. Clearly such arbitrage was not possible (nor was it necessary) before the advent of multiple trading centres in the same stock. These arbitrageurs perform a function much like that of the IDBs who arbitrage between competing dealers. In other words, they enable a fragmented market to function more like a concentrated market where all buy orders can meet all sell orders. However, they function not as brokers but as dealers since they have actually to buy shares in one market and sell in another and thus they employ capital.

### ETF certificate arbitrage against underlying basket of shares

In Chapter 18 we examine the liquidity mechanism used by ETFs in comparison to that of mutual funds. We will note that ETFs always trade close to the underlying value of the shares which they represent. This is achieved as a result of HFT arbitrageurs buying the ETFs when they are priced below the underlying basket of shares, converting into shares and selling those shares in the market at a profit and vice-versa.

### Statistical (deterministic) arbitrage (stat-arb)

This type of arbitrage **could at one time** generate a sure profit by, for example, buying dollars at a low price in New York with pounds and selling them for pounds in London at a higher price (or vice versa). Such certain arbitrages no longer exist. Today, arbitrages are more likely to be statistical in the sense that there is a mispricing of two assets on the basis of some statistical model. Stat-arb suggests statistical mispricings that will be true if the expectations in the model are correct over the long run, when the strategy is repeated many times. In order words, it has to be correct more than 50% of the time. Essentially stat-arb involves **mean-reversion strategies**, i.e. the expectation that price relationships between securities will revert to previous levels. Such strategies involve trading in hundreds and often thousands of securities and derivative contracts, with holding periods varying from seconds to a few days. Long Term Capital Management, the world's largest hedge fund at the time, was an example of a stat-arb hedge fund which for many years generated exceptional returns – sometimes 40% in a year. Eventually (in 1998) it failed – losing almost $5 billion. It had to be rescued by a US Treasury organised bailout.

### Directional strategies

Directional strategies involve unhedged positions being carried in anticipation of small intraday price changes. One such strategy would involve taking positions based on news announcements. These announcements could be macroeconomic, industry related or related to a single corporate. The news might be 'machine read',[8] as it would take too long for humans to read it and try to assess its implications. Based on past patterns it can be seen that such news generates recognisable and statistically robust patterns. HFT firms will then estimate expected price responses to such anticipated events. By acting 'ahead of the crowd', such HFTs are taking positions **ahead of such news being impounded into a market price**. Once the market as a whole has reacted to the news, which might take seconds, minutes or hours, the trade is reversed at a profit if the expected price response materialises.

## THE MERGING OF 'EXCHANGE' AND DEALER MARKETS

Today traditional market making in the form we described in the last chapter is on a much reduced scale, at least in the high market capitalisation (large cap) equities traded on the major markets. Instead, electronic market making offered both by the proprietary trading divisions of broker-dealers and by proprietary trading firms has developed to provide an alternative source of liquidity. The important distinction as we noted earlier is that these electronic market makers do not provide liquidity in bilateral transactions with their clients but simply by putting their limit orders (their quotes) into a lit venue, i.e. an exchange or ECN/ MTF. Thus the two seemingly conceptually distinct types of trading centre that we covered in the last chapter – the auction mechanism and the dealer mechanism – have merged in the form of HFT liquidity providers. This type of market which combines auction and dealer market in one trading platform is a so-called **hybrid structure.**

In fact the dealer model and the order-driven market are not conceptually distinct, since limit orders and dealer quotes are no different in concept from each other. Both are simply an offer of liquidity, i.e. a price and a quantity, to other traders. Indeed, when we looked at Level II prices on the LSE and the yellow strip of old, the dealer quotes were actually called orders. On an order-driven market, dealers can put their offers of liquidity into the auction simply by entering limit orders either on one side of the market or on both (two-way price). Rather than putting out bids and offers on their own screens and waiting for clients to call, they are simply putting them on to the order book of an auction market where any market orders on the other side of the book can interact with them.

---

[8] Thomson Reuters Machine Readable News is the industry's most advanced service for automating the consumption and systematic analysis of news. It delivers deep historical news archives, ultra-low latency structured news and leading edge news analytics directly to applications. This enables algorithms to exploit the power of news to seize opportunities, capitalise on market inefficiencies and manage event risk.

## Exchange mergers: a case study of NYSE Euronext

High cost traditional airlines such as British Airways have found it difficult to compete on cost with new entrants such as Ryanair and easyJet. They have had to achieve cost savings themselves in order to lower their prices. They have also had initiate mergers to gain scale economies. The increasing success of new, low cost exchanges such as chi-x and BATS has created a problem for incumbent exchanges whose costs are much higher. The first attempt to create a grouping of exchanges (which when it started was not because of low cost competition) was Euronext, which came into existence in 2000. This was a grouping of three European exchanges – Paris, Brussels and Amsterdam. The Euronext Group then acquired the Lisbon Exchange and LIFFE. Since then the group has merged with the NYSE to create NYSE Euronext. In 2011 it planned to merge with Deutsche Borse but in early 2012 the European competition authorities prohibited the merger. Their reason was the combination of the two company's derivative markets in Europe would have 90% European market share. This was thought to be unacceptable.

## The economics of exchange mergers

In most industries, mergers take place between companies in the same industry in the same country. Thus, for example, in the UK, T-Mobile and Orange merged to gain economies of scale and also to reduce competition in UK mobile phone services and thereby, hopefully, reduce the erosion of price margins. However, in the case of exchanges, each country had only one exchange (the US is an exception with the NYSE and NASDAQ). Thus mergers, to gain economies of scale, could not take place within a country but **had** to take place cross-border. Like all mergers the NYSE Euronext group had the potential to generate costs savings from the use of a single 'platform', i.e. systems which run the exchange. The various mergers involved did not raise competition concerns in any country until 2011, since the various component exchanges operated markets in quite different regions of the globe. The proposed merger with Deutsche Borse does raise competition issues because it would involve combining the two largest (competing) derivatives exchanges in Europe, LIFFE and Eurex. Thus in my view, the economic logic of merging exchanges cross-border is not the achievement of 'a global liquidity pool' (this is nothing more than marketing speak) but economies of scale in technology.

While at one time exchanges offered either cash market products (mainly equities) or derivative contracts, today most exchanges offer both. In fact, the economics of exchanges as for-profit companies increasingly depends on having a successful derivatives platform as well as the more traditional cash market platform. This is because it has become increasingly clear that cash market trading is subject to declining margins due to high levels of competition from the new, lost cost exchanges, whereas derivative markets have much higher margins. This is because of an essential difference between cash and equity products.

An equity (or bond) is a contract between a company and an investor. The company has little reason to object to this contract being traded on any venue and thus new low cost exchanges and MTFs can easily compete in equities and bonds with the established exchanges. An equity derivative (or any derivative contract), however, is a contract between an exchange and an investor. A derivative contract is designed by an exchange which has 'copyright' on the product design. If the exchange can maintain a monopoly of trading this contract it can obtain higher margins than in more competitive cash markets. It can achieve a monopoly if the contract is cleared through a clearing house (a central counterparty) which it controls and if the competition authorities allow it to refuse access to competitive exchanges or simply to charge an excessive fee for access.

In the case of contracts based on an index, control of licensing rights to use the index to create a derivative product based on the index depends on who owns the index. If the exchange itself has created the index it may refuse to license it to other exchanges and thus prevent them from offering to investors the same, or a **fungible**, contract, i.e. a contract capable of being opened on one exchange and closed on another.

The NYSE Euronext estimated that cost savings (synergies) of $583 million per year would have been realised if their merger with Deutsche Borse had been permitted to go ahead. In addition there would have been revenue gains (also synergies) of $146 million per year. Morningstar (an analyst firm) estimates that these merger synergies, net of implementation costs, would add over $2.5 billion to the market capitalisation (shareholder value) of the combined companies.

When examining mergers we have to consider possible benefits and drawbacks to two sets of interested parties. The first are the users of the exchange, who may or may not benefit. The cost savings may or may not accrue to them. They may alternatively accrue to shareholders. We must therefore secondly consider stock exchange companies also as shareholder investments. Have they been good investments for the institutional (or retail) equity investor? In practice they have underperformed the global market. This could be because gains have accrued to customers rather than shareholders through lower pricing.

To date there have no major cross-country exchange mergers in Asia. It is very likely, however, that despite domestic political objections to mergers with exchanges in other countries, such consolidation will occur. Initially, though, it is likely to be through agreements for sharing technology and access rather than through mergers between exchange companies. An example of this is given in the report of six emerging-market exchanges announcing a cross-listing alliance:

> Under the alliance, Hong Kong Exchanges and Clearing, BM&F Bovespa of Brazil, the National Stock Exchange of India, the Bombay Stock Exchange, Johannesburg Stock Exchange and the two Russian exchanges that are in the process of merging – Micex and RTS – will cross-list each others' stock index futures and index options contracts. They would be listed on each exchange in its local currency.
>
> *Financial Times*, 13 October 2011

# 14 CLEARING AND SETTLEMENT OF SECURITIES TRANSACTIONS

The previous chapters covered trading. However, a trade is nothing more than a **contract** made between two parties. The contract confirms that the parties have agreed on the price at which a particular asset will be exchanged for cash. However, a well-known aphorism in the market is that '**a trade is not a trade until it is settled**'. Clearing and settlement – the post-trade processes – are critical to trading and have become a much greater focus of attention within Europe for investment banks, employment in the investment banking industry, regulators, academics and trade bodies relative to the front-end (trading) of the industry since 2000. Much of this attention has been due to the fact that costs on the trading side had, by that time, already been reduced substantially over the previous decade, while post-trade costs (particularly in cross-border trades in Europe) had not.

More recently, the collapse of Lehman Brothers has made market participants and regulators more aware of counterparty risk. Such risk is particularly great on OTC trades which are conducted between a client and an investment (or commercial) bank or, even more so, in the case of interbank transactions. This has led to regulators agreeing new proposals for OTC trades, specifically derivative trades, to be cleared centrally (thus requiring collateral) and if possible to be transacted on an electronic trading platform which can provide transparency to regulators and the market as a whole.

A securities transaction involves a payment of funds in one direction and a movement of securities in the opposite direction. It thus involves the payment system but also a **securities settlement system** (SSS). In addition, if the transaction is cross-border it may involve a foreign exchange transaction. After a transaction there are three levels at which settlement may need to take place:

- Settlement between two broker/dealers operating in the OTC markets (interbank transactions);
- Settlement between a broker/dealer and his or her institutional/retail investor client;
- Settlements between institutional investors and their retail clients, for example mutual fund settlement systems.

We will focus on settlement between brokers/dealers (interbank) as this is the key area in terms of volume of transactions and systemic risk. The reason for this is that if a large institutional order arrives on a broker/dealer trading desk, it is unlikely that a single broker/dealer can fill it. The dealer may sell short or buy without an immediate offset on the other side and over time needs to undertake multiple transactions to offset his or her original client transaction. For risk management purposes, banks also undertake a high volume of transactions.

## SETTLEMENT OF SECURITIES TRANSACTIONS

Settlement of a securities transaction means the completion of the transaction: the seller transfers securities to the buyer and the buyer transfers money to the seller. Commercial banks are the key providers of the funds transfer side of a securities settlement. However, the securities side is handled by a different type of organisation. The principal providers of SSSs are:

- Domestic central securities depositories (CSDs);
- International central securities depositories (ICSDs).

A **CSD** is a facility (or an institution) for holding securities, which enables securities transactions to be processed by **book entry** (i.e. electronically). Physical securities (pieces of paper) may be **immobilised** (held in one place and not moved between owners) by the depository or **dematerialised** (so that they exist only as electronic records). CSDs also perform a **notary function**, i.e. as the registration of ownership of securities on a legal record, except, as in a number of countries such as the UK, where **company registrars, for example,** Capita are used. In China the securities settlement organisation are The China Securities Depository and Clearing Co. and the China Government Securities Depository Trust & Clearing Co.

CSDs were originally organised on a national basis. They were responsible for the settlement of securities traded on their respective domestic markets and indeed were frequently part of the exchange in that country. The two **ICSDs** in Europe are **Euroclear** in Brussels and **Clearstream** in Luxembourg. They were originally created to clear and settle Eurobond (international capital market) transactions – the first ever international securities without a domestic market. Over time the ICSDs have come to provide a wide range of services for the clearance of domestic and international securities, both equity and debt, as well as some intermediary functions. CSDs and ICSDs have developed links with each other to facilitate cross-border settlement. But as part of the internationalisation of the securities market, Euroclear has also acquired the domestic CSDs of France, the Netherlands, the UK, Belgium and Ireland and is thus both an ICSD and a CSD. These acquisitions should enable it to provide a service at lower cost than each country operating its own CSD as a result of economies of scale, though in practice such lower pricing may or may not materialise as benefits may accrue to shareholders or employees.

Securities transactions involve two legs – a transfer of funds and a transfer of securities. Understanding settlement requires, therefore, an understanding of both:

1. **Payment systems**, i.e. the combination of commercial banks, central bank and payment networks;

2. **SSSs**, i.e. the systems which arrange for securities to be transferred from seller to buyer and payment to be made through payment systems from buyer to seller.

In everyday commerce, we require only payment systems and not also special settlement systems. This is because in commerce the provision of goods and services happens simultaneously with the transfer of funds. For example, when you buy something in a shop, the goods are handed to you and you hand over notes and coin or a debit/credit card which effects payment simultaneously with the transfer of the goods. You are not at risk of not receiving the goods and the store-keeper is not at risk of not receiving payment (unless you run out of the store without paying). Of course, if you purchase goods from a website and transfer your cash to the merchant at that point, you are still at risk of a delivery failure if the white van does not deliver the purchase to your home.

In securities transactions we need systems to ensure that the payment of funds for securities being bought only happens if, at the same time, the securities are delivered. We call such systems **exchange for value systems** because we are receiving the equivalent value of our funds when we receive securities. The critical matter if we are selling is to find a way of ensuring that, just as we are handing over the securities, the purchaser does not, metaphorically, grab hold of the securities and run without paying over the value of the securities, as a thief might do in a store. Exchange for value systems ensure against **principal risk**, i.e. the risk of losing the whole amount of the transaction. In securities markets, the exchange for value mechanism is known as **delivery versus payment (DvP)**, where, in exchange for a payment of cash, there should be a delivery of securities made simultaneously. In order to achieve this we need to have a trusted third party standing between the two sides to confirm that our funds have been received before handing over our securities. This is the key role of the securities settlement system which arranges payment in return for delivery of securities. An analogy would be the **escrow agent** in the United States who takes control of a buyer's funds in a house purchase and receives the title deeds from the seller. Not until he or she has the title deeds will the funds be released to the seller.

## What is securities clearing and settlement?

Clearing and settlement of a typical securities transaction involves the following basic steps of the settlement cycle:

- Confirmation of the terms of the securities trade from a broker followed by affirmation by the other side of the transaction;
- Clearance of the trade by which the respective obligations (financial and specific securities) from the buyer and seller are established;
- Delivery of the securities from the seller to the buyer (one leg of settlement);
- Reciprocal payment of the funds (other leg of settlement);
- Custody, safekeeping and administration of the securities (post-settlement);
- Registration of ownership of securities on a legal record: notary function (post-settlement).

As a result of historically different starting points and organic development, the entities involved in the clearing and settlement process vary from country to country. Thus I will describe mostly functions, rather than specific organisational forms.

### Confirmation/trade matching

When a trade is executed, the first step is for the **counterparties**, i.e. the two parties to the trade, to confirm that they agree on the details of the execution. This may be achieved bilaterally through one counterparty sending the other a **confirmation** and the other sending back an **affirmation**. The confirmation would include the security code, the quantity, whether buy or sell, the price, the place for delivery and the bank account details. In the case of an electronic market transaction (as distinct from a telephone trade) the trade details would be captured automatically and basic trade data entry is not needed. In the case of international securities (bonds) most trades are confirmed through what was originally the ICMA trade confirmation system, TRAX II,[1] now part of Euroclear.

## CLEARING

Trading financial assets creates debit and credit positions. **Clearing** is the calculation of the bilateral or multilateral obligations of market participants. If most transactions in markets were between 'customers', i.e. buy-side users of the market, clearing would be undertaken, transaction by transaction, between dealer and client. In practice, however, the majority of financial transactions, particularly in an OTC market, are between large financial institutions. Many of these transactions are a result of interdealer transactions, i.e. dealers moving excess positions amongst themselves, subsequent to a large transaction coming to one of them. As a result, during a trading day, dealers will have large volumes of transactions amongst themselves – some buy, some sell, and, although the gross volume of transactions will be large, the net positions between them may be small and the net transfers in individual securities required may also be relatively small. It is thus possible to offset buys and sells on **both** the cash side of transaction and also on the securities side. This gives fewer securities movements and even fewer cash payments, thus saving cost and potentially reducing risk. Bilateral netting of this type can be undertaken by the parties themselves or multilateral netting (amongst all parties) can be organised by the settlement organisation. **Settlement netting** refers to situations when a clearing house or an SSS computes net positions without taking risk itself. It determines the respective obligations, i.e. it calculates the amounts to be settled. The settlement is then undertaken through SSSs.

---

[1] In 2009 Euroclear acquired Xtrakter Ltd, the ICMA subsidiary which owns TRAX, the trade matching and reporting system which is a key source for fixed-income business and reference data.

## CENTRAL COUNTERPARTY CLEARING AND NETTING

**Central counterparty (CCP) clearing** refers to situations when a clearing house interposes itself as a buyer to the seller and as a seller to the buyer. Thus it creates two new contracts that replace the original single contract. The legal process of replacing the original counterparties and becoming the single counterparty for all participants is called '**novation**'. Novation results in the CCP taking on all counterparty risk. CCPs were introduced first in derivative markets because, given the length of such contracts perhaps 12 months, a counterparty could easily become insolvent in the interim.

A CCP provides a number of advantages over contracts directly between the original counterparties. The first is that it allows an electronic order-driven market to function much better. If traders were forced to make transactions with counterparties of whom they had no business knowledge, trading volumes would be very limited due to counterparty risk. As the CCP becomes the counterparty to all transactions through the process of novation, i.e. the CCP takes over the obligations for the trade immediately it has been undertaken, traders take on the risk of the CCP alone. The CCP has, of course, undertaken a prior evaluation of the counterparty in order to satisfy itself that the risk it is taking on is not excessive. It is much more efficient for a single entity, the CCP, to undertake the credit evaluation of all potential counterparties than for each to have to do it themselves.

In a market with a CCP there is no disclosure of the name of the counterparty when trading. Moreover there is no disclosure at the point of settlement (since each trader settles only with the CCP). This anonymity of trading is advantageous for traders who do not wish to have their trades disclosed to others in the market. For example, hedge fund traders would not wish their strategies to be leaked into the market.

Figure 14.1 shows the Eurex trading, clearing and settlement processes which illustrate clearly that traders do not interact with each other. Instead they interact through the trading platform with Eurex Clearing (as a result of novation), and once the CCP has become the counterparty it can pass settlement instructions on to (in this case) one of the two ICSDs or the CSD with whom it has agreements.

As a CCP takes on all counterparty risk, it needs to have a mechanism to reduce the extent of this risk. The mechanism used is the provision of margin by members. There are two types of margin. The first is initial margin which has a similar function to a haircut in securities markets – an amount is transferred to the CCP for each trade, based on the volatility of the instrument being traded, and held by it until trade completion in order to cover the risk that prices move before the completion of the settlement process. The second is variation margin which provides for additional cash sums to be transferred if the price of the instrument moves by a greater amount than is covered by the initial margin. In the case of derivatives transactions, margins paid by the losing side of a contract to the CCP are continually paid out by the CCP to those on the other side of the contract, or repaid via the CCP to the other side if the contract value reverses.

As the CCP is the counterparty to all transactions, it is possible for it to net-off all cash payments to and from each member as a result of trades during a day. This is multilateral cash netting. It can also undertake multilateral contract or securities netting whereby all buy and sell transactions between any one member and all

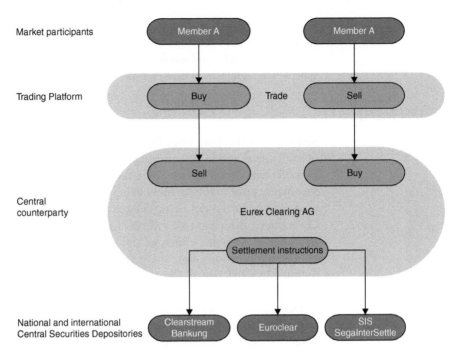

**Figure 14.1**    Eurex trading, clearing and settlement
*Source*: Eurex Clearing.

other members in a particular security can be netted down to one single securities movement, either to or from the member. It is important to understand, however, that multilateral netting of this type only works efficiently in markets where securities firms trade actively with each other, creating a high volume of transactions.

Multilateral netting has a further advantage for such firms. It allows them to show smaller gross positions on their balance sheets since only the net of all debits and credits comes through. This may have the advantage of reducing the amount of regulatory capital that has to be held against risk positions on the balance sheet. It should also reduce the amount of net margin collateral it needs to provide to the clearing house. If the Eurex/LIFFE merger had been permitted by the regulators, who are examining the NYSE Euronext/Deutsche Boerse merger, the proponents of the merger argue that this would create substantial economies for customers. This is because 90% of all derivatives transactions in Europe would then take place through the new entity and thus the extent of the offsetting of positions, and consequently the reduction in regulatory capital requirements, would be substantial. However, it would clearly also reduce competition which could have cost implications for traders.

It should be noted that derivatives exchanges have always operated using a CCP. Today almost all stock exchanges do so as well and, increasingly, CCPs are offering their services to investment banks for OTC transactions. Since the financial crisis regulators have also been trying to force a high proportion of OTC derivative trades (standardised contracts), in particular those in CDSs and interest rate swaps, to be cleared through a CCP and not bilaterally and if they are so cleared to be traded on an electronic swap execution facility, SEF as they are known in the US or organised trading facility (OTF) in the EU). Doing this would enable greater transparency for regulators and market participants than is currently available on OTC trades and would thus reduce counterparty and systemic risk of the type which materialised when Lehman Brothers collapsed.

## SETTLEMENT

Settlement is the delivery of the securities from the seller to the buyer (one leg of settlement) and the reciprocal payment of funds (the other leg). A key issue in settlement is how to overcome the risk that securities are transferred to the new owner prior to the payment being received in good funds or payment being made and securities not being delivered, i.e. principal risk on the counterparty. Overcoming principal risk involves finding a mechanism for **delivery versus payment**, as we noted above, i.e. delivery of securities **contingent on simultaneous payment** for them. There are three different models of DvP which are outlined in a BIS paper[2] *Clearing and Settlement of Exchange Traded Derivative Transactions*

Derivative contracts give rise to some different settlement issues from securities. The reason is that a derivative contract is a deferred contract, i.e. performance under the contract is contingent on events intervening between the date of the contract and its maturity. While at the time of entering a contract no payment (except in the case of an option contract) is made (in contrast to most contracts), the contract is made in the expectation of a subsequent transfer in one direction or the other by the time it matures. There is thus substantial counterparty risk over extended periods of time in such contracts. Without a CCP, exchange-based derivatives markets would not have developed to the extent they have.

## SETTLEMENT BY OFFSET

One of the major benefits of a CCP in exchange-traded derivatives markets (but not in cash markets) is the ability to **settle contracts by offset**. Without offset, contracts would not be nearly so liquid. In an exchange-traded derivative, a contract at any time in the opposite direction to the initial contract will settle the first contract since the counterparties become the same at the point of trade – namely the CCP itself. Without this, closing a trade would require an opposite trade with the same counterparty as the original trade which would be difficult to effect and probably be at a disadvantageous price. This contrasts with OTC derivatives contracts where the only party with whom it is possible to close out the contract is the investment bank which wrote it.

---

[2] There are three different models of delivery versus payment, which are outlined in *Clearing and Settlement of Exchange Traded Derivative Transactions*, Bank for International Settlements *Delivery versus Payment in Securities Settlement Systems* September 1992, Basel.

# MARKET FAILURE: SUB-OPTIMAL ALLOCATION OF RESOURCES BY CREDIT AND CAPITAL MARKETS AND CONSEQUENT BANKING AND SOVEREIGN DEBT CRISES

**15**

## MARKET FAILURE

In earlier chapters we have noted that the purpose of primary markets, both credit and capital, is to allocate resources efficiently –*optimal resource allocation* as it is known. In particular the function of the capital market is to allocate resources to a household, a corporate, a bank or a sovereign on the basis of a 'business plan' which demonstrates a high probability that the entity raising funds will be able to meet the P&I or return-on-equity requirements of the particular entity undertaking the financing. If the P&I payments are met on the due dates or the required rate of return is achieved then we conclude that the allocation of resources has been optimal. Some households and some corporates will, of course, fail to meet their P&I payments for 'idiosyncratic' reasons, i.e. just because in the normal course of events some households have bad luck or some companies make mistakes. Such cash flow losses to the lender are to be expected but can be met out of the risk premium paid by all borrowers.

A much larger issue is when investors as a whole fail to analyse a sector properly, underestimate risk and thus misprice that risk. This can occur both in the primary market and in the secondary market. Underpricing the risk of lending or investing leads to asset prices being higher than they would be if investors made valuations on the basis of rational expectations. **Overestimating future cash flows** or **underestimating the risk of such cash flows** due to collective investor euphoria can lead to assets being overvalued. Such overvaluations are often called asset price **bubbles**, which simply means that valuations have become overinflated. A good example of such a bubble was the dot.com or internet boom which peaked in March 2000.

Figure 15.1 shows the bubble in NASDAQ technology stocks expanding from 1999 to its peak in March 2000. The bubble in the **secondary market prices** of existing tech companies resulted in issues in the **primary market**, both IPOs

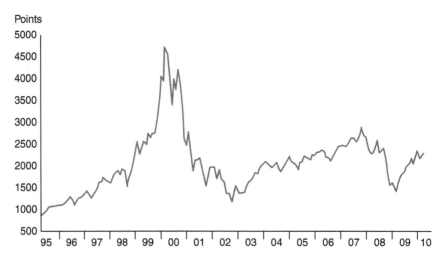

**Figure 15.1**  NASDAQ index from 1995 to 2010

*Source*: Data from NASDAQ.

and secondary issues (follow-on issues), being equally mispriced and thus new scarce resources – savings, brainpower, office space, etc. – being misallocated to these activities. As we now know, most of these resources were simply wasted as the companies which had attracted cash so cheaply went into liquidation shortly after.

The NASDAQ index subsequently fell to half its value as the bubble burst and it has not recovered since. Thus any investor buying into this index in 1999/2000 is still suffering from, at best, no gain at all or, at worst, showing a loss of 50% of value of his or her shares over a 12/13-year period.

The irrational euphoria surrounding tech stocks at that time is reflected in the following excerpt from an analyst's report from a major broker/dealer:

> An analyst who was with Prudential Securities was convinced the Nasdaq would smash through the 6,000-level within 12 to 18 months. 'If you're an astute observer, your portfolio will reflect what's new and exciting and dynamic,' he said at the time.
>
> BBC News Channel, 10 March 2010

Economic history shows that mispricings (**bubbles**) happen frequently. This suggests that it is not uncommon for markets to suffer from **market failure** and indeed bubbles in asset prices have probably existed since long before the well-known **South Sea Bubble**[1] and the subsequent failure of the South Sea Company.

Both the South Sea Bubble and the NASDAQ tech stock bubble occurred in the primary (IPO) market. The mispricing occurred at the point when these stocks were first issued. But often bubbles occur in the secondary market. For

---

[1] The South Sea Company share price rose from £128 in January 1720, to £175 in February, to £330 in March, to £550 at the end of May, and on up to £1,000 by early August. By December the price was back to £100 before the company collapsed.

some reason investors start bidding up the value of shares or bonds (or houses) above their fundamental value, based on rational expectations of cash flows and appropriate risk adjusted discount rates. At the time it may not be apparent that prices reflect a bubble but a subsequent collapse will generally be confirmation that it was a bubble and not a rational price increase followed by a rational price decrease.

Bubbles should not occur if capital markets function in the way textbooks describe, since prices of financial assets should always reflect 'true' risk and rational expectations. When a bubble is developing, what is happening is that prices in the secondary market, where repricing happens continuously (since most secondary markets are continuous), move away from the price that reflects true cash flows and risk. This of itself would not have fundamental consequences for the economy since all it does is transfer wealth between investors. However, if it impacts on pricing in primary markets, as it almost certainly will do, then it is likely to impact on resource allocation. Thus it is when resources are subsequently raised in primary markets at a price which does not reflect 'true' risk (either too cheaply or too expensively) or rationally expected cash flows, that we are likely, in consequence, to have a misallocation of real resources.

Such misallocation has occurred a number of times since 2000. We have already covered 'internet stocks' (the dot.com boom). But subsequent to this we had a house price boom in many Western countries resulting in house prices rising well above their equivalent (and rational) rental prices to which they should always have a close relationship. The high house prices resulted in the creation of mortgage assets based on underlying collateral values which were inflated (bubble prices). The prices of bank shares then rose to a level not supported by potential cash flows from bank assets. This resulted in the price/ book ratios for bank shares reaching 4 (see Figure 1.2) in the period 1999–2001 before falling to around 0.5 in 2011. Overvaluation also occurred in the prices at which banks were selling securitised assets based on underlying mortgages to investors and other banks.

Mispricing has also occurred in the case of eurozone sovereign debt in the period 1999–2010/11. The eurozone came into existence only in 1999 but in the period leading up to its creation interest rates of countries which had, prior to this time, been highly divergent, started to converge. For traders in sovereign debt at this time, the resulting so-called **convergence trade** was highly profitable. The trade was based on the assumption that all eurozone countries would have virtually the same interest rate as that of the least risky country, Germany, from 1 January 1999 onwards. When additional countries joined the eurozone – Greece for example joined in 2001 – its sovereign borrowing costs converged towards those of Germany. Thus investors clearly believed that the risk of lending to the sovereign states of Greece or Portugal or Ireland was very similar to the risks of lending to Germany. We will consider shortly why investors may have made this assumption and why it was a collective error on their part.

Inflated prices for such sovereign debt resulted in eurozone countries being able to rollover their debt at ever-lower interest rates in the primary market as prices rose in the secondary market. We now know that for many eurozone countries these secondary market prices reflected a bubble, and when investors appreciated their mistake, prices fell to such a low level that for some countries the primary market effectively shut. In the case of Greece, it was then unable to rollover its debt in the primary market and was therefore forced to default.

Appropriate pricing should be achieved as a result of the capital market acting as a 'governance'[2] mechanism. In the case of an equity issue for example, investors will evaluate the company to try to confirm that the price of its share offering (at the time of an IPO or in the secondary market) reflects its expected cash flows and thus that the share will generate the required risk-adjusted return to investors, for a company of that particular level of risk. If, subsequently, it seems to investors that the directors of the company are not managing it in an appropriate way in order to realise this expected return, they have it in their power (as the owners) to dismiss them and appoint directors who will manage the company in an appropriate way.

In the case of the debt markets also there is this 'gatekeeper' function, i.e. a constraint on access to the market by households, governments, banks and corporates. If the borrower can pass the gatekeeper's tests, then subsequently there will be a disciplining process if they deviate from their promises. If these gatekeeper and subsequent financial disciplining functions are not effective, the outcome may be market failure. In this case capital market governance will have failed to ensure an optimal allocation of scarce resources. The market should ensure that:

**Households** are constrained in their mortgage borrowing (access to the market) by rules on, for example, loan/value ratios, loan/income ratios and confirmation that the stated income of the borrower, age, household outgoings, etc. are 'true and correct', though clearly many were not prior to the 'subprime' crisis.

**Governments** are constrained by 'norms' for annual government borrowing/ GDP ratio, total stock of debt/GDP ratio, cyclically adjusted primary balance/ GDP, ratio of foreign finance of deficit to domestic financing, etc. In the case of the eurozone, the constraints were in the form of the **stability and growth pact** agreed by all member states of the zone which provided for financial sanctions (fines) against states which ran budget deficits exceeding 3% of GDP or had debt greater than 60% of GDP. However, after both France and Germany exceeded these limits without imposing fines on themselves, smaller countries felt no need to conform to the rules either.

**Banks** are constrained by capital ratios (debt/equity) and rising cost of funds, including that of equity, if leverage ratios are too high but clearly managed to overcome leverage constraints, partly through the use of derivatives and partly through using over-optimistic risk adjustment factors in their calculations of equity/risk-adjusted debt.

**Corporates** are constrained by the maximum debt/equity ratio that lenders will permit and rising cost of additional funds, including equity capital, as this ratio rises. In the decade of the 2000s, companies, with the exception of portfolio companies, held within private equity funds have not had excessive leverage ratios. Indeed, many corporations have built up large cash holdings as a result

---

[2] Governance can be achieved through the use of markets where competition serves to effect the allocation of resources or through governments and state bureaucracy.

of not being willing to commit cash to real investment for expansion or new ventures.

Subsequent to the acquisition by investors of new liabilities issued by any of the above classes of debtor, any changed likelihood of default should be reflected in a change in the price of an asset in the secondary market. If this change were a fall in price due to perceived increased risk, the debtor would know that on trying to refinance the loan (rollover) at its final maturity, the interest rate would be higher than before and that, *in extremis*, it would be impossible to rollover the loan. If the market is working efficiently this mechanism should discipline borrowers.

In fact, many borrowers from the year 2000 including governments, banks and households do have seemed to have been constrained by lenders. Thus we then have to ask why the market failed to price risk correctly at the time of issuance of new debt or exert discipline during the life of that debt until it was too late. Why did lenders (institutional investors, banks, sovereign wealth funds, overseas governments, etc.) invest in internet stocks, bank equity, shadow bank CDOs and peripheral eurozone government debt with such enthusiasm? Why were they subsequently unable to discipline debtors? Why did the market fail to operate in the way described by economist's descriptions of the efficient market mechanism?

Are the financial and eurozone debt crises in fact the 'fault' of the creditors, i.e. the investors rather than the debtors? Is it lenders who are responsible for debt crises? This would imply that the problem arose from a failure by creditors to undertake or apply effective risk analysis prior to lending, rather than being the 'fault' of the debtors. Answering this question helps in a consideration of a further question: who should pay the price for defaults on bank and sovereign debt? Should it be investors or should it be taxpayers? If we choose taxpayers we need to consider the moral hazard implications of selecting them rather than investors.

## WHY DO ASSET PRICES SUDDENLY FALL?

Our starting point for trying to answer some of the questions relating to market failure is to look at periods during which the prices of financial assets fall sharply (subsequent to a price boom or **bubble**), resulting in a loss of wealth for their holders. If asset prices fall there are three possible scenarios.

### Rational price fall

It might be simply that **real fundamentals have changed**. The following are all fundamental factors affecting future cash flows and the appropriate rates at which to discount such flows: a flu pandemic that kills millions of people; a volcanic cloud which shuts out sunlight and reduces crop yields and hence the availability of food; an earthquake in Japan or a tsunami which disrupts global supply chains; a severe flood in Thailand which causes cessation of camera production by Nikon and other firms; a prolonged and global cessation of flights due to volcanic ash as in northern Europe in May 2010; a rise in world wheat prices due to a hot dry summer in Russia, Canada and Ukraine; a sharp rise in the price of oil which makes much of the manufacturing industry, the travel industry, the existing stock of buildings, etc. uneconomic; or a regional war which disrupts commerce.

All of these causes of a decline in asset prices are simply reflections of reality – for example that there is less food in the world, meaning some will die, others will be malnourished, a higher proportion of income will be spent by everyone on food and therefore less money is available to spend on the output of other industries. Another cause could be that employees and consumers have been killed by a flu virus and therefore cannot produce or consume. Yet another could be that many assets, including motor-car factories, out-of-town supermarkets, etc. no longer have the same economic value given the change in the price of energy.

Changes in prices caused by fundamental factors do not confound the EMH. Indeed such price changes are an example of the **rational expectations hypothesis** that we examined in Chapters 1 and 12 working well.

## Irrational price rise preceding an irrationally large fall

A second reason for a fall in asset prices might be that in the prior period **prices have gone well above their 'fundamental' value**, i.e. their value derived by discounting rationally expected cash flows at an appropriate risk adjusted discount rate. This could be a price rise driven by euphoria. At some point investors realise that prices do not reflect rational expectations and prices then collapse, usually not just to a level reflecting fundamentals but to a level below this due to a sudden switch from euphoria to collective disillusion – the greed followed by fear analysis. Sir John Templeton[3] (died on 8 July 2010, aged 95) is famous for the following quotation which reflects this second reason for market price collapses: 'Bull markets are born on pessimism, grow on scepticism, mature on optimism and die on euphoria'. This phenomenon is a good description of **market failure** since investors are not pricing assets rationally, which confounds the EMH. Instead of valuing rationally, they are allowing emotion to cloud their judgement.

The EMH is based on the assumption that, in their economic life, people behave rationally (economic rationality). They will thus try to maximise their utility (their enjoyment of life) or profits. Since in many economic situations the outcome will depend partly on what people expect to happen, expectations of the future are important in decision-making. The price of an agricultural commodity, for example, depends on how many acres are planted, which in turn depends on the price farmers expect to realise when they harvest and sell their crops. Thus each farmer develops an expectation of the future price of, for example, wheat and decides how much to plant based on this estimate. If we assume people are rational in the meaning used above, then we have the basis of the rational expectations hypothesis. This assumption does not deny that people often make forecasting errors, but it does suggest that errors will not **persistently** occur on one side or the other. Thus outcomes will not differ **systematically** (regularly or predictably) from what people expected them to be. This is similar to the thinking that led the

---

[3] Templeton pioneered globally diversified mutual funds. In 1999 *Money* magazine called him 'arguably the greatest global stock picker of the century'

US President, Abraham Lincoln, to assert, 'You can fool some of the people all of the time, and all of the people some of the time, but you cannot fool all of the people all of the time'.

In the field of stock markets, the EMH would suggest that on average the population of investors is correct in its forecasts even though individual investors' predictions of future values may be wrong. Also, if investors as a group make errors, they are not systematically wrong, i.e. over long periods of time in one direction, and thus errors in forecasts are random (hence the **random walk theory** of share prices).

If we have periods of investor euphoria, such as in the case of internet stocks, bank stock prices or CDO prices, risk premia fall to levels that do not reflect true risk, i.e. asset prices rise, and at some point people start to spot the mispricing and asset prices suddenly fall to the level appropriate to the risk or, much more likely, given the herd mentality of investors (and also the fact that many investors will be highly leveraged and thus must sell regardless of price), prices fall considerably below their fundamental value. Thus are asset price cycles exaggerated by the majority of people not behaving as rational expectations would predict and magnified by leverage financing their portfolios.

In such circumstances one would expect that arbitrageurs would enter the market having spotted mispricing and that their actions would prevent a bubble growing. An example of such an arbitrageur would be a value investor such as John Paulson who bet against what he believed to be excessively high prices for subprime debt and generated many billions of dollars of gain from so doing. He is an example of one of the people not fooled in the language of Abraham Lincoln. But what if he, and others like him, had insufficient resources to take the risk of huge short positions against everyone else's long positions in the market? In this case prices would still not reflect rational expectations.

The case of sharp falls in government debt prices (in distinction to private debt prices) needs a slightly different analysis. Normally the yield on government debt in OECD countries reflects the time value of money without any (or minimal) credit risk premium. The reason is that investors believe that there is no credit risk in lending to such governments, i.e. no risk of not receiving P&I payments when they fall due. In the case of peripheral eurozone country debt, investors seemed to have believed the political rhetoric about the eurozone and 'all standing together', i.e. some type of eurozone guarantee of all debt, even though in fact it was very clear that this was in fact prohibited under the Treaty. Thus prices remained close to levels at the time of issue, despite it being clear to some that this was irrational. This is analogous to investors in Fannie Mae and Freddie Mac securities believing that they would be bailed out by the US Treasury, even though it was explicit that there was no US government guarantee of such debt. This is an example of contractual language stating explicitly that there will be no bail-out, yet expectations (often correctly) being that there will be a bail-out. This is, therefore, an example of moral hazard creating the problem rather than simply investor euphoria and thus the source of the problem could be government rather than investors or borrowers.

The eurozone was not set up as a transfer union, i.e. a union where a budgetary problem in one country would be resolved through help from all the others.

Instead it was designed on the basis of each country having full autonomy, i.e. sovereignty in its fiscal affairs. Unfortunately, countries had no autonomy in monetary affairs – these being controlled by the European Central Bank. Thus countries in the single currency zone could not:

1. Control their own interest rate;
2. Control their own money supply;
3. Devalue their currency if, due to wage and cost rises, their exports were becoming uncompetitive.

These facts were known by investors, yet collective investor belief seemed to disregard them.

## Price falls that seem to be induced by market structure – independently of fundamentals

A third type of fall is one where there is no obvious cause, i.e. **no fundamental factors** seem to have changed and there is no evidence of previous **bull market euphoria** (no mispricing). Such a market fall occurred on Monday 19 October 1987 – **Black Monday** as it was called. Stock markets around the world crashed. Hong Kong crashed first then Europe, and finally the United States. The Dow Jones Industrial Average fell by over 22%. By the end of October, the stock market in Hong Kong had fallen 45%, the United Kingdom by 26% and the United States by 23% from the 1987 peak. Black Monday resulted in the sharpest ever global decline in stock market history. I was working in the stock broking company Hoare Govett at that time and no one in the company could see any obvious cause for such a dramatic decline. II, unfortunately, was given the task of marking the trading and investment books to market to see how our loss compared with the market. At one point we had lost 40% of the value of all our inventory. However, by the end of the year, most of the world's markets were showing a gain, year-on-year. It appeared, therefore, that this was a crash without any underlying cause. The market's subsequent recovery raises issues relating to complex computer systems and their interactions with the 'human interface', economic rationality and the assumptions behind the EMH.

More recently, in 2010, the **Flash Crash** as it has been called resulted in the prices of some shares on the NYSE falling suddenly to a few pence before recovering to their 'correct' price. This type of mispricing is not related to irrationality in investors but to factors **endogenous** (internal) to the market structure of secondary trading markets in securities. (See chapter 25 for more on the Flash Crash.) Yet more recently, on 23 March 2012, BATS had severe problems. On the day it launched the IPO of BATS itself, its shares trading on its own system fell from the issue price of $16 to less than a penny. Shares in Apple also fell by 9% at one point. The problems were so severe that BATS pulled its new issue, i.e. withdrew it, even though it had been allocated and had started trading.

Figure 15.2 shows a **real house price index**, i.e. house prices adjusted for general inflation for the US for the period since 1890 based on an index of American house prices created by Professor Robert Schiller of Yale University.

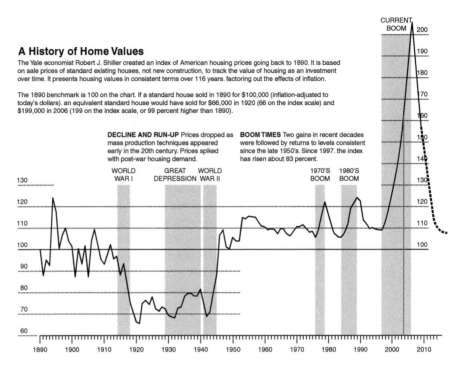

**A History of Home Values**

The Yale economist Robert J. Shiller created an index of American housing prices going back to 1890. It is based on sale prices of standard existing houses, not new construction, to track the value of housing as an investment over time. It presents housing values in consistent terms over 116 years. factoring out the effects of inflation.

The 1890 benchmark is 100 on the chart. If a standard house sold in 1890 for $100,000 (inflation-adjusted to today's dollars). an equivalent standard house would have sold for $66,000 in 1920 (66 on the index scale) and $199,000 in 2006 (199 on the index scale, or 99 percent higher than 1890).

**DECLINE AND RUN-UP** Prices dropped as mass production techniques appeared early in the 20th century. Prices spiked with post-war housing demand.

**BOOM TIMES** Two gains in recent decades were followed by returns to levels consistent since the late 1950's. Since 1997. the index has risen about 83 percent.

**Figure 15.2** US housing bubble

*Source*: Schiller, Robert, J, *Irrational Exuberance*, 2nd edn, 2005 © Princeton University Press, reprinted by permission of Princeton University Press.

The question to ask when looking at this graph is 'had I seen this graph in, say, 2006, would I have thought it possible that there was a bubble in house prices?' Clearly John Paulson thought so and was willing to make his 'big short' on CDOs based on mortgage assets. So too did some departments in Goldman Sachs. Most people looking at this graph today would ask: **but why did everyone not realise there was a bubble?** This is almost the same question that was asked by the Queen Elizabeth of England when meeting a group of economists shortly after the crash. **That is a key question to ask and it is one which is asked after EVERY bubble!** Perhaps too many people have a vested interest in the continuation of a bubble and therefore choose just not to see it. But equally importantly, many people have believed that the market is always right and should not be second guessed. Whether the market can arrive at the wrong price in its price discovery process, is a question considered below.

## EFFICIENT MARKETS CAN BE IRRATIONAL

Financial markets in many countries, particularly emerging market countries, do not function well – they are illiquid and fail to price assets appropriately. A key goal of regulation in the UK and the US has been to remove the impediments which might cause markets to be inefficient and illiquid. Much academic research over many years has been devoted to demonstrating that in well-regulated liquid markets share prices follow a **random walk**. With a wide range of **independently**

**acting** participants in markets who are in general economically rational in their assessment of future prospects, prices of individual securities **and** the overall level of prices in a market, have a strong tendency towards a rational equilibrium. This is known as the EMH. What is clear in practice is that there are many occasions in history when people act like a herd – they operate in panic mode – either desperate to get a share of the latest great idea or to get out of some asset that they suddenly believe is overvalued. Such herd behaviour conflicts with a key assumption of the EMH, namely the wide range of **independently** acting participants.

The EMH forms the basis of the **dominant market paradigm**, i.e. the thought process or model which underlies the actions of market participants, regulators and academics. But it has always been subject to some challenge. In his General Theory, Keynes says that 'we have reached the point ... where we devote our intelligence to anticipating what average opinion expects average opinion to be' in a similar way to that by which we might make judgements at a beauty contest. If that is so, then of course the assumption we have in the paragraph above of 'independently acting' agents is not a correct reflection of reality.

Charles Kindelberger, one of the world's most famous economists, in his book *Manias, Panics and Markets* illustrates how the tendency towards occasional speculative excess has spanned different markets, different countries and different centuries. In other words, one might conclude that speculative manias are not occasional events that can be disregarded when thinking about markets but very much part of normal market behaviour. Yet that is what market participants, regulators and many academics have done – disregarded 'normal market behaviour'. What we have observed in market behaviour since 2007 may, therefore, not be an aberration but something that must be expected given human nature and the regulatory framework we have employed to date based on the rational expectations theory and hence the EMH.

In contrast to the Keynes/Kindelberger/Minsky understanding of markets, the predominant tendency of researchers in financial market theory over the last 20 or even 30 years has been to assert (to claim but without producing evidence which can 'prove' it) that:

1. Efficient and liquid financial markets deliver **allocative efficiency benefits**, i.e. allocation of scarce resources to projects, by making possible a full range of contracts (**market completion**[4]), thus enabling providers and users of funds more effectively to meet their preferences for risk, return *and* liquidity.
2. This belief has ensured that in the United States in particular the development of derivative markets has been looked on favourably by regulators and legislators and has resulted in, for example, the Chairman of the Federal Reserve Bank of the United States, Alan Greenspan, using his moral authority to minimise the

---

[4] A **complete market** is one in which the complete set of possible gambles on future states-of-the-world can be constructed with existing assets. Every trader is able to exchange every good with every other agent and there are no transaction costs. Goods are state-contingent which means that is, a good includes the time and state of the world in which it is consumed.

extent of regulation of derivative markets, on the basis that it is unnecessary, since rational man will on average make rational economic decisions.

3. Markets are sufficiently rational to justify a strong presumption in **favour of market deregulation**, and in fact legislators have generally taken a strong line against 'excessive' regulation even of CDSs (in the US) and in the UK in favour of **light touch** regulation.

That even if markets are theoretically capable of irrational behaviour, policy-makers will never be able to judge when and how far they are irrational with sufficient confidence and therefore **cannot justify market intervention**. A policy of leaning against a rapid credit expansion and asset price rises would contrast with that followed by Alan Greenspan in the period leading up to the crisis. He maintained that it was not possible for a central bank to observe the development of a 'bubble' in asset prices and therefore it should not try to spot and deflate them. Instead it should restrict itself to 'cleaning up the mess' caused by any bubble deflating – hence the question is: should the central bank **lean** (against the wind) **or clean** (up the mess afterwards)? Indeed, monetary policy as practised by the Fed during the period 1987–2006, during which Greenspan was Chairman, was intentionally highly asymmetrical, which meant that when financial disturbance threatened growth prospects, monetary policy in the US was always eased, i.e. interest rates were reduced. For example, under Greenspan's reign, rates were reduced in 1987 (following the stock market crash), 1990–91 (following the property price crash and savings and loan crisis), 1998 (following the collapse of the world's largest hedge fund, LTCM) and 2001–04 (following the NASDAQ technology stock collapse).However, when it seemed to some observers that credit was growing too fast and asset prices, including house prices, were rising too quickly and were likely to generate imbalances in the economy (a bubble or Keynesian mania), rates were not raised because Greenspan (and other monetary regulators) believed that monetary policy should focus only on general price inflation, which was not showing any sign of being out of control, and thus rapidly rising real estate prices (asset prices) were not considered to be indicative of either inflation or potential financial instability.[5] The issue of whether rapidly rising asset prices are an indicator that the monetary authorities should pay attention to or not is still an open issue.

The financial crisis has caused a rethink by some market participants, regulators worldwide, European legislators, some parts of the legislature in the US, some academics and even Greenspan himself. The main criticisms of the EMH are that:

• **Market efficiency does not imply rationality**: The fact that security prices move as random walks and cannot be predicted from prior movements does not deny the possibility of self-reinforcing **herd effects** and of prices overshooting or undershooting rational equilibrium levels.[6]

---

[5] See William White 'Should Monetary Policy Lean or Clean?', the Federal Reserve Bank of Dallas, 2009.
[6] A good coverage of this issue is given in chapter 9 of Robert Shiller's *Irrational Exuberance* (Princeton University Press 2005).

- **Individual rationality does not ensure collective rationality**: Even if individuals behave in an economically rational fashion, imperfect information and agency relationships can still lead to price movements characterised by self-reinforcing momentum.
- **Individual behaviour is not entirely rational**: In addition to the above, according to insights from behavioural finance, cognitive psychology and the neurosciences, people often do not use the rational part of their brain for decision-making, as is assumed by the neoclassical economics paradigm (which in this case leads to the assumption of rational expectations) but make decisions instinctively which, at the collective level of the market, will produce herd effects and thus irrational momentum swings.
- **There is empirical evidence of large scale herd effects and market overshoots.** Economists such as Robert Shiller have provided empirical evidence showing that financial market prices can diverge substantially and for long periods of time from estimated economic values with the divergences at times so large that policy-makers can reasonably conclude that prices have become irrational (for example, this may have been the case for domestic house prices in a number of countries and some mortgage securities by 2006).

While creating '**complete**' **markets** is, in theory, desirable, in practice, beyond a certain degree of liquidity and **market completion**, further benefits may be small and may in practice be outweighed by the additional instability risks which increasing liquidity or complexity might itself create. For example, the liquidity benefits of HFT are debated while the drawbacks of CDO squared securities are probably undoubted since the crisis.

The evidence of so many crises since 2000 (the dot.com crash, the financial crisis, the eurozone sovereign debt crisis) and the empirical evidence now available on these has shown the fallacy of the accepted market paradigm – the EMH – in times of investor exuberance and investor depression. There has been a realisation by regulators that their mindset, i.e. the market paradigm they have used to understand markets, did not recognise that liquid traded markets are capable of acting irrationally and can be susceptible to self-reinforcing herd and momentum effects. This is also known as the **greed and fear** scenario, i.e. people are greedy and their collective greed may push up share prices. At some point, however, knowing that prices probably overvalue the asset in question, greed turns to fear of loss and investors, in a herd-like fashion, start selling, so bringing about the collapse that they fear. But this is not to deny that efficient and liquid markets do provide useful and accurate price signals as to the **relative attractiveness of different equity shares or credit instruments even if the OVERALL level of prices is subject to irrational over and undershoots**. There would seem to be no question that (irrational) emotion is important in determining asset prices and, indeed, in determining many outcomes in society, including election results.

If regulators accept that markets are inherently susceptible to irrational momentum effects, then one of the conclusions that follows is that attempts by the industry to move to ever greater liquidity in instruments and ever greater 'market completion' through the development of derivative and structured instruments results in potential disadvantages arising from **periodic and inherent instabilities in what are normally liquid markets**. This phenomenon may have been an important cause of financial crises such as that which commenced in 2008. Another important conclusion is that market regulatory policy would have to shift from the efficient market mindset to the exuberance/depression mindset.

It is interesting to note that in October 2011, two of the economists most involved in empirical work on the rational expectations hypothesis and its practical (but flawed) application, the EMH, were awarded the Nobel Prize in economics. According to the *Financial Times*[7] Professor Thomas Sargent has long said that rational expectations should not be seen as a school of thought or an ideological statement, but as a way of modelling how people think and react to policy changes and events. Sargent has observed that today's economic developments such as the eurozone crisis are driven strongly by expectations. The *Financial Times* goes on to say, however, that 'perhaps the main application of rational expectations theory is the efficient market hypothesis (EMH) which asserts that the price of an asset contains all relevant information and cannot systematically be over or undervalued. It was the widespread belief in this theory that led to the view that the credit bubble before the financial crisis did not exist'.

I leave it to you to ponder the question of whether the fact that rational expectations theory has been the predominant paradigm of how markets function is the cause of the financial crisis or whether it is human nature or one of many other factors that can be adduced as being 'the' cause.

## SOVEREIGN DEBT ASSET BUBBLES: FISCAL SUSTAINABILITY

Just as markets overpriced bank debt, bank equity and CDOs from 2000 to 2007, i.e. the period leading up to the financial crisis, so also they overpriced the debt of some countries in the eurozone during the same period and after, and thus, once the bubble in certain European sovereign debt assets burst, investors suffered large losses.

One reason for this mispricing may have been the mental process employed by investors, using an analogy with the 'too large to fail' doctrine whereby governments think large banks are too important to be allowed to fail. Investors may have thought that the strong governments within the eurozone would believe that peripheral eurozone countries – Greece, Ireland and Portugal – would bring down the whole single currency project if they were allowed to default on their debt. Thus the expectation was that despite the eurozone not being a **fiscal transfer union**, i.e. a union where taxpayers in one eurozone country would automatically provide support for those in another, investors believed that in practice they would help a country suffering from an unsustainable fiscal policy. This would involve fiscal transfers from countries such as Germany to countries such as Greece. If investors ultimately lose faith in the ability of a country to service its debt and believe that other sovereigns will not intervene to prevent default, then clearly the price of that debt will collapse. For investors, therefore, the question is how to analyse a country on a 'stand-alone' basis rather than as a country supported by other members of the eurozone, just as we should analyse banks on a stand-

---

[7] See 'Rational Expectations Theory Gets Nobel Nod' 11 October 2011.

alone basis as well as on the basis of being companies that governments will always rescue. To do this analysis involves trying to answer three questions:

1. How much public spending is optimal?
2. What is the optimal taxation rate on households and corporates?
3. How much borrowing is sustainable?

## HOW MUCH SPENDING IS OPTIMAL?

The decision that governments have to make as to 'optimal' spending involves two issues:

First, what is the optimal level of government spending to achieve the wishes of the population in terms of:

**public services** (also known as **public goods**) such as infrastructure, policing and external defence which individuals cannot provide for themselves; and

**transfer payments** such as pensions, state health provision, unemployment benefit, disability allowances.

Second, what is the maximum level of taxation that is optimal (with any revenue shortage made up by borrowing) given that the imposition of higher taxes by a government may result in them losing the subsequent election? In an age of mobility of both intellectual and financial capital, higher corporate and personal taxes may also result in overseas companies failing to locate in a country and to companies (including domestic companies) choosing to move abroad.

Unfortunately there is no arithmetical answer to these questions. One view of government spending as a percentage of GDP is that up to 40% is accepted without many people questioning it. At 50%, i.e. the government is spending, on behalf of its citizens, half of all GDP, many citizens would say 'enough, no more' i.e. that this is the maximum that they would tolerate.

When we examine historical levels of government spending we find that in the 1870s, spending as a proportion of GDP was only around 10% on average. By the time of the outbreak of the financial crisis it had risen on average to close to 50% for Eurozone countries and even for the US was creeping over 40%. Today, as GDP has fallen in many countries and transfer payments have increased due to unemployment rising, spending-to-GDP ratios are in some cases above 50%. France would be a good example of a country breaking the 50% level, having reached almost 55% in 2012. In some countries it is the cost of bank rescues which has pushed up government spending, Ireland being a good example of this. Equally important, of course, is how the financing of such spending is split between taxation and sovereign borrowing. At this point it is worth noting that China is what we might call an 'outlier' in the public spending league i.e. a country that has a very different ratio from almost every other developed economy with a public spending ratio (by the central authorities only and not local authorities) of only 20%. Many would argue that the Chinese economy would benefit strongly from this ratio rising in contrast to some European economies where a fall would be likely to be beneficial.

## WHAT IS THE OPTIMAL TAXATION RATE?

Once again there is no answer to this question. There are, however, many questions we might ask about taxation and undertake research on, of which the following are only four. First, there are many different taxes that a government can levy, so in what proportion should taxes be raised through income tax, corporation tax, sales tax and inheritance tax? Second, the **incidence** of taxation is also important, i.e. who should it mostly fall on – the poor, the middle income group, the rich or companies? Third, does a rise in income tax encourage those who are in work to work more in order to maintain their income or, by making leisure relatively more attractive, does it cause a reduction in work effort (the income or substitution effect)? If people are discouraged by income tax, is there a 'threshold' rate at which this effect becomes pronounced? Fourth, do capital gains taxes discourage enterprise and investment? If so, is there a 'threshold' rate at which this effect becomes important?

## HOW MUCH BORROWING IS SUSTAINABLE?

This is the key question. Just as households and companies have to consider how to finance spending, so too do governments. They have two choices: either from current tax revenue or from borrowing against the security of future tax revenues and hence future generations of taxpayers (intergenerational transfers). Making this choice depends, firstly, on what are thought to be the maximum levels of corporate and household taxation that are acceptable (or possible) in a democracy. But secondly, the proportion of spending that can be raised from borrowing also depends on the total stock of existing debt.

Some would argue that once the total public debt of a country rises above 90%[8] it starts to have deleterious effects on the economy and slows growth. This may also be the point at which investors, particularly overseas investors, start to consider whether the fiscal policy of the country is sustainable. But the true answer is that **once investor confidence is lost it has an unsustainable fiscal position**. What determines whether or not investors retain or lose confidence (and are therefore willing to **rollover** sovereign debt) depends on many things, but four in particular stand out.

• First, there is the faith that investors have in the **coherence of government policy** in relation to spending and taxation and the degree of interparty agreement on the need for appropriate stabilising measures. In the case of the eurozone, this is the degree of investor belief in the coherence of the monetary policy being followed by the European Central Bank and the fiscal policies being followed by the treasury in each country. Since there is no common fiscal policy in the eurozone, it is quite possible that there is incoherence in fiscal matters within the zone.

---

[8] It is important to be aware that in some countries, including Greece, official statistics on GDP may greatly underestimate actual output, since a considerable proportion of this is produced in the unrecorded 'black market'.

- In the case of Italy, there has been little belief in the willingness of different parties, representing different sections of the population, to come together to forge a joint, agreed, way forward, at least prior to the departure of the prime minister, Silvio Berlusconi.
- In the US there is no evidence that the opposing political parties, the Republicans and the Democrats, can in any way agree on any of the major issues with Democrats defending public spending and Republicans refusing to sanction any tax increase. In consequence US sovereign debt rises inexorably. In the UK, the fact that the two major groupings, the Conservative/Liberal Democrat coalition on the one hand and the Labour Party on the other, have no major ideological differences at least in the early years of the coalition has resulted in the UK being able to borrow at an interest rate comparable to that of Germany, despite the UK's large public sector deficit.
- Second, if a country's debt has become unsustainable, the **willingness of the population to suffer a fall in welfare** from reduced government spending, higher taxation and possibly lower incomes and levels of employment without resorting to civil action or violence, must be questioned.
- Third, there is the factor of the proportion of the total public debt held by **non-resident investors**. These are less likely to hold debt if they are concerned about debt sustainability.
- Fourth, there is the factor of the extent to which additional debt is self-financing i.e. generates its own P&I as a consequence of it being used to improve the efficiency of the economy (new roads, railways, water supplies, etc.) and which will result in higher tax revenues in future years rather than being used for transfer payments such as social security.

There is certainly no doubt that if 'too high' a proportion of spending is financed not from taxation but from borrowing, there may come a point at which lenders will refuse to buy government debt or the cost of it rises so much that the country enters a **debt trap**. This happens when the policy that is being pursued leads to an ever-growing debt burden (as a percentage of GDP) **as the interest cost on debt rises above the growth rate of the economy**. By this point, fiscal policy clearly is not **sustainable**.

Celasun et al.[9] define a **sustainable fiscal position** in the following terms:

> To be deemed solvent, a government must be expected to honour current and future financial obligations including the implicit commitment to continue providing certain public goods, services and transfers in the future.

This is actually very similar to a definition we used earlier in respect of households. Households must be able to service their debts as well as feed and clothe themselves and meet any other 'necessary' expenditure.

---

[9] O. Celasun, X. Debrun and J. D. Ostry, 'Primary Surplus Behaviour and Risks to Fiscal Sustainability' IMF Working Paper 06/67 (2006).

# ASSESSING FISCAL SUSTAINABILITY

There are a number of types of analysis and distinctions used to try to determine a country's fiscal sustainability. The first of these requires an understanding of the difference between **stock, flow** and **financing need:**

- **Stock:** the total stock of government debt outstanding, assessed relative to the GDP of the country, sometimes just called 'debt';
- **Flow adding to the existing stock:** the annual deficit that has to be financed, also measured relative to GDP, generally called the budget deficit;
- **Financing need:** the annual flow plus the amount of maturing debt which has to be rolled over during the year (depends on the maturity schedule of existing debt), i.e. annual deficit plus rollovers.

The second type of analysis considers two components of the annual deficit:

- **Structural deficit:** any deficit which remains throughout the economic cycle despite the economy operating at or close to full capacity;
- **Cyclical deficit:** any deficit which is a result of automatic stabilisers or additional borrowing undertaken at the low point of the economic cycle to prevent an amplification of the cycle.

If governments were to act the way they often declare they intend to, then the **structural deficit over a business cycle would be zero.** There would be a cyclical deficit in times of economic downturn (mostly from automatic stabilisers such as falling tax revenue and rising spending on unemployment benefit) that would be recovered from taxpayers in the next upswing of the economy when government tax yield would exceed government spending. Finland is a good example of a country which uses this approach.

The third tool of analysis, the primary balance, is based on the type of expenditure. Public spending has three components:

- **Current expenditure:** payment for health services, schooling, income support, armed forces, etc.
- **Capital expenditure:** investment (capital) expenditure on items which will raise the efficiency of the economy, support growth and thus generate increased tax revenue in future. Thus, roads, railways, port facilities, telecoms infrastructure (if these are state owned), advanced research, education and training programmes, etc. might be expected to raise the productive potential of the country.
- **Debt servicing:** the **interest payments** on the national debt.

The primary balance is the difference between tax revenue and current and capital expenditure combined, i.e. not including any interest cost:

Primary balance = total tax revenue – (current + capital) expenditure.

If the primary balance is not able to cover interest costs then it will result in the stock of outstanding debt increasing since some of the interest then has to be paid by issuing new debt. Only if there is a primary surplus and it at least equals the interest payments will the debt stay constant or fall. Alternatively, if the economy is growing and thus tax revenues are growing, then provided spending does not also rise, it may be possible to move to a positive primary balance.

Trying to get a feel for the probability of default of a sovereign is very difficult, never more so than when the politics of a country or a regional grouping, such as the eurozone, are also uncertain. In trying to assess sustainability and hence the likelihood that a country can continue to service its debt, an investor would consider the various measures we have looked at above. Clearly investors in the sovereign debt of some eurozone countries have, in the past, failed to do this analysis or the necessary political analysis (as have the ratings agencies) and thus have sustained losses.

If the primary balance is negative then ultimately it must be turned positive to make fiscal policy sustainable in the long-run. To do this requires some combination of:

a rise in taxation, or;
a cut in public spending, or;
economic growth which increases GDP while not increasing public spending as
  the economy grows.

Unfortunately, **structural adjustment measures** as the first two of these measures are described may actually make the primary balance more negative as they are likely to reduce demand and hence GDP and therefore tax revenue falls while transfer payments rise. Sadly, the third option is not really an option for countries which are already in recession and suffering from falling GDP.

Can contractionary fiscal policy i.e. structural adjustment measures, be expansionary? This is a question which is often asked. One side of the political debate, both in Europe and in the US, believes it can. The other side says, 'no, it will always be contractionary.' A good summary of the issues involved is provided in the excerpt below from a study[10] prepared by the Congressional Research Service, for Members and Committees of the US Congress to help them understand the issues:

> As Congress considers policies to foster economic growth, arguments have been made that the traditional expectations of fiscal policy, namely that cutting spending will contract the economy in the short run, should be reversed. Proponents of this view also argue that cutting spending rather than raising taxes would be a more effective means of increasing economic growth (or at least avoiding contractions). These arguments often refer to recent empirical studies of deficit reductions across countries.
>
> This view contrasts with that held by most economists and found in conventional models. In those models cutting spending will contract the economy. Chairman Bernanke of the Federal Reserve was referring to this view when he cautioned against large and immediate spending cuts. Most multipliers (measures of the effect of deficits on the economy) indicate that spending cuts contract the economy more than do similarly sized tax increases.
>
> Just as economists generally consider spending cuts to be contractionary in the short run in an underemployed economy, they believe that deficits can be harmful in

---

[10] *Can Contractionary Fiscal Policy be Expansive?* A study prepared by Jane G. Gravelle, Senior Specialist in Economic Policy, and Thomas L. Hungerford, Specialist in Public Finance, 6 June 2011, Congressional Research Service, 7-5700, www.crs.gov R41849

the long run by crowding out private investment. There is considerable agreement that the continuation of current tax and spending policies (*this means in the US*) will lead to an unsustainable path of the national debt, largely because of the growth of mandates arising from the aging of the population and the growth in health care costs. Thus, to most economists current macroeconomic policy challenges involve a trade-off between the benefits of starting to address the debt problem earlier versus risking damage to a still-fragile economy by engaging in contractionary fiscal policy, or failure to continue with expansionary fiscal policy.

The reason for concern about calls for spending cuts is that cutting government demand for goods and services by cutting the provision of public goods or cutting transfer payments will reduce incomes and cause household demand to fall. Equally, tax rises, by removing demand from the economy, are likely to cause a decline in GDP, i.e. negative growth, and hence worsen the various ratios which analysts look at. In the Eurozone, if all its members which are in financial difficulty try to cut back their fiscal deficits (and also their trade deficits) at the same time, the result is likely to be a fall in total demand across the eurozone. Only if countries in balance of payments surplus such as Germany, Austria and the Netherlands were to increase their total expenditure, perhaps by cutting taxes and increasing government spending, with some of this spending spilling over into other eurozone countries, is it likely that the eurozone as a whole could avoid falling demand and hence a worsening of the fiscal position of countries such as Greece, Italy, Spain and Portugal.

This problem is one to which we have referred earlier – the **fallacy of composition** – namely, what one country can do, all can't do. If all eurozone countries impose austerity measures to try to cut their budget deficit this will lead to them all suffering **a rise in their budget deficits.** This happens because austerity is likely to cause a decline in GDP (as in Greece, Portugal and Ireland) and in consequence a fall in tax revenues and a rise in unemployment benefits and other government (stabilising) spending which rises in a recession. Thus this approach is self-defeating. Ultimately Germany and the other trade surplus countries accept the need to finance other eurozone states which run payments deficits by means of fiscal transfers (subsidy), or the eurozone will break up. The reason why fiscal (public sector) transfers are now needed to finance the trade deficits of other countries is that German banks, which until now have been financing these deficits through lending to household and corporate debtors, have ceased being willing to continue to do so due to ever increasing credit risk.

An alternative solution would be to reduce the imbalances between countries with different cultural approaches to spending, saving, deficits and inflation, by splitting the eurozone in two. Indeed some German analysts are already talking about creating a new currency for Germany and other prudent countries which would be called the Thaler while the unstable countries could retain the existing euro. The euro would then, of course, devalue substantially but as that would be the aim of such a change, it would be a welcome development. This idea has quite wide support in Germany as the excerpt from a newspaper article[11] below, published in June 2012, indicates:

---

[11] Ambrose Evans-Pritchard *Eurozone Rescue Plan Is Sure to Backfire without Overwhelming Force, Daily Telegraph* (London), 20 June 2012.

Unease over escalating euro rescues is building by the day in Germany. Forty economists and professors have written a joint letter to Mrs Merkel, the Chancellor (the German prime minister), proposing a break-away 'Northern Euro', exhorting her to step back from the brink before making the 'even greater error' of ratifying the ESM [this is the creation of the so-called European Stability Mechanism].

The group said Berlin must clarify exactly how much Germany could stand to lose from the ECBs internal payments system, known as Target 2. Bundesbank claims on fellow central banks have exploded to €700bn or 27% of German GDP.

The idea of a North euro or 'Thaler', the coin of the late Holy Roman Empire, was first mooted by the former chief of the German Industry Federation, Hans-Olaf Henkel. It would allow southern EMU [European monetary union] states to keep the euro and uphold debt contracts. The region could reflate and regain trade competitiveness with a weaker exchange rate.

The market adjustment in price between the two currencies – the euro and the Thaler would minimise the build-up of financial imbalances between the two regions. Alternatively, to achieve an even better market adjustment mechanism across Europe, each eurozone country could revert to its own currency of a decade ago though this might have an even more disruptive effect on commerce. If this latter solution were adopted, the democratically elected government of each country would then be free to run its own monetary and fiscal policy as laid out in its election manifesto and stand or fall on its ability to achieve the objectives set out therein. Markets would adjust exchange rates and interest rates rather than these being set centrally by the existing eurozone institutions. One further additional possibility would be for Italy to split into two zones (effectively countries) with the northern part (where support for the Northern League political party is strong) joining the German block and the southern part joining what is sometimes known as the 'Club Med' group of countries.

## FINANCIAL FRAGILITY

The cause of **systemic** debt problems, which means problems which are not simply **idiosyncratic** but are the manifestation of cycles in which large numbers of debtors get into financial difficulty and are unable to make P & I payments, is something that has interested economists for many decades. Such problems worsen as the economic cycle turns down and employment and output fall. But it is equally important to look at the upturn of the cycle and ask why such high levels of debt are extended by creditors in an upturn when, almost inevitably, many debtors will not be able to meet their loan commitments in the downturn. This is suggestive of market failure, i.e. investors are making wrong risk assessments and therefore pricing wrongly.

The economist Hyman Minsky has produced a theory of financial fragility, i.e. the condition of a debtor which is likely to give rise to financial distress if the cycle turns down, which focuses on the means used to support debt, i.e. to provide the P&I payments necessary to **service** it. The theory focuses on firms (including banks) rather than countries or households, but is equally applicable to all three sectors. It is also an approach that was developed well before the current crisis but is probably applicable to all crises and in particular to the crises which commenced in 2008 and 2010. He defines three approaches to financing which he calls: hedge finance, speculative finance, and Ponzi finance.

- For **hedge finance**, income flows (personal income, company income or tax revenue) are expected to meet financial obligations in every period, including both the P&I on loans. The word 'hedge' in this context means that the liabilities due on the loan (P&I) are clearly expected to be **matched** by the cash that will flow to the borrower in future periods to meet P&I obligations. Required cash outflows are matched by expected cash inflows.
- For **speculative finance**, a borrower knows that he or she does not have sufficient income to meet both P&I payments. Income flows are expected to cover only interest costs. None of the principal can be paid off from income. A borrower must therefore roll-over debt when it becomes due, i.e. arrange a new loan prior to the old loan redemption date, in order to make the redemption payment. This is, in fact, the way in which most Western governments run their finances in normal times.
- For **Ponzi**[12] **finance**, a borrower's expected income flows will not even cover interest cost. As a result, the borrower can only make interest payments on existing debt by incurring additional debt and using the proceeds to pay the interest on the original and the new debt. The hope is that the market value of assets (such as a house which can be refinanced with a larger mortgage) or income will rise enough to pay interest in future periods and repay principal.

When a lender reviews a borrower's capability to service his debt he or she is trying to ascertain if the borrower is a hedge financier, i.e. can the borrower's income be expected to meet all P&I payments when due, while leaving sufficient income for **other costs**. If so, he they is likely to lend. This approach is relevant to bankers and bond investors lending on the basis of:

- Earned income of individuals where the **other costs** are living expenses;
- Revenues of firms where the **other costs** are costs of production;

---

[12] Charles Ponzi, a famous crook in the 1920s, swindled people out of their wealth by using new money coming in to pay interest and make repayments of capital. Today, of course, we have our very own Charles Ponzi in the form of Bernard Madoff who in 2009 was sentenced to 150 years in prison. I guess he will die in prison. By some estimates he had swindled people out of $65 billion (other estimates are 'only' around $23 billion) through a fund that people thought was genuine and which paid good returns (and repaid capital when requested). In fact there was no investment fund at all. All payments of interest and repayments of capital were achieved by using new funds coming in. The relevance of Ponzi financing today is firstly that the subprime problem in the United States is a good example of credit being overextended to people who were unlikely to be able to meet principal payments when due and also unlikely even to be able to meet interest payments. It would seem that lenders persuaded themselves that if the borrower could not repay then they could foreclose on the property without loss. But equally, Greek and Irish, and probably other sovereign, borrowing in the financial markets has been such that it was unlikely that even interest could be paid without raising new money to pay interest on the old, i.e. Ponzi financing.

- Net interest income and fee income of banks (revenue) where **other costs** are mainly remuneration costs, i.e. salaries and bonuses;
- Tax revenue in the case of countries where the **other costs** are the expected cost of necessary public services and income transfers.

The bank lender or bond investor wants to know if the borrower is likely to generate sufficient cash to meet P&I payments when they fall due. If the borrower is taking the risk of providing speculative financing, such a loan is clearly more risky than a hedge finance loan, where both interest and capital repayments can be met out of income. An interest-only mortgage (where capital is expected to be repaid from another source such as a with-profits endowment policy in the UK) is an example of speculative finance and has led to many borrower defaults when a with-profits endowment (investment product) fails to generate sufficient principal to redeem a loan.

Firms and governments continually use speculative finance rather than hedge finance as they borrow with the intention of paying interest only and assuming that loans can be rolled over, i.e. repaid to the borrower from the proceeds of a new issue of debt. Virtually no government, for example, has ever repaid all its debt on a net basis as governments repay maturing loans by issuing fresh ones. Thus governments almost universally employ speculative finance as their guiding principle. Companies, if they maintain a constant debt/equity ratio as they grow, are never repaying debt on a net basis, just rolling over their existing debt AND adding new debt. However, when a government is trying to reduce its debt/GDP ratio, is must for a while at least be a hedge financier.

A good example of speculative financing can be found in the position of euro-zone banks in mid-2011.[13] The structure of the eurozone system has encouraged, and enabled, banks in this region to fund themselves with short-term loans. For the 90 banks covered by the European Banking Authority stress tests, there is a need to refinance €5,400 billion of debt within two years from mid-2011. This is equal to 45% of the eurozone GDP. If they cannot achieve this because investors no longer think eurozone banks are safe then, without official intervention, they will collapse. The only alternative is for the European Central Bank to finance them. This is indeed what has happened. As the private markets ceased re-financing the banks, the ECB had to step in with its newly created Long Term Refinancing Operation (LTRO).

The next step on what some might describe as 'the road to perdition'[14] is when a company, a bank or a country can only pay interest on its loans by raising additional borrowing and using that cash to make interest payments, since it cannot pay interest from its income. This is, of course, **Ponzi finance**. A country suffering from the type of problems that have become manifest in Greece has been to employing Ponzi financing, i.e. these countries may not have enough tax revenue remaining after meeting even greatly reduced public spending to make all contractual interest payments in the years ahead without raising additional borrowing just to pay interest.

---

[13] See an excellent paper from the Peterson Institute 'Europe on the Brink' July 2011.

[14] *Road to Perdition* was originally a comic book and subsequently a film starring Tom Hanks (2002). 'Perdition' means hell in the Christian religion.

# 16 ASSESSING RISK AND RETURN FOR INVESTORS IN BANK AND SOVEREIGN DEBT

Global bank and sovereign debt together comprise by far the largest sector of the investment market. By comparison the global equity market is smaller. The relative importance of each sector can be seen Figure 1.1. Sovereign debt has also, the eurozone excepted, been the asset class which has given by far the highest return to investors since 2000. In contrast equities have been a great disappointment to almost all investors over that period as has bank debt. Any investor, therefore, has to consider these two large asset classes – sovereign debt and bank debt – as potentially important components of any portfolio. Though I have noted that sovereign debt has been the best performing asset class, within that class clearly eurozone debt has proved to be very risky, quite the opposite of what traditional finance assumes about developed market sovereign debt, i.e. being the riskless asset. Equally, bank debt or at least senior debt, has been assumed to be almost riskless due to the 'too large to fail' doctrine employed by governments. However, that doctrine is in the course of being modified in ways that may in future lead to losses even on senior debt but certainly on junior debt. Any investor, therefore, has to know how to assess risk on individual instruments within these two asset classes and to know when it may be appropriate to disinvest from them and, equally, to spot opportunities when they arise for highly profitable trades.

Chapter 15 covered the issue of market failure. This normally involves a 'bubble' in asset prices which then collapses. In the case of the financial and eurozone debt crises it has been banks and sovereigns that have had a problem in meeting their liabilities as they fall due, and the collapse in the value of their debt from 'bubble' levels can then result in the failure of leveraged entities which hold those assets. Even where a sovereign would seem to be solvent, markets may so over-price risk due to uncertainty (political uncertainty) that the high rates sovereigns then have to pay to refinance their debt does give rise to the possibility of default.

Any investor in any debt – corporate, bank or sovereign – needs to try to evaluate, firstly, the **probability of default** of the debt in question and, secondly, the probable **loss given default**. This is similar to the case of bank loans where the loan arranger has to calculate these probabilities before pricing a bank loan. We are concerned with how to assess risk on sovereign and bank debt and how this affects pricing from the point of view of possible investors in these kinds of debt. Our interest also arises from the fact that the financial and eurozone crises also provide opportunities for substantial profits to be made by choosing the right side of the trade to be on in the bonds comprising these asset classes. For example some debt investors in 2010/11 will have executed the inverse of the euro area convergence trade (in the lead up to 1999) by putting in place divergence trades or relative value trades, e.g. short Italy and long Germany, well before the Italian crisis came to a head.

The value of capital assets depends on both future expected cash flows from those assets, i.e. P&I flows and the discount rate used to account for the time value of money and perceived risk. If these cash flows cease or payment is late, the value of the capital asset will be reduced. It is the risk of non or late payment of cash or forced roll-over or extension of the final maturity of a bond due that gives rise to **credit risk in debt investments**, both for loans and bonds.

## A BANK OR SOVEREIGN DEFAULT

We noted in Chapter 7 that a bank would set the price, i.e. set an interest rate, on a loan starting with some reference rate, perhaps LIBOR and add to this the expected loss rate on loans of the particular type it was pricing. If this expected loss rate was wrong, and if in consequence unexpected losses were high as they were for quite a number of US, UK and European banks from 2007 onwards, then they may be sufficient to wipe out the value of the bank's equity.

In this event, in the case of a normal company (a corporate), it is likely that it would be unable to meet its liabilities as they fell due and thus would be insolvent. At this point its creditors would appeal to a court for a winding-up order, i.e. an insolvency procedure through which the company's assets would be sold (liquidation sale) and the proceeds distributed according to the ranking of the liabilities. Lehman Brothers, for example, is still in the process of being wound-up after becoming insolvent, a process that will in practice take at least a decade due to its complexity.

In the case of a bank, the liabilities are to depositors, senior debt holders, junior debt holders, equity holders, holders of derivative contracts, secured asset holders, interbank lenders, the European Central Bank and the European Stabilisation Facility (within the eurozone), the internal revenue service (tax authorities) and others. However, as we will see below, the state also has an additional interest in bank insolvency. The state may be unwilling to allow a large bank to collapse, even though it is insolvent. This adds a new, and critical, dimension to the issue, since, if the bank is insolvent but is not put through a liquidation process, then there is no agreed legal procedure to resolve the interests of the bank's various creditors. Only in a legal court ordered winding up is there a set of agreed procedures in law.

In the case of a country we have the same questions to ask. While at one time it was assumed that developed world debt was default free, today it has become clear from the eurozone sovereign debt crisis that this is not so. Thus estimating probability of default and loss given default on sovereign debt, as well as bank debt, has suddenly become of critical importance for investors worldwide – a new experience for most of them.

## RESOLVING INSOLVENCY

Insolvency can be defined in two different ways:

- **Cash flow insolvency** (illiquid debtor): unable or unwilling to pay debts as they fall due;
- **Balance sheet insolvency** (insolvent debtor): having negative net assets – in other words, liabilities exceed assets.

Whether the debtor is an individual, a non-financial company, a bank or a country (a **sovereign**), the question which always arises for a creditor in an **event of default**, i.e. missed or delayed payment of interest or principal, is whether or not the default arises from cash flow insolvency or balance sheet insolvency. Given the default, the creditor will normally make a decision on how best to **resolve the debtor's default** with the aim of minimising his or her **loss given default**. This requires that the creditor evaluate whether the debtor is suffering from **financial distress** has 'only' a cash flow problem or in fact has a balance sheet problem, i.e. is balance sheet insolvent and likely to remain so for the foreseeable future? If the former, the creditor may minimise his or her loss given default by employing **forbearance**, i.e. holding back on bankruptcy proceedings. This may involve rescheduling, i.e. extending the P&I payment flow in such a way that the debtor will be likely to be able to make payments under the new schedule. If the latter, then forbearance may, or may not, be the best strategy.

Forbearance could, for example, involve extending the period of the loan to reduce the rate of principal repayments or reducing the interest rate on the loan, either of which would reduce cash outflows in future time periods. Such forbearance might involve the creditor in a loss or, alternatively, the new cash flow structure could be designed to have the same present value as the original cash flows would have had by, for example, requiring a larger final cash payment at the end of the loan. In the case of Greece, the proposal put to investors holding Greek bonds is to 'voluntarily' accept an exchange of €1,000 Greek bonds for say €500 bonds, possibly guaranteed by some European entity or government(s). Such a haircut (50%) involves a choice between accepting a definite loss of 50% of value (in terms of NPV) in exchange for an asset of guaranteed value or continuing to hold Greek debt in the hope that its market value rises above that of 50% of face value or, alternatively, falls to zero.

I have talked of 'the creditor'. But in practice the problem is that there may be many different classes of creditor, each with different, and competing, interests (divided interest). Also, even within a creditor class, there are likely to be many conflicting interests rather than just one **collective interest** of the group as a whole. Indeed, there may be those who hold credit default swaps which will pay out on an event of default and thus may be keen to encourage the country to default. Thus obtaining agreement on how to 'forbear' may be difficult. This problem brings to the fore the issue of 'voluntarism'. If a debt restructuring is voluntary, then there is no event of default. If this is the case, those who hold credit default swaps against such debt cannot demand repayment at par from the swap counterparty since a voluntary restructuring is not a 'credit event', i.e. the trigger is not pulled by it.

In the event that the creditor deems that the problem is one of balance sheet insolvency, i.e. the debtor (an individual or a company) does not have sufficient assets to sell to meet its liabilities, now or in the foreseeable future, the best course of action for creditors may be to ask the courts for a winding up order. However, forbearance may be the best course of action if there is reason to believe that, for example, the debtor will obtain an asset at some point in the future (in the case of an individual, perhaps an elderly mother has a valuable house which is willed to the person). Such procedures can be initiated for individuals and for companies, including banks. However, for countries (sovereigns) there is no such process, as a sovereign's assets cannot normally be seized in lieu of scheduled payments on debt. Indeed developed country sovereigns generally have very few assets, as most public assets in Western countries have already been sold-off in privatisations (with Greece and Italy being exceptions). Thus for sovereigns the processes involved in resolving non-payment are very different.

## REPAYMENT OF DEBT PRINCIPAL: HOUSEHOLDS, SOVEREIGNS AND COMPANIES

When evaluating an individual or a couple's ability to support a mortgage, i.e. assessing the size of mortgage that is sustainable by this particular person or couple on a hedge finance basis, a lender will look at current income, expected future income, risk of redundancy, risk of cessation of income due to ill health and, also very importantly, age. The assessment of sustainability of the mortgage P&I payments involves calculating the likelihood that the person or couple can pay interest on the loan **and** repay the capital amount of the loan within their income earning lifetime. This would be hedge financing as we defined it in Chapter 15.

A couple in their early twenties can have a slower capital repayment schedule (perhaps 30 years) and hence lower monthly debt service cost (interest plus a small component of capital repayment) than a couple who are in their fifties (probably only five years). This difference within the category of **natural persons** (humans) in terms of cash-earning lifetime is one distinction that bankers must make. But the distinction between natural persons and the other two categories of entities which borrow – companies, which are classified as **legal persons** and **sovereigns** ('sovereignty' is the quality of having supreme, independent authority over a territory) – are even greater. The key difference is that natural persons have a limited lifespan (on average somewhere around 80 years, but an income-earning life of perhaps only 40 years), whereas companies and sovereigns have, in theory, an indefinite life.

This leads to the key difference in terms of borrowing. Natural persons must repay capital during their lifetime and normally within their likely income-earning lifetime (or on death from sale of assets), while companies and sovereigns always hope to **roll-over** their debt, i.e. to finance capital repayments from new debt that they raise (**speculative financing**). Indeed, sovereigns have in the past issued perpetual bonds that have no redemption date. For example, in the UK, War Loan bonds were issued some hundreds of years ago to help finance wars and these remain available on the market today. Sovereigns almost never repay all debt, though they do sometimes reduce the ratio of debt/GDP as a result of GDP rising due to economic growth, while still maintaining existing debt levels. In the next decade, however, it is likely that many Western countries will have to actively reduce their debt/GDP ratios in order to revert to sustainable fiscal policies in an era of low economic growth rates.

Given that speculative finance is the standard modus operandi of virtually all Western sovereigns, then in terms of fiscal sustainability, i.e. the ability to continue to service debt without ceasing essential public services and entitlements, the question that investors have to ask in respect of a sovereign borrower is *not* **whether it will be able to repay its debt** in the future but whether or not it will **be able to refinance its existing debt (roll-over its debt)** in the future, without a large increase in the interest rate due to a large rise in the risk spread attached to it. Such an increase in the interest rate could easily send a country into a so-called **debt trap**, i.e. be unable to meet interest payments if the new higher interest rate exceeded the growth rate of the economy. In 2012, Italy and Spain, suffered interest rates for new debt at levels which, if they continue at that level for a sustained period, will undoubtedly cause them to fall into a debt trap. This is despite the fact that these countries probably have sustainable fiscal positions if their sovereign debt can be issued at the same yield as that on German sovereign debt. This is known as a 'dual equilibrium' position – the country may end up either solvent or insolvent depending simply on the risk spread on their sovereign debt.

Once a country is unable to make interest payments on its loans from the tax revenue remaining after necessary public spending, it has to try to borrow just to pay interest and, in the case of Greece, even to pay the salaries of public servants such as teachers. Investors were asking in mid-2010 whether Greece had got to this point and their answer was clearly yes – Greece was at the Ponzi finance stage – and no, investors were not willing to refinance maturing Greek sovereign debt and lend additional amounts in order to enable the Greek government to pay them the interest due on the rolled-over debt. At this point the country would normally be forced to default on its debt and seek a resolution (restructuring) unless the IMF or the EU intervened to delay such an outcome.

The IMF and the EU did intervene and provided the required financing. The stated reason was that, given time (**forbearance**), cuts in government spending and tax rises as part of the **conditionality** of EU help, Greece would in future be able to repay the IMF and the EU and resume raising capital at normal rates in the private markets. Put differently, Greece was said to be suffering from a temporary problem and therefore forbearance, combined with public spending cuts, tax rises and more effective tax gathering was the solution. This has not proven to be the case and it is doubtful if anyone ever actually believed it was. Greece has been unable to return to the private markets.

In the case of Ireland, the cause is not traditional public spending or large deficits before the crisis but the guarantees provided by the sovereign on all Irish bank debt. Thus, in effect, bank debt becomes sovereign debt. The problems of banks and sovereigns then become closely linked. However, Ireland does look as if it will resolve its crisis with the limited help it has received.

## BANK FUNDING

In the case of companies, these are assumed to be **going concerns**, i.e. to have an indefinite life, unless the company **auditor**, an independent agent whose duty it is to report to the shareholders on the financial health of the company, decides to the contrary. In this case the auditor's report on the company will (in the UK at least) include a so-called **emphasis of matter** paragraph drawing attention to uncertainty about its status as a going concern. This would be done before the company was declared to be a **gone concern**. In the case of banks, which is the class of company in which we are most interested, audit firms[1] take a view on **whether or not they believe the bank is able to access sufficient funding for at least a year – the minimum for it to be viewed as a going concern**.

An important issue in respect of this assessment is whether or not the government of the country in which the bank is headquartered (or, in the eurozone, the ECB) is willing to provide that funding in the event that private lenders (depositors, other banks, bond market investors, etc.) are unwilling to provide it. Thus, the viability of a bank is as much a function of the certainty of official sector support in the event of financial distress as it is of the bank's actual balance sheet position. If an auditor qualified its audit statement of a bank by implying that it was heading towards gone-concern status, it would collapse immediately. Thus auditors are reluctant to qualify a bank's accounts in this way.

Figures 16.1a and 16.1b from the Bank of England (which we repeat from Chapter 8) show just how much the rating of bank debt depends on government support.

For example, if Irish senior bank debt had not been assumed to be protected by the Irish state as a result of the 'too large to fail' doctrine then Irish bank debt would have been rated Ba2, which is below investment grade, rather than A2 on the scale used above. This would have indicated that Irish banks had a real problem and therefore investors and bondholders might have taken action sooner to try to stop the banks from behaving so stupidly. The total implicit support to UK banks is estimated at an annual amount of over £100 billion. The support which governments give to banks in this way is an example of moral hazard leading to lending that might not otherwise be undertaken and hence a possible misallocation of resources within a market economy.

## RESOLVING NATURAL PERSON DEFAULT

Bankruptcy is a process initiated by a court when a person (or a company) is suffering financial distress. If the creditor cannot find a means of **resolving the default in negotiations with the debtor** (forbearance), then, subsequent to this, the appropriate court may agree to the initiation of a bankruptcy procedure. This procedure would normally involve the debtor's assets being seized and sold to make good the default (usually it would only partially make good). As an individual does not have limited liability (in contrast to a company), whilst the loan (for example credit card debt) may not have been collateralised, all the debtor's

---

[1] The so-called big-four audit firms are KPMG, Deloitte, Ernst and Young, and Price Waterhouse Cooper.

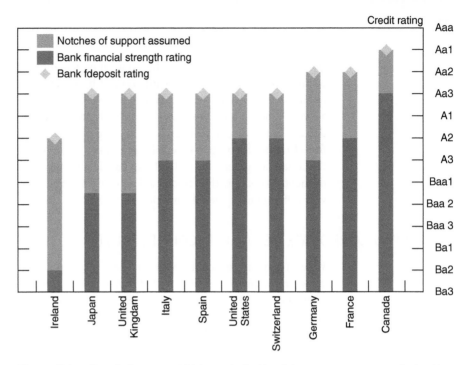

**Figure 16.1a** Benefit (in terms of higher rating) of implicit government support for banking firms (too big to fail, doctrine)

*Sources*: Bank of England Financial Stability Report June 2010 Chart 3.21, http://www.bankofengland.co.uk/publications/Documents/fsr/2010/fsrfull1006.pdf (accessed 2 February 2012), Moody's.

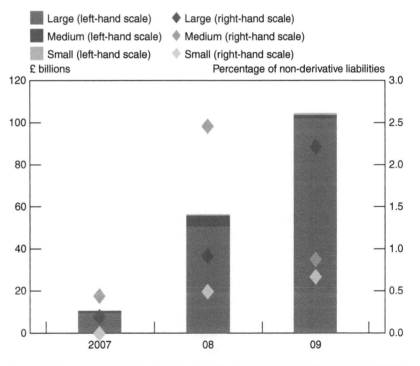

**Figure 16.1b** Estimated size of total implicit funding subsidy to UK banks and building

*Sources*: Bank of England Financial Stability Report December 2010 Chart 5.9 (p. 51), http://www.bankofengland.co.uk/publications/fsr/2010/fsrfull1012.pdf (accessed 2 February 2012). Bank of America Merrill Lynch, Bankscope published by Bureau van Dijk Electronic Publishing, Moody's and Bank calculations.

assets do become collateral in the event of personal bankruptcy being declared. Many people who use credit cards do not have many assets that could be sold to enable the bank to recover its debt and so in effect much of this kind of debt, as well as being unsecured, is also unlikely to see any recovery in the event of default. In the case of collateralised lending such as a mortgage, the creditor can **foreclose** on the property, i.e. take its rights to ownership of the property under the collateral agreement, and sell it to enable it to make good, at least partially, on the debtor's default. Thus credit card debt and mortgage debt in normal times have very different loss given default percentages.

## RESOLVING CORPORATE (LEGAL PERSONS) DEFAULT

When a company is unable to meet its debt payments as they fall due, its creditors can come to an arrangement with it if they believe the company is suffering from a cash flow, rather than a balance sheet, problem. In the United States, there is a special process in the bankruptcy law which permits a 'stay of execution' of bankruptcy under the so-called Chapter 11 arrangements of the US bankruptcy code. This allows the company time to try to work out the most satisfactory resolution of its problems.

The key difference between a legal person (a company) and a natural person (in addition to the difference in lifespan) is that, as owners of a company, the shareholders have limited liability for the company's debts, whereas a natural person without the protection of a company cannot have limited liability for his or her own debts. Thus whereas an individual is liable for **all** his or her debts, a company's shareholders are only liable for the company's debts up to the amount of their shareholding. Thus, in bankruptcy, when a company's assets are sold off, if the amount of cash realised in the liquidation does not meet the total amount of the liabilities, then the creditors suffer some degree of loss, i.e. loss given default. If anything remains from the value of the assets after paying off all liabilities, this is repaid to shareholders (the residual interest holders).

## THE RESOLUTION OF BANKS AND SOVEREIGNS

Resolution procedures for banks (which are, of course, companies) and also sovereigns are complex. The reason for this in the case of banks is that governments generally **will not permit** a systemically important bank to go into liquidation; and in the case of a sovereign it **cannot** go into liquidation. Thus the key difference between natural persons and non-bank companies on the one hand and banking companies and sovereigns on the other is that with the former there is a **clear legal procedure** in the event that the debtor breaks a contract with a creditor – the personal bankruptcy procedure for people and the corporate bankruptcy procedure for companies. With a bank which has reached the zombie stage i.e. kept artificially alive so it is a living dead bank, and sovereigns there is not.

If governments will not allow a bank, which is clearly in financial distress, to head towards corporate bankruptcy, and if sovereigns cannot declare bankruptcy, in the event of financial distress, there may be no clear procedures for resolving the situation. In particular there is an absence of a clear **trigger** which would enable the **resolution** of the insolvency to commence. This trigger is normally an **event of default** which is the point at which the debtor fails to make the required P or I payment when it falls due. But for a sovereign there is no agreed process beyond this point of failure to pay. For a bank there would be normal insolvency procedures, but, if the government intervenes to prevent this, there is also no agreed procedure.

The reason that governments will not allow most banks to collapse is a consequence of the government's responsibility for **financial stability**, which means ensuring that banks continue to be able to provide credit, deposit services and payment services. The collapse of any bank deemed 'too large to fail' and the fear of a systemic crisis, i.e. that the problem will spread to the banking system as a whole, means that governments will almost always rescue banks which are suffering **financial distress**.

Governments have in place arrangements to provide liquidity to banks which are suffering from liquidity problems, i.e. cannot raise funds from private lenders. This **lender of last resort** function of the central bank is the first weapon in the armoury of governments in the event of a bank experiencing liquidity difficulties. Unfortunately, distinguishing illiquidity from balance sheet insolvency is a difficult matter in the case of households, non-financial companies and countries, but even more so for banks: 'a classic problem in financial crises is to distinguish between problems of illiquidity and insolvency. Distinguishing between them is critical to the design of an effective response, but it is very hard to do'.[2]

This problem is one we covered briefly in Chapter 1, where we considered the problems of valuing financial assets and the distinction between historic cost valuation and market (fair value) valuation. In reference to the problem of Northern Rock, the first UK bank which had to be rescued by the government at the start of the financial crisis in 2007, the Governor of the central bank in the UK (the Bank of England), in a letter to a Treasury Select Committee of MPs, noted that central banks, in their traditional LOLR role, can lend to commercial banks: 'against good collateral at a penalty rate to an individual bank facing temporary liquidity problems, but that is otherwise regarded as solvent'. Shortly after this, Willem H. Buiter, the well-informed author of the website Maverecon, observed:

> It is by no means obvious that Northern Rock (total assets £113 billion as of 30 June 2007) suffered just from illiquidity rather than from the threat of insolvency. The organization has followed an extremely aggressive and high-risk strategy of expansion and increasing market share, funding itself in the expensive wholesale markets for 75% of its total funding needs, and making mortgage loans at low and ultra-competitive effective rates of interest. No matter how efficient you are, or how safe your assets are, if the effective interest rate on your borrowing exceeds that on your investments, you are unlikely to be a long-term viable proposition, no matter how impressive the growth of your turnover. Northern Rock's share price had been in steep decline since February of this year, well before the financial market turmoil hit.
>
> Maverecon, July 2007 http://maverecon.blogspot.co.uk/

---

[2] Tim Geithner, Chairman of the US Federal Reserve Bank, Speech at San Francisco Federal Reserve, June 2007.

Clearly, therefore, there were different views at the time of the Northern Rock rescue (around August 2007) as to whether the bank was illiquid or insolvent. Indeed, there was also the view that the problem was an idiosyncratic (or micro-liquidity/solvency) one, i.e. just one single bank in the whole country and not most of the banks in the country, implying that it was not a systemic problem. But as we now know, it was in fact the first evidence of a systemic problem in the UK financial system and more widely. Also, as we now know, Northern Rock was in fact insolvent at the time of its bailout, as Maverecon hints above. However, at the time these events materialised and in the period prior to this, it was hard to answer the key questions – is the bank solvent and is the problem related to just this one bank?

It is such uncertainties that can lead to the problem of risk changing from being measurable to being immeasurable. This is also described as risk changing into uncertainty (not capable of statistical analysis) based on the Frank Knight analysis I have already reviewed in the Preface. When this happens, investors simply take no chances and refuse to refinance loans to a bank, a company or a government. It is this uncertainty that can result in market failure, leading to undervaluation of assets, i.e. the value of debt in a situation of uncertainty may fall well below its EMH value simply because the information needed for it to be valid is just not available. This can also lead to lenders simply refusing to renew loans because, in the absence of risk that is measurable, they sensibly will not lend into a situation of uncertainty.

Figure 16.2 shows Northern Rock's capital structure. In the period from 2000 to its collapse in 2007, its balance sheet increased in size from around £20 billion

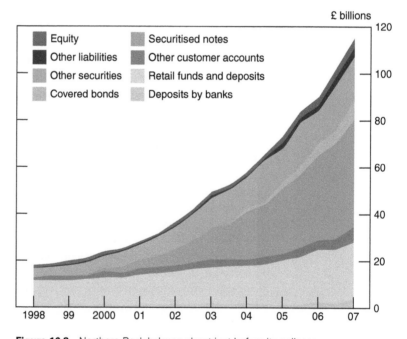

**Figure 16.2**  Northern Rock balance sheet just before its collapse

*Source*: Bank of England, Financial Stability Report October 2007 Chart 1 (p. 10) http://www.bankofengland.co.uk/publications/fsr/2007/fsrfull0710.pdf (accessed 2 February 2012).

to almost £120 billion. It achieved this by under-pricing mortgages and paying high fees to brokers to provide it with borrowers (a poor business model). It then financed this asset growth, mostly not on the basis of deposits, which being guaranteed are relatively 'sticky' (and low cost), but on the basis of issuing securitised notes (a risky and more expensive strategy). As we noted earlier these are not guaranteed and therefore do not provide 'sticky' funding. The bank did this because it could not find additional depositors to provide the liabilities required to fund its ever-increasing assets. It can also be seen that the bank's equity capital grew much more slowly than the rate of total balance sheet growth and indeed barely changed during this whole growth phase.

## BANK RESOLUTION

The question of bank resolution has come to the fore globally since the financial crisis. Given the difficulties that bank collapses presented to the authorities during the crisis a number of national and international bodies are now trying to develop new procedures for bank **recovery and resolution**, i.e. resolving the problem of a bank suffering financial distress. Regulators and legislators trying to develop appropriate procedures all have to face the challenge that if governments insist on preventing banks in financial distress from going through normal corporate bankruptcy procedures, then it is difficult to force liability holders to accept losses on their bank debt holdings. What this means is that whereas in a corporate bankruptcy there is a clear **event of default** which initiates a legal procedure, if a bank is kept alive despite being insolvent, this normal procedure cannot be used. Without bankruptcy, it is difficult to force liability holders to take losses and if they cannot be 'persuaded' then the government has to make good the losses to the point at which the bank is recapitalised adequately according to the Basel rules.

The question for a resolution framework is quite simple: in the event of a bank having assets worth less than its liabilities, and with a government determined to keep the 'living dead' (a zombie bank) alive, who should take the losses in order to reduce liabilities to a level appropriate to the value of the assets, i.e. to reduce liabilities to an amount which can restore the appropriate level of capital to the bank? Should it be the equity investors, the junior bondholders, the senior bondholders, the depositors, the deposit guarantee fund or the state (taxpayers)? The question might be simple but the solution is not. In the case of Greece, the same issues arose – how should private sector holders of Greek debt be **bailed in**, i.e. to make them take losses and how should these losses be distributed? In fact politicians were able to make private sector lenders accept losses by using the threat of forcing even greater losses on the banks which would have happened if Greece had simply been declared Greece insolvent.

## RESOLVING THE ISSUES RAISED BY A BANK SUFFERING FINANCIAL DISTRESS

A bank resolution regime is a set of procedures taken by the authorities to resolve the situation that an unviable bank finds itself in. 'Unviable' does not necessarily mean that it has collapsed. It means that the regulatory authority has come to the opinion that the bank is no longer able to continue in business because, for example, it no longer has the confidence of depositors and wholesale lenders, and as a result it no longer meets its conditions for authorisation as a deposit taking institution. In addition, the authorities have to believe that there is no reasonable prospect of the management of the bank being able to take actions which would correct the situation within a reasonable time frame, an action such as a secondary offering of shares to increase its share capital being an obvious one. The **trigger** for resolution, therefore, is likely to be the **withdrawal of its deposit taking licence**. However, as this alone is not a default, it does not trigger normal insolvency procedures.

There are a number of possible resolution schemes:

1. Closure of the bank and repayment of deposits to deposit holders;
2. Maintain the bank as a going concern (the bank remains open) through assistance from the authorities, such as the provision of liquidity or equity capital;
3. Government intervention, for example to nationalise the bank;
4. The organisation of a merger with another bank (frequently used for small banks);
5. The use of a 'bridge bank' to take the bank into temporary state ownership;
6. Splitting the bank into a 'good bank' and a 'bad bank', i.e. one which is viable and one which is not;
7. Forbearance and hope.

The key features of most of these schemes is that **they give the central bank the right to override the normal protections provided to creditors under corporate insolvency law**. Conversely, however, in most countries there are also protections through the courts against abuse of the law by the authorities. One normal protection under the law is that no creditor should find itself worse off under a resolution mechanism than under a bankruptcy procedure unless it agrees to the action being taken.

Today the debate on bank resolution revolves around a few key issues:

• If a bank remains a going concern, i.e. absent the required trigger which starts the normal process of corporate bankruptcy, should junior debt-holders still be required to suffer a 'haircut' or even complete loss on the value of their debt as they would in a corporate insolvency procedure, in order to avoid the taxpayer having to absorb the whole cost? Should even senior debt-holders suffer some haircut? If this were done, it would involve what is known as bailing-in private sector holders of bank debt. If they don't suffer any losses and instead the taxpayer takes on all the losses, private sector holders of bank debt have thereby been bailed out.[3]

---

[3] 'Bailing out' is an expression used in the seafaring world when a boat is in difficulty due to taking water on board. Initially passengers and crew will try to bail out the water from the ship to stop it capsizing. If they fail the ship will sink. If a ship is in danger of sinking, some passengers will believe their best course of action is for they themselves to 'bail-out' of the boat and swim for the shore, leaving the boat and any remaining passengers to sink beneath the waves.

- Should senior debt holders who are considered to have the same rights as deposit holders (but no deposit insurance) also have to contribute to 'returning the zombie to a normal life'?
- If a bank is not just a national SIFI but a global SIFI, (G-SIFI) how could a cross-border resolution be achieved?
- How can the process of resolution be 'pre-arranged' in order that it can be undertaken easily and quickly – normally over a weekend so that on the Monday morning depositors do not find that when they put a card into a cash machine the machine shows a message reading – 'sorry, the bank is bankrupt – we have no cash?

At the present time, the authorities in a number of countries are working with their banks to ensure that each produces its own resolution plan while it is a going concern so that, in the event of insolvency, this plan could be put into action quickly. This is also known as a '**living will**' in the sense that it is similar to a person providing in advance of death a listing of how his or her property should be disposed of to his or her relatives after death in order to avoid disputes.

In the international arena the problem of cross-border resolution is also being worked on by, for example, the Financial Stability Board which represents all the major countries and meets at the offices of the Bank for International Settlements in Basel.

## BURDEN SHARING BETWEEN PRIVATE AND PUBLIC SECTORS FOR BANKS SUFFERING FINANCIAL DISTRESS

Many commentators have said that banks should not be bailed-out, i.e. the majority of their security holders should not be saved from loss but instead even senior security holders should have to accept that they would be bailed-in, i.e. contribute to the cost of a bank rescue by incurring losses from a haircut. The Association of Financial Markets in Europe (AFME), in the case study below, shows how debt holders of Lehman could have been bailed-in had this been possible and how this would have reduced the losses which bankruptcy (the change from going concern to gone concern) inflicts.

### Case study: Lehman – what might have been

1. Old equity capital is written-off (becomes valueless) due to asset write-downs, but in exchange shareholders may be offered warrants which can convert into equity in the future if the company does well. New equity capital is created by converting Lehman's preferred, subordinated and a portion of senior unsecured debt into equity. This would be sufficient to achieve a tier 1 ratio above 20% (purposely conservative (high) to engender market confidence).
2. Investors in Lehman would have to recognise embedded losses of roughly $25 billion under a bail-in, considerably less than the estimated $150 billion in market losses that occurred. (The market loss estimate is based on post-bankruptcy trading levels for Lehman equity, preferred and subordinated debt – essentially worthless – and unsecured debt securities trading at approximately

20% of face value.) Some argue that these losses were especially high due to the disorderly nature of the Lehman bankruptcy filing. While it is difficult to determine the exact components of this loss, most believe that even an orderly transition to gone-concern will destroy substantial value.

3. Although the bail-in would have reduced claims and subordinated many investors, they should still be better off in economic terms than under a liquidation. Bail-in avoids the large, unnecessary, additional losses that arise in the transition from going concern to gone concern, known as bankruptcy costs. If Lehman had undergone a bail-in, senior unsecured creditors might have retained value equal to 85 to 95% of their original claim, rather than the 10 to 20% recovery values indicated by post-bankruptcy market trading levels.

4. The reduction in losses has important systemic implications. If the loss to creditors can be reduced from the severe levels implied by liquidation to a more modest (5 to 15%) level, stress on investing institutions will be much reduced. For example, one practical outcome of a lower loss level might have been to avoid the 'breaking the buck' event that occurred at The Reserve Fund, which led to significant contagion in that sector after the Lehman bankruptcy.

## THE SOVEREIGN DEBT RESTRUCTURING MECHANISM

In the case of a country, debt is issued by what is defined as a 'sovereign entity'. Being a sovereign entity means that those who hold sovereign debt are not entitled to seize any assets the government might own if it is in default (at least not within its territory). Thus in the case of a sovereign, the definition of solvency is based purely on the cash flow definition. A useful summary is:

> To be deemed solvent, a government must be expected to honour current and future financial obligations including the implicit commitment to continue providing certain public goods, services and transfers in the future (i.e. other costs apart from debt service costs).[4]

If, for any reason, a government cannot meet its interest obligation, it is technically not insolvent but is '**in default**'.

The fundamental difference between sovereign debt, i.e. debt issued by a sovereign authority which is the recognised government of a country, and corporate (including bank) debt is the more limited ability of creditors to take legal action against the debtor in the case of sovereigns and the very limited ability to achieve legal enforcement. In the past gunboats and marines might have been used as an enforcement weapon but today that is less likely to be the resolution mechanism. Traditionally, indeed, it was often assumed that there was **absolute sovereign immunity** from pursuit by creditors through the courts. For example, sovereigns cannot be sued in foreign courts. But changes in the law, and in particular US law, have resulted in a situation where sovereign immunity no longer plays an important role in shielding sovereign debtors from creditor law suits.

---

[4]  http://www.imf.org/external/pubs/ft/wp/2006/wp0667.pdf

Despite this, creditor litigation has been rare. One interesting reason for this has been that until the 1990s, most creditor-held sovereign debt was bank debt and often developing country debt. Banks holding distressed sovereign debt had a regulatory incentive not to declare the debtor in default, i.e. to create a **trigger**, since this would also require them, and any other bank holding such debt, to write down their loans at this point, which might lead to their own insolvency.

This willingness to offer forbearance has decreased as banks have increasingly chosen to, or been required to, write down debt to reflect prices in the new secondary markets that were developing from the 1980s onwards. Also, increasingly bank debt has been securitised and countries have borrowed through capital markets rather than through bank lending.

A key question in respect of sovereign debt is what sanctions banks or international investors have against a creditor in default. Traditionally the only weapon was permanent exclusion of that debtor from the international bank credit and capital markets. In practice, however, many debtors have been able to return to the markets after coming to an agreement with their creditors. The key question then is what kind of agreements can be made that overcome debtor insolvency while ensuring that creditors suffer the minimum loss given default.

The whole shift from bank credit to capital market credit has resulted in difficulties in debt restructuring negotiations. When the whole of a credit was owned by banks, the process of negotiation was conducted between the sovereign and a so-called **Bank Advisory Committee** for this loan. This committee had representatives from each of the major bank creditors. As banks generally had the same interests as each other since the debt was **undivided**, i.e. all on the same terms, it was relatively easy to come to an agreement that was 'satisfactory' to both sides. Today, however, debt in the form of securities is held by a very wide range of institutions, which often have quite different interests. In particular, there are so-called **vulture funds** which are investment funds which invest in **distressed debt**, i.e. debt which they purchase when it is trading at a low price – a price below fundamental value, whose interests may be quite different from banks and pension funds who have bought the debt at par (100) and are sitting on a large loss which is unrealised (historic cost) but will suddenly have to be realised if there is a declared default. There may also be holders of CDSs (protection buyers) who will **profit** if sovereign debt falls in value. They may also hold a small amount of the debt in order to be on the panel which is deciding on what action to take in respect of the debt. But their real interest is in default since this will require the CDS protection seller to pay out. The existence of these different interests amongst the creditors has led to what is known as the **collective action problem**.

## SOVEREIGN DEBT DEFAULT AND COLLECTIVE ACTION CLAUSES

The legal standing of sovereign debt is a complex area and therefore I am not going to try to cover it in detail. All I will cover is the issue of **collective action**. This is a means by which it might be possible for creditors and debtors to come an agreement, as is done in the case of corporate bankruptcies, but which is harder in the case of sovereigns. A **collective action clause (CAC)** in a debt contract is explained by the Bank of England as follows:

> The potential advantages of collective action clauses (CACs) to facilitate the restructuring of debts have long been recognised and have been standard in bonds under English law since the 19th century. Collective action clauses allow a contractually specified super-majority of bondholders to agree on a revision to the payment terms that is binding on all, even those who voted against. But until recently it has been the market convention in New York not to include collective action clauses. Achieving a comprehensive debt restructuring has required the unanimous agreement of all bondholders. This is generally felt to be suboptimal. Unanimous agreement means that debt restructurings are potentially held hostage to the actions of recalcitrant or rogue creditors who hope to receive better terms in subsequent offers. This can delay restructuring deals that are to the benefit of the majority of creditors and the debtor and can leave the debtor vulnerable to opportunistic legal action.
>
> Andrew G. Haldane, Adrian Penalver, Victoria Saporta and Hyun Song Shin, 'Optimal Collective Action Clause Thresholds', Bank of England working paper, 2004.

Developed market sovereign bonds have not, in the recent past, defaulted, in contrast to emerging market bonds which frequently have. Examples include Argentina, Mexico and Russia. But the agreement to create a legal route to default from 2013, concluded at the end of March 2011 at a European Union summit, has made it clear that **in future European sovereign defaults are a possibility**. The reforms will force private investors to share the burden of defaults just as bail-ins are designed to do in the case of banks.

The question, however, is: with whom are they sharing this burden? The main provider of official funds will be the **European Stability Mechanism** (ESM) which countries experiencing financial problems can draw upon for emergency loans. Critically, the **ESM will have senior creditor status over private sector fund managers, meaning private investors will be last in the queue for the recovery of money**. In other words eurozone countries will, for the first time, have '**structured financing**', i.e. funding with different levels of seniority, just like CDOs. If ESM funding fails to 'solve' a country's problem, the ESM will have first call on repayment of its loans (priority) before other (private sector) creditors.

In addition, all eurozone government bonds from July 2013 will have CACs written into them, which will outline a framework for default and give a majority of creditors, probably about 70%, the chance to trigger a restructuring, even against the wishes of the others. CACs are designed to avoid a situation where some bondholders 'hold out' for more or for special terms and by doing so hold up the final resolution of a default. CACs have worked well in emerging markets such as Mexico in 2003. They were included in new Mexican bonds after that date because of the difficulties experienced in trying to resolve the Argentinean default two years earlier (it took nearly a decade to resolve). Including a CAC is now standard practice in most emerging markets in Latin America, Asia and central and Eastern Europe.

# Case study: Greece – insolvent and near default in 2011

Many eurozone banks have been holding assets such as Greek sovereign debt at historic cost even though in the market such debt may be trading at a 50% discount. They will not, however, take a write-down on their balance sheets and through their profit and loss accounts until forced to do so through some '**trigger**' event, as this debt will be held on the banking book. Thus many European banks have managed to avoid disclosing that they have negative net worth by simply refusing to revalue loans which they know have fallen substantially in value. In the case of Greek debt held by banks, this was made very clear at the time of the eurozone summit in October 2011 at which Charles Dallara, as the managing director of the Institute of International Finance (IIF), was present as the chief negotiator on behalf of the banks on the issue of Greek debt:

> For weeks Dallara has said that banks would not agree to take any more losses on their Greek bonds than the 21% haircut already agreed in the summer. Any further losses could be dangerous. Angela Merkel, the German chancellor, however, had called repeatedly for banks to lose at least 60% on their Greek bonds. It was only fair for creditors to pay.
>
> Shortly after midnight, Dallara was called into the summit room and offered an ultimatum. If the banks would not agree to a 50% cut on their Greek bonds Europe would let Athens default. Merkel described the offer as 'the last word'. Jean-Claude Juncker, Luxembourg's prime minister said 'that if a voluntary agreement with banks was not possible, we wouldn't resist for one second, to move toward a scenario of the total insolvency of Greece'. Such a move 'would have cost states a lot of money and would have ruined the banks' he added.
>
> *Sunday Times* 30 October 2011

After the summit, the banks issued the following statement indicating that they had acquiesced to eurozone government demands.

**Press Statement on Euro Area Stablization Measures**

October 27, 2011: The following statement was issued by Mr. Charles Dallara, Managing Director of the Institute of International Finance:

We welcome the announcement by the leaders of the Euro Area of a comprehensive package of measures to stabilize Europe, to strengthen the European banking system and to support Greece's reform effort. On behalf of the private investor community, the IIF agrees to work with Greece, Euro Area authorities and the IMF to develop a concrete voluntary agreement on the firm basis of a nominal discount of 50% on notional Greek debt held by private investors with the support of a 30 billion Euro official package. This should set the basis for the decline of the Greek debt to GDP ratio with an objective of reaching 120% by 2020. The specific terms and conditions of the voluntary private sector involvement (PSI) will be agreed by all relevant parties in the coming period and implemented with immediacy and force. The structure of the new Greek claims will need to be based on terms and conditions that ensure an NPV loss for investors fully consistent with a voluntary agreement.

It should be noted that when Dallara says 'banks would not agree to take any more losses on their Greek bonds than the 21% haircut already agreed in the summer', it is very much Alice in Wonderland speak.[5] The debt has in fact lost most of its value (clearly Greece cannot pay) and thus it is not a question of agreeing or not, but simply what 'fictitious' numbers banks use on their balance sheets and whether or not this gives them a negative net worth. For any bank where it does, the bank then has to be declared insolvent or someone has to provide capital to replace that which has been written off as a result of the larger haircut. It should be noted that, in addition to losses on Greek debt, some banks have been protection sellers of CDSs on Greece sovereign debt. If the default is voluntary, no trigger has been pulled and thus no payout is required on the CDS. If however there is a default, many banks which are long Greek credit risk, will have to pay out very large sums. However, those who bought protection will benefit.

## Case study: Italy – illiquid or insolvent in 2011?

Italy at the end of 2011 had two problems:

- An international (current account) payments financing problem;
- A competitiveness problem due to political and social structural impediments to improving efficiency and hence productivity, and higher prices relative to firms in other eurozone countries due to inflation of cost levels relative to those countries.

The first problem is technically soluble through financial transfers from other countries through European agencies, though in practice this may prove politically impossible. The second, with its two components, may be insoluble within the eurozone. This is because the system of governance of Italy may be incapable of reform and, without currency devaluation, it may not be possible to improve price competitiveness without inducing unacceptable unemployment levels to achieve falling labour costs. If this is so, then finding an answer to the financing problem will not result in a long-term solution and hence the financing problem will simply reappear. The real problem is that Italy appears to have a balance of payments on current account problem, which temporary financing cannot correct. Only a reduction in its price level can possibly achieve a real solution to this problem and this is probably not achievable without a currency devaluation or cuts in wages and pensions so drastic that it would probably result in riots in the streets.

During the initial crisis period of November 2011 Germany stalled discussions on agreeing a financing solution for Italy in the belief that if one was offered too soon and too easily, Italy would renege on any structural adjustment plan to which

---

[5] Dallara speak (which is, more generally, bank speak or bank asset valuation principles) is similar to that of Humpty Dumpty in Alice in Wonderland: 'When I use a word,' Humpty Dumpty said in rather a scornful tone, 'it means just what I choose it to mean – neither more nor less.' 'The question is,' said Alice, 'whether you can make words mean so many different things.' 'The question is,' said Humpty Dumpty, 'which is to be master, words or me – that's all.' (*Through the Looking Glass*, chapter 6, slightly modified)

it committed in exchange for the financing. Thus structural adjustment commitments would have to come first, followed by staged financial assistance dependent on the IMF or another supervisor confirming that the required structural adjustments had been undertaken and their objectives achieved.

## ITALY'S FINANCING PROBLEM

The key problem for Italy is that if investors believe that its stock of debt will continue to rise as a result of Ponzi financing it will be unable to exit the debt trap which it is approaching. If so, investors will then cease to rollover their loans to the country. Thus fiscal policy becomes unsustainable. At the end of 2011 that looked like a possible scenario, though the resignation of the prime minister and the installation of a 'technocratic' government which has started to undertake the necessary structural reforms may temporarily at least give Italy some breathing space.

To understand how fiscal policy might become unsustainable, we use the following equation:

Change in Debt Stock = (Existing Stock of Debt – Primary Budget Surplus) $\times$ (Average Nominal Borrowing Costs – Nominal GDP Growth).

Let's make the following assumptions in relation to the above equation:

- GDP growth will have fallen to zero or be negative,
- The primary budget balance which in 2011 was reported to be around 0.5% of GDP will have fallen to zero (or become negative) due to falling growth, leading to higher government expenditure and falling tax revenue;
- The ten-year interest rate will remain at 7%;
- The whole of the outstanding debt, not just the €350 billion which needs to be issued in 2012, has to be refinanced within seven years at 7%.

On the basis of these assumptions let's try to put the arithmetic together for Italy. With sovereign debt currently at 120% of GDP, the interest bill alone on these assumptions would be 8.4% of GDP. If GDP starts falling rather than rising or the primary surplus becomes a deficit, then the figures become even more stark with the *interest bill* rising to as much as 10% of the reduced GDP. Even if most of Italy's debt does not need to be refinanced next year, as each year goes by, the interest rate that the market would demand for reinvesting in Italian debt would rise dramatically, just as it has for Greece, to levels that would be clearly unsustainable.

Unless investors in sovereign debt believe that Italy can increase its primary surplus dramatically, in order to at least stabilise its debt, they will not invest. While the above calculation assumes the interest rate remains at its peak (November 2011) of 7% and that all debt is refinanced next year, even on less aggressive assumptions Italy still needs to generate a primary surplus of around 5% just to shift from Ponzi financing (the need to raise money from lenders in order to pay them their interest) to speculative financing (able to pay interest from tax revenue but not repay capital).

If, on the other hand, Italy paid approximately the same rate of interest as Germany, say 2%, then it only needs to increase its primary surplus slightly to match this interest rate. Thus its overall budget including interest payments would be in balance. Thus fear of an unsustainable fiscal policy can itself drive up interest rates and thereby cause a country which **is** solvent to move towards insolvency. This is because we have moved from a position of measurable risk, where investors feel they can assess the risk of not being repaid in full, to uncertainty (i.e. risk that cannot be scientifically assessed), caused by conflicts within the eurozone governance institutions – national governments, the European Union, the European Central Bank and the European Financial Stability Fund and also structural and governance issues in Italy. If these latter issues are not addressed, then the lack of competitiveness will lead to a continuing increase in the debt/GDP ratio. When risk becomes uncertainty, interest rates incorporate a high uncertainty premium.

## IS THERE A SOLUTION FOR ITALY?

One solution is for the European Central Bank (ECB) to act as LOLR. Bagehot, who first defined the LOLR role for central banks, put it this way: 'Lend without limit, to solvent firms, against good collateral, at high rates'. In this case, 'firms' means 'banks'. If we substitute the word 'country' for 'firm' and substitute 'provide funding liquidity' for 'lend against good collateral' , then we have a solution: 'Provide funding liquidity without limit, to solvent counties, at a sustainable rate'.

Such lending would be done by the central bank (ECB) funding the whole of Italy's refinancing year by year starting with €350 billion for 2012. It would do this through monetary financing, i.e. monetisation of debt, otherwise known as quantitative easing. Quite simply, it would buy all of Italy's new issues of sovereign debt (if investors would not) and pay for it by crediting the cost to the country's central bank account in euros. Technically it can easily do this as the ECB is the institution that creates euros. As they are simply a book entry which can be created any time the ECB chooses (just as any central bank can create money), it is easy to do. It would lend at an interest rate only a little over that of Germany and, as markets gained confidence that there was a buyer of last resort in the market, prices of Italian debt would rise until the yield on existing debt was close to the yield on new debt. Gradually the ECB could stop buying new issues as private investors would be happy to buy, knowing that there was a buyer of last resort in the wings.

Unfortunately, the solution cannot currently be put into effect. The Lisbon Treaty prohibits such monetary financing, partly on the grounds that it is potentially inflationary. There would need to be either a treaty change or some 'fudge' to enable this type of quantitative easing strategy, currently being used by, for example, the Bank of England and the Federal Reserve System, to be employed by the ECB. Given that the ECB has already bought eurozone government bonds in large numbers in the *secondary market*, there is no technical reason why it should not also buy primary market issues. The only difficulty is the constraints of the governance system of the eurozone which are, rightly in my view, designed to minimise moral hazard within the zone. There is also, of course, total opposition of Germany to any such moral hazard inducing moves. Nonetheless, if the eurozone problem is to be solved, Germany must accept that as a surplus country a symmetric approach to solving the problem requires that it provide stimulation to the European economy even as others (the deficit countries) put their finances in order. To date, there is little sign of a willingness to accept the need for moves to stimulate demand and encourage growth as the only solution to the eurozone crisis apart from break-up.

## THE COMPETITIVENESS PROBLEM

Within a single currency zone such as the US (52 states), the UK (four countries – England, Scotland, Wales and Northern Ireland) or the eurozone (17 countries) it had been assumed by some that it was not possible to have a balance of international payments problem between the constituent parts. It was expected that any payments deficit within a single country or state or zone would be financed automatically by the others through the banking system. While this works quite effectively in currency unions which are also fiscal and political unions such as the US and the UK (note both have the word 'united' in their name), it may not work within a single currency zone which does not have fiscal or political union. It may be that eventually the banking systems of countries in surplus will cease to be willing to finance countries which are in deficit. If the economic performance of the countries continues to diverge then the payments imbalances will certainly cease to be financed by the private sector.

The central problem, however, is cultural. Two countries cannot share a single currency if one is ill-disciplined and the other well-disciplined. The consequence is likely to be a growing price level divergence between them which changes their relative competitiveness and hence leads to the need to finance ever growing trade imbalances between them. Italy has a political/business/cultural 'heritage' which militates against maintaining the same price level and rate of productivity growth as Germany which has a very different heritage. The Italians do, of course, have a democratic right to choose politicians who operate this way. That is their choice. But it may not be compatible with membership of the fixed exchange rate currency regime (the eurozone) of which it is currently a member.

The modus operandi of Italy is often referred to as the 'Italian Problem'. Here is a good summary of this structural governance problem which leads to its competitiveness problem:

> The system, or myriad systems that govern Italian life at every level, are in fact highly organized and impervious to change. They are almost impossible for outsiders to comprehend. It goes without saying that these sophisticated and interdependent webs of power and influence are not confined to the world of politics. Corporate Italy also abounds with these structures of tribal capitalism. In spite of everything the system does not want reform.
>
> Moving south, the Italian Treasury's insistence on maintaining 'controlling' stakes in the country's few national champions – electricity utility Enel, oil and gas group ENI and aerospace and defence company Finmeccanica – results in the three-yearly lottery of the government appointing these groups' senior managements. This particular

network, with its unhealthy temptation to dispense patronage, is one of the most public examples of networked Italy in action.

But the real war to turn Italy around will only be won if enough Italian insiders can be convinced that they no longer have everything to gain from perpetuating their undemocratic system of self-referential capitalism.

Paul Betts, 'Ill-judged Smirks about Italy Miss the Deeper Truth',
*Financial Times*, 11 November 2011

If Paul Betts, as a close observer of European life is correct, then it seems unlikely that the long-run competitiveness problem, which is in fact a cultural problem, can be solved by means of financing mechanisms. Italy has already agreed to let the IMF have observers in Rome and to give them access to the information required to monitor its compliance with promised austerity measures. In the longer run, if it allows the surplus countries of Europe, essentially Germany and the Netherlands, to dictate its fiscal policy and other related economic and social policies, then it may be able to stay within the single currency system. Otherwise, it seems unlikely that it can remain a member, regardless of the amount of financing provided in times of crisis. Even France, which in 2011 has been able to retain its AAA rating, is moving inexorably towards a financing crisis brought on by an unsustainable fiscal position – unless it can halt what looks like an inexorable rise in the ratio of debt/GDP.

The lack of competitiveness due to high labour costs and structural rigidities applies to a number of countries in the eurozone. This is shown quite clearly in Figure 16.3. It can be seen that Greece's labour costs had risen by more than 40%

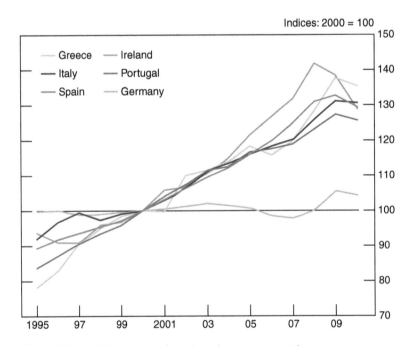

**Figure 16.3** Unit labour costs for selected eurozone countries

*Source*: Eurosat and Bank of England Financial Stability Report Chart 3.3 (p. 33), data sourced from Eurostat, http://www.bankofengland.co.uk/publications/fsr/2011/fsrfull1112.pdf (accessed 10 February 2012).

relative to Germany over a period of only 8 years. However, the other countries on the chart are not far behind Greece. Thus it could be said that the problem these eurozone countries have is not a 'fiscal' one but a balance of payments one caused by lack of price competitiveness brought on by the inability to devalue within the single currency zone. They can't sell enough exports or attract enough tourists and their own manufacturers have become uncompetitive relative to those in Germany. If this is so, the eurozone is not sustainable with its present membership.

# PART IV

# ASSESSING AND MANAGING RISK IN ASSET PORTFOLIOS

# 17 INVESTMENT MANAGEMENT AND PORTFOLIO STRUCTURING

## WHAT ARE THE RISKS INVOLVED IN INVESTMENT?

If asked: what is the purpose of investment management?, the average man in the street would probably say that it is to 'beat the market' i.e. to select shares that will outperform the market as a whole. Self-directed investors (households) generally operate on the basis that this is what they are trying to achieve for themselves and will read magazines such as *Investors Chronicle* in order to pick up 'stock tips' which they hope will lead to investment success – outperformance relative to some **benchmark** they have chosen. Households which do not want to do this themselves will employ a professional investment manager – a wealth manager – often because they believe a professional can achieve 'outperformance' on their behalf. Certainly the ability to generate outperformance is the **marketing claim** that many professional investment managers make. But despite this belief in outperformance being what investment management is about, **generating outperformance is not in fact the purpose of investment management** and indeed is also very seldom achieved consistently. The purpose of investment management is risk management, which in this case means creating portfolios which give the **highest expected return for any given level of risk** chosen by the underlying investors. The major types of risk facing the equity investor are the following.

### Risk of catastrophic loss

If an investor holds all his or her wealth in the shares of only one company, they take the risk that due to some event peculiar to this company such as its founder dying and no one being able to replace her, the company collapses and the investment falls to zero value. This type of risk is known as non-systematic risk, company-specific risk or idiosyncratic risk.

For most investors, losing all or a large proportion of their wealth is their biggest fear. For an equity investor, one obvious way to reduce this risk is by not holding all one's wealth in the shares of only one company which could collapse, resulting in a total loss of financial wealth. The old aphorism 'don't put all your eggs in one basket' is as applicable in asset management as in any other field. Risk can be spread across a number of firms so that if one firm does badly, it is quite likely that another will do well. Risk can also be spread over a range of industries and countries. By building a **diversified** portfolio of shares, risk can be spread across companies, industries and economies, and the risk of catastrophic loss will be reduced. Diversification can eliminate most idiosyncratic risk, i.e. the risk peculiar to just a single company, industry or country. **Diversification is sometimes called the only cost free risk management tool** because it enables risk to be reduced without having to pay for insurance or give up anything. Generally it is suggested that in one country's equity market, a portfolio of around 40 shares covering all major sectors takes out most of the company specific risk. The process of selecting these 40 shares diversified over sectors is known as the **security selection process**. One of the conclusions of what is known as the **capital asset pricing model (CAPM)** is that because any rational investor would diversify his or her portfolio in order to protect against the risk of a particular company doing particularly badly, the market does not provide any compensation for taking on such a risk. This is because, in a diversified portfolio, the probability of any particular company doing particularly badly is likely to be offset by another doing particularly well.

## Risk from a collapse of the equity market

In addition to all shares being subject to non-systematic risk, they are also all subject to general market influences known as **systematic risk, market risk**, or **beta ($\beta$)**, which arises from factors such as a change in the growth rate of the economy relative to what was expected, which affects all companies to a greater or lesser extent.

Whereas non-systematic risks are **uncorrelated** to each other, market risk affects all shares and therefore the performance of all shares is to some extent **correlated**. It is therefore not possible to eliminate systematic (market risk) through diversification within a single market. Indeed, the greatest amount of diversification possible – holding every share in the market – would not eliminate it, but simply allow an investor to have a portfolio which had exactly the same risk as the market.

Having minimised non-systematic risk by avoiding small, non-diversified portfolios, the next issue is now to reduce systematic risk, i.e. the risk of suffering a loss proportionate to the market if the market in which one is invested suddenly collapses, as happened, for example, in each of the years 1987, 2001, 2008 and 2011, when many markets collapsed by as much as 40%.

The simplest response to this risk is to diversify further, this time by splitting the portfolio between the equity market and another market with which it is not generally closely correlated. The fixed income debt market is normally such a market and thus most portfolios attempt to reduce the systematic risk of the total portfolio by holding a portfolio divided between these two asset classes which have a correlation of much less than one. The process by which allocations of total financial resources to different asset classes is determined is known as the **asset allocation process**.[1]

---

[1] There are many approaches to asset allocation which are well covered in single topic texts such as that written by David Darst, *The Art of Asset Allocation: Principles and Investment Strategies for any Market* (McGraw Hill, 2008).

Fixed income investment has a potential drawback for many investors. The volatility of the fixed income market is normally much less than that of equity markets. Thus its risk, as measured by volatility, is lower than for equities. Lower risk equates to lower expected return. Thus to generate the same expected annual return from a fixed income portfolio one needs to acquire a larger investment fund. For a person saving for retirement, this would mean saving a higher proportion of income over a lifetime in order to generate the same expected annual pension. It has to be noted, however, that since 2000, fixed income, apart from sovereign debt issued by the PIIGS (Portugal, Italy, Ireland, Greece and Spain) has, somewhat surprisingly, provided returns **very much higher than equity**, thus inverting the expected risk/return relationship.[2]

## Risk from not matching risk profile of assets against risk profile of liabilities

This risk is one that traditionally asset managers have chosen not to consider. The reason is that most investment managers, whether professional or self-directed individuals, choose to focus on managing financial **assets** without reference to the underlying **liabilities** to which the assets are related. Most managers are comfortable with assets, i.e. shares and bonds, but not with the concept of liabilities. A good example of the need for asset/liability matching would be a person building up a portfolio of assets to enable a comfortable retirement. Such a person will expect to be able to live off the income generated by the portfolio or to purchase an annuity to provide a regular income until death. However, if retirement happens to coincide with a market collapse, then the expected income either from dividends or capital may not materialise. This type of risk arises from mismatching the characteristics of the assets in a portfolio with those of the liabilities. **Asset and liability management** which aims to minimise this mismatch is often achieved through what is known as **liability driven investment**.

## STRUCTURING A PORTFOLIO

The portfolio structuring process can be undertaken in a number of ways. Normally, however, the first step would be to decide which **asset classes** to hold based on their expected return, risk and correlation with each other. This would be followed by the **asset allocation** decision, i.e. the proportions of each of the chosen asset classes to hold and then by **security selection** for each of the selected asset classes.

### Asset allocation

Having chosen the asset classes that the investor will include in his or her universe, e.g. domestic equity, foreign equity, long term debt securities, short term debt, real estate, art, commodities, precious metals, alternative assets, alternative investment

---

[2] A good study of the relative return on fixed income and equity markets over long periods of time is provided by the *Credit Suisse Global Investment Returns Yearbook*.

strategies, overseas assets, the investor then has to **determine the proportion** of each asset class to hold.

The optimal proportions of each possible asset class in a portfolio can, in theory, be determined on the basis of the expected return and risk characteristics of each market and the correlations between markets. However, in practice these approaches have not proven to be robust and, in periods when correlations between all markets are high as has been the case in this millennium, their utility is very much in doubt. Heuristic[3] processes for asset allocation may be as effective and are in common use even by many professionals.

## Security selection: implementing the asset allocation strategy

Having made the asset allocation decision, there are two ways to implement security selection within each asset class that comprises the portfolio. The first is for the investor to create his or her own portfolio within each asset class by buying securities in the market. The investor undertakes **security selection** and makes **direct investments** in individual securities by buying in the market through a stockbroker.

The second way to achieve the desired asset allocation is to employ specialist asset managers within each asset class who will undertake the asset selection on behalf of the investor. This involves using **collective investment funds (pooled funds)** which are covered in the next chapter, in order to obtain exposure to particular asset classes, e.g. domestic equities, domestic bonds, overseas equity, overseas bonds and real estate.

## Security selection: what determines the rate of return on a particular security

The **CAPM** is a very well-known model that can be used to determine the rate of return that investors require of an asset, i.e. to value it, on the assumption that the asset is to be added to an already well-diversified portfolio. I referred to this model in Appendix 1.1 where we looked briefly at how to value **uncertain** cash flows. The model assumes that any rational investor would hold a security only as part of a diversified portfolio and not as a single investment asset, since it is irrational not to diversify away company specific risk. There is, therefore, no reward (return) in the market for assuming **diversifiable** risk (catastrophic loss risk). CAPM uses the asset's sensitivity to **non-diversifiable** risk, i.e. systematic or market risk, which is often represented by the symbol beta $(\beta)$ to estimate expected return. Thus in this model, the investor will not receive any compensation for company specific risk, only for the risk of the particular share relative to the market as a whole. CAPM therefore uses the beta of a particular share as a measure of risk of this share, not the volatility of the share as a stand-alone investment.

In consequence, the valuation of any particular share in the market depends on whether it makes a market portfolio more volatile or not. The beta of a share

---

[3] 'Heuristic' means a 'rule of thumb', an educated guess, intuitive judgment or common sense – any means which makes decision making less brainpower intensive.

is the relationship between the return on a share and the return on the market as a whole, i.e. whether or not the share is adding to or reducing the volatility of a market portfolio. If the market rises or falls by 10% and the share also rises or falls by the same percentage, the share has the same beta as the market, i.e. a beta of 1. A beta of 2 would mean that if the market rose 10% this share would rise by 20% (or fall by 20% if the market fell by 10%), thus this is a risky share and would add risk to the portfolio. A share which would provide good diversification and hence would reduce risk if added to a portfolio would be one with a negative beta, say –0.5. Such a share would rise in price when the market was going down and so would reduce the overall volatility of the portfolio, even though its 'stand-alone' risk might be high (though equally it would fall in price when the market as a whole rose). The equation we use to calculate the required return on an investment relative to its risk (as measured by beta and not by standard deviation) is:

Required return = risk free rate + risk premium = risk free rate + [beta of the share x (market return – risk free rate)].

This is shown in Figure 17.1 where the market return (beta = 1) is 12%, comprised of the riskless rate of return (beta = 0) of 4%, representing the time value of money plus 8% for bearing market risk.

## THE IMPORTANCE OF INVESTOR BELIEFS IN DETERMINING THE APPROACH TO SECURITY SELECTION

Beliefs about the **sources of returns** within equity (or bond) markets, i.e. **the risk factors** for which the investor is being rewarded and about the efficiency or lack of efficiency of the price discovery process (the beliefs about the **EMH** which we considered earlier), are key in determining the strategy that the investor is likely to follow in his or her security selection process. We will start by considering the outcomes of two different sets of investor beliefs about market efficiency.

The first type of investor believes that markets are not efficient and thus diligent security selection can enable the construction of portfolios which will outperform

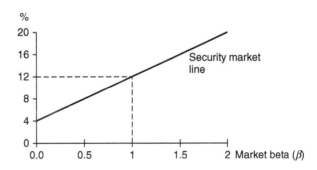

**Figure 17.1**  The security market line shows the required return on any equity security as a function of its beta

*Source*:  thisMatter.com, http://thismatter.com/money/investments/capital-asset-pricing-model.htm (accessed 29 March 2012); author: William C. Spaulding.

those which are constructed purely on the basis of simple diversification by sector, size of company, etc. Such asset managers, known as active managers, believe that they can generate what is known as **alpha**, which is outperformance of a portfolio relative to some **benchmark** and where superior investment results arise from **manager skill**.

The second type of investor believes that markets are efficient and therefore shares are correctly priced in terms of their risk – a belief in the EMH. Thus any share has the expected return for its level of risk. If this is the case, it is not economic to allocate resources to **stock picking**, i.e. trying to select over and under-priced stocks. Such investors, therefore, are likely to wish to find the lowest cost means of investing in a market to enable them to generate the market beta, i.e. the market return, but do not expect to generate alpha (from stock picking skill).

These two beliefs give rise to two different approaches to investment management as a result of the two different philosophies.

## Active management: attempting to generate alpha

Traditionally, most equity fund managers have claimed to be **active managers**, i.e. they believe their role is to seek out undervalued securities to add to their portfolio and, once these securities have realised their expected price appreciation, to sell them and acquire other securities which are expected to appreciate more rapidly than the market. This decision process is known as **stock-picking** and the fund manager who undertakes it is known as an **active** (fund) **manager** and the fund is known as a **managed fund**. It is also known as a **bottom-up approach** to portfolio construction, i.e. seeking out individual shares and using this selection of under-priced shares to build up an overall portfolio of shares. Such a portfolio may not be well diversified in terms of sectors or size of company. It may also have a level of risk quite different from the market as a whole.

Most retail investors operate in this way. They read blogs on the internet to try to discover which share is likely to be 'a winner' and should thus be added to a portfolio. The process is an active one in the sense that it involves continual research and subsequent regular sales and purchases. Both research and transacting with a broker cost money, which has to be deducted from the value of the assets under management.

## Passive management: being satisfied with getting close to beta

A passive investor does not believe that she can select under or overpriced shares and therefore she simply wishes to hold a scientifically diversified portfolio. She is likely to take a 'top-down' approach to investment. This means she will invest in each major sector of the economy, e.g. retail, engineering, electrical, and within each sector will invest in a number of firms so that even if one firm or one sector does worse than average, the others are likely to do better than average.

## MARKET PRICING OF SHARES

Are shares generally correctly priced or are markets **inefficient** and likely to misprice shares? It should be noted that we are considering only developed markets. Emerging markets may not correspond closely to this model and it is indeed likely that there are substantial pricing inefficiencies in such markets due to the lack of investor research, inside information, etc.

If an asset is trading in a market, investors are valuing it continually and this valuation we call the '**price**' of an asset or, more specifically, we normally use the expression **market price**. We can also consider the **value** of an asset in a different sense, which we might call its **fundamental value**. This is something which may deviate from market price (market value). Indeed, a security analyst's (researcher's) job is to try to **evaluate if the fundamental value of a share or bond differs from its market price**. He would then recommend a **trade**, i.e. buying or selling the security. By recommending trades to investors, he is helping his employer, usually a broker/dealer, to generate commission and trading income and hence the ability to remunerate him.

An obvious question is: why do prices in secondary markets change continuously if it is likely that price does not equal value? Do prices change to reflect changes in the fundamental value of a security? The answer is yes. As new information which is relevant to the fundamental value of an asset becomes available, it is **impounded** into the price, i.e. it is incorporated into the valuation model being used by investors and causes them to change their valuation of the asset and hence the prices at which they are willing to trade. In active markets **in developed economies in stable market conditions**, it is generally believed that new information is impounded into asset prices almost immediately (though HFTs may be ahead of others in the market). If this is so, then we have the foundations of the EMH, which is the proposition that the current price of an asset fully reflects all **publicly available information** about future fundamentals that could affect the value of the asset, i.e. its price in the market changes to reflect any change in its fundamental value. These fundamentals could include information on changes in market demand, higher raw material prices, changes in government regulations, exchange rate changes, interest rate changes, etc. and, of course, company specific changes such as a large orders or the firing of the managing director.

If the EMH is correct, then the price of any security is as likely to rise as fall in a subsequent period since at any point in time it is correctly priced in terms of what is known at that date. Consequently, there is little point in an asset manager devoting resources to trying to 'beat the market'. However, it is clear from the observed behaviour of most investors that they do not believe that this theory is valid. Some 80% of retail investors and almost as high a proportion of professional investors believe that active management can generate enhanced returns, even after allowing for the cost of researching stocks.

Generally outperformance is assessed as a return higher than the relevant index while holding stocks which on average are **no more risky** than the index portfolio. Frequently, however, a portfolio which generates a return higher than the market turns out, in fact, to be simply a riskier portfolio. In times of rising markets this would rise faster than the market but in times when markets are falling it would perform worse than the market as a whole. As markets are a **zero sum game**, i.e. what one wins another loses, then clearly everyone cannot be above average or beat the market. Once fund management fees are factored in, it is a negative sum game, as we have observed already.

There is substantial evidence that there are times when markets are not efficient and consequently the EMH does not hold. Such periods of mispricing include the pricing of peripheral eurozone government bonds at yields very close to those of the strongest country, Germany in the lead up to the eurozone crisis. Another example is the overpricing of mortgage assets including CDOs which led to the financial crisis. Nonetheless, the prices of shares or other assets relative to each other may be 'correct'. In emerging markets there is often no reason to believe that the market is efficient in pricing.

## DO ACTIVE MANAGERS OUTPERFORM THE MARKET?

Before we can evaluate the performance of an active manager **relative to** 'the market', we have to define what we mean by 'the market'. Today, relative performance is measured against an index (it was once measured relative to a peer group, such as all pension fund managers). If the relevant index falls by 20% over a year while the fund falls by only 15%, this is viewed as superior (relative) performance. However, **absolute performance**, i.e. the actual gain in value, is clearly highly negative if markets are falling and consequently portfolios are falling in value. Thus even though an asset manager may outperform the market on the downside, he or she has not provided capital protection. Against a **benchmark** (index), what he or she has achieved could be viewed as a good performance, outperforming an index even if it falls substantially. Thus **relative performance** managers as they are known protect against non-systematic risk, but not against systematic risk. If the manager has matched the market return as measured by an index, he or she is said to have generated a **beta** return, i.e. the return on the market. If however the manager does achieve a higher return than the market (after fees) then the active manager will be said to have generated **alpha**. Alpha is simply the excess return over the market (for the same level of risk as the market), which is assumed to be a result of manager skill. The manager could, for example, have predicted that markets were about to fall (or is this not possible?) and sold all holdings of shares and simply held cash. That would certainly give a very superior performance. Such behaviour by a manager has almost never been seen in practice.

The search for alpha is the holy grail of active fund managers. The problem with measuring performance this way, i.e. relative return, is that even if a market collapses and thus the investor has lost a great deal of money, provided the manager has beaten the market, he or she is said to have generated alpha and therefore achieved a good performance for his or her client. One can just imagine the conversation between manager and client along the following lines:

*Investment manager to client*: 'I've done really well for you – I've beaten the market by 2%'.
*Client to investment manager*: 'But you have lost me 20% of the money I invested with you!'

In practice, research suggests that few, if any, fund managers actually achieve alpha consistently over a number of years, though clearly by good luck or skill some will generate alpha in some years since, if we don't consider transaction costs, then in any market, 50% of investors must perform above average and 50% below average just due to chance (law of large numbers in a large population of investors). To demonstrate how this must happen statistically, we can imagine an experiment where we give 100 people a coin and ask them to toss it. At each iteration of the experiment, we eliminate those whose coin comes up with tails. On the first iteration (investment year) 50 people's coins will randomly come up heads (since heads and tails are equally likely). On the next toss by those 50, 25 come up heads. On the next toss it is 12 (to be exact 12 or 13). The next one six, the next one three. At this point each of the three can claim to have a 'secret' formula for success (generating alpha consistently) since these three have now had five heads in a row. Clearly they are geniuses!

Well over 50% of active fund managers, including self-directed retail investors, actually generate returns less than the market when measured over extended investment periods such as five to ten years, once investor fees and transaction costs are factored in unless, of course, like the bank in the run up to the 2008 collapse, they take more risk than the market i.e. ß. This does not mean that they will never generate alpha. In some years they will be lucky or skilful. But since investment is a long-term activity, what matters is returns over extended periods. In this regard, investment is similar to gambling. Sometimes a gambler will be lucky and boast of his success. But when measured over an extended number of years the amount that the casino takes out of the stake will ensure that gamblers don't generally achieve outperformance over longer periods of time. In investment management the 'house take' is the fees of the investment management firm plus the fees it pays to brokers for execution of trades. These costs can substantially reduce the returns realised by the underlying investor.

If most fund managers are unable to generate alpha, why might this be? Apart from the fact that investment outperformance is, as we have already noted, a zero sum game, the answer is that in a developed country in a liquid market an investor has to always know something that the rest of the market does not know, or latch on to an economic trend that others have not yet recognised, in order to beat the market **consistently**, where consistently means over five years at a minimum. If markets are **efficient**, i.e. prices always incorporate known information and new information is incorporated into prices very quickly as suggested by finance theory, then this, as we noted above, leads to the conclusion that prices in efficient markets follow a **random walk**, i.e. price changes are random and unpredictable.[4] Thus the historical record of stock prices is not a guide to future prices since all current information about a company or an economy is already incorporated in the price.

The only other thing apart from known information the impact of which should already be incorporated into the market price is unknown information becoming known in the future. Thus today's market price must be the best estimate of the **true** price. Only if someone has some information that is not **publicly** known, could they predict prices. This could be **insider information**, i.e. information that someone knows as a result of being a director of the company or an advisor to the company. Using insider information for investment purposes is illegal in most countries. Thus **consistent**, year by year, generation of alpha is unusual in

---

[4] Note that prices are not random in the sense of taking any value but random in the sense that movements up are no more likely than movements down, i.e. they are unpredictable.

traditional active portfolios. **Also, past success is generally no indicator of future success**. However, there are people who do believe that past **prices** and **patterns of prices** can help predict future prices. Such people make use of what is known as **technical analysis** which looks at patterns of price movements over a previous period. Some investors claim that this gives rise to superior performance.

## PASSIVE MANAGEMENT: BETA PRODUCTS

An alternative approach to active management is to accept the EMH as true (even if it is not) and therefore to accept market prices as given – to be price takers. An investor with such a belief will simply try to replicate the return of the market itself by holding the shares in the index which best represents the market. Alternatively he or she will use the services of asset managers who create index tracking funds, i.e. funds which try to replicate the wide range of indices which investors use as benchmarks to assess their performance. Such funds hold either all the shares in an **index** or a representative selection of them.

An index is an average of some subset of shares, or of all the shares, in a market. In the US, the index that would normally be used to judge performance (the benchmark) is either the **Dow Jones Industrial Average**, which includes 100 stocks equally weighted or, more normally, the **Standard and Poor's Corporation 500 (S&P 500)**, which gives a broader range of stocks, capitalisation weighted, than the Dow Jones. The **Russell 2000** and many other indices are also used. In the UK the indices that are frequently used are the **Financial Times/Stock Exchange 100 (FTSE 100)** or the **FTSE 350** (pronounced 'Footsie'). An index of the top European stocks is the **FTSE Eurofirst 300**. If the portfolio is international and includes both fixed income and equity then a possible index to use would be one of the global financial market opportunity set, for example the Morgan Stanley Capital International **MSCI Global Capital Markets Index**.[5] This index is designed to allow measurement of the diversification offered by global markets to investors allocating across the core asset classes of equity and debt. It provides a representation of the core financial investment opportunities available to all investors, regardless of their domicile. Index tracking funds are popular because of their low cost and are available as mutual funds and as ETFs.

---

[5] Morgan Stanley, on 25 April 2005, announced the following: 'The MSCI Global Capital Markets Index combines, on a market capitalization weighted basis, the components of the MSCI All Country World Equity Index[SM] and the MSCI Global Total Bond Index[SM], providing an objective representation of the global capital markets for research, communication and benchmarking. Designed to help both professional and high net worth investors, among others, the MSCI Global Capital Markets Index enables a more comprehensive, objective and easy comparison of individual portfolios versus the investable global opportunity set. The index provides a better understanding of the risk/return characteristics and diversification benefits of different asset classes and thus serves the investor's asset allocation process. Importantly, this index also helps articulate the added value provided by a strategic policy benchmark or other forms of asset allocation decisions' (http://www.msci.com/)

## THE ANTITHESIS OF BETA PRODUCTS: ABSOLUTE RETURN STRATEGIES

As we noted above, a traditional portfolio, whether actively managed or passive (index tracking), replicates the market approximately, and thus the risk to which it is subject is market risk (beta). The extent to which a managed fund (active fund manager) improves on the market return is its **relative performance**, i.e. how it performs relative to the market index. A fund attempting to generate alpha can collapse in value because the market itself collapses; yet if it collapses even slightly less than the market, the manager is said to be adding value (alpha). This is a very odd view of risk and it would seem unlikely that most investors realise that traditional managers make virtually no attempt to protect their investors from beta (systematic) risk, which in a diversified portfolio is the main risk.

An alternative investment strategy is to try to manage a portfolio to achieve **absolute performance** rather than relative performance. Absolute performance means simply the **actual return** which a fund achieves. Another way of looking at absolute performance funds is to view the investment objective as being to outperform the riskless rate, i.e. the Treasury bill rate, by an amount reflecting the additional risk taken by the fund. A key objective would be to avoid losing money in any month (if possible) and certainly over a period of a year, even if the stock market declines substantially. When we talk about absolute return funds, what we mean is funds which have the possibility and indeed the intention of using **short positions** and **derivatives** to offset downside risk and which may also use leverage achieved from borrowing or through derivative positions. Absolute return funds differ from conventional funds which are called '**long only**' meaning that the fund holds only 'long' positions in shares in contrast to an absolute return fund which is likely to hold 'short' positions as well.

## HOW TO OFFSET DOWNSIDE RISK: SHORT POSITIONS

An important way to change the risk profile of a portfolio is by employing **short positions**. Generating a short position in securities involves the asset manager selling shares he or she does not already own, just like a dealer taking a short position. . Anyone selling shares (whether an **outright** sale or a **short** sale) must deliver them to the buyer (and will receive cash in return). In order to **sell short**, i.e. to sell without actually owning shares, a fund has to borrow the shares from another investor who has them in his or her portfolio in order to deliver them to the buyer. On delivery of these borrowed shares, the short-seller is paid for them just as he or she would be if selling out a long position. There is an active market in secured **stock lending** (from institutional investors which own the particular share) which allows this **stock borrowing** to be undertaken for a fee. However, when the fund chooses to return the borrowed shares, it then has to purchase them in the market (at the market price at that point in time) in order to deliver them back to the lender.

The strategy of taking short positions involves not just randomly choosing to short a few shares. It involves research into which shares are most likely to fall in value relative to others. Indeed, if a fund manager thought that the whole market was going to fall, he or she could simply short the whole market, perhaps through a derivative product. Figure 17.2 shows the process of going short and subsequently closing the short position.

## LONG/SHORT FUND

Long/short is the most used strategy for absolute return funds using what is called **pairs trading**. In this strategy, all that matters is that the chosen shares in which the short positions are taken fall **relative** to those in which long positions are taken.. They do not need to decline in an **absolute** sense in a **long/short pairs strategy**. The objective is to try to trade pairs of stocks where research suggests that in the case of two very similar companies, i.e. in the same industry, the shares of one of them will underperform **relative** to the other over the chosen period **even if both rise absolutely**. Such pairs trading is designed to virtually eliminate market risk (beta), which means that, if the market collapses or shoots up, investor portfolios will **not** follow the market, since the rise in the long position will offset much of the fall in the value of the short position. However, it leaves the opportunity for a profit on the differential movement between the two shares, regardless of whether the market rises or falls. It does, however, create a new type of risk. The long-short portfolio is subject to **double stock selection risk**, i.e. the risk of wrong selection on both the long and short sides of the pairs trade, as it is differential performance in stocks in the portfolio that is generating value. Stock selection risk is, in effect, **manager risk**, i.e. the risk of selecting a manager who underperforms in his or her chosen strategy.

A strategy that a fund might employ is to research an industry sector such as soft drinks and to try to evaluate the likely relative performance of two companies in that sector. The analysis might suggest that PepsiCo Inc. is going to perform

**Figure 17.2** Opening and closing a short position

better than the Coca-Cola company as a result of Pepsi's lower exposure to cola drinks (more diversified). A portfolio might then contain a $1 million long position in Pepsi and a $1 million short position in Coke. If the stock market as a whole rises 10% while Pepsi rises 12% and Coke rises 4%, then the portfolio has made a return of 12% profit on Pepsi and a 4% loss on Coke, giving a net 8% return. However, had the market portfolio been held, the return would have been 10%.

It might seem unsatisfactory to have a portfolio that does worse than the market. However, that is only if the market as a whole **rises**. If the market falls 10% while Coke falls 12% and Pepsi only falls by 4% then the net return on the portfolio is a loss of 4% on the long position, offset by a gain on the short of 12%, giving a net gain of 8% compared with a market fall of 10%. It is quite possible that in practice, however, when the market rises by 10%, Pepsi increases in price by only 4% while Coke rises 12% despite research and analysis suggested that the opposite should happen.

The long/short strategy or pairs trading, when it works, is **achieving a reduction in volatility**, i.e. a low beta, by trying to extract the alpha from both the long and the short positions and by hedging most of the beta. **However, low beta portfolios cannot be expected to outperform the market on the upside.**

Figure 17.3 shows two types of fund. The first is a long only and the second has a substantial proportion (but not 50%) of short positions. It can be seen that, when the market rises by 10%, the long-only fund also rises by 10%, and when the market falls by 10%, the fund falls by 10%. In the long-short (but long-biased) fund, in contrast, the fund suffers when the market rises. If the market goes up by 10%, the fund only rises by 5%. But the great benefit in terms of stability is that if the market falls by 10%, the fund declines by only 5%. Explaining to a client why an investment in such a fund is not keeping up with the market when the market is roaring ahead, can prove to be a challenging mission.

The attraction of long-short absolute return funds is that they can be expected to reduce market risk (beta). This means that they reduce the extent of downside when the market declines but, equally, on the upside they will not generate as high a return as the market. They are sometimes described as funds which give

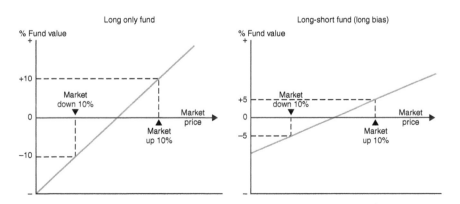

**Figure 17.3** Reduced volatility in a long/short fund compared with a long-only fund

bond market volatility (i.e. low volatility) with equity market returns (i.e. high returns). In practice they may not give as high a return as an equity market on the upside but, during the various equity market collapses and periods of high volatility during this century, they have generated much lower losses than most long-only portfolios.

# INVESTMENT MANAGEMENT PRACTICE (FUNDS): PENSION, INSURANCE, SOVEREIGN WEALTH, LONG-ONLY, HEDGE, MUTUAL, CASH, ETF'S, SYNTHETIC ETFS AND DELTA ONE TRADING DESKS

**18**

## FUNDS

The word fund is used with two meanings:

- **Investment institution funds**, or simply **the institutions**, all have the word 'fund' in their name – pension fund, insurance fund, endowment fund (including charities) and sovereign wealth fund. They hold a wide range of asset classes, often through the use of collective investment funds to achieve their diversification aims.
- **Collective investment funds**, also known as **pooled funds**, offer units or shares to investors. Examples include mutual funds, hedge funds, private equity funds, real estate funds, commodity funds, foreign exchange funds and exchange traded funds. These are generally funds which specialise in one asset class only and thus would comprise only a part of a retail or institutional portfolio.

The **institutions** are often known as **real money funds**, which is not a precise term but is generally taken to mean those investors whose funds have been set up for a specific purpose, for example the provision of pensions or insurance services, or the support for a charity or future generations of the population (sovereign wealth fund). Such funds are very seldom leveraged i.e. they don't borrow other's money.

On the other hand collective investment funds are set up to enable the real money institutional funds and households (either self-directed investors or those advised by wealth managers) to access specialised investment expertise. They are purely investment funds which do not serve other purposes directly, such as providing pensions or insurance or income to future generations. But it is important to understand that they are used to achieve these purposes by real money funds as they provide the specialised asset class sub-portfolios that these funds need for their overall, diversified portfolio. Once real money funds have decided on the asset classes to invest in, and the proportions to allocate to the different asset classes have been made (asset allocation), they can then invest in collective investment funds to achieve their overall portfolio objectives.

Collective investment funds do not have liabilities of the nature of real money funds. Instead they have unit holders who are simply participants in the 'equity' issued in unit form by the fund, i.e. they are just like shareholders in a company.

# INVESTMENT INSTITUTION FUNDS

## Pension funds

These are **funds** to which people contribute a proportion of their income during their working life and from which they expect to draw a pension at the time of retirement. While there are many variations, there are essentially two types of private pension scheme which have very different characteristics in terms of who bears the three most important risks. These risks are:

- **Investment risk:** the risk that the value of the fund collapses just as someone is about to retire;
- **Unexpected inflation risk:** the risk that inflation is higher than expected, either before or after retirement;
- **Longevity risk:** the risk that the pensioner has an unexpectedly long lifetime and thus requires a pension income for more years than he or she expected.

Pension funds can be of two types which differ very substantially in terms of who bears the above risks. The **defined benefit (DB)** is a pension scheme in which the employer is the 'sponsor'. The scheme rules determine the amount of an annual pension that will be payable to any particular individual from a pre-agreed retirement age until death and are laid out in a contract between the employer and the employee at the time of employment. Personal contributions into a pension scheme from salary deductions are normally free of income tax, though income from a scheme after retirement is generally taxed in the same way as income from employment.

In a DB scheme, the scheme (and thus ultimately the employer who is the scheme sponsor and has a legal requirement imposed on it to ensure that the fund meets its liabilities) is responsible for meeting its contract with the employee – which is to pay the pension as agreed. **Thus the three key risks – investment risk (adverse price changes), the inflation risk (higher than expected) and the longevity risk (living longer than predicted) – must all be borne by the scheme**. As a result of these risks, the employer may find at some point that it is required to make unexpected additional contributions to the fund because a pension regulator has declared that the fund has insufficient assets to cover its liabilities, due to one or more of the above risks materialising.

Today, many people do not have a DB scheme available to them but instead have a **defined contribution (DC)** scheme operated by their employer or, if self-employed, have their own DC scheme. These schemes are called 'defined contribution' in contrast to 'defined benefit' because only the amount the employer will pay into the scheme each year is agreed in advance, not what an employee will get out after retirement. Thus there is no contractual agreement for the amount of annual benefit from the time of retirement. On retirement, the retiree receives in cash this capital sum or cash accumulation – or pension pot as it is sometimes called. In DC schemes, the **employee** bears the investment and inflation risk and, unless he or she takes out an annuity contract, also longevity risk.

## The two sides of the pension/life assurance[1] industry (DC schemes)

A life assurer providing pension plans provides two services to households:

- **Accumulation services:** accumulation and management of assets to provide a fund;
- **Decumulation services:** the use of accumulated assets saved in such a fund to provide income in retirement.

The first of the above functions is relatively straightforward (asset management) and simply involves an individual directly, or through an employer, putting aside a regular sum of money. This is invested by an asset manager or a life assurance company in a range of assets which has been chosen either by the asset manager or by the individual. The asset manager has no liability to the individual except to transfer the total accumulated sum to the bank account of the individual at the time of retirement. The sum accumulated will depend on the contributions made to the fund, the rate of return on the assets and the charges by the management company of the fund. The pensioner can then choose to invest that accumulated sum in a portfolio of his or her choice and live off the income.

If the income is not sufficient to support the desired lifestyle then the individual can liquidate some of the fund on a regular basis, i.e. spend the capital. However, this results in income from the fund falling over the years and eventually the capital will all have been consumed. At that point the individual may still have very many years to live but will have no income. To overcome this basic uncertainty of life – the year of death – assurance companies offer decumulation products which take advantage of the law of large numbers to 'socialise' this risk.

The decumulation services of a life assurance company are designed to overcome the uncertainty of the year of death. The main product is the **annuity** – an annual payment every month until death. This is much more complex to create than the accumulation product. Clearly the year of death of any particular individual is uncertain, but more importantly the average year of death of a cohort of

---

[1] Insurance generally refers to providing coverage for an event that might happen – fire, theft, flood, etc. i.e. property or general insurance while assurance is the provision of coverage for an event that is certain to happen such as death – life assurance, annuity and pension products. In the United States both forms of coverage are called insurance.

the population, i.e. age grouping or class grouping, is uncertain. While the law of large numbers is the basis of calculations, as in so many other parts of the finance industry, in this case we are working with a statistic – the longevity of particular cohorts – which is not stable. This instability is known as longevity risk. Life expectancy in many Western countries has been rising rapidly due to better health care, a massive reduction in the proportion of the population which smokes and, until relatively recently, an improvement in diet. This increase may continue or it may be that high fat, salt and sugar diets in the West, combined with sedentary lifestyles, will lead to life expectancy falling in future years.

Figure 18.1 shows that the average life expectancy of a UK male aged 65 had increased from 11.5 years in 1940 to around 16.5 years by 2000. Thus any assurer offering an annuity in 1940 would expect to make monthly income payments for 11.5 years, whereas by 2000 it would expect to have to make these payments for 16.5 years. Unfortunately for assurers (though good for the individuals themselves), life expectancy has continued to rise since 2000 and thus, even if the assurer used up-to-date statistics, it could easily underestimate the life expectancy of the cohort of 65-year-olds.

There is another, very substantial, risk that an annuity provider is also taking on. This is investment risk. The provider may have to pay out a monthly sum on an annuity for a 65-year-old male for 35 years if, as is not uncommon these days, the person lives to be 100. It is impossible to forecast investment returns as far ahead as that. One way of reducing investment risk is for the provider to invest the lump sum in a relatively stable asset, i.e. not in equities. An investment fund for annuities (the asset side of the fund balance sheet) can be matched reasonably well to the liability side (payments on average for 20–25 years) by investing in long-dated fixed income securities. Since a life assurer holds such assets to maturity (regardless of the acquisition price, the redemption price is thus par), the (nominal) investment return can be known with relative certainty but not of course the real return since that depends on inflation over the period. The second aspect of pricing, therefore, involves relating the average annuity rate offered to a pensioner to the yield on a fixed income portfolio. In Figure 18.2 it can be seen that in the very turbulent period of the first eight months of 2011, when investors

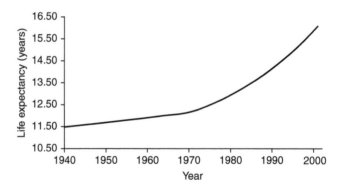

**Figure 18.1**   Male life expectancy at 65

*Source*: William Pomroy, Aviva. Provided to the author.

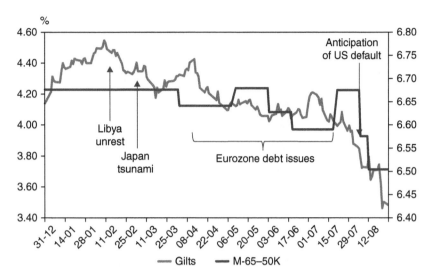

**Figure 18.2**   Gilt yields versus annuity rate

*Source*: William Pomroy, Aviva. Provided to the author.

*Note*: The vertical axis on the graph above, on the left hand side is the yield of the UK 20 year gilt (sovereign debt). It can be seen that its yield fell (its price rose) by over 1% over much less than a year. On the right hand axis is the annuity rate that would be offered to a 65-year-old male.

were seeking 'safe' assets, UK sovereign debt yields (gilt yields) fell substantially. In consequence, assurers were forced to reduce annuity rates (the line which is mostly horizontal) is for a male aged 65.

Table 18.1 shows how sharply UK annuity rates have fallen since 1994, in large part because of the fall in the UK gilts yield but also because of the increase in longevity of the population.

As of August 2011 for every £10,000 provided to the life assurer, it would provide an annual income of £650 (look at the right hand side of the graph in Figure 18.2. The annuity is a larger amount than the annual interest the assurer receives (£360) because the assurer is using up the capital that the annuitant has provided. The benefit of the assurer doing this, rather than the pensioner, is that thanks to the averaging effect of the law of large numbers, the assurer can calculate the average rate (over all its annuitants) at which it can deplete capital whereas an individual cannot calculate his date of death. Today, the best annuity rate on the market is closer to £590 because yields on UK government bonds (gilts) have fallen even further, By early May 2012 the 20 year bond yield had fallen to 2.93% compared with around 3.7% while the 10 year gilt had fallen to levels below that of the last 300 years at only 1.78%.

## Charities and endowment funds

Endowments are charitable funds derived from money given as a gift from one individual or built up over time from small donations. Such funds are intended to be maintained in perpetuity and thus have restrictions on how much they may pay out each year. University endowments are typical of endowments generally and

**Table 18.1**   Change in annuity rates over 15 years

|  | Average annuity rate<br>Male age 65 | Average annuity rate<br>Female age 65 |
|---|---|---|
| November 1994 | £1,145 | £1,016 |
| November 2008 | £701 | £658 |
| November 2009 | £625 | £585 |
| 1-year change | −10.8% | −11% |
| 15-year change | −45.4% | −42.4% |

*Notes*: Figures show gross annual payable monthly in advance. Figures based on an annuitant aged 65 buying a standard 'level without guarantee' annuity for a purchase price of £10K.

*Source*: Investment Life and Pension Moneyfacts, http://www.moneyfactsgroup.co.uk/ (10 February 2012).

in the US were also noted for having had the best investment performance over some decades compared with other managed funds (funds managed by commercial banks have generally had the poorest performance). Other examples are religious charities, welfare charities and organisations like Médecins Sans Frontières which help in relief work.

## Sovereign wealth funds (SWFs)

The first problem in analysing SWFs is trying to define what an SWF is. The term was first used as recently as 2005 by Andrew Rozanov.[2] What he was describing was a shift by some countries from traditional foreign exchange reserve management to something more like traditional investment management. The difference is that foreign exchange reserve management is traditionally very conservative. The assets held would normally be foreign currency government bonds and bills, usually denominated in US dollars, euro or sterling. In contrast, what Rozanov defined as SWFs held equities, whole companies and alternative assets in their portfolios. SWFs have become amongst the most important investors in developed equity markets. While many pension funds in Europe and the US (and also insurance and assurance companies) have been reducing equity holdings in preference to bonds (to try to achieve better asset and liability matching and reduce risk) by running down their equity holdings, their counterparties in the market in such sales have been the SWFs who have been increasing their holdings of shares in western companies.

## Assurance and insurance funds

There are two types of insurance company – life companies and general insurers. Life assurance companies do provide life insurance (insurance against the risk of death) but their main activity is, in practice, providing long-term savings products

---

[2]  Rozanov, Andrew (2005), 'Who Holds the Wealth of Nations?', *Central Banking Journal*, vol. 15, no. 4.

(accumulation products) and pensions and annuities (decumulation products). Life assurers build up a fund from the accumulated savings of their policyholders which is invested in appropriate assets and, at the agreed date, is paid out to the policyholder along with any investment returns that have been generated (as we saw in the section above on pensions) General insurance on the other hand provides cover on non-life risks by providing products such as car, home and earthquake insurance. General insurers take in premium income from their policyholders and use this to create a fund which, along with the investment returns on the fund, is used to cover expected claims and profit.

Life assurers generally seek long maturity assets. Clearly equities are long maturity but more usually long-term bonds, such as government bonds with a final maturity of 20–30 years. This asset class provides a better match for the average maturity of the liabilities that a pension fund, particularly a fund with many young members, may have. Such funds may also buy government bonds which are index linked. These provide a predetermined real yield plus the inflation rate in the previous year.

General insurers, and in particular those who insure against earthquake damage, hurricane damage, environmental disasters such as the 2010 BP oil spillage in the Gulf of Mexico, may unexpectedly need immediate access to cash to pay out on claims. Thus such investors need also to hold liquid assets. This is very different from pension funds or life assurers which can map out future cash outflows from pension payments with some certainty and can thus hold assets which are less liquid.

## COLLECTIVE INVESTMENT FUNDS (POOLED FUNDS)

### Funds: legal structures, regulatory framework and liquidity

**Collective investment schemes**, often known simply as funds or pooled funds, are vehicles which allow investors to benefit from the skills of an investment manager by participating as shareholders or unit holders in an investment company or trust which is managed by a separate management company.

Collective investment schemes potentially provide substantial benefits to investors, both institutional and retail. These should include:

- **Diversification (risk management)**: the ability to diversify widely within a market – something which is difficult for retail investors to achieve without incurring transaction costs at a level which might eliminate much of the benefit from equity investment. But the same benefit applies to wholesale (institutional) investors though to a lesser degree.
- **Access for wholesale and retail investors**: the ability to access specialised asset classes or segments of markets which require specialised investment expertise such as overseas markets, real estate and private equity.
- **Delegated monitoring**: the investment manager is expected to undertake all **due diligence** of proposed investments, including both IPOs and secondary market investments, to monitor their performance and the behaviour of the directors of the companies held in their portfolio, all on behalf of the underlying investors (the beneficiaries).

- **Transaction cost reduction**: the end benefit of using a delegated monitor to undertake most aspects of the investment process. However, there is some debate about whether investment managers do provide value for money. Transactions costs include not only the explicit management fees paid to the investment manager but also the dealing costs that they incur, which are not disclosed separately but simply deducted directly from net asset value.

It should be noted that in the above list of benefits of collective investment, the generation of above average returns (alpha) is not listed as it is not a principal function and indeed cannot be a function for the industry overall due to this part of the industry participating in a negative sum game (as we have already noted). For individual funds, however, in some years alpha may be an outcome.

## The two separate entities involved in collective funds

Figure 18.3 shows how collective fund structures operate. The most important idea to be clear about is that the fund is something quite separate from the management company. The fund is a trust or company belonging to its shareholders who are households and the real money funds. They finance this company (the fund) by buying equity units in it, for example, mutual fund units. The fund then employs an asset management company to acquire and manage appropriate assets within the fund which are purchased by use of the funding that households and real money funds provided when they purchased the fund's equity shares (units). In some structures (if for example the fund is a pension fund for the employees of one company only and can choose its manager), then the fund trustees will change the manager if he does not perform satisfactorily.

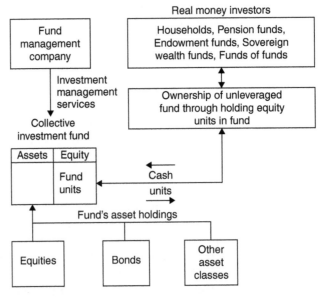

**Figure 18.3**    Generic collective investment fund structure

*Source*: Author.

## Collective fund structures

Funds can be structured in different ways:

- **CLOSED-ENDED FUNDS** exchange or OTC traded
  - investment trusts
  - investment companies
- **OPEN-ENDED FUNDS**
  **Traded through the manager**
  - mutual fund/ unit trust
  **Traded on exchange or OTC traded**
  - exchange-traded funds (ETFs) which trade on an exchange (as would be expected given their name) or over-the-counter through dealers (which might not be expected but is in the fact the predominant mode of trade)

## Closed-ended funds

These are investment trusts or investment companies which issue shares through an IPO just like any other company. Once the fund has been launched and taken up by investors, no further shares are issued nor will they be redeemed by the company. Closed-end funds are also known as **permanent capital vehicles**. However, they do have a considerable drawback – their values on the stock market may not equate to the value of the assets they hold.

A collective fund is one which can be viewed as having two 'values'. First, it can be valued by adding up the values of the underlying assets in the fund using current market prices of, for example the individual shares in the fund. This valuation is known as the fund's net asset value (NAV), i.e. the value of its underlying assets if it were to be broken up and sold on the market at that time. However, the value which is actually transacted by an investor in such funds is a second valuation which is that of the **units** in the fund not the underlying shares held (and of course the units also trade on the market. There is no reason why these units should necessarily trade at the NAV. They might trade higher or lower. In practice closed-end fund units (investment trusts) often trade at a discount to NAV.[3]

The problem with closed-ended (permanent capital) funds such as investment trusts is that there is no mechanism, as there is with mutual funds (or ETFs which we cover below), to try to ensure that the fund always trades in the stock market

---

[3] For example, a very high profile investment company fund – Fidelity International's 0.5 billion pound sterling China Special Situations investment trust, managed by the renowned Anthony Bolton – was issued in an IPO at 100 pence per share in April 2010. By November 2010, when investors still thought it was a good way to employ Bolton's expertise, it was trading at a 13% premium to NAV. By September 2011 it was trading at a 5% discount to NAV. Thus any investor who bought in at the time when there was such a large premium and sold when it went to a discount would have lost 18% simply as a result of the difference between market price and NAV. In addition, by November 2011, it was trading at 83.25 pence, well below its issue price of 100 pence. It has in fact fallen much more than the two indices with which it might be compared, the Shanghai Composite or the Hong Kong Hang Sen index.

at the NAV, i.e. the value of the underlying shares in the fund. Investment trusts frequently trade on the stock exchange at a discount to NAV and often at a substantial one. Thus those who buy shares in an investment trust at the time of its IPO may find that their investment falls rapidly to a discount to NAV. The reason for this discrepancy between fund value and NAV is that there is no arbitrage mechanism to relate the price of shares in the fund which trade on the stock market to the value of the underlying shares also trading on the stock market. If there is a large discount, someone could in theory buy the whole trust, sell the underlying shares held within it and take the profit from the difference between the market price and NAV. But in practice this does not happen very often and simply trying to buy all the fund shares would, anyway, probably drive the fund price back up to NAV, thus eliminating the arbitrage profit. Thus despite the advantages of closed-ended funds, they are not as popular as mutual funds.

An advantage of closed-end funds from the manager's point of view is that they are **permanent capital vehicles**, which means that investors in aggregate cannot 'escape' from the fund. The manager will always have a fund with the same number of units and will therefore always generate his or her asset management fee of 1 or 2% of NAV from the whole fund. In contrast, with a mutual fund which investors no longer find attractive, capital will leave the fund as in this type of fund the investor can sell back to the manager. The fund will thus eventually disappear completely if all investors ask for their units to be redeemed.

From the point of view of the investor, one advantage of closed-end funds is that they can be leveraged, i.e. the fund can borrow additional resources to invest in the underlying shares that the fund holds. If markets are rising faster than the interest rate on the borrowing then the returns on the units in the fund are leveraged up (but vice versa if markets fall). A second advantage for the investor is that it is possible to sell the units at any time when the stock exchange is open or at any time an investment bank will transact OTC. In contrast, all mutual fund redemptions and purchases take place at one time, normally at market close at 4 p.m. Thus, if markets are collapsing, investors must sit idly by waiting until the 4 o'clock close before being able to halt further losses. This feature is attractive to many investors, in particular institutional investors, who believe they can 'market time' and thus exit from an investment in the morning if they believe it will have fallen by 4pm.

## Open-ended funds: mutual funds

The attraction of open-ended funds, in contrast to closed-ended funds, is that they employ mechanisms to facilitate arbitrage between the fund units and the underlying assets if supply and demand for the **units** of the fund is mis-matched. However, the two types of open-ended fund – mutual and exchange traded – achieve this in different ways.

The difference between them lies in the different way in which liquidity is provided to the investor and through which the unit price is thereby kept in line with the NAV. In the former it is the manager, i.e. the fund management company, which redeems units or sells new units (provides liquidity). The stock market is not directly involved except to the extent that there is a **net imbalance** between unit sales to and unit purchases from investors at the end of the day. If sales to the manager are larger than purchases from the manager, he or she will sell the net amount of underlying shares on the stock market in order to redeem the net balance of units. If, on balance, investors want to buy units in the fund, i.e. more investors want to buy than sell, then the manager has to enter the stock market to buy the underlying shares in an amount that reflects that balance between new purchases and redemptions. Thus all liquidity has to be generated by the manager either from redemptions and purchases being equal (no net balance) or by buying or selling the net balance of a representative selection of the fund's securities on a market such as the NYSE. In consequence, mutual funds/unit trusts, should always be redeemable at the NAV of the underlying shares as this is the price at which the manager can obtain liquidity from buying or selling the underlying shares.

## Open-ended funds: ETFs

ETFs are shares in a fund vehicle which has been set up in a way that is similar to any company. They can thus trade on an exchange as do any company shares or investment trust shares. Surprisingly, however, given their name they also trade OTC and indeed it is reported that up to 70% of transactions are OTC. But in this respect they are no different from any company shares which are listed on an exchange but also trade OTC.

The ETF was developed to provide a vehicle which, by trading on exchange or OTC, could be bought and sold at any time of day, whereas mutual funds could only be redeemed at (normally) 4 p.m. each day. Thus, if a market was moving rapidly up or down, it would not be possible to invest or disinvest in mutual fund units until 4 p.m., by which time a substantial price movement might have taken place since the decision to invest was made. The liquidity problem for such funds is that the manager, or ETF sponsor as it is known in this case, is no longer available to perform the function of matching-off buyers and sellers and transacting any balance in the stock market to increase or reduce the size of the fund. There thus needs to be another mechanism which can ensure that such funds trade close to the NAV. The mechanism used involves the role of the 'authorised participant' (AP).

An ETF sponsor, such as Blackrock (iShares), having designed an ETF, arranges for two types of financial institution – electronic market makers and institutional investors – to become APs in the ETF. The APs actually start the creation process for the ETFs by delivering to the ETF sponsor a basket of shares (a creation unit of securities) which they have bought in the stock market and which represent the content of the ETF as specified in documentation provided by the sponsor, at its NAV at that time. In return for the basket of shares underlying the ETF (the creation unit of securities), the sponsor (iShares) delivers creation units of ETF certificates to the authorised participants. At this point the APs can sell the ETF in small (retail sized) units to investors via brokers on the stock exchange (see Figure 18.4).

An obvious question is how these units can remain at NAV, i.e. exactly the value of the underlying shares, whereas investment trust units don't. The answer

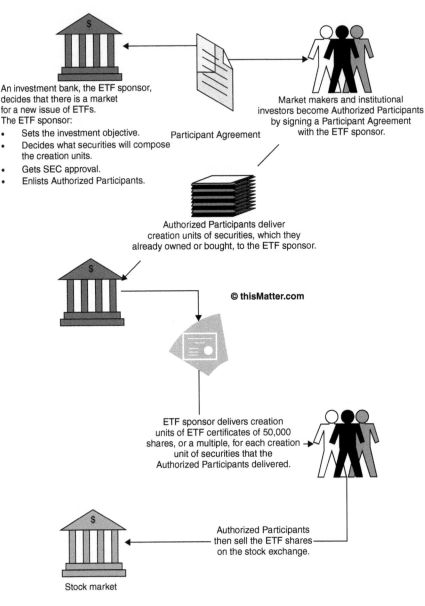

An investment bank, the ETF sponsor, decides that there is a market for a new issue of ETFs.
The ETF sponsor:
- Sets the investment objective.
- Decides what securities will compose the creation units.
- Gets SEC approval.
- Enlists Authorized Participants.

Participant Agreement

Market makers and institutional investors become Authorized Participants by signing a Participant Agreement with the ETF sponsor.

Authorized Participants deliver creation units of securities, which they already owned or bought, to the ETF sponsor.

© thisMatter.com

ETF sponsor delivers creation units of ETF certificates of 50,000 shares, or a multiple, for each creation unit of securities that the Authorized Participants delivered.

Authorized Participants then sell the ETF shares on the stock exchange.

Stock market

**Figure 18.4**   The ETF creation process

*Source*: thisMatter.com, http://thismatter.com/money/mutual-funds/etf.htm (accessed 10 February 2012); author: William C. Spaulding.

is that those APs who are market makers are HFT electronic market makers (See Chapter 13.) who make their profit from detecting deviations between the value of the ETF trading on the stock exchange and the NAV of the underlying basket of stocks (it takes only a few microseconds to detect any arbitrage and make the appropriate trades). Their job is to arbitrage between the two ways of holding this basket of shares, either as a collection of, say, 100 company shares or as a unit of a fund company.

If the ETF is selling at a discount to the price at which the same shares can be bought on the stock market, the APs will buy ETFs on the market. They then deliver these units to the sponsor (Blackrock iShares) which exchanges them back into the underlying company shares which the AP can sell for a higher price in the market, thus generating an arbitrage profit. Units in the fund are destroyed in this process(thus the fund reduces in size) since they have been returned to the sponsor who has destroyed them when he or she exchanges them for the underlying shares This arbitrage process can also work in reverse when the ETFs sell for more than the NAV. At that point the APs will deliver (cheap) shares to the sponsor in return for ETF certificates which the sponsor creates and the AP then sells through stockbrokers to investors for a higher price than the creation cost.

In Figure 18.5 (just a different way of looking at the same process as illustrated in Figure 18.4) you can see once again that the starting point for the initial creation of ETFs (let's say it's an ETF based on the FTSE 100 index) is investors asking their brokers to invest their cash in this ETF. The brokers pass the cash to the ETF market maker who then purchases the shares which are the constituents of the iShares FTSE 100 basket (essentially the top 100 UK shares) in the market. The market maker then delivers this basket of securities to the ETF fund advisor (iShares) who, in exchange, provides FTSE 100 iShare certificates, i.e. certificates

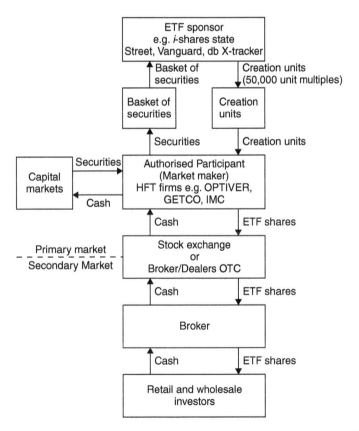

**Figure 18.5** The ETF creation (primary market) and secondary trading (exchange & OTC)

which represent the underlying FTSE 100 company shares. The ETF market maker then provides these certificates to the brokers in exchange for the investor cash. That's the creation process. If an investor now wishes to sell, he or she goes to his or her broker who will sell them to another investor via the stock market and return the market value of the iShares to the investor. But if there is an imbalance in supply and demand for the certificates on the stock market, say more want to sell than buy, then the value of the certificates will start to fall slightly below that of the underlying shares. It is at this point that the HFT market makers will detect the spread between the two and start the arbitrage process to eliminate it.

## Synthetic ETFs

In Chapter 9 I covered synthetic CDOs. There are three reasons why investment banks liked to offer these to clients rather than cash CDOs. First, they enable a CDO to be created very quickly. It does not require the investment bank to source the necessary securities in order to create a tranche. Second, they hoped to make a larger profit from the derivatives trades which they undertook when creating such securities than they could in 'simple' cash securities. But there is also an important third reason. Synthetic CDOs do not contain the actual bonds being referenced. Thus the collateral can be anything the investment bank chooses and the client is willing to accept. Thus it can be securities being held by the investment bank on their own account which are difficult to finance in the repo market but which can be financed easily from the cash provided by the investor to pay for a synthetic CDO. It may be difficult to finance such securities in the repo market but investors in the CDO are financing these holdings possibly without being aware of the risks involved. The main risk is that if the investment bank which structured the synthetic CDO (for example, Lehman Brothers), collapses, then the synthetic CDO contract may be valueless. However, the collateral should be available to re-imburse the investor. If, however, it is illiquid and has also fallen substantially in value, then the investor may suffer a large loss.

Synthetic ETFs follow a similar principal to synthetic CDOs in their construction. Since they are index tracking funds, investment banks have asked themselves why bother with trying to assemble a cash fund with all the problems of buying each individual security in an index when it is so much easier to simply buy a swap on an index! The fund might use a total return swap which matches the return from the dividend flow combined with the change in market value on, for example, the S&P 500 to achieve the required investment return. Of course the cash handed over by the investor will still have to be invested in some asset, i.e. collateral. What has become apparent is that in the construction of such synthetic ETFs, just as in the case of CDOs, the collateral may not be what the investor expects. It may be any asset, illiquid or liquid, which the ETF sponsor chooses. It might, in other words, be illiquid mortgage backed securities or CDO tranches which the sponsor is holding on his or her balance sheet but cannot sell. Investor cash is an attractive means of financing such illiquid holdings that an investment bank already has when the repo and interbank markets are effectively shut.

Figure 18.6 is meant to point out the illogic of this development from what was meant to be a simple and easily understood product with few risks, except market price risk, to one which may have substantial risks to the investor and may in addition present regulators with a systemic risk issue.

Figure 18.7 indicates how a synthetic ETF is constructed. The ETF is a product offering a return which closely matches that on some index such as the S&P 500 or the FTSE 100. The investor pays cash to buy the ETF units. This cash is not, however, invested in shares. Instead it is used to finance collateral which is designed to give (some) security to the investor. Bank 1 (the ETF sponsor) receives the cash and can then use it to, for example, finance some of its holdings of illiquid securities on its balance sheet which are difficult to finance in the repo or other markets.

The return required by the investor is generated by a swap, for example a total return swap (dividend plus capital gain), issued by Bank 2. In practice Bank 2 is the same bank as Bank 1, just different departments. The department of the bank which offers the swap is generally the so-called 'Delta One desk', i.e. the desk which creates derivative products that replicate cash products.

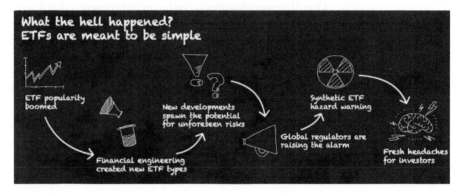

**Figure 18.6**  How ETFs changed from simple funds to ones which were very risky to investors and raised systemic risk questions

*Source*: Monevator.com, http://monevator.com/2011/04/26/synthetic-etf-risks/ (accessed 10 February 2012).

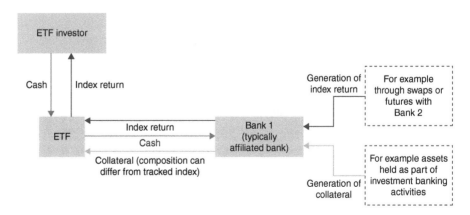

**Figure 18.7**  Stylised example of a synthetic ETF

*Source*: Bank of England Financial Stability Report June 2011, figure 1 (p. 15), http://www.bankofengland.co.uk/publications/fsr/2011/fsrfull1106.pdf (accessed 10 February 2012).

One attraction of synthetic ETFs is that the bank can generate additional revenues from synthetic ETFs compared with cash ETFs from, for example, financing cost gains made by financing illiquid collateral in a low-cost way. . Part of this lower cost or additional profit is given away to the client, but much is kept by the bank itself. In fact, ETFs have proven to be more profitable for investment management houses than traditional managed funds, despite their lower fees, with synthetic ETFs being the most profitable of all.

Kweku Adoboli, the trader who in September 2011 created fictitious transactions in ETFs to hide losses of over $2.3 billion on derivative positions, was working in the Delta One department of UBS, London. This is the department which provided the synthetic returns (total return swaps) required to construct these ETFs and which was believed to be a department with a relatively low risk profile.

## ETFs and the Delta One department of an investment bank

One of the peculiarities of the financial business is that it is not only asset managers who manage money. Investment banks also have a strong position in this market. First, many of them have traditional asset management subsidiaries. **In addition**, however, they can compete with traditional asset managers, including their own asset management subsidiaries, by creating products using derivatives from their investment banking departments such as the Delta One desk. The three basic types of 'structured' product they create are (1) capital protected products, (2) synthetic products such as ETFs created using, for example, total return swaps, and (3) synthetic CDOs. The dramatic growth of synthetic ETFs is shown in Figure 18.8. It should be noted, however, that the majority of BlackRock i-share funds are cash, not synthetic, ETFs.

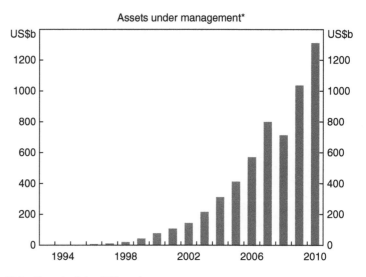

**Figure 18.8**  Growth of the ETF market

*Excludes exchange-traded commodities.

*Source*:  BlackRock, Reserve Bank of Australia, http://www.rba.gov.au/publications/bulletin/2011/mar/8.html (accessed 5 April 2012).

This growth in synthetic ETFs has been an important source of business to the Delta One desks. It was not only UBS which had such a desk. The French banks were particularly strong in this area. However, a year before the Adoboli losses at UBS, a trader in SocGen, also based in the Delta One department, lost the firm almost €5 billion in another trading fraud. Thus both recent trading frauds occurred in this division which was previously believed to be unglamorous, low risk and low growth. The following article, written a year before the Adoboli losses, suggests otherwise:

### Delta One Back in the Spotlight

When news broke that Jérôme Kerviel, a young trader at French bank Société Générale, had lost the firm €4.9bn on unauthorized trades, the spotlight fell on what had been one of the bank's least glamorous trading desks and, until then, considered a low-risk operation. The desk is known as Delta One.

Such units look after routine business and take their name from the flow of equity derivatives that closely track their underlying asset. If that moves by 10%, the derivative will move by very close to 10%, meaning it has a delta of one. Products that exhibit these characteristics include futures, forwards, equity swaps, dividend swaps, index arbitrage and exchange-traded funds. Delta One can be difficult to define, as it encompasses a broad range of activities, and where they sit varies between banks. It involves everything from intraday index arbitrage to inventory financing, and in certain houses it also covers long-term dividend trading activity.

Despite this lack of clarity and their conservative image, the units are tipped for growth in revenues over the next three years. In September, top-rated JP Morgan Cazenove analyst Kian Abouhossein caused a stir when he predicted Delta One would be an important part of future revenue growth in the investment banking sector. He said Société Générale, BNP Paribas and Goldman Sachs would be key participants and predicted a 9% compound annual growth rate from 2010 to 2012 in Delta One, versus a 5% growth in flow equity derivatives.

Revenues derived from Delta One will rise from $9.9bn in 2010 to $10.8bn in 2011 and $11.8bn in 2012, according to Abouhossein's estimates. Return on equity from Delta One is estimated to be 40% post regulatory changes, ahead of the total equity derivatives average of 22%.

Matt Turner, *Financial News*, 30 November 2010.

It is clear from the above why large investment banks have expanded their Delta One department and why they are enthusiastic about increasing the size of the synthetic ETF market as a means of increasing the flow of business to Delta One. For the investment banks it is a key way in which they can expand into investment management territory with products that conventional asset managers cannot easily replicate. It is equally clear that the risk management procedures within these departments have not been adequate given the opportunities traders within them have had for taking out multi-billion dollar positions.

## Absolute return funds: hedge funds

Within the open-ended fund category are absolute return funds. The range of strategies that these employ are very varied and have, until recently, been implemented mostly by what have become known as hedge funds. It is important, however, to appreciate that many absolute return strategies can also be implemented by funds which are **not** described as hedge funds. Indeed, under the UCITS framework which is the EU regulatory framework for funds, it is now possible to offer to the general public, funds which employ what are traditionally thought of as hedge fund techniques. In many cases it is even possible for a traditional fund to use ETFs to achieve the long/short positions across markets or market sectors which a hedge fund might wish to hold.

It is important to understand that the term 'hedge fund' is more of a legal definition than anything to do with particular strategies. Essentially the legal definition results from the attempts by regulatory authorities in the major countries to prevent small or uninformed investors being able to invest in such funds. The reason for the prohibition was that alternative funds, and specifically hedge funds, were thought to be much more risky than traditional funds. However, as it has increasingly become evident that hedge funds in general are not more risky but simply view risk in a different way to traditional funds (absolute risk versus relative risk), the regulatory authorities have increasingly allowed retail investors to have access to strategies that at one time would be described as hedge fund strategies, i.e. absolute return strategies.

The SEC in the United States (the statutory regulator of US markets) has in fact produced its own definition of hedge funds:

> 'Hedge fund' is a general, non-legal term that was originally used to describe a type of **private and unregistered investment pool** that employed sophisticated hedging and arbitrage techniques to trade in the corporate equity markets. Hedge funds have traditionally been limited to sophisticated, wealthy investors. Over time, the activities of hedge funds broadened into other financial instruments and activities. Today, the term 'hedge fund' refers not so much to hedging techniques, which hedge funds may or may not employ, as it does to their **status as private and unregistered investment pools**.
>
> Hedge funds are **similar to mutual funds in that they are both pooled investment vehicles** that accept investors' money and generally invest it on a collective basis. Hedge funds differ significantly from mutual funds, however, because hedge funds are not required to register under the federal securities laws. They are not required to register because they generally only accept financially sophisticated investors and do not publicly offer their securities. In addition, some, but not all, types of hedge funds are limited to no more than 100 investors.
>
> Hedge funds also are not subject to the numerous regulations that apply to mutual funds for the protection of investors including liquidity requirements, fairness in pricing, disclosure and use of leverage.
>
> This freedom from regulation permits hedge funds to engage in leverage and other investment techniques to a much greater extent than mutual funds. Although hedge funds are not subject to registration and the regulations that apply to mutual funds, hedge funds are subject to the antifraud provisions of the federal securities laws.

Because alternative funds are available only to **eligible investors**, such funds, and in particular hedge funds, operate under different, and less restrictive, rules than traditional funds. To be considered an eligible investor, an individual would generally have to have substantial net worth or be a 'professional' investor. The actual qualifications vary by country. Normally such **funds** operate **offshore**, i.e.

they are registered outside the US or the EU in, for example, the Cayman Islands, Netherlands Antilles, Bermuda or the Channel Islands. As a result they are able to employ a wider range of strategies than onshore funds where regulation is more restrictive. Although the actual fund (a fund is a company) is located outside the major financial centres, the fund management company is almost certainly in a major financial centre. Thus the people who manage such funds are located **onshore**, i.e. mainly in New York, London, Zurich, Frankfurt, etc., but increasingly in other countries. The strategies employed by such funds are also increasingly being copied by the more traditional funds. It is important to understand that the expression **'hedge fund' describes an organisational form *not* an asset class**.

In 2006, the Chairman of the UK regulatory authority, the FSA, made a speech about hedge funds which emphasised this problem of definition:

> Discussion of any subject should start with agreement as to what is being discussed. Nowhere is this truism more relevant than in a discussion of hedge funds, for the definition of hedge funds is far from clear. There is, for example, no legal definition of a hedge fund in either the UK or Germany. Indeed, when IOSCO carried out a survey, none of the responding jurisdictions reported a legal definition. So the phenomenon we are discussing is not a legally defined class. But the features which distinguish hedge funds are generally accepted to be:
>
> - They tend to be unregulated collective investment schemes – but share this characteristic in the UK with, for example, some occupational pension schemes;
> - They make extensive use of derivatives – but share this characteristic with banks, insurance and securities companies;
> - They use shorting techniques – as do others;
> - They use extensive leverage – again not a characteristic unique to them;
> - They have a charging policy which is typically described as 2 and 20 – that is an annual charge of 2 per cent plus 20 per cent of the increase in the value of assets under management. It is worth observing that this charging policy is not confined to what are normally thought to be hedge funds: in a recent interview, Blake Grossman, CEO of Barclays Global Investors, normally regarded as a mainstream asset management company, reported that about a fifth of its actively managed funds were managed against a fee structure which is comparable to what is normally regarded as hedge fund fees;
> - They tend to seek investment opportunities across the market widely, looking not only at established markets in equities and bonds (and their derivatives), but also at commodities, and at more esoteric investment opportunities: catastrophe insurance contracts, film finance and other non-mainstream asset classes. In that, of course, they are again not unique: banks, insurance companies and securities firms all pursue these opportunities.
>
> So my first point is that hedge funds are an ill-defined asset class. Indeed, the categorisation of hedge funds as an asset class is really rather odd. They are asset managers who utilize an investment approach (shared by many), who call themselves hedge funds. I find it difficult, if not impossible, to identify an activity carried out by a hedge fund manager which is not also carried out by the proprietary trading desk within a large bank, insurance company or broker dealer.
>
> Speech by Callum McCarthy, Chairman, FSA, SUERF
> (European Money & Finance Forum), 7 December 2006

## Hedge fund strategies

One of the problems when analysing hedge funds is to develop a taxonomy for (to categorise) their strategies. Without this it is difficult for investors to understand the characteristics of the investments they hold or to know how to compare the investment performance of a fund against some type of benchmark. The following provides a very useful taxonomy:

> The purpose of most classification schemes to date has been to identify the observable attributes of funds that are believed to determine return patterns. Then, using these proxies for returns, indices are created which group funds with similar attributes. The indices created are then put to various uses including benchmarking, portfolio construction and, where the funds are investable, direct trading. The most common proxy is a fund's self-described strategy.

> Bank of New York and Oxford Metrica,
> 'An Emerging Taxonomy for Hedge Funds',
> *Hedge Fund Journal*, Thought Leadership Series,
> November 2007

Figure 18.9 shows one generic way of categorising hedge funds. There are three basic 'hedge fund management styles' shown. The first uses arbitrage, which is a very different technique from the long-only fund. Alfred Jones was the first person to use the phrase '*hedged*' fund when he created a hedged fund structure in 1949. To neutralise the effect of overall market movement (to achieve a market beta close to zero) Jones bought assets whose price he expected to increase, and sold short assets whose price he expected to decrease. He referred to his fund as being 'hedged' in order to manage risk exposure from overall market movement. This type of portfolio became known as a hedge fund.

The word 'hedge' in Jones's terminology means that market risks were hedged. However, if we look at the third style (Directional) in Figure 18.9, the strategies employed are the reverse of hedging. In fact they may employ styles which magnify market movements, i.e. a beta that may be substantially greater than one. Thus the beta of hedge funds could vary from, for example, as little as $-2$ (leveraged and highly negatively correlated) to $+2$ (highly positively correlated to the market through leverage). A key aspect of performance, therefore, is the extent to which the portfolio is expected to be exposed to market beta, i.e. systematic

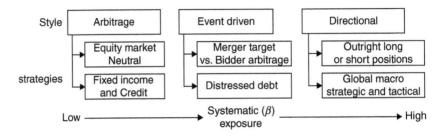

**Figure 18.9**   Investment techniques employed by different hedge fund sectors

market exposure, as shown at the bottom of the figure. Event-driven strategies are somewhere in-between. Merger arbitrage, for example, involves trying to predict the likelihood of success of an acquisition bid and arbitraging between the shares of the bidder and the target. Distressed asset investors are hoping to buy assets which others in the markets are selling at 'low' prices in the expectation that they will soon rise sharply in price.

Unfortunately, there is not sufficient scope within this book to cover all these strategies in detail.

Overall, an investor wishing to add hedge funds to his or her long-only portfolio, investing perhaps through a fund of funds, would be hoping to shift his or her expected risk/return profile from the point at the bottom right of Figure 18.10, labelled '100% traditional portfolio' (long-only), to anywhere on the curve from the extreme left point to the upper point '100% hedge funds', depending on their attitude to risk. Any point on this part of the curve is superior to any point directly below it, since it gives a higher return for the same risk. That is the aim of hedge fund portfolios designed to hedge risk.

One of the worst, if not the worst, year on record for hedge funds was 2008. On average, from the indices shown in Table 18.2, if someone had invested through 2008 across the universe of hedge fund strategies he or she would have lost nearly 19% of his or her investment. Thus the absolute return on funds was highly negative. As can also be seen from this table, apart from managed futures (which has

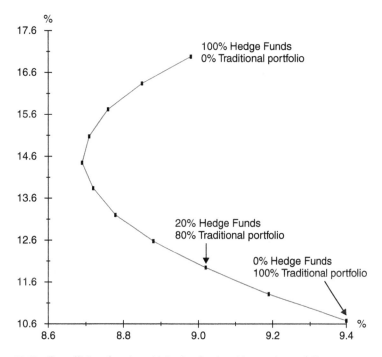

**Figure 18.10**  The efficient frontier with hedge fund and long-only portfolios

*Source*: Michelle Learned Banque Syz and François-Serge, L'Habitant Edhec et HEC Université de Lausanne.

**Table 18.2** Comparison of performance of various hedge fund strategies and other indices

| Index | Dec-08 (%) | 2008 (%) |
|---|---|---|
| **Credit Suisse/Tremont Hedge Fund Index** | **0.30** | **−18.80** |
| Convertible Arbitrage | −1.27 | −31.79 |
| Dedicated Short Bias | −2.55 | 13.87 |
| Emerging Markets | 0.25 | −30.38 |
| Equity Market Neutral | 1.89 | −39.44 |
| Event Driven | −0.26 | −16.91 |
|   Distressed | −1.37 | −19.52 |
|   Event Driven Multi-Strategy | 0.28 | −15.60 |
|   Risk Arbitrage | 1.49 | −3.37 |
| Fixed Income Arbitrage | 0.72 | −27.72 |
| Global Macro | 1.04 | −4.69 |
| Long/Short Equity | 0.85 | −19.92 |
| Managed Futures | 2.28 | 18.23 |
| Multi-Strategy | −1.66 | −23.74 |
| MSCI World | 3.06 | −42.08 |
| Barclays Capital Aggregate Bond Index | 6.21 | 4.79 |
| DJ AIG Commodities Index | −4.48 | −35.65 |

*Source*: MarketFolly.com, http://www.marketfolly.com/2009/01/2008-hedge-fund-performance-numbers.
html (accessed 21 February 2012).

not performed as well since), it was Dedicated Short Bias that led in performance – not very difficult to work out, since 2008 was the worst year for markets in decades, i.e. for long-only investors, and therefore investors who are net short should do relatively well.

If hedge funds could not protect investors from a loss does this mean that they did not perform as expected? There is no answer to this question since different people have different expectations. It also depends on which strategy you choose (in particular the degree of systematic market exposure) and, within a particular strategy, which particular manager you choose. But if you look towards the bottom of Table 18.2, you will see that the MSCI World Markets index showed a fall of 42% (the S&P declined by 37%). Thus, despite poor performance, hedge funds (on average across many funds and many strategies) performed much better than long-only funds would have done. By contrast, however, hedge funds in 2011 generally performed much worse than the major indices. Anyone invested in funds within the Credit Suisse Tremont Equity Market Neutral funds index in 2008 would also have been invested in funds which clearly did not perform better than the market (they should not have suffered a fall) but in fact lost almost 40%. Clearly strategies advertised as equity market neutral may not in fact be market neutral at all.

One particular hedge fund manager who, unlike most, did very well in the period of the financial crisis, including 2008, was John Paulson (unrelated to Hank Paulson, US Secretary to the Treasury and formerly CEO of Goldman Sachs). He was the manager who, prior to the collapse in the US housing market in 2007, took very substantial short positions in mortgage assets and indeed was on the opposite side of CDS trades with many investors, including investment banks and funds such as IKB (the German bank which lost so much from the subprime collapse). He is credited with engineering the 'greatest trade in history' which earned his firm $20 billion by betting against the housing market. In 2007, Paulson personally took home almost $4 billion – the largest one-year payout ever in finance.

Clearly Poulson's fund was not hedging risk and was in fact taking an outright and leveraged directional bet, quite the opposite of the original hedge fund idea. This worried quite a number of observers, one of whom made the following comment in February 2011:

> What I struggle with is how you know whether a guy like Paulson is capable of repeated genius or if he simply made one successful trade[4] on which he placed a much larger bet than anyone else. Don't get me wrong, I fully believe that an investor really only needs one big successful bet to outperform over a lifetime of investing. Make that one big fat pitch count when it comes your way and then follow it up by making sure to never lose that big amount of capital you have won. That is all it takes.

> www.gurufocus.com/news/120811/the-big-short-john –
> paulson – becoming-the-long-long-in-bubble-area-real-estate

The above reported concern was not misplaced. In 2011 (up to the end of September), Paulson's new funds have lost $6 billion. His 'Advantage Plus' fund, for example, is down 52% on the year to December 2011. This is in sharp contrast to the almost 600% return he made on his subprime bet. The bad bet in 2011 was on the likelihood of a sharp recovery of the US economy after the slowdown following the subprime crisis. He believed that after the collapse of 2008 there would, as in previous downturns, be a sharp rally and many distressed investment opportunities. Paulson had expected his leveraged long investments in US recovery to show returns in multiples of hundreds of per cent just like his earlier Big Short bet on US real estate. This leverage is reflected in an estimate of the beta of his fund of 1.4[5] compared with the market beta which is obviously 1.0. In order to minimise possible further falls in his fund, later in 2011 he took out hedges against such declines. However, hedges are expensive to purchase – normally they involve purchasing options. It is believed that the fund now needs to gain 90% just to return it to the level at the beginning of 2011.

---

[4] You might want to read an excellent book entitled *The Big Short* by Michael Lewis (Allen Lane, 2010). Lewis describes how, when Paulson was sitting on this investment idea and was certain he was correct, he kept thinking of George Soros and his advice to 'go for the jugular'. It takes some real guts to make a big bet that not many others are seeing – but that is how you make outsized returns.

[5] Quoted in an article entitled 'Paulson's Costly Bet on America's Rebound Unravels' In the *Financial Times*, 12 October 2011.

The above case study tells us, yet again, that past performance is not necessarily a guide to future performance – a well-known statement. It also tells us that an outright leveraged bet strategy is very different from a hedged investment strategy. It should tell us that taking grossly oversized bets is not really what the investment business is about.

Another of the world's most successful investors, this time in bonds rather than real estate assets, is Bill Gross of Pimco, the world's largest bond fund at around $250 billion in assets. His performance over many years has been truly exceptional. However, at the start of 2011, he took the view that over 2011, US Treasuries would decline substantially in price, having risen so much in previous years. He therefore sold his long-term US Treasury securities and moved into cash. His reasoning was that the US government was borrowing too much and monetising debt through quantitative easing and that this would lead to inflation and rising interest rates.

In fact, the eurozone crisis contributed to a global economic slowdown and to investors worldwide buying US Treasuries as a 'safe haven' and pushing interest rates down to a 65-year low. In consequence Pimco's Total Return Fund was up only 1.1% at the end of September against the relevant index of 6%. To try to recover lost ground, Bill Gross has greatly extended the duration of his fund, i.e. swung from a very low average maturity of bond to a long average maturity. He is therefore betting on a continuation of the downward movement in bond yields – something that few others would bet on after their already very sharp decline over 2011. You should check out what has happened to long-term US Treasury bond yields in 2012 to see if this second bet has worked out better than his first.

The rarity of continual outperformance by a manager is clearly demonstrated by some statistics in a report from Thames River Multimanager.[6] Their research showed that only 16 funds (not hedge funds but all types of funds) out of the 1,188 that it surveys were in the top quartile (top 25%) for performance in three consecutive 12-month periods to the end of March 2011. As this is only 1.3% of funds in the sample, it is a clear demonstration that previous year performance is little guide to future year performance.

## Fund liquidity

In normal times, liquidity, i.e. returning investor cash on demand, is not a problem for **mutual funds** (because their investments are generally highly liquid), though it has proven to be a very severe problem for real estate and hedge funds.

Hedge funds employ a variety of strategies, some of which involve trying to capture the liquidity premium in illiquid securities. Capturing this premium involves accepting that it may not be possible to sell the investments without incurring an unacceptable loss. Realising the premium without loss might involve holding the security until maturity (redemption) or only selling when market conditions are highly favourable. In late 2008, hedge funds were hit by very high levels of requests for redemptions. This gave them severe problems and many were forced to shut their doors (metaphorically speaking) in practice just refusing to

---

[6] www.thamesrivermm.co.uk/Home.aspx

redeem – rather as a bank suffering a run has to do once it has paid out its first few depositors.

To minimise the problem of illiquidity in the underlying assets, hedge funds have traditionally employed a number of mechanisms which try to minimise one of the greatest risks that affects hedge funds, namely the desire by their investors to have liquidity comparable to that of mutual funds. The methods they use include:

- **Lock-ups:** Traditionally, hedge funds have offered only quarterly or semi-annual liquidity. This is available only after an initial one-year lock up. More recently, hedge fund managers have begun to move from one-year lockups to two, three or occasionally more years.
- **Gates:** A gate is designed to limit outflows of funds in the event that too many investors wish to exit at the same time. Gates are limits on the percentage of total capital that can be withdrawn from a fund in a period. The limit could be 5, 10 or 20% at a liquidity date. From the point of view of the manager (and hence potentially of the underlying investors), gate provisions allow the manager to increase exposure to illiquid assets with less risk of a liquidity crisis at a redemption date. It should be noted, however, that the great advantage to the manager is that, while assets are under management, he or she earns a management fee (normally 2%) which would be lost if assets exited. There is therefore potential for a conflict here between the agent and the principal.
- **Side pockets:** A particular problem for funds which invest in less liquid assets (this was a particular problem for some funds invested in collateralized debt instruments) is that reliable valuations are difficult to find. One solution to this problem, which involves a structure which delays valuation until realization, is the side-pocket or side-car. A side pocket is in some ways similar to a separate, but attached, private equity fund. Assets held in a side pocket are not redeemed when an investor exits the fund, i.e. he or she still remains invested in the assets in the side pocket. New investors entering the fund after launch don't participate in the outcome of the investments in the side pocket.

I will not cover hedge fund strategies and performance in any detail. However, in Figure 18.11 there is a graph of performance over a particular period of time, of the basic asset classes – money, bonds and equities, compared with the major hedge fund classes. The spread of returns is, as can be seen, very wide.

The first thing to note in Figure 18.11 is that, as expected from finance theory, a line drawn between the three basic investment classes – money, bonds and equities – is a straight line, i.e. risk (as measured by volatility) is proportional to return (performance). The proxies for these three basic asset classes are LIBOR USD 1-month, SSB[7] World Government Bond Index and the S&P 500.

The second thing which is expected is that the average of all alternative strategies, measured as the Hedge Fund Index, is on almost the same line between bonds and equities, i.e. equity market return (11%), but closer to bond market volatility (9%).

---

[7] 'SSB' is Salomon Smith Barney, which was the investment banking arm of Citigroup.

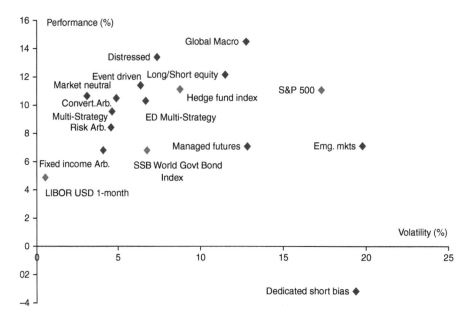

**Figure 18.11**   Performance of various hedge fund strategies over a period of time

*Source*: Michelle Learned Banque Syz and François-Serge, L'habitant Edhec et HEC Université de Lausanne.

It is when we look at the individual strategies that we find large variations in risk and return. However, it is not possible to say which is the 'best' strategy. That depends on an investor's trade-off between risk and return. If risk and return were expected to be the same in subsequent years (which they are very unlikely to be), some investors might choose Global Macro as the best trade-off, given their personal utility function (i.e. willingness to take risk). But others might choose Long/Short Equity, Distressed or Emerging Markets. But what we do know is that Global Macro dominates Managed Futures, since it has the same level of risk but a much higher return. However, the figure above relates to one historical period only. Figures based on the last five or two years would show very different patterns. Indeed, if you can observe which strategy gave the worst return (it's actually quite easy to miss it on this figure), you can also work out what was the likely period for measuring the risk versus return for these varied strategies. Note: its performance was negative.

An obvious question is whether or not alternative strategies do succeed in achieving a superior trade-off on the risk/return/liquidity spectrum and also in achieving a low correlation with the main market. There is certainly evidence that suggests that over a long period of time hedge funds have weathered domestic equity market downturns much better than the S&P index (as would be expected if they took large short positions when markets were turning down) – but that the extent of out-performance seems to have been diminishing since around 2003. One important issue is that actual funds do not on average perform at the level of hedge fund indices. Indices are not reliable indicators of actual performance and can over-estimate true returns to investors by as much as 5 percentage points.

The turbulent period for markets in August 2011 (normally August is a quiet period as so many investors are on vacation), provided a good test of hedge fund performance. In only the first ten days of August, the HFRX equity hedge index declined from around 94 to 84. From January 2011, up to 11 August, it was down from an index level of 100. Although this clearly shows that equity hedge funds find it hard to avoid losses when markets are falling, the index did fall less than the major equity market indices. One reason for the smaller fall was simply that many hedge fund managers had been hedging by keeping a large amount of cash out of the market, believed by some to be around 30% of their total funds.

Considering the difficulty of choosing an appropriate strategy for an alternative investment within a portfolio, and also the difficulty of choosing a good fund manager given that manager risk is probably the biggest risk in the hedge fund universe, many investors choose to make use of the services of a fund-of-funds. This is a fund which does not create hedge funds but selects perhaps as many as 100 funds from the universe that now numbers some thousands. A fund of funds selects only funds which have been in existence for many years, where due diligence can demonstrate that the fund has good systems and where the manager can clearly explain the strategy that has generated the results.

## Regulation of funds in the EU: undertakings for collective investments in transferable securities (UCITS) funds

The logic of preventing retail investors from purchasing investments which attempt to limit risk by hedging (hedge funds), and are in practice generally less volatile than traditional long-only funds, has been increasingly questioned. As a result, the new rules for collective investment funds, organised under the EU UCITS III framework, allows both short positions and the use of derivatives. As a result, there is an increasing number of products available which resemble traditional hedge funds in terms of strategy, but which are available under the UCITS banner. For some reason these are often known as NEWCITS.

The European Union has had the same difficulty in trying to define what a hedge fund is and hence to subject such funds to a different form of regulation from traditional funds. However, by creating a category of funds, UCITS funds, which may be freely sold across the whole of the European Union to unsophisticated (retail) investors, any fund not registered as a UCITS fund becomes a non-UCITS or non-harmonised fund. As hedge funds, private equity funds and other alternative funds cannot meet the requirements for UCITS registration (factors such as daily liquidity, use of depositories, audit and transparency) they are, consequently, non-UCITS funds. This gets around the problem of trying to define a hedge fund.

The original UCITS Directive[8] was adopted, i.e. became required for all countries in the EU, in 1985. As part of the objective of creating a single market in the EU, the Directive was aimed at ensuring that open-end funds were subject to

---

[8] A Directive is a legislative act of the European Union which requires member states to achieve a particular result. Directives have to be adopted into the legislative framework within each EU member state.

the same regulation in every member state. This was to encourage competition between suppliers based in different countries within the EU. The latest set of regulations, UCITS III, has two parts – one applies to the **fund management companies** and the other to the **funds** themselves (we have already noted the importance of distinguishing these two separate entities):

- **Management Directive**: seeks to give management companies a 'European passport' to operate throughout the EU, and widens the activities which they are allowed to undertake.
- **Product Directive**: the primary aim of this is to remove barriers to the cross-border marketing of units of collective investment funds by allowing funds to invest in a wider range of financial instruments (including derivatives). Within Europe, approximately three-quarters of all collective funds are UCITS.

At the end of 2010, the EU authorities finally agreed a new regulatory framework for non-UCITS funds, known as the Alternative Investment Fund Managers Directive (AIFMD). This is designed to try to create the same cross-border uniformity in alternative investments as in UCITS funds. Thus hedge funds, private equity funds, commodity funds and other previously non-harmonised funds will come under a new regulatory framework within the EU from 2013.

## Alternative assets: hedge funds and private equity compared

It is often assumed that because hedge funds and private equity are both classified as 'alternatives' that in consequence their characteristics are similar. In fact they are quite dissimilar. In particular, hedge funds should in principle be relatively liquid, while private equity is potentially quite illiquid except for trading through private markets. Secondaries, as they are known, are an important market in their own right to transfer existing holdings in a hedge fund, but, except at times of market exuberance, participations in funds may sell at a substantial discount to net asset value in these private markets.

Table 18.3 is a summary of some of the differences. In addition, it is important to remember that the heading 'Hedge fund' does not mean an investment strategy – there are many very different hedge fund strategies. Equally, 'Private equity' may mean buyouts or it may mean venture capital.

## The new approach to real money fund management for the new millennium

As a result of the poor performance of managed **relative performance long-only** funds compared with **alternative investment strategies**, new models for asset management have increased in popularity. In developed markets we are increasingly seeing traditional active fund managers being squeezed out on one side by index tracking funds, both mutual funds and exchange traded funds which have very low charges, and on the other side by specialist products, i.e. **asset classes** which have different characteristics to public equity and fixed income market securities and to **investment strategies** that are quite different from those traditionally

**Table 18.3**  Comparison of two alternative investments: private equity and hedge funds

| Features | Private equity | Hedge fund |
|---|---|---|
| Type of asset | Illiquid | Liquid |
| Amount of trading | Virtually none | Very active |
| Gearing | Highly geared | May be geared |
| Use of derivatives | Unlikely | Probably |
| Control or not | Control | No control |
| Investors | Institutional | Institutional |
| Life of fund | 7–10 years | Evergreen* |
| Liquidity for investor | Private market only | From manager |
| Terms of exit | At liquidation | Every 3m (+ notice) |
| Gate | Yes: always shut | Sometimes |
| Sidepockets | No need | Sometimes |
| Liquidity for assets | From IPO or trade sale | From public markets |
| Risk of capital call | Ongoing | None |

*'Evergreen' just means 'has potentially an infinite life', unlike a private equity fund which has a finite life.

employed and are frequently referred to as hedge fund strategies. In a research report issued in 2005, Morgan Stanley noted a

> polarisation of the asset management industry – our 'asset management barbell'.
> Traditional core investing is under siege on two fronts. On one side, quantitative houses offering cheap and effective ways to track market indices are increasingly encroaching into active money management with their enhanced products. On the other side, there is strong demand for spicier strategies such as hedge funds, property, commodities, private equity and specialist products.
>
> Morgan Stanley European Investment Research – Hedge Funds:
> Notes from the Investment Frontier, 27 September 2005

The above clearly failed to anticipate the sharp decline in property markets and private equity returns in many countries which was about to start at that time. But in overall terms what it foresaw was correct.

## Core/satellite

The so-called core/satellite approach to constructing a portfolio, what Morgan Stanley call the asset management barbell, is one that has been widely adopted by both institutional and retail investors as a means of avoiding the high cost of investing 100% in a managed fund. This strategy utilises index tracking funds for, perhaps, 80% of the portfolio, but tries to obtain diversification plus 'a gamble on the side' by including in the balance of the portfolio assets, such as hedge funds and individual stocks. However, the strategy could equally be implemented using low cost mutual funds where these were available:

'Core/satellite portfolio construction combines the most effective characteristics of index and alpha-generating strategies offering flexibility and lower costs than more conventional approaches. The broad range of market exposures offered by exchange traded funds allows for a significant role in the implementation of core/satellite strategies, used both as efficient core investments as well as satellites.

Core/satellite investing is based on the simple concept of splitting a portfolio into two segments. The first is the core. This forms the foundation of the strategy and provides the axis around which the more specialized satellite investments can be added. The core usually takes the form of a low risk, pooled investment vehicle. This is typically an index tracking fund, such as an ETF, that offers low cost, broadly diversified exposure to a market or index. The aim is to deliver a return in line with the market's performance – this is often referred to as the beta return.

The second segment of the portfolio is made up of the satellites. These are typically more specialized investments that are designed to generate additional returns (alpha) and further diversification. This can be achieved through exposure to specific markets, specialist ETFs, actively managed funds, investment themes and individual securities. Satellite investments typically carry higher risk and fees than core investments.

Many different types of professional investors are now using core/satellite strategies including pension fund managers, wealth managers and asset managers. The building block nature of ETFs makes them ideal for use as a Core element of a portfolio, or as satellite investments in specialist areas such as emerging markets or clean energy.'

# 19 WEALTH MANAGEMENT AND PRIVATE BANKING

## WEALTH MANAGEMENT/PRIVATE BANKING

I include wealth management in Part IV since, at its core, it is simply the use of an agent to manage risk for an individual or a family. Wealth managers make use of collective investment funds, as described in the previous chapter, to achieve the risk management objectives of their clients; or they may create their own portfolios in-house.

'Wealth management' is a relatively new term which came to prominence only in the last 30 years as more people in developed countries had a surplus of income over expenditure (savings) in an amount which might benefit from professional management. Prior to that those few who were rich enough to be able to save substantial sums employed the services of a private bank. Today, the main area of growth in wealth management/private banking is Asia which, due its rapid economic growth and increasing numbers of entrepreneurs generating wealth, is providing huge opportunities for financial services firms.

Private banking will always involve the provision of banking services, i.e. deposit and loan services, but private banks are as much involved in asset management advice as are wealth management firms. Private banks, however, generally target only the most wealthy individuals and not those with modest amounts of wealth. Wealth managers do not offer banking services, only asset management and advisory services.

In terms of types of client, these are often distinguished by the size of their **liquid assets holdings** available for investment, i.e. not including domestic residences. A common classification is to start with **ultra high net worth (UHNW)** individuals, which might be defined as having investable assets of $50 million or above. **Very high net worth (very HNW)** might be from $5–50 million. **High net worth (HNW)** might be defined as $500,000–5 million. Finally, many would include a category known as **mass affluent**, which would be those with around $100,000–500,000 to invest.

These categories represent a wide range of people in terms of where their wealth has come from and consequently in terms of their approach to managing their wealth. Coutts, one of the oldest private banks, makes this point in its literature by considering the background of potential clients and trying to appeal to them from the angle of understanding 'where they are coming from':

● **Executives:** demand on your time increasing so little time for your own financial affairs;

- **Professionals:** we understand your career path within your profession and how this affects your personal financial needs;
- **Entrepreneurs:** we understand the challenges of running your own business;
- **Acquired wealth:** we understand that this gives you countless financial questions, options and decisions;
- **Sports and entertainment:** our relationship manager (RM) understands your world and that you may not have time to actively engage with managing your wealth;
- **International:** we have always looked after individuals who are resident in more than one country;
- **Retired:** we understand the issues of retiring and will help you plan for the day you do retire to make sure your financial plans are robust and flexible.

This should enable Coutts to segment its client base thus:

- **Client segmentation definition**: the art and science of tailoring and delivering products and services to distinct client groups;
- **Know your client:** not just for regulatory reasons
  - Style of relationship manager that best meets his/her needs;
  - Products and services that best meet client's needs;
  - Model for segmenting clients: complex and proprietary.

Each segment, depending on degree of wealth and business background, requires a different type of service in terms of the actual client requirements. The economics of providing services to that segment, and hence the appropriate business model, is also different for each. Clearly at the top end of the market it is economic to devote considerable resources to individual clients and to have a very **bespoke**, i.e. personally tailored, service, whereas at the lowest end of the market it is not. At the lower end it might be a web-based service with a charge for telephone advice.

Individuals have different approaches to risk which at any level of net worth must be taken account of. Barclays Wealth, for example, emphasises this issue of **'financial personality'**. On the basis of this type of analysis of financial personality, a wealth manager can try to achieve congruence between the understanding the client has of risk and how it can affect him or her and the types of product that are available and the possible outcomes in terms of adverse market movements.

**Wealth management** may be part of a commercial/investment bank group but there are some hundreds or thousands of small wealth managers/independent financial advisors/financial consultants who provide advice to individuals on how to manage their financial assets. Wealth management is an industry which does not require much capital and is the most fragmented part of the financial services industry. What it requires as employees is people who have a basic understanding of finance but equally importantly either good contacts with the wealthy or good human relations skills that enables them to convince customers to do business and to remain with them as advisors. These people are known as relationship managers. Wealth managers recommend a portfolio structure to clients – traditionally perhaps 40% domestic equity, 20% overseas equity, 30% fixed income and 10% in cash equivalents – and then execute the necessary transactions by using either brokers or, more probably, the mutual fund and ETF products created by the asset management industry. Some wealth managers also have both the expertise and the access to alternative assets such as hedge funds and private equity on which they will provide advice to clients. Increasingly it is likely that the successful wealth managers will be those that understand the structures and investment characteristics of different alternative strategies and are able to explain these convincingly to potential clients.

The wealth management industry has two components:

- The '**manufacture**' of products, for example mutual funds, structured products and tax efficient investments. These are created by the asset management and investment banking industries. Some wealth managers have an asset management company and an investment bank within the group (for example Barclays, Credit Suisse and Morgan Stanley) and as a result can suggest their own in-house products to clients.
- The **distribution** of these products to clients. This is the role of RMs operating within a wealth management firm, whether this is an integrated firm, i.e. one which combines manufacture and distribution such as Barclays, or is a pure advisory firm.

The large wealth managers will generally have a wide range of products manufactured in-house, i.e. by their own asset manager or investment bankers, while smaller wealth managers provide only distribution through RMs. This latter type of wealth manager will access a wide range of manufacturers and ought to choose those products which he or she thinks provide the best solution to a client's problems rather than those providing the highest commission rates.

## CASE STUDY: THE UK MARKET LEADER, BARCLAYS WEALTH

Barclays Wealth is owned by Barclays Bank plc, a UK high street bank which has chosen to develop its wealth management arm into a major part of the parent company's operations (which also includes Barclays Capital). Barclays Wealth is the UK's largest wealth manager with total client assets of £164billion, as at 31 December 2011. With offices in over 20 countries, Barclays Wealth focuses on private and intermediary clients worldwide, providing international and private banking, investment management, fiduciary services and brokerage. The services it provides to clients are categorised as below:

- Banking and finance
  - Day to day banking;
  - Liquidity management service;
  - Lending;
  - Foreign exchange;
- Brokerage;
- Financial planning;
- Investment management
  - Discretionary;
  - Non-discretionary;

- Investment products;
- Retirement and protection;
- Trusts and estates.

Like most good private wealth managers, Barclays emphasises the importance of clients understanding their own **investment philosophy** and thus of understanding their own financial personality and investment style and the implications for them, as individuals, of studies into behavioural finance. Barclays Wealth produces research on personal investment of which the executive summary from a Barclays Wealth Insight, below, is a good example of work which attempts to help clients understand their personal investment philosophy.

> **Desire for discipline:** Despite being wealthy, nearly half of the investors polled in this report acknowledged that they want more self-control of their financial behaviour. Women were more likely than men to have a greater desire for self-control. Desire for discipline also changes with source of wealth. Those whose wealth has come from earned or investment income are less likely to want more control. However, where wealth is derived from inheritance, high net worth individuals are aware of a need for discipline, perhaps due to their need to be accountable for the legacy they are managing. Similarly, entrepreneurs and those whose wealth comes from property or large bonuses are more likely to have a high need for discipline.
>
> **The trading paradox:** The survey exposes an interesting contradiction on the theme of overtrading. Previous research has shown that excess trading can compromise returns; however, many high net worth individuals believe that you must trade frequently to do well in the markets. These same individuals suspect that they overdo it because they are over three times more likely to believe they trade too much. In fact, almost 50% of traders who believe you have to trade often to do well think they buy and sell investments too frequently. This overtrading is associated with a desire for a more disciplined approach to their finances. In addition, low composure, concern about preventing bad things from happening and a high appetite for risk increase the likelihood of trading too much.
>
> **The gender difference:** Whilst the research finds differences between individuals within all the groups, there are several robust personality differences between men and women when looking at these groups in aggregate. Men tend to have a higher risk tolerance, being more likely to label themselves 'financial risk takers' and having a greater openness to choosing high risk investments. Men have more positive views on the benefits of frequent trading and timing the market, yet – consistent with the trading paradox – they are more likely to believe they trade too much. Men have higher composure than women; that is, they are less likely to believe they are easily stressed. Women tend to have lower composure and a greater desire for financial self-control, which is associated with a desire to use self-control strategies, and women are more likely to believe that these strategies are effective.
>
> **Age really does make you wiser:** The adage that we mellow with age rings true in this report. Age is characterised by calm, acceptance and satisfaction. The data suggest the idea of happiness in old age also transfers to the way we approach our finances. In fact, even if wealth levels do not change, with increasing age the wealthy gained a calmness and confidence in their approach to financial management.
>
> **High stakes:** A significant difference emerges when we look at the relationship between worth and financial personality traits. Those with greater income and wealth have

higher risk tolerance levels. The pattern behind this observation is extremely robust. Having a risk-seeking personality has its own challenges – it is clearly related to a higher desire for financial self-control.

**Rules rule**: The report shows that investors use many types of decision-making strategies to control their decision-making process. The most popular include setting deadlines to avoid procrastination and using cooling-off periods to reflect on decisions. Respondents believe that rules are more effective in their financial lives rather than in life more generally.

# PART V

# INTERNAL CAPITAL ALLOCATION: THE ROLE OF DIRECTORS, INVESTORS AND THE MARKET FOR CORPORATE CONTROL

# 20 THE INTERNAL CAPITAL MARKET AND INVESTOR GOVERNANCE OF CAPITAL ALLOCATION

Part I of this book covered the credit and 'external' capital markets. The governance mechanism for the external capital market revolves around the need for the company to persuade potential investors in an IPO that they will, in fact, earn not less than the required market return for a project or company in its particular risk class. However, the main source of financing for new investment projects in companies subsequent to an IPO is **not the external capital markets but the so-called internal capital market**. The reason is that after undertaking an IPO on the primary capital market most companies never again raise equity on the public markets. **Secondary offerings**, i.e. an offering of additional shares sometime after the initial offering (meaning a second, primary offering and nothing to do with the secondary market), are relatively rare. In fact, most equity financing for new projects or expansion of existing ones comes from retained profits. Only banks which have eaten through their equity capital have had to access the equity market for additional funds. Companies may of course access the debt markets on a continuing basis both to re-finance their maturing debt (rollover) and to maintain the debt/equity ratio as equity increases due to retained earnings.

There is a very key difference between funds raised in the external capital market through an IPO (or secondary offering) and funds generated from retained earnings. While both are equity, the governance of the approval process for such new investment is different:

- **Funds raised in capital market**. The company has to make a case to investors in terms of expected return and risk. If it cannot make a good case that it can generate the required rate of return (at least equal to its cost of capital) on any additional capital that investors supply, it will not be able to raise fresh equity. Thus the capital market is a rationing mechanism designed to ensure optimal use of society's scarce resources.
- **Retained earnings**. The company does not need to make a case to investors since it already has additional funds belonging to them simply by not paying out all profits to them. Thus it does not need to demonstrate that this additional funding will earn at least the cost of capital and therefore there is a greater chance than with external financing that it will not. This arises from the agency problems that exist when we separate ownership and control in a company and

when the incentives of the management of the company are not fully aligned with those of the owners (the shareholders). The capital market is no longer performing its important function of external governance and discipline and, instead, when retained earnings are used for financing new investment, we have an internal capital market making capital allocations.

There are in fact three different models of internal capital allocation.

- The first is profit retention. Any company running a single business which does not pay out 100% of its profits to its owners (the shareholders) then has to have an internal capital allocation mechanism. This is the capital budgeting process, the same process as is employed to generate the information required to persuade investors in the external capital markets to provide funds. When employed on internally generated funds, however, the criteria applied to decision-making may be different and there is no longer the discipline of needing to persuade 'outsiders' of the investment case for employing funds in the way that has been decided internally.
- The second also involves profit retention but this time in a multi-product or conglomerate company. Such companies have a number of divisions operating in different industries in which some divisions are described as 'cash cows' (cash generative and not requiring much new investment, as the market growth rate is slow) and some are described as 'stars' (while they do generate cash, because they are in a high growth sector, they also require more cash than they generate). There are in addition so-called 'dogs' (which are divisions in an company with a low growth rate and low cash generation) and 'questions marks' (which are those where market growth rate might be high but with only a small market share and the particular subsidiary is not generating the cash necessary to a become major player in that sector). (see Figure 20.1).[1]
- Finally we have the private equity model which also involves a group with a number of companies within it, each in a different industry but **not** a conglomerate. A key distinction between private equity and a conglomerate is that each so-called portfolio company within the private equity fund structure has to stand on its own. The fund manager of the portfolio of companies held within a private equity fund does not reallocate capital from one company to another. Most of the cash generated is likely to be used to pay interest on the high level of debt employed in private equity. Any surplus cash generated by company A within the portfolio is returned to the fund, and from there to the investors in the fund. It will not be used to provide financing to company B or company C within the fund. Thus while the initial capital raised by private equity from external investors is allocated by the fund managers (on the basis of the prospectus issued to fund investors) subsequent surplus cash flows from portfolio companies are not reallocated within the fund but returned to the external investors. This should be a way of avoiding a common problem with

---

[1] This framework for thinking about different businesses was developed by The Boston Consulting Group (The Product Portfolio) in 1970.

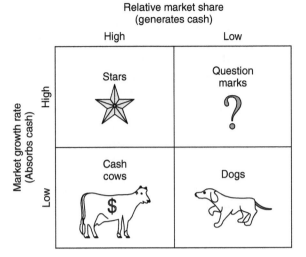

**Figure 20.1**   The Boston Consulting Group Product Portfolio matrix

*Source*: Adapted from the BCG Portfolio Matrix from the Product Portfolio Matrix,(c)1970, The Boston Consulting Group; http://www.bcg.com/ (accessed 4 April 2012).

multi-divisional companies which is that those who generate the resources without the group feel less included to do so if they see that such resources are simply given to those who cannot generate surpluses themselves. Those not generating surpluses then come to rely on others within the group to subsidise them and so do not bother to try to overcome the lack of profitability through greater effort or a more effective business strategy.

# AFTER AN IPO

The need for good corporate governance after an IPO arises from the fact that once a company has raised funds in an IPO, it is no longer directly subject to market discipline over its (real) investment behaviour. The key issue for investors (and also for society more widely) is whether or not the resources it controls continue to be used in the most productive manner, as was expected by the initial investors when they provided the original financing. If resources are not being used efficiently, there is a risk that lenders will not be repaid or that shareholders will not achieve the expected rate of return on their investment. This potential problem may arise because of agency issues between the directors and the shareholders. Directors are responsible for ensuring the most productive use of resources but may not have their incentives aligned with those of the owners. They may choose to overpay themselves (though the meaning of this is hard to define) as many CEOs of banks may have done. This seemed to be the case just at the time when they could be said to be misusing shareholder funds in acquiring risky assets such as CDOs or by making risky acquisitions such as RBS's purchase of ABN Amro – an acquisition at the top of the market which, shortly after, resulted in RBS becoming insolvent and being rescued by the UK government.

The question is how to ensure that CEOs and other officers of companies are paid 'fairly', are incentivised to act in the interests of shareholders and are disincentivised from undertaking projects, in particular acquisitions of other companies, that on an objective assessment would seem to be unlikely to be able to earn the bank's cost of capital and may indeed lead to the acquiring company becoming insolvent. The great incentive for directors here comes from the fact that the larger the company, the more prestigious is the job of running it, the higher the salary and bonuses, and the lower the risk of another company bidding for it, as it may be so big that the acquirer would get indigestion from trying to swallow it. In addition, in companies with a number of divisions or subsidiaries, some of which generate a lot of cash and others which do not, the directors are likely to transfer funds between the cash generators and cash absorbers and in so doing they may be likely to support 'dogs' and also too many 'question marks' which never, in fact, become stars but are held on to for emotional reasons.

Another way of looking at this issue is that, in any enterprise, there are two distinct roles:

- The management of the business both from a day to day point of view and from a strategic point of view;
- Risk bearing through equity investment, i.e. ownership of the business and through providing loans to the company.

In a sole trader business, clearly ownership and control of the business are totally integrated in the same individual. Thus when the owner makes a decision involving risk (such as additional investment in the business) he or she is also responsible for ensuring that the new investment is effectively used. In a small private company, the owners may also coincide with the managers.

As an example, investment banks until some 20 years ago were private partnerships[2] in which the partners were the owners of the investment bank, provided all the equity finance, made all the key decisions and had **unlimited financial liability**. In such a business it is unlikely that the partners would have taken the risks that Merrill Lynch, Morgan Stanley, Goldman Sachs and others took from 2000 to 2007 since any liability that resulted from those decisions would have fallen on the partners personally. It is interesting to note the extent to which risk-taking would seem to have increased in Goldman Sachs from the year 2000 onwards – the year of transition from private partnership to public company.

In the public company, it is of the essence that risk bearing (ownership) and control (management) are separated. Indeed, it is a central tenet of capitalism that this is the most effective way to organise production. **Separation of ownership and control** is the 'innovation' which allowed such a massive expansion of industrial capacity in the Western world. Without this separation and the creation of public companies able to access public saving, the private wealth of those who owned firms would not have been adequate to enable the massive expansion of industry in the 18th and 19th centuries. Indeed, one of the problems before the

---

[2] Goldman Sachs, for example, was a private partnership for 130 years until it undertook an IPO in 1999.

invention of the public company was that the rich, often the landed gentry and aristocrats may not have had the brains required for successful management and innovation while those who had the intelligence and education to manage companies successfully did not have the wealth to own their own companies. **It was the invention of the public company (separation of ownership and control) and the pooling of funds through capital markets that have been the keystones of economic development since the Industrial Revolution commenced at the end of the 1700s in the United Kingdom and shifted the world into the industrial age.**

However, once the two key functions in the capitalist system are allocated to different sets of people, an agency problem may arise between them unless there is a mechanism to try to ensure an alignment of interests between the two groups. Such a mechanism might be profit sharing. This would mean that directors and managers would be incentivised to maximise profit for shareholders since this would also benefit them financially. In practice schemes of this type, including share option provision to directors, have **not** worked as well as expected in achieving a congruence of interests. Even if interests are congruent, there still needs to be a mechanism to monitor the directors and managers to ensure that they are making the capital allocation decisions which are expected to maximise shareholder wealth. In particular, the use of share options for bankers where this year's declared profits can easily disappear in subsequent years through unexpected losses relating to previous year's 'profits', as has happened to profits generated by banks from 2000–07. This may result in bankers seeking short-term profit but departing from the bank before unexpected losses materialise.

A further reason why there needs to be some mechanism to hold the management of public companies to account is that the world changes continuously. This leads to an ongoing need for change within a company. The **configuration of assets under the control of the company** may need to be changed to reflect changes in demand patterns, new technology, prices of inputs (costs) and outputs (revenues), exchange rates, interest rates, inflation rates, etc. If the board of directors is to meet its obligation as agents of the shareholders (the principals) to maximise shareholder value, the directors need to respond to changes in the external environment by making changes to the processes within their firm, the range of industries in which they are involved, the asset structure of the firm, the liability structure of the firm, etc. This involves understanding corporate strategy. While shareholders will generally not try to second-guess the directors they will still want to review what is being done in their name to reflect economic change.

If the directors did always act in the shareholders' interest and responded appropriately to changes in the external environment, there would be little need to monitor their performance. But in practice, what was once known as 'x-inefficiency', which simply means that directors and managers prefer an easy life to one where the work/life balance is in favour of the company, rather than the company employee, means that there is likely to be a need for monitoring.

One type of X-inefficiency can arise from a growing scale and scope of a company. The reason for this is that a larger, more diverse, company may be less efficient than a smaller, more focused one. But for the directors, the larger a company, the higher their remuneration is likely to be. The prestige of the chief executive will also be greater. But perhaps even more relevant is that one of the mechanisms for overcoming misuse of resources in a company is the takeover option and in particular the purchase of a company from its shareholders by private equity. If this happens, the directors are likely to lose their jobs. However, the larger the company, the harder it is for private equity firms to garner the resources necessary to make an acquisition. Thus for the directors of a company personally, growing in size by acquisition may make it less vulnerable to being acquired itself, at which point the directors would be likely to lose their employment. Thus becoming larger is advantageous to them, but may not be so to shareholders. It reduces the ability of external governance mechanisms to function appropriately. Citigroup, for example, which was once the largest bank in the world, demonstrated many times before its ultimate nationalisation by the US government that it was 'too large to manage'. Bank of America, with severe problems in many of its business areas and with 250,000 employees, is said by some to be too large to manage. Its size is, in considerable part, a result of two major acquisitions, Countrywide Home Loans and Merrill Lynch – both of which have proved problematic. Our interest is in how these agency problems can be minimised and what financial mechanisms there are that may help to overcome them in the event that corporate governance does not achieve this.

## MECHANISMS TO OVERCOME A FAILURE OF CORPORATE GOVERNANCE

Frequently the corporate governance mechanism fails to achieve the objectives set for it in, for example, the **OECD Principles of Corporate Governance**. The question then is: what mechanisms are there to try to remove and replace incumbent directors or to persuade them to act in a fashion which is in accord with the interests of the company and its shareholders? Shareholder action is the first stage in this process.

In theory, it should be possible for shareholders to dismiss the board and elect a new one. Indeed, there is no reason why shareholders themselves should not be elected to the board. But there are a considerable number of difficulties in the way of achieving change by this means.

The first problem is that companies are owned by three types of shareholder:

1. individual investors;
2. institutional investors, and;
3. short-term traders such as HFT traders who attempt not to hold overnight positions.

An individual investor has no power unless he or she can pool support from, normally, thousands of others – something which would be hard to do. They would need to have voting rights amounting to a relatively high proportion of total shareholders (ideally more than 50%) in order to force through change. They might try to change the directors, but in many countries the directors have periods of office that do not coincide. Thus it is difficult to remove a complete board of directors at one time. In addition, today many investors are located outside the home country of the company and are unlikely to wish to be involved in governance at all.

There is also the fundamental difficulty that many investors, retail and institutional, if they are unhappy with the performance of a company, **simply sell their shares**. The reason they do this is that secondary markets provide an alternative, and in many ways much easier, mechanism for investors who are not content with the way in which a company is being managed to express their dissatisfaction. In countries where it is possible to sell shares short, even if they don't have shares in the company to sell, they may take out a short position in the belief that the market is over-valuing the shares. Long/short hedge funds, for example, would be likely to short such a company if they detected a problem. To the extent that selling pressure on the shares of a company causes them to fall substantially, this alerts even sleepy shareholders to the fact that something may be wrong with the management of the company. If more investors had been willing to short bank shares (this implies that they had researched them and realised that their values were unsustainably high), or analysts to have advised traders to go short, the directors might have reined in their risky activities (though equally, many boards would not). Nonetheless a falling share price, due to investors fleeing a company, is part of the overall governance mechanism.

In the case of institutional investors, particularly those with a large percentage holding in a company, it might seem that it would be relatively easy to persuade the directors to change a policy that the shareholders thought was not maximising their wealth. In practice, however, many institutional investors would seem to take little interest in corporate governance and effective shareholder action. Instead, they believe their function is to select shares which they think are undervalued and buy them and sell those they think are correctly priced or have become overvalued. Many institutional shareholders are simply not interested in trying to change corporate behaviour – they would much rather just sell out. They don't behave as we might expect 'owners' to behave.

A further problem arises from the fact that many shareholders are **indexed mutual funds** or **exchange traded funds** which undertake no research and simply ensure that their fund holds the shares (or a representative selection of shares) in an index. As passive shareholders, they have no interest in activism. They do not even sell if the directors of the company are clearly acting against shareholder interests. Thus these shareholders, in their trading activity, are **price takers** (they simply accept the market price as 'the price') and buy or sell purely on the basis of whether a share is, or is not, in an index which they are replicating. Hedge fund shareholders, on the other hand, are **price makers who only trade if they believe that the current market price is wrong**.

Short-term traders such as those who use HFTs have no interest in the fundamentals of companies. Their interest is in **short-term mispricing arising from frictions in the trading process**. Many will not hold positions overnight. Thus such shareholders have no interest whatever in taking action regarding corporate governance.

There are a number of funds, in particular hedge funds, who hope to generate alpha (outperformance) from shareholder activism. Such funds target a particular company where they believe that they have spotted a strategy for the company to follow, which it is not following, and which could result in greater shareholder value. By buying into the company they hope to influence its strategy, ideally by obtaining a place on the board. Such **activism** can be effective, but there is relatively little capital employed in this activity and thus its benefits are likely to be marginal.

Given that existing shareholders do not in general take a proprietorial approach to the companies in which they are investors, society needs some other mechanism which may enable the transfer of control of assets which are not being properly managed to a different group of managers. This mechanism is the **market in corporate control** which we cover in the next chapter.

# 21 THE MARKET FOR CORPORATE CONTROL: MERGERS AND ACQUISITIONS

## MERGERS AND ACQUISITIONS

We noted in the last chapter that many investors will sell their shareholding in a company rather than trying to change the management if they believe it is not employing the company's assets in the most productive way. Sales by large investors are likely to drive down the price of a company's shares. As more people become aware of the problem another company may come to the conclusion that it could manage the assets better and make them more productive (profitable). It thus may make a bid in the stock market for all the shares (or at least 51%) to give it control of the company and will hope to profit from the changes it believes it can make.

In the stock market, small parcels of shares are exchanged between investors. In the **mergers and acquisitions market** on the other hand, the whole share capital or at least a large part of it, i.e. ownership of a company, is transferred – and with this ownership comes **control**, which is the ability to make decisions on resource allocation within the company. That is a key difference between, for example, a private equity fund (which takes control of companies) and a hedge fund or mutual fund (which have no interest in control). Thus the mergers and acquisitions business is often called the **market in corporate control**. While technically the firms which advise on mergers and acquisitions (M&A) need not be financial intermediaries (in theory M&A is just an advisory service), in practice investment banks long ago extended their activities from just arranging primary market financings to also providing advice on corporate acquisitions. More recently, many investment/commercial banks have also become involved not just as agents in such transactions but as principals. As well as offering advice they have offered the temporary financing which is necessary to pay for an acquisition at the time of completion of the deal and subsequently arranged the permanent financing which will substitute, at lower cost, for the interim financing. One of the first innovative forms of interim financing promise, i.e. something to persuade shareholders that a bid can be financed, was that provided by the **highly confident letter**.[1]

---

[1] The **highly confident letter** was a financing tool created in the 1980s by Drexel Burnham Lambert, and specifically by Michael Milken. It enabled corporate raiders to launch LBO offers without the debt component of their financing package fully in place.

M&A is the activity dealing with mergers between firms and acquisition of other firms. The difference between mergers and acquisitions may only be in terms of the language used. Mergers are very rare, with the British Airways/Iberia merger in 2010 to create International Airline Group (IAG) being one of the few in recent years. Most M&A transactions are acquisitions since only with a true acquisition is it clear who (in terms of management) has control of the combined company. For that reason I will focus on acquisitions. The management of the company being bid for may recommend to its shareholders that they accept a bid, as it considers this course of action to be in the shareholders' best interest (**an agreed bid**), or it may reject the bid on behalf of its shareholders on the grounds that it will not be as economically valuable to the shareholders as continuing to hold the shares would be (and continuing with the present management). Bids which are rejected by the management of the bid-for company (**unfriendly bids**) lead to each side putting forward to shareholders its proposals to make the company more efficient and thus worth more to them. It is important to appreciate that ultimately it is not the managers or directors who decide whether or not to accept a bid. It is the exclusive province of the owners of the company – the shareholders. Nonetheless the incumbent management will try to influence shareholder decisions.

M&A can be an important revenue generating area for investment banks. Until securities trading became the most profitable area in the decade starting in 2000, M&A was often the major source of profit. It was also one of the most prestigious areas in which to work, as those managing M&A departments were in regular contact with the senior people in the largest corporations. However, although most investment banks undertake M&A activity, it is not a principal activity, i.e. **it is not a banking activity, a securities activity or a financing activity**. It is an agency activity – giving advice to senior corporate executives and advising on pricing and structuring deals. It may, however, subsequently give rise to financing business.

Traditionally corporate finance houses were independent and worked as agents for their clients. Corporate finance became part of investment banking as a result of M&A activity generally requiring financing, both temporary loans and permanent equity capital and long-term debt. Thus in order to increase the opportunity of obtaining the mandate for the financing (potentially very profitable), investment banks would offer advice in this area. However, the conflicts of interest that arise from combining these two activities has led to an increasing number of M&A specialists moving out of investment banks and setting up independent boutiques which do not provide financing, but only advice.

It also has to be appreciated that M&A bankers are continually 'touting for business', i.e. approaching companies with proposals for deals that they hope to execute. They are not passive employees who wait until a company knocks on the door asking for advice. Thus it is possibly often the case that the pressure to do a deal comes less from the initiative of the company than from forceful persuasion

---

Although the 'highly confident letter' had no legal status, Milken, had a reputation for being able to sell such bonds and also to provide a secondary market and thus bids were able to go ahead much more quickly than with traditional financing.

and stroking the ego of the chief executive (good salesmanship) by investment bankers. Many of the acquisitions in the financial services sector which destroyed shareholder value instead of enhancing it were pushed by M&A departments working with hubristic CEOs.

## WHO BENEFITS FROM A TAKEOVER?

In a takeover, there are two sets of shareholders to consider:

• Those of the bidding company, also called the **acquirer** or bidder;
• Those of the company being bid for, also called the **target**.

We need to consider what happens to shareholder wealth, for both sets of shareholders, depending on whether the bid succeeds or fails. We also need to consider to which set of shareholders any subsequent **efficiency gains** made by the new owners accrue.

Our starting point for analysis is that if the stock market values capital assets (company shares) correctly, then a bid at above this price, i.e. **a bid premium**, would, other things being equal, reduce shareholder wealth of the **acquiring** shareholders by transferring wealth to the shareholders of the **target** company. Thus we have to explain why bidders may be willing to pay more than the market price. There are a number of possibilities:

• The market has made wrong estimates of expected future cash flows;
• The market has made a wrong estimate of the appropriate risk adjusted discount rate;
• The acquiring company believes that there are **synergies**, i.e. gains from integration, that can be generated from the acquisition which are at least equal to the bid premium and, if in excess of the bid premium, will generate an **increase in shareholder value** for the acquiring shareholders (i.e. a rise in share price);
• The acquiring company believes that its intended strategy is superior to that of the incumbent management and will generate much higher returns;
• The directors of the bidding company are not concerned that there will be a loss of shareholder value as frequently happens in the case of large companies making bids, since their bid may be simply to increase the bidding company's size to protect it from being bid for.

Academic research suggests that **most acquirers overpay and thus destroy their own shareholder value** by transferring it to the selling shareholders. Reasons why company boards may act in this way include:

• The larger a company, the higher the pay of its executives tends to be;
• More prestige will accrue to the chief executive of the larger company;
• The company, being larger, is less likely to be bid for by another company or targeted by private equity which might result in the board members losing their jobs.

The shareholders of the target company may realise a gain from the bid premium. Whether or not they do and how large the gain is depends on the '**currency**' used to pay existing shareholders i.e. whether the bid is a:

- **Cash bid** so that the selling shareholders receive an all **cash** payment (i.e. a fixed and guaranteed amount) in exchange for their shares;
- **Paper bid** in which the currency being offered is new shares (traditionally paper certificates) in the acquirer which will be given to the selling shareholders (or it could be a cash and paper bid).

If it is a paper bid, then the questions that need to be asked are:

- Will the price of those shares decline between the date the bid is first made and when the shares are received – as happened in the case of Barclays Bank bid for ABN AMRO which was predominantly paper and unsuccessful (fortunately for them) compared with RBS's successful bid in cash?
- Will those who receive the new shares hold them or sell them immediately in the market?
- If the new shareholders do not sell the shares (perhaps because this would trigger a tax liability on the capital gain) will the synergies being claimed by the bidder be realised and subsequently reflected in the price of the bidder's shares?

## ACQUIRERS: TRADE, CONGLOMERATE AND FINANCIAL BUYERS IN ACQUISITIONS

In any acquisition there are different types of potential buyer. **Trade buyers** are those in the same industry; **conglomerate buyers** are usually those in a different industry. But both are companies either in the manufacturing or service sectors. On the other hand there are so-called **financial buyers** which are companies whose sole objective is to own a company for a defined period during which they plan to increase value before reselling. Such buyers raise the funds required for acquisitions from investors and also from banks and other lenders. This latter type of buyer is normally a **private equity** firm which is undertaking what is known as an **LBO**.

### Trade buyers

A **trade buyer** will normally be in the same or a closely related industry. There are two main motivations for such a purchase. The first is to **attain economies of scale or scope** by combining the acquired company with its existing operations in the hope of gaining efficiencies, generally known as synergies. It may be that the industry is one where the larger the scale, the lower the unit cost. Or it may be that by acquiring a firm which produces complementary products or operates in related markets, there are efficiencies of scope to be gained. Provided the benefits of these new efficiencies accrue to customers, and not simply as excess return on shareholder capital (supernormal profit), then society as a whole benefits. An example of trade buyers would be Cadbury's acquisition of another small chocolate company, Green and Blacks, and the subsequent acquisition of Cadbury by Kraft, another food company. In both cases, arguments were made to shareholders about economies of scale and scope which would lead to economic gains.

The second reason is to reduce competition and, thereby, hopefully to **improve pricing power**, i.e. expecting that shareholders, not consumers, will benefit. For example, in the investment banking industry, the failure of important firms – Lehman, Bear Stearns and Washington Mutual – and the nationalisation of others – such as AIG and Royal Bank of Scotland – has reduced competitive pricing pressures in the industry. In the case of Lehman, by acquiring its US assets, Barclays Capital was able to increase its product range and its geographical scope and, with this, potentially improve its profitability. It is to be presumed that when JP Morgan Chase acquired Bear Stearns and Washington Mutual it hoped that this additional scale and scope, in a market which had suddenly become less competitive, would lead to an enhanced rate of return on capital employed. It also, of course, made JP Morgan, more than ever, 'too large to fail'.

## Conglomerate buyers

Conglomerate buyers (or firms which are diversified over many business areas) are not common today, but at one time were thought to be the way of the future. General Electric is one of the few remaining US conglomerates. It has a very diverse product range. The logic of such conglomerates was not efficiencies of scale and scope but diversification of investments, which was said to benefit investors. In addition, the use of an internal capital market was said to overcome the problem of capital constraints on investment arising from imperfections in external capital markets.

In practice there has been little evidence of such benefits (hence a principal reason why most conglomerates were broken up) though General Electric would seem to be an exception. Also, and most importantly, investors can achieve their own diversification at little cost just by acquiring a diversified portfolio of companies. The unpopularity of conglomerates is indicated by statistics which suggest that conglomerates in Europe and the US suffer a discount to 'pure play' companies of around 10%. Interestingly, in Latin America they would seem to trade at a 12% premium.[2] This would also seem to apply in India and perhaps in China. One reason suggested for this according to Tarun Khanna[3] is that in those countries capital markets are not nearly as well developed as in the West and risk capital is difficult to access. In such a capital-constrained environment with less-developed capital markets, it may be entirely appropriate for diversified companies to finance projects using their internal group capital market by using profits generated in one part of the group for investment in another. A further reason is that it can be much harder to get permissions for new factories and permits in emerging markets, hence expertise in navigating bureaucracies is important. Spreading this cost over a large diverse group could be called 'regulatory synergies'.

---

[2] 'Company Chiefs Look to Divide and Rule', *Financial Times*, 24 September 2011.
[3] *Winning in Emerging Markets* (Harvard Business Press, 2010).

## Financial buyers

A high proportion of total acquisitions in the M&A market is made by private equity funds which buy companies across a wide range of industries with the intention of reselling within a few years, during which they hope to generate value by making the acquired company more efficient in terms both of its financing and its physical structure.

Buy-outs of companies or parts of companies by private equity have accounted for 50% or more of the total M&A activity in the UK through most of the decade. Indeed in the first half of 2010, when M&A activity was much lower than usual, private equity buy-outs amounted to 73% of all such activity.[4] The importance of private equity as acquirers means that an understanding of this part of the finance industry is important for anyone involved in an M&A department of an investment bank. Not only are they important M&A clients but they are also important clients for the banking (financing) side of an investment bank because they also need to raise funding to make acquisitions. Finally they are very important clients for the IPO department since within a few years they must dispose of all their acquisitions, and an IPO is one route to disposal. Thus private equity firms have contributed substantially to the profits of investment banks over the period 2000–07.

---

[4] 'News and Updates Quarter Three 2010', Centre for Management Buy-Out Research, University of Nottingham (supported by Barclays Private Equity).

# 22

# PRIVATE EQUITY

A private equity (PE) fund is a **pool of capital** raised mainly from institutional investors and then invested by a PE firm. Rather than creating a highly diversified fund, such as a mutual fund, by investing many small amounts in a large number of companies, a PE fund invests large amounts in the entire share capital of a small number of companies. The important thing to appreciate about PE is that, by acquiring the whole share capital of a company (or a minimum of 51%), the fund manager also obtains control of (the ability to direct) the companies which it has acquired.

The **fund** is normally structured as a **limited liability partnership**. The fund is, in turn, controlled by a **general partner**, which is the **management company** or PE firm. The capital in the fund is managed by the **general partner**, while the **limited partners,** who are qualified investors such as pension funds, financial institutions and wealthy individuals, provide the bulk of the funds (though the general partner should also put in funds to help align interests and reduce the agency problems in such firms). The limited partners are not involved in investment decisions, as it is the general partner which manages the fund's investments. The limited partners are, however, involved in the advisory committee which is empowered to decide on some matters. Examples of general partners are the large private equity firms such as KKR, Alchemy, Apollo and CVC Partners.

In Figure 22.1 it should be noted that we show a management company managing the assets of only one fund. In practice the management company is likely to manage many funds (possibly even some dozens) since each fund is liquidated after 7–10 years and thus there needs to be a succession of funds if the private equity management company is to stay in business. The figure is intended to make clear, (as with the 'Generic Collective Fund Structure diagram in Chapter 18) that the fund is a separate legal entity from the private equity management company i.e. the general partner. Within each fund managed by the general partner are what are known as the **portfolio companies** (as shown in the Figure 22.1).

On average, a fund has a life of around ten years. In the first five years, the fund is empowered to acquire investments (companies). In the next five years it should dispose of them, so that by year ten all the portfolio companies have been sold and all cash generated has been returned to investors. The fund will acquire 10–20 companies (both public and private) over the first few years of its life (**the**

**investment period**) and will **liquidate** them, i.e. turn them back into cash, over the last few years of the life of the fund, either through an IPO or a trade sale, or even through sale to another PE company. Thus at the end of this period, the fund itself 'expires'. Thus PE funds are not evergreen funds as hedge funds are.

It is important to appreciate that a new fund cannot immediately invest all the funds it raises since suitable investments (companies) may not be available. PE funds, therefore, draw down cash from the limited partners in the fund in stages. There is thus an initial cash transfer from the limited partners leaving an unfunded commitment to the fund. As a result of this, Figure 18.3 notes that with private equity there is an ongoing risk of 'capital call' i.e. at any time over the five years subsequent to the signing of the limited partnership agreement, even at a time when an limited partner might be short of cash, the general partner can demand another instalment of the committed investment. As portfolio investments (companies to be bought by the fund) are about to be acquired, the manager will call on its limited partners to provide the necessary cash.

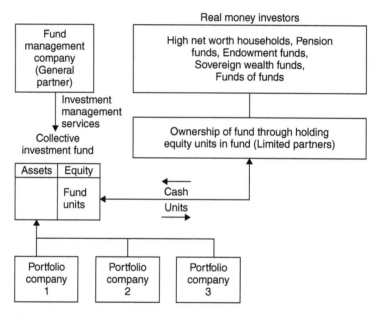

**Figure 22.1**  Private equity fund generic structure of private equity collective investment fund

## TYPES OF PRIVATE EQUITY FUND

**Buyout funds** are the largest funds in the private equity category. These are active in acquiring 100% of (mostly) large public companies or at least a controlling interest of not less than 51%. They generally acquire a company in the public market and frequently sell it back into the public market.

**Growth capital** is another important type of fund which is not necessarily acquiring control but is likely to have active involvement in a company which needs additional resources, perhaps to take a new product it has developed from prototype stage to full production or to expand output of an existing product.

Venture capital (VC) is the third type of private equity. This would involve providing financing to a company which has still not generated profits or even any revenue. It is thus the most risky type of financing since the company has no history as a trading company. Many venture capital investments fail to generate any return and, indeed, may suffer a complete loss of the investment. For this reason there are generally more portfolio companies in a venture capital fund than others in order to provide diversification.

Turnaround is the final type of fund which looks to buy under-performing companies or those in financial difficulties which may be available at a discounted price given the risk that it may not be possible to turn them round.

## WHAT DETERMINES THE PRICE THAT A BIDDER CAN PAY FOR A COMPANY?

One problem for any investor in any company is the asymmetric information problem that we have touched on before. This is the inevitable asymmetry between outsiders and insiders, i.e. between potential investors and the management who run the company. In the case of portfolio investors, they have to rely on their own analysis or that of securities analysts, most of which is undertaken without any 'inside' access. It is unlikely, however, that any private equity investor will consider acquiring a controlling interest in a company without overcoming this asymmetry. They will normally be able to undertake due diligence inside the company, including employing accounting and legal firms to 'look over the books and contracts', and to interview management. By doing this PE investors can reduce the risk they are taking by paying above the market price for a public company or paying the wrong price for a private company.

## ACQUISITION OF A PUBLIC COMPANY

In the case of a bid for a public company, the company already has a valuation which is likely to be close to its 'true' value as perceived by its shareholders. This is the 'fundamental' value of the company given its current management and strategy. To buy the whole company (rather than just the marginal quantity of shares that shareholders happen to want to sell) will require that the bidder offer a price higher than the market price. The reason, obviously, is that many existing shareholders are happy with their investment and they always have the option to sell at any time in the stock market at the current market price. They are therefore likely to sell to a bidder only if they receive a premium. The question for the bidder, therefore, is the size of premium it feels able to offer. Determining this, i.e. the price which will persuade all shareholders to sell yet will enable the fund to generate an adequate return on its investment, is a key skill in the PE business.

## ACQUISITION OF A PRIVATE COMPANY OR A DIVISION OF A PUBLIC COMPANY

A PE fund will also be interested in acquiring private companies. A private company's shares have no market price, although shares may change hands between family members or others at a price based on NAV or on any basis that can be agreed, not in a market place but in a bilateral transaction. More usually, however, the price would be based on a multiple of **earnings before interest, taxation, depreciation and amortisation (EBITDA)**. For PE buyouts this measure of earnings is more relevant than the more normal earnings measure. The multiple to calculate the purchase price would normally be around 6–7 times this amount.

In the case of a division of a public company, the existing owners (in effect the directors of that public company as agents of the shareholders) are unlikely to be willing to sell if they receive from the sale only the pure economic value to the parent. Thus just as with a public company there is a need to pay a premium. The first step for both sides in a potential sale is to make a valuation of the division as it currently exists and the contribution it makes to the share price of the public company which owns it. Thus as in making a bid in a public market, once again the question for any bidder is how much of a premium it is able to pay and still extract value from the transaction.

In order to bid a higher price than the existing (pre-bid) economic value, it is necessary that the bidder have a strategy that will allow it to increase the value of the asset. Such strategies may involve:

## FINANCIAL CHANGES

- Making more efficient use of equity capital by financing much of the acquisition from debt which may have a lower cost than equity.
- Consequently achieving a tax shelter from the fact that debt interest payments are tax deductible, whereas dividend payments are not.
- Issuing additional debt and using the proceeds to buy back equity thus increasing earnings per share.
- Selling off the real estate assets of the company (such as the buildings owned by a hotel chain or the stores owned by a retailer) and then renting the real estate back from the new owner. The capital released can then be paid out to the new owners, i.e. the private equity fund, as a cash dividend.

## REAL CHANGES

PE is, or should be, more about real changes effected within the company than about any financial changes on the balance sheet. In the case of the buyout of a public company, PE is about transferring control of a company from absent shareholders who are not motivated to intervene in company affairs even if poor decisions are being taken since, as we noted earlier, they prefer just to sell out., Control is transferred to a new 'owner', the PE general partner, which can then implement an incentivisation structure within which the agency problem between owners and managers can be minimised. In the case of medium-sized enterprises, public or private, being acquired by a PE firm, there should be an additional benefit of access to a higher level of skills from the general partner than is available within a medium-sized firm. In effect, the managers in the general partnership act like activist shareholders

Employing a more focused and incentivised managerial team who believe they can increase economic value through better management should be the key to

PE. A new management team, motivated with incentives in the form of options on the shares of the company they are managing and no 'legacy' attachments to under-performing parts of the business, are likely to find ways to overcome the x-inefficiencies that exist in most companies such as

● Selling parts of the company where the return on invested capital from that part of the company is less than the overall target;
● Achieving **synergies** by combining the company with another within the private equity portfolio, i.e. undertaking mergers between companies within the portfolio;
● Shutting down loss-making parts of the business which the existing managers were unwilling to do;
● Improving the efficiency of processes in order to cut costs.

If the business which is for sale is securities brokerage, for example, and the PE firm already owns such a business, it is often the case that: the back office of the acquired business can be closed down and staff moved to the existing office; the back office can be closed completely and all the work handled by existing staff; or one computer system can be expanded to run the whole operation. In addition, such an acquisition allows the new owners to fire underperforming brokers in the acquired operation, possibly also in its existing investment, and thus to increase revenue generation per head in the combined business. Equally, clients of the acquired broker who do not generate adequate revenue or who are costly to service may be dropped in a way that would have been difficult prior to takeover.

## FINANCING A PE ACQUISITION

When the company being acquired has been **conservatively financed**, i.e. with a relatively low debt/equity ratio, there may be scope for much more aggressive leverage in the new venture. The funding structure of a deal would involve the following components:

● Senior debt;
● Mezzanine debt;
● Private equity (limited partners) investment;
● Management (management company or individual managers) equity investment.

**Senior debt** is normally secured on the assets of the venture and has first call on the assets in the event of liquidation. It would generally be supplied by a commercial bank and would be subject to conventional ratios such as:

● **Interest cover:** how many times more than the annual interest payment is the pre-tax profit? Today interest cover is often measured in terms of a multiple of earnings before interest, taxation, depreciation and amortisation (EBITDA).
● **Debt/equity ratio:** how much debt relative to equity is there? Banks might enforce a maximum 1:1 ratio, thus limiting how much senior debt could be raised.

- **Collateral:** what assets are available for liquidation in the event of bankruptcy? In the case of service businesses, there are frequently very few realisable assets.

**Mezzanine debt** is so called because it occupies the mid-tier between debt and equity (as in the mezzanine floor in a building between the ground and the first floor). This type of financing is particularly useful in service businesses with few assets which could be used as collateral where traditional bank lenders are unlikely to lend enough to make an acceptable bid possible. This type of lender is likely to be a specialised institution which lends not on the basis of collateral but on expected cash flow and the likelihood that cash flow can support the additional debt. However, given that mezzanine finance is likely to be much more risky than senior debt, the price charged will be considerably higher, probably between that of senior debt and the expected return on the equity component. Often this type of financing will be provided partly as a **pay-in-kind** loan. This is similar to a zero coupon bond. Rather than paying interest year by year the interest is rolled up and compounded year by year and paid at the final maturity. This type of financing might involve an interest rate of 15% (which if all paid in cash would be very high indeed and almost an equity return) but only 50% (a 7.5% rate of return) is paid in cash. The remaining 7.5% is rolled up and not paid until maturity.

**PE limited partnership investment** is the equity component of the financing provided by the limited partners in the PE fund. This may be as little as 30% of the total financing but more normally would be 50% (a 1:1 debt to equity ratio). Even a 30:70 proportion of equity to debt, while it is a much lower proportion of equity than most public companies, is still very substantially lower than is employed by banks which prior to the crisis had, in some cases, a 3: 97 proportion of equity to debt!

**Management equity investment** is any equity investment made by the managers of the portfolio company which has been acquired by the PE company. This is designed to demonstrate a congruence of interests between the outside investors and the senior employees of the management company.

A PE fund bidder may be willing to offer a higher price than a trade buyer despite the synergies that the trade buyer may be able to realise simply because the private equity bid will involve less equity investment as it is financed by a higher proportion of debt. Such a capital structure will leverage up the return on equity capital for a given return on assets if the investment is a success but equally, of course, if it is not, it will reduce the ROE compared with what it would have been with a less leveraged structure due to the mandatory interest payments.

Just as it is important to understand the distinction between the fund itself as a company and the management company it is also important to understand that there are two levels of company on the fund side. At the first level, the fund itself. This is simply a holding company for the second level which is the PE investments i.e. the portfolio companies which are the actual operating companies which the PE manager has acquired on behalf of the fund. The fund (which in turn is owned by the institutional investors) owns all the companies at portfolio level though each of these companies **is itself a limited liability company**. This means that if its liabilities exceed its assets and its creditors force it into liquidation, once the value of shareholder funds invested in the acquisition has been lost, the portfolio company's shareholder (the fund itself) can lose no more. Any further losses fall on the creditors, i.e. the debt holders. To achieve this, **the debt required to finance the acquisition of a portfolio company is actually raised by the portfolio company itself, not by the fund**. This means that each venture (portfolio company) stands alone and is not supported by the fund in the event of losses beyond the invested equity in that company alone. If this were not the case and borrowing were undertaken at the fund level, lenders to each of the companies in the portfolio would have the right to force the fund itself and hence any company in the fund into liquidation in order to recover their losses. Thus when an acquisition is being financed, the company being acquired raises the debt to pay for its own purchase secured on its own assets. There must therefore be simultaneity between the transfer of ownership and the raising of 'leveraged debt' to finance the acquisition. Figure 22.2 shows a financing structure, though it does not make it clear that the debt financing is actually issued by the portfolio companies (target companies) and not by the fund.

Ultimately the objective of private equity is to generate higher returns than the public market and, ideally, returns not highly correlated with the public market. Whether this is achieved or not is an open question. Some research suggests it does achieve both objectives. Other studies suggest not. To a great extent it depends on being in the right fund at the right time. On average it would be surprising if funds, which buy out from the public market at a premium, sell back into the public market at a later date, and meantime take out a 2% annual management fee, and 20% of all returns generated, were to provide a return in excess of the public market even given any real improvements in the operation of the company. In addition, if the fund buys in the public market and sells back to the public market, it is quite likely that its returns are quite highly correlated with the public market rather than providing an 'alternative' investment to the market.

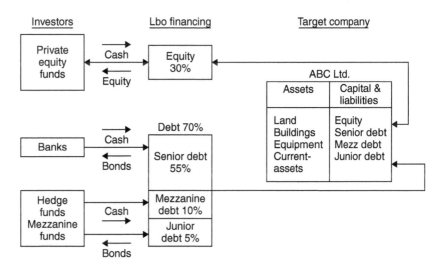

**Figure 22.2**   Financing a leveraged buyout (LBO) by a PE fund

# THE SECONDARY MARKET IN PE PARTICIPATIONS (SECONDARIES)

Holders of participations in PE funds hold an illiquid asset. There is no liquidity provided by the manager of such a fund for the obvious reason that it is whole companies that the fund invests in, not marginal percentages of the share capital, as in the case of hedge funds. The investor in PE has an additional problem compared with the investor in hedge funds. He or she agrees to participate in a PE fund but is only required to provide the actual funds once the manager has found suitable assets to purchase. Such unfunded commitments give rise to the possibility that, at the time of a call for funds, the investor has its own liquidity problem and is unable to meet the commitment. In this case the manager is entitled to sell the participation in the fund for whatever price can be realised. This could result in the investor making substantial losses.

The alternative is to try to sell the participation, and the unfunded commitment, to another investor. In fact the market in secondaries is reasonably large (around $20 billion of transactions each year) and some funds specialise in buying secondaries. In good times these may sell at a premium to NAV while, in difficult times, they are likely to sell at a discount.

# A COMPARISON OF TWO ALTERNATIVE ASSET CLASSES

In this chapter I have considered mostly the management and control issues associated with PE. However, this asset class has been created because it is believed to provide investors with an alternative which, within a diversified portfolio, offers good investment opportunities (higher return than the market and low correlation with the market)

As with hedge funds, a key problem for investors is that while top quartile funds have in the past generated returns well in excess of 'the market' other funds have at best only equalled it. Thus manager selection is critical. For this reason, any investor intending to add this asset class to a portfolio should consider accessing it through a fund-of-funds rather than through direct investment in individual PE funds. Choosing a fund-of-funds also involves manager selection risk. The role of the fund of funds manager is threefold. One is to select, from the total universe of PE funds, particular funds which the manager believes are likely to be in the top quartile of performance. Another is to eliminate from these, those where there are issues raised by the due diligence process. Finally, the aim is to create a portfolio of funds to achieve a desired risk/expected return outcome.

Selecting funds and selecting fund of fund managers is made somewhat easier by the fact that PE is (or should be) a real asset management activity and not a financial asset management activity. The ability to be a good real asset manager is something at which people improve over time through a learning process. Thus there is some 'persistence' of a succession of good returns from particular general partnerships. This is in contrast to active long-only fund managers and hedge funds where there is little persistence of superior performance. The reason is that long-only and hedge fund managers operate in relatively efficient financial markets where luck is often a key component of periodic success, whereas PE managers operate in relatively inefficient real markets where (real management) skill is important and can be learned and improved on. However, at times when new investors are anxious to acquire participations in the new fund of a particular general partner which has had outstanding returns in the past, it is likely that it will be fully subscribed by existing investors in its older funds. Such investors are generally keen to 'rollover' their realisation from one fund which has just been liquidated into the new fund being offered by the same manager. Thus access is likely to be limited to just this group of which fund-of-fund companies are a substantial part. Table 18.3 which compares the different features of – hedge and PE, emphasises the importance of investors appreciating the very substantial differences between these two alternative asset classes.

PART
**VI**

# INTERNAL RISK MANAGEMENT AND EXTERNAL REGULATION OF FINANCIAL INTERMEDIARIES AND MARKETS

# 23

# RISK MANAGEMENT IN CREDIT INTERMEDIARIES AND INVESTMENT BANKS

All companies need to undertake risk management in order to minimise the possibility of unexpected events having catastrophic outcomes. Banks and investment banks are in the business of dealing in risk – it is their 'stock-in-trade' – through their activities in securities and derivatives markets. If they are to be able to provide risk management services to clients they need to manage their own risks in order to ensure that they stay in business. Also, banks are much more highly leveraged than any other type of company and thus a relatively small fall in the value of their assets can easily wipe out their capital.

Prior to the financial crisis, many banks had invested in the debt of other banks and financial intermediaries and also in sovereign debt. As the market prices of such debt rose, banks which held such debt on their **trading** books were able to record gains. As such gains accrue to shareholders, this means that the bank's capital increased. On the basis of this increase in total capital, banks were able to acquire further debt (without having to increase leverage) and thus to increase the total size of their balance sheets. However, once the price of such assets collapses, this process reverses. Such a fall in the value of assets in a leveraged institution quickly generates losses which may exceed the amount of capital the bank has. Thus market failure, i.e. mispricing of assets causing an unwarranted rise in price followed by an excessive decline in price, can easily lead to the failure of financial institutions.

Governments rarely intervene to save corporates if they are likely to collapse but frequently intervene to save banks. This is because if a non-bank company is forced out of business as a result of an unexpected risk, it may have little impact on the wider economy. However, if a large bank goes out of business, it impacts the provision of credit and payment services which has more severe consequences than the cessation of output by other types of company. Governments may believe that as a result they have to follow the **too large to fail** doctrine, which means providing support to banks in financial distress.

It is not only that individual banks may collapse. Even more important is the fact that banks are much more interlinked with each other than other types of company, through, for example, the interbank market and derivative contracts, and thus there is greater **systemic risk** in the banking system, i.e. the risk of one bank's actions impacting on others and leading to financial instability and crisis with implications for the wider economy that don't apply to any other sector. As we shall also see, even if there are no **direct** links between financial companies, the impact of the actions of one bank or investment firm through its decisions on the market value of assets held on its balance sheet (and in particular asset sales which generate a true market price), can impact on many other financial institutions as it may cause them to have to mark-to-market at the same levels. When they do this it may lead to them being balance sheet insolvent.

Financial instability of this type causes problems in credit provision, the functioning of the payments system and in the risk management services available to corporates and households. Because of this, one key role of government is the maintenance of financial stability which is the **on-going provision of credit intermediation (deposit taking and lending), risk management and payments systems** by setting up mechanisms to minimise such risks. A key weapon is trying to ensure that they have appropriate internal governance. Since the business of banking is dealing in risk, the management of risk in banking is a key management function.

## RISK MANAGEMENT AND RISK MEASUREMENT

Too often risk management becomes confused with mathematical models or with a set of regulatory requirements which happen to be in force in a particular country at a particular time, such as Basel II regulations. While models are critical and the regulatory framework lays down **minimum** standards, risk management starts as a management process rather than as a set of techniques or regulatory compliance. Risk management in a bank is a process which starts at the very top of a company by:

- Defining a business strategy;
- Developing a business model;
- Identifying the risks to the company from this model (and its potential returns);
- Quantifying the risks;
- Ensuring that senior management and all lower management levels in the company understand the risks and take account of them.

It also involves having a reward system for employees (a bonus system) which does not amplify risk by encouraging excessive risk taking. Thus the remuneration structure has to be consonant with the risk management objectives.

The risk management process involves the checks and balances the company employs to try to ensure that the business model and the risks to which it subjects the company do not destroy it. This involves having, amongst other things, a risk management unit in the company that is 'independent' of the operating units, a process of risk reporting and an oversight process by senior managers and the board of the company.

A good example of a financial company which did not have such processes in place was Northern Rock. It had a business model which involved expanding its lending much faster than any other lender in the UK (using brokers who were incentivised to bring in lending business for a fee but without bearing any risk), financing the balance sheet mainly from wholesale sources of funds which are not 'sticky', lending at higher (borrower) income multiples and higher loan to value ratios than any other lender (thus creating more risky loans), and generating smaller realised lending spreads from loans than any other bank which in some cases would seem to have been negative.

This was probably not a viable business model in any economic environment, and once the UK economy witnessed an increase in liquidity preference (i.e. savers and lenders wanted to conserve their own liquidity), the model simply collapsed. Clearly the risk assessment processes in that bank and the management oversight of them were not appropriate for such a business. In addition, however, it is clear that the regulator was not taking note of the 'outlier' nature of this business model, i.e. a model being used by other banks but not to the extreme limits that Northern Rock took it to. Alternatively, of course, the supervisors from the FSA were unwilling to try to second-guess management and intervene, even when they saw a 'red flag', particularly given the aggressive nature of the CEO towards anyone who took a different view from him. Equally, shareholders were either not aware of the outlier nature of the business model or were also not willing to second guess management or were quite happy as long as 'profits' seemed to roll in. Today the FSA has said it will evaluate business models and come to a view on whether or not a strategy is viable.

It could be said that Northern Rock collapsed because its business model was not viable. Alternatively it could be said that it was able to employ this business model because the checks and balances within the capitalist system – the board with its independent directors, the regulatory supervisor with its powers of intervention, analysts with their power to make valuations that differed from the current share price and shareholders with their power to dismiss directors – did not function as mechanisms to control and manage risk. That is, **the governance system failed**.

## WHAT IS RISK IN A BANK?

Banks, as we noted earlier, hold risky assets on two parts of their balance sheet:

- The **banking book** which is where, traditionally, commercial banks held loans;
- The **trading book** which is where, traditionally, investment banks held trading positions which would include positions long and short in fixed income, forwards, swaps and options.

Today, commercial banks are also heavily involved in trading as well as lending. Investment banks may also be involved in lending as well as trading and may in addition have extensive proprietary investments on their balance sheet. Thus for either type of bank both locations on the balance sheet are relevant and give rise to risks. It should be understood, however, that these 'locations' on the balance sheet are simply different line entries. **But it is the different regulatory classification of possibly the same asset which may determine how risk is assessed and the** amount of capital required to be held against the assessed risk. This can give rise to management choosing to arbitrage between the two books.

## THE MAJOR BANKING RISKS

### Credit and counterparty risk

I have put these two categories of risk under the same heading as both are risks that result from having an outstanding contract between the bank and a third party. In the case of credit risk, the contract is between the bank and a borrower, and in the case of counterparty risk it is a contract between one bank and another bank or financial institution in respect of a securities trade, a derivative trade or an interbank loan. Such contracts give rise to a creditor/debtor (i.e. asset/liability) position on the balance sheet which may be short term but is still very real. Credit and counterparty risks are the risk that the customer or counterparty does not pay amounts due under a contract on the due date. Generally the risk of such default arises from financial difficulties of the borrower or counterparty, and such difficulties obviously include bankruptcy. Lehman's bankruptcy is the classic case of counterparty risk manifesting itself on the balance sheets of its counterparties leading to large write-offs on their profit and loss accounts.

Clearly the senior management in a bank needs to take measures to limit such risks and to try to ensure that credit and counterparty risk cannot result in their bank failing. In the case of **counterparty exposure** one element in minimising the risk of such exposure involves having **counterparty limits** which are designed to avoid too much outstanding risk with a single counterparty, i.e. to limit the amount that will be lost if a particular counterparty defaults to an amount that will not put the bank in danger. In the case of **lending**, there are rules on the total amount (relative to total lending or to bank capital) that can be lent to a single borrower, and also industry limits and country limits. Such limits reduce **concentration risk**. In addition, of course, loan pricing is designed to try to ensure that the credit spread covers expected loss. That is a key protection against credit risk. However, if risk estimates are substantially below the outturn, then the unexpected loss can threaten the survival of the bank.

### Market or price risk

Market risk arises from holding assets which have a **market price** as distinct from loan assets which do not trade on a market and thus do not have a market price. Market risk is the risk of the price of an asset changing during the holding period. However, the definition of 'market price' has become flexible. Many OTC instruments do not trade actively on a market and thus there is no continuous price history of trading as there might be with a widely traded equity. Even more problematic is assets which nominally are traded but which actually virtually never trade (for example many CDOs) and where transaction prices, if any, are not disclosed to the public. Such assets may be priced using mathematical models and are said to be **marked-to model**-rather than marked-to-market. Indeed, so obscure are some of the models pricing using them is sometimes described as **marked-to-myth**.

There are a number of different market risks including equity price risk, commodity price risk, foreign exchange price risk, derivative price risk and interest rate risk.

## MEASURING AND MANAGING MARKET RISK: VALUE AT RISK (VAR)

While assets held on the banking book (which are intended to be held to maturity) are valued on the basis of historic cost adjusted for any actual losses, assets held on the trading book are valued daily at their market price. This daily **MTM** leads to a potentially high volatility in the value of the trading book assets. Any change in the market value of the portfolio (either an increase or a decrease) has to be transferred daily to the profit and loss account which in turn is reflected by a change in the amount of equity capital on the balance sheet. Thus while an increase in asset values over a day will give a gain in profit from that day's trading, falling asset values result in a write-off to the profit and loss account and hence a reduction in shareholders' funds.

**VAR** tries to estimate for each area of market risk (equities, fixed income, commodities, currencies) how much each portfolio might lose (with a given percentage probability) over a time period. Thus if the bank holds a portfolio of equities worth £100 million, and if the managers of the bank want to know at a 99% confidence level what loss they might expect over a ten-day trading period, then VAR will give them that information. For example, it might be that at the time in question there is a 99% probability that there will, on average, be a loss of £7 million **or more** during one out of every 100 ten-day trading periods.

But how can this be known? The answer is that we look at the past to see just how volatile the asset price was. We take the statistics for each type of asset we hold and gather the information on its past volatility. **If we assume the future is like the past**, then we can know the likelihood of making such losses. An important caveat which greatly reduces the value of VAR as a useful measure of risk, however, is that if we use volatility over a recent, very calm, period in the market, it will not include periods when markets suddenly crash. Thus it may underestimate the chance of a large loss. VAR does **not** tell us the maximum loss we can make – only that the loss is likely to be the VAR amount **or more**. Thus VAR has severe limitations. These limitations are brutally exposed in a postscript to Chapter 28 (pp ....) where I note that JP Morgan reported a loss of $2bn (supposedly from hedging activities) in May 2012 at a time when VAR was reported as $67m.

The value of VAR, however, is that since it can be used right across a bank's various business areas (and it can now also be used for credit risk), it provides a way of aggregating risk. It is thus a useful measure, at least in the sense that it should show if the overall risk of a bank is suddenly increasing, which enables management to take action to reduce risk to bring VAR back down to a lower level. Unfortunately, in the run-up to the financial crisis in 2007, VAR showed risk as declining when in fact it was rising sharply! This was because volatility of asset prices had been falling since the turn of the millennium ('**The Great Moderation**') and VAR calculations based on previous years during an upturn of the cycle did not reflect the fact that cycles also, and perhaps inevitably, turn down at some point. Thus the historical record that was being used for VAR calculations, rather than covering a whole cycle – up and down – only covered the up-phase. This is known as point-in-time volatility, as distinct from **through-the-cycle volatility**. Figure 23.1 gives an indication of just how mis-leading volatility indexes were in the run-up to the financial crisis. Volatility was clearly very high around 2001 at the time of the dot.com crash but fell from that point on until the crisis hit.

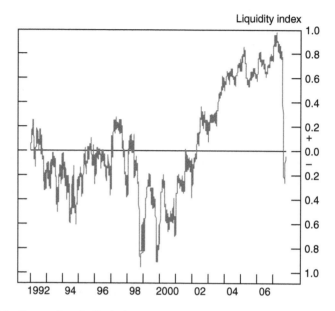

**Figure 23.1** Composite volatility index

*Note*: The liquidity index shows the number of standard deviations from the mean. It is a simple unweighted average of nine liquidity measures, normalised on the period 1999–2004. Data shown are an exponentially weighted moving average. The indicator is more reliable after 1997 as it is based on a greater number of underlying measures. Data have been revised following methodological changes. See April 2007 Report, box 2: Financial market liquidity, p. 18.

*Source*: Bank of England Financial Stability Report October 2007 (p. 44), http://www.bankofengland.co.uk/publications/Documents/fsr/2007/fsrfull0710.pdf (accessed 6 March 2012); Bloomberg, Chicago Board Options Exchange, Debt Management Office, London Stock Exchange, Merrill Lynch, Thomson DataStream and Bank calculations.

# BALANCE SHEET RISKS

## Interest rate risk and asset and liability management (ALM)

Traditionally, **apart from credit risk**, the main risk in running a bank was that the relationship between assets and liabilities could change in a way that caused substantial variations in profit. Thus while credit risk management and market risk management involve managing principally the asset side of the balance sheet, in ALM the objective is to match the two sides of the balance sheet to keep mismatch risk to an appropriate level. This is very similar in concept to the use of liability driven investment in asset portfolios such as pension funds where the objective is to avoid dramatic changes in the value of assets relative to the liabilities (pension payments).

Interest rate risk arises when a bank finances a long-term loan (asset) with a short-term liability. Since short-term interest rates can vary continuously, it is quite possible for the interest received on the loan to fall below that on the liability that is financing the loan. This is known as **negative carry**, i.e. the spread position is long the asset and short the liability which has a **carrying cost**: a negative spread instead of a positive one. If this happens, the bank will lose money on the loan. Banks operate, as we have already noted, by borrowing short and lending long. Thus if all bank loans were at a fixed-rate for long terms, while all financing was short-term at variable rates, a sharp rise in interest rates would cause the bank to start to show losses on all its loans.

The normal risk management method to avoid this mismatch is to link the interest rate on the loan (asset) to the bank's borrowing cost (cost of liabilities). Thus, most longer-term loans are priced at what are known as **floating rates** which means on the basis of 1, 3, 6 or 12 month **LIBOR + a spread** to reflect the level of risk. Simultaneously with the loan being arranged, the bank or the borrower could take out an interest rate swap which converts a fixed rate to a floating rate or vice versa if either of them wished to change the nature of the risk they had taken on.

In practice, of course, bank balance sheets are much more complex than this. But the principle is the same – there is a need to calculate the mismatches between the two sides of the balance sheet and decide whether the implied risks are greater than the bank wishes to accept. One of the most used techniques for doing this is known as **gap analysis**. The meaning of 'gap' is the difference between interest sensitive assets and interest sensitive liabilities in a given time interval. The gap method involves categorising assets and liabilities according to how often they are repriced, for example, a one-month deposit is repriced every month. Thus at the end of the month, the bank might have to pay a higher interest rate on it. A five-year loan might have annual repricing. The periods for analysis might start at 'overnight' money, moving on to one week, one month, three months, six months and twelve months. In each of these periods, the ideal from the point of view of minimising gap risk would be for the assets and liabilities in each time period to be equal, i.e. no gaps.

Of course, if there are no gaps, it is very unlikely that the bank can make much profit since it makes profits from taking a maturity mismatch risk when the **yield curve** is upward sloping, i.e. when long-term interest rates are above short-term ones. Thus ALM risk management is about deciding how much **mismatch** risk the bank is willing to take.

## Managing liquidity risk

A similar approach can be taken to managing liquidity risk. Here the gap is defined in terms of **net liquid assets**. This is the difference between liquid assets (which can be sold to realise cash) and volatile liabilities (liabilities that might run-off). Managing the gap is designed to ensure that the bank is not taken unawares by a liquidity problem of its own making. However, it is much harder for it to protect itself against systemic risk problems such as those that arose during the financial crisis, i.e. extreme and rare scenarios. Such scenarios can give rise to **funding risk** which is the risk that the liquidity it expects to be able to raise from the wholesale market becomes unavailable just at the time when it is needed.

## Other risks

There are many other risks to which banks and other financial institutions are subject. These include settlement/payment risk, operational risk, reputational risk and sovereign and political risks on assets in the form of government securities or loans to countries where political risk is high.

## MANAGING THE BANK

The directors of a bank have a responsibility to manage it in such a way as to maximise 'shareholder value'. As in any business it is necessary to take risks in order to generate a satisfactory return. Banking is rather different from other industries, however, in that there are substantial **externalities** if a bank is heading to insolvency. This arises for two reasons. First, if a large bank goes out of business there is a withdrawal of credit and payment facilities from existing customers who may have outstanding arrangements with the bank. Replacing credit facilities is likely to prove costly for many customers, which is much less so than for the products of other companies such as motor cars. Second, and most importantly, because the central bank has a responsibility to maintain financial stability, this may mean that a bank in difficulty may have to be rescued at public expense. Thus in the case of banks, the costs of excessive risk-taking may be passed on to customers and taxpayers and not all assumed by shareholders and bondholders.

In order to minimise the risk of insolvency or illiquidity, the directors of a bank should:

1. Allocate funds to assets based on the level of risk, including both credit and liquidity risk, so that the return on assets is expected to be appropriate for the level of risk taken;
2. Ensure that the bank has adequate liquidity for all but the most extreme, and rare, scenarios;
3. Ensure that the total risk to which the bank (or other financial institution) is subject is not so great in relation to its total capital and its liquidity position that, in the event of a change in market environment, the bank could become insolvent (bankrupt) or illiquid and unable to overcome the problem through management action.

## CAPITAL AND LIQUIDITY RATIOS

We have noted a number of times that capital is what provides protection to creditors. It is the assurance that investors need in order to persuade them to lend. Charles Bean of the Bank of England describes the role of capital thus:

> Capital is essential because it is the means by which intermediaries persuade creditors that they will almost surely get their money back ... Extending guarantees on funding,

whether retail or wholesale is another way to make creditors believe that they will get their money back.

The Great Moderation, the Great Panic and<br>
the Great Contraction – Speech given in Barcelona on<br>
25 August 2009[1]

But the question remains: how much equity capital is sufficient? Unfortunately there is no answer to this question. On the question of how much liquidity is required, unfortunately there is also no answer. In the first instance it is up to the directors of a bank, as the agents of the shareholders, to decide how much capital to employ (i.e. how much leverage, since the remainder of the balance sheet must be liabilities) and also how much maturity mismatch to allow and hence how to decide if the balance sheet is adequately liquid. The requirements of regulators should be only the second line of defence.

Evidence from bank insolvency over decades suggests that some boards of directors and managers will take more risk of insolvency and more risk of illiquidity than society might deem appropriate, given society's interest in financial stability. What this means is the public – taxpayers and voters – have an economic interest in every bank's capital and liquidity decisions. Private decisions by directors in these two areas generate the possibility of externalities, i.e. costs which accrue to others than the shareholders. However, directors and managers are concerned only with the private costs of failure. Given the substantial additional costs that have to be borne by society as a whole (negative externalities) in the event of a bank collapsing, most countries have chosen, through laws on bank capital and liquidity, to limit the degree of risk-taking by this particular type of company (banks) and to regulate their capital structure. This disparity between public and private costs is an example of one type of **market failure** which is a situation in which the pursuit of one set of individuals' self-interest can lead to results which are not efficient for another set of individuals (in this case taxpayers) and where state intervention (in this case by regulation of capital and liquidity ratios) can lead to a better chance of an optimal outcome from the point of view of society as a whole.

## MINIMUM CAPITAL REQUIREMENTS

We have noted above that it is the duty of directors of a company as agents of the owners (shareholders) to optimise the trade-off between risk and return, including the decision on the appropriate debt/equity ratio. However, to ensure that all banks have at least **a minimum** percentage of capital, banks worldwide are required to follow a set of rules agreed by the Basel Committee of Banking Supervisors which specify the required minimum amount of capital a bank must hold relative to its (risk-weighted) assets. Before we look in more detail at the Basel framework, however, we need to understand how banks actually operate

---

[1] http://www.bankofengland.co.uk/publications/Documents/speeches/2009/speech399.pdf

in practice in order to see why they have very precise regulations on government capital and liquidity.

## HOW BANKS GENERATE THEIR RETURN ON EQUITY CAPITAL

Banks are financial intermediaries that take on various types of risk in order to meet the needs of the household and corporate sectors. By managing those risks in an appropriate way, they generate utility for their two sets of customers who are on opposite sides of the balance sheet (remember that banks are financial intermediaries who make profits by standing between the two sides of the balance sheet, i.e. two sets of customers):

- **Depositors** who accept that they have to pay a price in terms of a relatively low rate of return on an asset (a bank demand deposit) which has the features of being of fixed value, instantly redeemable for cash (instantly liquid) and instantly transferable to others through the bank's payment systems (demand deposit);
- **Borrowers** who are willing to pay interest costs and fees in excess of the amount paid out to depositors in order to obtain (funding) liquidity which enables the bank to generate a return on capital which is acceptable to its investors.

Many banks start their planning process with a target return on equity which they believe is required to satisfy shareholders. The minimum return required is the market return for an equity of comparable risk to the bank's shares and might be, say, 12%. But the economics of banking is such that the **return on assets** is relatively small. Thus to achieve such target rates of return on equity requires a high degree of leverage.

Leverage, i.e. the use of debt rather than equity to finance asset holdings, is higher in banking than in other industries. Leverage involves risk (risk of insolvency and illiquidity) but also amplifies return. In the two hypothetical examples below, the first represents a conservative bank which has a low implied leverage. The second is one with a leverage ratio that was not unusual a few years ago but clearly suggests a high degree of risk of bank failure.

The appropriate leverage ratio is one of the key decision variables for the board as agents of the shareholders. However, in this industry, unlike others, regulators also take a particular interest in capital structure because of the public interest concerns if a bank should become illiquid or insolvent. They do this by setting a minimum capital requirement that, indirectly, sets a maximum leverage ratio. Much of a bank's income is not interest income but fee income, which does not require the use of the balance sheet. The leverage ratios are, therefore, only indicative. Also, the leverage ratio traditionally used by regulators is not a simple equity/

**Table 23.1** Bank ROA, ROE and leverage

| | Return on assets (%) | Return on capital (%) | Implied leverage (debt/equity ratio) |
|---|---|---|---|
| Bank A | 2 | 12 | 6 times |
| Bank B | 0.4 | 16 | 40 times |

total assets ratio, but equity as a percentage of **risk-adjusted assets**. This means that if a bank holds assets which, for whatever reason, are viewed as low risk, then the true debt/equity ratio can be **very** much higher than for a bank where the same volume of assets are viewed as highly risky. The bank may also appear to be low risk when in practice it is a high risk business due to assets being (intentionally) classified as lower risk than they really are in order to make the capital ratio appear better than it really is. In-house risk models can be very effective at achieving this objective.

Increasingly regulators are starting to take cognisance of non risk-adjusted leverage ratios, i.e. using the ratio of equity to total assets rather than to risk-adjusted assets. Just how highly leveraged many banks were is shown in Figure 23.2. The average ratio in mid-2008 was close to 50 times. Some banks were at over 60 times. By 2011 ratios are more reasonable but can be seen to be rising again in 2011. You might consider whether regulators should have intervened in the case of banks which were clearly 'outliers' in the period from 2004–08. It was not difficult for them to spot (for example Northern Rock must be the bank at the very top of the chart with a ratio approaching 70 times). However, it might have been harder to do anything about it, given the UK regulator's so-called 'light-touch' approach. It was believed back in those days that large banks knew what they were doing and that market forces would prevent them behaving in ways which could threaten their survival and thus regulators were reluctant to intervene.

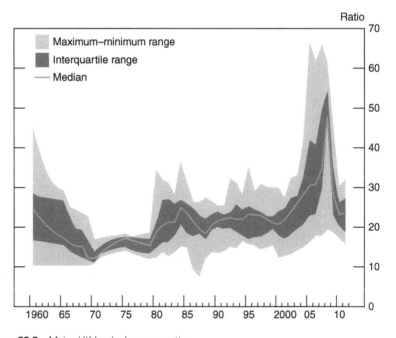

**Figure 23.2**  Major UK banks leverage ratios

*Source*: Bank of England, Financial Stability Report, December 2010 (p. 52), http://www.bankofengland.co.uk/publications/Documents/fsr/2010/fsrfull1012.pdf (accessed 6 March 2012), published accounts and Bank calculations.

# 24

# REGULATION OF BANKS AND INVESTMENT BANKS: BASEL I, II AND III

A director of a company owes the company a **duty of care** and a **duty of loyalty**. In general, under the 'business judgement rule', if a board of directors exercises these duties appropriately, the members of the board will be protected from liability (to shareholders) for their actions. In effect, there is a presumption that, in making business decisions, directors act on an informed basis. However, this presumption can be overcome by showing that the board was grossly negligent in its decision-making. The directors and officers of a bank thus have the responsibility of, amongst other things, minimising the chance of their company failing due to liquidity or solvency problems which they could have anticipated. This responsibility arises from general company law. However, because of the importance of banks to the economic stability and growth of an economy, governments generally do not just rely on company law. Instead they have set up a regulatory framework which banks must follow. This framework is designed not only to minimise the risk of a bank collapsing and the cost of rescue should it collapse, but also to try to ensure that it does not act against the interests of its customers. That banks may do this, even with regulation, is emphasised in a statement by the Governor of the Bank of England in an interview in 2011:

> Since 'Big Bang' in financial services in the 1980s, Mr King goes on, too many in financial services have thought 'if it's possible to make money out of gullible or unsuspecting customers, particularly institutional customers, that is perfectly acceptable.
>
> Interview with Charles Moore,
> *The Daily Telegraph*, 5 March 2011.

Financial regulation is, therefore, trying to achieve two things – fair behaviour towards customers and, most importantly from the point of view of this text, financial stability.

## WHAT IS FINANCIAL SERVICES REGULATION?

Regulation is of two types:

- **Conduct of business** to provide protection to clients of financial services firms who are not as well informed as employees of these firms in matters such as whether or not the product being sold to them is appropriate for their needs (an example of asymmetric information);

* **Prudential (also called safety and soundness)** to protect clients from the possibility of the financial services firm going out of business before it has met its contractual obligations to its customers.

## Conduct of business rules

The key difference between financial services and products purchased in a store or even a motor car is that only the **expected** benefits of a financial services product are known at the time of contract and, in comparison with other purchases, obtaining redress is much harder. The main reasons for this are:

1. The firm may be dishonest in its marketing and may mis-sell products and therefore the expected benefits may not materialise;
2. Investment returns (what is being purchased) are unknown and can only finally be known at a date well into the future, i.e. at the maturity of the product;
3. The product may have flaws in its design;
4. The firm may go out of business before it delivers the expected benefits.

In these regards financial products and services, like most professional services, are different, at least in degree, from most manufactured products, where it is relatively easy to judge quality in advance or where means are available to insure against poor quality (third-party backed guarantees on products and extended warranties on cars, for example).

As a result of these differences, there are regulations such as: **know your customer (KYC)** which require firms to ask an extensive set of questions prior to suggesting a financial solution; **suitability tests** to ensure that the product is suitable for the needs of the particular customer; or the requirement to have a **cooling off period** of perhaps a week during which an already signed contract can be rescinded by the customer.

Conduct of business rules are generally very detailed and are often developed by lawyers working for regulatory authorities. They are also in considerable part developed with reference to the sale of products to **retail clients** rather than to **professional** investors through wholesale markets. But the division between the two may not be as clear as was once thought. The fraud case brought by the SEC against Goldman Sachs in April 2010 in relation to the sale of CDOs hinged on whether or not a counterparty in such a transaction (in this case IKB, a German bank) was a **professional counterparty**. If so, it should have understood the product being sold to it, i.e. there would have been no asymmetry of knowledge between the counterparties. Alternatively, if IKB had been a **retail client**, i.e. which could be interpreted as one which would be assumed to have less knowledge than Goldman, there would have been an asymmetry of information.[1] Unfortunately

---

[1] This question of the duty that an investment banker owes towards clients and counterparties is not a new one. In 1994, Proctor and Gamble, one of the world's largest companies, lost $195 million on interest rate swap contracts it had taken out with Bankers Trust

the case was settled out of court with a record fine paid by Goldman to the SEC of half a billion dollars and thus no US case law came into existence to suggest how courts would make such a distinction between investors in the future. The distinction between retail and sophisticated investors may be changed if not by regulators then by securities firms themselves.

## Prudential regulation

Prudential regulations are imposed by the state in almost every country to try to ensure that the directors and officers of firms, in particular banks, behave prudently, i.e. that they do not take excessive risk which could threaten the survival of the firm and hence, given the need to ensure financial stability, lead to costs that taxpayers had to meet. These rules focus on the **capital structure** of the institution and also to a lesser extent, at least to date, on the **amount of liquidity** it holds – aspects of business that are **not** regulated in other industries.

**Prudential regulation** is enforced for banks and other types of financial institution for two reasons:

• To protect retail and wholesale customers directly from the collapse of the financial institution with which they have a contract (customers of the particular financial institution) and from which they might suffer loss;
• To minimise the risk of the failure of one bank from insolvency – causing the failure of others (**systemic risk**) that would not otherwise fail through insolvency – and thereby to protect customers of other financial institutions and taxpayers from the cost of bank rescues.

The detailed prudential regulation and the close supervision of banks in contrast to other industries is imposed because it is believed that there is the possibility of **market failure**[2] which requires action by the state to minimise **spillover** effects if a bank collapses. A spillover is an effect on others which the shareholders and directors of the bank are unlikely to take account of in their consideration of how much risk the bank should bear (because it does not impose direct costs on them or their shareholders).

Prudential regulation is mainly concerned with ensuring that the firm is able to remain in business even if there is a fall in revenue, a fall in the value of financial

---

(now Deutsche Bank) and refused to pay BT this amount (being an OTC contract, BT had not required margin payments even when the contract went against Proctor and Gamble). Proctor and Gamble claimed that BT did not fully explain the potential risks of the swaps. An out-of-court settlement was reached, thus we do not have case law arising from this transaction. But prior to the settlement, the judge in the case said that BT had a duty of good faith under New York State commercial law. Such a duty arises if one party has superior information and this information is not available to the other party.

[2] Government intervention may be appropriate when markets do not work optimally, i.e. there is a Pareto sub-optimal allocation of resources in a market/industry. Markets may not always allocate scarce resources efficiently in a manner which achieves the highest total social welfare.

assets held by the firm, an increase in its liabilities or a problem with liquidity. It is, in other words, principally concerned with the following four things:

- The need to have adequate **capital** to cover losses on **customer assets (bank loans)** on the banking book if adverse unexpected outcomes materialise, i.e. to protect against insolvency;
- The need to have adequate capital to cover **mark-to-market losses** on the trading book;
- The need to have adequate **liquidity** to meet depositor demand for cash in exchange for **deposit liabilities** when they fall due, and to minimise the risk of illiquidity;
- The need to have adequate **liquidity** to enable the bank to survive if it is having a temporary problem rolling over its wholesale liabilities.

**Regulation of capital** is designed to reduce the likelihood of a bank becoming insolvent. Insolvency arises from the value of a bank's assets falling below the value of its liabilities. The more equity a bank has relative to debt the safer it will be, but the more debt it has relative to equity, the more profitable it will be as it is then more highly leveraged. In order to achieve high returns on equity banks naturally include substantial debt, i.e. deposits and other forms of debt such as bonds, commercial paper, sale and repurchase agreements (repo) and interbank loans on their balance sheet. They are thus enabled to leverage up the return on equity from the relatively small return which they generate on assets.

More equity financing relative to debt makes a bank safer but may raise the cost of funding and hence the price at which it lends. The question for regulators is, first, how to measure risk and, second, what is the optimal trade-off between risk and additional capital to provide protection to depositors, debt holders and taxpayers if the state expects to have to rescue banks which are deemed 'too large to fail'. The regulator also has to consider what the relationship is between the amount of equity capital they require banks to hold and the amount of credit that a bank will be willing and able to provide to the economy, i.e. if capital ratios are too high, banks may not be able to provide as much credit through credit intermediation as they could with lower ratios and thus growth and employment might be lower.

In asking such questions, the answer has to be that the only capital structure that almost guarantees that a bank will not collapse is 100% equity (just like a mutual fund), since then there is no debt and therefore no creditors able to apply to the courts for a winding-up order. But at any level below this, there is still a possibility of collapse. This was clearly manifested in the financial crisis when a number of banks collapsed despite having levels of capital that were deemed more than adequate by regulators. It should be noted, however, that this capital was deemed adequate measured not against total assets but against risk-adjusted assets which may be a much smaller measure and may be artificially lowered by faulty risk models.

If each country set its own bank regulatory standards, it is likely that many banks would choose to locate in the country with the least onerous regulation, in particular capital and liquidity requirements. This would result in banks in such locations being at a competitive advantage (at least until they collapsed) relative to those in countries with more rigorous standards. To avoid this problem of competitive advantage arising not from lower operating costs (which is good) but from taking greater balance sheet risk, capital and liquidity standards are globally coordinated through an international body called the **Basel Committee on Banking Supervision (BCBS)** which comprises regulators from around the world. The Secretariat for this body is located in the Bank for International Settlements (BIS) building in Basel, Switzerland. This is the clearing house for the central banks of the world and in addition provides them with various other services. The BCBS is not an executive body and thus it can only make recommendations. However, most countries then use the rules that are developed by this committee, such as the Basel II rules under which international banks currently operate, as a basis for their own banking legislation. In the European Union, the European Commission first creates a **Directive**, i.e. a law which all member states must reflect in their own regulatory framework, based on the Basel rules (in the case of the EU, the **Capital Requirements Directive (CRD)**), which, in yet another step, has to be **transposed into national legislation** in each member state.

## BASEL II

Unlike the previous Basel regulations (Basel I), Basel II uses a methodology which is risk sensitive, i.e. various asset types are allocated an appropriate risk factor (risk-adjusted assets). Basel II also considers not just credit risk (as was the case under Basel I) but also market risk and operational risk.

Basel II also reinforced the importance of **supervision**, i.e. the role of regulators in trying to detect if banks are, in fact, following the rules and behaving in an appropriate way. It also tried to use the power of self-interest of various parties by introducing the concept of **market discipline** to try to ensure that, for example, counterparties are aware of the extent of risk-taking by the bank to which they are lending. As a result of these improvements (they were thought to be improvements at the time but in practice have proven to be a contributory factor in the financial crisis), Basel II has three 'Pillars':

1. **Pillar 1** is concerned with assessing the **level of risk to which the bank is exposed** – from credit risk, market risk and operational risk – and with assigning an appropriate amount of (equity) capital to protect debt holders from these risks. In the case of credit risk, this can be measured using a so-called 'standardised approach' which relies on external credit assessments (such as rating agency measures of credit risk) or alternatively they may be allowed to use their own internal systems for assessing risk. Market risk would normally be assessed using the VAR methodology. Operational risk is the risk of loss from inadequate or failed internal processes, people, systems or external events. Loss of computer data, for example, is an operational risk.
2. **Pillar 2** is the **supervisory review process**, undertaken in the case of the UK by officials from the Financial Services Authority (FSA) or in the US by the Federal Reserve, the Office of the Controller of the Currency, FINRA or other regulators. However, it is important to note that this pillar requires financial institutions to have their own internal processes to assess their capital adequacy in relation to their risk.

Under this pillar, the supervisor can also examine other risks that a bank may face such as concentration risk (too high a proportion of total lending to one customer), reputation risk, liquidity risk and legal risk. These are known as residual risks, under the Basel system. The supervisor also has the power to review the risk management systems employed by the bank.

3. **Pillar 3** is known as **market discipline**. The objective is to try to use market forces as a means of disciplining banks known to be willing to employ higher levels of leverage and take on more credit, market and liquidity risk than might be appropriate given the 'spillover' effects of a bank collapse. Pillar 3 works through provisions that require banks to disclose to the market, information which is relevant to counterparties assessing the risk of lending to, or otherwise transacting with, a counterparty bank.

## BASEL III

The official name for Basel III[3] which covers bank capital, liquidity and related matters is 'Basel III: A Global Regulatory Framework for More Resilient Banks and Banking Systems'. Basel III is in part an outcome of the Group of 20 (G20)[4] meetings that took place for the first time in 2008 and again in 2009 during the heat of the financial crisis when the heads of state of 20 major countries met together to consider how best to avoid a repeat of the crisis. They debated the measures that were necessary. It is important to understand that the measures included more than simply higher capital and new liquidity requirements, important though these were.

Basel III is not yet in force. But it has already become the focus for banks to ensure that they can meet its complex requirements by the due date. Based on the Basel II rules, the draft Basel III regulations, which will start to come into force in 2012/13, have a phase-in period up to 2019.

## CALIBRATION OF THE CAPITAL FRAMEWORK

We have noted a number of times that the role of capital is to absorb loss in order that the liability holders of the bank – depositors, senior debt holders, junior debt holders and others – do not have to absorb losses. However, there is virtually no amount of capital that guarantees the liability holders against suffering any loss. The percentages of capital required under the new rules are much higher than under the old, **but some banks will still become insolvent**. This is not designed to be a regime in which failure is impossible. However, the new rules do increase the amount of the highest quality capital, namely equity, from only 2% of risk adjusted assets to 7%, as shown in Table 24.1 In the UK, it is intended that the capital requirement for banks located in the UK should be even higher, up to an additional 3%. It should be noted that we use the expression **risk-adjusted assets**, not total assets. Risk adjusted means that risk factors have been applied to each

---

[3] See www.bis.org/publ/bcbs189.pdf (published in December 2010).

[4] Argentina, Australia, Brazil, Canada, China, the European Union, France, Germany, India, Indonesia, Italy, Japan, Mexico, Russia, Saudi Arabia, South Africa, the Republic of Korea, Turkey, the United Kingdom and the United States of America.

asset type and therefore the risk adjusted total is likely to be lower than the actual asset total. In fact, according to the Independent Banking Commission in the UK,[5] once an adjustment is made for risk, risk adjusted assets are only around 50% of the actual total of assets on the balance sheet. Thus a 7% risk adjusted asset ratio would be, if this is correct, a 3½% ratio of equity to total assets.

## THE 3X3 MATRIX PLUS PLUS PLUS

Table 24.1 is a little complex and requires some explanation. First, we have the categories of capital along the top of the table. Under the new rules, there are three types of capital:

- **Common equity** (the US term) or ordinary share capital (the UK term) is the best type of capital to absorb losses and prevent the bank becoming a gone concern. **After deductions** means mainly two things. First, that any accounting 'goodwill' resulting from an acquisition, which is on the balance sheet as an asset, has to be deducted from equity. Second, tax loss assets, i.e. the expectation that tax losses from previous years will be of future value if the bank ever again makes profits, have to be deducted from assets. Any deduction from assets reduces equity since equity equals assets minus liabilities. Common equity is what would have been described as 'Core Tier 1' under Basel II.
- Additional Tier 1 capital (the amount above common equity that makes up Tier 1 total) must be perpetual, like common equity, but might be items such as amounts on the 'share premium' account. The Basel III document gives full details of what may be included.
- Tier 2 is capital (which makes up the difference between Tier 1 and Total Capital) which is not perpetual but nonetheless is subordinated to depositors and general creditors and has an original maturity of at least five years. The Basel III document gives full details of what may be included.

**Table 24.1**   Calibration of the capital framework under Basel III

| Capital requirements and buffers (all numbers in per cent) | | |
| --- | --- | --- |
| | **Common Equity (after deductions)** | **Tier 1 Capital** | **Total Capital** |
| Minimum | 4.5 | 6.0 | 8.0 |
| Conservation buffer | 2.5 | | |
| Minimum plus conservation buffer | 7.0 | 8.5 | 10.5 |
| Countercyclical buffer range* | 0–2.5 | | |

\* The requirements for countercyclical additions to, or deductions from capital depending on the stage of the economic cycle, have not yet been defined.

*Source*: Basel III: A global regulatory framework for more resilient banks and banking systems, December 2010 (rev June 2011) Basel Committee on Banking Supervision.

---

[5] See. http://bankingcommission.independent.gov.uk/

The total capital requirement on the top line of the table is 8% of which 2% can be Tier 2 (least good type of capital). The maximum for 'Additional Tier 1' is 3.5% and this would bring the total up to 8% by using the second best type of capital (Additional Tier 1) and no third best (Tier 2). If any of the above minima were breached, the regulator would withdraw the bank's licence. This 'trigger' would then mean the bank could be subject to whatever resolution regime was in force in the particular country.

A bank also has to have a **conservation buffer** which is simply an additional amount of equity it is expected to have in normal times. This gives the bank a 'grace period' if capital is falling but has not yet reached the point at which its licence will be withdrawn. At the level of an additional 2.5% of equity, this gives a total amount of required common equity of 7%. For total capital the ratio is 10.5%. If its equity falls below 7% or either of the other ratios is breached, then the regulator can prohibit it from paying dividends. It might also be able to limit bonus payments since if dividends and bonuses are restricted, more profit remains within the bank and becomes retained capital (equity). There is thus an appropriate incentive structure within the bank to encourage adequate capital since otherwise shareholders will suffer and employees could also lose out.

*Plus*: In addition to the 7% common equity it is expected that banks will be subject to a so-called **countercyclical buffer which will vary with the credit cycle**. Thus if credit is growing much faster than the economy as a whole, the regulator can start to require this additional amount of capital up to an expected level of 2.5% and therefore reduce the leverage available to the banks, thereby hoping to reduce credit growth. If the economy was winding down, and in particular if credit was growing more slowly than the economy, the regulator could reduce this buffer to zero, thus increasing the leverage available to the banks to increase the supply of credit.

*Plus*: Those banks which are considered **systemic**, i.e. a SIFI which is any large bank in a country, or a G-SIFI which is a large bank which operates globally, may have to hold an additional capital surcharge to reflect the danger to the economy as a whole if it were to collapse and hence the cost to the taxpayer to resolve it without it becoming a gone concern. Thus this additional capital is designed to encourage large systemically dangerous banks either to split up into a number of independent smaller companies (and therefore avoid the additional capital requirement) or to accept the additional capital requirement but thus be less likely to suffer **firm specific stress**, i.e. the possibility of collapse.

It should be noted that all the above ratios of capital to total assets measure assets not as valued on the balance sheet but in terms of how risky they are deemed to be. Thus the asset measure is **risk adjusted**. A bank can therefore hold more low risk assets for a given amount of capital, as we noted before, than it could high risk assets to reflect the fact that some assets may be more likely to cause banks to become insolvent than others. Unfortunately, however, different banks assess risk differently. We also know that the risk measures used under Basel II (and continued in Basel III) did not really estimate many risks appropriately.

*Plus*: Regulators were very concerned to discover just how high the **non-risk adjusted** leverage ratio of many banks was. Some had a leverage ratio of 66 times, i.e. only around 1.5% of equity to **total** assets. To prevent a recurrence of such high ratios, regulators are likely to require banks to conform also to an unadjusted leverage ratio which might be 3% equity to total assets. This would give an unadjusted leverage of 33 times.

## LIQUIDITY REQUIREMENTS

The official name for the second half of Basel III on liquidity standards is 'Basel III: International Framework for Liquidity Risk Measurement, Standards and Monitoring'. The first thing to note is that under Basel II (the framework which has been followed until the time of writing), the rules on liquidity were relatively lax. In fact the view of regulators was that, provided a bank was solvent, the efficient market pricing of trading book assets (meaning they would always be priced at their fundamental value and therefore would be easy to sell for their fundamental value) would ensure that there would be no bank runs as a result of their not being able to sell assets. Thus the job of regulators and supervisors was to ensure that banks were solvent and, if this was successfully achieved, liquidity standards were only a secondary consideration. This was so strongly believed to be a valid approach that banks were permitted to hold much less capital against their trading book, compared with their banking book, on the grounds that tradable assets could easily be sold and thus generate liquidity. This was despite the fact that many 'tradable' assets on the trading book were virtually non-traded CDOs. In practice this expected liquidity dried up just when it was most needed. This is one of the negative aspects of the 'efficient market belief' which, at least until now, has been the paradigm which 'regulates' the thinking of regulators.

A major reason why this approach to liquidity management was erroneous was that bank directors, regulators and supervisors seemed to have operated on the basis of ignorance of a very important concept in economics – the '**paradox of aggregation**' also known as the '**fallacy of composition**'. What this means is that what one can do, all cannot do. If all banks are hit at the same time with a liquidity crunch and all try to sell their assets to generate liquidity from secondary markets (**market liquidity**), the price of those assets is likely to fall well below their fundamental value. Thus the assumptions of the EMH do not hold once a market is 'one-sided'. The EMH assumes that this cannot happen – that there will always be sufficient arbitrage capital on the other side of the market willing and able to take advantage of mispricing and thus acting on the assumption of reversion to mean, i.e. returning to the 'correct' fundamental value. In reality this simply does not happen. Thus once assets have to be revalued at these new market prices (because they are held on the trading book), it is quite possible that all of a bank's capital has been wiped out and the bank is therefore insolvent. Not only that but when all banks are trying to raise new capital at the same time to replenish their liquidity by trying to generate liquidity from primary markets (i.e. **funding liquidity**), investors take fright and refuse to provide the necessary liquidity at almost any price. These problems have arisen because of the increasingly integrated global network that links banks worldwide and the increasingly similar asset structure of many banks which has resulted in systemic problems (problems for all banks), much more than in the past.

As a result of the financial crisis, regulators have formulated a new set of liquidity regulations for banks. These liquidity ratios are designed to minimise the chance of a liquidity crisis and, in the event of an individual bank problem, to give it more time to find a resolution.

Basel III has two separate sets of rules on liquidity.[6] These are known as the **liquidity coverage ratio (LCR)** and the **net stable funding ratio (SFR)**. The first of these is concerned with ensuring that in the short term a bank is holding sufficient high quality liquid assets to withstand an acute stress scenario lasting for one month. The second is designed to encourage banks to fund themselves with liabilities which match the assets they are financing so that they could survive for longer, i.e. to avoid the situation of required cash outflows exceeding actual cash inflows.

Any bank makes a schedule of cash inflows and outflows on a daily basis. Inflows come from borrowers paying interest and repaying loans. Outflows arise from interest payments the bank has to make plus running costs such as salaries. In uncertain times, outflows may rise substantially as a result of one of more of the following possible shocks to a bank:

- A significant downgrade of a bank's credit rating;
- A significant outflow of deposits;
- The loss of unsecured wholesale funding;
- A significant increase in secured funding haircuts (for example on repo financing);
- A call for an increase in margin (collateral) on derivative transactions;
- An increase in calls for stand-by facilities, such as overdrafts and lines of credit.

The first line of defence for a bank in the event of liquidity problems is not funding liquidity but market liquidity. Thus banks will be required to assess the amount of liquidity they need in the event of a shock and to hold sufficient liquid assets to finance this net outflow (liquidity coverage ratio). Liquid assets would include notes and coin, deposits at the central bank, short-dated sovereign debt and certain categories of corporate debt (though with appropriate haircuts).

## NET STABLE FUNDING RATIO (NSFR)

To complement the liquidity coverage ratio (LCR), the Basel Committee developed the concept of the net stable funding ratio which establishes a minimum acceptable amount of stable funding based on the liquidity characteristics of an institution's assets over a one-year horizon. It is designed to **promote structural changes in the liquidity risk profile of institutions away from short-term funding mismatches and towards more stable, longer-term funding of assets**. It is, in other words, trying to change the structure of bank balance sheets. Like capital ratios which should be set at an appropriate level by the directors of a bank regardless of any regulation, liquidity ratios are something which bank directors have always had responsibility for as agents of the owners of the bank. The net

---

[6] See www.bis.org/publ/bcbs188.pdf

stable funding ratio has therefore built on two traditional methodologies used by international banks and rating agencies – 'net liquid assets' and 'cash capital'.

If banks comply with these new rules, it is likely that they will have much greater liquidity and hence much greater ability to survive idiosyncratic stress, i.e. stress peculiar to that particular bank, than on the ratios that most banks employed prior to the financial crisis. These new ratios are designed to prevent a repetition of liquidity problems at **specific** firms, such as the scenario which played out from August 2007, as firm specific crises became a **systemic** liquidity crisis. If these new liquidity regulations manage to prevent this scenario repeating, they will be performing the task they have been set.

## BASEL III: CAPITAL AND LIQUIDITY RULES – WILL THEY DAMAGE THE GLOBAL ECONOMY?

At the time of writing, the EU was planning that the Capital Requirements Directive, which would implement the new Basel rules across Europe, to be known as CAD IV, would require banks to hold 7% of capital against their risk adjusted assets (implying approximately a 3.5% capital to total assets ratio). It was reported in the *Financial Times* on 13 October 2011 that some European banks were 'threatening' to meet the new capital requirement, not by increasing their capital through a capital raising issue of equity or through cutting bonuses or through cutting dividends, but by selling off assets and reducing future lending. Thus, rather than increasing the numerator (capital) in the ratio capital/assets, they would reduce the denominator.

One head of a European bank was quoted in the same *Financial Times* article as saying: 'Why should we raise capital at these depressed share price levels?' His complaint reflected the fact that bank shares sell at around 60% of NAV as given on the balance sheet. Another senior banker is quoted as saying: 'It's fundamentally wrong to increase capital at the moment. Deleveraging needs to happen.'

The problem is that European companies rely on banks for as much as 75% of their funding, compared with only 25% for US companies. If banks cut back lending it could have severe repercussions for the economic recovery of the eurozone from its 2011 levels. To overcome banks' unwillingness to raise new capital, the president of the European Commission, Jose Manuel Barroso, has said that banks supported by the eurozone bailout fund should be stopped from paying dividends or bonuses.

One reason why investors are likely to be unwilling to buy new bank shares is, of course, that the additional capital will simply be used to allow banks to write off the huge losses they have not yet been willing to disclose, were they to value assets at true, mark-to-market prices, particularly on the sovereign bonds which they hold. Thus the new capital would simply 'disappear'. It would, however, enable the banks to continue as going concerns which they could not do were these losses to be written off without additional capital having been supplied. Two French banks, BNP and SocGen, have already indicated that they intend to dispose of assets valued at €150 billion (at risk weighted values). It is expected that UniCredit of Italy and Commerzbank of Germany might make comparable disposals.

The new liquidity ratios raise some fundamental issues. They require banks in each country to hold more of their own sovereign debt as a highly liquid asset. However, as we now know, sovereign debt is not in fact credit-risk free. A further, and important consideration for even the most solvent countries, is that the new liquidity proposals have the effect of forcing banks to fund government deficits. In an era when some might argue that running budget surpluses should be on the agenda in order to reduce the government debt/GDP ratio, forced funding is possibly undesirable. For countries which have balanced budgets or small deficits, the new rules present the problem of an inadequate supply of government bonds. It is clear, therefore, that the new rules on capital and liquidity, while possibly reducing the risk of financial instability, also raise a number of issues of equally fundamental importance, i.e. the possibility of a fall in the rate of growth and an encouragement to governments to run deficits.

# 25 REGULATION OF SECURITIES MARKETS

Market regulation tries to achieve two objectives: one is to protect investors and the other is to ensure that markets function as well as possible. The market regulator in the United States, the SEC describes its mission as: 'to protect investors, maintain fair, orderly, and efficient markets, and facilitate capital formation'. Note the '**facilitate capital formation**'. This emphasises that the function of securities secondary markets is not to offer a casino within which people can gamble but to provide market liquidity in the secondary market without which the primary (financing) market would not function properly, i.e. the secondary market contributes to the financing function.

It is particularly apposite at this time to be analysing the regulation of markets as reviews of market regulation were undertaken in 2011 by the SEC, the European Union and the Australian market regulator. In particular, given that some analysts have blamed the lack of regulation of derivatives markets in the United States for being a contributory factor in the 2007 financial crisis, market regulation can be seen as not just an investor protection or an orderly market issue, but as a systemic one. Not everyone agrees, however. The former Chairman of the Federal Reserve System, Alan Greenspan was, during his tenure, one of the cheerleaders for a financial system with less, rather than more, regulation. In 1999, in a speech to the Futures Industry Association, he argued that exchange-traded derivative markets should have reduced regulation, just like OTC markets:

> The fact that OTC markets function quite effectively without the benefits of CFTC[1] regulation provides a strong argument for development of a less burdensome regime for exchange-traded financial derivatives.

From 1999–2007 the OTC derivatives markets may have seemed to be functioning effectively but in fact they were creating hidden problems which only came to be realised post-2007. At a more general level, Greenspan's underlying belief in free markets is emphasised in this excerpt from a speech to Congress in 2002:

> Those of us who support market capitalism in its more competitive forms might argue that unfettered markets create a degree of wealth that fosters a more civilised existence. I have always found that insight compelling.

---

[1] CFTC is the Commodities Futures and Trading Commission which is the regulator for exchange traded commodity and financial futures.

It is important to realise, therefore, that the need for regulation of securities markets is not self-evident. It needs to be argued for in terms of **market failure**. However, the outcome of the 2007 crisis may convince you that there were market failures. Whether regulation would have prevented such failures is another issue.

## THE START OF MARKET REGULATION

In the US, before the Great Crash of 1929, there was little support for federal regulation of securities markets. When the stock market crashed in October 1929, public confidence in the markets plummeted. Investors large and small, as well as the banks which had made loans to them, lost great sums of money in the ensuing Great Depression. **There was a consensus that, for the economy to recover, the public's faith in the capital markets needed to be restored.** Congress held hearings to identify the problems and search for solutions. Based on the findings in those hearings, Congress passed the Securities Act of 1933 and the Securities Exchange Act of 1934, which created the SEC.

### Exchange Act requirements for a national market system

In the Securities Exchange Act, 1934 Congress, for the first time, directed the SEC to facilitate the establishment of a **national market system**. In 1975 with improvements in technology becoming available, Congress updated the Act by mandating a national market system composed of multiple competing markets linked through technology. At this time Congress found that it was in the public interest and appropriate for the protection of investors and the maintenance of fair and orderly markets to assure five objectives:

1. Economically efficient execution of securities transactions;
2. Fair competition amongst brokers and dealers, amongst exchange markets, and between exchange markets and markets other than exchange markets;
3. The availability to brokers, dealers and investors of information with respect to quotations and transactions in securities;
4. The practicability of brokers executing investors' orders in the best market;
5. An opportunity, consistent with efficiency and best execution, for investors' orders to be executed without the participation of a dealer (this would mean through a multilateral trading system, for example).

The final Congressional finding was that these five objectives would be fostered by the linking of all markets for qualified securities through communication and data processing. Specifically, Congress found that such linkages would foster efficiency; enhance competition; increase the information available to brokers, dealers and investors; facilitate the offsetting (matching) of investors' orders; and contribute to the best execution of investors' orders.

Over the years, these findings and objectives have guided the Commission as it has sought to keep market structure rules up-to-date with continually changing economic conditions and technology advances. This task has presented certain challenges because the five objectives set forth can be difficult to reconcile. In particular, the objective of matching investor orders, or 'order interaction', can be difficult to reconcile with the objective of promoting competition amongst markets – something we have already noted.

Order interaction promotes a system that 'maximises the opportunities for the most willing seller to meet the most willing buyer'. However, when many trading centres compete for order flow in the same stock, such competition can lead to the fragmentation of order flow in that stock. Fragmentation can inhibit the interaction of investor orders and thereby impair certain efficiencies and the best execution of investors' orders. Competition among trading centres to provide specialised services for investors can also lead to practices that may detract from public price transparency. On the other hand, mandating the consolidation of order flow in a single venue would create a monopoly and thereby lose the important benefits of competition amongst markets. The benefits of such competition include incentives for trading centres to create new products, provide high quality trading services that meet the needs of investors, and keep trading fees low.

## EUROPE

Unlike the US, Europe is not a single country and, until relatively recently, there was little attempt to create a single regulatory framework across the whole region. As a result, the regulation of markets prior to 1993 was the remit of national authorities. In the UK for example, until 1987, shortly after the reforms of the LSE were introduced (Big Bang), there was virtually no statutory regulation of securities markets which were, instead, governed by the rules of the LSE operating as a self-regulatory body.

The **Investment Services Directive (ISD)** was the first regulatory framework developed in Europe and came into force in 1996. Its objective was:

> to create a 'European Passport' for non-bank investment firms to carry out in all Member States a wide range of investment business (i.e. order collecting, execution of orders on an agency basis, dealing, portfolio management and underwriting) as well as certain additional services (such as investment advice, advice on mergers and acquisitions, safekeeping and administration of securities and foreign exchange transactions) if mentioned specifically in the authorisation.
>
> www.europa.eu

Thus this Directive[2] is less concerned with investor protection, market integrity and capital formation than with trying to create what Congress in the US in 1934 called a national market system. The ISD was, therefore, one aspect of the attempt by the EU to effect a shift from the original concept of a 'Common Market' in Europe towards the creation of a 'Single Market' across all EU countries. The belief was that, by analogy with the US, the EU would achieve efficiency gains from the economies of scale that a single market would facilitate. The creation of the single currency, the euro, was another important objective, in that it was believed

---

[2]  A Directive is a legislative act of the European Union which then has to be implemented in every member state.

that by reducing exchange risk and the possibility of competitive devaluation, the interests of the Community as a whole would be enhanced. The ISD had within it a provision in respect of financial markets, permitting the domestic regulator to enforce a 'concentration rule', i.e. to prohibit competition in the trading of equities. Since 1996, it would seem that the Commission has come round to the view that **the concentration provision** was not achieving the right balance between competition amongst orders and competition amongst venues.

The replacement for the ISD was the **Markets in Financial Instruments Directive (MiFID)** which came into effect in all EU countries in November 2007. Under the ISD, European regulation recognised two entities which provided trading venues – **regulated markets** (for example a stock exchange) and **investment firms** (broker/dealers, not investment managers). Under MiFID the latter category has been renamed **systematic internaliser**, and a third one has been added - the, **multilateral trading facility (MTF),** similar to an electronic communication network (ETN )or alternative trading system (ATS),. While also concerned with the 'single market', MiFID is much closer to the Exchange Acts in the US compared with the ISD, as it focuses, as they do, on investor protection, competition and cost of capital.

The focus on the role of markets in contributing to economic growth and job creation and on competition as a means of contributing to this represents a considerable shift in thinking by the Commission. Unfortunately, as we know from an earlier chapter, competition between trading centres, unless properly regulated, can give rise to **market fragmentation**. Thus, although MiFID was introduced only in 2007, by 2010 the Commission was starting to examine possible changes to MiFID (namely MiFID II).

## MIFID II AND MIFIR

MiFID II will not come into force for some time yet. However, the public consultation document issued at the end of 2010 makes it clear that it will be concerned, inter alia, with:

- The growth of dark trading in broker crossing networks in particular and the extent to which this damages price discovery in lit markets;
- The extent to which it may be necessary to mandate a 'consolidated tape', i.e. a single data source, which reveals all trade executions in a security, as in the US, rather than trades being published in an unconsolidated manner;
- Whether there are any issues raised by automated trading and in particular how these are peculiar to, and did not pertain prior to, HFT;
- Whether the regulatory structures for MTFs and regulated markets should be harmonised, given that they perform essentially the same function.

MiFID II also now has a little brother, MiFIR which incorporates much of the regulation in the European Market Infrastructure Regulation. MiFIR is not a **Directive** which each European state must implement, to being a **Regulation** which will be implemented centrally from Brussels rather than being allowed to be individually (and less uniformly) implemented by national regulators. This is to overcome the problem of previous Directives which have been diluted or even ignored by some member states. It thus avoids uneven implementation across the Union.

At the time of writing, the final MiFID II regulations have not been published.[3] However, it is clear from the draft legislation that one important aspect of the new regulations concerns HFT as a possible source of financial instability, independent of that which can be generated by banking systems. The following gives an idea of some of the likely proposals in the final MiFID II/MiFIR regulatory framework:

### 'Final' MiFID II Draft Curbs HFT, Bans Prop Flow from Broker Crossing Networks (BCNs)

The final draft of the European Commission's proposed revisions to MiFID will impose new restrictions on high-frequency trading (HFT), confirm a ban on organized trading facilities crossing against prop trading flow, and define new rules for access criteria between central counterparties (CCPs) and trading venues.

Among the most substantial additions is a new liquidity requirement that seeks to stem HFT by forcing market making algorithms to operate continually during market hours. According to the draft report, 'an algorithmic trading strategy shall be in continuous operation during trading hours of the trading venue to which it sends orders or through the systems of which it executes transactions. The trading parameters or limits of an algorithmic trading strategy shall ensure that the strategy posts firm quotes at competitive prices with the result of providing liquidity on a regular and ongoing basis to these trading venues at all times, regardless of prevailing market conditions'.

According to the draft, operators of the new category of market the so-called Organized Trading Facility (OTF) which at the time of writing included broker-crossing networks (BCNs) cannot trade against their own proprietary capital – referred to as prop trading – while systematic internalizers (SIs) can. SIs are not, however, permitted to bring together third-party buying and selling interests 'in functionally the same way' as a regulated market, multilateral trading facility (MTF) or OTF.

The final MiFID II draft also introduces new index licensing requirements, which assert that trading venues 'should not be able to claim exclusive rights in relation to any derivatives subject to this obligation preventing other trading venues from offering trading in these [index and benchmark] instruments'. Such an amendment could open the door for exchanges to trade indices licenced by rival bourses, for instance the

---

[3] As had been widely expected, the draft legislation is split into two separate documents. Provisions dealing with pre- and post-trade transparency, exchange trading of derivatives, product intervention by national authorities and provision of certain services without a branch by non-EU firms are contained in a regulation (MiFIR) that will have direct effect in member states without the ability for member states to put their own interpretation on the provisions in implementing legislation. The remaining provisions dealing with matters such as authorization and operating conditions for investment firms, passporting of activities across the EU, conduct of business rules, including investor protection, and powers of national authorities and the European Securities and Markets Authority (ESMA) are contained in a directive (MiFID II) that will need to be implemented by member states through national legislation (www.mofo.com/files/Uploads/Images/111031-EU-Publishes-MiFID-II-MiFIR.pdf).

London Stock Exchange could offer derivatives based on EuroSTOXX indices, which it has been so far prevented from doing by Deutsche Börse.

*Trade News* 10 October 2011
(www.thetradenews.com/trading-venues/6869)

It is quite clear from the above that regulation of markets is becoming ever more complex and hard to understand as regulators try to forestall market crashes or instability caused by features of markets themselves, such as feedback loops, and at the same time try to ensure fairness and competition in markets.

## THE FLASH CRASH: US MARKET EVENTS OF 6 MAY 2010

One of the key functions of market regulation as we noted at the start of this chapter is to try to prevent the occurrence of 'disorderly' markets. Rather like the expression 'keeping a disorderly house',[4] we may know what it means when we see it, but in law it is difficult to define.

The huge increase in trading volumes, speed of execution and use of automated algorithms to generate orders has for some time caused regulators some concern. On 6 May 2010 at around 2.30, the S&P volatility index (VIX) rose sharply. The Dow Jones Industrial Average (DJIA) had fallen around 2.5%. At the same time, liquidity available in two of the most actively traded instruments – the E-Mini S&P 500, which is a futures contract that enables hedging or speculation in the S&P 500 index, and the S&P 500 SPDR exchange traded fund (SPY), which is the most popular of all US ETFs and is based on the S&P 500 – fell. From then on, one of the 'unexplained' crashes in US security markets started to develop. On 30 September 2010, the SEC (which regulates cash equity markets) and the Commodity Futures Trading Commission which regulates derivatives markets issued a joint report of over 100 pages entitled 'Findings Regarding the Market Events of May 6, 2010'.

The following is a summary of the SEC explanation of the event.[5]

At 2.32 a mutual fund (a long-term institutional investor) initiated a programme to sell 75,000 E-Mini contracts to hedge a cash equity position. Such a programme represents a substantial proportion of the normal turnover of this contract. On the morning of 6 May, the volume of contracts over the half hour period from 9.30 a.m. to 10 a.m. was around 100,000 contracts. Thus any attempt to sell 75,000 contracts in 30 minutes would be likely to lead to a dramatic decline in prices. Traders in large size therefore considered the amount of turnover in a contract or security before deciding how to undertake a sell programme of this size. Clearly, one approach is to try to sell a quantity representing, say, 10% of the turnover in the previous period and when that order is completed to enter another order for another 10% of the turnover in the previous

---

[4]  A Disorderly House, in English law, is a house in which the conduct of its inmates is such as to become a public nuisance. In England, by the Disorderly Houses Act 1751, the term includes common bawdy houses or brothels, common gaming houses, common betting houses and disorderly places of entertainment.

[5]  From the joint SEC/ CFTC Report entitled 'Findings Regarding the Market Events of May 6', Issued 30 September 2010.

period. The trader would continue to do this until the whole order had been executed, hopefully without having moved the price against him or herself.

Today it is not only professional traders who use algorithms to place orders. Buyside investors do also. This particular buyside investor, a large mutual fund called Waddell & Reed Financial, uses an algorithm to decide when to send orders to a trading centre and in what size. Clearly the volume that has gone through the market in a previous period is a key consideration. However, there might be other parameters programmed. These would include time: over what maximum period should the trade be fed into the market? Should a high proportion of the order be executed at the opening and at the close when volumes are often at their highest? At what point should a price decline in the market cause a cessation of sell order entry? If price falls by a large percentage, should sell orders be changed to buy orders? These are all factors that a human buyside trader would consider.

In fact, the algorithm used by Waddell was programmed to consider only volume in previous periods. It was programmed to feed orders into the June 2010 E-Mini market to target an execution rate of 9% of the trading volume in the previous minute. This was to be executed regardless of time or price. Unlike a previous large sell order which this mutual fund had executed, which took five hours to execute 75,000 contracts and took account of time, price and volume, this one took just 20 minutes.

If an investor is selling in this size, there need to be others willing to buy, otherwise there can be no executions. The possible buyers are real money funds ones (for example mutual funds similar to Wadell itself) who take a different view of the likely direction of the S&P over the days or weeks ahead. There are also cross-market arbitrageurs who will try to transfer some of the selling pressure from the futures market to the cash market. In this case the two markets are, firstly, the ETF which tracks the S&P (SPY) and, secondly, the underlying stocks in the S&P. The third group of possible buyers are HFTs which are active in the futures market.

Initially it might be expected that the HFTs would be first into action to buy from this seller, prior to realising how much more there was still 'to go', i.e. that the first batch of orders was only the tip of the iceberg of a hugh hidden order. According to the Report, the HFTs bought around 3,300 contracts. Immediately after this, not surprisingly, they started selling since they don't generally hold large net positions. This set of traders is said to have sold 2,200 contracts. However, the total trades (not the net change in positions) of the HFT amounted to nearly 140,000 contracts, which was 33% of the total. Indeed, between 2:45:13 and 2:45:17 (during a period of four seconds), HFTs traded over 27,000 contracts, though only buying in total a net 200 contracts. **Unfortunately, the Waddell algorithm viewed the increase in volume of trading as a reason to increase sales, even though the volume was not sales to end buyers, i.e. fundamental investors.**

This type of trading is described by the report as 'hot potato' trading, i.e. always passing on a position as quickly as possible. One outcome was a decline in both price and liquidity since fundamental buyers and cross-market arbitrageurs were unable or unwilling to supply enough buyside liquidity.

A second liquidity crisis was happening in the cash equity market. When market prices decline so rapidly, the trading algorithms of liquidity providers in the cash market halted trading so that human traders could consider what was happening.

It could, for example, be that a large trader had gone out of business or a bank had collapsed. In some individual securities liquidity simply evaporated. As a result, trades were executed at what are known as stub quotes, which are prices entered by liquidity provides into their systems far away from realistic prices, in order to meet their obligation to an exchange to always provide a quote. In order to minimise any chance of their quotes being executed against when the 'true' price was unknown, these stub bid-offer quotes had a huge spread between them. In some cases the bid was as low as a penny (one cent) to sell, and the offer $1,000 to buy.

The conclusion of the report is that the interaction between automated execution programs and algorithmic trading strategies can quickly erode liquidity and result in disorderly markets – something which Congress requires the SEC to prevent. In particular, in times of extreme volatility, high trading volume in markets where HFTs are active is not necessarily a reliable indicator of market liquidity.

Was the Waddell order the only cause of the turmoil in the markets? Some suggest that other factors were involved. A report in the *Wall Street Journal* gave an alternative view and suggested that HFT selling was also an important factor. As with most market crashes, different analyses lead to different conclusions. But the key insight is that future market crashes of this nature are quite likely as the interaction of algorithms can lead to unexpected outcomes.

In the UK, the Government Office for Science in 2011 set up a study programme into 'The Future of Computer Trading in Financial Markets'[6]. One of its conclusions was that feedback effects could be important in causing unexpected outcomes in computer based trading markets. These could result from the non-linear dynamics of the financial system, where a change in one variable could lead to a small or large change in another variable, depending on the current level of the first variable – sometimes known as the butterfly effect. This is the observation that, in theory, given non-linear systems, a butterfly flapping its wings in Tokyo could cause a hurricane in the US.

European regulators are now trying to make sure that a 'flash crash' does not happen in Europe, and one of the measures they may take to try to prevent it is requiring all users of algorithms to submit them to the regulator for review! This seems an improbable 'solution'.

In terms of what might be done to prevent a repetition of the 'flash crash', a 'limit up, limit down' rule may have to be implemented. This would cause trading in any particular security to stop for five minutes if the price moved more than a certain percentage in a period of time. This five-minute period (or whatever period is chosen) would allow human traders to reassess the fundamentals of the security and decide if there were good reasons for the sharp price movement.

---

[6] http://www.bis.gov.uk/assets/foresight/docs/computer-trading/11-1276-the-future-of-computer-trading-in-financial-markets

PART

# THE ROLE OF GOVERNANCE AND STRATEGY IN RESOURCE ALLOCATION AND FIRM AND INDUSTRY STRUCTURE: CASE STUDIES IN FINANCIAL SERVICES

# BUSINESS UNIT AND CORPORATE STRATEGY, GOVERNANCE AND FIRM AND INDUSTRY STRUCTURE

Optimal use of society's scarce resources requires that financial intermediaries, as well as corporates, employ the resources available to them, including human resources, in their most productive configuration. Corporate strategy is one important aspect of this. Without appropriate strategy and its effective implementation, resources will not be appropriately allocated by public capital markets or 'internal' capital market allocation.

It is noticeable that in all the textbooks available in the field of strategy, there would seem to be none focussed on financial services. The principal reason for this is that very few people who are interested in strategy come from a financial services background. When they look at our industry they find it difficult to come to grips with its complexities and 'dematerialised' nature. They are used to dealing with firms which make 'things' and where it is easier to understand what the firm is trying to do. I cannot cover strategy issues in this book in depth,[1] but a brief overview is given below.

## BUSINESS UNIT AND CORPORATE STRATEGY

Business unit strategy:
*analyses how a business can compete most successfully in the market in a particular product or service. It includes strategic decisions about choice of products to meet customer needs in an economic fashion by gaining advantage over competitors, exploiting or creating new opportunities etc.*

Corporate strategy:
*analyses the direction and scope of an organisation over the long-term which achieves competitive advantage in a changing environment through its configuration of resources and competences with the aim of fulfilling stakeholder expectations*[2]

---

[1]  My next book, **Management of Complex Financial Institutions**: *The Economics of, and Strategy Development in, Wholesale and Investment Banking, Asset Management, Insurance and Financial Companies,* will cover these issues.

[2]  Adapted from *Fundamentals of Strategy* by G. Johnson *et al.*, FT Prentice Hall, 2010.

So what does this latter definition mean in practice? 'Scope' is a critical concept here, being the range of products, markets, countries, etc. and hence the overall size and complexity of the organisation. 'Configuring resources' refers both to human capital and equity capital. Thus high cost and difficult to manage human traders might continue to be replaced by automated systems while capital would be moved out of businesses which are not performing as hoped or where requirements for increased regulatory capital make them less attractive and into business areas with greater potential. 'Stakeholder expectations' refers to the expected rate of return on equity and the growth rate of earnings from it, but in the case of banks in particular it should also include expectations of debt holders, taxpayers and society as a whole.

## STRATEGIC MANAGEMENT

A good, and more detailed, definition is:

*For managers, strategic management involves a greater scope than that of any one area of operational management such as derivatives trading or asset management. Strategic management is concerned with complexity arising out of ambiguous and non-routine situations with organisation-wide rather than operation-specific implications.*

*This is a major challenge for managers who are used only to managing, on a day-to-day basis, the resources they control directly. The manager who aspires to manage or influence corporate strategy needs to develop a capability to take an overview, to conceive of the whole rather than just the parts of a situation facing an organisation.*

*Because strategic management is characterised by its complexity, it is also necessary to make decisions and judgements on the **conceptualisation** of difficult issues. Yet the early training and experience of managers is often about taking action, or about detailed **planning** or **analysis**.*[3]

This definition is useful in emphasising that the 'silo' approach to initial training in the industry and its focus on specialisms (such as risk management, trading strategy, investment strategy and IT management) is not a good background for acquiring the skills necessary to be successful in senior management posts which require skills of strategic analysis beyond those of business unit strategy development. It is for this reason that those who are 'rainmakers', i.e. those who generate substantial revenue, often fail when promoted to senior management positions. Thus even though the words 'strategy' or 'management' appear in a number of these specialisms, it is a very different kind of strategy or management from business unit strategy or business unit management and is instead what we call 'strategic management'. **This latter type of management is one which relates closely to the purpose of this whole book, as described in the Preface It is about taking a 'helicopter view' of the business rather than a 'nose to the grindstone' type of view.**

A good example of the possible cost to an individual of being seen by a chief executive to have experience and understanding of only one part of the business

---

[3] Ibid.

would be the sacking, in 2011, of the head of investment banking at JP Morgan, Bill Winters, after a record year for the investment banking division of JP Morgan. Winters was a possible successor to the CEO Jamie Dimon. When he dismissed him, Dimon's explanation was that a career investment banker such as Mr Winters could never head a diversified financial group such as JP Morgan without a wider experience and understanding. Winters dismissal arose from the fact that he had not gained experience of the industry as a whole and all its parts to enable him in later life to consider how the parts might best be fitted together to achieve JP Morgan's 'mission'. This may be the true reason for him being fired or, of course, it may not. The true reason may have been that he disagreed with Dimon over the issue of how much risk was being taken by the bank. We now know, since a large loss disclosed by JP Morgan in May 2012, that in fact the bank as a whole was not being appropriately run and that would seem to have been a failing of Mr Dimon's overall management. The shock of an estimated $2bn loss in the so-called chief investment office (CIO) from trading in a business area which was supposed to be hedging the bank's overall risk (a loss estimated by some as likely to be $7bn by the time positions are wound down), cost shareholders a 17% fall in the value of the company's shares.[4]

We have, in fact, already covered many of the strategic issues in the industry at many points in the text up to this point.. Indeed, much of strategy is nothing more than straightforward economic analysis of products, sectors and industries. But in this chapter we will consider the role of strategic management more closely. Figure 26.1 shows the three important areas of strategic management: analysis, followed by choice, then implementation.

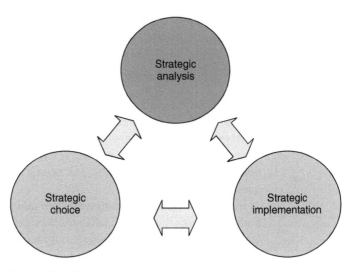

**Figure 26.1**  The strategy process

---

[4] This case is so important for the future regulatory and governance structure of the industry that I cover it in more detail in Chapter 28 in a Postscript.

Some of the analytical tools that are normally used in such analysis are:

- **PEST analysis:** to help understand the 'environment' in which a business operates and its implications for strategy. PEST (sometimes called PESTLE) stands for Political, Economic, Social and Technological. To this, particularly in the case of banking, we should add 'regulatory'.
- **Scenario planning:** a technique that builds various plausible views of possible futures for a business which in banking might include stress tests on the balance sheet, given scenarios that might be generated from the economic analysis undertaken using a PEST approach.
- **Market segmentation:** seeks to identify similarities and differences between groups of customers or users.
- **Competitor analysis:** a wide range of techniques and analyses that seek to summarise a business's overall competitive position.
- **Critical success factor analysis:** to identify those areas in which a business must outperform the competition in order to succeed.
- **SWOT analysis:** a useful technique for summarising the key issues arising from an assessment of 'internal' position and 'external' environmental influences on a business. SWOT stands for Strengths, Weaknesses, Opportunities and Threats.
- **Five forces analysis:** some 30 years ago Professor Michael Porter of Harvard Business School developed a technique for identifying the forces which affect the level of competition in an industry. **As the level of competition is the key factor in determining profitability**, this type of analysis is critical in strategic management.

There are two basic approaches to achieving competitive advantage, according to Porter. These are either cost leadership or differentiation of some type – product features, distribution, service, image. An example of a company that has focussed very successfully on image is Apple. Their products may be no better in terms of features or quality than, for example, Samsung, HTC, Google or Dell. But despite this Apple products sell for a large price premium over others. It is obtaining this additional premium over cost that enables Apple to be such a profitable company i.e. to generate a return on equity well in excess of its cost of capital. Apple uses design, good integration between products and services and ease of use as its differentiating factors and is able to extract a large premium over cost as a consequence of this.

In the case of finance, differentiation generally results from holding some limited monopoly power. Exchanges may generate premium margins in areas where there is limited or no competition, such as derivative contracts which they have designed and own, based on indices they also own. In this regard, it was reported in December 2011 that the LSE had purchased 50% of the FTSE index company that it did not already own and hoped to create more contracts based on 'its' indices. Investment banks generate premium margins in OTC derivative contracts for similar reasons – there is more limited competition in investment bank bilateral trading than in exchange multilateral trading.

## CORPORATE GOVERNANCE

We have looked at the influence of the environment and other factors on an organisation's strategic position. But we also have to be concerned about the overall purpose of the strategy being pursued and with providing a mechanism to ensure that this overall purpose is being achieved. One element of this involves defining who the **stakeholders** are in an organisation. Is it just the shareholders? Do they have absolute primacy over every other group involved in some way with the organisation? 'Other groups' include bondholders, suppliers of bank credit, other suppliers, taxpayers, society as a whole and, last but certainly not least in the case of financial services firms, the employees. This last category of stakeholder is one which can benefit very substantially from successful strategy implementation. In the case of financial services, this set of stakeholders believes it should take a major share of the gains from such successful strategies through bonus payments, but not a share of the losses when the strategy fails. The ability not to take losses arises from limited liability of companies for their debts, the asymmetry in returns between shareholders (dividends) and employees (bonuses) in times of financial stress and the existence of the 'too large to fail' doctrine. It can also give rise to conflict with regulators over capital ratios **as any profit not paid out in dividends or bonuses (retained profit) increases capital ratios**.

## THE CORPORATE GOVERNANCE PROCESS

Corporate governance[5] is a system of checks and balances that is designed to try to help minimise agency problems, such as those between the directors and managers on the one hand and shareholders on the other hand, and thereby achieve the optimal use of scarce resources. The corporate governance system has similarities to the political system in democracies where there are checks and balances built into the system (separation of powers) to try to ensure the optimal governance of a country. Corporate governance is the means by which we try to maximise the likelihood of companies being well managed. It involves a system which tries to ensure that the board of directors of the firm acts solely in the economic interests of the shareholders and any other relevant stakeholders but, if it does not so act, that there are mechanisms to monitor and then challenge the incumbent management (just like an opposition party in a parliament). Figure 26.2 indicates some of the processes involved in effective governance.

There are two types of director. There are those who work full-time for the company and are called executive directors, and there are also non-executive directors who do not work for the company. It is these non-executive (in theory independent) directors who are supposed to ensure that the executive directors act in the interest of the shareholders. In some countries all, or a majority of, the directors are non-executive and a number may be nominated by employees or trades unions. The board would normally also have a chairman and a **chief executive officer (CEO)** who is the person at the top of the company responsible for

---

[5] For a detailed coverage of corporate governance with good case studies, see Carol Padgett *Corporate Governance – Theory and Practice*, Palgrave Macmillan, 2011

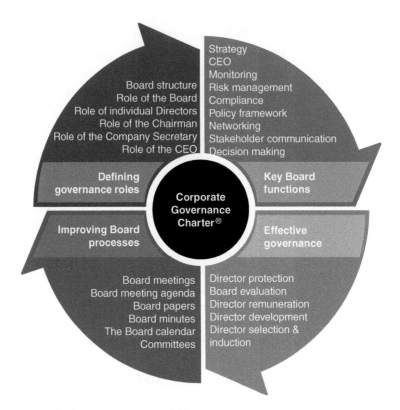

**Figure 26.2**   Corporate governance activities

*Source*: Kiel, G & Nicholson, G, *Boards that Work: A New Guide for Directors*, McGraw-Hill Australia Pty Ltd, 2003; registered trademark of 'Effective Governance Pty Ltd (Australia)', http://www.effectivegovernance.com.au/Board-Charter.html (accessed 2 March 2012).

strategy. The board also appoints an audit committee, which is a sub-committee of the board whose responsibility is to deal with financial reporting and disclosure issues and a remuneration committee to decide on directors' remuneration (salary and bonus). In the case of banks and most financial institutions the board also appoints some of its members to a risk committee.

The principles of governance apply (at the present time) only to public companies, i.e. to ones whose securities (shares and bonds) are quoted in a public market. The best explanation of corporate governance principles and why they are important is that published by the Organisation for Economic Co-operation and Development:[6]

---

[6]   The OECD groups 34 member countries sharing a commitment to democratic government and the market economy. With active relationships with some 70 other countries and economies, NGOs and civil society, it has a global reach. Its 30 member countries are: Australia, Austria, Belgium, Canada, Chile, Czech Republic, Denmark, Estonia, Finland, France, Germany, Greece, Hungary, Iceland, Ireland, Israel, Italy, Japan, Korea, Luxembourg, Mexico, the Netherlands, New Zealand, Norway, Poland, Portugal, Slovak Republic, Slovenia, Spain, Sweden, Switzerland, Turkey, the United Kingdom and the United States.

Corporate governance is one key element in **improving economic efficiency** and growth as well as **enhancing investor confidence**. Corporate governance involves a set of relationships between a company's management, its board, its shareholders and other stakeholders. Corporate governance also provides the structure through which the objectives of the company are set and the means of attaining those objectives and monitoring performance. Good corporate governance should provide proper incentives for the board and management to pursue objectives that are **in the interests of the company and its shareholders** and should facilitate effective monitoring. The presence of an effective corporate governance system within an individual company and across an economy as a whole, helps to provide a degree of confidence that is **necessary for the proper functioning of a market economy**. As a result, the cost of capital is lower and firms are encouraged to use resources more efficiently thereby underpinning growth.

Corporate governance is only part of the larger economic context in which firms operate that includes, for example, **macroeconomic policies** and **the degree of competition in product and factor (labour, capital) markets**. The corporate governance framework also depends on the **legal, regulatory** and institutional environment. In addition, factors such as business ethics and corporate awareness of the environmental and societal interests of the communities in which a company operates can also have an impact on its reputation and its long-term success.

OECD, Principles of Corporate Governance, 2004.
http://www.oecd.org/dataoecd/32/18/31557724.pdf

## SCALE AND SCOPE IN FINANCIAL SERVICES

Previous chapters have focused on the functions of the financial services industry – financing, liquidity provision, risk management, asset management, payments, clearing and settlement, etc. We have not spent much time on the institutional structure within which particular companies offer their products and services. This structure includes the range of products and services offered, the organisation of value chains and the size of particular financial companies, generally measured as balance sheet size.

For any company its size, whether measured as total revenue, profits or as market capitalisation, results from:

- The number of stages in the value chain which it has **integrated**;
- Its product scope (range of products and services);
- The **scale of operation** (market share in each product);
- **Geographical scope**, i.e. the range of countries in which it operates.
- The profitability of each business area in which it operates and its expected growth rate which determines **overall profitability** and market capitalisation

The financial services industry can be analysed in a very similar way to any other industry. First, it can first be broken down into broad categories of product: retail banking, wholesale banking, investment banking (i.e. corporate finance), broker/dealer activities, insurance, asset management and wealth management. If we take each of these sectors then, in addition, within each we have a variety of products and services that may be offered to customers. We then have the geographical scope, i.e. some companies operate only in their local region, others are national, while yet others have operations in the United States, Europe, South America and Asia. The product range, market share and geographical scope in turn determine the size of the company. Important questions following from this are whether these factors affect the rate of return on capital (private benefit), customer satisfaction (customer benefit), pricing power (shareholder benefit) and moral hazard (public concerns). Thus:

- Does integration of the value chain reduce costs, provide diversification benefits for investors or enable a superior service to be delivered to customers?
- Are large firms more efficient than small ones, i.e. are their costs lower? If their costs are lower, are prices to customers lower, i.e. do customers (and thus the economy more widely) benefit directly or do the benefits of lower costs accrue only to shareholders and employees (from bonus payments)?
- Are there benefits from integrating a wide range of activities? If there are, do the benefits flow to customers or to employees and shareholders?
- Does global reach enable firms to generate a higher return on capital employed and does it provide customers with a service that domestic firms cannot provide by simply accessing a range of firms across the globe?
- If the industry has fewer large firms, does this give them a better control of the prices they can charge, i.e. does it give them monopolistic/oligopolistic pricing control at the expense of their customers and society in general?
- If firms are very large, does this raise public interest questions? First, can such firms be too large to manage and thus give rise to risks from management failures? Regardless of management failures, does the **too large to fail doctrine** result in moral hazard in such large firms?

## INTEGRATION

All industries have some element of specialisation by the firms which operate in it. In a previous age there were specialised greengrocers, butchers, fishmongers, furnishers, dry goods stores, chemists, retail banks, telephone system providers, etc. This meant that a customer requiring all these services would have to visit and transact with a range of independent firms. Today, on the other hand, supermarkets try to offer 'one-stop shopping', i.e. every type of foodstuff plus clothing and perhaps home furnishings, banking, chemist's products, insurance services, email accounts, mobile phone services, petrol station services, etc., even though there are few connections between these different (non-food) products. The cost of providing a full-service shopping experience of this type is probably lower than for the aggregate of specialists and thus the prices charged to customers could be lower than for specialist stores.

In practice customers might be willing to pay the same or **higher** prices just because of the convenience of one-stop shopping. If this were so, the benefits of integration would flow to shareholders (and perhaps also employees) rather than to customers and thus society as a whole. If, however, there were many similar supermarket chains, competition between them would almost certainly drive prices down to a level which reflected the lower costs of an integrated service.

Thus the benefits would flow to customers (as a result of competition) and thus to society as a whole.

In the financial world, it is not simply a question of offering a wide range of products. It is also a question of whether or not different activities that need to be combined to offer a single product or service such as equity trading (broking + dealing + research) should be combined in one company or offered through separate companies. This is a question which is analysed in economics in terms of **integration through the market** (i.e. contractual relationships between independent companies in the value chain leading to the final product) or **integration through a hierarchy** (i.e. bringing all elements of the value chain in-house, within the same parent company and employing a bureaucratic structure and internal transfer pricing contracts between the different departments in the value chain to offer a similar service). There is also a much more fundamental question which is whether or not customers benefit from using a **full-service, integrated company** to supply the majority of their financial services. An analogy can be made with a different industry – electric power. In the UK this was once an integrated industry in which a single (nationalised) company owned and controlled power generation, the national grid which distributed the power across the nation and the retail supply to customers. The same company also had retail showrooms for appliances. Today UK power generation is in the hands of a number of competing companies. The national grid is controlled by a different company. Finally, the distribution of electricity to households is offered by many competing suppliers. There is also a need to consider the issue of conflicts of interest between the firm and its customers and between different sets of customers which the firm serves. Conflicts of interest have become a key issue in financial services firms as a result of the integration of a wide range of services.

*Integration through the market.* In this industry structure, each company within the industry specialises in one small part of the business – for example there are many securities brokerages, wealth managers, independent research houses, securities dealers and asset managers who specialise in only one business area. At one time there were also many specialist corporate finance advisory houses (these have reappeared in the last decade) and trading houses and of course insurance companies and commercial banks. For the financial **system** to work well, some of these different specialised firms providing particular functions have to be linked together as they are parts of a chain leading to the final service provided to clients. For example, a stockbroker needs to be linked to securities traders and to researchers. A corporate finance advisor needs to be linked to commercial banking and investment banking services in order to be able to recommend possible suppliers of these services. A wealth manager needs to be linked to asset managers to obtain 'product' to retail to customers. An investment bank (corporate facing) needs to be linked to securities distribution firms (investor facing) but the two activities and sets of customers do not need to be integrated within a single company. In the past, these different activities, though organised through separate companies, were integrated through **market relationships**, i.e. contracts under which business was undertaken between separate firms. It was thus possible for a firm at one stage in the value chain to choose the 'best of breed' company in another stage of the chain with which it would then cooperate.

Prior to 1986 in the UK, it was illegal for a single firm to offer both brokerage and dealing, i.e. **only integration through the market was allowed by law**. Such a form of industrial organisation was presumably thought to avoid conflict of interest but, importantly, it was also said to work well in many respects.

*Integration through a hierarchy.* Today financial activities are mostly integrated through what is known as a '**hierarchy**', i.e. internal organisation within a single enterprise with multiple departments doing business with each other under a set of company rules, rather than through contracts between independent companies. This gives rise to the problem of ensuring that all parts of such companies operate as a single team when appropriate in order to realise any possible benefits from synergies. This, however, often gives rise to conflicts.

A potentially important objection to integration through a hierarchy is that there is a clear incentive for a company to try to keep all business in-house, thereby avoiding competition, with the aim of increasing pricing power and hence margins. In contrast, market integration involves competition for business at each stage in the chain and a best of breed supplier can be chosen. Highly integrated firms are also likely to have far greater conflicts of interest within the firm (many of which will be irresolvable) than would be the case when integration is between separate firms. It has been reported, for example, that when Goldman Sachs was asked by a regulator around the turn of the millennium to list all the potential conflicts of interest in their business, they came up with a list of 500 such possible conflicts. In 2010, the case against Goldman by the SEC in respect of conflicts of interest in its sales of CDOs to IKB in Germany makes it clear just how conflict-ridden the investment banking business is.

Most financial companies started life as specialists and gradually extended the scope of their business, their size and geographical spread. Thus, when we look at today's financial conglomerates which have the major share of revenues in this industry we find that they have generally been created by the **acquisition** of many specialised firms rather than through **organic** (internal) **growth**.

When we look at investment banks, we observe that it is only relatively recently that each of the very different constituent components of the securities industry – the investment bank (corporate facing), broker (investor facing), securities trading (principal activity-making markets) – have come together to offer a full range of functions through one company, thus creating what is sometimes known as a **broker/dealer** or, more generally and somewhat misleadingly, as an **investment bank**. The name 'investment bank' may not be historically correct but it is the normal term now used for this type of institution. It is also only relatively recently that such companies have offered services from offices in all the major continents of the world.

An example of this process of moving from being a single purpose partnership which started as a corporate finance house, i.e. a traditional investment bank, is Morgan Stanley. Until 1997, Morgan Stanley would have had market relationships with a range of **wire houses**, i.e. national brokerage chains, of which one would have been Dean Witter.

In 1997 Morgan Stanley, which until then had been principally an investment bank in the traditional meaning of the word (organising new issues for corporations), acquired Dean Witter in order to allow it to distribute to retail and institutional investors a considerable proportion of those issues which it origi-nated. This acquisition, in historical terms, is very recent. The question we should ask is whether or not this acquisition and others it has made benefitted employees, shareholders or customers, i.e. did any potential benefits from the acquisition accrue to employees and shareholders rather than to customers? If they accrue to customers, that represents the public interest. If the benefits accrue to employees, in the form of higher bonuses and shareholders in the form of higher dividends, that represents private benefits.

Until 1997 Morgan Stanley was a very successful investment bank. An acquisi-tion such as Dean Witter (and subsequently Smith Barney) is an example of **inor-ganic growth**, i.e. growth resulting from acquisition rather than from starting up from scratch. On the other hand, Merrill Lynch, which was originally principally a nationwide brokerage (wirehouse), decided to expand its investment banking capability **organically**, i.e. not through acquisition but by internal diversification and rapid expansion in new and risky business areas, in particular mortgage secu-ritisation, in order to build a fully integrated firm of similar size to its competitors. Sadly, this was a failure due to the hubris of chief executive Stan O'Neil (2003–07) who was willing to take on a level of risk that his counterparts in other firms were unwilling to do. He seems to have believed that if such risks led to higher returns he would be a hero. Today Merrill Lynch is part of Bank of America, as the invest-ment banking activities it had expanded into under O'Neil led to such large losses that it was no longer viable as a stand-alone company. Many would say that it was actually insolvent prior to takeover.

**Bancassurance** is a term used to describe conglomerates which combine retail banking and insurance and which employ the bank's retail network to distribute insurance products – life insurance and general insurance. The bancassurer may also manufacture insurance, i.e. do the underwriting (liability side of the balance sheet) and investment functions (asset side of the balance sheet) required to run an insurance operation. The logic of bancassurance is that both sets of products are sold to retail clients and thus both can be sold through bank high street branches. Despite this, the bancassurance model is one without sound conceptual underpin-nings and may not survive as the standard business model, even in Continental Europe where it has long been popular.

One reason it may not survive is that, in practice, cross-selling between insur-ance and banking products is difficult as many customers do not like having a bank clerk suddenly ask them about insurance when they are making an enquiry about their bank account. Equally, there is no necessary logic in insurance underwriting being combined with retail insurance selling. They are different businesses with quite different skill sets. There is also no necessary logic in combining the liability side of insurance, i.e. underwriting risk, with the asset management side of insur-ance which involves portfolio management. Indeed smaller insurance companies contract out this business. Thus any bancassurance firm could be broken down into a retail bank selling bank products, an insurance company selling retail products through comparison websites such as gocompare.com, an insurance underwriting company and an asset management company which manages insurance portfo-lios for a range of insurers as well as managing in-house funds. In turn, the asset manager might choose to contract out trade execution to firms which specialise in this function. Thus 'dis-integration' of the value chain might be a better operating model than a highly integrated one.

Recently, one of the key proponents of the bancassurance model – ING bank – started the process of separating its insurance side from its banking side. This was partly due to a requirement of a regulator but also because there is no necessary logic in the combination. This is discussed in the next chapter.

## RETAIL BANKING AND INVESTMENT BANKING

We should not really cover this topic under the heading 'integration' since there is no obvious need for these two different businesses to be integrated. There is little obvious economic connection between them. When they are integrated within a single firm or holding company the reason is normally to take advantage of low cost insured retail consumer deposits for investment in banking assets, something which is clearly against the public interest, or for reasons of capital or liquidity regulatory arbitrage which is also likely to be against the public interest. It has also been argued by some firms that it enables the wealth management division to sell investment banking products to its customers (the wealth manager could of course buy-in such products). It is because of the lack of any obvious beneficial synergies between these two businesses that the UK Chancellor the Exchequer announced in December 2011 that the UK would enforce a ring fencing of UK retail banking from investment banking following the recommendations of the Vickers Report (which is covered in more detail in Chapter 28).

# 27 CASE STUDIES IN FINANCIAL SERVICES: SUCCESS AND FAILURES

Keeping investment banks alive in difficult times is challenging. Many have failed to survive. Bear Stearns and Lehman are only the latest in a long line of investment banks which have failed over the past decades. Royal Bank of Scotland and Citigroup are examples of those which survive, but in a much weakened state and only through temporary state ownership. Indeed the failure rate of investment banks over decades has made some rating agencies view them as not being eligible for 'investment grade status' in their company ratings. JP Morgan Chase is one which came through the financial crisis strengthened relative to its competitors. Even harder is the creation of a new 'bulge bracket' investment bank able to challenge the other major houses. I will now offer a contrast between a successful challenger and an unsuccessful one, before looking at some of the walking wounded from the war of attrition of 2007–12.

## A TALE OF TWO COMPANIES: BARCLAYS PLC AND NOMURA

### Barclays Capital: a case study of the successful creation of a bulge-bracket investment bank

In the UK, it was illegal to combine commercial banking with 100% of a securities broking or dealing firm until a reform of the law in 1986 which became known as Big Bang. In that year Barclays acquired a broker (de Zoete & Bevan) and a dealer (Wedd Durlacher). These were combined (something else which was illegal until 1986) into Barclays de Zoete Wedd, or BZW as it was known. BZW was not a success. Like many UK-owned firms in broking and dealing, trying to compete with US bulge-bracket firms, which had so much more experience, was difficult or impossible.

In 1996, BZW was headed by Martin Taylor who in that year hired an American, Bob Diamond, to help build an investment bank out of the small brokerage and dealing firms they had purchased ten years earlier. But within two years, by 1998, Taylor lost confidence in the ability of a UK commercial bank to build an investment bank, given how risky it was, and tried to shut it down. The reason for his change of mind was the loss of £250 million in the Russian bond market meltdown of 1998. Taylor's comment in 2002 about the circumstances at that time was: 'the board was attached to this fantasy of a UK investment banking champion. It was absurd, absolutely absurd'.[1] Not surprisingly, he left the bank in 1998 to be replaced by his hire of two years previously, Bob Diamond. In contrast to Taylor, Diamond told the *Financial Times* in an interview on 18 June, 2009 after the Lehman acquisition: 'our aim is clear. It's to be the premier global investment bank over the next couple of years'.

The first strategy that Diamond had employed to expand BZW when he still worked for Taylor, was to take large proprietary trading bets to try to generate revenue as a short-cut to growth. One of these bets was on Russian bonds, a move which led to the losses mentioned above. One manager who was there at the time is quoted by the *Financial Times* on 14 March 2010 as saying: 'we had a large prop desk – that was one way to cover the costs of setting up an investment bank. But we lost a fortune'. Soon after this loss, BarCap, as it was now called, was cut down to being essentially a fixed income house without equity trading, IPOs or merger and acquisition capability.

Focus such as this is clearly one possible strategy which may be successful. It may seem surprising to learn that a bank such as Barclays would **bet the bank** on the price of Russian or any other securities. However, a few years before this I was present at a meeting with the Bank of England with colleagues from Security Pacific Bank. We complained about the impossibility of building an investment bank because there was insufficient profit in either originating eurobonds or in trading UK gilts. The response of the Bank of England was simply that it was necessary to take a speculative view on prices based on research and market knowledge in order to have a chance of success. Thus Diamond's strategy was not unusual and was, indeed, standard practice in US investment banks but not in UK ones.

In 2002, Enron, the world's premier commodity and energy company, collapsed due to fraud. As its demise meant a sudden reduction in competition in these trading markets, Barclays moved rapidly to enlarge very substantially its commodities business, in part by taking on staff who had previously been employed by Enron. Commodity trading has, of course, seen dramatic growth in activity since that date to the benefit of Barclays profit and loss account.

Over time BarCap has also returned to equities and M&A but it was the opportunity to acquire Lehman Brothers which was the '**game changer**'. Originally the US Treasury wanted Barclays to acquire Lehman (the company), but without knowing its true value it was impossible for Barclays to offer a price that would be attractive to the Treasury unless the Treasury also gave a guarantee. In the end the Treasury found no alternative but to offer to sell Lehman in pieces. Barclays bought the US operation while Nomura bought the European and Asian parts.

In 2000, BarCap had a balance sheet of approximately £160 billion. By 2008, i.e. post-Lehman, it had grown to £1,600 billion (it is now somewhat smaller, like almost all investment banks). By then it was employing around 23,000 staff compared with around 4,000 a decade earlier. There is little doubt that today BarCap is a success, though in this business fortunes can change very quickly, and it has indeed become one of the bulge-bracket houses since the Lehman acquisition.

---

[1]  'Taylor Salvo for Barclays', 4 March 2002, http://www.telegraph.co.uk/finance/2755580/Taylor-salvo-for-Barclays.html

## Nomura: a case study in which the ability to create a global investment bank is still unproven

The other acquirer of Lehman assets in 2008 was Nomura whose story has worked out differently. You should note the change in fortune that is perceived by the financial press between 2010 and 2011 in the excerpts from the *Financial Times* below.

### Nomura's Challenge Is Winning Market Share

Building a global investment bank in the aftermath of the worst financial crisis in generations would probably be viewed as a step too far for most institutions. Not, however, for **Nomura**, the Japanese securities group that snapped up most of Lehman Brothers' European and Asian assets when the US investment bank collapsed in September 2008. At the time, analysts and investors queried whether Nomura, as a Japanese house, would be able to bed down an acquisition that added 8,000 people accustomed to operating in Lehman's no-holds-barred culture, virtually overnight. Two years on, with the integration having gone better than many senior executives expected, Nomura's challenge is winning market share and revenues.

At the time of the Lehman purchase, Nomura's management believed there would be big opportunities for a 'pure play' investment bank, i.e. one without a commercial bank parent, as several big US and European rivals faltered or were forced to accept government handouts to survive. But many of those institutions, such as UBS and Bank of America, recovered far more quickly than expected, limiting Nomura's ability to gain share in areas such as equity and debt capital markets – especially when it still lacks critical mass in the US.

Having tried and failed to crack the US market several times before, Nomura has spent the past 18 months adding hundreds of staff to its North American business. The group now employs nearly 2,000 people there, up from just 650 two years ago. Some executives would like to boost that number dramatically, potentially through the acquisition of a mid-tier US investment bank – although Nomura is quick to stress that no suitable target has been identified, nor is any deal in the offing. Investors are increasingly clamouring for the bank to deliver on an international growth strategy that continues to drag on profits. [Figure 27.1] shows Nomura's corporate structure.

*Financial Times*, 21 December 2010

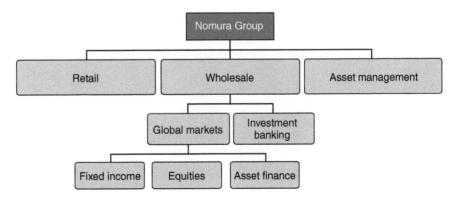

**Figure 27.1**   Nomura corporate structure
*Source*: Nomura.

### Lehman benefits still elude Nomura

Nomura's chief executive admitted the Japanese investment bank's overseas businesses had not met expectations, as it unveiled results showing it is still not reaping the benefits of its Lehman Brothers takeover. Kenichi Watanabe said the bank's goal this year was turning round the global wholesale business. 'Nomura's performance in global markets was a bit disappointing,' said Shigeru Oshita, chief fund manager of Japanese equities at Chuo Mitsui Asset Trust and Banking.

'What we have to do is, firstly, make profits where we invested,' Mr Watanabe said, referring to the European, Middle Eastern and Asian operations of Lehman that Nomura acquired in 2008. The bank does not break down its profits geographically, but it said businesses in the US, Europe and Asia were loss making in the year to March.

It had shifted its focus to business areas where it could be competitive and enforced a pay-for-performance culture to rein in compensation costs, he said. Nomura now expects the wholesale division to achieve revenue growth of 15 per cent annually, and pre-tax margins of 10–15 per cent, compared with 1 per cent last year. Nomura managed to cut compensation costs, which had surged to 48 per cent of net revenues in the third quarter, as the bank continued to hire aggressively, particularly in the US, to build up its presence there.

*Financial Times*, 28 April 2011

### Nomura: the only way is up

Quarter after quarter, Nomura's results seem to confirm an immutable law of investment banking: a good deal for bankers, a bad one for investors. Take the dividend for the year to March – Y8 ($0.10) per share. At the same stage in 2008, before Japan's premier brokerage started sifting through the wreckage of Lehman Brothers, it was paying out Y34 per share. Meanwhile, compensation and benefits as a proportion of revenue from broking, investment banking and asset management are now 75 per cent, up from 58 per cent immediately pre-Lehman. No prizes for identifying the real beneficiaries of chief executive Kenichi Watanabe's vision to build a top-five global investment bank.

It is little wonder, then, that a more sober tone has taken hold among management. Executives won't disclose internal targets for profitability, but they are talking, at last, of providing a better return for shareholders. The US platform is more or less complete; wholesale division chief Jesse Bhattal has reshuffled a few lieutenants elsewhere. While rivals are preparing investors for the shock of single-digit returns on equity rather than the 15–20% they have become used to, Nomura's remain stuck in the 1–2 per cent range. The only way, surely, is up.

*Financial Times*, 28 April 2011

### Nomura's Global Goal Faces Steep Challenge

Nomura has reached a critical point in its struggle to become a global powerhouse as its share price hovers around a 37-year low and after Moody's warned its credit rating could be lowered to one notch above junk.

While Nomura still dominates in Japan – thanks to its retail and asset management units – the overseas wholesale business is sagging under the weight of high costs, and is losing large amounts of money as a result. Between July and September, its retail operations generated Y10.7bn ($137m) in pre-tax profits while its wholesale business made a Y73bn loss. 'They are taking money from their best business and putting it into overseas investment banking, where they have no edge,' says one Singapore-based hedge fund manager. Nomura's shares are trading at a mere 0.4 times book value – similar to some of Europe's weakest banks – reflecting concerns about a further deterioration of its balance sheet and poor profitability, says a Tokyo-based analyst.

Although the globalization of its Japanese clients means Nomura needs to maintain an overseas presence, analysts and financial industry officials increasingly believe the bank will have to scale back its overseas ambitions to maintain a better balance with its ability to generate profits at home.

*Financial Times*, 28 November 2011

## Why has the outcome for these two companies, Barclays and Nomura, been so different?

Like most questions of this type there is no comprehensive answer. But we can cover some of the areas that may be relevant. But first it is important to understand that there are always two possibilities which may lead either to success or to failure. One is good (or bad) strategic analysis and choice and the other is effective (or ineffective) strategy implementation It is sometimes difficult to know which of these factors is most important in determining success or failure. In addition, of course, there is the issue of luck – good or bad, which in practice may be the most important factor.

The first difference between these two companies is that Barclays was a commercial bank before branching out into securities and then into investment banking, whereas Nomura was essentially a broker which has, over many years, tried to become an international investment bank. It might seem that the latter would be more likely to succeed than the former given that they would seem to be in the same business area as investment banking, whereas commercial and investment banking are considered by many to be quite different businesses. But in fact a brokerage background, particularly retail brokerage in which it has its roots, is probably the worst possible starting point for building an investment banking franchise. Brokers don't think in terms of risk and spreads. They think in terms of commissions. It can be almost impossible for those who have climbed the seniority ladder to become senior managers in a brokerage business (agency) to change their entire mindset and to think instead as principals. Without this, success is unlikely.

A second difference is the nationality of the two companies and the respective outlook of society in the two countries in which they have their head offices. The UK has always had a liberal approach to granting work visas to foreign nationals. Investment banks in the UK are unlikely to have a majority of UK citizens working for them, and the range of countries from which people are hired is very wide. In addition, English is the international language which most business people speak and therefore it is not difficult for a foreigner to become a manager or a director in the home country of a UK bank. Most importantly, in the UK, as in the US, promotion is based on ability, not tenure: as a meritocracy, remuneration is performance-based and not a fixed salary, as it is frequently in Japan.

Japan has a more insular culture than the UK or the US, is more hierarchical and less meritocratic. It also has not, traditionally, paid people based on the amount of revenue or profits they generate but on the basis of 'rank' and seniority. Most people in Japan do not speak English as a second language and cultural differences between Japan on the one hand and Europe and the US on the other are very substantial. Trying to create a global investment banking franchise is, consequently, an uphill struggle. For financial institutions from other countries trying to build a global franchise, this is an important lesson to learn.

Barclays was a pure commercial (retail and wholesale) bank in 1986. Commercial bankers, like brokers, are also not generally good at running investment banks. But by the time of the Russian crisis in 1998, Barclays would seem to have created a separate investment bank which was no longer run by ex-stock brokers or UK citizens alone. Thus the hiring of Americans such as Bob Diamond at that time may have been an important factor in moving BarCap away from a commercial banking, stock broking and UK mindset.

Nomura, on the other hand, remains essentially a stockbroker with a broking mindset rather than a dealing mindset. It is also essentially a domestic firm and in large part retail, in a country which is mainly interested in domestic securities and not international securities. It has not managed to introduce Western style management and in consequence has found it difficult to attract the best performers. Without the entrepreneurial approach taken by US investment banks (or those which copy US practices) it may not succeed in building a global investment banking franchise, regardless of whether the chosen strategy is logical or not. In terms of the City of London as a whole, success as a centre for international investment banking was not achieved until old traditions were swept away after the reform of the stock exchange in 1986 and until US citizens with deep experience of investment banking and principal businesses started to take senior positions in UK investment banking institutions.

## UBS: WITHDRAWING FROM THE RACE?

UBS had long been known as the major asset and wealth manager in Switzerland and was extremely successful in this activity. Rates of return were high and risk was low. UBS had also had a successful eurobond underwriting and trading operation in London for many years. In 2001, it decided to try to become one of the bulge-bracket underwriters able to compete with the major US investment banks. By 2003, UBS had moved to fourth in the investment banking league table from seventh. Over the subsequent four years, UBS consistently ranked in the top four in the global fee pool and for 20 consecutive quarters it had reported rising profits. Of course, these turned out, in practice, not to be profits since the degree of risk attached to them had not been properly estimated in terms of expected loss. In early 2009, UBS reported that it had lost 20 billion Swiss francs (US$17.2 billion) in 2008, the biggest loss of any Swiss company ever. The crisis resulted in it taking a total write-down of around $50 billion, mainly on mortgage related assets.

UBS had long talked about the benefit to clients and shareholders of its integrated structure comprising investment banking, asset and wealth management, and commercial banking. But in August 2008, the newly appointed chairman,

Peter Kurer, admitted that there were flaws in this business model when he said that his **strategic review** had 'clearly revealed the weaknesses associated with the integrated "one firm" business model'.

### Integration Loses its Attraction

UBS has long been amongst the most vocal cheerleaders for the integrated banking model combining investment banking and wealth management. But after more than $42bn of write-downs in its investment bank, Switzerland's largest financial institution is publicly questioning that model. The big unknown is whether this will lead to a break-up.

The admission that investment banking and wealth management are not necessarily complementary businesses is a seismic shift for UBS. It also flies in the face of the integrated strategies that its peers are pursuing. But Peter Kurer, the new chairman, changed the group's tune on Tuesday when he said a strategic review had 'clearly revealed the weaknesses associated with the integrated "one firm" business model'.

It is hard to imagine Marcel Ospel, his predecessor and the architect of the modern day UBS, ever saying such a thing. Right up to his departure Mr Ospel was arguing in favour of UBS's integrated future. But UBS is returning to the drawing board because the subprime mortgage crisis has hit it harder than any other European bank. **Most worryingly, the losses have prompted clients to withdraw cash from UBS's core wealth management business.** To cap it all, UBS is coming under pressure from **activist shareholders** to take radical action.

UBS's answer is to establish its three main business units – investment banking, private banking and asset management – as standalone entities that will no longer share each other's infrastructure, people or capital. They will not be legally established as subsidiary companies, but will effectively function as such. All they will share is the UBS brand, and ultimate oversight by the group management. The idea has two goals. The first is to ensure that all of UBS's businesses – but mainly the investment bank – take risks in a calculated way. The idea is to prevent the investment bank falling into the trap of taking big gambles for small rewards, because the group has access to cheap funding.

'The rationale of imposing greater capital discipline on the business units by this separation is obviously a good thing,' says Matt Spick, analyst at Deutsche Bank.

All the same, UBS has let a genie out of the bottle in **floating the possibility of a full-scale divorce between investment banking and wealth management**. Insiders say it intends to usher in a major cultural shift by forcing staff to work in a more segregated way. If that succeeds, it may be hard for UBS to renew its wedding vows with the integrated model.

*Financial Times*, 13 August 2008

### UBS Charts Aggressive Course

Few institutions have faced a greater challenge in investment banking than **UBS**, the Swiss group that was forced to write off $50bn in mortgage related losses at the height of the financial crisis. Having long touted the benefits of an 'integrated' model that was supposed to profit from synergies between its three main businesses – investment banking, wealth management and asset management – UBS's securities division was exposed as a teetering house of cards built on toxic assets.

Like many of its rivals, UBS believes tighter global capital and liquidity requirements will benefit those banks which trade predominantly on behalf of clients, rather than for their own 'proprietary' desks. The group has added about 750 people across its fixed-income and equities divisions during 2010, boosting capacity but also driving up the cost-to-income ratio in its investment bank to 80 per cent. The group needs to hit its medium-term targets of SFr20bn ($20.7bn) in revenues and SFr6bn in profit before tax – targets it will fall far short of this year. Is ratcheting up risk in an expanded investment bank the answer? Investors were repeatedly told at a conference in London last month that **UBS, in contrast to some rivals, will be more aggressive with its bets over the coming months**. Its next chapter may be just as interesting as the last.

*Financial Times*, 21 December 2010

The next few months certainly were interesting. Within just over six months of the above statement (in bold), the *Financial Times* reported:

### UBS Pulls Back on Investment Banking

'UBS is downsizing its investment bank.' The Chief Executive told the FT that UBS's investment banking arm would focus on supporting its flagship wealth management business rather than competing with global rivals in capital intensive areas such as fixed income trading. 'The question we really had to ask ourselves', he said, 'was how much trading do we need in our investment bank to satisfy the needs of our wealth management business and how much do we need to build on top of that to be relevant as an investment bank.'

After barely surviving the financial crisis, UBS is pinning its future on continued growth in private banking, particularly in Asia and other fast-growing markets, rather than more volatile trading profits. Analysts and investors have long agreed that the wealth management arm, which in 2009 settled a long-running tax evasion probe with US regulators, is the jewel in UBS's crown.

The investment bank, by contrast, has lost momentum in spite of hiring hundreds of bankers over the past two years. The division's pre-tax profits slumped 71 per cent during the second quarter, to SFr376m, compared with the same period last year.

Several analysts questioned, however, whether a rather limited restructuring of the investment banking, as opposed to a full break-up, would solve UBS's woes. 'While a partial downsizing of some investment banking activities may be positive for leverage and mix, it leaves the tough question of how viable and how profitable a mid-sized investment bank can be,' said analysts at Barclays Capital. 'Memories of ABN AMRO come to mind.'

*Financial Times*, 27 July 2011

The following year a dramatically large loss hit the bank as a result of an unauthorised trading bet going wrong. Such events often trigger a dramatic re-structuring as observed below.

### UBS revamp goes back to Warburg roots

In September 2011, UBS announced that it has suffered a loss in its so-called Delta One department as a result of a single trader taking large bets using derivatives (up to $10 billion in positions) and in consequence losing the firm $2.3 billion. This suggests to observers that despite reporting that it had totally overhauled its risk management system, it had actually failed to do this adequately. The result may be that UBS further downscales its investment banking division. However, when we examine the future structure of the industry an important issue is the use of in-house investment banking products to support the wealth management business. It may be argued that wealth managers would be more successful if free to buy 'best of breed' products from any investment bank supplier rather than being forced to buy in-house.

Since UBS announced its loss, its CEO, Oswald Grübel, has resigned over the issue of the extent to which UBS should retain its investment banking operations. One reason for scaling back is given by the statistics in a report by RBC Capital markets which analyses the Group's business mix and (internal) capital allocation. The report notes that in 2010 the investment banking division accounted for **60% of allocated capital or risk-weighted assets but for only 35% of pre-tax profits**. In contrast the wealth management business accounted for **33% of pre-tax profits but only 8% of allocated capital and risk-weighted assets**. The imbalance is clear

The rapid change in fortunes of UBS since the financial crisis is likely, in fact, to take it back to being more like S.G. Warburg, the UK merchant bank it purchased in the mid-1990s:

Warburg's words hark back to a different time in which the reputation of an institution 'for integrity, generosity and thorough service' was its 'most important asset'. For UBS's board, these founding principles would be a good place to start as they refocus the Swiss institution's investment bank.

In Saturday's statement announcing the departure of chief executive Oswald Grübel from the bank, it was revealed that the board of directors had asked the group executive board to accelerate the implementation of the investment bank's client-centric strategy, concentrating on advisory, capital markets, and client flow and solutions businesses. The word 'client' was repeated no less than four times in the short statement, while a quick examination of UBS's most recent quarterly results shows client was mentioned 55 times in the document.

Outgoing chairman Kaspar Villiger said in Saturday's statement: 'In the future, the investment bank will be less complex, carry less risk and use less capital to produce reliable returns and contribute more optimally to UBS's overall objectives.'

While the bank will continue to utilize its vast equity research, sales and trading platform and aspects of the fixed income business, not least to service its own wealth management clients, there appears to have been a shift of focus back towards the old advisory business that UBS acquired in 1998 when it merged with Swiss Banking Corporation, which had three years before acquired SG Warburg.

*Matt Turner, Financial News, 27 Sep 2011*[2]

## The UBS investor day: 18 November 2011

This was the day when UBS finally announced that proprietary trading within UBS had effectively ceased. Fixed income trading activities would be wound down because the return that could be generated by a second-tier player such as UBS was not commensurate with the capital that had to be committed to this activity.

On this day, UBS committed to cutting the total of risk-weighted assets on its balance sheet in half by selling them to investors or other banks. Two particular

---

[2] *Financial News*, 27 September 2011 (www.efinancialnews.com/story/2011–09–27/ubs-revamp-back-to-sg-warburg-roots?ref=email_35883).

areas the bank said it would exit were asset securitisation and complex structured products. Essentially the bank would revert to what it once was, i.e. essentially a wealth manager. However, the parts of the investment bank that facilitated this function, and could produce good risk adjusted return on capital, would be retained. UBS will be smaller and less risky in future. One has to assume that, as well as being under pressure from investors, they were also under pressure from the central bank and the regulator in Switzerland. It is quite possible that they made it clear that a country the size of Switzerland (small) could no longer afford to have 'too large to fail' banks in the country since they gave rise to the risk that they were 'too large to save'.

Although the future of UBS's investment banking division as a full-service, bulge bracket house might have looked bleak at the time of the UBS investor day referred to above, since then, the arrival of a new co-head of investment banking would seem to have enabled the bank to generate synergies from his previous contacts and the bank's access to funding as reported by the FT:

### UBS puts armoury at Orcel's disposal

UBS is gearing up to use its balance sheet heft to back its new co-head of investment banking as the Swiss group steps up efforts to revive its status in the market.

Sergio Ermotti, chief executive, last week hired Andrea Orcel– a 20-year veteran of Bank of America Merrill Lynch – to jointly run UBS's investment banking operations in an early sign of the direction of his strategic ambition. According to people close to the chief executive, Mr Ermotti is committed to backing the client relationships that Mr Orcel will bring with funding commitments on a par with those made available by BofA. 'We need to take risk. We will have the same kind of risk appetite as BofA,' one banker said. The news will come as a surprise to those who have written off UBS as a force in European investment banking after a rogue trading scandal last year and political pressure in Switzerland for the bank to retrench.

In the €7.5bn rights issue for UniCredit, which BofA led – a deal Mr Orcel described as the 'scariest of my career' – BofA stunned rivals with its preparedness to take on such a risk amid a volatile eurozone financial environment.

It has emerged that some of BofA's biggest clients in Europe are set to desert the bank and are gearing up to follow Mr Orcel to UBS. Both Santander and UniCredit, two clients with which Mr Orcel has close longstanding relationships, are preparing to shift business from Merrill to UBS, the Financial Times has learnt.

Mr Orcel is seen as one of the best-connected advisory bankers in Europe thanks to close relationships with chief executives and other top executives. Intesa Sanpaulo and Monte dei Pasche de Siena in Italy, as well as VTB and Oleg Deripaska in Russia, are among his other clients.

UBS's hiring of the man dubbed the 'George Clooney of banking' and its commitment to support clients with financing emphasises the shift the Swiss group is looking to make at its investment bank as it retreats from certain activities, particularly in fixed income.

But insiders say it would be wrong to view the strategy as new, particularly in Mr Orcel's specialist area of financial institutions. UBS led Deutsche Bank's €10bn rights issue 18 months ago and has underwritten fundraisings that include the UniCredit cash call and others at Commerzbank, BBVA, Santander and Bank of Ireland.

*Financial Times*, 26 March 2012

## MERRILL LYNCH: CASE STUDY OF ASSET MANAGER/WEALTH MANAGER/ NEW ISSUE HOUSE THAT TRIED TO BREAK INTO THE INVESTMENT BANKING BULGE BRACKET

In November 2007, Stanley O'Neil resigned as CEO of Merrill Lynch after large losses on subprime securities. A month later John Thane, the former CEO of the NYSE, was appointed CEO but was forced to resign a little more than a year later as losses mounted and he was found to have acted in inappropriate ways in regard to staff bonuses and other matters. Speaking to US business network CNBC a few months before he resigned, however, he picked on the wealth management business to get him out of a tight spot:

> We believe we will shortly be back at profitability. The good news is that we have a very different mix of business than a pure investment bank. Our wealth management business, which is about **half our revenues, doesn't use very much capital, doesn't take very much risk, has great return on equity and margins, and it has been pretty much immune to the ups and downs of the marketplace**.

> CNBC, 8 August 2008

One has to wonder why Merrill, which clearly had an extremely good business model in its wealth management area at that time, should then, under the 'leadership' of Stan O'Neil, set upon a strategy to build up a business – the mortgage securitisation business – which eventually destroyed it. The mortgage securitisation business, in contrast to wealth management, could be described as using a lot of capital and being very risky.

In practice it gave negative returns on equity (huge losses) and indeed the whole CDO structured finance business virtually disappeared after the financial crisis. For Merrill it resulted in its having to be acquired (by Bank of America) in order to save it from collapse. As in so many cases of corporate problems, they arise from the governance mechanisms in a company not being able to constrain the ego of the CEO despite clear evidence that their 'strategy' does not represent a business model which is viable in the longer-run. Thus even though the CEO may propose a strategy, it should be the role of the board to examine the logic of the strategy, for example, potential reward versus risk, and prevent it being implemented if they believe it is not in the interests of the shareholders.

## CITIGROUP: A CASE STUDY OF A FIRM WHICH WANTED TO BE ALL THINGS TO ALL MEN AND WOMEN

An important question is whether a very large widely diversified company in terms of both products and geographical locations is able to achieve economies of scope and scale (synergies) which enable it to generate either greater economic value for shareholders or higher pay-outs for employees or whether its complexity actually leads to a loss of economic value. Citigroup, for example, has been proposed as the paradigm (a very good example of a particular model) of the 'complex financial institution' as regulators describe such companies. As we now know it failed and had to be nationalised, in part because of over-complexity leading to an 'unusual' corporate government structure.

The '**Company Perspectives**' below from the Citigroup website in 2003 suggests that the company is a model of a safe and profitable enterprise. As we now know, at the time this was written, it was actually heading towards bankruptcy and subsequent nationalisation by the US government.

### Company Perspectives

We are an economic enterprise with ... a relentless focus on growth, aiming to increase earnings by double digits on average; a global orientation, but with deep local roots in every market where we operate; a highly diversified base of earnings that enables us to prosper under difficult market conditions; capital employed in higher-margin businesses, each one of which is capable of profitable growth on a stand-alone basis; financial strength protected by financial discipline, enabling us to take risks commensurate with rewards to capture attractive opportunities; a close watch on our overhead costs, but with a willingness to invest prudently in our infrastructure – we spend money like it's our own; a focus on technological innovation, seamlessly delivering value to our customers across multiple platforms.

Clearly the above statement was no more than a marketing 'puff' for the company. In fact the real truth was exactly the opposite to what is written above.

## ING: A CASE STUDY OF THE ABSENCE OF EXPECTED SYNERGIES, DIVERSIFICATION AND CROSS-SELLING OPPORTUNITIES

INGs banking arm was the thirteenth largest in Europe and its insurance business was ranked sixth in the world. However, what has become clear since the financial crisis is that the basis of ING's success, as for other bancassurance groups, was as much as anything a result of 'arbitraging' the regulatory capital requirements of banking businesses and insurance businesses. It was commonly believed, and believed by regulators, that these two types of business were not closely correlated. If this were so then the regulatory capital required by one side of the business could also be used by the other side since supposed lack of correlation between banking and insurance means that both would be unlikely to be hit by a crisis at the same time. Since the financial crisis, when the assets of both parts of bancassurers were hit at the same time, it became clear to regulators that their assumption of a lack of correlation was mistaken. Today, European bancassurers have to capitalise each part of their business separately according to the requirements of the Capital Requirements Directive (banks) and the Solvency II Directive (capital requirements of European insurance firms).

The two parts of the business are being completely separated with the insurance and asset management business being sold. The explicit reason for this is that on becoming insolvent and obtaining state aid to enable it to survive as a going concern after the 2008 financial crisis, the competition requirements of the European Union which prohibit state aid required the company to split in two to avoid action by the European competition authorities. However, the implicit reason is that there is no obvious benefit to shareholders from combining the two businesses once the previous capital advantage was eliminated.

The benefits of cross-selling insurance products to banking customers are often given as a reason for believing in the bancassurance model beyond that which was supposed to be achieved from diversification benefits. However, in practice these are often difficult to realise. Apparently only 13% of the total sales of the insurance side of the business came through the banking side. In addition, it is not clear that there are true customer benefits. The benefits may all accrue to employees and shareholders.

## Other businesses without obvious synergies

Other insurers have, for various reasons, chosen to sell their insurance arms or their banking arms. Allianz, one of the world's largest insurers (€1 trillion of assets under management) acquired Dresdner Bank some years ago, partly for diversification reasons. In practice the merger did not work and in 2008 Allianz sold Dresdner to Commerzbank. Allianz now holds 20% of Commerzbank as an investment but the previous concept of creating a bancassurer has not been pursued further.

Rabobank, a major Dutch bank, acquired 39% ownership of Eureko – a large insurance and asset management business in 2005. It appeared that the intention was to create an Allfinanz business which is one step further in combining financial services than bancassurance. The logic is that a bank has a large branch network and can therefore sell banking products, insurance products, mutual funds and other asset management services. In practice this concept would also not appear to have worked as intended. One factor has been that in the financial crisis, Rabobank had to, or chose to, inject its share of a €1 billion capital raising into Eureko just to avoid it becoming insolvent and to retain its proportional share ownership.

In November 2011, Deutsche Bank reported that it was conducting a strategic review of its US and other asset management divisions due to regulatory changes and associated costs. The division is ranked twelfth globally by Pensions & Investments. While asset management has been profitable for Deutsche Bank more recently, the division has struggled for years to gain scale, lagging behind much of the industry. Deutsche Bank acquired much of its current asset management business through its purchase of Bankers Trust, a US commercial/investment bank in the late 1990s, and also the US-based asset manager Scudder Investments in 2002. They believed the deal would help push Deutsche to the top of the global rankings in asset management. However, the bank's lack of experience in the US, which is the most competitive of all regions, has made the achievement of this aim difficult. It has also been reported that the division had high costs relative to other global asset managers.

What is certainly clear from what has happened since the crisis is that merging different financial businesses within one holding company may not bring the expected benefits. One reason is that if a bank owns one insurer it is likely to offer its customers only that insurer's products. Consumers generally do not like such a model and are likely to shop around elsewhere for the best product or the best value, such as may be found on a comparison website or via a broker. Thus cross-selling, also known as 'one-stop shopping', is not necessarily what customers want, in contrast to the situation for supermarkets. In addition, product distribution (of insurance for example) simply does not require ownership of the insurance underwriter itself. There is no obvious reason why combining these two activities should result in a business being more profitable than either part separately.

It is also the case that, increasingly, insurance companies are splitting their underwriting activities (the liability side of their balance sheet) from the asset management side of their business (the asset side of the balance sheet). The reason for this is that these two sides of the business involve very different skills, and in the latter there are very considerable economies of scale and specialisation which can be achieved from large asset management businesses. Thus smaller insurers now may contract out the asset management side of insurance. The larger insurers now frequently set up a separate asset management company to manage their own (in-house) funds, and this company is then also free to offer third-party asset management to outside customers.

# 28 THE FUTURE STRUCTURE OF THE INDUSTRY: IMPLICATIONS OF RE-REGULATION

The following quotation from Henry Kaufman, one of the best known bankers of the last 30 years (he was on the board of Salomon Brothers which is now part of Citigroup and latterly Lehman Brothers) suggests that the conglomerate structure of the financial services industry that has developed since the 1990s has led to the creation of companies which have a risk incentive structure that is inappropriate for society's needs:

> Meanwhile, top managers at many financial institutions will find themselves in unfamiliar territory. Their mode of operating, their business culture, has been to pursue aggressive growth targets for profits and market share by diversifying operations into new financial domains and by swallowing up competitors. Wielding generous compensation incentives, managers of leading banks encouraged employees to take big risks. As institutions grew and diversified, their activities became too wide-ranging and complex for senior managers to oversee effectively. At the same time, risk-taking came to rely more and more on quantitative risk-modelling, which tended to marginalize qualitative investment judgment. As we now know, econometric risk-modelling failed when it was most needed.
>
> Henry Kaufman, 'Prepare for Change on Wall Street',
> *Financial Times*, 2 June 2010.

Growth by acquisition, diversification and conglomeration and the shift from partnership structure to public company status have certainly changed the nature of firms in the industry and the industry itself. The incentive structures that have been created may have resulted in a heads we (the bankers) win, tails you (society) lose. A belief that the new business model which has led to the conglomeration of so many different types of business in G-SIFIs and a skewed incentive structure within these large complex firms has led to many proposals for change by governments, supranational bodies and regulatory agencies.

A key question is whether these large 'conglomerate' financial institutions are now too large and complex to manage as well as being too large to fail but possibly also too large to save. These issues were explored in a paper by Michael von Bretano,[1] former senior investment banker and chairman of ICMA until 1992.

---

[1] 'Too Big to Fail: Too Big to Manage', LSE FMG Paper, May 2010.

He notes that the management structures of some financial groups, Citigroup in particular, as a result of their enormous size and diverse range of businesses, have had to change from the model which is generally understood as the governance structure of public companies. Such governance structures are designed to ensure that the 'buck stops here' at the main board level. As was discovered by a US Senate Committee, this is not the case in such 'complex financial institutions':

> Some of the complexities of such a system were quite vividly demonstrated recently when top executives of Citibank appeared before a Committee of the US Senate. The bankers clearly baffled the Committee members when they seemed to suggest they were not personally responsible for the bad risks in their balance sheet as this responsibility had been delegated to a highly capable executive on a lower level.
>
> A critical result of these developments appears to have been hardly noticed so far: the fact that the executive boards of the parent company of such 'banking conglomerates' no longer control day-day-day operations.
>
> The traditional two-tier structure of the executive and the non-executive boards has been superseded by a three-tier structure; beneath the traditional structure a third level has been established consisting of the division/product heads who are responsible for the various operating units. It follows that the boards of directors of such an organisation are no longer supervising the executives in the traditional way because they are mainly dealing with the executives of the second tier whose primary role is to supervise the executives on the third level who in reality manage the bank.

'Too Big to Fail: Too Big to Manage',
LSE FMG Paper, May 2010.

Clearly Citigroup was a company which flouted a basic rule of corporate governance – that the buck stops here with the directors on the board who are responsible for everything that happens at a lower management level. The board members are indeed responsible for the bad risks in their balance sheet and this responsibility cannot be delegated. Clearly Citigroup was **too big to manage**. For a country the size of the United States it was not too big to save but, had it been based in the UK or Switzerland, it is unlikely the state would have had the resources to save it.

In analysing these issues, the question of what 'society' thinks is important. Commercial and investment banks exist only at the behest of the population of a country. Their purpose within society, as we have noted a number of times, is to facilitate the process of economic change leading to higher living standards for the population of a country through economic growth and the maintenance of full employment. They do this by meeting the financing, saving and investment needs of households and companies. Commercial banks, in particular, are different from other companies in that their 'compact with society' – the various support mechanisms provided to them in the form of liquidity insurance, deposit insurance, the 'too large to fail doctrine' and lower financing costs due to explicit and implicit government support – means that they are not in fact operating as typical private companies. However, one cannot just assume that a small number of profit-maximising companies (banks and other financial institutions) operating within a country actually do provide appropriate financial services to their corporate and personal customers and to society at large. This is clearly a highly complex issue. We can only cover the question of firm and industry structure briefly in this short chapter but I hope that it will provide readers with some thought provoking ideas.

The financial services industry will be greatly changed by new regulations mostly consequent on the failings within financial institutions and in regulation and supervision that became apparent during the financial crisis. But in addition, the realisation in Europe that there is a symbiosis between the eurozone banking problem and the eurozone sovereign debt problem has raised further issues. That problem manifests itself most obviously when legislators suggest 'force-feeding' government debt into the banking sector to solve sovereign debt problems (via, for example, the LTRO programme of the ECB) at the same time as they are proposing to inject government equity capital into such banks in order to make them strong enough to hold such risky sovereign debt. Unfortunately if a country itself is in financial difficulty, and indeed the EU itself also, it is unlikely it can provide the 'too large to fail' financial support that its banks may need.

The key policy change in respect of banks has been the acceptance of the need to reduce the risk of their collapse through higher capital and liquidity requirements as detailed in the Basel III proposals. While these changes, of themselves, will not eliminate the possibility of crisis or collapse, along with changes in the nature of regulatory supervision and industry structure they will certainly strengthen the system. Policy changes are aimed at reducing the probability of:

- *The collapse of a single bank*: through tougher prudential controls on capital and liquidity to reduce the likelihood of a financial institution collapsing;
- *A systemic crisis*: *through* a reduction of systemic connections to minimise the risk of a systemic crisis and to reduce the likelihood that a single bank collapse impacts on other financial institutions in such a way as to risk their collapse;

And, if a bank does collapse, reducing the cost of:

- *Resolving a single bank collapse*: *through* changes in banks' corporate structure and activities to ensure that if a financial institution does collapse that its 'resolution' is unlikely to require a call on taxpayer resources.

Following from these three types of policy change, there are four factors likely to impact on the future structure of the banking industry in the US and in Europe. These are:

- The need for additional capital to replace capital wiped out by the financial and eurozone crises and in addition the increase in regulatory capital that is required under the Basel III rules;
- Competition concerns of governments and competition authorities consequent on the observed supernormal levels of profitability and consequent large bonus payments prior to the crisis;
- A desire by governments never again to have to face the issue of 'banks which are too big to fail' and which can only be rescued using taxpayer funds;
- The perceived changing economics of the industry and any benefits or drawbacks resulting from large scale or extensive scope.

From the regulatory viewpoint, the key objective is to prevent another systemic crisis which puts domestic economies and the global economy at risk. Trying to prevent such a repetition involves, at the level of the individual firm, trying to ensure that the risk taken by investment and commercial banks is reduced or that the capital and liquidity requirements imposed on investment banks to protect against risk are increased or some balance between these two. Regulators world-wide are currently working on an appropriate framework (Basel III) designed to reduce the risk of a repetition of the crisis.

In terms of sources of investment banking revenue, bulge-bracket investment banks in particular Goldman Sachs, in the run-up to the crisis had changed from being mainly agency firms providing client services to corporates on the one hand and investors on the other to being proprietary risk-taking companies in many ways similar to hedge funds. This is clear from the huge proportion of revenue attribut-able to 'trading and principal activities' which can be seen by looking at profit and loss accounts up until around 2008. One reason why there would seem to have been this shift was the realisation that it was possible for such firms to generate enor-mous revenue from risk-taking and to ensure that a very high proportion of such revenue accrued to employees – 50% of revenue being a frequently quoted figure. This incentive structure meant that a focus on short-term profits by managers and employees was entirely logical, even at the cost of creating huge 'tail risks', i.e. risks which might seem unlikely to materialise but which do in fact materialise much more frequently than might be expected. One key change made by regulators in a number of countries to minimise skewed incentive structures has been a require-ment that a high proportion of total bonus based on revenue generation must be paid to employees in the form of shares with a vesting period of at least five years or only at the point of retirement (as was the case in partnerships).

## NEW REGULATIONS AND THE STRUCTURE OF THE INDUSTRY

In the United States, the Dodd Frank Act (based on the Volcker proposals), signed into law in July 2010, is to some a reversal of the Gramm–Leach–Bliley Act of 1999 and a re-enactment of the 1933 Glass Steagall Act. In fact that would be an over-simplification. Its aim is:

> To promote the financial stability of the United States by improving accountability and transparency in the financial system, to end 'too big to fail', to protect the American taxpayer by ending bailouts, to protect consumers from abusive financial services prac-tices, and for other purposes.

While it will not be known for some years how the Act will, in practice, affect financial firms it is certainly designed to reduce the extent to which banks can be involved in proprietary activities as distinct from client-related activities. Its overall purpose is to improve financial stability. However, its success can only be judged many years into the future.

## NEW REGULATIONS IN THE UK

There are many aspects to the 're-regulation' of financial firms in the UK but we will explore only one – the proposals published by the Independent Banking

Commission in September 2011, which is likely to lead to the enactment of legislation in 2012. The Commission, chaired by Sir John Vickers, was established by the Chancellor of the Exchequer (the UK finance minister) in June 2010 to recommend changes to the UK banking industry structure following the worst financial crisis in living memory. The Commission was asked to consider reforms to the UK banking sector to promote financial stability and also to make the market in the provision of retail bank services more competitive.

The twin objectives, 'financial stability' and 'competition', are key. Financial stability means avoiding another banking collapse. Its opposite, instability, is something that, were it to happen again, would probably topple any government on whose watch it happened. But, more importantly, the problem faced by the authorities is that they no longer have the firepower to put out the flames from another banking fiasco. Banks, as we have discovered recently, have a symbiotic relationship with governments and could cause the collapse of the sovereign authority itself.

The need for more competition in (retail) banking markets is to avoid the banks generating excessive profits (economic rents) and simply making their employees increasingly better off by exploiting the consumer, thanks to an uncompetitive market for retail services. Competition is key to reforming the banks since without it they may become lazy, impose unjustified charges and try to ensure that pay for employees comes before customer service and low charges – just like any company would do.

The recommendations of the Commission in respect financial stability fall essentially into two areas:

- 'Ring fencing' the UK high street retail banking business from the City of London wholesale and investment banking business within any banking group;
- Increasing the amount of equity capital which retail banks must employ to finance their operations in order to provide more protection to depositors and hence to the taxpayer.

Ring fencing is thought by many analysts and commentators to be, on balance, a worthwhile step despite the objections that the major banks have raised in respect of the proposal. It would do no more than take us back to earlier times before 1986 when banks and investment banking were separate and when the economy was actually growing much faster than it is today. It would also force the retail component of the bank with its now required separate board of directors to focus on the 'real economy', i.e. lending to businesses and households rather than trying to find ways to create assets to trade independently of what might be happening in the real sector.

The proposals would be effected by creating a separate company to provide UK retail banking services. A new holding company would also be formed which would own both the retail bank and the wholesale/investment bank. The two companies would be required to have separate capital and liquidity reserves. With ring fencing, if the retail part of the bank got into difficulties it could be rescued by the government, 'resolved' to use the jargon, at much lower cost to the taxpayer than the banking conglomerates we have today. On the other hand if the trading part of the bank collapsed, there might (should) be no need to rescue it. It could be allowed to collapse. It seems likely to me that once domestic retail banking is offered to customers through a separately capitalised company from investment banking that the likely outcome is for the two, very different, businesses to be completely separated. This could be achieved either through a flotation of the retail bank in an IPO or through a distribution to the shareholders of the group which holds shares in the retail bank.

In summary, the outcome of the deliberations of the Vickers Commission probably represents a good step in the right direction towards returning retail banking to its former role – helping the growth of the real economy. But equally, it is only one set of the many reforms that needs to be taken over the years ahead to provide the UK with a banking system that will also be safe and not liable to plunge the country yet again into a state of financial instability. It should also be noted that it is unlikely to have any impact on competition in investment banking. In this business area, government policy in a number of countries, such as forced mergers post-2007, combined with the collapse of a number of investment banks during the financial crisis, means that competition in investment banking is now much less than before 2007. Unfortunately, new entrants into the field have had only limited success, as we noted in the case study of Nomura. Equally, UBS has decided that it is not going to succeed as a bulge-bracket investment bank and is withdrawing from many activities.

## TRANSACTION TAXES: A TOBIN TAX

Many politicians and voters feel that the financial industry has changed from being one which provides services to households, small firms and large enterprises to being one which generates revenues indirectly from households and firms through structured transactions and trading. In consequence there have been attempts a number of times in the past to introduce a tax on transactions, often known as a transaction tax or 'Tobin tax' after the original promoter of such a tax. The latest attempt to introduce such a tax has come from the European Union which in September 2011 proposed the introduction of a rate of 0.1% for cash market transactions and 0.01% for derivative transactions. It is not clear if the purpose of such a tax is principally as a revenue source for governments or if it is designed to reduce trading, which is seen as unproductive – but it is probably the former. It might also be seen as an alternative to introducing value added tax on financial transactions, a tax which is currently not imposed within the EU. However, the introduction of a transaction tax would require all EU countries to vote in favour and the UK, not surprisingly as it has the largest financial sector, has said it will vote against the proposal.

## WHAT WILL BE THE INDUSTRY STRUCTURE IN 2020?

The board of directors and senior managers in commercial and investment banks focus on return on equity as a measure of their success. Since banks have a very low return on assets it is necessary to leverage such returns in order to achieve an ROE in excess of the bank's cost of equity capital. Regulators were very concerned that under the previous Basel rules it was possible for banks and investment banks to have leverage ratios, i.e. the total balance sheet size divided by the tangible equity, of 60 times. Under the new rules the minimum leverage ratio will be 3% (33 times leveraged). Thus banks will have to increase their return on assets (or generate more fee income) if they are to achieve previous ROEs. One way to do this is to automate more bank processes to reduce costs. A good example of a bank which is trying to achieve this is Santander UK, an offshoot of the major Spanish bank:

> Speaking at Santander's annual investor conference in London, Ms Botín predicted that the UK business would deliver a return on tangible equity (RoTE) – a measure of profitability than excludes goodwill write-offs – of about 11 per cent in 2012 and 2013, down from 15 per cent this year.
>
> Meanwhile its cost to income ratio – a measure of how much it has to spend to generate revenue – was expected to jump from 45 per cent this year to 48–50 per cent by 2013.
>
> The bank plans to invest £490m over the next two years, roughly half of which will be used to improve its service for small and medium-sized businesses and the rest on upgrading systems and overhauling its retail arm. That is expected to start paying off in 2014, when Ms Botín forecasts a RoTE of at least 16 per cent – a number that exceeds the targets of other UK banks. Ms Botín said the bank faced 'strong headwinds' over the next two years, including a weaker than expected economy, higher funding costs and what she called an 'increasingly onerous and uncertain regulatory environment'.
>
> 'Santander UK Chief Warns on Profitability',
> *Financial Times*, 29 September 2011

I have to say that I think it is unlikely that banks in general will achieve a 16% ROE. If they do, it would suggest that the banking industry is either very uncompetitive (thereby generating supernormal profit) or that it is taking a very high, and unacceptable to the taxpayer, level of risk. We should expect the ROE to be comparable to that of other companies in the UK and not very much higher. Bill Winters, former co-head of JP Morgan's investment bank, thinks that the best-run banks will be able to generate an ROE of maybe 13%, compared with 20–25% historically. He also thinks there will be a middle tier which achieve a 9–11% return with the weakest ones below that.

## DERIVATIVES TRADING AND CLEARING

In the case of investment banks it seems likely that many of the activities that were able to generate high returns, either because of lack of transparency for clients (and hence high profit margins) or because they involved high leverage or excessive risk taking, will no longer be sources of high profit due to the changing regulatory structure. An example would be derivatives trading where bilateral trading, in some cases without a competing dealer market structure or much transparency, has led to high profit margins in the past. New regulations on both sides of the Atlantic to try to force most 'standardised' transactions on to multilateral trading platforms, with trades then going through a clearing house, should both reduce margins and make transactions more transparent both to customers and to regulators.

It would seem likely that the investment banking industry will decline in total size, i.e. in terms of the number of employees, profit generation, percentage of GDP, etc. However, even if that happens, it is still likely to be a much larger industry than it was at the start of the 2000s. But for those looking for a career in the industry, it is vital to understand the changing business model of the industry and to seek out the areas of business that are expanding and are, if only for a few years, highly profitable.

## WILL RE-REGULATION OF THE INDUSTRY PREVENT ANOTHER FINANCIAL CRISIS?

The short answer to this difficult question is: no. It is not possible to make a completely safe financial system without greatly reducing the availability of funding for valuable projects that would benefit society. As with most things in life it is a question of balance, in this case on the one hand between making the system safe and, on the other, ensuring economic growth and full employment.

The unfortunate aspect of re-regulation is that at the date of writing financial industry lobbying seems to have persuaded legislators that the balance should tilt towards the minimum change in substance in order that the industry can carry on as before without having to curtail many of the practices that have led to difficulty in the past. At the same time, some areas are in danger of being over-regulated, yet without any guarantee against failure. All I can say at this point, therefore, is that I believe there will be future crises, both banking and sovereign debt related, and the most we can hope for is that the severity of them, and the cost to taxpayers, will be reduced by the measures taken by bankers, governments and regulators.

## POSTSCRIPT – THE JP MORGAN CIO LOSS AND ITS IMPLICATIONS FOR GOVERNANCE AND REGULATION

As this book went to print, it was announced (on 11 May 2012) that JP Morgan had suffered a trading loss over only a few weeks, of at least $2 billion but with a final cost to the bank expected by some to be as much as $7bn. What was alarming was that this was not the result of unauthorised trading by a so-called 'rogue trader' such as Leeson (Barings), Kerviel (Soc Gen) or Adoboli (UBS) but by traders within the so-called Chief Investment Office (CIO) which was supposedly hedging the bank's overall risk. Thus it was supposed to be the office which reduced the risk to which the bank was exposed.

The loss within this department will hit directly at the attempts by banks to limit the extent to which the Volcker rules will be loosened by legislators. Banks have been lobbying strongly to try to prevent the proposed rules reducing their proprietary trading by more than a token amount. Indeed, JP Morgan has tried to argue in the past that the Volcker rules could severely damage the ability of its Chief Investment Office (CIO) to manage the bank's risk i.e. to reduce the risk of loss and hence the possibility of collapse. It would seem that although the chief investment office was supposed to be hedging risk, it also functioned as a profit centre, taking on what seem in retrospect to have been exceptionally large positions.

It was reported in the Daily Telegraph:[2]

> Senior executives at JP Morgan were given repeated warnings about the controversial unit responsible for a shock $2bn trading loss at the bank. Staff from the bank's investment banking arm privately told the management – including chief executive Jamie Dimon – that the bank's Chief Investment Office was 'an accident waiting to happen'.
>
> Bill Winters, the former co-chief executive of JP Morgan's investment banking division is among senior staff at the bank who made clear their concerns about the risks being taken by the CIO.
>
> One source with knowledge of the situation said: 'This had been red-flagged for at least a year, there was no way Jamie did not know about the concerns many people had.'

Commentators have in the past deemed JP Morgan to be the best run bank in the world with the best risk systems as it was the one which best survived the financial crisis. If this is so, then it raises questions about the quality of strategic management and risk management in others. It also raises the possibility that bankers have already, post crisis, returned to what they like doing best – taking outsized risks with other people's money. I say this because the function of the 400 staff in the CIO was to hedge positions and invest 'excess deposits'. Of these 400 staff, many were former proprietary traders. It would seem possible that as the impending Volcker rules made it harder to hold large risky positions on proprietary books such risk positions were moved under cover into the CIO. It is said that the office held $360 billion of securities and had become the major player on one side of a CDS index trade. The system to measure risk in this office was also reported as giving a Value at Risk (VAR) of $67m when in fact it was $129m. Clearly even if the VAR figure had been correct, it did not give anything like a useful indication of the possible loss. Interestingly, you will note that one of the key people giving early warning about the risks being taken by this office was none other than Bill Winters[3] – the man who Mr Dimon said was not adequately skilled to be responsible for the commercial banking side of a universal bank. You might like to consider what conclusions you come to after considering this case in more detail.[4]

The excerpt from a *New York Times* article below, also raises the question of why regulators were not aware of potential problems in the CIO. The suggestion is that regulatory capture i.e. regulators being too close to those they are regulating and supervising, was one possible reason for the loss:

### Regulators are under scrutiny in JPMorgan trading loss

Scores of federal regulators are stationed inside JPMorgan Chase's Manhattan headquarters, but none of them was assigned to the powerful unit that recently disclosed a

---

[2] 'Accident Waiting to Happen at JP Morgan', *Daily Telegraph*, 12 May 2012.

[3] http://www.telegraph.co.uk/finance/newsbysector/banksandfinance/9262085/The-day-JP-Morgans-Jamie-Dimon-lost-his-sparkle.html

[4] 'How Dimon Was Knocked Off His Pedestal by the London Whale' Http://www.telegraph.co.uk/finance/newsbysector/banksandfinance/9260941/JP-Morgan-2bn-loss-Dimons-in-the-rough.html

multibillion-dollar trading loss. Roughly 40 examiners from the Federal Reserve Bank of New York and 70 staff members from the Office of the Comptroller of the Currency are embedded in the nation's largest bank. They are typically assigned to the departments undertaking the greatest risks, like the structured products trading desk. Even as the chief investment office swelled in size and made increasingly large bets, regulators did not put any examiners in the unit's offices in London or New York, according to current and former regulators who spoke only on the condition of anonymity.... The lapses have raised questions about who, if anyone, was policing the chief investment office and whether regulators were sufficiently independent. Instead of putting the JPMorgan unit under regular watch, the comptroller's office and the Fed chose to examine it periodically.

### Regulatory influence

The bank pushback also suggests that JPMorgan had sway over its regulators, an influence that several said was enhanced by the bank's charismatic chief executive, Jamie Dimon, long considered Washington's favourite banker. Now, as regulators scramble to determine whether the chief investment office took inappropriate risks, some former Fed officials are asking whether the investigation should be spearheaded by the New York Fed, where Dimon has a seat on the board. Some lawmakers and former regulators also have reservations about the comptroller's office, which is investigating the trade and was the primary regulator for JPMorgan's chief investment unit. 'The central question is why Jamie Dimon was able to so successfully convince both its regulators that there was nothing to see at the chief investment office,' said Mark Williams, a professor of finance at Boston University, who also served as a Federal Reserve Bank examiner in Boston and San Francisco. 'To me, it suggests that he is too close to his regulators.'

Regulators are not typically stationed at divisions like JPMorgan's chief investment office. Such divisions are known as treasury units. The units hedge risk and invest extra money on hand, and tend to make short-term investments. But JPMorgan's office, with a portfolio of nearly $400 billion, had become a profit center that made large bets and recorded $5 billion in profit over the three years through 2011 ......Long before the recent trading blunder, JPMorgan had a pattern of pushing back on regulators, according to more than a dozen current and former regulators interviewed for this article. That resistance increased after Dimon steered JPMorgan through the financial crisis in better shape than virtually all its rivals.

Jessica Silver-Greenberg and Ben Protess /
*New York Times News Service* 26 May 2012

# THE FATAL FLAW IN CAPITAL ALLOCATION: THE SHIFT FROM A TRUST MODEL TO A TRANSACTIONAL MODEL

We have examined the problems to which individual financial firms became subject during the financial crisis. But we also need to consider wider factors that were driving the industry as a whole in the direction that it was taking over a long period of time. To understand this narrative it is necessary to think in terms of how firms compete over time and what happens when the regulatory framework results in the rules of competition being changed – not just in the current period of regulatory change but stretching back to the first steps towards deregulation.

Financial market regulators until the 1970s and 1980s were generally opposed to competition between banks or at least to what they considered to be 'excessive' competition. In the early 1970s financial systems were characterised by important restrictions on market forces which included controls on the prices or quantities of business conducted by financial institutions, restrictions on market access, and, in some cases, controls on the allocation of finance amongst alternative borrowers. These regulatory restrictions served a number of social and economic policy objectives of governments. Direct controls were used in many countries to allocate finance to preferred industries during the post-war period; restrictions on market access and competition were partly motivated by a concern for financial stability; protection of small savers with limited financial knowledge was an important objective of controls on banks; and controls on banks were frequently used as instruments of macroeconomic management.[1]

In the case of equity markets, most countries permitted stock exchanges to have what was known as a 'fixed commission structure' which meant that competition for trading business on the basis of the percentage commission charged was not permitted. Thus the commission on a large trade was a very large cash amount even though the cost of executing it might be no more than for a small trade. This structure did, in fact, subsidise retail trades at the expense of wholesale trades.

Fixed commissions were abolished in New York on 1 May 1975, known as 'Mayday'. In London fixed commissions were abolished on 27 October 1986, a

---

[1] Malcolm Edey and Ketil Hviding, 'An Assessment of Financial Reform in OECD Countries', OECD Economics Department, Working Papers nos 154 (1995).

date known as 'Big Bang' when, also, UK brokers were for the first time allowed to combine with jobbers (dealers and market makers) to create integrated broker/dealers. Abolishing fixed commissions immediately resulted in brokers competing on price for the first time and led to lower profitability in brokerage in both countries.

The so-called agency broking model became much less attractive to broker/dealers since the fee that could be charged in the newly competitive market for this type of service no longer covered its cost. But over time the business based on the capital commitment model (dealer side of the business) also became much more competitive as a result of competition leading to falling spreads (partly as a result of the greater transparency arising from information vendor price feeds). As a result, the return on capital committed to helping clients execute trades fell.

There was also a shift in the types of client for whom the banks were willing to provide capital to facilitate business. The first of these new types of client was the hedge fund. Hedge funds wanted excellent execution services and, most importantly, were willing to pay appropriately for that service as well as for other 'prime brokerage' services. At the same time, another type of client, private equity, was proving extremely profitable, provided the investment bank was willing to commit capital. In this case the capital was for bridge loans at high margins to enable private equity firms to make acquisitions followed later by long-term financing in the capital markets to replace the bridge financing. These financings brought interest rate spread income followed by fee income. Subsequent to this there would be an IPO or trade sale which also generated high levels of fees for the investment banks. Thus both sets of new clients, hedge funds and private equity, proved to be much more profitable to service than traditional mutual funds or pensions funds (which were always trying to drive down transaction costs) or smaller companies trying to go public but where fees charged might barely cover costs and which were unlikely to make use of investment bank services subsequent to the IPO.

Realising that the business model of hedge funds and private equity was potentially a much more profitable one than investment banking itself, many investment banks, started to shift their own business model from just servicing these new clients to employing their own capital in these same activities. Traditional client trade execution for mutual funds and pension funds continued to be important, but more for the information flow that such trades generated which enabled the bank's proprietary desk to have a greater insight into market direction and hence which side of a trade they should be on.

In this new business model, security analysis (research) was increasingly seen as a luxury since the revenue generated from falling trading commission income and ever tightening trading spreads was not sufficient to support the type of research that had been undertaken in the days of fixed commissions. In consequence research became more focused on encouraging (hyper) active trading (often known as 'churning') with counterparties rather than actually enabling them to generate alpha.

Alpha generating research increasingly became a hedge fund activity or, to the extent that it was produced within investment banks was not shared immediately with their clients but used on the proprietary trading desk. Also, as brokerage commission from investor clients became increasingly unable to support in-depth research, the corporate finance side of the investment bank began to use researchers as an adjunct to IPO activity. By taking researchers onto the corporate finance payroll the corporate finance staff were able to ensure that the research produced would support the (high) pricing of the new issues they were undertaking (he who pays the piper plays the tune). As a result, broker research became much less independent. Indeed a number of brokerage houses have been prosecuted for issuing research which claims that a company is a great investment while internal emails describe those same companies as 'a piece of s---'.

The role of the investment banking division (which arranges IPOs) within an integrated firm has traditionally been to act as a gatekeeper and an 'endorser' of companies which are being taken public. When a major issuing house such as Morgan Stanley or Goldman Sachs brought out a new issue, the name of such 'white shoe'[2] issuing houses (as the lead manager) on the prospectus was like a 'good housekeeping' seal of approval. The function is similar to that which a bank performs when it reviews potential borrowers, decides whether to lend or not and then determines the appropriate interest spread (price) for a loan with that level of risk. This 'underwriting' function traditionally has been one of the key factors in overcoming the asymmetry of information between investors and companies at the time of an IPO. In this regard it is similar to the function of the rating agency in respect of debt issues where the rating is a 'good housekeeping' seal of approval and helps overcome the inability of investors to perform a detailed credit analysis of the borrower. Traditionally, therefore, reputation was the key to the success of an investment bank in its primary market function. We now know that revenue generation for shareholders (and staff bonus payments) came increasingly before the fiduciary[3] role that we might have assumed brokers or broker/dealers and rating agencies performed for their clients.

In addition to the abolition of fixed commissions potentially leading to broker/dealers becoming unprofitable, a second factor since 1975 was the increasing power of the computer. Improved and lower cost technology developed by information providers such as Thomson Reuters and Bloomberg led to greater transparency of markets through display screens in investor offices showing prices (pre- and post-trade transparency) which led to a lowering of margins on principal (market making) transactions. This was in addition to the reduction in commission margins on the broking side. However, computerisation also enabled more trades to be conducted without raising the cost base of the firm proportionately and facilitated a great increase in trading volumes. As with so many business, it then became a question of whether or not an investment bank could lower its costs and raise its transaction volumes fast enough to keep ahead of falling margins.

The on-going reduction in the unit profitability of executing trades for clients, whether as agents or principals, resulted in the boards of some investment banks

---

[2] 'White shoe' meaning a long established firm with a high reputation (originally those populated by White Anglo Saxon Protestants (WASPS) but now used more widely for any firm of high repute.

[3] A fiduciary is some who has a relationship of trust with someone another party. The fiduciary has a duty to act at all times for the sole benefit and interest of the party who has put his trust in the fiduciary.

deciding increasingly to employ their own capital to generate capital gains for the bank rather than simply using their capital to intermediate client trades and enable clients to (hopefully) make capital gains. This use of own capital is known as **proprietary trading**. This business model involved the best trading ideas that were developed in-house then being executed by the house. In such trades, it was most likely that the investment bank would be on the winning side and not the counterparty and thus despite trading being a zero-sum game the bank would hope to be on the winning side more than half the time.

It might seem strange that an investment bank would knowingly put its counterparty on the wrong side of a trade. But today it would seem that investment bankers believe they owe no, or little, fiduciary duty to their counterparties. In a series of interviews in April 2010, the US Senate's Permanent Subcommittee on Investigations tried to understand the role of fiduciary duty in an investment bank and to understand if investment banks still believed they owed clients such a duty. One of those they interviewed was the CEO of Goldman Sachs, Lloyd Blankfein, and their questioning was at least in part in relation to the Abacus CDO transaction to which I referred earlier. Blankfein seemed puzzled by the line of questioning. His Senate interlocutor, Carl Levin, seemed frustrated that Blankfein did not acknowledge that a bank may be conflicted if it is selling securities to clients but also itself, betting on a sharp fall in their value at the same time on its own account:

> *Levin*: When you sell something to a client, they have a right to believe that you want that security to work for them. In example after example ... we're talking about betting against the very thing you're selling, without disclosing that to the client. Do you think people would buy securities from you if you said, 'you know, we want you to know this, we're going to sell you this, but we're going out and buying insurance against this security succeeding. We're taking a short position' ... That's a totally different thing from selling a security and no longer having an interest in it ... Is it not a conflict when you sell something to someone, and then are determined to bet against that same security, and you don't disclose that to the person you're selling to?

> *Blankfein*: In the context of market making, that is not a conflict. What clients are buying ... is they are buying an exposure. The thing that we are selling to them is supposed to give them the risk they want. They are not coming to us to represent what our views are. They probably, the institutional clients we have, wouldn't care what our views are, they shouldn't care. We do other things at the firm ... where we are fiduciaries.

> *Levin*: And that's the part that's very confusing to folks ...

> *Blankfein*: I know.

> *Levin*: ... because they think you're fiduciaries.

> *Blankfein*: Not in the market making context.

> *Levin*: Yeah but they are not told that not only are you not a fiduciary, you are betting against the same security that you are selling to them, you don't disclose that. That's worse than not being a fiduciary. That's being in a conflict of interest position.

> *Blankfein*: The markets work on transparency with respect to what the item is. It doesn't carry representations of what position the seller has. Just think of buying from ... a stock exchange, or a futures market. You don't even know, you're not even supposed to know

who's on the other side. You could have the biggest mutual fund in the world selling all its position in something, they could hate it. You would never know that if you were a buyer of a stock... Liquidity in the market demands transparency that the thing is supposed to do what it is supposed to do. The people who were coming to us for risk in the housing market, wanted to have a security that gave them exposure to the housing market, and that's what they got. The unfortunate thing... is that the housing market went south very quickly... and so people lost money in it. But the security itself delivered the specific exposure that the client wanted to have.

The above exchange seems to confirm a somewhat different view as between legislators and investment bankers of what investment banks do. The model in the mind of legislators seems to be the old one; and the model in the mind of the investment banker is the new one. The investment banker seems unable to understand why the legislator does not realise that it is 'inevitable' that the contemporary investment bank is conflicted and is not, or perhaps never was, a fiduciary.

A key reason for the change from one business model to another was that investment banks had changed their ownership structure from private to public and their risk capital, instead of all being held by partners, came to be held mostly by outside investors. This leads to a different approach to both risk management governance. There were two main reasons for the move to public corporation status. First, the increasing cost of automation/computerisation, Second, the need for capital to enable increasing volumes of proprietary trading, merchant bank type activities (providing loan financing for business) and in-house hedge fund and private equity business. These all required ever more equity capital to support an ever growing balance sheet. In consequence, by 1999 (the year Goldman went public), every bulge-bracket investment bank had changed from being a private partnership to being a public company.

This new structure seems to have brought with it demands from the providers of capital for an ROE that was two or three times that expected of other industries (in 2006, the average ROE for investment banks was 23% and for Goldman Sachs it was 33%). It also brought a change in the business model from a trust-based one to a transactional one. Developments in computers and software had an important role in this change. Increasingly computers were being put to a new use, not simply to make business processes less costly. This new use was to enable the application of pricing models developed in academia to be useful in a practical setting. The Black Scholes option-pricing model was one of these. Computers and their associated programs also enabled the securitisation of loans and hence enabled the growth of the shadow banking system. It was in the creation and, more particularly the sale, of structured securities that the difference between the trust model of an earlier era and the transactional model of the new era manifested itself,[4] as demonstrated by Senator Levin's inquisition above.

Even Alan Greenspan, the greatest booster of the virtues of free markets and market self-regulation, appears to have been shocked by this change: 'in a market

---

[4] Suzanne McGee, *Chasing Goldman Sachs* (Crown Business/Random House, 2010) is an excellent book which helps to explain the changes in business models in banking.

system based on trust, reputation has a significant economic value. I am therefore distressed at how far we have let concern for reputation slip in recent years.'[5]

A very good summary of the **fatal flaw** – the shift from so-called **trust-based relationships** between an investment bank and its clients to the current **trans-actional-based model** – is given in the following, which was an analysis of the Goldman Sachs Abacus deal, a securitisation deal on which IKB (a German bank) lost most of its investment in Abacus assets while John Paulson's hedge fund made a very large return from being on the other side of the trade (see pp. 000–000). Both were **clients** of Goldman or, as Goldman would argue, both were **professional counterparties** in the transactions: they undertook with it.

The investment bank's historic raison d'être was in resolving conflict in situations where the formal law was ineffective. It did so by staking its **reputation** on promises to both parties to a transaction. Because both parties **trusted** it, the investment bank received fees for making these promises and, because it valued the fees that sprang from its continued trustworthiness, it worked hard to make meaningful promises, and to maintain its reputation.

This type of intermediation is also practiced by investment banks when, for example, they undertake to provide accurate information about a securities offering or about the quality of a stock tender offer. It is also central to the credit ratings industry, to auditing, and even to the news media.

It is highly unlikely that the firm would undergo a cultural shift from a trust-based, relationship-oriented business model to a more transactional one accidentally, and without a great deal of thought and introspection. To the extent that this change has occurred, it reflects economic imperatives. In particular, it is a response to technological change and, in particular, to changes in information technology.

Powerful desktop computers enabled wholesale banks to measure and to record data that previously had to be taken on trust. It enabled banks to adopt academic models like the Black Scholes formula for option valuation, and to build financial engineering businesses that rested upon these models. Financial engineering and better information technology both substituted for the **trust-based intermediation** that formerly was at the heart of investment banking business. Activities that previously had been the sole preserve of the relationship banker shifted increasingly to the trading room.

Within their dealing rooms investment banks rely upon a transactional, arm's-length model of business, so that they need a reputation for competence and transparency, but not for their ability to sustain private, trust-based trade. These technological and economic imperatives have caused changes to investment bank culture.[6]

---

[5]  Speech given at the Markets and the Judiciary Conference, Georgetown University, 2 October 2008.

[6]  Alan D. Morrison and Steven Davidoff. *Computerization and the ABACUS: Reputation, Trust, and Fiduciary Responsibility in Investment Banking* Centre for Corporate Reputation, Said Business School, working paper, 2010).

## WINNERS AND LOSERS IN THE NEW BUSINESS MODEL

The discussion in Chapter 27 suggests that the change in the investment banking industry business model described above has led to winners and losers within the industry. Goldman Sachs and JP Morgan Chase in particular would seem at this point to be winners. Others such as UBS, Nomura, Royal Bank of Scotland, Lehman Bros., Bear Stearns, Citigroup and Merrill Lynch have clearly been the losers. They latched on to the new model but when markets turned down they did not seem able to deploy the necessary risk management skills to minimise losses in this new capital intensive and highly geared transactional business model. It could also be argued, as it is in the following excerpt, that the type of leader of the large organisation has also changed, and this is what has enabled this new business model to flourish until it causes corporate collapse. Indeed, in the case of almost all investment banks, a key change in the business model was from that which held until the 1990s in which the CEO or chairman or both came from a corporate finance background (relationship business) to the model in the new millennium when almost all have come from a trading background (transactional business). The following excerpt from an academic paper suggests that some companies may have been run by those from the 1% of the population who have little conscience or empathy and who care little for anyone other than themselves.

When presented to management academics in discussion, the Corporate Psychopaths Theory of the Global Financial Crisis is accepted as being plausible and highly relevant. It provides a theory which unifies many of the individual interpretations of the reasons for the Global Financial Crisis and as such is worthy of further development. The message that psychopaths are to be found in corporations and other organisations **may be important for the future longevity of capitalism and for corporate and social justice and even for world financial stability and longevity**.

Stemming from this belief that the message concerning psychopaths in corporations is important, an aim of this paper has been to get the work that psychologists have been doing on psychopathy, and on 'successful psychopaths' and Corporate Psychopaths in particular more widely known to management researchers and to managers themselves. In particular the paper presents a theory concerning the Global Financial Crisis which may throw considerable light on its origins.[7]

An article in the Guardian[8] newspaper considers whether the CEO of Lehman at the time of its collapse might be the archetype of such a person

> I've never met Dick Fuld, the former CEO of Lehman Brothers and the architect of its downfall, but I've seen him on video and it's terrifying. He snarled to Lehman staff that he wanted to 'rip out their [his competitors] hearts and eat them before they died'. So how did someone like Mr Fuld get to the top of Lehman? You don't need to see the video to conclude he was weird; you could take a little more time and read a 2,200-page report by Anton Valukas, the Chicago-based lawyer hired by a US court to

---

[7] Clive R. Boddy, 'The Corporate Psychopaths Theory of the Global Financial Crisis', *Journal of Business Ethics* (2011) 102: 255 - 259

[8] *Guardian*, 29 December, 2011: 'Beware Corporate Psychopaths – They Are Still Occupying Positions of Power' by Brian Basham

investigate Lehman's failure. Mr Valukas revealed systemic chicanery within the bank; he described management failures and a destructive, internal culture of reckless risk-taking worthy of any psychopath.

So why wasn't Mr Fuld spotted and stopped? As I see it, in its search for never-ending growth, the financial services sector has actively sought out monsters with natures like Mr Fuld and nurtured them with bonuses and praise.

If one asks more generally why such people would even have been hired, it has been suggested by some in the industry that they are especially sought out in good times because of the revenue they can generate in such an environment. They are often described as rainmakers who are very valuable in good times but need to be subject to particularly close and effective governance during difficult times in the market. Equally, of course, some rainmakers are people with high-level social skills who can develop good business relationships. The value of such people comes from their ability to develop and maintain such relationships.

## INDUSTRY EFFICIENCY

In Chapter 15 and other parts of this text I have considered the extent to which the capital allocation mechanism, i.e. the financial services industry, performs the task of resource allocation in an appropriate fashion. A second relevant question about the industry is the resource cost of the 'machinery' which enables this allocation process.

I noted in Chapter 1 that The Turner Review[9] calculates a figure for the value added of monetary and other financial institutions to be 3.5% of GDP in 2000, rising to almost 6% of GDP by 2007. Thus the financial services sector in the UK which, alternatively, we can call the capital allocation machinery, used almost twice the proportion of society's resources to achieve this allocation process by the time of the financial crisis, compared to prior to the build-up period. In the US the proportion in 1960 was 3% of GDP (for labour alone) while 50 years later it was at least 7% of GDP.[10] Not only is this a very large component of GDP just to allocate resources in the new, high tech and intellectually complex world of finance, it also involves employing many of the best minds available in society. These same people could be employed by other industries producing outputs such as health care, education or manufacturing. It is partly in consequence of this shift of resources, both real and financial into this industry, that regulators, legislators and voters have started to examine more closely what society obtains from this use of resources. Clearly the industry performs a very important function but society is concerned also with the cost of providing those functions and with whether or not the business model being employed increases the likelihood of financial instability. I do not have space to consider these issues in detail but I would expect them to feature on the news pages of the press and in the debates in legislatures.

---

[9] The Turner Review: A Regulatory Response to the Global Banking Crisis, March 2009, Financial Services Authority.

[10] See Benjamin Friedman, *Is Our Financial System Serving Us Well?* (Daedalus, 2010).

# 30 The Global Economic And Financial Outlook: 2020 Vision

The English language has an expression '20/20 vision' which means perfect vision. The year 2020 may be the end of the current decade but the surest way for an economist to lose his or her reputation is by making forecasts particularly as far out as that. Economists can no more predict the future than can anyone else. Thus I will not try to predict the financial or economic world in 2020. What economists can do, however, is to point to developing trends, inconsistencies in policy, changes in underlying fundamentals and other factors that might impact on the firms whose activities they help to finance and hence impact on the providers of financial services. But the outcome of these factors will remain uncertain and will not be subject to statistical risk analysis. Nonetheless, for politicians, regulators and bankers it is necessary to try make sense of developments and take steps to try to protect countries, financial firms and financial assets, respectively, from these uncertainties.

## THE GLOBAL FINANCIAL SITUATION

In December 2011, the managing director of the IMF, the body which more than any other is in touch with global economic and financial developments and their implications, said:

> There is no economy in the world, whether low-income countries, emerging markets, middle-income or super-advanced that will be immune to the crisis that we see, not only unfolding but escalating.[1]

The crisis she foresees arises in considerable part from the global and regional imbalances that I have covered in earlier chapters and to the absence of any indication that nations can agree between themselves, or through regional groupings such as the eurozone, as to how to reduce them. In fact these imbalances are

---

[1] 'IMF Chief Warns Over 1930s Style Threats', speech by Christine Lagarde, *Financial Times*, 16 December 2012.

likely to widen. In December 2011, the Bank of England published a paper[2] which strongly suggests that, even though global imbalances helped create the financial crisis, they have not declined and are likely to become larger, not smaller. The Bank estimates that between 2000 and 2007 annual gross international capital flows increased from 5% of global GDP to 17%. Corresponding with this increase, global current account imbalances (deficits plus surpluses) rose from 3% of global GDP to 6%. They expect this to rise to 8%, which is more than double the level before the 2008 peak of the financial crisis. Much of this is due to the growth in real incomes and changing demographics in emerging market economies. It should also be noted, however, that in 2011, China's current account surplus fell greatly and in the early months of 2012, Japan which has almost always been in surplus, went into deficit.

## THE US OUTLOOK

The US has until now been the second largest global economy (the EU is the largest) and, in consequence, has been a key driver of global demand. Today the US would appear to be stuck in a battle between competing ideologies regarding how to rescue it from low economic growth, rising unemployment and falling real incomes for a high proportion of the population.

Since the Ronald Reagan era, the US has followed a strategy of believing that low taxes, particularly for high income earners and for those owning capital assets, would stimulate the economy to grow faster. However, government spending has not been reduced to match the declining revenue (as a propor-tion of GDP) and in consequence budget deficits have increased. Spending has, indeed, been cut – in many of the so-called 'supply-side' areas where the private sector is less likely to invest and which, it might be thought, would help boost growth rates in the future. These include education programmes at all levels from nursery to advanced technical training and university education and, of course, science and technology research. In addition spending on infrastruc-ture, which in the US is in considerable part a Federal responsibility, has also been sharply reduced, leading for example to poor quality roads. In contrast, in northern Europe (Norway, Sweden, Denmark, Germany, Holland, Austria, the UK and even northern Italy) a different model has been followed. The tax/GDP ratio has risen, perhaps too much, but with outcomes that are generally believed to be better than those in the US. Geoffrey Sachs,[3] one of the world's best known development economists, has noted that the US model has led to higher unemployment, larger budget deficits, greater poverty, larger trade defi-cits, lower social mobility, shorter life expectancy and lower reported life satis-faction in the US, compared with northern Europe. Even for a practical and very applied development economist like Sachs, the US problem looks intractable in anything shorter than the very long term.

---

[2] 'The Future of International Capital Flows', Bank of England Financial Stability Paper, December 2011.

[3] 'Death by Strangling: The Demise of State Spending', *Financial Times*, 16 December 2011.

A key problem for the US is that there are two opposing philosophies in that country as to how to achieve economic success. One believes that government gets in the way of economic success and the other believes that it can be an important contributor to it and to the contentment of the people of the country. In consequence those who believe in the first philosophy want to cut taxes and government spending even further than they have already been, almost regardless of any budget deficit that arises in consequence, while the other wants to increase taxes and government spending. Until the country as a whole comes to a single understanding of how to overcome its problems, it seems unlikely that the US will be able to progress as it has in the past.

## THE CHINA OUTLOOK

China has clearly been the economic development model par excellence if one considers simply the rate of change of GDP and not issues to do with personal freedom, income distribution or pollution. However, much of the growth of this economy has been predicated on US and European demand for products made in China and on a construction boom that many believe is no longer sustainable. Nonetheless, the Chinese model of a 'directed market economy' or 'state capitalism' does seem to have performed in many respects better than economies where the state has withdrawn from any attempt to stimulate growth in output or to enable supply side reforms.

In Chapter 1 I discussed the contrast between the price system in a free market economy as a means of allocating scarce resources and the alternative, Marxist, system of a central authority undertaking this direction. I noted that Chinese economic output grew dramatically and rapidly after Deng Xiaoping took over the leadership and instituted reforms to shift the country from the latter system to the former. However, not everything is as it seems:

> Contrast the U.S. and its free market economy with China's system. For years now, that country has experienced double digit growth. Many observers would say that China's embrace of capitalism since 1978, and especially since joining the World Trade Organization in 2001, has been responsible for its boom. They would be mostly wrong. In fact, **a new study prepared for the U.S. government says it's not capitalism that's powering China, but state capitalism** – China's massive, centrally directed industrial policy, where the government positions huge amounts of capital and labor in economic sectors it intends to nurture. The study,[4] prepared by consultants Capital Trade for the US–China Economic and Security Review Commission in the United States, reads in part:
>
> > In a world in which central planning has been so utterly discredited, it would be natural to conclude that the Chinese government and, by extension, the Chinese Communist Party have been abandoning the institutions associated with the communist economic system, such as reliance on state owned enterprises (SOEs), as fast as possible. Such a conclusion would be wrong.[5]

---

[4]  See www.uscc.gov/researchpapers/2011/10_26_11_CapitalTradeSOEStudy.pdf

[5]  Ian Bremmer, 'The Secret to China's Boom: State Capitalism', Reuters webnews, 4 November 2011.

With the Chinese economy moving rapidly to parity in GNP terms with that of the US (though per capita incomes will remain at much lower levels), a setback in China, whether from the real estate market or from political developments, would have severely deleterious effects on the global economy in a way it would not have had in 2000.

## THE EUROZONE CRISIS

At the time of writing, the eurozone presents the most immediate threat to the global economy. The possibility of a breakup of the zone is now openly discussed whereas before late 2011 European politicians would not discuss this possibility, even sotto voce. Already all the major European legal practices have issued briefing notes to their financial services clients on the implications of a breakup and all financial services firms have taken steps to minimise the impact on themselves and their clients were it to happen. I would assume, also, that the Greek authorities have already given an order to Thomas de la Rue (the UK firm that prints most countries' banknotes) to print 'new' drachma so that they are available in the event that the country exits the eurozone.

More alarmingly, perhaps, but also very realistically, the European Financial Stability Facility is reported[6] as having prepared a draft prospectus which includes explicit warnings to investors that the euro could break apart or even cease to be a 'lawful currency' entirely. It has also been noted that one bond issuer has already provided such a warning. Petrobras, the Brazilian national oil company in a US-filed prospectus for a €1.85 billion bond issue in Dec 2011, warned that 'market perceptions concerning the instability of the euro, the potential reintroduction of individual currencies within the eurozone or the potential dissolution of the euro entirely could adversely affect the value of these euro denominated notes'.

The desire to preserve the euro 'at all costs', an expression that politicians often use, is predicated on the belief that 'without the euro there can be no Europe' – a statement made in 2011 by the then leaders of France and Germany, Nicolas Sarkozy and Angela Merkel. Such a statement is clearly untrue since the European Union was 'Europe' from its foundation in the 1950s until 1999 (when the euro became an accounting currency) and 2002 when notes and coin were issued. To resolve the eurozone crisis, these politicians have focused on fiscal aspects of the crisis and temporary official financing of states and banks which are in difficulty. Overcoming the fiscal issues (overspending and undertaxing by some countries) involves applying IMF-type 'conditionality' which we have already covered. It involves dictating to countries in difficulty what they may and may not do in the areas of spending and taxation if they are to be 'saved' by bailout funds. Such 'direction' is potentially undemocratic and in practice is likely to be highly deflationary, i.e. likely to reduce GDP and employment even further consequently leading to fiscal deficits increasing, not reducing. Thus conditionality has the potential to lead to 'difficulties' of a type which democracies are not expected to experience, namely political unrest. The rating agency Fitch, in mid-December 2011,

---

[6] 'EFSF Ponders Euro Warning Clause', *Financial* Times, 16 December 2011.

concluded that: 'a comprehensive solution to the eurozone crisis was technically and politically beyond reach'. In other words, while there may be solutions (of which a reversion to the 1999 status quo ante is one), the politics of a group of 27 disparate countries trying to agree on what to do to overcome the single currency crisis is not conducive to success. Decision-making in such groups is much harder than in markets where everyone simply votes to buy or to sell and the adjustment to a new reality is 'discovered' by the market, for example the foreign exchange market, through a price change.

Many would also argue that the problem is not a fiscal one and that in fact the European leaders are tackling the wrong problem. A number of researchers have come to the view that the eurozone problem is caused by divergence of competitiveness over 13 years, not simply by budget deficits'. If that statement is correct then the problem is financial imbalances, and the consequent need for capital flows, induced by fixed (non-market determined) exchange rates between countries with very different social and economic structures which results in substantial imbalances between northern and southern European countries. If this is so, then overcoming eurozone difficulties, while also needing fiscal adjustment in a number of countries, essentially requires a choice between exchange rate flexibility (allowing countries to leave the eurozone or breaking up the zone) or massive deflation in a number of countries to reduce price disparities within the zone. It is because of the economic logic behind this statement that even the European Financial Stability Facility, whose function is to preserve the euro, feels obliged by the law of disclosure to warn that the currency may not be forever.

The symbiosis between the eurozone crisis and the European banking problem is an issue that I have referred to in earlier chapters. It has come to fore at the end of 2011 with an expectation by politicians that the European Central Bank's announcement that it would offer low-cost three-year funding to European banks (the so-called Long Term Refinancing Operation or LTRO) would result in those banks using the additional funds to buy eurozone sovereign debt. For many banks, however, that would be difficult due to their already inadequate levels of equity capital which would have to be boosted to enable the acquisition of additional assets. Nicolas Sarkozy was reported in mid-December as suggesting that banks could use the funds to 'backstop' their governments.

Barclays Capital in a note to investors on this matter said that 'in extremis, bulls argue that pumping ECB liquidity into banks effectively creates a buyer of last resort for sovereign debt – thereby ending the current crisis. That view is wrong'.

The CEO of UniCredit said: 'it would not be logical to use ECB funding to buy more government debt and I would prefer to lend to the real economy'.

A senior French banker was reporting as saying 'the French banks are not going to go out and say it explicitly but the general feeling is it's not a good idea'.[7]

One of the problems with all the financial solutions suggested by politicians to end the eurozone crisis is that they neglect the 'real' side of the economy. The quotation above by the UniCredit CEO clearly suggests that if he had to use the

---

[7] Banks shouldn't buy government bonds with extra cash – UniCredit, Reuters UK, 14 December 2011.

ECB money to lend to governments, then he would have less to lend to the real economy. The real economy would be **crowded-out**. That remains a real problem. Not only that, but politicians seem to have shifted from the view we covered in Chapter 1 that 'money is a veil' over the real economy to the view that 'money is what drives the real economy and economic growth'. By this we mean that increasing the money supply by quantitative easing, and providing loans through the central bank to enable commercial banks to buy government bonds represents the limit of some EU government thinking.

One of the few bankers/politicians to appreciate the central importance of the real side of the economy and the need for the state to be involved in it is, surprisingly, Jean-Claude Trichet, onetime President of the European Central Bank. In 2006 (before the financial or sovereign debt crises) when the European and global economies seemed to be performing in a miraculous way, he made a speech which provides a good summary of these issues relating to competitiveness and possible solutions. Given that Trichet's own job is simply to try to ensure financial and economic stability rather than economic dynamism, and that this was written before the financial crisis caused such high levels of unemployment in the EU, it is clear that he considers the **real economy** issues, not just the **financial economy** issues, as vital in 'creating an entrepreneurial-friendly economic environment and lowering administrative costs imposed by the public sector'. Here is an excerpt from the speech:

> There are **four key priorities** for reform in Europe, namely, getting people into work, increasing competition, unlocking business potential and supporting an innovative environment.
>
> • First of all, **well-functioning** labour markets are needed. Necessary labour supply-side measures include the reform of tax and benefit systems to increase incentives to work. Measures aimed at reconciling family with professional life, such as the provision of childcare, may also raise participation rates. Furthermore, the use of flexible forms of work, such as part-time and temporary work, may also provide further working incentives. To stimulate labour demand, there is a need to promote wage flexibility and address labour market rigidities.
> • **Increasing competition** is the second prerequisite for better economic performance. Europe should step up measures to boost services market competition in order to support a higher level and growth rate of labour productivity and promote a more dynamic economy. In this context, an internal market for services and the adoption of the EU Services Directive would constitute an important step forward.
> • The third prerequisite for higher growth in the euro area is the unlocking of business potential by creating an entrepreneurial-friendly economic environment and **lowering administrative costs imposed by the public sector**. The immense importance of this issue is increasingly appreciated and several initiatives at national or EU level aim at 'better regulation'.
> • Fourth, to fully exploit productivity potential, labour and product market reforms need to be complemented by **policies that help to diffuse innovation**, including measures to support higher investment in research and development. To be most effective, these measures need to be accompanied by efforts to improve the labour force's level of **education and expertise** in such a way that **human capital** is continuously adjusted to labour market needs.

Applying comprehensive structural reforms is of particular importance for the euro area countries, in order to increase wage and price flexibility and the resilience to shocks, facilitate structural adjustment, raise potential output growth and job creation, and reduce price pressures, thereby facilitating the task of the single monetary policy.[8]

While in Italy, few people are confident that the **political system** has the ability to reform itself and achieve the objectives outlined above, one private sector firm and **one individual** in particular, has achieved much against great odds:

Mario Monti's government of technocrats is battling entrenched interests in trying to take even modest steps to liberalise Italy's moribund economy, but some would say the nation's real reformer is the lone figure of Sergio Marchionne of Fiat.

By breaking the mould of labour relations set through collective national bargaining, the chief executive of Italy's largest industrial group has taken on two powerful lobbies – Confindustria, the main employers association which Fiat is quitting next month, as well as the trade unions.

Mr Marchionne hailed Fiat's agreement on more flexible contracts with all major unions bar one this week as 'historic'. In return, the carmaker is pressing ahead with billions of euros of investments in Italy – its roots for more than a century – even though its chief executive says it would make more financial sense for the merging Fiat-Chrysler group to focus on operations abroad.

Mr Marchionne has a divisive image in Italy, a country he describes as one where 'he who shouts loudest wins, where people speak a lot, listen little and do even less, where more efforts are made in front of the TV camera than in real life'.

Mr Marchionne was speaking at the launch of the new Panda model at Fiat's Pomigliano plant near Naples on Wednesday. Infamous in times gone by for its low productivity and high rate of absenteeism, where workers often had second day jobs, a gleaming Pomigliano has been transformed at a cost of more than €800m into the group's most state-of-the-art, automated plant worldwide.

Workers there call it a 'revolution'. Those that have jobs – a rare commodity in Italy's blighted south – seem happy with the new deal, accepting higher wages for shorter breaks, more night shifts and tougher conditions on sick leave and the right to strike.

Gianluca Spina, dean of Politecnico di Milano school of management, says the terms of Fiat's new labour contracts are not so revolutionary as such, but the challenging of Italy's status quo has set a trend that other big companies are likely to follow.

'It seems that Marchionne is the only real reformer in the country, maybe because he's not really Italian and is prepared to do Thatcherish things,' commented James Walston, political scientist at the American University of Rome.[9]

What is unfortunate is that the politicians in Europe do not seem able to achieve such agreements or real reforms. Nor, it seems, are politicians in the US able to achieve agreement between the two parties on how to stimulate job growth and economic growth.

---

[8]  Structural Reforms in Europe OECD Observer, July 2006 http://www.oecdobserver.org/news/fullstory.php/aid/1847/Structural_reforms_in_Europe.html

[9]  'Fiat's Jumper-clad Revolutionary', *Financial Times*, 17–18 December 2011.

The state's role in relation to growth and employment in most economies today (China is one of the exceptions as it is actively involved in economic activity) is as a **facilitator**. Facilitation involves providing:

- A **dynamic facilitating structure** in terms of an absence of unnecessary bureaucracy, support for innovation and higher education, agencies to support new enterprise, etc., within which the private sector can operate;
- A **stable financial and economic environment** within which the private sector can operate. Unfortunately, until governments in Europe and the US take Mr Trichet's recommendations from 2006 seriously, and even take time to consider how China has achieved its economic dynamism through state directed capitalism, it is possible that neither Europe nor the US will return to full employment or a satisfactory growth rate. Clearly this has serious implications for all sectors of society as well as for the financial services industry based in Europe and the US. We have to hope that the issues I have outlined above are resolved and do not change from 'unfolding to escalating', as in the December 2011 comment by the Managing Director of the IMF quoted at the start of this chapter.

# INDEX

# DH

332
QUI